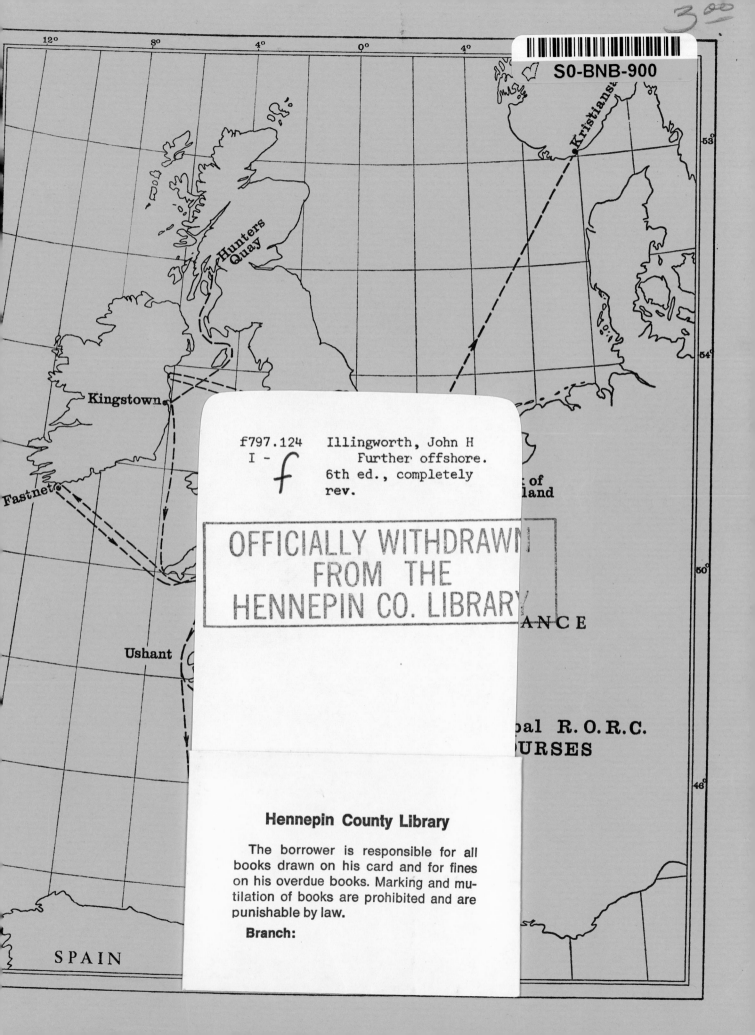

S0-BNB-900

f797.124   Illingworth, John H
I - f   Further offshore.
            6th ed., completely
            rev.

OFFICIALLY WITHDRAWN
FROM THE
HENNEPIN CO. LIBRARY

Hennepin County Library

The borrower is responsible for all books drawn on his card and for fines on his overdue books. Marking and mutilation of books are prohibited and are punishable by law.

Branch:

Further Offshore

FURTHER OFFSHORE

Ocean Racing, Fast Cruising

Modern Yacht Handling and Equipment

CAPTAIN J. H. ILLINGWORTH

R.N. RTD.

ADLARD COLES LTD LONDON

TO MY FATHER
in appreciation of unfailing help and encouragement

© *J. H. Illingworth, 1958, 1963, 1969*
First published as Offshore, *1949*
Second Edition, 1950
Third and Revised Edition, 1955
Fourth and Revised Edition, 1958
Fifth and Revised Edition, 1963
Sixth Edition, completely revised, 1969

Published by Adlard Coles Ltd
3 Upper James Street Golden Square London W1

SBN 229 63890 2

Printed in Great Britain by Ebenezer Baylis and Son, Ltd
The Trinity Press, Worcester, and London

CONTENTS

FURTHER OFFSHORE
ERRATA

Page 4,   col. 2, para. 5, line 2 should read: or 30-square metre

Page 5,   col. 1, para. 6, line 4: for '8' read '9'

Page 51, col. 1, para. 3, line 3 should read: 10, 11, 12, 13, 14, shown with two cutter layouts on pages 52–3.

Page 54, col. 1, para. 3, line 3 should read: the ratio of the hoist to the length of the foot on the boom is 3.1 to 1.

Page 60, col. 2, para. 5, line 7 should read: Diagram 18 shows the rig of *Robert Gordon*, a 66′ schooner built of steel in Holland.

Page 64, col. 1, para. 4, line 12: for 'crew' read 'clew'

Page 67, col. 2, para. 1, line 16: for 'XVI' read 'IV'

Page 69, col. 2, para. 4, line 2: for '*Maid*' read '*Monk*'

Page 74, col. 1, para. 6, line 7: for '38' read '37'

Page 81, col. 2, para. 4, line 14: for '17' read '15–16'

Page 96, col. 2, para. 6 line 2: for '25' read '24'

Page 98, col. 2, para. 4, line 4: for 'crew' read 'clew'

Page 132, col. 2, para. 3, line 2 should read: 6 × 37, and to a lesser extent the 6 × 24, is not so . . .

Page 134, col. 2, para. 7, line 5: for '36' read '34'

Page 136, col. 2, para. 5, line 2: for '37' read '35'

Page 140, col. 2, para. 1, line 6: for '40' read '37'; para. 3, line 2: for '39' read '37'; line 6, for '10' read '11'

Page 170, col. 1, para. 4, line 15: for '86' read '87'

Page 193, col. 1, para. 2, line 2: for '71' read '73'

Page 197, col. 2, para. 4, line 6: for '69' read '74'

Page 200, col. 1, para. 2, line 8: for 'radio' read 'ratio'

Page 207, col. 1, para. 3, line 4: for '60' read '80'

LIST OF PLATES

LIST OF DIAGRAMS

FOREWORD

The fifth edition of *Offshore* was completely revised and considerably enlarged, but the pace of development in the sport of ocean racing has become so rapid that yet another more complete revision has been called for. This revision has been so massive, and includes new drawings new chapters and new appendices, that I have felt it should have the new title of *Further Offshore*. The techniques of sailing and offshore racing are slowly changing. But hull form, rigging, and fittings have improved at ever increasing speed, especially over the last few years. Gear has improved enormously.

All these developments have been covered in this new edition, and a great number of new designs and photographs have been added to illustrate the latest trends. I have drawn principally from the hard facts and figures which are available to me from many yachts of my own design; rather than offering generalisations about boats of which I have not so intimate a knowledge. But thanks to the generous co-operation of other naval architects in the U.S.A. and France as well as in Britain there is a good cross section of the world's best yachts.

One of the features of modern ocean racing is the general improvement in keenness of competition both in the yachts themselves and in their sailing and handling. It is this that keeps us designers on our toes, giving us scope for experiment, development, and improvement in every direction. Today the hull design must be right, the sail plan and rigging must be right, and above all skippers and crews must be keyed up to get the best out of their boats. Competition in ocean racing is hotter than ever before, and what is more, it is more international in character, as is evidenced by the toughness and success of overseas challenges for the Admirals Cup, by the strength of the foreign entries in the Fastnet and Bermuda races, and by the French successes in winning the R.O.R.C. overall points championship.

In short, ocean racing is now a major sport; the major sport for many of us. I hope this new book *Further Offshore* will help further to encourage it, and that it will prove useful especially to the new blood which is vitalizing the sport. Good luck and good sailing to all of you.

J.H.I

I

OCEAN RACING—THE BACKGROUND

There is of course nothing new about racing across oceans. Ever since the dawn of history sailing vessels have vied with one another to make the faster passage. The great races from China in the tea clippers; the cracking competition to be first home with the wool from Australia; those and many others leap to mind. But these, one and all, were passages made by vessels in the course of commerce; and by relatively big vessels manned by large professional crews.

The dawn of ocean yacht racing may perhaps be said to have begun with the three notable transatlantic matches which were sailed in the mid-nineteenth century and later—sometimes in the depths of the winter. But here again the yachts were generally ships manned primarily by professional seamen.

History was made by the splendid transatlantic race of 1905, which was won from five other yachts by the schooner *Atlantic* in the record time of 12 days, 4 hrs., 1 min. 19 secs. from Sandy Hook to the Lizard: a yacht which incidentally still survived in the training service of the United States until 1948.

Among the first of the modern ocean races was the Bermuda Race, first run in 1906. The course was 660 miles of ocean from New York to Bermuda. Interrupted by the First World War the series was resumed by the Cruising Club of America in 1923. In 1926 the races became biennial, later alternating with the Fastnet Races, which meanwhile had been started in 1925 in British waters by the Ocean Racing Club; also over a 600-mile course finishing at Plymouth, after rounding the rock off the south-west corner of Ireland from which the race takes its name.

We had to wait twenty years for the third, now famous, event to be instituted, this time in the Southern Hemisphere—the Sydney to Hobart race. This is run under the aegis of the Cruising Yacht Club of Australia over a course of about the same distance.

You will note that I make a definite distinction at the point where we arrived at the modern ocean races. And this is done with intent, because these modern blue riband events and the great

number of shorter races offshore—more of these later—are indeed different. The essential ingredients are small yachts and amateur crews. And an indefatigable spirit of keenness mixed with an indefinable spirit of good sportsmanship. Shake up well in a big wet seaway for some days, and you have the essence of ocean racing as we know it today.

One of the early problems which arose was that of allocating fair time allowances. The Atlantic race of 1905 was sailed without allowance which clearly did not give the smaller yachts any chance. On the other hand arbitrary handicapping was obviously undesirable. Search was made for a system of measurement readily applicable to yachts afloat, from which could be deduced a speed figure or 'rating' fairly representing the speed capabilities of that hull, and from which the time allowances between yachts of various sizes could be readily and directly calculated. Thus was born the R.O.R.C. Rating Rule. This was largely the work of Major Malden Heckstall Smith in collaboration with Dick McLean Buckley, then and for twelve years subsequently Secretary and later Admiral of the R.O.R.C. The rating rule, though subject to constant development in points of detail, has remained substantially unchanged.

Essentially the system of a rating rule is that those factors, notably length and sail area and small freeboard, which increase the speed, are 'pluses' in the formula and those which tend to decrease the speed, such as extra beam and depth of hull, are minus or dividers in the formula. Added to the formula are a number of 'safeguards' penalising what the committee feel to be unfair or unhealthy ways of increasing the speed, such as excessively long masts, or excessive ballast ratios.

This formula was at first also used in America. But later they felt they wanted a formula to encourage a definite type and the traditionally large beam of American boats, and introduced the Cruising Club of America Rule which arrives at a somewhat similar answer by different means.

At the time of going to press, a new international rating rule is in a well-advanced stage. Based on the R.O.R.C. rule it will not penalise so heavily rather fuller quarters. The scantling allowances have been revised and may be in part replaced by an inclining test. The measurement of sail area is likely to follow the C.C.A. pattern, giving an overlap of around 160 per cent base of triangle. It remains to be seen whether this will be accepted in the U.S.A.—the new rule, virtually complete, is included in Appendix VII.

These rating rules and their time scales are discussed in detail elsewhere in the book; this brief reference to them here is however necessary because their success in enabling boats of all sizes to race together is an essential feature in ocean racing as we know it.

The R.O.R.C. rule was used throughout European and Mediterranean waters, and by the C.Y.C.A. in Australia.

All the Royal Ocean Racing Club races are open to yachts of 24ft. water-line and over. Most of the races are for yachts with ratings of from 19 to 70 ft. R.O.R.C. Rating. Occasionally smaller yachts are accepted.

Twelve or thirteen races of between 200 miles and 600 miles each are given each year by the R.O.R.C.—enough for any offshore racing glutton! Many of the races finish at ports abroad, and the great majority of races are entered by yachts from many continental countries as well as from Great Britain or Eire.

The races are normally subdivided into three classes according to ratings, which are of course roughly proportional to their size. The large Class I is now 70 ft. to 29 ft.; Class II is below 29 ft. to 22½ ft., and the small yachts in Class III have ratings below 22½ ft. to 19 ft. Class II and Class III are in certain races subdivided into (A) and (B) sections according to rating: for 1969 Class II is 25 ft. to 29 ft. and 22½ ft. to 25 ft., for Class III it is 21 ft. to 22½ ft. and 19 ft. to 21 ft.

In these races, apart from the principal open prizes in each class, there are subdivisions—Alpha and Beta divisions. The latter consists principally of yachts which either are older racing types or have not the advantage of being designed for offshore racing.

Eligibility for 'Beta' division depends on age and results, though the rating is done in the same way for all yachts and all are eligible for the open prizes. Details concerning 'Beta' division and the rules governing them vary from year to year.

Yachts built before 1st January, 1963, and any one-design or yacht with standard hull of which the first of the series was completed before that date, will be given an allowance of 1 per cent. deducted from her T.C.F. The rating will not be changed.

The aggregate results for the whole season in each class are totalled by a special system of points to determine the champion yacht of the year in each class. In the same way the aggregate of points won in R.O.R.C races by each club, to which total certain competing yacht belonging to a member of that club contributes, determines the winner of the Annual Inter Club Championship.

The Junior Offshore Group, and the Groupe Croisière Legère in France, each arrange similar programmes of about ten races: of from 40 to 180 miles again under the R.O.R.C. Rating Rule, which may shortly be superseded by the 'new' Rule.

Apart from the principal Royal Ocean Racing Club events there are every year a very great number of extremely sporting events over shorter offshore courses given by other clubs all around the coasts of Great Britain, Ireland, and France. Many are open to boats of less than 24-ft. water-line. The majority are, like the R.O.R.C. events themselves, run under R.O.R.C. rating and time allowance. Typical of these is the Island Sailing Club's race round the Isle of Wight for the Crankshaw and Windler Bowls, attracting two hundred entries. Aside from the fun which they offer, these races constitute a remarkably fine training ground for the longer and more serious events. A typical list of some of these races is given in Appendix X, together with a R.O.R.C. programme. Long-distance races also are organised by Norwegian and Swedish clubs in the Baltic.

The Bermuda Race is at present open to yachts of from 26-ft rating to 73 ft. in length over-all provided not more than one-third of that length is in the overhangs. The minimum waterline length in practice is around 28 ft. (See Appendix XII.) In the U.S.A. the C.C.A.'s primary racing activity is the Biennial Bermuda Race. A good deal of the remainder of the offshore racing is on a semi-regional basis, various clubs giving important races. For instance in non-Bermuda years the New York Yacht Club gives the Annapolis Race.

Some of the clubs use the C.C.A. rule of measurement, but on account of the amount of work involved in measuring, many clubs have their own simple rules. The number of fine races given both on the east and west coasts, in the West Indies early in the season and on the Great Lakes, is very considerable.

The Cruising Yacht Club of Australia has a 24-ft. low limit for the waterline of yachts for the Sydney–Hobart and lower limits for their shorter races. In the Australian programme is sometimes the Montague Island Race from Sydney over a 370-mile course, given by the Prince Alfred Club. The Hobart Race starts on Boxing Day.

In some years the C.Y.C. gives a 1,100-mile race from Sydney to the French colony of Noumea. Among many clubs giving good shorter races off shore, the Royal Yacht Club of Tasmania have two well-established events, and there is a 200-mile race in Western Australia.

In South America ocean racing is making steady progress, with a triennial race from Buenos Aires to Rio de Janeiro. More of this anon.

In the Mediterranean a series of well-organised offshore events is held every year, starting as a rule in mid-July. 'Le petit Fastnet de la Mediterranée' is a race round the Giraglia Rock (or sometimes a vessel anchored nearby) off Corsica. The race is from Toulon to San Remo in odd years and generally the reverse in even years. The start is given on about 14 July. From Lisbon the Associacao Naval occasionally race 500 miles to Madeira. In July this is mostly on a reaching or quartering breeze. In Greece, the Athens to Rhodes race is gaining stature.

There are three other races which are notable and very long, which have been held at irregular intervals, and which have produced some tremendous adventures, though naturally the racing is not always so close and competitive as in the other events. I have already referred to the early Transatlantic races. Since then we have had races across the pond in 1928, 1931, 1935, 1936, 1950, 1952, 1955, 1963, and 1966. The races are run in an easterly direction, which is usually downhill with the westerlies.

Then there are the Trans-Pacific Yacht Club's famous California to Honolulu races which have been mostly held to alternate with the Bermuda races. Often also a downhill slide, mostly in fair weather, it is a great distance to race over.

There is the trans-Tasman Race—1,500 miles odd from New Zealand to Australia. Many races have been sailed over this stormy course.

In 1950 I formed the Junior Offshore Group in England to race boats of between 16- and 24-ft. water-line length—real midget racers, some of these. Their races run up to 250 miles in length. M.O.R.C.—the Midget Ocean Racing Club of America followed close in the same line.

At the other end of the scale, in 1955 I set up in England a committee to promote racing between the remaining great sailing vessels, nowadays used for training purposes. As the S.T.A.—Sail Training Association—we ran the Torbay–Lisbon Race in 1956 (600 miles) and in 1958 the Brest–Madeira–Canaries Race (1,300 miles). In 1960 they raced from Oslo to Ostend, and from Cannes to Naples. Eight square riggers were engaged, apart from the big schooners and the yachts. In 1962 the course was from Torbay round a vessel off Ushant to Rotterdam. Her Majesty the Queen fired the starting gun, from the Royal Yacht Britannia. Since then the S.T.A. has run a big ship Transatlantic race—east to west. Apart from the main squadrons, classes are included for vessels of over 30-ft. water-line and under 100 tons; in each case carrying 50 per cent trainees.

Space has precluded the mention of many splendid events, but I have, I think, said enough to show that the great business of ocean racing is going from strength to strength in almost every corner of the world, and to indicate to you that almost wherever you happen to be or care to go, there will be racing available to you; and tremendous things to tilt at.

But in case you should leave this chapter with the feeling that the big races and the sizy yachts were the things that counted most, I would as a tail-piece like to tell you that of the many races I have sailed, the one I always think of with as much pleasure as any, and as having been one of the more sporting events in the proper sense of offshore racing, was the 50-mile race round the Island of Malta, in 1939, in which the great majority of the entrants, including my own boat, were between 16 and 18 ft. on the waterline length.

This contest had all those essential things which make up a fine race off shore; moonlit night sailing; changes in the weather from calms to all the breeze we wanted; a stretch of inhospitable coast with no port and a fair chance to drown oneself if one did not do the right thing; running, reaching and a real go to windward to finish up with, which left most of the crews with a wet neck under their oilskins, and a feeling when ashore that no whisky and soda had ever tasted so good, and that no hot bath had ever been so welcome.

2

CHOOSING AND TUNING A BOAT

Every now and then a comparatively elderly yacht stages the most magnificent come-back in offshore racing. Most people are surprised; everybody is pleased. Alternatively a new yacht that has done well in her first season slips back among the 'also rans'. Some will say she is out-dated, but they are probably wrong. The explanation is much more likely to be that the nice gear with which she started life has got out of order: she has changed owners perhaps and fallen into the hands of men who knew her not, and maybe had not the time or inclination to take the trouble to find out.

The point of this is that the condition and tune of the boat is almost as important as the design.

Success Factors. To turn to the specific question of boat selection, I have sometimes tried to evaluate the factors which contribute to success in ocean racing, and must admit that it is a pretty subject for debate. I suggest you can simplify the problem by dividing it into three parts. The first we will call the hull; this embraces the original design and construction. If you assume, as in general one may, that the construction is adequate to the job, it really boils down, as a success factor, to basic lines and ballast ratio.

The second part I call fitting and tuning. I use fitting out in the widest sense, being everything and anything one could do to a hull, the equipment, the layout and arrangement of the rig and sails, or alterations to the accommodation and interior fittings. In other words anything which could be done between laying up and the first race next season.

The third part of our success or otherwise is what we do with the equipped and tuned ship after the ten minute preparatory gun. In other words, the way we sail the race. This obviously includes the quality of the helmsmanship, the strategy employed by the skipper, the efficiency of hands in setting, handing and trimming sail, and the accuracy of the pilotage and navigation. In this third, the cook contributes his important quota to the efficiency or otherwise of the *équipe*.

Now if we assume, as I think we may, that these parts are of roughly equal importance, we see that two-thirds of the success is up to the owner rather

than the original designer. If we reckon in the possibility of minor modifications to the hull—the rudder, propeller, aperture, ballast and so on—the proportion is even higher.

In this case it is clear that by intelligent purchase of an existing, even quite elderly, hull we can, provided we are prepared to take sufficient trouble with the rig and equipment, quite probably put ourselves among the front rank of the 'Beta' class racers, with a sporting chance of a prize in the open division. If the hull is reasonably modern our chances are clearly even better.

So let us proceed to the business of examining the question of purchasing our hull. The 1957 R.O.R.C. rule gave almost all types of boat a fair chance and the new rule is likely to do the same. So what we have to do is to find a hull which is *good of its type*. For instance if you fancy a Norwegian pilot cutter you must get a good example of this type. For still strictly within a type, one can draw a nice or a shocking set of lines.

Outside this there are a lot of good boats which don't conform definitely to any type, and you may well ask how one is to judge these. There are so many special cases that generalisations on such a subject must necessarily have exceptions, but I think one safe line of thought is that the boat should have 'useful ends'. I don't mean necessarily long ends or short ends; I mean that the ends should contribute usefully to the performance, to an extent which is comparable with their lengths. I know a few boats who have fancy sheer lines and bows which reach out in front of them to no very good purpose. This overhang is going to put the ratings up just the same.

On the other hand you have boats like very old *Cynthia*, or thirty-square *Tre-Sang*, which have long overhangs which materially add to their performance—are in fact a logical part of the boat—and which raise their rating nearly in proportion to the performance added. These boats do well though R.O.R.C. ratings are 3 to 6 ft. more than their waterline length. But they are 'young men's' boats; fast and wet with not too much room in them. They give you a very sporting ride, and it is good to think that these boats, built to other rules and conceived under other stars, can still win, in almost any weather, if they have a determined crew and skipper.

It is worth remembering that if one has big freeboard one should have for R.O.R.C. races conservative 'ends', otherwise the measured length gets pushed out unduly. This does not mean that one cannot have a shapely boat. The 'Foxhound' group of yachts to Camper & Nicholson's designs have biggish freeboard but moderate ends, and almost invariably did well. *Bloodhound*, which I rigged in 1962, is still a prize winner in Class I.

There are now available, second-hand, numbers of genuine ocean racing boats designed by Holman, Nicholson, Clark, Giles, Robb, or ourselves, virtually all of which are in a general sense good boats; though the 'end test' should be applied. Many of them have never yet shown their best form, and if a firm of architects specialising in ocean racers is chosen to alter and modernise their rigs they may well come out in the first flight. Their racing record is not an infallible guide, because previous owners may never have had the time and facilities to tune or race them consistently.

Having now chosen and, after survey, bought one's boat, one must not sit back and accept her as she is. If one can, one wants to buy a boat early in the winter so that one has the winter to work out, arrange, and complete such alterations as may be necessary. Nearly everything in the other chapters has a bearing on existing boats, but, in order to make things easy, here in very brief are a few of the things you can get right on with.

Immediately you have bought her get an accurate up-to-date sail plan. Should there be an R.O.R.C. Certificate you can get the dimensions there. If there is none, measure the spars in the loft, and get 'J' from the deck. Nine old sail plans out of ten which one finds in the hands of owners, builders, and sailmakers are inaccurate, so a newly made plan is a nice clean start.

Review of the Sail Plan. Then review in conjunction with an expert friend or naval architect, this sail plan, to see where it can be improved. Work out from the formula in the rig chapter (8) the area of sail you need for offshore racing; and then see how this can be arranged with the minimum rating and maximum efficiency, making the best use of existing spars and sails. It is imperative that the rig should be compact, with every square foot of the sails best placed to do the job, but concentrated as near its mast as maybe. The rules, be they C.C.A. or R.O.R.C. are hard on sail area, and small sails hung on the end of attenuated bowsprits are no good to you. You must keep the rig in board as far as you can, and exploit such overlaps as are

allowed to you without penalty. There is a good deal about these things in other chapters.

Tuning up Existing Boats. Take trouble with the ship's bottom. Very few people get down to producing a really nice bottom. Yet the drag due to wrinkled dirty paint is just as great off shore as racing in the Solent. I prefer a bronze anti-foul, because it can be rubbed down after application. Don't forget to fair up, with rasp and cement, the underside of your keel, if it be of lead.

It is impossible properly to estimate the residual life of standing rigging. All we can do is to check that there are no obvious defects and then renew it if history indicates that it has had the equivalent of six full seasons, unless it is stainless steel when it should last a minimum of twelve seasons.

In old boats have special examination made of the shroud, runner and preventer chain plates, and the forestay and bobstay anchorages. Go over the spars with the foreman of the rigging loft just as soon as the boat is yours; and particularly the mast iron work. In the masting chapter (15) there is some information about alterations. Hollow wood spars near twenty years old must be suspect.

Reducing Leaks from the Deck. Remember that few cruising boats are constantly driven as hard as ocean racers and consequently few get water over their decks in the same regular quantity. Therefore however smart she is, check with a hose test that the deck and superstructure are made watertight, because there is nothing more discouraging than constantly wet berths. One expects a damp bed now and then, but not running water. For instance if necessary in an old boat canvas the decks; plenty of good paint under and over the canvas; cheap and effective. Make the sky-lights watertight with really good covers, or alternatively do away with the openings and fit a fixed light in place. The ordinary cover is often useless. The canvas needs to come down to deck level and be hauled taut by a draw-string in the hem under a projecting beading all round. The cover itself should be proofed either with a patent process or special solution, or by soaking in a mixture of three parts kerosene and one of boiled linseed oil. Some plastic covers are translucent.

Fore hatches mostly leak, but much can be done by thin rubber circular section jointing, and ensuring that there is a thumb-screw or screws to pull down on four sides—or one central man-sized screw and a strong back will do it. Remember that rubber is virtually incompressible and that it gets its jointing value by distorting. So by having a semi-circular section butting on a flat surface, or in some similar way, give it a chance to distort and

2

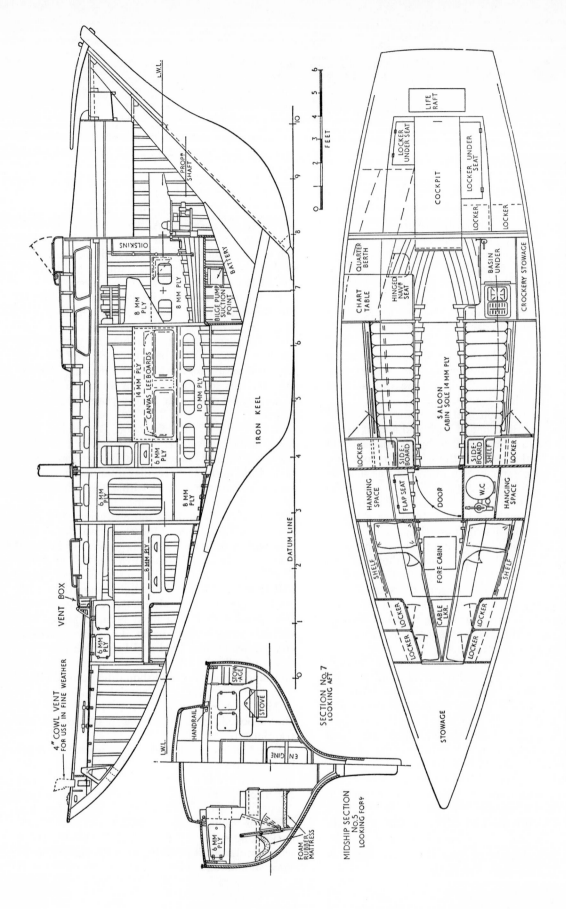

Diagram 1—*Maica*, won the British R.O.R.C. Class III and the French U.N.C. open offshore championship in 1962. Designed by Illingworth & Primrose and built by Burns of Bosham for Monsieur Henri Ronault. *Dimensions:* L.O.A. 33 ft.; L.W.L. 24 ft.; beam 8 ft. 11 in.; draft, 5 ft. 10 in. *Sail Measurements:* fore triangle, 226 sq. ft.; mainsail, 258 sq. ft.; total measured area, 484 sq. ft. I = 37 ft.; J = 12.2 ft.; B = 13.25 ft.; P = 39 ft.

make a tight joint. Rubazote gaskets are very good for this job. (But see drawing of our threecoaming-forehatch).

Bad leaks can sometimes be permanently cured by careful injections of jointing compound with a pressure gun, particularly in the case of a recessed or grooved joint.

Sliding hatches are less easy to make tight. But a proofed canvas envelope to cover the whole of the hatch-open portion, plus a slight projection aft, is a big help. For stopping up casual leaky seams after commissioning, electric light cable gland-sealing compound, which never hardens, is extremely handy. For making good any leaky ports and similar openings for race purposes only, heavy lanolin or mineral grease smeared on the *outside* of the joint is almost 100 per cent.

One way and another, for comparatively little expense the leakage in most boats can be reduced to an acceptable amount.

As regards old headsails one can do quite a bit about their cut by setting them up and sheeting them in moderate breezes from a flag pole in the garden, taking one halyard leg a long way back as a preventer. Spinnakers, too, can have a full power trial this way. In the case of all the sails if the canvas proves sound, but they are really old, have them completely re-stitched; the stitching almost invariably goes before good canvas, and I don't believe you can ever really test the stitching by hand throughout the sail.

Bad headsails with hard lines in the leech can sometimes be improved by fitting battens; or even cutting it bodily out into a curve. Other defects in their set will need the attention of the sailmaker. But don't be content with an ill-shaped sail. Old or new, it can be improved. Conversely, I have won races with a threadbare mainsail, which had been well looked after; so thin that you could see the opposing boats nicely through it.

Take every available chance to view your boat, with one expert friend perhaps, from outside. Get her really trimmed for racing—it is not much good otherwise—and have her sailing her best to windward, in charge of the mate. Then make repeated circuits round her in a motor boat critically studying the sails, rigging, and spars. If this can't be arranged get a tow astern on a long painter in the dinghy, giving her in turn, a sheer to weather and to leeward with a paddle.

For the rest, look through the notes on the various parts of the ship in other chapters of the book and see what can be done in an existing boat and within the scope of a reasonable budget. Don't as a rule make any alteration that is not necessary to the efficiency of the ship. Every alteration costs money,

is a worry, and a risk; well justified if you have an object clearly in mind, and often not otherwise.

Ordering a New Boat. Just a few words about ordering a new boat. As a sort of general rule decide on the size of ocean-racing boat you want and can afford, and then cut its length by 10 per cent. You may then have a little over when the boat is finished, to keep her up to concert pitch. A smaller boat better maintained is nearly always more satisfactory and more pleasure to own, as a racer, than one you just can't afford to keep properly.

However, there are the low limits of size, which one wants to watch, to ensure acceptability; specially in the U.S.A. where unfortunately the limit is changeable, and often based on rating.

If you have a good idea of what you want, give your naval architect the whole works on paper; but tell him that it is for guidance not a bible, and that the underwater part is all his affair. So often I hear people say—'the boat was not what I really wanted' or 'I don't really think he understood what I asked for'. Poor man, erudite as he may be, he has not second sight and in the absence of some decent directive can only guess at what the owners really mean.

You may on the other hand not be entirely certain of the shape of the ship you want. In this case go to an architect well up in ocean racing and after subtracting 20 per cent from your original estimate, tell him what you can afford to lay out, and which races you want to tilt at. Then give him a completely free hand to prepare outline drawings. Have a look at these and make minor amendments to the accommodation and superstructure as you wish, and he can then fair things up in detail.

Standardisation. As a third alternative you can choose a repeat of a successful boat, or one of the standard ocean racing designs, of which there are many examples in this book.

More trouble and thought has gone into these designs and their equipment than the ordinary owner would be able to muster. In the Maica class, for instance, built at C.M.N. and at Chevertons, the keels, bulkheads and so on are batch-produced for cheapness, while moulds and drawings serve again. But the specification and the equipment are still of the highest class. So an owner gets a better boat for his money than otherwise, and he can fit up the inside, the deck and rig, within limits, to his pleasure.

Production at the Chantiers Mécaniques de Normandie at Cherbourg is one of the boldest and, to date, the best-executed scheme in Europe for series production of ocean racers. Here Class II or Class III yachts are laid down in batches of ten and J.O.G. boats in batches of twenty-five, in a shed as big as a cathedral, with overall travelling cranes for moving complete yachts, special painting bays, and a separate bay for applying fibreglass under controlled temperature. Thus a considerable economy is achieved.

In Italy at Offanengo, near Milan, Alpa have in recent years created a similar enterprise for the production of glass fibre yachts. At the time of writing one offshore yacht to our design comes off the line about every four days; either the Alpa '11', the Alpa '9' or the Alpa '8'; to Class III, IV, and V respectively.

As time goes on we shall see more of these first-class batch-produced boats for offshore work, just as we have seen them for inshore racing in the past, because they offer the best chance of reducing the cost of building and equipping boats.

3

THE CONDUCT OF A RACE

The day approaches for the first big event; our weeks of thought and preparation are nearly complete. At this point the skipper and his navigtor should spend some little while on their pilots and charts, unless they are unusually familiar with the course, refreshing their minds concerning the strength and direction of the tidal sets at various periods and in various places, such as off headlands and in narrow places, which are likely to be important; memorising the relative strengths in- and off-shore and so on. The relative positions of the marks and leading obstructions to searoom should be briefly studied so that one sees the chart nicely in one's mind's eye. A few notes, including the direct magnetic courses between marks, may be made.

Getting to terms with the course details is more helpful than many people accustomed to chart work might imagine. It often enables one to arrive much more quickly at a decision as to the proper course of action, on a sudden change of wind or weather, or in case of temporary accident to some gear.

Of course, the time you will require will depend on the unfamiliarity of the waters and the nature of the course. Before the first Sydney–Hobart race in 1945 I was a complete stranger to the Australian waters south of Sydney, in which there are important seasonal sets. As it was the first race over this course there was no previous race data to call on. So I spent several complete evenings on the charts and sailing directions and made fairly copious notes. I also sought out and talked to a good number of coastal skippers, including the trawler men. I was glad to have had time to do this; in the race I felt as I came to the various landmarks that they were already old friends appearing very much as one had expected.

If the start is in the morning, one gets the food, all except the fresh bread, and possibly greens, on board and stowed at least the day before and if possible one gets those crew members who are sleeping on board early to their bunks. It is generally better to leave inessential work than to have all hands toiling on the last night. But if there should be a last minute job to do, detail one or two hands to do it and encourage the rest to turn in. If the morning start is early, call the crew in good time and preferably get the dinghy stowed and lashed and things squared off while the cook is getting the breakfast. If it is wet or threatening keep the mainsail coat on; otherwise get that stowed too. Where necessary bring the sails out of their less accessible lockers into their proper sea stowages. Sometimes the fo'c'sle bunks are handy for this purpose, since at sea the crew will be sleeping in 'hot bunks' farther aft. If your interior arrangements are good there should be little other difference between harbour stowage and sea stowage. But get the boat tidy to start with. Then one can have a meal in peace.

The only excuse for a late trip ashore should be to fetch a late weather forecast, fresh bread and green vegetables, but if this is going to risk delay do it the night before. Unless you have a long sail to the start you can leave your headsails until you see what the conditions are to be like. Scuttles should be screwed up and greased round where necessary, that is to say, where rubber jointing is shaky.

As we make sail and blow up towards the marks, tension rises for the big moment of the start is at hand. It is wise to get down towards the start in good time to get one's meal decently digested and have time to look around and size things up. But longer than this at the start is unnecessary, and wearisome to the crew who will be keyed up.

One by one fellow competitors appear. One recognises old friends, some re-rigged, and looks around to spot the newcomers; the thrill of seeing the offshore fleet assemble is ever fresh.

If you know your own boat's capabilities don't pay too much attention to the canvas that other people are carrying. They may be sailing shorthanded; or making a wrong appreciation.

Every boat will be different, with different stability and different balance, and in any case one does not want to copy the other man's mistakes; besides he may be busy changing his mind. One will have studied the weather reports and possibly been able to get a last minute forecast from some local meteorological authority; one reserves judgment till, say, quarter of an hour before the five-minute gun and then after having a good look round and taking everything into consideration including the degree of protection which the early portion of the race will enjoy, perhaps in an estuary, one makes a decision as to the canvas to be carried. In a big boat, or where a reef is in question, decision is called for a few minutes earlier.

On the other hand if the start is in really light weather it is as well to have the sails (except when the spinnaker is in question), all set and broken out before the start, so that the wrinkles are given a chance to stretch out: in moderate fresh conditions you may chose to defer setting, for instance, the staysail, if you have two headsails, until just before the start, more particularly if it is a genoa staysail with a big overlap and likely to decrease one's manoeuvrability and visibility.

In the smaller sizes of racers, I am not convinced of the necessity for stopping up sails. It is often not possible to restop them at sea, on account of conditions generally, or because the sail is not dry. It involves therefore two different drills for setting sail, in addition to considerable extra preparation. If one does stop up sails it is important to use multiple turns only in way of and near the clew; with bigger sails put four turns at the clew, three next door, two next to that, then all single turns. There should be no turn within 3 ft. of the head of a headsail, or within 5 ft. in the case of a spinnaker.

And the Start! One's start should be made as keenly as if one's race was to be over a 6-mile instead of a 600-mile course, partly because one never knows how close the finish is going to be and partly because it sets the standard by which one is going to sail the whole race. A few seconds saved here and there soon in the course of days add up to many minutes. In the 1931 Channel Race of some 230 miles we won the Forsyth Cup for the first home in *Lo III* by 55 secs. from *Spica*. In the same year *Patience* led *Highland Light* over the Fastnet finish by about the same distance. In the 1937 race from St. Nazaire to Benodet *Maid of Malham* finished about two lengths ahead of *Ortac*. In the Giraglia in 1953 we had an overlap on *Swallow* 100 yds. from the finish.

Moreover, particularly under light conditions, there is always at the start a chance to get clear of the fleet, and keep for a time out of a lot of other chaps' foul wind. In 1947 at Plymouth, in the start of the race to La Rochelle *Latifa*, *Myth of Malham* and *Cohoe* were the only ones to drop their kedges really adjacent to the line. In the fickle breezes which came up after the start the few yards advantage which these three had was converted into almost as many miles lead over their class mates.

The start will generally be made in sheltered or semi-sheltered waters. If you judge that once outside, oilskins will be required, it is advisable to get the crew to put on trousers, at least, before the start, otherwise with the interest and incident of the start and the first leg of the course skins may be donned too late and half the crew will start the race in wet togs. If the crew are oilskin covered, one can station some of them, and directly after the start, forward on deck. Otherwise the whole crew will be in or about the cockpit and she will be down by the stern until one settles down to watches.

Settling Down. Once clear of the start and the ensuing incidents settle down to watches as soon as convenient. Otherwise one finds the natural tendency is for everyone to spend the first eight hours on deck and then all to be comparatively weary at once.

Night sailing is specially important and many races are lost at night. One has known boats that habitually get behind their proper place in the race during the night watches. At night it is difficult to be certain that one's sails are trimmed correctly on the wind; helmsmanship needs special attention. And it is very easy to pinch a boat at night, partly because the speed through the water seems deceptively greater than it really is.

For all these reasons special vigilance and alertness are required during the dark hours. Moreover one never knows when an emergency may arise, such as a sprung spar needing repair, or a torn sail which requires the watch below to sit up stitching. So it is up to the skipper tactfully to insist that crew members off watch get into their bunks and get all the proper rest they can, right from the early stages of any long race.

One will be comparing one's performance with other boats against which one has sailed before. If one's own speed is better or worse than usual one must at once try to see why; study the set of the sails in both boats and learn from it. But it is when out of sight of the other boats that difficulty arises in keeping up the interest of one's watches; and let it be said one's own interest, if one is skippering! Everyone should be sail trimming and steering with the same meticulous care that would be employed if a rival boat were creeping up on the weather quarter; and it is quite a nice test to ask oneself from time to time whether one is in fact doing this.

If every boat in an ocean race were sailed as hard and carefully throughout the race as it is for the first few hours after the start and generally the last few minutes before the finish, what a lot of time would be saved in the course of a season!

Talking of sail trimming, one must impress on

one's crew that one can hardly give too much attention to this. The mate of the watch or if the mate happens to be steering, someone else with the necessary knowledge, should repeatedly go forward and examine critically what is going on. And the emphasis should be on the 'critical'; not just a glance and thought that all is well, but a searching desire to better the set and propulsive efficiency of the sails.

The actual technique of sail trimming is discussed in detail in three other chapters, but it is as well to recall that it is not just a matter of adjusting the sheet. The position of the headsail sheet lead may need adjustment, probably forward or aft, but possibly even inboard or outboard. The leech line may need easing, to get rid of a hard ridge, or tautened to quell a bad quiver.

Different wind strengths and small changes in the direction call for sail trimming; but also the moisture content in the air and the temperature will be varying, all of which will affect the set of the sails. As the season progresses all sails will in addition be progressively stretching, and so the position of the sheet lead will need continual adjustment.

When one has a long reach or run under fairly steady conditions it is fun to get keen competition going between the port and starboard watches to see which watch can make the most miles by the patent log during their respective spells. Everyone in the watch should be encouraged to take an interest in the set of the sails, and to make suggestions with a view to improving their set. The decision as to an adjustment, other than simple sheeting will still rest with the mate of the watch, but the fact that several minds are working on the problem stimulates everybody. A little competition is healthy here, as in most other places.

The mate may be taking a look at the chart. I should be glad to hear a call from a hand on deck 'Mr. Mate, I think the Yankee sheet lead can be moved a foot aft'—comes the mate to have a critical look. 'I believe you're right' and back she goes.

At this point I can hear you, gentle reader, saying to yourself that if you follow all this advice, life at sea is going to be pure hard work instead of fun, and that you would rather sail along more peacefully. I can only reply that the keenest crews I have met have generally been the happiest; though truth to tell, I can hardly remember an unhappy one, offshore racing.

The Post Mortem. Apart from paying unrelaxed attention to the job of ship driving, the thing which wins races is not so much brilliant strokes of tactical genius as the business of avoiding mistakes. After a race I try and tot up the cost of mistakes I

have made. They come to a surprising total of time, and they serve to keep one humble and, one hopes, to assist in avoiding a repetition at least of these particular faults.

In the case of the Fastnet of 1947 which we won with *Myth of Malham*, here, from my notebook, are a list of mistakes and the time I estimate they cost us.

(1) Starting too close under the starting vessel and late at the line.—$\frac{3}{4}$ min.

(2) Working the Isle of Wight shore too close after rounding St. Catherine's (misreading of tidal information on chart).—Direct loss, 18 mins.

(3) Indirect loss due to getting too close to Dorset shore—difficult to calculate—perhaps—1 hr.

(4) Hanging on too long to the ghosting genoa when wind freshened and came ahead off the Lizard.—4 mins.

(5) Snarl-up when changing a headsail at night turning to windward due to failure of a halyard winch, etc.—6 mins.

(6) Landfall made 8 miles too far to the west of Scillies due to use of steel winch handle near to the compass.—1 hr. 15 mins.

If one can lose time this way in light and moderate weather, how much more time can one lose in heavy weather. Snarl-ups of gear are apt to be more serious and time-consuming, because the heavy motion and the water coming over slows one's movements on deck. And in heavy weather there is an awful temptation to let things be when one knows some adjustment or sail change should be made. In general very little time is lost by reducing sail a little early—a little before the optimum point—in freshening conditions. The change will be more readily and quickly accomplished, and you will not carry any running gear as you might by hanging on. Much more time is, on the whole, lost by delay in setting more sail when the wind lightens. One is apt to hang back to make sure the change in wind has come to stay; then by the time the new sail is up on deck and hanked on and the change has been accomplished, the wind is quite light and one realised with an inward prick of conscience that it was an overdue change.

On the other hand, just because one has made mistakes, all is not lost, for clearly the other chaps are making their quota of errors, and having their share of ill luck. Almost anything may happen to turn the tables, so unless one can see several smaller vessels ahead, one need never assume that one is out of the running. And in British racing, every boat you beat makes another point for your own club in the ocean racing Inter Club Championship; even if you are the penultimate finisher.

I remember very well making our way at night

up the Derwent river towards the finish of the first Sydney–Hobart Race, and the state of doubt and apprehension of the crew, as to our position. We encountered wind of gale force from right ahead for about thirty hours on the second and third days. We knew that at the time the southerly buster broke, several of the bigger yachts were well ahead of us, and we had seen no other boat for five days. Our wireless had chucked its hand in, and we had no news. We were of very small displacement and had made very slow progress to windward in the gale; I felt the bigger boats must have got away from us then. Moreover we had had calms some of the time towards the finish—the sort of maddening calms that conjure up before one's eyes visions of the crews of bigger rivals already popping the champagne corks ashore.

A launch full of chaps came down the river to identify us and gave us a very hearty cheer. I hailed back and asked them how many boats were in ahead of us, which was greeted with more cheers and loud laughter. I could feel a sort of inaudible groan go up from the crew, as repeated inquiries only brought more laughter. We did not realise that they in the launch thought they were having their legs quietly pulled, and it took us some moments to find out the truth—that we were first home. As it turned out the next boat was 23 hrs. behind us. So you see, one can never tell.

Taking Shelter. Talking of heavy weather, brings one to the question of taking shelter during a race. There is no doubt that there are times when it pays to shelter for a short while—for effecting repairs, giving the crew a short respite or some other specific purpose. As an instance I recall Lyn Martin with Don Robertson and his brother as mates, turning *Janet* in behind the handy shelter of a prominent headland, after running up the New South Wales coast in a strong southerly blow during the 1946 Lion Island Race. He had a full mainsail set and was going like a train close behind us; and we wondered at his action. As he reached shelter he shot her up into the wind, downed the big mainsail and hoisted the smaller hardweather sail. Almost before we realised what he was doing, he was out at sea again; a fine bit of seamanship. A mile or two later when we had rounded Lion Island we came hard on the wind for a dead beat to windward in the same southerly, and *Janet* was nicely canvassed for the job, and went on to win handsomely. Meanwhile we were wrestling with a whole plethora of trouble—a split mainsail, then a split jib; and finally a clean carry away of the forestays, due to a bolt letting go, which eased the stick neatly over the side under rather trying conditions, with a big sea running.

Permitting ourselves another digression, this race afforded a most interesting example of the use of twin spinnakers. We had come out of Sydney Harbour to a strong southerly breeze with a dead run up the New South Wales coast and a fair bit of sea running. I set two genoas as spinnakers from the usual head of the fore triangle which was some 11 ft. or so below the masthead; one sheeted to the main boom and the other to the spinnaker boom, and lowered the mainsail. We were able to run straight and comfortably for the mark way up the coast, while almost everyone else was unable to keep the wind dead aft in that seaway and had to run miles up to windward, gybe, and turn back. Probably lack of proper fore guys to the booms contributed to their difficulties. Anyway, when we got up to Lion Island we were ahead of a great many larger faster boats. Twin spinnakers were, I believe, barred the following year. But if the leeward headsail were hanked on to a stay it would set equally well, and there should be no objection to lowering the mainsail, under R.Y.A. or R.O.R.C. rules.

Returning to the question of putting in during a race, when the shelter is very handy and where one goes in for a special reason for an essential job and for a limited time, no exception can be taken to such an action. But as a general rule all question of sheltering should be kept out of one's mind and out of the minds of the crew, because any such thoughts will clearly be bad for morale.

A good instance of a legitimate sheltering might be, early in a race, the necessity for re-reeving a halyard which could not be managed, probably, in the seaway with winds of gale force.

Apart from this, very occasionally there arises a time when general sea-sickness and crew exhaustion make sheltering almost the only alternative to retiring; and in such circumstances clearly the preferable one. These conditions are naturally more likely in a small boat. They are nothing to reproach oneself about and have, I fancy, happened to us all at some time or other. I suggest that in a case of this sort when you get into shelter, which need not necessarily be a harbour, but just a good quiet lee, that on dropping the hook, or on heaving to, the skipper makes up his mind as to the minimum length of time necessary to rehabilitate the crew and the yacht. Perhaps it is only time for a meal and pump out the boat. Maybe it is a meal plus a three-hour caulk. But in any case I feel it is important that the skipper tells the crew when they come in just how long they have to rest and does his best to stick to it, regardless of the weather. The business of coming in and waiting for weather to moderate is unsatisfactory because everyone is unsettled wondering what the programme is going to be; very likely it leads to unsatisfactory discussion as to the proper moment to proceed.

First Races Offshore. These thoughts lead one naturally to the consideration of a related matter as to when a new owner should feel ready to 'start entering' for races. Owners sometimes say to me something of this sort, 'I am keen to start ocean racing but feel I should do some more practice cruises first and perhaps enter next year.' The fear of the possibility of having to retire from races, entered in the early stages, deters some people. To them I say that by far the best way to get proficient is to start racing as soon as you, or your deckmaster, has sufficient experience to go offshore in safety; providing of course you have a nucleus of strong crew members and a well-found ship. You may learn as much in an average week-end offshore race, keenly sailed, as in a fortnight's cruising. There is always a competent crew hand or two to be had, if one gets round to searching for them in good time.

Provided the boat is seaworthy, has a crew suitable to her size and someone on board with a knowledge of coastal navigation, then there is no reason why one should not have a go. In R.O.R.C. or J.O.G. racing very possibly one will be relegated to the Beta division, which is intended for less modern racing and cruising boats, who are, perhaps not so completely fitted out for racing as the open division. Very possibly in the first season one may find in one or two races that one has to retire; but it is better to have sailed and put in, than never to have raced at all. And meanwhile one is having a great deal of fun, and amassing experience at a great rate.

4

AT THE HELM

This short chapter is addressed primarily to the newcomer to offshore racing. Helmsmanship is one of the most fascinating sides of any sailing and ocean racing is no exception. It is by no means a black art but one which can readily be learnt by a little patient study, understanding and practice.

The primary differences between inshore and offshore steering are that off shore we have to compete with the motion of the ship in a seaway, and we have under those conditions to learn to steer steadily by a compass.

About half the time the steering will be on a plain reach or run when no very special skill is needed. But what is required is a great deal of concentration, to keep the ship as close as possible to her course with the minimum use of the helm. This means a little more than simply watching the compass because we must learn to anticipate to a mild degree the swing of the ship's head and to meet it with early and small movements of the helm; things which in time will become automatic and second nature. A few people can steer indefinitely without apparently tiring, having acquired the habit of subconscious concentration. But as a general rule when reaching or running it pays to work tricks of half an hour, so that during this period one can concentrate completely. And to help the helmsman concentrate, don't chat to him; nor to others in a loud distracting way.

It is a strange thing how many people don't realise when they are steering a zig-zag course. Occasionally, one can get the helmsman to look behind him in fine weather. The sight of the wiggly wake, showing a few hundred yards astern very often, and thrown into relief by the foreshortened view, has a salutary effect on a self-satisfied steersman. Equally strange is that some people who have a great deal of sailing experience have not acquired the knack—it is no more—of steering with the minimum use of helm. They let the boat swing away from her course; jam the helm down; she comes up and past the course and the helm is tweaked violently to weather. Conversely, some people take to steering on a reach in a few minutes and having acquired the knack hardly ever go wrong.

It is worth remembering that in many circumstances, the deviations from course are due to the waves passing under her and lifting first her quarter and then her bow, or vice versa. If left to herself she will, to a large extent, keep a steady mean course, and fighting the helm in attempting to avoid these undulations will only make her roll, and retard her.

When reaching or running it is preferable for the racing helmsman to occupy himself solely with steering and to have someone else to do the sail trimming and lookout, so that he may give his whole attention to holding carefully to the course.

Getting to Windward. Getting a boat to windward is of course a different thing, and does to some extent require real experience, though often less concentration than on a reach. It also requires some knowledge of the boat; the best of helmsmen take some little while to get the feel of a strange boat; and having got it in one weight of wind he may find further experience and guidance is necessary under other circumstances. So I am always glad in a strange boat to have an older crew hand give one frank advice, 'Now we are into the lop more you won't be able to hold her up that high' or 'her best speed under these conditions should be just six knots'—looking at the speed variation indicator. And by the same token I try and sit, in my own boats, with the new helmsman for a little while and see what he makes of it and whether I can help him.

While naturally one wants everyone in the crew to get some steering, should there be a complete beginner say in each watch, it is, when the yacht is on the wind, best for him to be occupied with other tasks; to await more steering experience when cruising. Meanwhile when racing he can learn by noting carefully how the helmsman gets her along, what indications the helmsman is using; sometimes his shroud tell-tales, sometimes his masthead flag, or by watching a certain point in the luff of the mainsail; or again he may in light weather be sitting to leeward and watching the luff of a jib. By sitting quietly alongside a good helmsman one unconsciously absorbs the technique; the rhythm or timing of his helm movements with respect to the boat in the seaway, and the correct reactions to the small variations in wind and sea.

When you take over a boat on the wind in fresh or strong conditions in a seaway, ask the last incumbent what speed he has been registering on the speed indicator, if you have one. Then sail her for a few moments jolly full; get her tramping along first; then very quietly edge her up towards the wind, giving her time after each edgement to settle down to a steady speed. So after a little while you will find out how she will go best for you, and you will be able to confirm the best speedometer speed. At night the ability to turn the light on the speed and check that you are doing your knots and therefore not pinching her, is a great help and comfort, because speed at night is deceptive; you may think you are going a great rate and not realise that you are a knot and a half under the optimum.

On the wind in moderate conditions some helmsmen are so afraid of being labelled pinchers that they habitually sail the boat too full. I am of the opinion that, in general in good modern yachts, more time is lost in this way than by pinching. The latter condition generally announces itself by the lifting or slatting of headsails. If lifting does not occur as soon as you pinch it means that the headsail or sails are sheeted too hard.

But the converse does not apply; one can happily sail too full without any noisy or very obvious signs manifesting themselves.

It is a fact which can readily be demonstrated by instruments at rest, that the wind is rarely constant in direction for more than a few seconds. Thus it is probable that any helmsman who holds an absolutely steady course on a moderate wind for long periods is not in fact getting the best out of the boat.

He should have been testing the wind by very gently working her up and letting her come off again so that after a while he is constantly making tiny alterations of course, almost subconsciously, to suit the small drifts in wind direction. But at this point it must be emphasised that we are speaking of moderate conditions of wind and sea. In heavier conditions or a tumble of sea we cannot afford to luff, because quite a loss of speed occurs quickly when we momentarily get too close on the wind.

On the other hand it must be borne in mind that in any reasonably close-winded yacht (carrying overlapping headsails in anything of a breeze to windward) the luff of the mainsail will be continuously alift, and that this does not mean that the sail is unhappy, especially with terylene sails. If we sailed off to fill the sail we would probably be sailing much too full.

Exceptions to this rule are less weatherly craft that cannot stand the sails pinned in, and yachts with very flat mainsails; either gaff sails or bermudian sails with insufficient curve or flow in them.

Except in very small yachts or in exceptionally heavy weather, you will generally find it best to drive her to windward at the same speed off shore in a seaway, as you would in calm water with the same amount of wind. That is to say sail her at the same speed, but owing to the sea, not so close.

Naturally this is only a general rule and cannot invariably be applied. But it is certainly a good guide and guards against what sometimes is done, which is to trim the sheets and sail her as though she were in calm water, and travel at literally half the speed.

Some boats with long full bow overhangs, pound like billy-oh going to windward. The boat feels as though she is being dropped on the pavement every few seconds. One wonders that every fastening in the boat is not loosened. After half a day of it, one is sure one's back teeth have been. Just occasionally by sailing a shade closer or a shade freer one can legitimately reduce the pounding, in that particular length of sea. But most generally any pandering to it spoils her performance; since reduction in pounding has generally been achieved either by luffing and slowing her unduly, or by bearing away more than is acceptable. You just have to stick it, and grin if you can.

Incidentally one need not feel that one is damaging the hull unduly. The worst you are likely to do is to disturb the caulking in the foreward part of the boat. The worst pounder I ever owned is now well over fifty years old and still racing! I do think however that in such boats one should keep an extra sharp lookout on one's standing rigging and associated fittings.

Heavy Weather Steering. Turning to the question of steering in heavy weather, one finds in books erudite instructions about watching the seas and easing her over the extra big ones, and so on; sometimes to luff a little, sometimes to bear away a shade, and so forth. In general I am not at all impressed with the necessity for this, nor for the advisability of it from a racing point of view. If she is anything like a good boat, and is properly canvassed for the weather, she will find her way up and over and down the other side of the biggest seas perfectly happily. The helmsman's time in general is better spent in keeping the boat sailing steadily and at her best speed, with the minimum of helm, rather than in trying clever dodges to ease her over the seas. If you doubt this think of the gale conditions in driving rain at night. It will then be virtually impossible to judge the oncoming seas, but your boat does not need eyes; if you have trimmed her sails reasonably, she will get right on with the job.

There is one partial exception to this rule which is with heavy quartering seas which look specially like breaking on board. I think that it is worth occasionally, if you happen to see a specially ominous one, putting the helm up and bringing her more or less stern on to it. But here again the thing is not as necessary as it appears; and when a dark night falls, then all the wave crests look about equally large and vague and whitely foam capped. Once again you have to leave it largely to the boat.

In bad weather, when heeled, there must be a taut line round the helmsman. This will leave both hands free for the tiller.

Rhythmic Rolling. Going downwind in a seaway in fresh or strong breezes, particularly with the spinnaker set, often produces a slow roll, which builds up in amplitude as successive seas pass under the boat, until the booms may dip each side. I have christened it rhythmic rolling. The sail trimming implications are dealt with in the chapter on spinnakers, but as this is a chapter for helmsmen, we must mention it here too. The fact that you have now been warned that it may take place to an apparently alarming degree has, I hope, itself reduced its terrors.

The phenomenon is due primarily to the action of the seas passing under the ship in lifting the weather quarter and letting down the lee bow and a moment later vice versa, at regular intervals. This starts a regular roll; the spinnaker being free to swing a good bit about its masthead incites the ship at each swing to a bigger and better roll, like one does as a child on a swing, until the swing rides high into the air. Only in the case of the boat things are reversed, and the mast swings farther at each roll towards the sea.

Some boats are worse rollers than others—those with a tendency to gripe, or run up into the wind, badly balanced boats, being generally bad culprits.

The palliatives are chiefly in the hands of the sail trimmer, but the helmsman can help quite a bit by fighting the roll as little as possible. If he fights it, four times out of five he will be unconsciously playing the swing game and, by making the boat sheer sharply, will be increasing the roll. As far as is feasible, that is to say without letting her broach to or gybe, let the boat find her own way out of the trouble.

Assessing the Course. It is absolutely necessary that at the end of his trick the helmsman should be able to assess accurately the mean course he has steered during his watch. It is clearly equally necessary that he should be honest about it; not simply report parrot-like the course that was ordered.

There may have been conditions of wind or sea which made it impracticable for him to keep exactly to his mean course; and a deviation from it during his trick is of small moment—provided he logs the actual course steered. In the same way on the wind be sure you are not guilty of wishful thinking, and reporting an optimistically high course for logging.

It is difficult at the end of an hour for the helmsman or men to remember exactly what happened earlier in the hour and to average up, particularly in variable windward conditions. So when racing I log the course made good every quarter or half hour, and there are always separate columns for course ordered and course made good.

And so even when on the wind, when the helmsman is steering by his sails, he will have to keep glancing at his compass so that he can report accurately on the mean course. And apart from this, in a seaway, particularly at night when the sails and tell-tales may be difficult to see, the compass is often a real help even on the wind. At night it is occasionally easier to steer on a star, checking your course now and then on the compass. And if there should be a landmark ahead, clearly you will use this, checking from time to time on your compass to see if you are being set off to one side or the other.

Some boats can have their masthead racing flags illuminated by small electric lights; it is particularly valuable in the larger ocean-racing yachts where the masthead flag will be up to 90 ft. above the deck. But if your racing flag is partly light in colour it is not too difficult in a smaller boat with a mast height under 60 ft. to flash a beam torch on the flag and/or the shroud tell-tales, from time to time. To leave the masthead light on continuously is contrary to the International Rule of the Road —when under sail only; unless it is shrouded.

In well-balanced boats it is sometimes desirable to let the tiller move to and fro a little when the sea puts the pressure on.

Mite needed it sometimes to do her best. And *Myth* is an interesting example. On occasions when going to windward one gets the sails exactly balanced; one can then let go the tiller and she will maintain her course, while the speed variation indicator will show a small but definite increase.

The tiller will move to and fro over a small arc, as though some kindly ghost were gently guiding her. Actually the rudder is simply reacting to the flow of the water leaving the underbody of the boat, and adjusting itself to cause the minimum of resistance; forming a sort of flexible streamlined tail. *Maica* will sometimes do the same.

Try, when at the helm, a variety of seating

positions until you find the best for each kind of steering. She may be heeled or on a level keel; maybe on the wind when you will need to be positioned so as to get a good sight of the sails and tell-tales, or on the reach when your chief thought will be for the compass. In a seaway try and get a position where you are well wedged in, so that you have good control over the wheel or tiller. For instance one of my favourite positions with tiller steering and with the boat heeled, is with my feet on the edge of the cockpit seat opposite, and my knees raised up so that I can steady my tiller arm on them. This in turn steadies the tiller under conditions when one can steer with an inch or two's movement each way.

It is well worth while to consider a small alteration to the cockpit—a higher seat or a footrest perhaps—to improve one's comfort and therefore efficiency when steering.

It is a help to have a reasonably stiff positive tiller, from which all back lash has been eliminated. Remember that the leverage you get is a function of the distance your hand is from the nearest point on the rudder stock, that is in a line at right angles to it, and not of the right length of tiller lying along the deck. So a short tiller growing out at near right angles to the stock from just above the cockpit floor, is advantageous; it is stiffer, lighter and takes up less boat room.

Wheel Steering. In the case of wheel steering there are some excellent gears on the market which give one quite a feel of the boat. But the smaller the boat the quicker she will need her helm applied, and the less will be the torque on the rudder necessary. So for smaller yachts the gear ratio of turns to operate must be less; three-quarters of a turn to hard-over from amidships should be plenty.

Another advantage of wheel steering is that it normally brings the helmsman farther aft, where he is clear of the sheet workers and where he can glance up at the masthead flag with less up-craning of the neck. On the other hand he will be able to see much less of the headsails to leeward for light weather and there will be a trace more motion right aft.

To sum up our conclusions on steering, on the wind miss no chance to sit beside a good helmsman and see the way things go; the manner in which indicators are used, and the small amount of helm necessary. On the reach or run, get into the habit of noting whether the boat is really off her course, or whether she is merely weaving a little, as she goes about her business, due to the action of the seaway. And be constantly trying to judge whether a boat is really doing her best; going as fast as conditions of wind and sea permit. This is a thing which repays continuous study.

5

THE CREW

Numerical Strength. The first problem is to decide the total strength of the crew. Many considerations enter into the question but at the outset I will say that in my view it is far better to have too large rather than too small a crew. When in doubt, take that extra hand, or couple of hands maybe, if the boat is a big one. Remember in the first place the guiding principle we have set ourselves—to give nothing away at any time. This presupposes a standard of handling comparable with inshore racing. Admittedly it may not actually be possible in practice, but anyway that is what in the first instance we must aim at. This means that one watch must be able to put the ship about, set up the backstays and sheet the headsails without any avoidable delay. And that requires that the watch on deck shall be fully sufficient to man the winch or winches.

Except in small boats, the helmsman should have nothing to do except steer, for almost every time he takes his attention off the helm to back up on the tail of a sheet, or to trim a sheet with both hands while the tiller is jammed by his stern, the boat will wander a bit. And if the crew is really up to strength it should be possible to perform any operation in the boat except reefing, without calling the watch below; except perhaps in very small boats.

If the skipper stands out of a watch, and there is much to recommend this, then we can allow that he will be on deck, as well as the watch for changes of headsail, setting and gybing the spinnaker. In fact we require one crew on deck and one crew on watch below; or at least the skipper and one watch should constitute an adequate crew, in the regatta sense. If the crew is too small and part of the watch below has to be called to change the larger headsails or to set the spinnaker, not only is time lost in getting the men turned out, but they are probably only half awake when they do come on deck. Moreover their eyes may not be accustomed to the dark as yet. Almost invariably they will be less than fully clad, and go back to their bunks cold and perhaps wet. Clearly as the race goes on the crew that is being continually turned out in their watch below may get progressively more tired and less efficient.

But worse in practice than that is the effect on the skipper of wondering whether he should call the extra hand or hands; it often results in delay in deciding on a change of sail or a gybe. This indecision would probably never have occurred had he had a sufficient team on deck and ready. The skipper should be able to feel that his crew is numerically strong enough to enable him to order all changes of sail and any other required work regardless of considerations of failing efficiency due to exhaustion.

Again a big crew provides a reserve against one or more members being incapacitated by minor injury, illness, seasickness, or even sore hands; and it helps to make the gap less serious, if at the last minute before the start someone does not show up. Obvious, you may say, but, taken along with other aspects, an argument you cannot afford to ignore.

Dyed-in-the-wool cruising men are often exponents of the small or moderate-sized crew. They have been accustomed to handling their ships in a seamanlike manner with limited hands. And maybe they, used to the space and ease of cruising, unconsciously resent the contrast of crowded conditions when racing with a big crew. However, seamanlike procedure often falls a good deal short of racing requirements.

Consider the case of a 6-metre racing in the class—a highly developed one—where you can bet your bottom dollar no unnecessary weight is tolerated. They carry five hands, in spite of having a very simple sail plan.

Systems of Watches. I have assumed that one is working the ship watch and watch, because I do not see that there is any serious alternative. Personally I work ordinary sea-going watches—that is to say four-hour watches except for the first and last dogs—the two-hour watches from four in the afternoon to six and from six to eight. This is of course designed to dodge the sequence which would otherwise bring the same watch on at the same time each day; one presumes the word 'dogs' is a corruption of 'dodge'. This system is good in that it involves changes of watch at convenient meal times; between the morning and forenoon watches at eight for breakfast, before the afternoon at noon for midday dinner, tea at four, and supper at 'twenty hundred' before the first.

I have heard the six hours night watches strongly argued; dividing the eight to eight stretch into two and relieving at 2 a.m. The pro is that each watch gets a chance of a straight five to five-and-a-half hours' sleep. The cons, and I fancy they very much outweigh the pros, revolve around the inability of the average crewman to remain alert for as long as six hours at night.

In heavy weather, that is to say with wind of gale force and with the boat reduced to storm canvas, I have occasionally broken temporarily into three watches of two hours each; but only on occasions when it was fairly clear that conditions were set for a long steady blow. With storm canvas set and trimmed there is not much to be done on deck, except to steer and keep a lookout. When cruising one would probably be hove-to and more comfortable, but racing one keeps the boat sailing as long as possible before heaving-to, and being on deck particularly in a small boat where the tops of the seas are falling on board frequently, is apt to become exhausting if the gale is a prolonged one. Under such circumstances these shorter two hour watches may pay. But I repeat only when things are set and settled.

The Skipper. There is a lot to be said for the skipper standing out of the watches. If he takes a watch he is sure to get called out frequently during his watch below, and may tire himself out. Or alternatively, if he is not shaken decisions have to be taken in his absence; or a decision delayed until his turn on deck is due. It is of the first importance that the skipper should be readily available, remain active, alert, and on the call whenever he is required, from starting gun to finishing gun, and to this end the ability to slip below for a few minutes or hours of rest whenever conditions allow, is of the greatest value. Anything less than full vitality on the part of the skipper subconsciously communicates itself to the crew and tones down their performance.

There is an old cliché that the skipper should never send a man on a job that he is not prepared to do himself. Perhaps it might be safer to say a job which the skipper would not have been prepared to do at the other man's age. But leaving that fine distinction aside, it is perhaps this and similar maxims which result in some skippers rushing into the fray at every opportunity; grabbing to secure a flogging sail, wrestling with a seized slide, or on the stem head, when the genoa has to come in and so on. The immediate result is that he can't take an overall view of proceedings and is unable to control the evolution in hand. The secondary effect is that he tires himself out before the race is over, and his efficiency falls off; his judgment may suffer; his decisions will certainly be less speedy; he may become irritable and upset himself and his crew.

He is probably older than most of his hands and will almost certainly be on deck a far larger proportion of the race than his crew, who if it is a well-organised boat will be getting their regular watch below. Therefore the skipper should save himself, remembering the fate of the armies where the generals tried to act as platoon commanders. And he should *from the start of the race* take every chance, when things are quiet, to snatch a little sleep. It is very tempting to stop on deck during the early parts of the race—both for the skipper and the crew—to see the fun; particularly tempting because often one is then in company with a good many of the fleet. The skipper must insist that within a few hours of the start the crew start regular watch-keeping, and by the same token must rest himself. To go below out of the wind and strong light, and relax, is worth-while rest even if one does not sleep.

One more point on this line—remember that it is more difficult to sail a boat perfectly at night than by day. An ill-trimmed sheet or a drop in speed from some similar cause is more liable to go for a time undetected. Sailing to windward is more difficult too, as all the 'aids' are less clearly distinguishable. And the natural habit of man being to sleep at night the crew are, though they might stoutly repudiate the suggestion, clearly liable to be less alert. For all these reasons the skipper wants to be about the deck at least as much if not more by night than by day. This applies with special force when the crew are not very experienced.

Which reminds me of an odd little happening. It was the last race of the season; there had been several changes from the regular crew, and on this account the crew was not fully acquainted with the boat. The course was only 110 miles, and so I decided to remain about throughout the race. Conditions were light and towards dawn, as I went below to write up the log, I was conscious of that accumulated tiredness which is apt to afflict one right at the end of a hard season. I remember making a desperate effort to write up the log and ward off sleep. A moment later I awoke still at the chart table aware that I had dreamt of the West Indies and sighting a strange sail. I went immediately on deck, reproving myself for having dozed off. I returned later to the chart table. No doubt obsessed with the necessity for writing up the log and not giving way to the charms of Morpheus, I found I had started, in my sleep, to record my dream in the log. In a drunken-like diagonal scrawl my hand had written of the sighting of a strange four-masted barque at dawn!

These remarks apply when there is the one skipper and deckmaster. There are of course other satisfactory alternative arrangements; for instance two partners in a syndicate may take charge of alternate watches. In this case it may be convenient for the navigator to stand out. If on the other hand the navigator keeps a watch it is very desirable that there should be a second plotter in the opposite watch. It is in fact entirely practicable to have the skipper indicating the course to be steered and the navigator of each watch simply plotting the vessel's position. If the skipper himself acts as a navigator, he should definitely stand out of watches, and unless the boat is a small one, allow a good deal of the sailing of the ship to devolve on the mates of the watches; the skipper saying *where* the boat is to go AND in addition plotting her exact position, and the mates attending in detail as to *how* to get her along the course as quickly as possible.

In a larger yacht both the skipper and the navigator should stand out of watches: say three in each watch and two out of the watches is a total of eight. Even in a crew of six, two out of the watches works well and allows of four for gybing ship without calling the watch below. In a larger yacht still one can stand three or four out of the watch—say in a total of twelve, four in each watch; and skipper, navigator, cook, and the paid hand (who knows the bosunary best) standing out.

Traditionally the owner is the skipper. But it would be far better for the owner in some instances to delegate this authority to another member of the afterguard. The make-up of a skipper should clearly include a fair knowledge of ocean racing in general, and an intimate knowledge of ship driving in particular; a capacity for taking charge, a reliable stomach, and tireless energy. These things are equally clearly not found in every owner. Though one does not question the owner's right to make his own mistakes, should that be his pleasure, it may well be in some cases that by transferring skippership to a more experienced friend, he would enjoy the racing more; have time to watch what was going on, to get those photos that he has always been meaning to take, and finish the race comparatively fresh into the bargain.

But having transferred skippership, let him for the sake of the ship and the happiness of the hands firstly make the position clear to the crew and subsequently give the skipper his head, and for better or for worse, not interfere or question his judgments.

Turning to the question of the duties of the individual crew members, it is the custom of inshore racing, and in some offshore racers, to allocate specific jobs on deck and to try to stick to them. Personally I have found that in practice, in the long run, this is impossible off shore. It is in consequence better for all the crew members to realise from the start that they may be required to do any job in the ship as the occasion arises. They will then take an interest in everything that is going on instead of specialising and finding themselves with a strange piece of gear in an emergency. Needless to say, during a particular evolution the skipper, mate or senior hand on the spot will spread the hands around on to specific jobs, one or two to the halyard, one on a guy, another two to the spinnaker boom and so on.

A completely new system of watches was suggested to me by David Parker. It is as follows. With a crew of five one has two on watch. Every one and a half hours a new man comes up. In case of need of a third man, for a sail change or reefing, one calls the next man on. This normally allows three hours on and four and a half hours below. If the third man is called, even very early, he still has had at least three hours below.

This system can only work with five very trained men, not needing continuously to seek the skipper's advice. The obvious advantage is the possibility of a higher proportion of time below in trying conditions; either of calm or heavy weather. But apart from this, having a new man on every one and a half hours may renew the watches' interest. It saves the scramble of several people changing into oilskins at the same moment, and all coming up temporarily night-blinded.

Variations of this system are to have five people watch-keeping, plus a stand out skipper, in a crew totalling six. Or in a big yacht to have two hands coming on every one and a half hours plus skipper and cook standing out of watches. The big snag is the timing of meals. I have not tried the system myself so I don't, out of hand, recommend it, but I consider it to be well worth considering in that it tends to assist that vital need: to help keep up the crews' attention on the job. As I have indicated, it is for the same reason that I don't, when racing, recommend the six-hour occasional watches.

Small Boat Organisation. Most of what I have written in this chapter applies to boats with crews of five to fifteen souls. Very small yachts racing at sea are to some extent a problem on their own. In *Tre-Sang*, which won the Class II British ocean racing championships in 1946, H. G. Hasler had a total of three hands. He had a 'watch' of one hand at the helm, who was able to trim the small sails at a pinch. He himself combined the duties of navigator, cook, and deckhand when required, snatching sleep when possible. This is a good organisation for a 20-ft. water-line J.O.G. yacht, which carries no spinnaker.

Merle of Malham my 1967 J.O.G. racer displaces 3 tons. One extra hand with his kit, the food necessary and the added four gallons of water would total at least 2.3 cwt., or a 4 per cent increase in primary displacement. Such a small crew would only be efficient when working with a very small and easily handled sail plan. *Merle*'s mainsail is about 200 sq. ft., or only a little under twice the size of a 14-ft. dinghy sail. And it has very efficient roller reefing. *Mouse of Malham*, R.O.R.C. Championship Class III winner, displaced even less—at 2.4 tons.

Specially built 24-ft. water-line light displacement ocean racers are boats of which we shall, I hope, see more as time goes on, with pockets becoming shallow with taxation and yachts' costs still increasing. For these boats a crew of four, which means two in a watch and the skipper not standing out, is a good organisation; or six for long races, when all the crew are not strong numbers.

Sea-sickness. If any reader considers this subject indelicate, I must ask him to turn over a few pages, for I propose to discuss frankly the ocean racing skippers' Public Enemy Number One. Quite a lot can be done if not to defeat him, at least to reduce the deadliness of his onslaughts.

Firstly, don't be shy about tackling the thing openly with the hands. This is necessary if we are to make the best of preparatory work, for I believe that quite a big proportion of sea-sickness is due either to an acid, or to an uncleared stomach. It is too late to tackle acidity adequately when we get to sea—it requires a week or ten days of quiet preparation ashore beforehand. This is clearly unnecessary for the fortunate ones with a cast-iron inside. But the trouble involved may be well worth while in other cases, and make all the difference between a happy ocean racing season and something of a penance. This method of approach to the problem was established in connection with landing operations in the 1914–18 war and confirmed again between 1940 and 1945.

The three principal culprits as regards acidity are fats, red meat, and alcohol. So during the season, we of the Queasy Brigade are to hold off greasy soups, fried things, and too much butter and marg. We eat fish in preference to beef and go easy on the booze during those ten days before the race, and particularly before the first race of the season.

Oranges are not acid, nor in general are stewed fruits, vegetables, salads or potatoes. I mistrust apples. Glucose is a valuable anti-acid and should be plentifully taken in tea, coffee, and puddings. A proportion of this is found in barley sugar and most boiled sweets. Some people find chewing-gum a big help. Sticks of barley sugar should be sucked, not chewed.

Turning to the question of a clear stomach, during the period of preparation, I advise regular dosings of liver mixture. Andrews Liver Salts has a good proportion of bicarbonate of soda in it and should assist in the anti-acid treatment as well. Milk of Magnesia is mildly laxative and alkaline also, and can be had in tablet as well as liquid form. It will of course take a little experience to find out what suits you, but a clear tummy gives one a fair chance to avoid the liveriness which is half-way to sickness.

As everyone knows life in a small yacht at sea tends to make one constipated. This is in part due to the diet, in which bread, buns, biscuits, and potatoes may predominate. But I guess the principal cause to be that one's body is rarely relaxed; the stomach muscles are in general tautened when balancing onself against the movement of the boat. This may be due to subconscious reactions, and may also apply when one is turned into one's bunk. In any case one's periods bunked down are short and sometimes irregular which probably disturbs the digestive routine.

Be all that as it may, 90 per cent of people are to some extent affected in this way at sea, and more so in bad weather, when one takes less liquid perhaps. And so everyone should bring with him a supply of his favourite small liver pills. In addition I personally always pass round the ship's pills and probably a supply of Milk of Magnesia as well, once or twice a day to tempt the people who have forgotten to look after themselves; a thing all too easy to do when one is beginning to get tired as well as wet.

Sea-sickness thrives on cold and dampness. So take extra care to clothe yourself adequately, and if circumstances allow, change out of your wet things as soon as you come off watch. Get into dry vest and underpants and sweater even if you know you will have to re-don some damp things before you go on watch again. If you are liable to seasickness, turn in right away with a handful of biscuits, perhaps with barley sugar, some cheese, and dried fruit. First-class tack this, if the tummy is not over-strong. If you have organized your watches, as I have suggested elsewhere, with a view to reducing the chance of the watch below being called, you will encourage people to change their cold wet gear before turning in.

In bad weather when the fore hatch (and probably other vents) are shut, the rule should be 'no smoking below'. Smokers as well as non-smokers will be the better for it, for the air below, with cooking inevitably going on, must not be further fouled.

If you are feeling a bit queasy and do have to sit about down below, try to avoid violent movement, and try keeping your back away from a settee, so that you can in part balance the motion of the ship by movement of the body above the hips. It is well worth while to keep a supply of air-sick bags in each compartment below (any large stout paper bags will serve) to avoid the necessity for having to go hurriedly on deck to be ill and getting wet and cold, for you won't have the time or inclination to don oilies. The bags can be passed up and over the side quite painlessly.

I subscribe to the idea that however sea-sick one is, one must make the effort to eat moderately, unless one has given up hope of keeping one's watch. I have mentioned a handful of biscuits and cheese and dried fruits before turning in; and a similar effort should be made before going on deck; or something popped in one's 'skin pocket to munch on watch.

As the season goes on, one will settle down, and sickness will worry one less.

Sea-sick Dopes. Among the accepted anti-sea-sick drugs, all of which can be recommended, are Avomine, Dramamine, Benadryl, Phenergan, and Hyoscine-Hydrobromide. Dramamine is an excellent American product but often not obtainable in Europe. The last three were tested against one another in 1951, very carefully, on sixty-eight soldiers, over tests lasting about two weeks in coastal force vessels. All three drugs were found to be fairly effective, with Hyoscine the best. This drug protected 96 per cent of the sick prone from vomiting and 77 per cent against both nausea 'feeling of sickness' and vomiting. The only weakness of the tests were that each test, of which there were a number, lasted only about two hours in 'bad weather conditions'. However, they were clearly important indications.

It is interesting to note that none of the drugs tested had any serious ill effects; that is to say disturbance of sight or confusion of senses. There was no unusual onset of giddiness, headaches, or drowsiness.

For the tests the dosage used was 1 mg. of Hyoscine, and 25 mg. for Phenerga and Benadryl. The doses were taken as capsules between $1\frac{1}{2}$ and 2 hours before the onset of bad weather. For ocean racing Dramamine should be taken only half an hour before proceeding in bad conditions, the dose being 50 mg., repeated every 5 hours. Some reports of Dramamine state that this specific drug tends to cause drowsiness. Avomine is another drug well liked by many people; Marzine is another very good one.

Prior to the tests referred to above I generally carried Hyoscine on board and always had the impression that it was a help to the sea-sick prone. I do believe, however, that if one is a sufferer one should try various drugs until one finds the most effective one that suits one; that is to say, is effective and has no ill effects. Avomine or Hyoscine do not seem to upset one; other dopes work excellently on some chaps and are death to others. Ancolan—a new B.D.H. product—has had some success in certain cases. An old and very sea-sick friend of mine once gave me as a present a couple of packets of a dope which had enabled him to survive two years in a destroyer without reversing one meal. This seemed a good enough recommendation, and so I gave one packet to a girl who was setting off for America and put the other by in my 'come in 'andy' locker. The opportunity soon arose to test it. We were starting in the Solent for a Cup race, leaving the Wight to port that year and thence to Cherbourg. It was blowing freshly from the southwest, knocking up a nice little sea off the Needles.

In general I had not been too fit, so thought I would try and make a certainty of my stomach by taking the appropriate dosage. To cut a long story short, and it seemed very long to me at the time, I was so ill and weak towards the end of the passage that I was making my way forward on all fours. A friend a little later made the passage to America in *Normandie* in nearly perfect weather and owing, I am convinced, to the dope was landed in New York on a stretcher. I have known of similar cases with other potions. So don't try new ones out in important events!

Feeding. All of which brings us to the question of feeding in general, when off shore. The main principles as I see it, should be that the food should be arranged so that it can be prepared with the minimum expenditure of fuel and crew energy. These considerations apply with greater force in small and medium-sized boats and are less important in larger vessels. If the menu is complex and requires a lot of preparing, or cooking, many man-hours will be used which can often be ill spared. The cook could be more profitably employed getting rest or giving a hand in his watch.

It depends of course to some extent on how one's cooking is organized, but it is seldom possible in a smallish yacht to carry a hand to cook only. It is generally better to have a cook or duty hand taking it in turns in each watch. In this way the full watch is still available for changing sail and so on, without calling hands in the watch below. But circumstances alter cases and it depends a lot on whether you have one or two born cooks in your crew.

In *Myth* I cooked breakfast and prepared tea and midnight supper. The navigator often did lunch and dinner; both non-watchkeepers.

But apart from the conservation of manpower aspect, it is still advisable to have simple meals, firstly because bad weather is much less likely to disorganise the cuisine, and secondly because in bad weather the less the cooking, the fresher will be the air in the boat. Also meals will be more quickly got ready after a job requiring all the available hands; and more quickly eaten too, which is a consideration when one is feeding by watches.

All this points to the benefit of having some ready cooked meats and quite a lot of meals out of tins, in the smaller craft at any rate. Some people are so imbued with the importance of adequately feeding the crew that they provide far more than is necessary. Over feeding makes the hands sleepy and less alert and perhaps livery and more prone to sea-sickness as well.

Turning to a choice of menus, I think that tinned soups are well worth their place, for in bad or cold weather they are stimulating, very comforting and easily made. There are also several new brands of dried soups which some owners prefer and are packed in watertight envelopes. With bread they make a light meal, but it is worth remembering that the food value of tinned soups and of so-called beef extracts for soup making, is generally very low indeed. Cocoa is equally easy to make and has more food value. At a change of night watch we generally have the kettle boiling and then make up cocoa, tea, Nescafé, or Bovril to choice. Among vegetables not requiring cooking on board, I greatly favour lettuce, tomatoes, small carrots, and beetroots. The latter in vinegar will keep fresh for long periods. Of these fresh things I find one can hardly have too much; however much is taken on board, none remains at the end of the passage.

With a view to making the eternal tinned meat and vegetable stews tasty, I favour alternatively or together, small fresh onions, which require little cooking, chives which for long passages can be kept growing in tin pots, oxo cubes, tinned macaroni and sweetcorn and our old friend H.P. sauce. It is not always possible to stick to one's menus, but I think it helpful to have a draft series to cover the whole race at its maximum length, made out in advance. The duty cook knows just what to get up from the store and it ensures making the best of what variety there is. These draft menus are also the easiest way accurately to assess the overall requirements of food for a race and any continuous passage, and thus to avoid carrying unnecessary stuff.

Generally when racing, I don't like the crew to take meals on deck. In practice it cultivates a slovenly attitude to crew's duties, and results either in neglect of the job, and/or bolting one's meal. Even in small yachts, unless sea-sickness is very prevalent, I think it better to eat comfortably and relaxed below.

In small boats, particularly in those of light and moderate displacement, it is desirable only to take the necessary food plus a small margin against delays and accident. Over-providing, for instance, stocking up with tins for the whole season, can easily load the boat with a quarter of a ton of unnecessary weight. In a boat like *Rani*, in which we did the Sydney to Hobart and other races, this represents a 3.7 per cent increase in the designed displacement!

For the same reason, it is desirable to arrange tinned food stowage low in the boat so that it acts as inside ballast. Nearly always it can be conveniently located under the cabin sole, if necessary in perforated 'zinc' trays or metal-wire baskets, or perhaps in more easily found plastic baskets. But in this case the labels should be removed and the contents indicated by scratchings on the tin. Otherwise the bilge water will in time soak the labels off and these will most likely sooner or later jam up the bilge pump suction. And almost certainly the bilge gremlin will chose a bad weather moment for this particular turn, because the bad weather will help him dislodge the labels from their nooks and crannies where they have temporarily lodged. It involves a lot of work to get these labels off dry. But a bucket of hot water will soon bring them off and quite neat abbreviated markings can be employed. One of my hands, for instance, for BREAST OF FINEST SURREY FOWL simply wrote HENTIT.

Brown bread keeps best. We usually carry sliced bread 'saves work, and crumbs' with loaves individually wrapped and put into plastic bags; stowed in any lockers not likely to be flooded.

It is often necessary to keep bread to the limit of edibility. Mouldy bread can have its outside cut off and be quite passable within, specially if toasted. But mould is liable to infect a wood locker and hasten the deterioration of the next lot of fresh loaves. The addition of salt when baking helps keeping properties and wrapping in cellophane is helpful if you can organise it. Alternatively grease-proof paper is a help. An entirely different approach to the problem is to keep bread ventilated in net bags instead of lockers; but space rarely permits, and it may get dripped on.

There is always a possibility of the race taking longer than the normal owing to being hove-to for exceptionally bad weather, or to delays due to gear carrying away; a badly torn mainsail for instance.

So one must provide emergency rations for the whole crew for, say 40 per cent longer than a normal weather passage: say for three extra days on a 650-mile race or one day for a 250-mile race. This assumes that light weather passages, for which normal rations will be on board, will be seven and three days respectively. In smaller yachts where food stowage is quite a problem, this emergency survival ration can conveniently be in the form of K rations, or similar tinned containers, such as are issued to the services for similar purposes. These tins contain everything essential for a day, including tea, sugar, and a cigarette, in the lightest and handiest form, which can be kept on board in the minimum of space.

Apart from these it is most important that a small supply of dry tack be assembled in an accessible place before a race, where in emergency tired crew members can have direct access to it. I have already mentioned biscuits (left in their packets), barley sugar, dried fruits, and cheese. Among the cheap dried fruits are dates, figs, prunes, raisins, pears, and apricots—the latter known as 'monkeys' ears'. The ordinary sorts, prepared for stewing, are O.K. provided they are of reasonable quality. Cheese has about the highest nutritive value of ordinary dry foods, and moreover it can be eaten alone, regularly without upsetting the balance of one's diet. Ryvita or Vita Wheat is a good alternative to biscuits.

Fresh Water Stowage. Turning to water stowage, this is sometimes quite a problem in the smallest boats. A very comfortable allowance for big yachts is a gallon a man a day, which is what we used to calculate in the early submarine days, which allows a quart or more a day for washing. If one forgoes this washing, for which (let's be honest) one has not much time when racing, three-quarters of a gallon per man per day is more than ample. Providing the cooking of spuds, onions, and carrots is done in sea water and provided the sea water is used for tooth mugs—vegetables cooked in sea water are entirely palatable—and if you also forgo the fresh water for washing up and go a bit careful on consumption generally, half a gallon per man is quite comfortable, even in warm weather. In cool conditions you need less. One should allow for a quart a day during the 'emergency 40 per cent' period. This means five gallons per head for a 650-mile race. The C.C.A. insist on twelve American, *i.e.* ten British gallons, per head, for the Bermuda Race, on account of the nature of the course.

I like the fresh water stowed in at least two separate tanks to afford an accurate check on consumption at half time. It also provides a standby against accidental pollution or leakage of one tank. If one has more than two tanks the suction pipework becomes rather complex in small craft. Breaking up into two tanks and using one tank 'right out' also reduces the amount of free surface liquid and has a beneficial effect on stability. For the same reason one tries to design deep narrow tanks rather than flat shallow ones. This also assists in keeping a suction towards the end when the vessel is moving in a seaway or heeled. Fortunately the natural shape of a bilge is such that suitable tanks can generally be accommodated under the cabin sole. In addition to dividing up the main stowage into two, I always carry a few bottles of emergency drinking-water, preferably one to each crew member. It is comforting to know that one of these, independent of pipe systems and other possible sources of loss, and one can at a pinch use up the main tanks, knowing that there is this last supply, under one's lee as it were. A separate emergency container(s) is now a R.O.R.C. requirement.

Tanks 'made to measure' with the necessary piping are quite expensive and lately we have successfully used instead in many Class III and all our J.O.G. designs, plastic jerry-cans. These keep the drinking water fresher than galvanised tanks. A two-gallon can will last a small galley most of the day. A portable plastic suction pipe from the fresh water pump in the galley, and similarly in the heads/wash-room, is dropped in when the can is changed. Two-gallon cans, or in J.O.G. racers one-gallon cans, stow under the cabin sole, or under the cockpit and bunks. Watering by dinghy is simple.

In Appendix XV is a typical overall food list, suitable for a three-day race with a crew of ten, which can be scaled up or down to suit the actual numbers and race length.

The researches of Dr. Bombard show that when short of water one can add a high percentage of sea water without harmful effects; but this must be done before one gets too thirsty and dried out.

Commander Erroll Bruce in his excellent book *Deep Sea Sailing* (Hutchinson) has a good chapter about feeding, which will be a useful guide to small and medium sized ocean racers for transatlantic events and the like.

Crew Fitness. It should be self evident that a physically fit crew will do better than a soft one. And yet one sees the keenest people—or they would say and feel that they were 100 per cent keen—making no effort to get fit before the season; appearing with soft hands and generally looking like something found under a stone.

I don't suggest that it is necessary to train as if one was going in for the Olympic quarter-mile or twelve rounds with Joe Louis, but if for the last few weeks before the season, one makes a point of walking a really brisk mile or two whenever the opportunity offers, wet or fine—perhaps using one station from home and walking the rest—or setting off half an hour early by foot instead of by bus—and if one limits one's alcoholic consumption, perhaps smokes less and gets to bed early for the last week, by these simple means one is at least in sufficient shape for three or four days' hard sailing to put one in real trim.

The job of hardening the hands is more difficult. The countryman won't be worried. But for those of us who have comparatively sedentary occupations, it is quite a problem; failure to do anything in preparation may result in raw hands and spoiling the fun of a full race, as well as becoming gradually less useful to the crew as the race goes on. Golf is valuable and of course is the best of general training as well. Any sort of carpentry and gardening is a help and, wood sawing and axe work are excellent for the hands and for the back muscles which are needed in sailing. One chap I knew kept a rope purchase at home and, having dipped his hands in brine, hoisted a scrap motor car engine, weighing a couple of hundredweight, two or three times each morning and evening to the highest suitable branch of the 'only' tree in his back yard. There are many other minor ways of assisting, such as always using an ash plant walking stick, with the bark still in place on the handle. Of course if we can do a little day sailing to start the season, 'nuff said'.

Training as a Crew. The best way to start the season is to enter for a few day races—regatta handicap events. This quickly gets people into the way of the boat, hardens their hands and muscles up their backs. It shows up weaknesses in the yacht's gear, or indicates minor deficiencies which can very likely be remedied overnight and tried again next day. Even if your boat is not fully tuned, or the crew worked up, have a go, the moment you can, at a short race. It will shake things down three times as quickly as ordinary day sailing, and get everyone on their toes as well.

It may possibly be the case that you can't get your full ocean racing crew together for these preliminary races. Or your may get some for each race perhaps. This is no great handicap to training, since at sea, one watch plus skipper will be required to set and hand sail, and with half to two-thirds crew available similar conditions will obtain. If the skipper owner is not available one of the mates of the watch should take her out and have a good crack at a local race.

During these preliminary events the skipper should give all hands an opportunity at the helm and carefully observe their capabilities. Many excellent crew hands are poor helmsmen and not infrequently one finds men, generally those with a good deal of class racing experience, who are reliable helmsmen and only moderately useful on the fore-deck. On the other hand many crew members without a great deal of experience to windward will steer the boat perfectly well on a quiet reach where ability to concentrate entirely on the job is more important than experience.

Having sized up their capabilities at the helm the skipper should discuss these with the mates of the watch. He will ensure that really bad helmsmen are told frankly that, except in an emergency or just for short periods, they are not to steer on the wind, until they have gained further experience in minor inshore races or cruising. He will arrange that passable, but not yet fully experienced helmsmen are given the necessary supervision and relieved at once when they strike a bad patch, or when steering conditions become too difficult for them. They will generally be the first to agree that it is not fair on the boat, or the other crew members, that their chances and all the work put into the race shall be jeopardised by inexperienced steering, any more than it would be fair to have a beginner practise his wire splicing on the main shrouds.

On the other hand, experience alone is no guarantee of efficiency at the helm. I know of at least one mate of the watch, who is a first-class deckmaster, but realising his shortcomings will if possible avoid steering the boat.

Stimulants at Sea. And now for a word or two concerning the use of 'drink' at sea. I say 'use' advisedly, because I propose to discuss it entirely on its merits, without reference to preconceived prejudice, that is to say, purely from the standpoint of utility.

In sport alcohol has its uses. For instance, taken at just the right moment, the right length of time before the start of a ski race or downhill run, quite a lot of us have found that it eases one's nerves and gives one the extra little bit of *élan* and flexibility, with which it is so valuable to start. And taken before the last or penultimate chukka of a hot and strenuous polo match, I have occasionally found a good brandy and soda to be of real value.

But in these cases the object is to gear oneself up for a special effort over a strictly limited period. In ocean racing the requirement is quite different and although there will be many strenuous moments, above all what is wanted of all the crew is steady, persistent application. This applies most particularly to the skipper and navigator, who are continually on the go and whose resting moments are less regular.

The effect of alcohol on a tired wet man is sometimes beneficial, provided he has come off watch. Alcohol stimulates the action of the heart which results in a temporary feeling of well-being, but does not actually warm one; by circulating the blood at a greater rate it exposes it to chilling if one's extremities are cold and in effect the final answer is actually to lower the body temperature. And so as a general rule, its use is only recommended in cases of exhaustion and cold when the man has come below and is definitely to remain below for a spell. And as I have indicated elsewhere, alcohol has an acid reaction on one's insides and in the long run may increase the tendency to seasickness.

To the man who ashore is accustomed to regular consumption of a noggin or two before his lunch and his dinner there would appear at first sight to be no valid reason why he should not partake as usual when racing. However, working on deck in a seaway demands the most acute balance, particularly to meet the unexpected movements of the ship. In this respect, the demands on one's senses and reactions are more acute than, shall we say, the demands made upon a rider of a bicycle. And whether it is the open air, or what, I don't know, but I believe that tots at sea are more powerful in their effects than the same ration taken at the club bar.

Naturally no one can take exception to the consumption of a reasonable quantity of beer, but if eight men drink two tins of beer a day, each, on a seven-day race, and each tin weighs one pound, then 1 cwt. of extra weight and displacement is involved. But water can be reduced accordingly.

So taken full and by in average racing, I hold that, except for the very occasional semi-medical use of a tot, alcohol is best left ashore, or at least in the locker until the hook is down and the sails are stowed; and then it will be all the more welcome. On the other hand, when a long spell of light fluky winds have frayed one's nerves, a tot all round may help restore good temper.

Clothing at Sea. Nothing very complex is called for in the way of seagoing clothing. On the other hand I have known of a case where unsuitable clothing has actually resulted in the withdrawal of a yacht from an ocean race, and there must be many intermediate cases where a severe loss of efficiency results from lack of the necessary togs.

During the last war, many special suits were devised for aircrews, coastal forces, submarines, and special operations, but I have yet to see one which beats well-designed oilskins worn over the necessary number of sweaters to match the temperature. Most of the padded suits are the very devil to dry once they become thoroughly damp, whereas oilskins soon drip themselves dry, and a supply of spare sweaters can be kept for use until a patch of light weather or down-wind sailing gives one a chance to hang them out, when they soon dry out in the wind.

For bad, really cold weather, I like a thick pair of cloth trousers worn over two pairs of underpants, one of these having long legs. On top a thick vest with long sleeves; a woollen shirt with sleeves; then two sweaters; one sleeveless; and a thin gaberdine canvas smock, of the type one pulls over the head; more or less waterproof. In this rig one can dash on deck in an emergency without oilskins and without getting soaked. Finally thin pliable oilskin trousers and a thin short oilskin coat, smock type or double-breasted, with a belt or other means of drawing it around one. I wear a small towel at the neck and it is necessary to make sure that this is of the right bulk and does not prevent the oily jacket from buttoning, nor half choke one.

Oilskin Trousers.—I think it most desirable that the oilskin trousers should be fitted with braces and come well up under the armpits. I would like to emphasise the need for pliable oilskins; the stiff ones not only make one clumsy, but are tiring and being uncomfortable there is a tendency to put off the evil moment of donning them until too late, when one is already part wet. And for the navigator or skipper, it may be necessary at times when one is likely to be called on deck, to sit below, or even sleep for short periods, in one's oilskin trousers. The skipper needs to be a bit dictatorial at times, in getting the watch to take timely steps to put on more clothing, and in particular their 'skins. Thin oilskin trousers are the better for doubled seats to take wear on the outer layer, while the inner remains waterproof.

A sou'wester or a hood is of course necessary. One of the troubles is that both these make it difficult to hear and a hole in the earflap of a sou'wester is worth while. The hoods which attach to one's jacket are snug, but most of them are too stiff and allow insufficient play to the neck so that one has to turn one's whole body round instead of glancing over one's shoulder. In cold weather it is most necessary to wear something on the head even when sou'westers are not needed to keep the wet off; because of the large blood circulation to the head, keeping it warm helps keep up one's general warmth and well-being. Conversely, an uncovered head will result in an excessive loss of warmth. For instance far more than results from bare feet.

The sleeves of the jacket should have storm cuffs; or stout rubber bands, office type, are sufficient. In *Maid* and *Myth* we had a tray of these located near the companionway in the chartroom. The bottom of the oilskin trousers should have a draw string in the hem. These can be pulled tight over short sea boots, or round the ankle. Strips of good quality towelling are generally necessary round one's neck under the oilskins. I make mine 7 in. × 34 in. At least two towels, for long races three, per head should be provided. Henri-Lloyd (Little Hulton, Worsley, Manchester) provide very good special light oilskins.

Messrs. Offshore Sailing, of Salcombe, South Devon (no relation to this book), market very good sea-going suits of very light but serviceable skins, smocks, and trousers. These incorporate very adequate (and special) buoyancy, which does not impede and does not need inflation.

Footwear. If you do wear sea boots, get the lightest soled pair you can find, or they will make you clumsy and very unpopular when you tread on other chaps wearing gym shoes. They should be an easy pull-on fit, readily kicked off in the water if need be. Heavy sea boots take up a lot of stowage room and weigh a good bit. Except for winter and spring sailing, I am not sure that they are worth their place in a small ship when racing. The Sperry Company of America make a really light sea boot—a gym shoe bottom and a light rubber leg, which are a joy.

Gym shoes, or sneakers, vary a good deal in their gripping properties. The American Topsiders, which have a closely serrated sole, and the English Dunlop non-skid, take a lot of beating. Dunlop—the Magister Model sole—is slightly superior in gripping power. Crêpe rubber soles are not as a rule good; the best thing one can do with them is to overheat them on a hot pipe and reduce them to a state of permanent tackiness. Rope soles grip fairly well, but they should not be worn ashore, as grit becomes embedded in the sole and liable to score varnish and other nice surfaces on board. Also they soak up the wet. In bad weather Magister shoes alone seem less cold than with soaking socks. Short, light, Dunlop sea boots are also available and are excellent.

Clothes Changes. In the old days of bowsprits, I used to tell my crews to bring a complete change of clothing to every hundred miles of the race; which meant six changes for a Fastnet. In bad weather one had sometimes to take off one's oilskins in order to change headsails, going to windward, at the end of a long sprit. This was necessary to lessen the weight of the sea on one when she put her nose well in, a tendency which was made much worse by the presence of half the crew forward and one chap 8 ft. beyond the stem head. However, when the change was over there was a peculiar feeling of satisfaction in having accomplished this without running the ship off her course, or heaving to, processes which when repeated two or three times during a long windward turn would quite likely drop one out of the prize list. Cruising, one could set the sails flying and have the tack go out on a traveller to the bowsprit end, but though this would answer fairly well with working sails, it was no good with a big yankee jib, which had to be hanked on to the stay to do much good to windward; otherwise the luff would sag away excessively.

With a more modern inboard rig one will not need quite such a big kit of spare clothing. But it is most desirable that everyone should be able to get into a dry change at the end of the watch on deck should this be necessary. Sitting about below, or turning in with wet clothing in cold weather gradually undermines one's resistance and encourages *mal de mer*. It may make sleep difficult. A complete change of clothing to every two hundred miles of the race is a minimum, and small or low freeboard yachts should have more.

Noise at Sea. Crew efficiency clearly requires that men off watch should get the maximum of sleep and rest. To this end unnecessary shouting on deck and loud conversation below should be avoided. Canvas curtains help deaden noise, and these, or in larger yachts doors, are often worth their nuisance value to divide the galley-cum-chart-table working space from the sleeping quarters.

Other things being equal, the quieter sheet winch should be chosen. Placing these abaft the helm, as we do in most of our new designs, also helps. Small staysail winches which may have to be placed on or near the roof can be fitted on a rubber pad, though the reduction in internal noise is by no means complete.

6

STRATEGY IN OCEAN RACING

Aside from pure navigation, which is dealt with briefly elsewhere, there may arise many questions on the answers to which depends the course to be steered, and these may conveniently be called strategy. They are closely related to navigation, and dependent to some extent on ship driving, or deckmastership. But it is in reality almost a separate subject. At any rate, to treat it separately will, I think, assist in making its messages clear. If one had to define strategy in offshore racing one might say it was the business of choosing the best series of courses when there are alternatives. You may say some of the questions are tactics, but where strategy ends and tactics start is difficult to say and so it's all lumped in together here.

Covering Rival Boats. Unlike considerations applying to regatta sailing, a lot of one's actions off shore do not deal with or concern the other competing yachts, because in most cases there will be a number of competing yachts, anything from six to one hundred and forty. In many cases they will be sailing widely different courses and it is not as a rule politic to concentrate on covering a particular boat; not unless you are convinced she is your most dangerous rival or that in covering her you are not going appreciably out of your way.

In class racing, without time allowance, covering usually consists of keeping between your rival and the mark. In ocean racing if you rate a little lower than the rival in question you may be able to cover him by dogging his course, so to speak. But if it is leading you into courses of which you do not approve—getting you too much to windward or to leeward perhaps—then it should not as a rule be continued, that is, unless you are near the finish; because although you may be holding your bigger rival nicely at the moment, a change in conditions later—such as a strengthening wind—may enable him to slip away and save his time under the changed conditions.

Weather Reports. Let us take now the question of weather reports. Some people refuse even to listen to these at sea, in case they are tempted to some rash course of action, while to others they are the very gospel on which all decision should be based. While I would certainly prefer the former

to the latter view, I hold that something of a compromise is best. The matter is dealt with from an elementary Met. angle in the chapter on wind and weather.

It is useful to remember that in fresh or strong winds the weather reports are as a rule more reliable as to the wind, than in moderate to light conditions, under which an unexpected small secondary effect may pop up and upset the predictions.

Deviations for Weather. Before embarking on the race one will have got all available information from the Meteorological Offices. For some reason the local British Met. forecasts seem sometimes less reliable than the head offices.

When listening to the weather reports one should have a pad in hand, and the rough noting should be fairly recorded immediately afterwards in writing in the log, in so far as they concern the race area. One then takes account of the probable local onshore and offshore breezes. In waters where temperatures are generally moderate these are only of moment fairly close to the shore. On these and the look of the sky one makes one's personal forecast of the weather for the next twelve hours.

It is then that the question arises, how much is one to allow this to influence the course to be steered? The answer should, I feel, generally be only to a limited extent. If there is any golden rule in offshore racing it is 'Don't gamble on the weather'. By gambling I mean committing yourself to a course which if the change in wind and weather predicted does not come off, one is completely 'sunk'. But by all means slightly modify your course, keeping a shade to windward or leeward of the direct course. As you will see from data given later in this chapter considerable deviations from the rhumb line can be made in cases where the next mark is a distance away, without adding much to the total mileage to be covered. But on average it is surprising how often the change turns out to be just sufficiently different from your forecast to make your gamble unworkable.

Accuracy of Weather Reports. Often in summer weather the change is later than was expected owing to the slowing up of 'the front'; sometimes the change is preceded by an unexpectedly long period of light variables, particularly if a reversal of breeze is awaited. Quite often the direction of the new wind is a couple of points off what you wanted.

Therefore on the whole and specially when in doubt it is far better to sail the wind and weather as you see it and find it. But I am not advocating a disregard of the weather reports. There are many occasions when they dictate slightly altered courses. Moreover they give one valuable information as to the probable strength and duration of a blow, even if the exact timing and direction are not always accurate.

For instance if one was from the forecast morally certain that the change when it did come was going to result in wind of gale force, rather than a short fresh blow, one would very probably when it breezed up keep her sailing on fair-sized head-sails and pull down a couple of reefs in good time. Thus one would get the job done more quickly and with less expenditure of effort than if one waited, in the expectation of it freshening no further, until she was staggering under a full mainsail and reduced to a rag of headsail; conditions under which there may be undue delay in getting her properly canvassed and sailing again, and during which times there is a risk of minor carry-aways.

When to go for a Gamble. When one is pretty sure of one's forecast, and if one is not at that time favourably placed, taking account of rating, compared to the others in sight or in known positions, then occasionally it may be worth while to take on a gamble. An interesting instance of this occurred in the 1937 Fastnet. Captain Franklin Ratsey took his big gaff-rigged pilot cutter *Zoraida* way outside the Scillies to find a forecast southwester. Incidentally, a fine sight she looked in that race, with a new suit of tan coloured sails, every sail perfect, and a tremendous area set. But of course she was an old-timer, and could not expect to hold the newest boats on the wind. Meanwhile the rest of the fleet were endeavouring to work their way against a foul tide and light airs past the Longships, on the much more direct route inside the Islands. He found his breeze; much fresher and some time before it reached us farther inshore; more than this, his gamble had placed him in a position many miles to windward. He was in a commanding position which would have enabled him to reach out for the Fastnet Rock, and as it turned out, reach nearly all the way home again on a fine soldier's wind; conditions under which he would take a lot of catching. He had, in fact, after the start, under similar conditions, led the whole fleet out of the Solent. The race seemed half-way into

the bag. However it was not to be; a slip with one of the preventers brought the topmast down, leaving him not only without his fine jackyarder, but without his great yankee masthead jib.

Maintaining Speed rather than Course. Before we pass on to consider the policy for various points of sailing, there is a point we must make in a general way about sailing towards one's next mark. Though naturally the direct course is a thing one must have clearly in mind, don't let's get bound to it. It is far more important to keep the boat sailing at a good speed towards a distant mark, pointing somewhere in the neighbourhood of the right direction, than to pinch on to the exact course and have the yacht doing a lot less than her best.

When sailing off to gain speed, the extra distance one travels, always speaking of making for a turning point off shore and a real stretch ahead of you, is much less than one might at first sight imagine. We will examine this in more detail later. Meanwhile we can say that the all but golden tactical rule is 'keep her moving regardless of the exact course'.

If you as skipper, or navigator, find your crew are badly inflicted with 'Rhumb Line Phobia', one of the childish but partially effective dodges is never to draw the complete rhumb line on the chart—simply plot one's D.R. position and read off one's course ordered and note it in the log. Be very clear that I am not advocating any relaxation in the navigation or plotting; I am simply suggesting that the hard black line—that prudish path from which we may fear to wander—is sometimes a false guide.

Ever Changing Rhumb Line. To take the matter a stage farther; to drive the spike well home as it were; consider this aspect. The rhumb line is the direct course between your last mark and your next. But with the tides, and maybe the necessity to steer off to keep up one's best speed, or to take a board on the wind which carries you off to one side or the other, with these things and others one is often going to get off the line. And as soon as you are appreciably off the line it ceases to have real significance, except for its academic value subsequently. What should interest you as skipper, or mate, is the new direct course from your present position to the next mark. The quickest way to the next mark becomes a problem in which one's previous direct courses are of no consequence. Very obvious you may say, and so it is when one sits down here to analyse it calmly. But just the same there are many cases on record where boats have painfully worked their way back on to the original rhumb line, as though it was some lovely smooth path.

There is, it is needless perhaps to say, another extreme; one can overdo the business of sailing off to find the fastest points of sailing; particularly in fresh conditions. Talking to other skippers after the 1945–6 Hobart Race I was under the distinct impression that most of them had on that occasion altered course an unnecessary amount with a view to working wind and set to the best advantage. The Australian yachtsmen are very speed-minded —and perhaps less navigation-minded than most of us in the old country. This was confirmed when the various track charts were superimposed. The breezes, apart from the gale period with wind from ahead, were mostly moderate to fresh commanding ones and our distance sailed was a good deal less than most. I fancy it was partly on this account that we managed to establish a big lead on *Winston Churchill*, who was just behind us when we cleared the New South Wales Coast, and a good deal bigger and faster than *Rani*.

Correcting for Tide. One's navigation manuals teach one to correct one's course for tide. And if one is likely to cross the area in question within the space of one flood or one ebb one must lay one's course corrected accordingly. But should the job involve crossing one or more complete tides it is quite important to make an overall plan. Supposing a crossing from the Sovereign light-vessel off

Beachy Head to the Le Havre lightship—which is part of the famous R.O.R.C. Channel Race—takes one flood and one ebb, it is far better to let the tides nearly cancel out, and to steer as though there were no tide, rather than to keep on the rhumb line by allowing for the tides, steering first to port and then to starboard.

The extra distance which one sails through the water by correcting for the tide can be got from the traverse tables, if one has them. A brief extract which will give you an equally good idea is given under the down-wind sailing section of this chapter. Strangely enough by steering direct the distance travelled *over the ground* is greater. Diagram 2 shows the specific case of a yacht doing about 6 knots on a commanding breeze with 72 miles to go between marks and covering it in just over the 12 hrs. or one complete tide. Sketch A on the left shows one's path over the ground steering direct allowing oneself to be swept athwart one's direct course and back again. B on the right is a vector diagram showing the courses which one would steer to keep near the rhumb line.

Naturally it is rare that the effect of one tide exactly cancels another, or that one makes the passage in exactly one tide. But the principle applies just the same—let as much as possible of the tides cancel out and only correct for what is left. This applies too for longer passages where 'several tides are crossed'.

Cutty Mason in his interesting book *Deep Sea Racing* studied tidal streams in relation to tactics in detail. But these will need to be studied, absorbed and evaluated well in advance.

Marks dead to Windward. Circumstances under which it is specially necessary to take account of impending wind changes include those when there is a long turn more or less dead to windward. So at this point we may consider the general strategy of sailing long distances to windward. Supposing one has, as we had in many of the Fastnet Races, 160 miles or so from the Longships to the Fastnet Rock with a nose end breeze and no special incentive in the way of tides, sets, or protected water to encourage one to go one side or other of the 'rhumb line course'. If the wind remains steady one can make the whole distance in two long legs on the port and starboard tacks, or alternatively one can make a succession of comparatively short tacks of say 15 miles a board.

The time taken will be the same in each case, but it is important to note that in general, the latter is much to be preferred. In practice one leg is generally very slightly more favourable than the other and one should plump for this one and go on sailing it until it becomes the unfavourable one by about

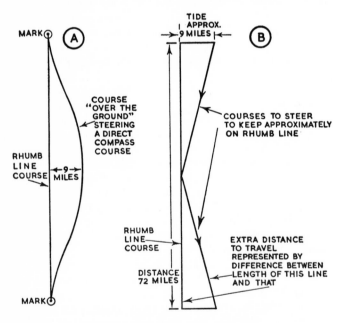

PASSAGE BETWEEN TWO MARKS ACROSS ONE TIDE (FLOOD & EBB)
ASSUMPTIONS MEAN SPEED OF TIDAL CURRENT 1½ KNOTS DISTANCE APART OF MARKS 72 MILES APPROXIMATE YACHTS SPEED 6 KNOTS

Diagram 2.

5 degrees. For instance suppose that in the seaway in question your experience indicates that your boat will lie within 46 degrees of the wind. The first time you tack, you will be able to check this figure by noting very carefully the mean course for 5 min. before and 5 min. after putting about, and halving the difference between these courses. Plot your D.R. position carefully on the chart, and continue on your tack until your objective (shall we continue to assume it is the 'Fastnet') bears 51 degrees on your weather bow. Then put about, and the Fastnet will, if you are correct in your estimate of 46 degrees steered, be 41 degrees on the other bow. Continue again on this new tack, with the Fastnet gradually coming broader on the beam, until on this tack likewise it bears about 51 degrees.

As you get nearer the mark, the boards will get gradually shorter. One is crossing and re-crossing the dead-to-windward line. The reason one should do this in the absence of other factors making it desirable to be more to one side than the other of the line, is to keep the Fastnet as near as makes no matter dead to windward, so that *any* chance shift of wind is advantageous. These theoretical courses are shown in Diagram 3.

Naturally, as one approaches very near the mark one need not make the number of boards to keep within the 10 degrees arc. But in any event one's

last pair of boards should be short ones, to avoid risk of overstanding the mark.

Of course this is the theoretical strategy assuming that the wind is constant. It does not quite work out that way, as there will be minor shifts in the wind direction. But this does not alter the fundamental soundness of the thesis which can then be very simply stated. 'In a wind varying in direction choose the leg which points you nearest your mark. Continue sailing this until it becomes definitely the less favourable one by more than 5 degrees. Then it is time to go about.' The word 'definitely' is important since, if one takes account of momentary changes in direction, one will under certain conditions be for ever tacking ship.

But if a shift of wind is forecast one stands more to the side from which the wind is to come. Going out to the Fastnet if the wind is expected to veer one stands more to the northward on the port tack until perhaps the Rock bears Red 61 degrees, then goes about and keeps on to the starboard tack until the Rock bears 51 degrees on the weather bow; then about again on the starboard tack. In this way you will be working always a little to the northward of the windward line. The moment the shift comes, you will be able to bang her round or to the starboard tack; or if you are on it, you may be able to free sheets a shade.

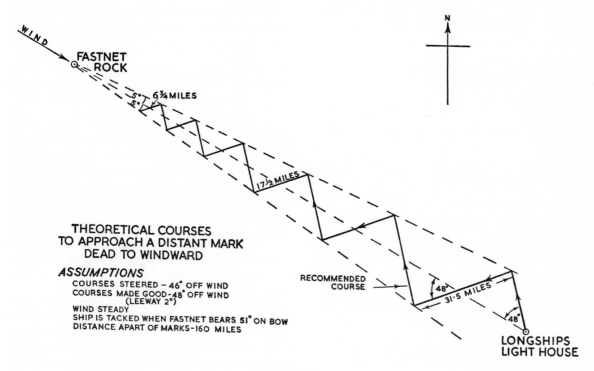

THEORETICAL COURSES
TO APPROACH A DISTANT MARK
DEAD TO WINDWARD

ASSUMPTIONS
COURSES STEERED – 46° OFF WIND
COURSES MADE GOOD – 48° OFF WIND
(LEEWAY 2°)
WIND STEADY
SHIP IS TACKED WHEN FASTNET BEARS 51° ON BOW
DISTANCE APART OF MARKS – 160 MILES

Diagram 3

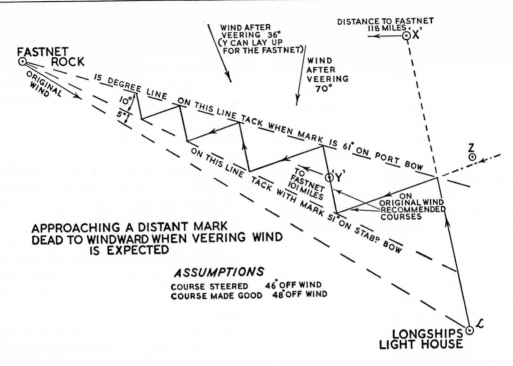

Diagram 4

Courses before a Wind Shift. If the shift does not come, no harm is done. But on the other hand it is unwise to stand too far to the north because if the veering shift turns out to be a big one, then one has overstood. Take a look at Diagram 4. Supposing one stands steadily on the port tack until one gets to position X, and the wind then veers 70 degrees, one is no less than 17 miles farther from the Fastnet Rock than the man at Y, who has sailed the same distance and both of them have the wind sufficiently free to make approximately their maximum reaching speed. And 17 miles is a matter of at least 2 and maybe 3 hrs.; it might well decide the race.

One can, if one is prepared to do rather shorter tacks, as a very good alternative, use the 15 degree line only, and make 1-hour boards to the south of it before coming back on to the port tack.

As soon as the wind has veered 36 degrees Y can point up straight for the mark, and as it probably veers gradually farther he will be freed and ahead of X. He has in fact got what northing is really required without over-committing himself. A four point shift in the wind is very usual in European waters—'the winds will be moderate, south-westerly veering to west later in the day' or something of that sort.

This recommendation applies equally when the course between marks is not direct up wind. For instance if one's last mark was at Z, instead of at L,

one would enter the tacking areas as shown and proceed as before.

So if you accept this thesis, the rule can be put: 'Turning to windward towards a distant mark in a steady breeze which is expected to veer, keep to the right of the direct windward course but not more than about 15 degrees. If the breeze is expected to back then keep to the left.' The words left and right are used in preference to port and starboard so that there shall be no confusion with the port and starboard tacks which one is making.

A Close Fetch to the Mark. Perhaps the most difficult problem, and also the most fascinating one, is to decide just how free to sail the boat. If the next mark is more or less dead to windward that is one thing; the tactics for these conditions have been discussed, while the technique of getting a boat to windward in a seaway is dealt with in another chapter. For the moment I refer to the situation where it is a close fetch to the mark; which is may-be 50 or 500 miles away. The close-hauled fetch may head you about direct for the mark, or just not enable you to point up for it, and the problem is whether to sail her hard on the wind or a good full—full and bye as the old seamen used to style it—though for them that meant farther off the wind than it does for our modern fore and aft rigs.

If one could assume that the wind was going to remain constant, then the problem is compara-tively easy because one sails close-hauled for the mark. But if there is going to be an unpredictable change in wind direction before you get to that mark, which if it is a considerable distance away, is more than likely, then your object is to get as close to the mark as possible by the time that the wind change occurs, regardless of whether that 'distance away' is to leeward related to the present wind.

To illustrate the point (Diagram 5) let us assume that under the conditions in question we can make 5 knots close-hauled and just lay the course, and that by sailing half a point off we can increase our speed to 5.4 knots. If we are clearing the Longships for the Fastnet 160 miles away, and if an appreciable change of wind comes 12 hrs. later then the difference in position between sailing a straight course and one half a point off is represented by the positions X and Y respectively. If you had sailed a whole point off and made good 5.7 knots, then you would find yourself at Z.

At this time the man who is a whole point off at Z is in the best position, nearest the Fastnet by $6\frac{1}{2}$ miles, though the half-pointer has scored over the direct-liner by 4 miles.

Now supposing the change of wind comes after 24 hours' steady sailing, then the respective position would be XX, YY, and ZZ. The half-pointer is nearer the mark by 7 miles, compared to the close-hauled man; if they both sail free to the Fastnet, he will be about an hour ahead. The 'whole-pointer' is just 1 mile nearer the Fastnet still—but at the expense of being very much to the leeward on the original wind.

If no shift in wind direction has come after 24 hrs. both the 'off course' skippers will be wise to come close-hauled. In fact few people would be prepared to risk carrying on a whole point off so far; they would limit their risk by turning on to the wind earlier, had they sailed that course. They should, however, after coming close-hauled continue on the port tack until it becomes the less favourable by 5 degrees unless there are considerations of current and sheltered water. The straight-liner will

of course have done best, but the half-pointer will not have lost much. The whole-pointer is likely to be over 3 hrs. behind the straight-liner if he comes close-hauled after 24 hours' sailing.

You may say, this is all a gamble on a change of weather—the thing you advised us against. In a way this is true, but between this form of gamble and the general case there is a big difference. In this form you are definitely getting something back, in any case, whether the gamble comes off or not, in the shape of increased speed. It is like backing both ways where your horse can't help being at least placed.

There is one point which though important is not self-evident from the theoretical point of view; that when one decides to sail, say, half a point off and starts one's sheets accordingly, one obviates the possibility of pinching due to poor helmsmanship.

The Rule for Close Fetching. The actual case worked out illustrates a truth: 'There is never much risk in sailing half a point off your close-hauled course to gain speed towards a mark at a considerable distance.'

When you come to think of the business of determining your most effective close-hauled course, it is always a matter of opinion and experiment to determine exactly how close it pays to sail. It is clear that one's experience reinforces the graphical conclusion; over a narrow arc of course in the neighbourhood of the optimum, there is not going to be much lost to windward by sailing off a few degrees.

Weighing up the advisability of sailing off wind, one has to bear in mind:

(*a*) The distance of the next mark.

(*b*) The characteristics of the boat under the prevailing conditions.

(*c*) The general steadiness or otherwise of the wind conditions in that area of the world at that time of the year.

(*d*) The particular weather report of the moment.

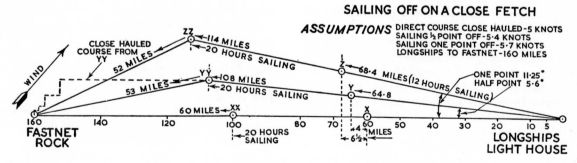

Diagram 5

As regards (*a*) it is obvious that we are only talking of distant marks. Any mark within 25 miles or so must be sailed for close-hauled, and unless there are rather strong indications of impending changes, or unless the conditions are generally variable. So in general must marks up to 40 miles away. In this connection one must bear in mind that should the shift be a slightly heading one, the close-hauled course has paid. Other things being the same the more distant the mark the more worth while is the gamble.

Concerning (*b*) it is generally the heavier cruising type which will gain most by being sailed off—boats of the Beta division under English rules.

The *actual* gain in speed by 'sailing off' a normal cruiser is possibly about the same as that in most modern ocean racers, but the gain *relative to the close-hauled speed* is greater.

Close Fetching with various Rigs. But more modern boats may score heavily under certain special circumstances. In a modern yawl rig, with a good gap between the mainsail leech and mizzen mast, if you were prepared to sail about a point and a quarter (about 14 degrees) off, you could set a mizzen staysail, increasing your total sail area by about 18 per cent. This would be very valuable in light weather.

It is largely a question of knowing your boat and how she will react to sailing off under the various wind and sea conditions, and it is important that one should take every opportunity of gaining data. If you have a speed variation indicator this will make things easier. If not, one can resort to half-hourly log readings, being careful regarding the time of reading, since a minute each side of the half-hour will give you a 2 in 30 or a 6.7 per cent error. Or in light weather one can use the Dutchman's log: a piece of wood or some object unaffected by the wind is dropped clear of the ship forward and timed between the stem and as it passes the counter end, with a stop-watch. Quite accurate results are obtained at speeds which are too low to be properly recorded by patent log. For convenience, I make out a table for the speeds 'for every second' so that the speed can be read off directly the time has been taken.

As an instance of the necessity for knowing one's boat's performance—lest one takes quite a wrong decision concerning the amount to 'sail off'—*Myth* sailing in light winds is an interesting example. In Force 1 her fastest point of sailing is five points off the wind. There is therefore no point, in this weather, in ramping her off.

Bermuda Race Conditions compared to Hobart Race. As regards item (*d*), concerning the general weather conditions for the time of the year, we may usefully compare the two big races in which there are long straight legs. The Bermuda Race is a direct course the whole of the 635 miles. The Sydney–Hobart, of 650 miles, has 570 miles or so in the same general direction with only minor alterations in courses to exploit the current. But the latter race has three sets of wind conditions in that distance; the first down the coast of New South Wales, the second across the Bass Straits, and then the south-eastern coast of Tasmania.

It is pretty clear that in the Hobart race we can generally count on a real wind shift a couple of times during the passage. But experience indicates that 65 to 70 per cent of the races will be sailed with the wind free and of this spinnakers will be set perhaps 35 per cent of the time.

In the Bermuda Race the crossing of the Gulf Stream (which often occupies a band some 120 miles wide towards the end of the first half of the race), generally results in fireworks of some sort or another, be it only a few mild squalls. But this does not alter the fact that most of the wind comes from the same school, and as often as not if you start on the starboard leg you sail most of the race on this tack. Therefore it will be by no means safe to bet on a fundamental wind change in the course of the race.

Fastnet Conditions. It is rare for the Fastnet Race to be sailed without some major wind change occurring in the course of the race. But then there is no leg as long as the others in question and it is often possible for the passage from the Scillies to the Fastnet to be made without a major shift. Similarly for the return trip; one cannot definitely count on a shift in that time. On the other hand one is somewhat more likely to have a wind change of some sort on the first long portion of the course, that is to say between clearing the Isle of Wight and arriving off the Lizard.

Our fourth factor (*d*) 'The particular weather report of the moment' needs no elaboration in the present connection.

Rough Rule for Sailing Off. If you decide to go in for a bit of 'sailing off', you will find the following additional general rule useful, particularly when conditions do not enable you to sit down to very extensive or accurate plotting: 'On a close fetch if you sail off a whole point to leeward, from close-hauled, to gain speed, and no shift of wind arrives or is in early prospect by the time you have sailed half the distance to your mark, you should then come close-hauled again. But if you have sailed off only half a point you can wait for your shift till you have sailed two-thirds of the distance.'

Diagram 6 gives you an idea of the extra distance you have to cover owing to various deviations from the direct course, resulting perhaps from a decision to sail fuller or more to windward; or perhaps to go looking for wind or for set, or for some other reason.

The direct distance between the two marks is assumed to be 100 miles. The actual distances covered shown in column A assume that one resumes the direct course after covering one-fifth of the distance; column B after two-fifths of the distance; C, three-fifths; and D, four-fifths. The explanatory sketch represents graphically the four different alternative courses, A, B, C, D, for a 15 degree initial deviation.

Tactics for Reaching. If the mark is at some distance it is very often permissible to make a slight deviation from the direct course in order to get a particular sail to draw. As already mentioned half a point off may well enable you to get the mizzen staysail set; and in light weather this may pay handsomely. For instance in *Orion*, the bigger mizzen staysail was 600 sq. ft. Similarly a slight alteration of course, perhaps to leeward, or maybe to windward, might well enable a particularly favourable combination of sails to draw between the masts of a schooner.

In light going and a beam wind, even with a sloop or cutter, it may well pay you to sail half the way to your mark with a genoa set, pointing say a point high of your mark (and travelling faster than with the wind just about the beam), and at half-way if the wind were still in the same direction, to turn on to a direct course for the mark which will then bring the wind a point abaft the beam, and set a spinnaker, which will under R.O.R.C. limits, have an area 80 per cent greater than the genoa. In connection with such deviations, Diagram 6 will be of interest.

The possibility of exploiting such advantages will depend on the particular rig and outfit of sails in your boat. But in any case they are light weather tactics: in fresher conditions it will normally pay to go straight for your mark.

The Weather Mark—Holding to Windward. There is another quite separate aspect of reaching, which applies only to approaching a fairly near mark, or obstruction to sea room—which is the question how much windwarding should be kept in hand. Allowance is normally made only for minor variation in wind direction and only for a small amount of 'heading' by the wind. When the wind is on or abaft the beam, no allowance need be made, since a minor change still leaves the wind free. With the wind $4\frac{1}{2}$ to $5\frac{1}{2}$ points on the bow, however, a heading of 1 to 2 points will result in being unable to lay the mark. Therefore it is customary to lay up for a while a little above the mark, perhaps half a

DISTANCES COVERED BETWEEN TWO MARKS ONE HUNDRED MILES APART DUE TO DEVIATIONS FROM A DIRECT COURSE

INITIAL DEVIATION MADE FROM THE DIRECT COURSE	PROPORTION OF DISTANCE COVERED BEFORE RESUMING THE DIRECT COURSE			
	A $\frac{1}{5}$	B $\frac{2}{5}$	C $\frac{3}{5}$	D $\frac{4}{5}$
5°	100·05	100·2	100·45	100·7
10°	100·53	101·0	102·4	105·8
15°	101·0	102·3	105·1	111·7
20°	101·7	104·3	109·3	120·0
25°	102·6	106·9	115·0	130·4
30°	104·6	110·3	121·8	143·0

NOTE:
IT WILL BE POSSIBLE TO INTERPOLATE FOR INTERMEDIATE COURSES AND FOR TURNS MADE AT OTHER POINTS. AS THE BASE DISTANCE IS 100, THE INCREASES IN DISTANCE CAN BE TREATED AS PERCENTAGES AND EASILY APPLIED TO OTHER BASE DISTANCES.

Diagram 6.

point, if it can be done without too much sacrifice of speed—this will depend on the boat and on the sea conditions. I say 'for a while' because when one has slowly worked to a safe distance to windward—and it should be slowly to avoid an undue deviation from the correct course—one resumes a direct course.

The exact action to be taken varies so much on circumstances that it is difficult to be more specific than this. The amount one works up may be increased if the mark is not in sight, perhaps owing to fog or weather, if one is uncertain of one's position, always provided there is no risk of sailing right past the mark. In the case of the Fastnet for instance there is no such risk, since the coast behind will come up. But if the mark is a lightship well off shore, then one can't afford to work to weather to an extent which will unduly increase the chance of missing it altogether.

It should be noted that this refers to marks which are being approached from, say, under 30 miles. When being approached from a considerable distance the chances of a change of weather make the speed aspect more important than that of the exact course for the mark.

Tactics in Down Wind Sailing. Let us first consider the conditions when the wind is dead aft or fine on the quarter. The one rule we must get firmly in our minds from the start is this 'never run by the lee'. You may say that this is obvious. But just the same, once the main boom is nicely guyed forward, one is apt to find the helmsman hanging on to the course ordered, carefully watching his compass; while he has failed to realise that the wind has crept round to his lee quarter.

In light or moderate weather running by the lee results in a serious loss of speed. In strong winds the effect is less serious, but one will not be tempted to do this on account of the discomfort and risk of gybing.

So as soon as there is any tendency to run by the lee, she should be quietly luffed to bring the wind fine on the proper quarter. This may take you out of your course, but the loss will be less than running by the lee. Should the change in the wind hold, one can eventually gybe. But while you are preparing to gybe, rigging fresh guys and so on, you should be luffed out and not running by the lee.

The apparent wind when astern is more changeable than when ahead, as we see in Diagram 7, and so one has to be continually on the look-out, and in light weather be prepared to steer a comparatively zigzag course in order to keep the wind slightly on the quarter.

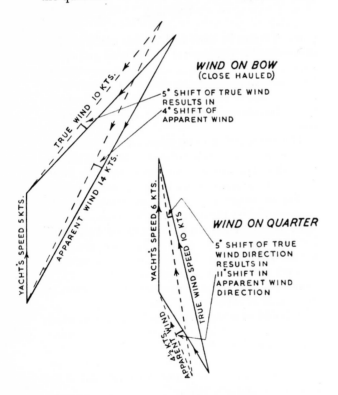

SHOWING CHANGES IN APPARENT WIND
DUE TO SHIFT OF TRUE WIND
NOTE - ORIGINAL WINDS IN FULL LINE
SHIFTED WINDS DOTTED

Diagram 7.

As we can see again from Diagram 7, the apparent wind is always more out on the quarter (farther ahead) than the true wind. This means that after gybing one has only to bring the true wind slightly on the new weather quarter for the sails to fill properly. The importance of this is in connection with the question of how soon to gybe. Tacking down wind will be dealt with separately, but the point I want to make at the moment is that only a relatively small change of course will bring the apparent wind from nicely out on one quarter to nicely out on the other. Therefore in moderate winds, where the question of sailing well up into the wind to increase speed does not arise, a gybe can profitably be made rather earlier than might be expected. This is not easy to understand, but it is worth a little study and thought.

In light winds one travels appreciably faster with the wind nicely out on the quarter, rather than with the wind fine on the quarter, because one's apparent wind speed is increased. The problem, and it is not an easy one to solve, is how much running up towards the wind pays?

Sailing Up to Light Breezes. The first thing to note is that unlike the problem of a close fetch, where we were also estimating how much off the direct track to sail to gain speed, the sideways deflection off the rhumb line course is not as a rule of any importance. Either the mark is so far away that the deflection is geometrically negligible, or if the mark is nearer, one can run into the rhumb line on the other gybe under the same conditions as one ran out. Gybing under light conditions is a comparatively easy business and should waste very little time; of course, without lowering the spinnaker.

Tacking Down Wind. If, as one can, one assumes that the deflection is to be neglected, then the ratio of the distance travelled when sailing off course to the direct distance is the secant of the angle between the courses. The extra distance to be covered expressed as a percentage for various courses, that is to say for various amounts of sailing off (down wind) course is as follows:

$$5 \text{ degrees} - 0.4 \text{ per cent}$$
$$10 \text{ degrees} - 1.5 \text{ per cent}$$
$$15 \text{ degrees} - 3.5 \text{ per cent}$$
$$20 \text{ degrees} - 6.4 \text{ per cent}$$
$$25 \text{ degrees} - 10.3 \text{ per cent}$$
$$30 \text{ degrees} - 15.5 \text{ per cent}$$
$$35 \text{ degrees} - 22.1 \text{ per cent}$$
$$40 \text{ degrees} - 30.5 \text{ per cent}$$

This table explains more quickly and definitely than any other way, why tacking down wind can pay. It is clear that the gain in speed necessary to make 20 degrees deviation is easily attained.

It pays to steer 20 degrees up if one's speed increases by more than one-sixteenth. If you are in light wind doing 3 knots this is one-fifth of a knot; and the actual gain might well be half a knot.

In some cases, with *very* light airs it does pay to sail as much as 25 degrees from the direct track. This will be a case where one's speedometer may help, or the use of a Dutchman's log. However, owing to the fact that the yacht's speed is reducing the apparent wind speed, a small variation in true wind speed strength will make a much larger relative change in apparent wind strength. We have already noted in the diagrams the same effect regarding direction and these effects result in great difficulty in getting steady comparable readings from which to estimate the gain in speed from 'sailing up'.

So difficult is it to get any practical speed figures, that it is better in very light winds to sail two points up and leave it at that. But this is only in light winds. At other times the sailing up should be confined to the amount necessary to ensure that the wind is just on the quarter rather than dead astern.

In fact with the spinnaker set in light airs the apparent wind is so variable that it is often best to sail so as to keep the *apparent* wind about 40 degrees out on the quarter and accept whatever course this gives one—a pretty zigzag one, but possibly the best speed you can get; and it may obviate the need for constant sail trimming and disturbing the spinnaker. A good deal will depend on the direction of the sea which may affect the steadiness or otherwise of the boat, and in turn the amount of wind one can hold in a spinnaker, which one is striving to keep full and drawing, in a tumble of sea.

With two-masted rigs the necessity for sailing up is often greater than with cutters or sloops, so as to put the 'tween-mast light sails to work. This is particularly so in the case of the schooner with the big light fisherman sail; this will be comparable in size with the spinnaker which can only be set from the foremast head in a schooner, under normal racing rules.

In the case of yawls and ketches if a $2\frac{1}{2}$ point alteration in course, to bring the wind from near astern to well out on the quarter, enables the mizzen staysail to be got to draw—then in very light winds this will probably pay. It won't do any worth-while work with the breeze right aft.

But finally one must make the point that this sailing up can only really pay when you have the proper full-allowed size of spinnakers, of modern parachute cut, and in the case of two-masted ships, light 'tween-mast sails of maximum area.

7

HEAVY WEATHER RACING

Some of the points made in this short chapter are to be found elsewhere in the book, in another context. They are covered again here for the sake of completeness, because thus assembled I feel them to be more easily digested and remembered.

Having got into our oilskins in good time, with a good strip of towelling inside round our necks, close-fitting cuffs, rubber bands round our ankles, and a couple of good sweaters under all this, we can face what's coming with equanimity, and settle down to deal with ship handling in strong and gale conditions.

Whereas in light and moderate weather the crew will be 'jumping to it', with the skipper striking the high note to keep everyone on their toes, the heavy weather tempo must be made deliberate. In addition to the immediate considerations of ship handling and ship serving, he will have in mind two paramount needs; to avoid accidents to personnel and equipment, and to conserve and maintain the health and strength of the crew, as may be necessary in relation to the length of the course.

The recommended measures in respect of heavy weather feeding, dosage, clothing, and bunking will not be recapitulated here, as they are too long to be repeated, but they should be considered in relation to the other aspects of heavy-weather racing.

Sail Changes. Let us first talk about the timing of sail changes. The general tendency of most people is to delay reductions of sail too long, and conversely to be too slow when the wind eases in setting more sail. One probably delays changing back to the larger or to full sail 'in case it is just a lull'. This can be a bad fault. But when a boat is being fairly hard pressed, very little speed is lost by a moderate reduction of sail; and if it is fairly obvious that it is going to be necessary to reef some time in the near future it is better to 'do it now', before she becomes hopelessly over-canvassed. The operation will then be more quickly and smartly done, and will take less out of the crew. The psychological effect will be good too; compared to waiting till the ship is really overpressed and then having a struggle to reef.

All this applies with special force when going to windward. Perhaps the only exception is on a reach, not too far from the finish, when it is permissible to hang on with the vessel over-canvassed.

Where one takes a reef in the mainsail early then one can hang on to large, or fairly large, headsails for a while. These keep her sailing while reefing, and when the full weight of the blow is upon one, they will be relatively quickly changed; specially in a cutter.

In sloops of the *Maica* type or in *Belmore* we generally roll down a couple or three rolls in the main before we change from genoa to working jib; and with the onset of still heavier weather we roll down a good deal more before changing from the working jib to the storm jib.

Reefing Cutters. In cutters like *Oryx* or *Outlaw*, when I am of the opinion that a moderate gale will be experienced, as the wind increases I change from a large yankee to second yankee. I then put a reef in the main; and keep set the second yankee —a sail reaching nearly to the masthead—and a moderate overlap genoa staysail. During this phase I hank on the storm jib and heavy staysail on to their stays and lash them down on deck; if the indications are that the gale is going to be a severe one, I pull down two reefs, together, at this time. In either case, except with roller reefing, to reef I lower the mainsail completely, a thing which at this stage, before the wind increases too much, can generally be done without altering course, and the boat continues at fair speed on her big headsails. In a masthead cutter rig where the mainsail is very moderate in size it is generally possible to lower the mainsail even when running before the wind. The mainsheet is hardened as much as proves feasible, keeping weight all the time on the main boom foreguy and the topping lift; and then lowering the sail as quickly as possible.

Where a boom crutch is available the boom is lowered into this. It is then a very quick operation to lace in a reef really neatly, and it requires very much less effort than pulling down a reef with the sail hoisted. If this technique is used it is not necessary to incur the windage of reef points; simply have a row of reef eyelets and pass a lacing. It is best to start lacing in the middle of the sail, the middle of the lacing being marked in colour (but not with a knot) so that two men can work together, one lacing forward and the other aft, each with an assistant to hold the sail and gather it up as necessary.

It is most necessary to have two or three sets of gear comprising the lacing cords and the two lashings, one for the clew and one for the tack, all prepared and put on one side; and never to use these for any other purpose so that they are ready to hand as soon as needed; and all in good condition also.

Here again we have another advantage of the cutter rig over the sloop; the relative ease of reefing. Of course, in the smaller sizes of yacht where roller reefing is used this question does not arise; or at least it is of less importance.

Handling Storm Sails. In a cutter in very heavy weather it is generally better to set two small headsails rather than one medium-sized one. Experience indicates that the two headsails and a reefed mainsail make her steadier; having less tendency to sheer off her course, and being easier to steer; in a word, carrying her sail better. Also the centre of effort of the sails will be low. Finally if one gets a severe prolonged squall one can then quickly lower the staysail and leave the ship well balanced.

The set of storm headsails requires study in advance. They should be properly tried out to determine the correct position of the sheet leads on deck. Often these require to be further inboard than those of the big sails.

In strong and gale force winds the leach of a headsail is very apt to quiver, and shake the whole mast, upsetting to some extent the set of all the sails. Moreover this vibration if prolonged puts extra fatigue, stress, and wear on all the fittings of the mast, and the rig generally. This tendency is particularly marked with terylene. With a view to reducing the tendency of leaches of storm sails to shake I now always fit them with three or four short thin plastic battens, permanently sewn into the sail. Then if necessary the leach line (which I specify in storm sails to be in strong terylene) can be tautened without pulling the sail into a baggy shape. As these sails will be small, the battens do not prevent the sails coming about and they do not catch up. If made in plastic they can be left in the sails when these are bagged without risk of breakage. In larger yachts where wood battens may be preferred these should preferably be made in ash. They must in this case be thoroughly varnished; if not they will retain wet and will not dry out when the sail is dried. A waterproofing agent may be applied to the wood prior to varnishing.

Down Wind in Heavy Weather. First, we must make the point that windward sailing in such conditions, although tough work, is in a sense relatively easy; easy in so much that having got the yacht trimmed down to proper storm canvas, well sheeted home, there should not be much to do, other than slog it out.

On the other hand hard down wind sailing from the skipper's point of view is a much more tricky problem. It calls in the first place for very nice judgment as to exactly what sail should be carried, and as to how it should be set. It requires a good deal of nerve and a certain amount of luck to keep a yacht sailing her fastest and safely down wind in gale conditions. The helmsman must be reliable, and alert. Also, one should add, not unnerved by the endless series of rushing, towering seas, which one after the other come up, hang seemingly poised over the counter and then, as she lifts, foam on under and around the yacht.

The risk of broach-to is ever present; a risk which is greater when the maximum of sail is being carried and when the boat is going her fastest; thus a risk which must be accepted.

Provided those on deck each have a line around them the damage to a well-found yacht resulting from a broach-to is not as a rule serious. And the chances of being pooped by a sea when one is well offshore are not very great. On the other hand when running in a big sea and gale force winds into soundings, that is from ocean into shore conditions, the probability of a sea breaking on board is considerable.

In the *Mouse of Malham* racing up Channel near Dover, and trying to carry a medium big spinnaker in too strong a wind (an error of judgment on my part) we broached good and properly. She ran out of control across the seas, until the breeze was on or just before the beam, and the masthead spinnaker pulled her over until she was more or less laid flat. I saw *Blue Disa* in 1949 do much the same thing; though in less wind but with a bigger spinnaker. In neither case was any damage done; except perhaps to the crew's nerves.

In 1955 racing round the Owers lightship in gale conditions in shallow water, *Mouse of Malham* was rolled over by a breaking sea well beyond the horizontal. Some things from the galley landed up in the coach roof, and on deck Mac McGrath and I looked down the line of the masts into the trough of the sea—glad to have a taut line round our chests. When the breaking sea had rolled on into the shallows *Mouse* came up and sailed on.

Running Sails. The sails to be used depend a good deal on the rig and characteristics of the hull. Often one arrives at the weather mark reefed after a turn to windward and has to decide where to put on extra sail. If she is at all hard headed and has broaching tendencies it will generally pay to leave the main sail reefed or rolled down and to put more sail on forward.

On the other hand a spinnaker when set increases the tendency to rhythmic rolling, so the two things have to be weighed up against one another, because either can become the limiting factor in hard driving down wind. Rhythmic rolling is discussed in detail elsewhere, but it is worth remembering that when conditions become marginal, in the sense that she is rolling so much that she can barely carry the canvas she has up, a slight alteration in course may enable you to bring the boat under control; perhaps by a slight luff when you are nearly 'dead before'.

Likewise, when broaching-to looks like requiring the handing of the spinnaker (and a big speed reduction) a slightly more down-wind course may enable you to continue carrying it. If the breeze eases later you will be glad to have the big bag still flying and you can luff up again. If later it hardens, you will not mind handing the spinnaker and you may then after luffing go faster with the wind further on to the beam rather than fine on the quarter.

Mastheads—Spinnaker Outfits. In masthead cutters which have short main booms, the full-size spinnakers are so large compared to the mainsail that some graduation in size and purpose of spinnaker is more necessary than in other rigs with smaller triangles. In *Monk of Malham* in 1967 we had four spinnakers; a full-size lightweight Terylene spinnaker for general use and particularly good for light reaching with the wind on the beam; then another full-sized vertically cut spinnaker in a little stronger nylon for harder running in winds, say, Force 5 or 6. In these strengths there is no need to attempt to carry such a sail with wind near the beam, so the need for a horizontally seamed sail is less and the vertically cut sail is much stronger.

The other two are storm spinnakers. The exact dimensions will depend on the aspect ratio of the fore triangle. I suggest that the larger storm spinnaker should be of the 'Wrens' Knickers' type (see the Spinnaker Design section), giving one a sail nominally 60 per cent of the full area.

In the modern 'six-sevenths' sloop, where the area of the fore triangle is nearly equal to that of the mainsail, I design the sail outfit to include two full-size spinnakers: *i.e.* full width and full length, but differently cut, plus the storm spinnaker referred to above.

The smaller storm spinnaker of a masthead

cutter—not needed in other rigs—can usefully be 70 per cent hoist and 55 per cent width, giving one a sail 38 per cent full area. We ran home from the Fastnet Rock very happily under such a sail in 1957. In each case these storm spinnakers should be set over at least one and preferably two small low headsails. The spinnaker pole heel should be as high up the mast as feasible. Both the C.C.A. and R.O.R.C. rules limit the height to which the boom heel can be set, and it should be feasible in most yachts to have the heel slid up by a hand standing on the main boom without resorting to heel purchases (except in larger yachts). A stop must be fitted at the top of the track in which the spinnaker boom heel fitting slides. Larger yachts will need a heel line led to a block above and down to winch; and a down haul.

When one gets settled in this manner with a small spinnaker drawing nicely over the top of two small headsails the boat is generally reasonably steady even in a seaway. The point in getting the boom as high as possible is to enable the head of the small spinnaker to be hoisted to, or at least near to, the masthead, thus reducing the spinnaker's tendency to increase rolling.

A boomed-out genoa can, if no storm spinnaker is available, serve. In practice it is less satisfactory than the smaller spinnaker; and if it is your best genoa, it can well get spoilt for its more important role.

These small spinnakers should be about 2 or 3 ounces heavier than the normally recommended spinnaker weight for the boat. (*See* Appendix IV as to exact weights.)

For higher aspect ratio fore triangles it will be necessary to increase the widths, but the hoist should not be less than 70 per cent full hoist or it will be difficult to get the head of the spinnaker near the masthead.

One of the small spinnakers should be capable of being hoisted on the staysail halyard, should in storm conditions it prove impracticable to set it to the masthead; should, for instance, the boat get very wild and difficult to control.

I have previously referred to the need under these conditions for all hands on deck to look after themselves, and if necessary clip their safety clips or belts to the ship. It is specially important for the helmsman to do this, as his attention and strength will be concentrated on his tiller or wheel.

Goosewinged Headsails. When the wind is too strong for even a small spinnaker, the spinnaker boom can be employed to boom out a small headsail. The boom should be rigged in the ordinary way with fore and aft guys and a lift, but instead of an outhaul the weather sheet of the headsail is led through the block eye or snatch hook in the end of the boom. The sail should be hanked on to its stay as usual, and then drawn out to the boom end by the weather sheet. A headsail cut low in the foot should be used for best results. By having the sail hanked on to the stay it is kept in better control. The tendency to make the ship roll, and even to start a rhythmic roll, which is evident with a free sail set to weather, is much reduced if the sail is either on a stay, or at least tacked in its usual place and hoisted with a taut luff.

In a cutter a genoa staysail (not a genoa jib) is an ideal sail for this purpose. Even light Terylene is quite strong enough. In the case of a sloop the genoa will be too large and the working jib may be too high in the foot. In this case two special low-cut sails with a modest hoist may be provided specially for running in hard weather.

When the ship becomes 'wild', sheering about when running in gale or near gale conditions, it often pays to lower the reefed mainsail and sheet a headsail to the main boom end, to leeward. Alternatively and better, if there is available on board a second spinnaker boom, this may be rigged to leeward and the leeward headsail sheeted out to this.

This is quite allowable under R.O.R.C. rules and rating—provided the sail is a genuine headsail or a hard weather running sail of not more than half the rated area of the vessel. In other words, provided this is not used as an excuse for setting twin spinnakers.

Incidentally twin spinnakers were allowed in 1937, and I used them with great success in my *Maid of Malham*. They enabled me in medium breezes downwind to outsail *Foxhound* or *Bloodhound*, in spite of their 10 ft. of extra waterline length. Later twin spinnakers were barred, principally on the very valid grounds of the expense involved, and also because with no mainsail set one is not very manœuvrable; it might, for instance, be difficult to pick up a man who had fallen overboard. But under twin spinnakers sailing a masthead cutter was a great thrill.

To return to our stormy muttons, I must emphasise again the advantage of running in very strong winds under two boomed-out headsails, either sheeted to one spinnaker boom and the main boom or to two spinnaker booms, which is the best arrangement. It seems to draw the ship along by her head, and has a wonderfully steadying effect.

Hull and Sail Balance. Some boats are so much easier to 'run hard' than others. It is more a matter of hull balance than length of keel. The *Mouse* though very short in the keel runs beautifully in strong winds—she planes like a dinghy, the tiller

'goes hard' and she is as easy as a lamb; and going knots faster than the heavier boats of the same size. *Artica II* is of much the same design, though bigger.

Many yachts of shallow draft with centre-plates are absolute bitches when running hard in a big seaway. Not to be confused with medium draft yachts where the plate is a mere extra, they sheer about all over the place and need constant watching.

I think it is an important general maxim for racing in strong wind conditions to carry a little less sail than seems the optimum up wind, and a little more than seems natural down wind.

To return again a moment to the sloop rig. In storm conditions when going to windward, some sloop yachts, particularly those with transom sterns or fine after bodies, develop serious lee helm when close reefed and setting a headsail on the usual stay. The remedy is to set a storm staysail on a special stay or flying, tacked to a point about one-third of the base of the fore triangle abaft the fore stay, and perhaps hoisted to a lower point. It is sometimes possible to use the spinnaker lift, if this is made good and strong, as a halyard. This will lead to the crosstrees and the well spaced out lower shrouds should take care of the extra fore and aft loading engendered. This staysail should have an extra stout luffwire, if it is to be set flying. There is a good deal to be said, in a sloop, for having an inner fore stay in lieu of two lower forward shrouds. It saves weight and cost and windage. It clears the sheets from the mast when tacking and it may well help in the above connection. Only in shifting the spinnaker boom over when gybing is it in the way. In a new sloop yacht this question should be studied early during the vessel's trials. And every new yacht, whatever her rig, should seek out heavy weather as a trial as soon as her sails are stretched.

Finally, a general word. I suggest that gale conditions should be considered as all part of the game; as a set of circumstances to be dealt with by careful forethought and preparation, and by logical handling at sea. If this outlook prevails among skipper, navigator, and crew, much of the terror of storm weather is removed, and one sets out happily knowing that in all probability one can readily cope with anything that comes along.

Optimum Angle of Heel. It is important to discover early in a yacht's racing life to what angle she can usefully be heeled when going to windward. *Mouse of Malham* and *Artica*, unbeatable in wind free conditions, start to slow up when heeled to more than 30 degrees. On the other hand *Belmore* and her several sisters will hurl themselves happily to windward at 40 degrees or more, and much the same can be said of the many *Maicas, Monk* and others.

8

NAVIGATION

Navigation is a complete subject in itself, and one which is very well covered in all its aspects by a variety of manuals. So the purpose of this short chapter is only to touch on a few points which are either peculiar to ocean racing or have a special aspect in the light of offshore racing requirements.

You may well wonder why navigation in ocean racing is any different from navigation during any other voyage. While the general principles of normal navigation hold good for this sport, one is faced with some particular problems.

The skipper requires to know his position, to the best of the available knowledge, absolutely bang up to the minute; so that he can take instant advantage of any change of wind or conditions of sea or weather.

The actual physical difficulty of taking and plotting bearings and sights in a small sailing vessel going to windward, while being driven to the limit of her capacity often in heavy weather, and carrying a large crew who take up most of the space, is increased beyond what one can imagine in the charthouse of a steamer, or even in a large cruising yacht, which will be taking things comparatively easy, without too much press of sail.

Finally, there is the difficulty of maintaining and estimating the course accurately, which is increased by the hard driving and by the necessity of gaining every inch to weather, and on many other occasions by the necessity for minor changes in course, to suit varying wind conditions, regardless of 'course ordered'.

At the other end of the scale there is the small boat cruising yachtsman. Although to some extent the conditions are alike, the problem is different because the degree of accuracy needed is lower and there is not the necessity for keeping the plot right up to date.

Before we get down to the job, we must study the tools a little. The first requirement is a serviceable chart table. It is quite remarkable how few yachts are adequately equipped in this respect. One finds large smart vessels with every sort of comfort and expensive equipment, and the owner at sea trying to do his plotting on the saloon table, off which the watch below are also getting their

meal, and which they have anointed with considerable dollops of that insidious commodity—marmalade. Every now and then his pencil runs half through the chart as it comes to the crack where the table leaf hinges. Finally, someone spills half a cup of tea on the chart, which in desperation is then double-folded and taken up into the cockpit, where someone puts his foot on it—after it has acquired more dampness. Is it any wonder that the plot is far from accurate?

Chart Table. Good plotting is essential, and every ocean racer must have a decent chart table, and it is possible to arrange this even in the smallest boat. In the three R.N.S.A. 'Twenty-Fours' built at Camper & Nicholsons in 1949 I arranged a chart table about 30 in. long fore and aft and about 28 in. broad athwartships. This chart table is hinged, and folds up vertically 'and a bit farther' to form the back of a settee when in harbour. Behind this are book racks, instruments, and stowages for dividers and pencils, also for india-rubbers and the magnifying glass.

The chart table folds down over the foot of the bunk. Opposite is a small flap seat. This seat is handy too in a general way, as it is clear of the two bunks which will be in use together a good part of the time at sea. The forward edge of the table has a canvas screen which 'folds in' when the table is vertical. It keeps the light of the chart table off the sleepers' faces. A similar sized chart table has been arranged in our 20-ft waterline J.O.G. racer *Wista*, without appreciable sacrifice of accommodation, so there is clearly no reason why any boat should be without one.

In *Rani*, where I had not the time fully to rearrange the accommodation, I fixed in a few minutes a perfectly good chart table consisting simply of a draughtsman's standard drawing board, hinged to the ship's side over the foot of a bunk, supported at its inboard edge by a pair of light chains which provided means of adjusting the slope, and of holding the board up against the side deck above when not in use.

As to the actual construction of the chart table, the principal consideration is to get material which will not warp. Quarter-inch plywood of good quality, framed and cross-battened with Western Red cedar is about the best and lightest job. There should be a small beading on the inboard edge with its edges well rounded to avoid cutting the chart. In large yachts which have a 4-ft. fronted chart table one can have a slot in the front of the table lip to drop the near edge of the chart through.

It is important that the navigator be, in all but the smallest yachts, in a place clear of the gangway through the accommodation. In *Belmore* we had a chart table running athwartships with the foot 'not head' of the navigator's berth under it and a seat on the edge of the berth. (*See* page 50.) *Maryca*'s table was similar but had 20 degrees of athwartship inclination adjustment.

British charts come in all sizes and shapes and therefore there is no ideal chart table size— roughly, the bigger the better. The *Minx* size, 28 in. by 30 in. is a good one to aim at in a very small yacht. One can often trim the edges of a chart to reduce its working size for small yachts. *Myth*'s table took up the whole space between two partial bulkheads about 3 ft. apart. *Merle of Malham* (1967) was similarly arranged. There was a 4-in. deep chart stowage under the working table, which gave one 6 in. into which one's knees could be slipped. The working table top hinged, and could be secured open to allow one to rummage with both hands in the chart stowage. This whole arrangement worked out well, and with one's knees pulled up under the chart table, and one's feet on the ship's side, one can steady oneself in a seaway, and have both hands available for the chart work. The *Myth*'s width athwartships of the table is 28 in. One other tiny point; the beading of the tables does not extend to the ends, leaving room to sweep the crumbs out when in harbour or cruising, when in use as a food table opposite the galley.

Although there is no standard size of chart spread out, all Admiralty Charts fold into the standard folio cover, which is 20 in. by 28 in. This is a handy size to know, so that suitable flat stowages for spare charts can be arranged an inch or two larger. However little room there is one can generally spare space to arrange a space an inch under the table which will stow a goodly number of charts. One can use the space between the mattress and a wood bunk bottom, provided the bunk is 21 in. or more wide, for stowing a thin folio, if nowhere else is available.

But practically all French charts will lie flat on a chart table 105 cm. by 78 cm. and will stow in a similar space; they do not fold.

As an *aide mémoire*, here is a suggested short list of chart table gear which you need:

Emergency chart table lighting.
One parallel ruler.
Six HB pencils.
Three small pieces of soft india-rubber (artist's grade).
Deck watch.
Two pairs of dividers, one long- and one short-legged.
Sextant.
Magnifying glass.
Binoculars.
Supply of soft tissue paper for cleaning lenses.
Barometer—temperature-compensated.
Deck log and Navigator's Notebook.
Hand-bearing compass.
Clock, eight-day (preferably with alarm for alerting one of weather radio broadcasts).
Torch, small, for identifying charts.
Navigational publications are given on the next page.

All this gear needs a proper stowage in the vicinity of the chart table, together with a rack for books. The deck log and navigator's work book and the tide atlas, which are being constantly used and are in consequence liable to be continually sculling about on the chart table, need a specially handy clip. In *Myth* we had two strips of $1\frac{1}{2}$ in. by $\frac{1}{8}$ in. Birmabright which lay parallel to the ship's side, leaving a slot into which the log could be thrust. The pencil and divider stowage is generally best arranged in vertical holes; or if they slope, the slope should be fore and aft rather than athwartships.

The clock should preferably be visible from the companionway, as well as from the chart table, so that the watch on deck, and in a small boat the helmsman, can see when it is time to read the log or call the watch. Since it also needs to be kept dry, the right position requires a little study.

Always keep a separate torch allocated for navigation and stowed accordingly; then if the normal lighting fails or is inadequate for any special task, you are not dependent on the deck torches, which may be in use. Better still have a powerful 6 volt battery lamp in a slip over the chart table, set downwards. This can well serve as a steamer scarer also.

Books and Sundries. The following is a list of books which we carried in *Myth*. Those marked with an asterisk are only needed for celestial navigation. Those marked with a dagger are useful but not essential:

Tables of Computed Altitude and Azimuth* (H.D. 486 or in U.S.A. H.O. 214); *Tidal Stream Atlas* (for the relevant areas); *Astro Stars for Air Navigation* (selected stars, A.P. 3270 or in U.S.A. H.O.

249)*; *Nautical Almanac* (of the relevant year); *Tide Tables*; *Sailing Directions* (to suit locality); *Lecky's Danger Angles*†; *Admiralty List of W/T Signals*; *'What Star Is It?*; *Admiralty List of Lights* (for seas in question).

Apart from these books I like to have the following posted up handy to the chart table:

Deviation Card (if there is any); Dutchman's Log Table (in two columns, seconds against knots for every second, worked for the overall length of the ship); Sail List (reference numbers, stowages, areas, weights of cloth); International Code of Flags (illustrated card); Speed by second bow wave table.

Speed, Distance and Depth Recording. The speed by second bow wave is obtained from the formula speed in knots equals four-thirds square root of distance in feet from stem at water to crest of second bow wave.

A useful but non-essential item is a Stuart's distance meter—a small instrument which is handier than a sextant for taking the angles subtended by an object of known height, and which by means of a cunning scale, reads off the distance away from the object. Although used generally to enable warships in company to keep station by observing the angle subtended by the next ahead's mast-height to the water, it is on occasions very welcome to the racer trying to skirt past a lighthouse, or cliff which has outlying dangers; in stemming a tide, to sneak round close to a headland may mean less current or cutting a little corner. This is really an easy short cut to the sextant angle and Lecky's Tables.

In the absence of echo-sounding gear a really useful item is the 'Harpoon' Depth Finder. This used to be made by Messrs. Thomas Walker, of Oxford Street, Birmingham, and as far as I know is the only trade-made one of its kind. It is a hand lead which records the depth, regardless of the angle at which the line descends, to that it can be used under way. A propeller-shaped vane revolves as the log descends and records on a small dial. At first it is difficult to believe that this device will function, but I have never detected any error in it. It is made in two sizes. The smaller Mark II is very adequate for the average yacht and is easier to handle. It is designed for 30 fathoms. With the larger one I have had soundings under way up to 40 fathoms. The principal difficulty is dealing with the line. In *Maid* we had a small drum under the bridge deck and used 2 lb. hemp line. This could only be used at quite low speeds. Still it was a big improvement on the hand lead. In *Myth* we had a better arrangement in the form of a drum off a Kelvin sounding machine. I reduced the amount of

wire to 100 fathoms, and fitted a brass knob which turned on its spigot bolted to the side flange of the drum; for winding in. The drum was kept in the bilge till needed, and then mounted on a permanent fixed vertical brass spigot on the counter.

More recently I have used with the harpoon depth finder a device designed by my father; an outsize salmon fishing reel mounted on a pistol grip with a special 100-lb.-breaking-strain line. It is essential to have a special wind-home handle.

Echo sounding was permitted for the first time in R.O.R.C. races in 1958. Where money is available it is worth its place in all but the smallest racers.

Deck Log. I have generally made out my own blank deck logs, because I have never found one of the standard ones quite suitable. In ocean racing I find it desirable to log the course actually steered at least every half hour, because if left longer in variable conditions, one cannot make an accurate estimate from memory of the mean course. I think it essential to have two separate columns for 'course ordered' and 'course actually steered' so as to make it clear to all that one wants the whole truth and nothing but the truth logged; not simply the course ordered.

As to speed and distance recorders, the Brooks and Gatehouse (Lymington, Hampshire) Harrier Speed-Com-Distance recorder seems without a peer. Very small propellers project port and starboard just forward of the fin keel. They, with repeaters for the cockpit and so on, are very expensive and if too dear our old friend the patent log takes pride of place. I normally use a Walker Excelsior Mark IV log. This comes in a handy box with spare log line, a tin of light oil for the recorder head, a spare spinner, and spare leads for the line. The log recording head should be mounted as near central as possible and as low, as near the water, as is convenient, on the transom. The next consideration is to get the correct length of line; that is to say the minimum length (and drag) to give accurate readings. Too short a line will cause the spinner to surface, or run in the disturbed water near the surface when going at full speed.

My rough rule for the length of log line is:

Length in ft. $= 10S + 5H - 30$

Where $S =$ maximum speed of boat (neglecting planing)

$H =$ height of instrument above water.

This will give you a line something less than that recommended by the makers, who are, of course, more concerned with the accuracy of their instrument than with the drag that results.

To reduce still further the drag, Messrs. Walker have supplied me with a special fine nylon log line. This has proved satisfactory.

I have sometimes carried an extra 40-ft. log line with a reduced weight sinker in light weather for low speed recording. But when it breezes up, one is generally busy doing other things—shifting sail and so on—and it may be inconvenient to spare a hand to change back to the normal line.

As to speedometers apart from the B. and G. there are three types. They are primarily of assistance in sail trimming but as they may also operate as distance recorders they are included in the navigation chapter. The most usual is that exemplified by the Kenyon, which has a small finger projecting from the hull, well below water, which is moved against a spring by the pressure of the water and transmits hydraulically the reading to a gauge in the charthouse or cockpit. These give fairly good results, but in some hulls, they vary their readings with the heel of the boat, no doubt owing to a change in the direction of the water flow relative to the fore and aft line, at the position of the finger.

For this reason some owners fit two Kenyons, one each side, and take the mean of the readings. Kenyons have also a distance recorder based on the mean reading of the speedometer.

The Kenyon type offers some constant resistance in the water, but it cannot be very much because the Americans, having access to all the recent tank test data, use them in their six-metres. The other snag is, of course, their vulnerability to damage when docking or slipping. There is no doubt that some maintenance is involved. American yacht stations run 'Kenyon service'.

The second type registers the pull of the patent log line. It has the advantage that it involves no extra drag or water resistance over that already resulting from the log; it can be made in such a form that it requires virtually no maintenance.

The B. & G. propeller type has been referred to already. There are others; and venturi types which work only fairly well in sheltered waters. This speed-distance log known as the Harrier records distance as in a car, and speed on a dial repeater, cockpit mounted at a distance. Two dial sizes are optional—automatic by-heel switched; port and starboard underwater units are normal. I now always use a Harrier; excellent as to reliability and accuracy but ghastly as regards their initial cost. You should carry a spare propeller unit, and calibrate the set early in the season. Also carry a set of the tiny spare batteries as there is no main battery connection. A 'real' and doubled speed scale is provided for sail trimming.

In 1955 Walkers introduced a new low drag 'Knotmaster' patent log. This is operated by a very small rotator to show distance run. It has an

excellent speed variation indicator; a 'damped voltmeter' calibrated in knots relaying speed to a dial mounted near the helmsman. This outfit is recommended for J.O.G. and small R.O.R.C. yachts. A repeater for distance can be installed in the chart house, but it needs a full yearly refit.

Hand-bearing Compasses. The normal form of hand-bearing compass has a bowl about 3 in. across fixed to a handle, like a mushroom to its stalk. In the handle is an electric torch to illuminate the card from underneath, so that bearings of lights can be taken at night. This is a desirable feature as the alternative use of a dimmed torch is clumsy.

These compasses are now made in several countries and by various makers. They require to be at least as dead-beat as the steering compass; a test for this is detailed in the steering compass section of the 'Equipment' chapter. The light must be cut down so as to provide the minimum illumination necessary; otherwise you will be dazzled and unable to see faint and distant lights. A red painted bulb is desirable as red is the least disturbing colour for night vision. If you have not time to mask your bulb you can temporarily achieve the same result by fitting a partly spent cell as one of the two in the torch. A spare bulb, which is of lower voltage than that of the ordinary torch, should be kept in the box, secured perhaps in a bit of fine cloth by a big drawing pin, if no proper stowage is provided. Ladies' nail varnish can be used to form an indelible translucent red coating. Unfortunately, for reasons unknown to me, and in spite of entreaties from me and others, most makers have never got round to making a really good dead beat 'handbearer'. Recently the French 'Mini Compass' has become available as a hand bearer, and a month's cruising trial on board *Monk of Malham* indicates superior performance. The price is reasonable and it can be obtained in Britain from Offshore Instruments Ltd. at 47 Upper Grosvenor Street, London W1.

The graduations of the tiny card are magnified by a prism and it is most important that the figures should come up good and clear, because otherwise, with the wetness due to spray, and tired eyes, you won't be able to take quick accurate bearings in bad conditions, particularly if you are long-sighted. It is as well to seal the joints with tape and wind some over the switch, unless these are of watertight type. Thin surgical plaster is best.

The cards are graduated as a rule, 0° to 360° but you can get the 0° to 90° type if you prefer them.

Care and Frequency of Plotting. So much for the equipment, and now for the job. The majority of offshore races are sailed partly in sight of land, and partly out of sight. The navigational requirement is clearly to know at any moment where one is and the direct course for the next mark. It is for the skipper, who may or may not be the navigator, to decide whether or not this course is to be used. The ability to go to the chart at any moment and to see exactly where one is, or to have such a recent position that one can make an accurate spot guess, is of the first importance. I know some people who get along quite nicely putting practically nothing on the chart, but as far as I myself am concerned, I should have a good deal of difficulty in making quick decisions as to the correct moment to go about in a change of wind, and on similar occasions, were I not 'on the map'.

Racing in coastal waters, if one is covering ground, one may normally plot one's position once an hour. Out of sight of land, when obstructions to sea-room and marks are distant, once a watch will often be enough. Never miss a chance to get a good fix. It may show up an unexpected set, or the visibility may close down suddenly. If you have acquired the habit of keeping yourself on the map you will have no trouble, but otherwise, two or three times a season maybe, you will be caught napping.

We had two interesting examples of these two things racing in America in 1948. We had cleared New London and the lighthouse beyond when we were all enveloped in a thick sudden mist, with two buoys to find in turn. There were about fifty boats racing with us, mostly getting lost. We kept our usual plot going, including radio direction finder and found our way round without delay.

The very next race we started outside Deering Harbour, and the first mark was out of sight off shore. We started taking back bearings shortly after the start, and found we were being set much more than the *Tidal Atlas* suggested was to be expected. This enabled us to sharpen up into the wind and when the mark came in sight, we were just enough up tide to weather the mark, though the wind went light. The other forty boats did not make it, and had a weary beat up against the tide. So we won that race too. We were paid some nice compliments about our cunning tactics, but of course it was not a matter of cunning but just of a little care in plotting.

Running Fixes. You will find a lot in navigation manuals about running fixes. While they may be useful when one is proceeding on a steady course at considerable speed with known and moderate tidal streams, under the average coastal sailing conditions with varying currents round the headland on which you are fixing, they should be accepted with reserve. As a rule even a moderate cross-bearing fix is to be preferred.

Next in importance to reasonable accuracy, and regularity in plotting one's position, comes ability to estimate the probable accuracy of one's position. This comes with practice in the particular boat and with a particular crew or type of crew; it is to some extent peculiar to the *équipe* as a whole, being dependent on a compound of care in steering, heeling errors of the compass, the boat's behaviour under various conditions, and so on.

Boats which carry a good deal of weather helm generally steer themselves a shade to windward of the estimated course made good. Or at least sufficient to nullify the leeway. For finely-balanced boats one has to allow normally 2° or 3° for leeway, making to windward, and more in bad weather. But it depends on the boat, and it takes time to find out.

Errors in Patent Log. As to the patent log, these are as a rule remarkably accurate in sheltered and semi-sheltered waters and in fine weather off shore; provided of course there is enough way on the boat to keep the log line streaming nicely out aft: say $2\frac{1}{4}$ knots or more for the Excelsior IV or $1\frac{1}{2}$ knots with the Knotmaster. Below this speed the drag becomes important and the readings less accurate, and the log should be handed.

In bad weather, or strong winds, and a big seaway, they suffer from errors which are not their fault, since they can only register the number of times the spinner revolves. The first error resulting in over reading is due to erratic steering, which can be reduced by a good and painstaking helmsman but not completely avoided by any amount of care when the wind is abaft the beam, in strong conditions. The counter of the boat will move over a wider arc of variation than the centre of the boat, probably increasing the error.

Then in really deep water sailing—this would be important in transatlantic racing and might affect a Bermuda or occasionally portions of a Fastnet race—there is the over-reading error caused by climbing up and down the seas.

It is hard to say how much to allow as so many things come into it, but if you want a guess I would say that with an Excelsior IV for deep sea, clear offshore ocean conditions, that 2 per cent over-reading should be assumed in fresh conditions, rising to 4 in strong and 6 per cent in a gale. This assumes steady conditions, giving rise to a sea commensurate with the wind.

In short strong blows in sheltered water, or in-shore, or wherever the land cuts down the sea, these errors will be cut accordingly, since they are seaway errors and not wind errors. They will be non-existent in smooth water.

But beware of too short a log line, when down

wind causes exactly opposite errors. If the spinner breaks surface, or comes up into broken water in a seaway, appreciable under-reading results. Knotmaster logs with smaller spinners are more liable to this trouble and care must be taken (1) always to use two lead weights on the line off shore—not a single weight as recommended by the makers for smaller yachts, (2) to have the line emerge low down, (3) that the orifice is well rounded, (4) that the register is regularly oiled.

If one is fortunate enough to have been able to go without a new suit for several years, and to have saved enough pennies to buy a Harrier, these problems will not pose themselves.

Surface Drift. When calculating one's dead reckoning position, one naturally applies the set of known tidal streams and ocean currents, details of which are given in the special charts, month by month, and one's leeway. What is often overlooked is the effect of surface drift or 'wind-induced current' which may be appreciable in vessels of small draught—which in this sense covers all small yachts. There seems little doubt that the effect decreases rapidly with the draught of the yacht. Surface set develops only gradually when the wind blows fresh or strong, more or less from the same direction for considerable periods. It is probably negligible for the first 12 hrs., and I doubt whether there are any sufficiently reliable rules for calculating it subsequently. However if one is aware of its possibility in open water one is less likely to be caught out by it.

All the races around the coasts including even the Fastnet and the Sydney–Hobart are frequently completed with success without celestial navigation —without taking sights. All the same it is an advantage on many occasions to be able to take an accurate sight, particularly after a spell of windward work or light weather and variable winds, which may throw the dead reckoning out. Under these conditions every chance of a patch of sunlight should be taken.

Sights from Small Vessels. To take good sights in small vessels requires special practice, even by someone used to sight-taking in ships, because the height of eye is so small that it is very easy to mistake the top of a wave or swell for the horizon. The difficulties are to know when one is getting a good horizon, and to get oneself balanced—poised against the motion of the vessel. Every foot higher you can get in the boat when taking your sight is valuable; it decreases the chance of false horizons. It is worth a little study to find places in the ship where you can get yourself secure by leaning your back against a boom crutch, a high life line, a mizzen mast or something of the sort. It will need

to be in the after third of the ship when you are going to windward, to keep spray off the sextant. In extreme cases it may be desirable to pay off the wind for an instant to keep a dry sextant.

The art of taking observations of celestial bodies is, I think, 75 per cent practice under the conditions in which you will expect to operate, and 25 per cent care of the sextant. You must ensure that your sextant is initially as free from error as possible before going to sea, if necessary call in the aid of an expert. While at sea handle the instrument with more care than you would a new born babe: after all you can always raise up more sons to your name, but a bad sight may put you on the rocks for keeps. Every time you take a sight, check that your side and index errors have not been altered by a chance knock. Whenever the sextant is exposed to spray or damp carefully clean all the lenses and shades. Strip down the telescope, dry it out, if necessary, and keep all the moving parts clean of verdigris.

The bodywork of bringing the sun or stars accurately down to the horizon is very like riding a horse. The hips and below must be glued to your mount—in this case the boat—by whatever means is suitable, wedging, lashing or balance. The waist remains perfectly supple so that the head and upper part of the body remain upright as though in gymbals making a perfect mounting for a steady sextant on the heaving ocean.

For ocean racing the stowage of the sextant, apart from being secure, must be as handy to the companion as a weatherproof position allows because one often only has a minute of sun to catch.

Star and lunar sights are much less easy in a small vessel, because of the increased difficulty of knowing when you have a decent horizon, from your relatively low position. Some people find it a help, equally with solar observations, to have a helper calling 'crest' and 'trough', as the ship rises and falls in a seaway. Never take less than four observations to enable a false one to be detected; in bad weather five or six.

Nowadays with the wireless available and its frequent time-checks one can dispense with the old-time chronometer and use a good deck or chronometer watch, provided it has been rated, preferably in the yacht, from the morning and evening time signals. If one's watch and wireless fail one, one can still get one's latitude at true noon from meridian altitude observations: taking a series of sights to find the maximum altitude. One should also remember the possibility of checking one's watch by taking a longitude sight when one's position is already known from other sources.

Radio Direction Finding. Provided the operator is in practice, direction finding on Radio Beacons can be an invaluable aid. The most practical sets are those which have a small aerial mounted on a compass. This enables a hand-bearing compass to be taken into the hatchway and operated above deck level. This reduces errors which are present even in wooden ships on certain bearings due to steel members such as chain plates, or stiffening in way of the mast, mast steps on deck; other instruments; lines of torches, etc., etc. As the bearing is read directly off the hand-bearing compass it also eliminates the error of calling to the helmsman for 'ship's head' and the nuisance of correcting for relative bearing.

Among the best of these sets is the Heron-Homer made by Brookes and Gatehouse of Lymington, Hants. It is very small and completely watertight. It is necessary to have a headphone attachment to avoid disturbing the ship with a loudspeaker. Make sure that you order enough length in the connection between the aerial and the set to enable the operator to sit on the coach roof in case of need, to avoid wave top interference. Apart from unreliable signals near dawn and dusk, with any good set, bearings 40 miles away should be accurate within 4 degrees. Often at 60 or more miles they are accurate, but the chance of a 'bent signal' is increased with range, or by intervening land, and sometimes by heavy non-uniform cloud. If your aerial is not compass-mounted an extra $5°$ error can result mostly from ship movement and the complication of having the ship's course read at the moment of taking the bearing on the loop instrument, which of course registers relative to the ship's head. This error will be less in calmish conditions.

In British waters with an ordinary non-directional but fairly powerful receiving set—a good aerial helps a lot—one can use 'Consol'. There are stations in Scandinavia, Northern Ireland, and Brittany of which one can sometimes get excellent bearings. It takes a bit of practice, and one has to have the special charts, which are easily obtained, showing the signal obtained on each line of bearing. Sets with a special circuit to receive these signals are even better.

Sometimes one can get one station and not the other, but the point is that while most radio direction beacons are by intention local this covers a much larger area.

Various other schemes such as the Decca need special receiving apparatus, which will add to the already formidable list of equipment. Most of these, including Decca and Loran, along with the use of transmitters and Radar, are banned in British

racing. Transmitters are allowed, however, for the Hobart and Bermuda races; some years they are mandatory equipment.

Very few of the small wireless sets are even driptight, let alone splash-tight, and it is worth having a canvas hood made with only apertures for the controls and the voice. The most frequent way in for wet is down the aerial lead—so lead this up to the set.

Deviation of Compasses. Compass errors that a cruising yacht would not worry about may make a good into a bad landfall for an ocean-racer. There are a few lucky racers who have no engines and no ferrous material in their construction who do not need to worry about deviation. Fortunately standing and running wire rope rigging at its usual distances does not seem to affect the compass, in boats of ordinary beam. The only likely culprits in narrow boats are the runners, and one can generally try these out in calm water at anchor, letting each go in turn and then both together, to check that they do not affect the compass. If they do affect it, the thing would be to re-arrange the run of them farther forward or farther aft; or replace in stainless steel.

Deviation can alter appreciably while a ship is laid up ashore, and so one should get her 'swung' each year for adjustment of compasses, if at any time she has had any deviation, by someone professional or amateur, who is accustomed to the job. If one finds this impracticable to arrange, one can get quite a good check by comparing the hand-bearing compass with the steering compass, while one is being towed around one's buoy slowly by a pulling boat or relatively small motor boat. A powerful boat will tow too fast and disturb the water, while at the moorings. Alternatively a tow round the harbour on gradually altering courses will do the trick; or one can give oneself a good swing between three or four piles or buoys, with a line out to each.

While taking the ship's head with a hand-bearing compass one should be standing on deck, or in a larger yacht on a skylight or some such deck erection, to get as far away as possible from hull interference. Select a position well clear of standing rigging and steel mast fittings and line up on something in the fore and aft line. Stretching a taut hemp between the masts or from the backstay(s) to the mast, just above the operator's head, enables him to keep his head central. If there are grave doubts about the steering compass take a second set, another complete swing, from another position forward in the ship.

Should the ship be of composite construction one will take special care to get well away from the deck, standing if necessary on a crate, discarded after storing ship perhaps.

The question of a steel yacht is of course more complex. One can get one's compass adjusted to give one a well corrected compass and a perfect deviation card, but there is no certainty that bad weather and pounding will not throw this out, particularly in a new yacht, so a re-check on reaching a sheltered place is no bad thing. More serious is the heeling error. In steam ships this cancels itself out, but if you have a long close-hauled leg, which may be 100 miles or so, it may result in landing up 10 miles to leeward of the Fastnet or Bermuda.

In a steel yacht I would make strenuous efforts when swinging for compass adjustment to get a swing while heeled, even if it means going to some lengths, such as filling one side deck with lead or stone ballast (not iron ballast!) and hanging a couple of mooring anchors on the main boom and spinnaker boom, and squaring them outboard. Or the dinghy filled with junk or even crew, would serve for weight in a small yacht.

It is amazingly easy to develop compass errors. Three specific cases that have happened to me were due firstly to a concealed steel tiller, canvas and brass covered; to a steel winch handle in a non-ferrous winch, not shipped at the time of

MYTH OF MALHAM
PILOTAGE TABLE   SINGLE HANDED RACE
S.B.C. CLUB LONG ISLAND SOUND U.S.A.

CLOCKWISE (SIGNAL WHITE BLUE)

FIRST LEG   S. 22° E. (KEEP CLEAR TO PORT OF LAND AHEAD)

TIDE	½ TIME	RED BUOY	TO PORT	2 CABLES
•8 KNTS. TO W.	⅚ TIME	RED BLACK BUOY	TO STBD.	3½ CABLES
	ROUND C13 TIDE 1 KNOT TO E. (BLACK)			

SECOND LEG   N. 78° W. (CAPT. IS. LIGHT FINE TO STBD.)

TIDE	½ TIME	BLACK BUOY ½ MILE	TO PORT	LLOYDS NECK
E. INSHORE				
W. OFFSHORE				
	ROUND 32A (FL. RED WHISTLE)			

THIRD LEG   N. 60° E. (ON GREEN LEDGE)

TIDE	⅓ TIME	RED BUOY	TO PORT	9 CABLES
DEAD AHEAD	½ TIME	RED BUOY	TO PORT	9 CABLES
	⅘ TIME	RED BUOY	TO PORT	2½ CABLES

ANTICLOCK (SIGNAL BLUE PETER)

FIRST LEG   S. 56° W. (ON RIGHT EDGE WIND)

TIDE	⅕ TIME	RED BUOY	TO STBD.	2½ CABLES
DEAD BEHIND	½ TIME	RED BUOY	TO STBD.	7 CABLES
	⅔ TIME	RED BUOY	TO STBD.	9 CABLES
	ROUND 32A (FL. RED WHISTLE)			

SECOND LEG   S. 78° E. (9 CABLES TO PORT OF EATON'S POINT)

TIDE	½ TIME	BLACK BUOY ½ MILE	TO STBD.	
E. INSHORE	⅚ TIME	RED BLACK BUOY	TO PORT	
W. OFFSHORE		½ MILE		
	ROUND C13 BLACK BUOY			

THIRD LEG   N. 18° W. (ON GREEN LEDGE)

TIDE TO W.	½ TIME	RED BUOY	TO STBD.	2 CABLES
WEAK EXCEPT				
E. GOING AT				
S. SHORE				

Diagram 8.

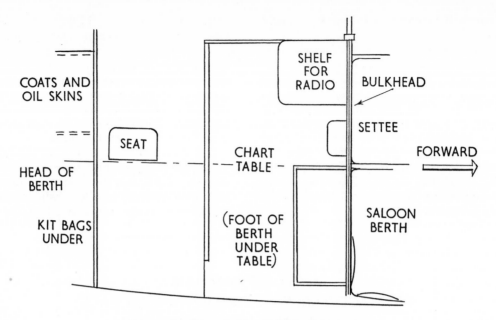

Diagram 9.—*Belmore's* Chart Table Arrangements.

swinging; and to the hanging of a bunch of shackles and I.I.B. blocks under the bridge deck on which the compass was fixed. So from time to time when a nice transit comes on in coastal waters, perhaps a lighthouse opens up on a distant point, or something of that sort, it is as well to get a check on the steering compass, by steering straight down the traverse. In the course of a forenoon's sail stretching in the Solent, for instance, it is possible to get traverses on half a dozen distant courses and to get quite a fair idea of the extent of the deviation there is in the compass. This will simply be a check; not a method of producing a deviation card.

Use of 'Tidal Atlas'. As to the *Tidal Atlas*, which gives one a diagram of the state of the tidal currents for every hour of the tide before and after high water, it is very necessary to go through it before the race and to put on each diagram in pencil the hours each day to which it applies, so that at any time in the race one can turn up the page which then applies without reference to the tide tables.

For short-handed racing it is as well to assemble beforehand on a card all the pilotage dope which is likely to be required; the courses and distances between marks, the bearings of prominent objects, the probable state of the tidal currents in each part of the course. This can then be given a lick of varnish and posted in the cockpit in sight of the helmsman. The card which I used in the 1948 Single-handed race from Norfolk Conn. is reproduced in Diagram 8.

Bubble Sextants. Airmen use a bubble in their sextants to get a horizontal line, in lieu of a horizon. High hopes were entertained that this would also improve the chances of getting sights from small yachts when conditions of weather, including false horizons due to heat haze, interfered with normal methods.

Experience suggests that these bubble sextants are not a great help. Although vertical movement of the ship or plane does not interfere too much with good results, lateral displacement of the observer, due to rolling or pitching of the ship, causes oscillations in the bubble. In practice the occasions when the ship is steady enough, and when the bubble shows to advantage over the normal method appear to be so infrequent as to make it not worth the complication of carrying and working an extra instrument.

9

RIGS AND SAIL PLANS

A little while ago I undertook to look into the problem of selecting a rig for a light displacement ocean-racing design 29 ft. 8 in. on the waterline and 38 ft. 9 in. overall, with a proviso that the counter could be shortened in the case where the rig did not require this. I commenced the examination with a 42-ft. mast, as we reckoned that this was the maximum length which could conveniently be designed without a forestay, other than the stay to the masthead. With this in view we assumed the lower of the two cross-trees would be well up the mast and that there would be a good fore and aft spread to the lower shrouds. The mast being fairly well into the boat in all the rigs, we had a just acceptable athwartships staying base.

I assumed that the R.O.R.C. sail area would be exactly 500 sq. ft. in all cases, and proceeded carefully to draw the most favourable ketch, yawl, and sloop.

Rigs Compared. These are referred to under the tallies EK, EY, and ES in the diagrams, numbers 9, 10, 11, 12, 13 and the table of dimensions and areas, Diagram 14. ES is not actually drawn as it resembles so closely EY. It will be seen that in order to avoid providing a bowsprit, the yawls and ketches have a slight overlap penalty. It is probable that in detailing the design the necessity for this penalty could be avoided, perhaps by moving the mizzen mast and the main mast aft. It does not however affect to any important degree the comparisons between rigs which we are making.

Passing to the cutters, I did three. EC has the high cross-trees with small 'panels' to the upper part of the mast, between them. This gives a man-size in staysails and a smaller jib, which has to be cut high in the foot to enable it to sheet clear of the big staysail.

This I consider to be quite a good rig. Then I drew a cutter rig ECM very much like that used successfully in *Maid of Malham*, which has a more moderate sized staysail. I passed on to ECH, not actually drawn out as it closely resembles the others in appearance, which represents virtually *Monk of Malham* sail plan on a slightly smaller scale. It has higher aspect ratios than the *Maid*, and the 44-ft. mast.

Then, assuming that the necessity for sailing without a forestay was waived, I postulated a 44-ft. mast for a sloop, and drew out ESH to see how she compared.

When I came to weigh up the advantages and disadvantages of the various rigs I was bound to admit that there was nothing much in it. I think every one of these layouts would have a good chance. I should be most interested to try out the various rigs on similar hulls. My belief is that there would not be a great deal in it, though under R.O.R.C. ruling, in all but the smaller yachts, I prefer the cutters to the sloops. The C.C.A. and the new International Rule allows greater overlaps, and the sloops benefit more than the cutters from this.

Ketch Rigs. Turning to detail considerations, the ketch rig shows its proverbial advantage of setting a good deal of sail off the wind. By virtue of being a moderate displacement hull, one has a longish length of deck, relative to the total area required, over which to spread one's sail plan. This clearly enables the ketch or yawl to exploit her mizzen staysails to advantage. The area of sail which the ketch can actually sport on a reach, with a 500 sq. ft. nominal total, is no less than 994 sq. ft. Of course, it cannot all be reckoned as 100 per cent efficient. Still, it is useful. Ketch rigs have got themselves a bad name in Europe, partly because very few people have tried the rig thoroughly, and partly because they have often been associated with hulls that are not weatherly.

We have rigged three new yachts very successfully as ketches: *Melusine*, 34 ft. W.L., *Talofa*, 47 ft. W.L., and *Stormvogel*, 60 ft. W.L. All have proved very good to windward and handy for cruising.

With the introduction of the 1957 R.O.R.C. rule the use of 'rig allowances' was dropped. A rig allowance was intended, and largely succeeded, in equalizing the real average value of the total area to a yacht when racing. But it could not in every case distinguish between a good example and a bad example. For instance although *on the average* a cutter's area may be worth 4 per cent more than a yawl's, a well laid out yawl will be worth more than a badly laid out cutter.

So in the later rule each part of each rig was

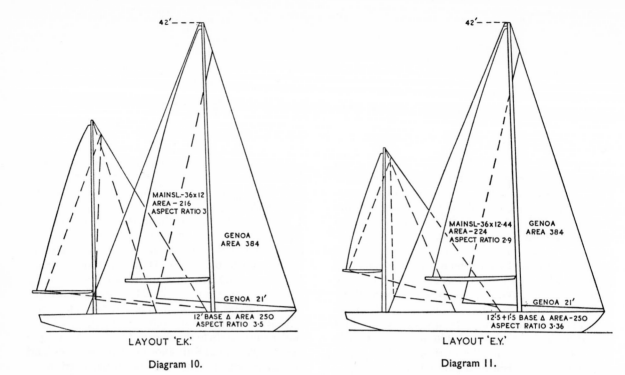

LAYOUT 'E.K.'

Diagram 10.

LAYOUT 'E.Y.'

Diagram 11.

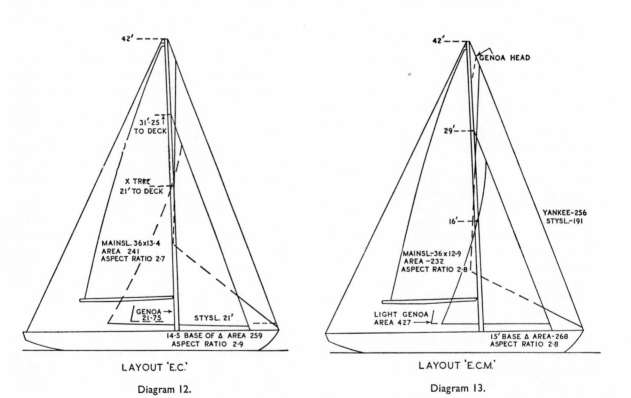

LAYOUT 'E.C.'

Diagram 12.

LAYOUT 'E.C.M.'

Diagram 13.

Rigs Compared.

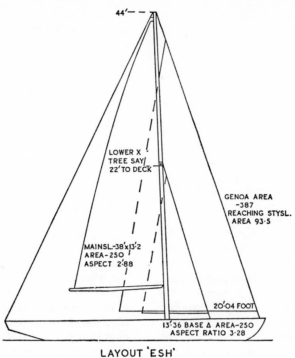

LAYOUT 'ESH'

Diagram 14.

measured individually. A yawl or ketch's mainmast sails were measured as though she were a cutter (or a sloop) and the mizzen was given what the rule makers assessed as its real value to help that cutter. Since the gap between the mainsail and mizzen mast is an asset to the mizzen staysail, this also is lightly taxed.

The C.C.A. follows very much the same principles. But there are important differences in the method of computing the rated areas of each part of the rig, which can be found in the relevant appendices. The 'new rule' in general follows the C.C.A. This method of sail measurement is likely to be used in the new international rule.

The Case for the Yawl. Most of what has been said about the ketch applies to a more limited extent in the case of the yawl. The total area of reaching sail including the larger mizzen staysail in the plans in question is 870 sq. ft.; but on the other hand with a little bigger base to her fore triangle she should be a shade faster to windward.

Previously the low limit of area for a mizzen was 9 per cent of the total area, R.O.R.C. (The British rule) defined a yawl as a vessel having the after side of her mizzen mast on or abaft the water-line ending. Now no such definition enters into the calculation of areas.

The mainsails of schooners and the mizzens of wishbone ketches are measured as for other main-sails. The area between the masts is measured at a percentage of actual area because there is no rig allowance.

Bermudan mainsails are measured at 50 per cent boom × hoist. With their roach they actually measure appreciably more. Gaff sails are measured as two triangles based on boom and diagonal again as before. With rig allowance. The fore triangles under R.O.R.C. rating are now in all rigs rated at 100 per cent area.

The C.C.A. method of measuring 'tween-mast areas is more complex, depending on the type of sail set within the area: and this is shortly sure to be increased.

It is important to note that a moderate displacement hull is required to enable a yawl or ketch rig to be exploited to the full. A heavy displacement type requires more sail and sometimes one has not the length to spread it out properly; that is to say, to fit a good gap between the mizzen mast and the leech of the mainsail.

One pays in rating, and in £ s. d. for that matter, at the same rate for a sq. ft. of sail area at deck level as high up, and that part of the sail which is less than half the beam of the boat above the deck does not do much good in a breeze, because it is foul winded by the hull. And in light weather it is clear that one wants one's area as high as one can get it: bearing in mind the wind gradient.

Where one is free to redraw the sail plan, to arrange the boom, half the beam above the deck is not a bad rough rule. No difficulty with a high boom should arise provided the goose-neck can slide down so that one can get at the sail to reef it; particularly in the case of the larger boats. Both the R.O.R.C. and the C.C.A. impose a limit on this height however. If you can't get your aspect ratio up to 2.8 with these heights, it will pay to carry the boom a little lower, speaking of predetermined sail area and mast heights, in order to raise the ratio.

This rig alteration is mentioned to show what can be done at a moderate cost to improve and modernise an existing rig.

Aspect Ratios and R.O.R.C. Rule. Myth of Malham's mainsail aspect ratio, that is to say, the ratio of the length of the foot on the boom to the hoist, is 3.1 to 1. *Mouse of Malham*'s is 3.2 and also in *Artica II*, which we designed. After many years, other designers 'saw the light' and even went a little further concerning aspect ratios. It worked satisfactorily and although this is at present thought to be as high as it pays to go, we do not know the limit until we try it. The *Blue Charm* has one of 3 to 1; it was not convenient to go higher in the mast on this design. That is really the limiting factor in ocean racing practice—above a certain height the extra mast rigging necessary is hardly worth it.

Myth of Malham has a fore triangle aspect ratio of 3.16, *Minx of Malham*, 3.34 and 1967 *Monk of Malham* 3.5. The *Blue Charm* class are 3.6, being light yachts; the various variations of the *Maica* clan from 3.0 to 3.4. In *Artica* and in *Mouse of Malham* we went up a lot; to about 4.2. I fancy this is about the efficient limit. The high aspect ratio also makes it easier, other things being the same, to keep the luff taut. But this involves a longer un-supported length of mast, in a fore and aft direc-tion, if it is a sloop; unless one faces up to the addition of an extra forestay, which may not be all that is required unless one has extra runners too. Weight and windage are going up all the time as one raises the point at which the forward stay leaves the mast. Moreover, and this is important, as the aspect ratio goes up, the difficulty of getting a genoa to sheet clear of the cross-trees is increased, and one has to fit an extra pair of cross-trees; to keep these short enough to avoid reducing the angle made by the shrouds with the mast. So here again the limit in offshore racing aspect ratio appears in practice to be the difficulty in getting the extra length of mast arranged, and as the ratio gets higher the advantages decrease and the draw-backs increase so that one comes to a sort of optimum point which appears to be between 3.0 and 4.2 according to displacement.

The R.O.R.C. light penalties on higher aspect ratios were reasonable as 'efficiency measures' but not serious deterrents when one is planning high ratio efficient sail plans. The 'new rule' penalties are more severe.

Aspect Ratios and C.C.A. Rule. All of the foregoing apply when the R.O.R.C. system of measurement is in vogue. When one comes to the C.C.A. method of rating sail area the position is different. There is a severe tax on aspect ratios both in the case of fore triangles and mainsails.

I have an open mind about which C.C.A. aspect ratios pay best. If I had to guess I would say about 2.8 in both cases (but I believe that expert opinion in America feels that it should be lower). Our *Belmore* was 2.8 and as she has been once overall third and once overall second in the Bermuda race, perhaps that reinforces this view.

Cutter versus Sloop. I would like to consider a little further the question of the cutter against the sloop; of two headsails against one. You will hear it said that the sloop is closer winded, and while there may be a grain of truth in it—I am not convinced of it myself—it does not apply with much force off-shore because in general the requirements of a seaway oblige one to sail fuller than for the average regatta windward work, inshore. I will agree that many cutters are not as close-winded as they might be because it is much more difficult to design the sails just right, *vis-à-vis* one another and the main-sail. It is partly a matter of stay arrangement but chiefly on account of the way the sails are drawn in the plan, and the way their sheeting is arranged in the boat. Another contributory factor is the arrangements made for keeping the luffs taut, which involves the whole mast design, and is more difficult in a cutter than a sloop.

In 1966 we had the exceptional opportunity of racing from Cherbourg to the Solent two modern ocean racers of 30 ft. water line with identical hulls; one sloop and the other cutter rigged; both of our design. I skippered the sloop and we were soundly beaten by the cutter; mostly in reaching conditions.

I have sailed *Myth* in a race which happened to coincide with the course of the old rule 8-metres racing in the class and she pointed just about with them. Her rated area is very much less than that of an 8-metre—I suppose round 150 sq. ft. short, apart from the important fact that they can use a very much bigger overlap than the R.O.R.C. rule allows, though *Myth*'s aspect ratio, one must mention, is higher. Her displacement must be about the same, and to approach their perform-ance does seem to indicate that a well-arranged cutter does not give away anything to a sloop. This is particularly the case when the R.O.R.C. rule is the yardstick, because the 150 per cent limit to the headsail foot length does not cut down your cutter's windward working area. But working with the larger (but taxed) overlap at present (1969) allowed by the C.C.A. rule you can make out a better case for a sloop, because this extra overlap can serve you as a working sail going to windward. *Myth*'s sail plan is shown in Diagram 20.

To take the specific case of *Monk of Malham* (1967) the big yankee (that is the high-cut large working jib set to the masthead—incidentally a term almost unknown in America) together with the big overlap staysail has an area of 600 sq. ft. which is around 80 sq. ft. more than that of her R.O.R.C. genoa. In other words for a given fore triangle a single headsail boat cannot set so much sail for reaching, though the single sail going to

windward in light weather will be equally efficient. The old 1957 rule rates the fore triangle at 100 per cent which offers no special incentive to return to the tiny fore triangle; this in spite of the fact that the mainsail with its roach is far bigger than it is measured.

Again the smaller mainsail of the cutter has the big advantage that it rarely needs reefing. And the two-sailed rig will stand longer in a strong breeze, before a change is needed, than an equivalent single sail.

Going back a bit, the Channel Race of 1947 is still a good example. It was a turn to windward from the Forts at Portsmouth to the Sovereign at Beachy Head in a breeze which gradually freshened from a whole sail one to a strong wind over Force 7. The mainsail has an area of 305 sq. ft. We reduced

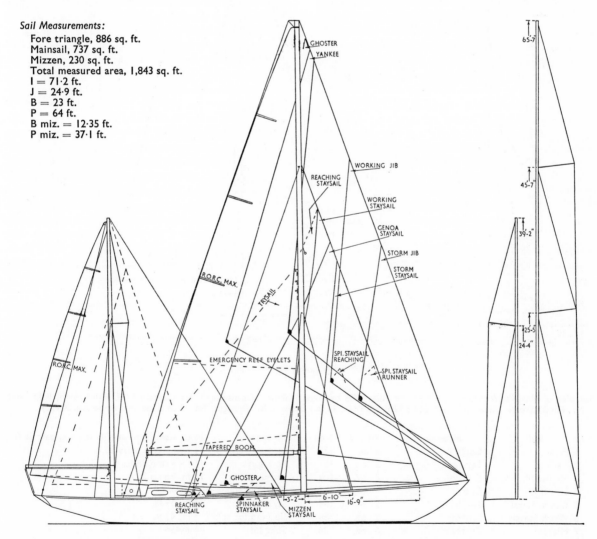

Sail Measurements:
Fore triangle, 886 sq. ft.
Mainsail, 737 sq. ft.
Mizzen, 230 sq. ft.
Total measured area, 1,843 sq. ft.
$I = 71 \cdot 2$ ft.
$J = 24 \cdot 9$ ft.
$B = 23$ ft.
$P = 64$ ft.
B miz. $= 12 \cdot 35$ ft.
P miz. $= 37 \cdot 1$ ft.

Diagram 15.—Monsieur Georges Lucas' ketch *Talofa*. Rig designed by Illingworth & Primrose. L.O.A., 67 ft. 3 in. Hull built by Chantier Naval Constantini, La Trinite Sur Mer, Morbihan, France, 1961.

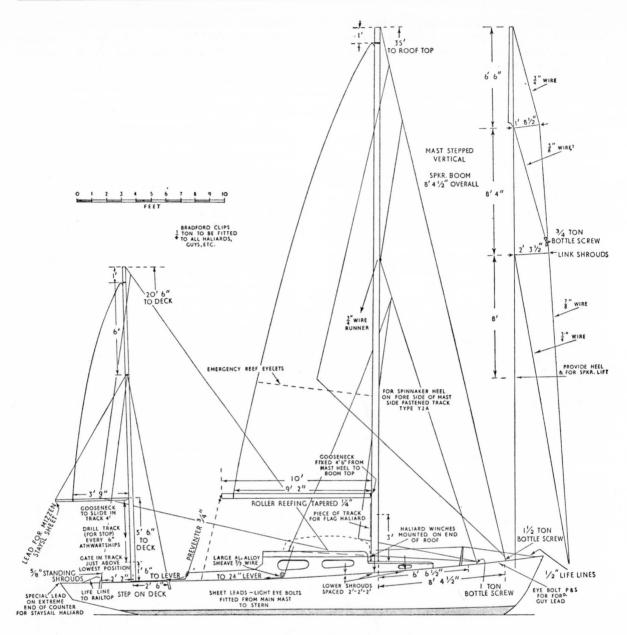

Diagram 16.

Sail plan of *Mouse of Malham*. Designed and built 1955 by Aero Marine, of Emsworth, for Captain J. H. Illingworth, R.N., and Mr. Peter Green. Dimensions:—*L.O.A.*: 32 ft.; *L.W.L.*: 24 ft.; *Beam*: 8 ft.; *Draught*: 5 ft. 9 in. (See also Appendix XVII.)

No.	Sail	Material	Weight	Area
1	Main	Cotton	8 oz.	135
2	Yankee	Terylene	5 oz.	157
3	Middle Jib	Cotton	8 oz.	108
4	Storm Jib	Cotton	9 oz.	51
5	Genoa Staysl	Terylene	5 oz.	106
6	Work Staysl	Cotton	9 oz.	64
7	Mizzen	Cotton	6 oz.	26
8	Mizzen Staysl	Terylene	$2\frac{1}{2}$ oz.	100
9	Spinnaker	Terylene or Nylon	$1\frac{1}{2}$ oz.	—

Jib sheet $1\frac{1}{2}$ in. hemp one pair 49 ft., one pair 38 ft.
Staysail sheet $1\frac{1}{4}$ hemp two pairs 30 ft.
Fore guys $1\frac{1}{4}$ in. hemp 38 ft.
Aft guys $1\frac{1}{4}$ in. hemp 36 ft.
Ghosting single sheets:—
Stysl $\frac{3}{4}$ in. 19 ft.
Jib (and for spkr) $\frac{3}{4}$ in. 42 ft.
Spkr lift $\frac{5}{8}$ nylon
Main sheet $1\frac{1}{4}$ ft.

headsails until we were down to our smallest jib of about 100 sq. ft. and no stay sail and she kept going nice and close, hard on the wind, and logged, if memory serves, exactly 100 miles in 16 hrs for an average speed of 6.25 miles an hour. The sloops all had to pull down one and in some cases two or three reefs, and lost quite a slab of time.

The time we saved was put to good use because we caught our tide around the Havre light-vessel and finished 16 hrs ahead of the next boat in; just one of those lucky things, because we were not that much faster than the other boats.

I must apologise for referring so repeatedly to *Myth*, but as later as in the 1961 season she was again champion of R.O.R.C. Class I.

1962 *C.C.A. Headsails.* The 'new rule' abolishes the unlimited headsails and measures the width of the sail to the clew at right angles to the luff with (in effect) 158 per cent base of triangle as the minimum width. Above this there is a modest tax on added width. I would guess that a genoa foot length of about 160 per cent base of triangle with the clew 2 to $3\frac{1}{2}$ ft. up off the deck (according to the size of yacht) would pay best, provided the yacht were in a general sense not short of area in her rig. If she were a bit short of overall area it might pay to have the foot length up to 180 per cent base triangle, with the clew a shade higher again.

As a bit of now old history in 1948 when I was Commodore of the Royal Ocean Racing Club, I agreed with the American Commodore that the R.O.R.C. should accept the 180 per cent C.C.A. spinnakers in lieu of our 150 per cent ones, and that the C.C.A. should accept the 150 per cent genoas; all of which was good in bringing rules together, and seemed a sensible compromise because R.O.R.C. spinnakers were ribbon narrow and C.C.A. genoas very large, unhandy and expensive.

We introduced the C.C.A. spinnaker in Britain, but the Commodore in the U.S.A. changed and the genoas did not. It is interesting to see that at long last the C.C.A. have limited their genoas, but sad that they have not seen fit to unify the measurement entirely. The 'new rule', although introducing other grave difficulties, should correct this.

But to return once again to general discussion of the merits of the two headsail versus a single headsail rig, there are two other considerations worth taking into account. In a relatively short-keeled boat, which is a necessity in a modern racer to keep the wetted area down, the presence of a second headsail does, I feel sure, steady the boat on the wind. It spreads out the sail-loading over several points and when the boat luffs, as she is bound to do at times in a seaway, the slightly different behaviour of the two headsails probably has a steadying effect. My experience in bad weather with *Wista* indicates that even in the smallest (J.O.G.) offshore racers this holds good.

A mizzen in a yawl has something of the same effect—steadying a boat on the wind. Some years ago in a fresh breeze and some sea *Stormy Weather* was tried out against *Dorade*; each in turn, with a reef down and the mizzen, and alternatively with a full mainsail and no mizzen set. Rod Stephens told me that it had shown that the mizzen sail did pay on the wind in a big seaway—adding to directional stability, a thing one has often wondered about and rarely had a chance to try.

More Cutter Considerations. The other thing about a two headsail rig is that when one is changing sail forward one is never bare-headed; the other sail carries on while the change is being made.

So the masthead cutter rig can justly claim to be a fine sea-going rig. No sail is too large and the mast is magnificently stayed, with two forestays and one or two standing preventer backstays. The overall height of the mast is at a minimum too.

Cutter versus Sloop again. However, in its modern racing form with the high narrow fore triangle it is not the easiest inshore racing rig because both headsails have a fair amount of overlap and need some getting about. Single part sheets are a big advantage here. On the other hand when one reduces for hard-weather racing or cruising to a pair of small headsails she is fine and easy to handle. And if it comes on to blow a bit harder, stow the staysail and there you are, provided the rig is high and narrow, sailing happily under jib and small main. But if your fore triangle is old style—too long on the base—maybe the jib will be too far away to play nicely with the main, even in fresh conditions.

However, when one gets down to the smaller sizes under 30-ft. water-line, the simplicity of the sloop rig has strong attractions. The fore deck is comparatively small, and space inside the boat for stowing the bigger wardrobe of sails required by the cutter is limited.

Sail Costs of Rigs. Diagram 19 shows the standard sail plan used with the original *Maicas* and with *Brigantine*. It is a good instance of a very economical layout, reducing to a bare minimum the number of headsails. This design has had a great many racing successes and makes a topping little cruising yacht. Of course the sail outfit can be elaborated with quadrilaterals, ghosters, and so on, but she will be quite raceworthy with only the compromise genoa, the larger of the two working jibs, storm jib, and spinnaker. On the score of cost of the sail outfit the sloop has the advantage. The mainsail may be 30 per cent bigger but against that there will probably

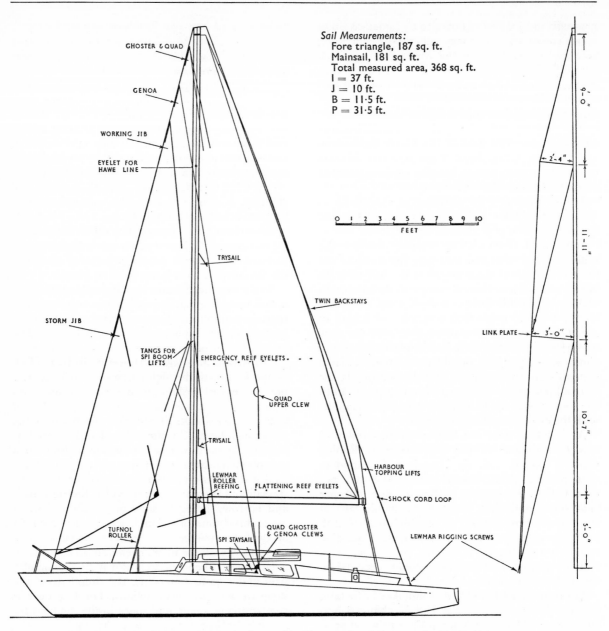

Diagram 17.—Sail plan of *Midnight*, designed by Illingworth and Primrose for Mr. D. McLennan.

be two or three headsails—the staysails in fact—and the jibs will be smaller. If you have a masthead genoa for a cutter, it will be much larger. The spinnaker will be much larger too. Against this you can sometimes set the fact that with a masthead rig the storm rig is simply a staysail and one may avoid carrying a trysail which is necessary for a sloop. The C.C.A., the J.O.G. and the R.O.R.C. rules all make adequate storm canvas compulsory.

Slutter Rig. Then there is another rig which is well worth considering, which partakes of something of the sloop and something of the cutter,

which I call, because it is most necessary to have a name, a SLUTTER rig. This is a rig where sail is set alternatively, but not normally at the same time, on two stays; one going to the masthead and the other from approximately the same point on deck to a point lower down the mast. The latter stay is used in fresh breezes and the masthead for lighter weather.

This has the advantage over the normal sloop that it sets a much bigger fore triangle and thus gets more total area for a given mast height. It has the advantage of a small mainsail, which will hardly ever need reefing, while at the same time it has not the complication of a cutter's rig with its third sail to handle when going about.

One must set against this the necessity when tacking either to disconnect the forestay with a lever, or to fight the masthead sail around through the narrow triangular gap between the stays. Experience indicates that unless an aluminium or an unduly heavy wood mast is used it will be difficult to get the masthead sail to stand in any weight of wind, or in a seaway, without the forestay. Because the headsail is set to alternative heights on the mast, this is less easy to keep straight.

I remember very vividly the business of getting *Orion*'s 1,800 sq. ft. genoa about under these circumstances when we were caught in puffy head winds in the channel between Largs and the Cumbrae. It was at night, during the 100-mile race round the Ailsa Craig. The channel looks wide enough by day but with an 80-ft. long yacht we seemed to be putting about every few seconds.

The slutter rig does increase the multiplicity of sails because it often means two masthead headsails to avoid the first reduction of headsail being too large—particularly since this is far the largest fore and aft sail in the boat. This is sometimes overcome by using a storm headsail as a baby jibtopsail set over the staysail, and is quite a good answer, though one is, of course, back to three sails. The sail used must be cut low in the clew or it will not sheet in the ship.

St. Barbara, the Gunners' old ocean racer, had her first season as a slutter, but on account of the difficulties referred to was converted to a sloop, setting sail only on the lower stay which was closer than most to the masthead. The more usual version has its stay well down the mast, at the next natural cross-tree position, and is applied mostly to smaller yachts.

Minimum Areas for Ocean Racing. In the above considerations we have assumed that the area of sail to be carried was known, since one has to start with a pre-determined figure to compare rigs. We will now consider the important question how much area is required.

Both C.C.A. and R.O.R.C. rules are hard on sail area. If one carries an oversize sail area, for the size of boat, the rating rises out of proportion to the advantage which it confers as regards speed. So the tricky thing is to decide at what level to set your area. The amount of sail normally carried in America is a little more than it is in England: this is largely a question of custom and partly on account of the amount of light weather they get on their eastern seaboards at certain times of the year.

The R.O.R.C. method of measuring sail area in detail is given in the appendix with the rating rule.

For rough calculations to avoid square roots you can take twice the reduction off the calculated sail area. For example instead of taking 2 per cent off the square root of the S.A. take 4 per cent off the area.

You will want to know just how an alteration of sail plan will affect your rating, and a very useful little rough rule to remember is that a difference of total sail area will result in about two-tenths of that change in rating.

For instance suppose you had an 8-metre approximately in class racing trim, with a mainsail hoist of 52 ft. and a mainsail foot of 21 ft. You want to convert her for ocean racing. You decide to keep the fore triangle at its present area with a hoist of 42 ft., and to reduce the mainsail to 48 ft. hoist, and the length on the boom to 16 ft. This gives you a 3 to 1 aspect ratio and still enough sail. You would have reduced the mainsail area from 546 to 384; and supposing the fore triangle base was 15 ft., you would have reduced the total rated area from 814 to 652 or by 20 per cent odd.

The reduction in rating would be four-tenths of 20, or by about 8 per cent. Thus if the rating had been originally 36 ft. it would now be down to about 33.12.

The area we want to arrive at is the minimum which will give us a reasonably good performance in light weather. It is therefore more or less independent of the stability of the boat.

Formula for Sail Area Necessary. Now we come to the business of actually calculating the sail area which is going to pay us best. As a new owner taking over a boat you will want a rough check on this and for this purpose I have developed the following formula, which assumes an average good shape and no special peculiarities of form; and gives the area for the R.O.R.C. rule. (For the Bermuda Race under C.C.A. rating it is probably wise further to increase the sail plan by 8 per cent.)

The total area of sail required equals:

$$25 + [44T + .85LB + 1.5M(3.1 - R) + J(3.3 - V)] \times \left[\frac{C - K + 100}{100} \right]$$

Where

Total Area is R.O.R.C. measured area. (There should be no great difference in the case of the new international rule).

T   Displacement in tons in sea-going trim (including food, water, crew, and clothes).

L   Length on water-line.

B   Beam.

M   Length of foot of mainsail.

R   Aspect ratio of mainsail.

J   Base of fore triangle.

V Aspect ratio of fore triangle.

C Constant between 0 and 8 depending on length and depth of keel (or for a short keel).

K Constant between 0 and 3 depending on section (3 being for very easy section, 0 for powerful section).

It is important, particularly in small yachts, to calculate carefully the weights of crew, food, etc., including, for instance, the weight of an engine if this was not allowed for in the initial design, and any extra gear which puts her down below her initial designed marks. Otherwise one's displacement is fictitious. A really stiff yacht of Class II or III can afford to carry with advantage up to 8 per cent more sail than this minimum which is calculated just to give a good light weather performance.

Ratio of Area in Fore Triangle. The present fashion for masthead rigs, that is to say, rigs in which the headsails are set to the mast head, is due primarily to three causes. In the first place the modern high-shouldered spinnaker set to the masthead gets wind from both sides of the top of a narrow-headed mainsail. Thus not only does it drive more when full, but it is less liable to fall in with the rolling or yawing of the yacht.

But there are two other good reasons independent of rating considerations. Reefing a mainsail is a time-wasting business in a seaway, and it is much quicker to shift to a different-sized headsail. If one has a masthead rig the bigger proportion of the area is in the fore triangle and the mainsail is relatively small and will not often need reefing.

The final and important reason is that offshore in light airs the headsails, square foot for square foot, do more work than the mainsail. I say offshore deliberately because under average light weather conditions there will be an old swell or some motion, and the mainsail, of comparatively heavy canvas, will have the wind rolled out of it by the motion of the ship, while the much lighter light-weather headsails will still be at work. Owing to there being less weight in their fibres, they will stay comparatively quiet under the gentle pressure of a light wind, which will not be strong enough to control the inertia of the heavy mainsail canvas.

There is a staying advantage in the case of a cutter or two headsail yawl or ketch, in having a masthead rig, because the preventers can be standing rigging.

For all these reasons, although it is not essential to go to the masthead rig, it is necessary to have a reasonable proportion of one's total area in the fore triangle; or in the 'tween-mast staysails plus the fore triangle in the case of a schooner. You will ask what is the minimum and that is a difficult question to answer specifically without reference to all the circumstances. I think one should certainly insist on the fore triangle (taken at its actual full area) being more than 40 per cent of the fore triangle plus mainsail; and 45 per cent would be a better minimum. As an instance, 47 per cent is the figure in the case of the hypothetical 8-metre which we cut down for ocean racing earlier in the chapter.

In the case of yawls and ketches one's mizzen staysails are useful light-weather reaching sails and on this ground one could, if the rig made a bigger fore triangle inconvenient to arrange, put up with a little less than the 45 per cent.

Masts for Masthead Rigs. But in this connection one must sound a word of warning about the strength of the mast. Having read the paragraphs above it would not necessarily be wise to gallop off and give the yard an order to convert your present rig into a mast-header with the existing stick, because very likely the top part was only meant for hanging the peak of the mainsail on, and not for taking the thumping compression which a big headsail inevitably puts in a mast. In the chapter no. 15 on masts there are some suggestions for dealing with these problems.

Reaching. Most of the development in the efficiency of sail plans, tall sails, reduced windage of spars and riggings and so on, has resulted in improvement virtually only in windward ability. Thus the total areas have been gradually cut, and still the boats go as well or better to windward. But it has resulted in many modern English designs being relatively slow on the reach in moderate conditions. This should be remembered when one is gunning for the Sydney–Hobart or Honolulu or other races where wind-free conditions predominate, and where more sail area may be advisable.

Schooners. You will be saying to yourself that I have said very little about schooners. And in truth they have little vogue on the European side of the Atlantic these days. All the same I feel that if the staysail schooner has a modern logically arranged rig there is no reason she should not do very well. Diagram 18 shows the rig of *Kalcarra*, a 25-ton schooner, which was built in Malta just before the war. The owner, Bill Greer, and I, designed this rig in 1939 to provide a layout that would be really well stayed, would take her well to windward, and, as a working rig, would be easily handled. You will see that the luffs of the headsails are nice and parallel, and the sails designed to work in with one another. All three working headsails are about the same size, and taking off the upper staysail leaves her nicely balanced. She crossed the Atlantic to Canada, via the West Indies, recently.

I have not sailed in her, as she was not rigged

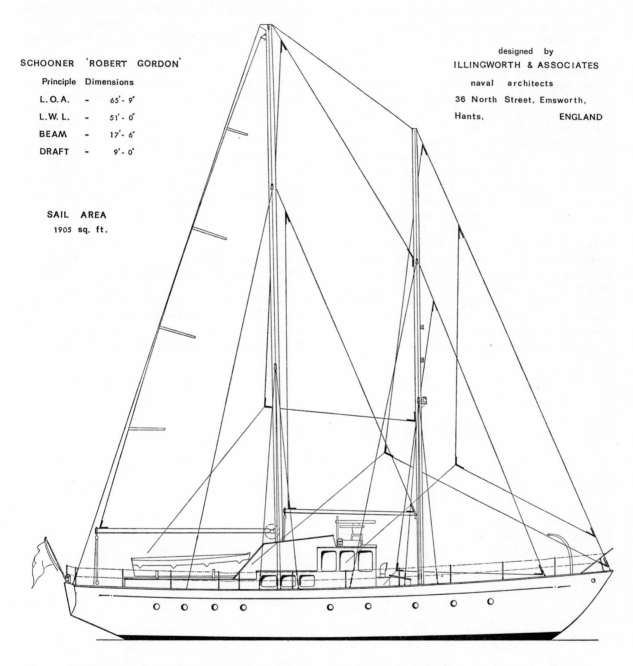

SCHOONER 'ROBERT GORDON'

Principle Dimensions

L.O.A. - 65'- 9"

L.W.L. - 51'- 0"

BEAM - 17'- 6"

DRAFT - 9'- 0"

SAIL AREA
1905 sq. ft.

designed by
ILLINGWORTH & ASSOCIATES
naval architects
36 North Street, Emsworth,
Hants, ENGLAND

Diagram 18.—*Robert Gordon*. A 67' schooner to Mr. Illingworth and Associates' designs, built in steel by Messrs. Van Bennekum near Schliedrecht in Holland and launched in May, 1968.

when Hitler marched into Poland, but Bill tells me she goes well. A similar rig, and more recent, has been successful also in Sir Leslie Kemp's schooner, *Daffodil*, of about the same size. A larger schooner under this rig was built successfully in 1968.

The essential feature of this rig, apart from keeping luffs roughly parallel, is to arrange for the upper staysail to be handed and set without going aloft. If this sail is tacked to a slide in a track which runs only to the foremast spreaders this is readily achieved; though set flying it can be kept under reasonable control with a tack downhaul. The forward lower shroud chain plates should be well forward of the mast. Alternatively it can be tacked through a sheave in the mast at the spreaders, the fall of the wire tack span being led to deck well forward of the mast on the centre-line; again with a downhaul line abaft the mast.

In a rig like this the foremast is a perfect job for an aluminium tubular mast. In a staysail schooner with no sail directly abaft the foremast, it is important to set the forward headsail to the masthead, to use the full length of the luff. This gives one 10 per cent extra sail area compared to the usual sail with clearance at the head.

Every rig has its own particular shortcoming and snags about all schooners are firstly the cost of the racing sail outfit which must be 30 to 40 per cent more than an equivalent sloop, and secondly, that one sets such a small spinnaker. One has to indulge in more tacking down-wind and try to keep the 'tween-mast sail drawing.

Concerning the schooner rig I wrote in *Offshore* 1949, 'with the measurement concession allowed to schooners 'tween-mast area, this rig should have a very sporting chance'. I tried very hard to get an owner of a larger yacht to let me do an up-to-date ocean-racing schooner rig; without success. When Eric Tabarly was building his ketch which was to win the 1964 single-handed Trans-Atlantic he asked me about rigs and I told him I still considered the schooner to have a bright chance in R.O.R.C. races; and very bright in single-handed racing. It was left to the enterprise of Eric, with his own design, to demonstrate the truth of my belief; he swept the board with a schooner rig in *Pen Duik III* in 1967; including winning the Fastnet.

The detail design of all headsails and their correct drawing out on the sail plan is discussed separately in the chapter no. 10 on headsail design, which in turn should read in conjunction with the chapter nos. 12, 13 and 14 on sail trimming.

THE DESIGN OF HEADSAILS

In a previous chapter we have considered at some length the relative merits of various rigs, and the layout in each case. Here we are concerned with drawing in the sails, in detail, on the sail plan. One sees each year new sails appearing in the fleet with the same old defects; insufficient clearance at the head, very likely sheeted too far inboard and too far forward, and perhaps set too high at the tack; sails set nearly on top of one another; or lying hard round the shrouds. With these and a lot of minor troubles one feels that, though each case has its own special problems, a few simple rules and precepts, based largely on experience and without too much reference to higher theory, can steer one clear of many of these snags.

We will concentrate for the time being on windward sailing. We need to provide the best sails for four different weights of wind : firstly light airs Force 0 to 2; secondly light to moderate breezes, Force 3–4; thirdly fresh to strong winds, Force 5–6; and finally storm canvas. As a general rule, one can say that it is necessary in a fully-found ocean racer to have a separate sail, or set of headsails, for each of those conditions. The exact wind strength at which the change-over is made will naturally vary. For instance class one may run from 0–1 and class two from 2–4.

Importance of Light Canvas. Although this may seem strange to those who are accustomed to think of ocean racers as tough-rigged storm-beaters, it is a fact that off shore one has to pay more attention to ghosting sails than when handicap racing in more sheltered conditions. Because of the extra movement of the boat in a seaway, the reduction of the inertia of the sail becomes most important. Moreover the overlapping part of a sail which in a steady boat you might in calm water and with care, be able to keep working, in a seaway in light airs may become just a tail to shake the rest of the sail unmercifully.

Headsail Layout. Quite apart from the general choice and layout of a rig, it is of the utmost importance that the sails should be carefully drawn exactly to suit the fore triangle and the available sheeting base, in each case bearing in mind the weight of wind for which they are designed. Before we

go on to consider the shape of individual sails to suit various rigs we can set out a few useful general rules.

The angle of the head of a cotton sail should never be less than $18.5°$, and $20°$ is a better minimum; $2°$ more in each case for Terylene. If the sail is narrower than this at the top, difficulty will be experienced in getting it to stand. In extra narrow sails, in order to prevent the upper part of the sail from lifting, the line of the sheet will be taken too far forward, giving too big a downward component to the pull, and spoiling the general shape of the sail. Terylene sails for strong breezes should aim at a minimum head angle of $24°$, and preferably not more than $28°$.

Clearance Above Headsails. One of the difficult things to determine is the amount of clearance to be left between the head of the sail and the top of the stay on which it is set. By the top I mean the point of intersection of the stay with the mast. If too little clearance is allowed, the mainsail will be back-winded excessively, and the air flow will be untidy. On the other hand if the clearance is too large, then one is losing area. The problem is further complicated by the fact that the necessary clearance depends not only on the length of luff of the triangle—the bigger the sail the more is wanted —but on the amount of overlap the sail has on the mast and on the maximum wind strength for which the sail is designed.

No formula is likely to meet every condition, but I have evolved one which gives a good guide as to the minimum clearance necessary (a little more will never do any harm) for windward sailing. Purely reaching sails can go much higher.

$$C = .018 \, I \, UO - .5h.$$

where C = clearance between sail head and top of stay.

I = Height of the triangle.

U = Maximum wind strength, Beaufort Scale, for which the sail is designed to set on the wind.

O = Overlap ratio.

h = Hollow (if any) in the leech.

The overlap in this formula is to be taken in the case of genoas and low-cut sails, in accordance with the R.O.R.C. method, which measures distance from the sail tack to the position of a perpendicular dropped from the clew of the sail, compared with the base of the triangle.

Thus a genoa that is 16 ft. long on the foot, set in a fore triangle with a base J of 10 ft., has an overlap ratio of 1.6.

In the case of high-cut sails it is necessary (for the purpose of our formula) to project the line of the luff downwards to a typical genoa sail foot-line, and measure the overlap to that point. The working of the formula depends very much on correct estimation of the maximum wind strength, and it will be convenient in some cases to use an intermediate figure, say $3\frac{1}{2}$ when it is estimated that Force 4 will be just beyond the proper range of the sail, working to windward.

Position of Headsail Tack. In general headsails should be tacked down as close to the deck as possible, to get the maximum amount of luff length. With this end in view the cringle can be worked into the sail, with a little care, though sailmakers don't fancy the job, as it may make wrinkles to the tack. There is another reason why the tack should be hooked or shackled direct to the deck fitting, and the tension put on the luff by the halyard. If one uses a tack tackle it is difficult in the haste of changing a sail at sea to make sure where the crew is going to finish up. If you attempt to set it up low to the deck you may find your hard down before you have got the necessary tension on, and have to slack off the tack tackle and sweat up a bit more on the halyard—all a time-wasting job. And if we agree that the clearance at the top of the sail is important, then clearly we must set the sail in a fixed position on the stay. Thus the use of a fixed tack and a good halyard is much to be preferred.

Most headsails have wire luff ropes, and generally this is to be preferred where yachts have to be raced, or cruised, by less than expert crews and at night. I have for very many years used hemp, later Terylene, luff ropes in light sails. I tried these in working sails in 1963 in *Outlaw*; in conjunction with small worm-operated tack winches to give accurate tensioning of the luff, and variation of the 'fullness' or curvature of the sail. Of recent years the 'stretchy luff' has been in vogue and in skilled hands is effective. But the ability, especially at night, to be able to hoist the headsail up good and hard without delay or worry, is indeed valuable.

Genoa Foot-Line. Turning to the drawing of the line of the foot, there is no doubt that in the case of the very low-cut genoa it is most difficult to get it to set perfectly. Still it has been done often enough. A slight rise from the tack, above the horizontal, to which must be added the sheer of the boat when thinking of the foot-line relative to the deck-line, does as a rule make the sail set better. It depends somewhat on the beam of a boat; a very narrow boat is not such a good sheeting base and the higher cut may be advisable. Likewise genoas with very big overlaps, for boats with their masts well into the boat (bringing up the clew to about abreast the helmsman) must be cut on the rise as the boat there is getting too narrow to sheet to, compared to the foot length of the sail.

If you look at photographs of boats trying to set genoas, which come too far aft, you will often see that the part of the sail near the clew is doing negative work, since it is inclining to weather.

It is normal and good practice to cut a genoa leech with a hollow in it. It goes some way towards preventing the line of the leech lipping in. Apart from this the amount of the hollow depends on a variety of things such as the necessity for clearing cross-trees or stays. A pronounced hollow can be used if necessary, and the sail will as a rule set all the better for it on the wind. Reaching, of course, one loses something.

One hears it said that a genoa is a windward sail and no good for reaching. While it is true that a genoa must be cut pretty flat to set well on the wind, such shape or flow as there is being mostly up in the forward third of the sail, the easing of the sheet on a reach gives it extra shape or flow; and it can in practice be used perfectly well on a reach. Hard weather genoas are cut flatter; light weather ones are normally given extra flow.

Nearly all the things we have said about a genoa apply to the quadrilateral jib, which can be considered as a genoa with its clew portion cut off. The layout of the cloths however needs special treatment. The upper clew cringle of a quad requires a very light nylon thimble and minimum roping. Unfortunately modern penalties have almost debarred these sails from racing, and totally under C.C.A. rules. How much better to have put on an appropriate penalty, commensurate with the speed advantage, rather than shut off a possible useful avenue of development.

It is true that these low-cut genoas and genoa staysails—for all that has been said applies pretty well to staysails as well as single headsails—obstruct the view, but that has often to be accepted. In the case of yachts that have a biggish coach roof, the extreme bottom of the low-cut sail is partly blanketed, and so there is not the same incentive to run the line of the foot down to the gunwale in designing one's sails. A genoa foot should be cut perfectly straight, but when considering the foot of a genoa, see that it clears the lifeline if it has to cross it, as the R.O.R.C. provides for lifelines at least 24 in.

above the deck all round the yacht. Another point is that the headsails can exceed 1.5 J at a modest penalty of 0.4 times the excess, providing that they do not exceed 1.8 J. *See* R.O.R.C. Measurement Rule V(14) (iii).

Genoa Details. Care must be taken to see that the clew of a genoa is carefully reinforced and doubled, the general scheme being to run it in a three-pronged fashion up the mitre and foot and leech. Local sailmakers, used to making working sails, of heavier canvas, sometimes neglect this on a 'jenny'. If you have to add it to a cotton sail later, try and use well-stretched cloth from a second-hand sail. After a sail has been set a time or two, and stretched, mark the places in red or blue pencil where the shrouds are rubbing and have these lightly doubled.

In big genoas, particularly in larger boats, it is helpful to have a becket sewn into the foot at half-foot length, which a crew member can man and haul forward to help get the sail about; sometimes with the aid of line and block near the tack.

R.O.R.C. Foot Length Limits. Although the new international rule of measurement is shortly to be brought into force in some countries, many clubs have opted to continue with the R.O.R.C. rating rule. By R.O.R.C. rule since January, 1949, one is allowed the same sized spinnaker as the Americans, that is to say with a width at base or higher of 180 per cent. The 'penalty' for headsails having a horizontal foot length clew to tack, of more than 150 per cent of the fore triangle base J, amounts to the addition of one-third of such excess to the measured base of the triangle. This also allows one to use a spinnaker and spinnaker pole, which in width or length is oversize by the same amount, without any further penalty. Since 1957 the area of the fore triangle, which is measured as half the product of the base (J) measured to the fore side of the mast and the height (I), is rated at 100 per cent of its actual area. The height I in the formula is measured to the point at which the highest stay on which sail is set intersects the fore side of the mast, or to the halyard block if the highest sail is set flying.

Staysails for Sloops. Of recent years, since the early editions of *Offshore* were written, I have found it well worth while to make use of a small light stay-sail under the genoa when reaching. This sail can be set as soon as the wind frees a full point, in moderate or light conditions. It is tacked down to an eyebolt to weather of the centre line, about 40 per cent base of fore triangle ahead of the mast, and hoisted flying by a halyard going up about 40 per cent of the genoa hoist. A spinnaker boom lift will often serve. This sail can also be usefully set under a high-riding spinnaker.

Ghosting Sails. It is important to note that for ghosting, that is to say for sailing in extremely light airs, sails with a very big overlap are definitely inferior to those with a moderate overlap, because the strength of the wind is insufficient to hold up the portion of the sail adjacent to the leech, which falls inboard and spoils the whole set of the sail. Taking this into consideration we can see why it hardly pays to design for R.O.R.C. races with a penalty overlap. This applies with special force to fore triangles with modest aspect ratios, that is to say, where there is a moderate hoist compared to the base.

For ghosters the weights of cloth recommended are shown in Appendix IV. If you wish to econo-mise by cutting the total number of sails, then you start your lightest sail a shade heavier. Unlike genoas and normal headsails which must have stout thimbles at each corner, ghosters should have a light clew thimble.

New International Rule and C.C.A. Headsails. Some different considerations apply though here too the spinnaker is allowed without penalty to be 180 per cent J in width at any height, which provides a nice shaped sail even with high aspect ratios.

But there is a light tax on the amount of genoa overlap beyond about 160 per cent, and fore triangle area is rated at 120 per cent of actual area. There is also quite a tax on fore triangles (and mainsails) whose aspect ratios exceed two to one, the penalty becoming about 15 per cent added area for rating as the ratio increases towards the present-day maxima.

A moderate amount of overlap is useful in enabling us to get the drive necessary out of a sail plan which is concentrated well inboard of the ends of the boat, and is consequently easy to handle; easy to change headsails on, or to reef the mainsail. Every foot we move the foremast stay inboard, the easier becomes the job of sail handling, for we have more deck space round our stay, and the motion becomes less violent. Moreover the team working there is not putting her head down so much.

This is one of the strong arguments against the 'measure the lot' thesis which has gained some ground of late; and a headsail which can only be 90 per cent of the area of its foretriangle looks a poor skinny affair when set for a reach in a nice moderate breeze.

But on all but the smallest racers, overlap beyond a reasonable point adds to the effort of working the ship, and to the area and cost of the sails, out of proportion to the extra speed gained. So perhaps the R.O.R.C. '150 per cent J' genoa is a good compromise: though the new rule which measures the base at right-angles to the stay, and results in a genoa of about 160 per cent J is not too different.

In this connection it must be remembered that ocean racers have to be handled and readily put about by one watch of the hands, by day or by night. Fighting an enormous masthead genoa around when going about inshore, with the race finish in sight, and all hands on the job, may be good fun, but it loses some of its attraction in the middle watch, when in a breeze it proves to be just a bit more than one watch can properly handle. More is said about this in the chapter no. 9 on rigs.

Special Sails for Reaching. We have in effect covered the question of the design of the outline of the genoa sail; because we have fixed the head and tack and discussed the clew position. It used to be the fashion to have special sails cut rather fuller for reaching, with flatter sails for windward work. In general I am doubtful whether this extra sail is justified, since one automatically increases the flow or curve of a sail when one eases sheets. And until the wind comes abaft the beam, and one's sails become stalled, one needs to have a nice flat leech even for reaching; a thing many of the old time balloon or reaching jibs did not show. How often, too, when one thinks one is settled for a reach, the breeze draws round ahead with the least warning, and puts one on the wind, and then perhaps frees again a few minutes later?

There are, however, two minor respects in which reaching headsails are superior in moderate breezes. Whereas it is good practice to cut some hollow into the leech of a genoa—it helps keep it flat—the reaching sail can be cut straight in the leech. And it can be cut with virtually no clearance at the head of the sail. An additional reaching staysail can be justified in sloops; when the owner's pocket is deep enough.

The larger, lighter, higher cut yankees or genoas will meet all requirements for use on the fore top-mast stays, for reaching.

Cloth Weight for Headsails. Now for the important question of choosing the correct weight of cloth. Appendix IV gives you full details of my suggestions on this subject.

In the case of headsails the answer in brief is to use the lightest weight of cloth which will keep its shape, in the wind strength for which the sail is designed.

This in turn divides itself into two aspects; that of keeping its shape through the season, which is partly a measure of its quality, and the require-ment that the shape or flow which the sailmaker has given it, be not exaggerated, or temporarily stretched in the puffs, so as to spoil its intended form.

Provided it will stand and keep shape, the advantages of light material are manifold. In light variable breezes it will fill more quickly; and the folds and creases will be smoothed out more thor-oughly in light going. In the motion of a seaway the reduced inertia of the lighter material will, as we have already mentioned, result in the limited wind pressure of light breezes being better able to keep the sail steady. Other things, such as the method of manufacture and form of finish, being the same, the lighter the cloth the finer will be the weave and texture, and the smoother the finish resulting in reduced friction loss when going to windward.

Light canvas takes up less stowage space and requires less effort and time to handle when setting and handing.

Speaking of a cotton sail for a moment, after getting a soaking at sea and going into strange shapes in its rack, when re-set the lighter sail will dry more quickly, and more rapidly resume its proper shape. In any material when the light chap is set, weight aloft is saved; and in the aggregate of spare sails it has some significance as a displace-ment factor too.

However, all these advantages are nullified if the sail is carried on the wind in too strong a breeze, in which it can't hold its shape. In a 35-ft. water-line boat our ghosting sails may be as light as 4 oz. The various headsails will graduate up through perhaps 10 oz. for the breezy genoa, to 13 oz. for the yankee and for the other jibs, as well as for the storm can-vas. But it depends a lot on how the rig is arranged; whether you plan to do any fresh weather sailing with a genoa, or whether with a masthead cutter rig, for instance, you intend going to the yankee for windward work in any breeze. The table in the no. IV Appendix should take care of most of these problems.

Storm Sail Canvas. Most sailmakers provide un-necessarily heavy canvas for storm sails. These weights may be of value for round the world voyag-ing, but the ordinary yachtsman and offshore racer makes only occasional use of them. For a given weight of material and weight of wind the stress in the fibres of a sail are about proportional to the square of the linear dimensions or to the area of the sail. Nearly but not quite, because the sail is not all in one piece but cut in cloths. Anyway the point is that a small storm sail in the same material as your much bigger second jib will probably ride out a gale quite nicely. The unnecessarily heavy sails cost more, take up more room and are more awk-ward to handle. But, I can hear you say, what about a margin for old age? To which I would reply that there is no bigger snare than a really heavy sail, which may be very old and have had little use and looks good; once it or its stitching gets ripe with age the extra weight won't stop it splitting. Further discussion of these questions will be found in the sections dealing with alterations and attention to worn sails; and in the chapter on sail setting and trimming.

Storm headsails, in general and more particularly Terylene ones, are prone to bad leech shiver which though it may not retard the vessel shivers the mainsail, frays the crew's nerves and must accelerate deterioration of mast fittings and rigging by fatigue stressing. Strong leech lines and sewn-in short tufnol battens should be provided.

Headsail Cloths. There is not much to be said about the lay of the cloths because experience shows that the mitre cut for headsails gives the most strength for weight, with a reasonable compromise as regards the cloths running in the same direction as the air flow. Earlier headsails, designed on considerations of strength and simplicity, often had their cloths vertically, and these were difficult to set, as they go into furrows. Some years ago there was a vogue for cutting genoas with horizontal cloths, to streamline the seams. These sails, however, lose their shape more quickly. Double gores or mitres have become fashionable in some quarters, but their value is not really established. When I have been stuck at times for the right lightweight of cloth, I have got the sailmaker to use the next available weight up the scale, and run wider cloths. With Terylene there is much to be said for wider cloths.

Nylon for Sails. For spinnakers I think it takes a lot of beating. A large spinnaker can be of $1\frac{1}{2}$ oz. nylon, which is exceptionally light.

Very fine nylon must be dressed to be windproof. If left with parachute finish, which is intended to pass air through the fibres, power is lost.

A heavier nylon yankee gives good results in wind Force 1–2 and fair results with wind Force 3. But all these sails, as soon as the wind freshens, start to shiver in the queerest places; an infinitesimal change in wind strength means the trimming of the sheet, and very likely a change in the sheet lead position.

To sum up, for spinnakers nylon is tops and stands more wind than Terylene. For other racing sails nylon, being fundamentally more elastic, is not recommended.

Terylene (Dacron). Is recommended for nearly all sails, other than spinnakers and storm sails. It is best until something better is invented. Its inherent smoothness makes for faster sailing to windward, and this smoothness is enhanced by special finishes. But over finishing reduces its

ultimate strength, and must be avoided particularly in spinnakers. It has approximately (in the better qualities) the strength of nylon and similar freedom from mildew. It is less elastic and equally unaffected by moisture. It appears less subject to deterioration from sunlight. As with nylon care must be taken to get the high-tenacity quality; say the 'M type'. The medium-tenacity Terylene is as elastic as nylon, and has only 70 per cent of the strength of the best qualities. The elasticity of best cotton is well below that of best Terylene, but it is still occassionally preferred for breezy headsails and because of the strong tendency of Terylene to flutter. The rougher fibres of cotton working over one another largely damp these flutters down. (As to weights *see* Appendix XVI.)

Good strong leach lines must be provided for all Terylene sails; and used, but to the minimum tension necessary, for reducing leach flutter. Terylene headsails intended for use in breezy conditions should have five short unbreakable battens fitted to the leach, and the pockets sewn up.

PLANNING THE SAIL OUTFIT

We now come to the important matter of planning the lady's complete trousseau of headsails; of deciding how many sails we need, or rather how few sails we can do with, to cover the requirements set out above. To take the simplest case first let us look at a small sloop.

The absolute minimum outfit, doing things as economically as possible will be a genoa, to the 150 per cent overlap, or 160 per cent if the new rule is in use; a big working sail with the clew drawn on to the shrouds, and a heavy weather sail about half that area. The storm headsail should not normally be more than 20 sq. ft. per ton of ballast keel, plus 20, or if you don't know your ballast weight, you can calculate in another way; $16\frac{1}{2}$ per cent of R.O.R.C. rated area or $13\frac{1}{2}$ per cent of the C.C.A. or new rule rated area.

As a full outfit we shall probably demand one headsail for each of the four conditions mentioned earlier. A keen owner of a larger craft might demand five. As the R.O.R.C. and the new rule is hard on sail area, designers, as we have observed in other chapters, should have based their total sail area on the minimum necessary to give their craft a decent performance in light weather. Thus it will come about that the total sail area will have been chosen with little regard to stability, and stability will vary a good deal between approximately similar sized boats according to the fullness of their ends, hardness of their bilges, the beam, ballast ratio, and the draft.

If she is a stiff craft, then both the Number One

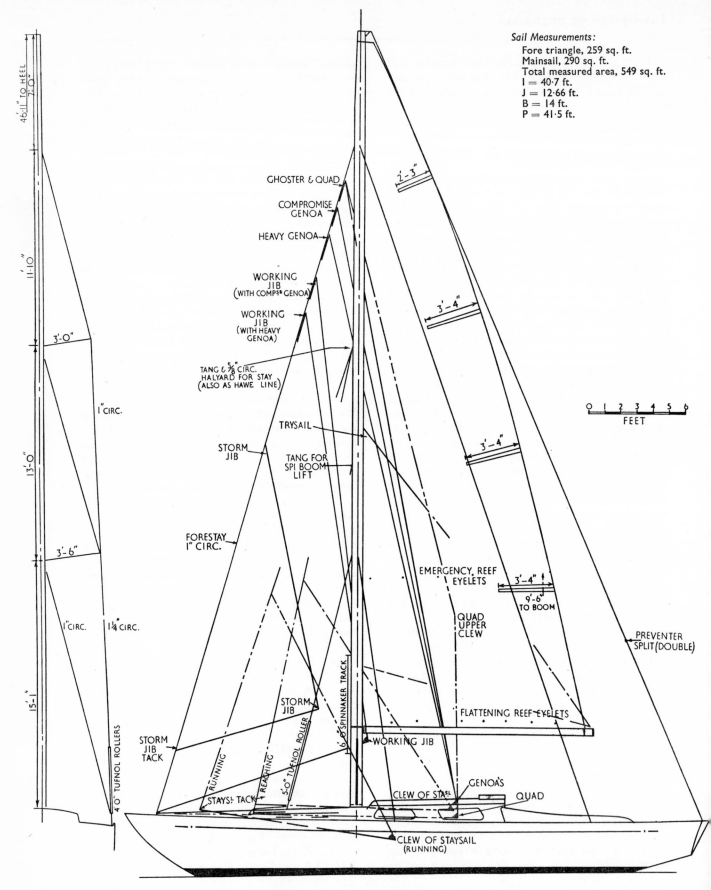

Sail Measurements:
Fore triangle, 259 sq. ft.
Mainsail, 290 sq. ft.
Total measured area, 549 sq. ft.
I = 40·7 ft.
J = 12·66 ft.
B = 14 ft.
P = 41·5 ft.

Diagram 19.—Sail plan of *Brigantine*, Class II ocean racer designed by Illingworth and Primrose. She won the Morgan Cup for 1963 and is owned by Messieurs Bernard Moureau and Pierre Mulot.

and Number Two headsails will be of about the same size, but the second will be of heavier material, cut flatter, with more clearance at the head. This in effect means a minimum outfit of four headsails to a stiff sloop. On the other hand if she will not take a full-sized jib in Force 4 breeze, you may reduce the designed size of the second headsail until she does.

Sloops: Steps in Area of Reduced Headsails. Each sail subsequently should be an equal reduction in area over the larger one. It would seem at first sight that one should go in percentage reductions. For example, 450 sq. ft., 300 sq. ft., 200 sq. ft., and 135 sq. ft. But in practice it is better to step it 450, 345, 240, and 135 sq. ft., partly because of the increased effect of the windage of the spars, as wind speed increases. If you decide you can only afford three sails you can still proceed on the same principle, but pitch your smallest sail a shade higher with a reef. The bigger the proportion of the total area you have in the fore triangle the greater is the necessity for making the steps more gradual; it may mean an extra sail.

Clew Positions for Heavy Weather Sails. The smaller sails will be cut higher in the foot, since this will make them easier to sheet, and they will stand better in hard winds and not collect the water.

Also one will get a longer length of luff for a given area. Yet another consideration; one wants to keep the flow up in lee of the mainsail in spite of the headsail being much reduced in area, and having the clew higher for a given area will help in this respect. It is extraordinary how far away a small jib can be and still achieve this, in strong winds. And when the ship is well heeled the flow off the jib probably spreads from the bottom upwards across the mainsail.

But in general these small sails should still be tacked fairly close to the deck; in this way the luff will be sagging off to leeward less than if the sail is set higher, and the centre of effort of the sail will be lower and will heel the boat less, which not only results in the boat having a more easily driven form under water, but in the sail having a bigger driving component and smaller 'depressing' one.

Sloops: Balance Under Storm Conditions. Sometimes in sloop-rigged yachts when they are close-reefed and sailing with a storm jib, the centre of effort of the sail plan moves so far forward that they carry a difficult amount of lee helm. This is particularly likely to occur in fine-sterned designs— metacentroids and the like. It is difficult to predict in advance whether this will occur, and an early trial should be attempted in a fresh breeze, or better, a strong breeze. A lower wire halyard to set the wire luffed jib to an inner tacking position

4

may be is needed. This halyard can also serve as a spinnaker pole lift. When used with the storm jib it will need to be set up with a tackle or winch; or alternatively a tack tackle must be used. Clearly it is best to set the storm jib, if the normal forestay cannot be used, to a lower cross-tree. A hole through the foredeck towing cleat (or a strop) will save an extra toe-stubbing eye-bolt.

Layout of Cutter Headsails. And so we come to perhaps the most difficult of all the problems—how to design the large working headsails of a cutter, the jib, and staysail; and how to get the maximum total effective area, in a given fore triangle. One must arrange that these two partners and mother mainsail all the while pull in accord, and not despoil one another with undue backwind and the like. The closer winded the ship is, as a hull, the more acute does this problem become. But there are many advantages to this rig, as we have noted in a previous chapter, and so the problem must be tackled.

There are roughly three modern ways to lay out the fore triangle with two headsails. One can have a comparatively insignificant staysail and use over it a sort of yankee-jib-topsail-nearly-genoa. *Bloodhound* sometimes sports this type of sail and seems to go all right under it. The J class *Whirlwind* had an extreme form of it which seemed to work pretty well too, though it was all but a sloop.

Then one can have the intermediate arrangement typified by *Maid* (*see* Diagram 21) where the clew of the yankee comes only to the main shroud, and the staysail under it has quite a big overlap on the mainsail, being a sizeable fellow. In the third method one has the staysail the principal partner and having arranged his stay well up the mast and the sail with a nice fat overlap, one draws a very high-cut narrow yankee jib topsail on the outer stay, which will terminate at deck not far forward of the forestay. One will hope to goodness one can somehow get the jib sheet past the staysail's belly, and probably end by accepting a 'hard line' across the leech of the staysail where the sheet bears. The limit in the height of the clew should be ability to sheet in the ship. The head angle will be minimal.

In spite of these difficulties, it is not a bad rig provided it is not made too extreme.

In the old days one's headsails used to converge to a point on the mast. Then we discovered that they set better with parallel luffs. Later with the tendency to increase the aspect ratio of the fore triangle the stays have started to converge towards the deck.

In the good cutters, like *Maid* or *Myth*, *Outlaw* or *Oryx*, while one can carry a pretty big yankee for

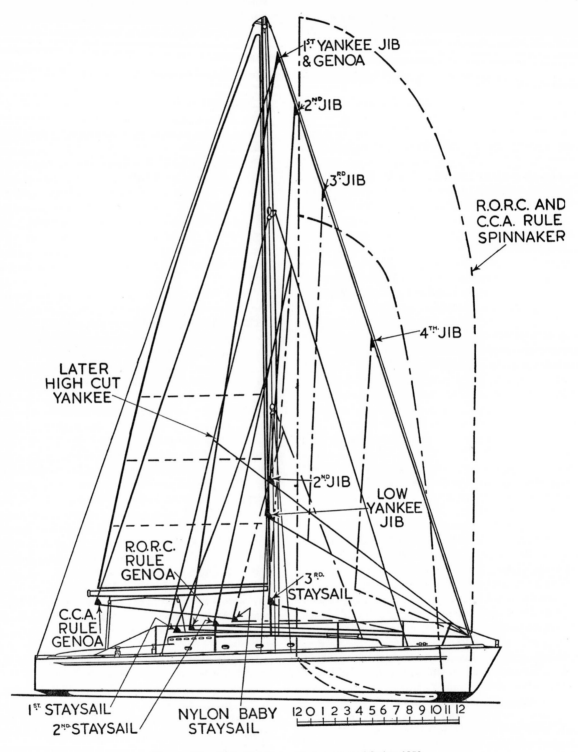

Diagram 20.—*Myth of Malham* sail plan, as modified in 1950.

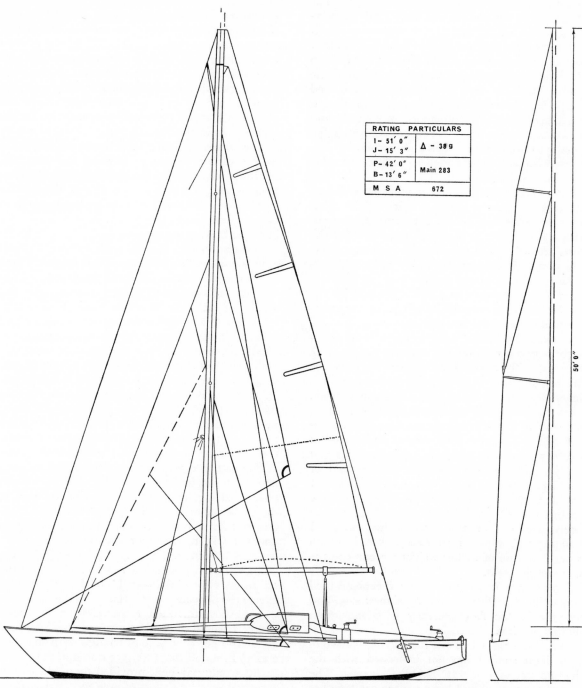

RATING PARTICULARS	
I – 51′ 0″ J – 15′ 3″	Δ – 38.9
P – 42′ 0″ B – 13′ 6″	Main 283
M S A	672

Diagram 21.—*Monk of Malham* built for John Illingworth by Raymond Labbé at St. Malo. Her principal dimensions are: L.O.A., 39·7 ft., L.W.L. 30·0 ft., beam 11 ft., 1 in., draft 6 ft., 9½ in. Rated sail area 672.

light windward work and for reaching, the serious heavy windward work is best served by having the biggest staysail that can properly be set and not being too greedy with the size of the yankee. The smaller high cut yankee will back-wind the staysail less, and the luff will stand straighter, so that it is driving more and burying her head less. Its clew on the wind should be a little forward rather than aft of the main cap shroud, and nearly a third of the total hoist off the deck. The clearance at the head can be had from the formula for a 4, 4½, or 5 wind Force according to the toughness of your rig and the stability of the boat. All this of course applies equally to two headsail yawls and ketches.

'Steps down' for the yankees follow the same principle as the sloops.

Cutter Staysail Design. Three staysails are sufficient in a racing cutter—the big one which will be about 9 oz. for a moderate-sized boat and will be cut with a big hollow to the leech so as to clear the lower cross-tree; a hollow of about 4 per cent of the hoist of the sail. You can if you want add a 'reacher'.

The clearance at the head will be 50 per cent more than that laid down in the formula for the jibs for the same reason—to help clear the cross-tree and increase the overlap—and because it will have to be sheeted extra flat in order to set effectively between the mainsail and the yankee. The leech should be cut only just to clear the cross-tree and this together with the other provisions mentioned should give you quite a sizeable overlap. From 1963 onwards the length of the foot of an overlapping staysail plus the distance between its tack and the fore top mast stay at deck may not exceed 150 per cent base of fore triangle; or about 160 per cent for the new rule. The second or working staysail will be of about 10 oz. for a Class II boat and the clew will come to the mast. The heavy weather sail will be about half that size: but a sail rarely needed. For the older racing cutters I designed a ghosting staysail and yankee. But with better Terylene of lighter weight we can use the light working sails.

Cutter Genoas. In a cutter, the word genoa is used to describe a headsail set on the highest stay, and cut low in the foot generally with maximum allowed overlap.

In a cutter rig where one has the big yankee of fairly light stuff, I am not impressed with the absolute necessity for an R.O.R.C. genoa. The area of the staysail and large yankee are together appreciably greater than the genoa; and I think one can manage nicely without a genoa: though a masthead ghoster—a very light genoa—is valuable.

But, still of course referring to twin headsail rigs, when one uses a big overlap under C.C.A. conditions, the genoa becomes more valuable, particularly when your mast is stepped not too far aft, and when in consequence your sheeting base is wider and more effective. One must decide whether one is sometimes going to sheet to the end of one's main boom; and if so definitely design for this with a suitably high clew. Remember that the clew will move forward quite a bit when actually set, compared to the position as drawn 'flat' on the sail plan, but that the boom will generally ride a little higher than in the flat sail plan.

The Americans with their masts stepped fairly well forward in the case of the yawls and with their relatively big beams can make very good use of their genoas. They won't work well in narrower yachts like *Bloodhound*, *Foxhound* or *Myth*, in a breeze. Apart from the small sheeting base, they bury the bow, going to windward.

Spinnaker Staysail. It is desirable to have a special light staysail with a small hoist and relatively long foot for use under a high-flying spinnaker in light weather with the wind on the quarter. This sail should be tacked a little way abaft the fore topmast stay to any convenient point, set flying and hoisted to a point about 40 per cent of spinnaker hoist. The luff should be 40 per cent of spinnaker hoist. The foot of sail should be 120 per cent J, *viz.* a little bigger than the base of the fore triangle. If you draw it in thus on your sail plan with the tack 10 per cent J below the deck you will determine the correct leech length. The R.O.R.C. is apt to change its mind about spinnaker staysail limits, —so check on the current rules before ordering one.

If in certain conditions this sail is found to interfere with keeping the spinnaker full, *e.g.* if the boat is rolling, and the spinnaker is unstable, it should be handed. It is important to avoid an unduly tall staysail which, though you won't perhaps notice it, will interfere with the spinnaker.

C.C.A. Headsails. The recent rules abolishes the unlimited headsails and measures the width of the sail to the clew at right-angles to the luff with (in effect) 160 per cent base of triangle as the minimum width. Above this there is a modest tax on added width. I would guess that a genoa foot length of about 160 per cent base of triangle with the clew 2 to 3½ ft. up off the deck (according to the size of yacht) would pay best, provided the yacht was in a general sense not short of area in her rig. If she was a bit short of overall area it might pay to have the foot length up to 180 per cent base triangle, with the clew a shade higher again.

11

THE DESIGN OF MAINSAILS, TRYSAILS AND SPINNAKERS

The proportions of mainsails are, more than in the case of the proportions of individual headsails, a matter fundamental to the rig, and therefore are dealt with under that chapter. There is some other comment concerning mainsail detail in the chapter no. 12 on sail setting and trimming, and the important question of slides is dealt with under the heading of mast fittings.

So it only remains, as far as mainsails are concerned, to deal with some minor matters. In the first place there are very heavy penalties, prohibitive ones in fact, on excess widths of headboards and on excess batten lengths. The allowed width of headboard without penalty, and these should be used, is 3 per cent length of boom as measured. The excess is added to the boom measurement in calculating the sail area.

Under R.O.R.C. rating the maximum number of battens allowed is five. They must divide the leech into approximately equal parts. If four or fewer are fitted the maximum length without penalty is 14 per cent of boom plus 1.5 ft. or 12 per cent plus 1 ft. if five are fitted. Twice the excess length of each batten is added to the boom measurement. Under the new international rule slightly different lengths are laid down, with permissive (at very slight penalty) R.O.R.C. lengths. See Appendix VIII for details. The use of five battens reduces the tendency of the leech to shiver. Battens may be of Tufnol, celeron, ash, or hickory. If of ash, young ash, as opposed to old or long-seasoned ash is to be preferred. Battens should be well tapered; edges and lanyard holes rounded off; and wood battens well varnished. Two sets, one thin and one thicker, should be provided.

Double-luffed mainsails, which in effect have a pocket into which the mast is laced, so as to streamline the flow on to the sail, are barred. Likewise special light-weather mainsails are prohibited because they would involve much extra expense without adding to the sporting character of the racing.

Mainsail Cloth Weight. As additional light-weather mains are barred, care must be taken to choose a mainsail cloth which will be fully adequate to its task but no heavier, since the tendency to shake the wind out of the sail in a seaway will be greater as the weight and inertia of the sail material increases.

The weight of cloth I recommend is shown in Appendix IV. These details are based on the average size of mainsails in ocean racers. If your mainsail is large for the boat, and is going therefore to require early reefing, you can base your size on a single-reefed sail; or just use 1 oz. lighter cloth. If the sail is exceptionally small for the stability of the boat, use 1 oz. heavier, since it will be carried longer, in heavier winds, before reefing.

Messrs. Ratsey at Cowes have been kind enough to furnish me with a list of the cloth weights they normally use for mainsails. These are from 1 to 3 oz. heavier than my scale.

Reefs. In small and medium-sized yachts fitted with boom gallows, either standing or folding, which are strong enough to enable the main boom to be strapped in there whilst reefing, a lacing may be passed, obviating the necessity for reef points and their attendant windage. But a lacing is very awkward to pass at sea with a free swinging boom. In bigger yachts the difficulty and delay of passing a reef lacing is greater and a case can be made out for 'reef points in any case'. The detail of reefing arrangements is considered under the heading of sail handling. Make sure that proper patching is fitted in way of your reef points; this is particularly important with the lighter sails now recommended.

It is useful to have a balance reef, curved so as to take some of the flow out of a full-cut sail when necessary. Apart from the foregoing, when reefing offshore is needed, a real reduction in sail is required. Where the mainsail is small in relation to the total sail area as in the case of a ketch, a schooner or a modern cutter, then a total of two reefs are sufficient. The elimination of a reef reduces friction windage on the sail and simplifies reefing sheaves and gear. In other cases three may be provided, though if you are going to have reef points with their attendant windage I would still have only two. In bad weather one rarely needs to mess about with small sail reductions. In any case I would advocate the deepest reef being about 35 per cent up the hoist of the sail. This makes the fully reefed mainsail, allowing for the roach, that is to say the outward curvature of the leech which is held out by the battens, about half its original size.

If you go in for a switch track in the mast, or a duplicate mast track, to enable you to hank on the trysail before lowering the main—then the trysail can be 50 per cent of the mainsail area and one deep reef in the mainsail only is necessary. The trysail in this case should have a reef in it, to bring it if necessary down to the size mentioned below. But if the trysail is used in its normal function, as a storm sail to be set when a reefed mainsail is too large, then I feel it should be a small sail; in area round about 25 sq. ft. per ton of ballast, plus 25 sq. ft. Or if you are not sure of the amount of ballast carried, you can use an alternative rule and make it 19 per cent of the R.O.R.C. rated sail area, or 16 per cent of the C.C.A. rated area. Trysail shape and cut are dealt with later on in the chapter.

A trysail is rarely used and if it is reduced to the small dimensions indicated above, purely on considerations of sailing requirements, there is a welcome reduction in initial cost and stowage space required on board.

GAFF MAINSAIL DESIGN

Turning to the question of gaff mainsails we may consider how we can improve their performance to make them a match for the now almost universal bermudan rig.

One of the difficulties we meet at once is that in order to carry masthead headsails we require either an unacceptably heavy mast, or to use a hollow spar with two or more pairs of cross-trees.

Now to have cross-trees means that the mast-hoops shall not be required to slide up past the lowest cross-tree, which will probably be impossible to arrange conveniently. In this case, a perfectly satisfactory arrangement would be to have the heel of the gaff slide up in a reinforced Y2A track, of which details are given in Diagram 38 in the mast fittings chapter no. 18. This track successfully carried the gooseneck of the boom of *Myth* and so, given a good long slide, would easily carry the gaff. The mainsail luff is attached to slides like a bermudan. I suggest the gaff and the topsail yards should be aluminium alloy tubes. The thrust of the gaff on the mast needs special rigging consideration.

'Dyarchy' Topsail. We now come to the important question of arranging the topsail in the pole mast to the best advantage. The arrangement (Diagram 22) which Laurent Giles & Partners have worked out for Roger Pinckney, formerly Commodore of the Royal Cruising Club, and which has proved successful in *Dyarchy* is as follows:

The upper part of the mast is pear-shaped, and on the after side is a groove which takes the extra large luff rope, in the same manner as is employed for some dinghy mainsails. Permanently inside the groove is a small bronze traveller, through which the wire topsail halyard runs freely. The halyard is attached to the sail by a screw-on fitting, so that it is a continuation of the luff rope. The metal traveller remains at the bottom of the groove, thus keeping the halyard in the right place until the head of the sail enters the bottom of the groove. The head of the sail then pushes the traveller up as it is hoisted, and once having entered the groove it cannot jam or escape. It is consequently under control when either setting or handing. Provided the wind is forward of the beam, the sail enters the groove: but with the wind aft, one may have to luff or go aloft just to start it.

Gaff Mainsails for Ketches. One of the ways of making a gaff rig pay its way under modern conditions is to rig it in a ketch. The mainsail and topsail are larger than a bermudan mainsail on the same mast and would rate about the same. The rig would show to advantage reaching and running, and should not be much slower on the wind. With a ketch rig a triatic stay can be carried between the mastheads and a standing preventer backstay arranged to the mizzen mast, which could set a bermudan sail.

The ketch rig also allows of the efficient use of a vang to the mizzen masthead—a most important consideration. This matter is dealt with in more detail in the appropriate chapter no. 9.

Much the same consideration but with less force applies to a gaff mainsailed yawl, in which, provided the gaff was arranged to be not too long, and for the head of the topsail to make a comparatively small angle with the mast, it would be just feasible to have a triatic stay, assuming as we may that the mizzen mast was half the height of the main mast, and stepped clear of the main boom end.

Running preventer backstays are of course needed as well in either case.

Booms and Reefing. We are now concerned with the question of whether to provide roller reefing or not. I had it in eight personal boats and we have used it in hundreds of the ocean racers designed by us in recent years. There is no doubt that on a great many occasions roller reefing was a great racing time saver, and I rarely remember being in any trouble with the gear. In cases of roller reefing with a bendy boom, a calliper-claw is required.

A bit of extra wear and tear to the sails must be accepted but with Terylene the distortion is acceptable.

The principal snag to roller reefing is the resultant difficulty in the layout of the boom and gear. One has to resort to less convenient arrangements for the main sheet and the topping lift, the fore guy, and also for the sail outhaul. Further, the kicking-strap can only be used with difficulty when one is reefed. The boom will weigh a little more and be a shade less efficient than a flat boom, with a full sail.

This is a fair price to pay, and the problem is to consider under what conditions it will be worth while. In small and medium-sized yachts—shall we say those with main-sails up to 600 sq. ft.—the answer depends, as I see it, on the amount of reefing one is going to do. If the boat has a big mainsail and a relatively small fore triangle, the liability to reef is increased. It is further increased when one has a moderate ballast ratio and a moderate beam, with an average or slack midship section; that is to say when she is not specially stiff.

In laying out a rig for ocean racing purposes one furnishes her with the minimum sail area that will give her an adequate light-weather performance. For reasonably good hulls, this performance depends primarily on the ratio between sail area and wetted surface, but with an eye also to displacement. Thus the sail area is likely to have very little direct relation to the stability of the boat; yachts of the same size will have roughly the same sail area, and one will be much stiffer than the other. The less stiff one will have a bigger scantling or stability component under any rule, and in consequence a smaller rating, so she will not necessarily be any less likely to succeed, but the point for the moment is that she will certainly reef more often.

Pros and Cons of Roller Reefing. And so one wants to weigh up the various factors. If she is likely to want fairly frequent reductions in mainsail area, then roller reefing is worth having. We use it in virtually all our new sloops.

Many other boats which I raced offshore, *Maid of Malham, Myth of Malham, Outlaw, Oryx, Stormvogel,* had relatively small mainsails, and were rarely reefed. None of them could justify the inclusion of roller reefing: most of the sail reduction can be done in the fore triangle.

Storm Sail Layouts. All offshore racing rules including the C.Y.C. of Australia call for adequate

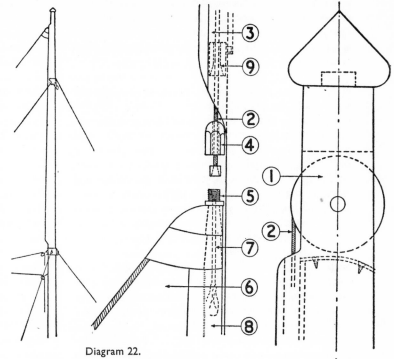

Diagram 22.

Details of *Dyarchy*'s Gaff Topsail Gear
Design by Laurent Giles & Partners

1. Topsail halyard sheave in mast-head.
2. Wire topsail halyard.
3. Groove in after side of mast above peak halyard block to take topsail luff-rope.
4. Screw fitting on halyard.
5. Screw fitting on continuation of top-sail luff-rope.
6. Topsail.
7. Wire joining screw fitting to luff-rope.
8. Italian hemp luff-rope.
9. Bronze traveller permanently inside mast groove to centre wire halyard.

storm canvas to be carried. A trysail is not specifically referred to, but is advisable when the mast is stepped well forward in the boat, and in general with a sloop rig. In the case of a cutter with the mast stepped well in to her, a good staysail will generally serve as storm canvas, and enable her to turn to windward under this sail alone, should one feel disinclined to the extra expense, weight, and stowage space occupied by a trysail.

Of yachts I have owned, *Queen Bee, Makeshift, Thalassa, Maid,* and *Wista* would all work tolerably under a staysail alone in fresh conditions. *Myth of Malham, Monk, Outlaw* and *Oryx* would go really well under a staysail alone. For instance in *Myth* we had a 200-sq. ft. staysail under which she would close-reach like a train in Force 8. If the wind increased further this could be changed to a 125- or 100-sq. ft. sail.

Under the C.C.A's regulations the carrying of a trysail is compulsory, and no relaxation from this rule is permitted. There is no doubt that the trysail is a useful sail. When in *Myth* we used it quite a bit cruising in strong winds and moderate gales.

Layout of a Boom. The main or mizzen boom, or, of course, the foresail boom of a schooner, should be as light as possible for three reasons. Firstly, everything in the ship must be as light as is reasonably consistent with the necessary strength; and particularly so with gear which is well above the deck. Secondly, light spars ease the stress and chafe on the gear and make topping up and reefing and working the ship generally, a lighter duty. Lastly, and very important, a lighter spar gives the sail a better chance in light weather, enabling it to take up its natural curve without being unduly borne down. One hears it said that a heavy boom helps keep the boom down in fresh breezes. But this is the function of a kicking purchase, combined with an adjustable slide to the horse. Aluminium alloy booms are now general in modern yachts. They cost less than a good hollow spruce boom, weigh less, and it is now generally accepted that the main sheet loading should preferably not be concentrated at the boom's outboard end. But if you opt for roller reefing, there is need for a claw ring. The reason why end-of-boom sheeting is not liked is because in strong winds the boom bends the wrong way and gives extra hollowness, or curvature to the sail; instead of flattening it as would be the tendency were the sheet loading applied near the middle of boom.

If you choose wood, hollow booms are well worth while in conjunction with roller reefing. But they do not show to such advantage as might be supposed in other cases. A hollow spar's principal virtue is its greatly increased strength for a given weight in compression. Unless a loose-footed sail is used, a boom has principally to resist a bending load, owing to the upward pull of the sail being distributed along its entire length while the downward pull of the sheet and the gooseneck are concentrated near the ends. The principal subsidiary loading in a boom is that due to striking the runner when the ship is gybed without hauling the main sheet aft, resulting in a bending stress in the other plane.

In consequence, except for roller reefing, a deep narrow-sectioned boom is generally used nowadays, pivoted so as to be free to turn on its gooseneck and lie in the same plane as the sail. The pivot of the gooseneck should be not too far below the top of the boom, or it will be a nuisance, having a tendency to 'flop over' when the sail is lowered. As with other spars silver spruce is preferred, though best Oregon

(Douglas fir) and many other woods can be used.

If wood booms are appreciably hollowed, much more care and some weight will have to be expended in the fastenings of the fittings to the sides of the boom. These will include two or three reef pennant sheaves and eyes to match opposite them, several sheet fittings, the boom guy fitting, perhaps two small winches for reefing, or attachment for the reefing tackle, and cleats, etc., for these; the sail outhaul and perhaps the topping lift. Extra thickness of walls should be left in way of these fittings. It is important to have sufficient wood in the boom top to enable the track to be secured by screws. With a swivelling boom the topping lift should preferably lead from its standing part on the masthead to a sheave in the boom centre-line, otherwise the boom will tend to cant on the swivel as soon as weight is put on the topping lift. If the standing part is on the boom end, the fall has to come down from the masthead, involving extra windage and weight aloft.

To carry a centre-line topping lift means either offsetting the sheave of the mainsail outhaul slightly—which is feasible—or mounting this forward of the topping lift sheave. One can have holes about 18 in. long leading the two wires out to each side of the boom, where the purchases or winches are arranged. This is a neat arrangement and works well. For the topping lift, the purchase of which is otherwise apt to hang-down, the moving block can be run on a track on the side of the boom. A cheaper dodge is to use a wood bull's-eye and tail instead of a moving block, in conjunction with a cleat sheave, in this case the lead being from the tail of the dead-eye to the cleat sheave, through the bull's-eye, and on to the cleat. The dead-eye is less objectionable when swinging below the boom than a block.

Sometimes one sees a single block on the end of the standing topping lift wire, which then finishes a few feet above the boom. This enables a wire pennant to be used through this block, the standing end of the pennant being on one side of the boom and the running leg through a sheave fixed on the other side of the boom. This gives extra power suitable for a larger yacht and leaves the centre of the boom free for the outhaul. But there is with this arrangement a slightly added risk of the topping lift fouling the preventer backstays; with a single lead it seems always to come clear in time. This risk is unacceptable when the single preventer is split into two legs, where the fouling can take place at the junction of the legs.

For cruising a topping lift is desirable; to facilitate handling with a weak crew. But I manage happily without when racing in yachts of up to

18 tons displacement—say 40 foot waterline—provided one can use a really good boom crutch for reefing. This saves not only weight and windage aloft, but a frequent source of snark-ups; round the batten ends, cross tree ends or backstays.

It is now usual to arrange a track on the top of the boom to take the slides attached to the foot of the sail, probably of the same type as that used for the mainsail luff. With roller reefing this slide should be recessed well into the boom so that the slide tops just show. In small and medium-sized yachts the slide carrying the clew of the sail can be arranged to slide in the same section, additional fastenings being provided in way of this section. It is certainly a convenience where this can be so fitted. Often a stronger type of track is available of the same section for use for the aftermost few feet where the clew slide works.

The remarks concerning the fastening of tracks, materials, and slide design, which are given under the chapter dealing with mast fittings, apply of course to boom tracks.

The ways of rigging main sheets are legion. For instance in one modern system, for a large yacht, the main sheet leads have the standing part on the deck, lead up to the boom, down to the horse or slide, up again to the boom, and forward through one or more bull's-eyes to keep it up against the boom, through another block, and down to a block on the coach roof—preferably at the break in the roof or some other strong point—thence aft to a winch; or simply to the hand and cleat. This is much handier in small and moderate-sized boats than having the main sheet handled on the side decks. Even in larger yachts, with a powerful geared winch, the number of parts of a main sheet can be severely reduced.

Very small mainsails as in *Myth* (of 300 sq. ft.) can have their standing part on the boom, lead down to the horse or slide and up to the boom, then forward.

I like the slide on the horse or the track to be controlled by a slide located by a plunger so that it can be fixed in any position or allowed limited movement.

Roller Reefing Details. Arrangements with roller reefing will be quite different. The primary thing is to ensure that one's gear is oversize for the job—plenty strong and plenty powerful.

It is curious how often one sees roller reefing gear of inadequate proportions on otherwise well-fitted yachts, which even if it does not break, results in a fiendish struggle to roll the sail. I prefer the worm-driven type. It is naturally important to keep it very well lubricated. The large size Merriman roller reefing gear has taken care, in yachts of

4*

my own design, of mainsails of over 1200 sq. ft. Lewmar Marine make several smaller sizes of good gear. The handles should be strong, extra long and detachable, and there should be at least one spare on board.

It is said to be an unkind system as far as the mainsail is concerned, but I have seen many sails which have done several seasons and survived quite happily. A fairly large diameter to the boom, which will then normally be hollow, probably helps in this respect, though it requires more power to roll it down. The mainsail luff track requires to terminate some little way above the boom, or to be fitted with a gate there, to let the slides out when reefing. The extreme forward end of the boom requires to be cleared away to accommodate the accumulation of luff rope when rolled down. It is very important that the boom should be slightly tapered, largest diameter aft.

If there is a 5/16th in. difference in diameter it raises the outboard end of the boom 1 in. at each roll, and the sail sets the better for it. For a very short boom, 13 ft. odd in the mainsail foot, such as for the Maicas, $\frac{1}{4}$in. taper is probably enough, and $\frac{1}{2}$ in. might be needed for a 30 ft boom tapered, to avoid odd results, since the error will be cumulative.

When roller reefing gear is fitted the arrangement of the topping lift and the main sheet is critical. The usual device of a plate taking the main sheet at the bottom and the topping lift at the top, secured by an axial bolt to the boom, and revolving on this bolt, is fairly all right for the smaller yachts, but is open to objections for ocean racing and deep-sea cruising. It is difficult to get a fair place to attach one's invaluable fore guy to the main boom, and the bolt soon wears at sea. The arrangement where there is a collar, rotating in a groove on a bronze fitting on the boom end, is much to be preferred—the topping lift, main sheet and fore guy can all take off lugs on the collar. I prefer to roll down reefs with no weight on the lift, which can really be dispensed with in small yachts.

The kicking-strap presents a problem, and this can only be used readily with a full sail. If a stout plate of galvanised steel, brass, or light alloy be slotted and sunk flush with the under side of the boom, a small catch can be passed into the slot from aft and the kicking-strap block, or lanyard if a winch is used, can be bent to this. The plate requires to be man enough to prevent distortion from very local loading. In making the slot the edges of the material may be flanged 'upwards' and in small sizes a ball-shaped catch can be used to give a little universal action. In mainsails above 250 sq. ft. a longer fitting is needed to spread the load. As an alternative, and a simpler one, a canvas strop can be passed over the boom and hauled down towards a rail sheet lead by a small purchase. Lewmar Marine, of Emsworth, Hants, make a specially good self-locking one. A portable calliper claw or a similar fitting is needed for use when the sail is rolled; to be shipped after rolling down has been completed; or, if one remembers, a stout canvas band can be rolled in.

As we have indicated earlier the main sheet is always less easy to arrange with roller reefing; the nice arrangement whereby the main sheet leads down on top of the coach roof is no longer feasible, and one has to resort to the more old-fashioned arrangement of having quarter blocks and a horse, or alternatively—and I prefer this—having one fixed point, on the rudder head, or clear of the tiller, and the remaining parts going to a horse, or slide. The position of the slide should be, I suggest, governed by stops, so that it can be pulled a-weather, fixed amidships, or allowed a limited travel to and fro, less than the full horse, if need be. In this connection reference may be made to chapter no. 12 on mainsail trimming.

One of the disadvantages of roller reefing is that, normally, one has to have a round boom which is heavier and less efficient, as to wind flow, than the now usual deep-sectioned rectangular beam-shaped boom, pivoted at the gooseneck. A rectangular roller reefing boom, with its corners well rounded *bien entendu*, I have used successfully in a small off-shore racer. But it needs extra power to roll down. One must however keep it of regular section, very slightly tapering towards the mast, and one cannot use the section with a 'steep double taper' away from the centre on the under side, which is efficient as a beam-loaded spar.

TRYSAIL DESIGN

Personally I like a trysail cut like a headsail, with a gore down the middle and the cloths arranged herring-bone fashion. It is also important that if the leech is roped, it should only be very lightly roped. If it is heavily roped the sail inevitably stretches more than the roping, and goes into a bag at the leech, and when you want to claw offshore, it won't serve to windward at all well. The sail that I drew for *Myth* which proved successful (I have used very similar sails on very many yachts since) was as follows:

Luff, 17 ft. 3 in.; Leech, 23 ft. 0 in.; Foot, 13 ft. 0 in.; Headboard, 10 in.; Material, 12½ oz. flax; Area, 120 sq. ft.

It was a parting present from the Greenock Sail and Tent Company, when we left the Clyde, and a really nice sail incidentally. The headboard reduces the hoist necessary, and in this case enables one to set it under the lower cross-trees. Had this not been a requirement, one would have had a cringle in the head, instead of a board, and 18 in. more hoist.

Normally one uses mast track slides, as for a mainsail; and keeps a collar or two of parrel beads and a lacing for use should the track be damaged and not available. In boats where the trysail is used regularly we provide a second track—or it is switched into the main track when necessary, above that portion of the track on which the mainsail is housed, so that one can have the trysail hanked on ready to hoist before the mainsail is lowered. A further refinement is to have the trysail hanks on a piece of 'magazine track' which is detachable from the mast with the sail. In modern aluminium alloy the weight of these fittings is not great, but to work conveniently they need a near plane surface, so in planning your mast you should, if you want these fittings allow for a swelling here on a wood mast, or a wood chock on alloy masts. To convert a wood mast to this system is however possible, since a filling piece can be glued to the mast, with cold water glue, and be as strong as a solid mast. A typical modern arrangement is that shown in Diagram 23.

In designing a trysail I think it important to have the tack well above the clew, otherwise it is difficult, if not impossible, to get it sheeted right, without the use of the boom; and one of the objects of a trysail is to provide an alternative sail for use in case of an accident to the boom or its attendant gear. *Myth* trysail can be clewed to the boom or sheeted to the quarter. In the latter case the spinnaker after guys are immediately available as sheets.

DESIGN OF SPINNAKERS

You may remark at this point that I have not dealt with the design of spinnakers. The maximum size of spinnaker that can be used without penalty is regulated by rule. At the time of writing both the R.O.R.C. and C.C.A. allow the following sizes, as does the new rule:

Headboard: Width not exceeding 5 per cent of spinnaker boom length.

Spinnaker Boom: Length measured at right-angles to centre-line of yacht from C.L. to outboard end not to exceed J.

Width of Spinnaker allowed (at any height)—$1 \cdot 8$ J.

Length of luff and leech allowed $\cdot 95 \sqrt{I^2 + J^2}$

where I = effective height of fore triangle or point to which spinnaker is hoisted from the deck.

J = base of fore triangle (from foreside of mast to the point where the luff stay of foremost headsail cuts the deck or bowsprit).

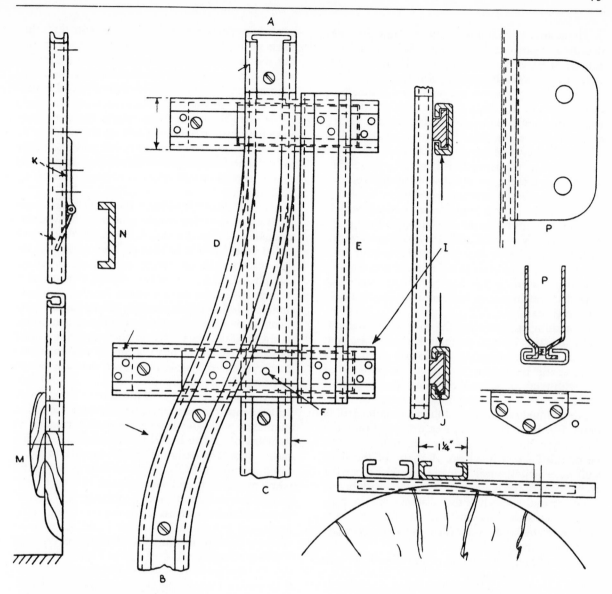

A. MAIN TRACK UP MAST
B. MAGAZINE TRACK
C. MAIN TRACK TO GOOSENECK, LENGTH TO
   SUIT NUMBER OF MAINSAIL HANKS
D. CURVED SWITCH
E. STRAIGHT SWITCH
F. HOLE FOR LOCKING PIN
H. CROSS TRACKS (Y.1 TRACK)
J. CROSS SLIDES
K. TONGUE AND CATCH TO RETAIN HANKS
M. TURN BUTTON
N. CHANNEL GUIDE, ¾" LONG (ONE AT EACH
   END, AND AT 2 FT. INTERVALS)
O. FISH PLATES FOR STRENGTHENING JOINTS
   IN TRACK
P. OVERHAUL FITTING
   MAGAZINE TRACK.   LENGTH TO SUIT
   NUMBER OF TRYSAIL HANKS.   POSITION ON
   THE MAST BY CHANNEL GUIDES, AND HELD
   IN PLACE BY TONGUE AND TURN BUTTON

SWITCH POINTS FOR Y.1 TRACK
                      Y.2   ,,
                      Y.3   ,,
B.   FOR Y.1   ,,
                      Y.2   ,,
                      Y.3   ,,
MAGAZINE TRACK FITTINGS:-
K.   GUNMETAL
M.   ,,
N.   ,,
(FOR ALL SIZES OF TRACK)
O. GUNMETAL   FOR   Y.1 TRACK
                      Y.2   ,,
                      Y.3   ,,
P. GUNMETAL   FOR   Y.1   ,,
                      Y.2   ,,
                      Y.3   ,,

Diagram 23.
Switch Track and Fittings.

There are additional restrictions under the rules designed to prevent the spinnaker being cut like a genoa; because the width allowed is greater than that of the maximum genoa permitted.

The weight of canvas recommended is shown in Appendix IV. It remains to be decided at what height the maximum width is to be, and the nature of the curve of the head of the spinnaker. The object is to have the spinnaker reach out when set, and collect as much wind as it can, by extending beyond the triangular area as far as possible, consistent with the sail remaining stable.

This will be especially important as one's largest headsail is appreciably smaller in width than one's spinnaker. My guess is that the maximum width should be carried 60 per cent up the height. Jean Jacques Herbulot has an intermediate cut of 'Chevron' cloths which has been very successful indeed in getting more balloon area in calm and moderate seas.

Something the same applies to drawing out the curve on the foot; I doubt whether it is very critical. I would guess that the lowest point of the belly should be drawn to be about 10 per cent of the width of the spinnaker below the tack and clew.

For spinnakers I don't think a headboard is necessary. It is, however, most necessary that the head clew and tacks of the spinnaker should be doubled and tripled up. A shape of the light stuff of which the sail is made should be carried 10 per cent of the hoist down from the head for the doubling and about half that distance for the tripling. About half these amounts can be put on the clew and tack. This spreads the loading away from the corners.

The luff and leech are of course identical—you can't tell t'other from which, except that they must be taped in distinctive colours to help sort out the sail. There should be a swivel, preferably a ball-bearing one, on the head of the sail. The swivels should be checked over for size and load—the size of the spinnaker halyard will give you a guide as to the strength necessary. Many of those supplied by sailmakers are not man enough.

I rather like a very fine wire luff and leech rope in horizontally-cut spinnakers to help the sail keep shape, though these are no longer required by C.C.A. rules.

Heavy-weather Spinnakers. We developed some years ago a completely new type of heavy-weather spinnaker which my assistant Sir David Mackworth called 'the Wren's knickers'. The design of the spinnaker has three objects. First of all, to reduce the full R.O.R.C. spinnaker by about one-third of its area. But still at the same time to maintain sufficient luff and leech length to enable the spinnaker to be set to the masthead. If one is not able to do this, that is to say, if there is a lot of free halyard between the head of the sail and the masthead rythmic rolling is very much encouraged. In addition it must be capable of being set over headsails without interfering too much with their proper performance on a reach. The width of the storm spinnaker must also bear a reasonable relation to its hoist, otherwise it will not be stable. Although rather specially designed it has proved to be, I think one can fairly say, brilliantly successful wherever it has been seriously used.

Transatlantic. For this and other races of several thousand miles, at least three full-sized spinnakers and two storm spinnakers are desirable on account of their liability to damage. (*See* Heavy Weather Racing, Chapter 7.)

12

HANDLING AND TRIMMING OF MAINSAILS AND TRYSAILS

Turning to the consideration of mainsails, let us deal first with bermudan sails, since they are used in 99 per cent of the ocean racing fleet nowadays. The layout of the gear is covered in other chapters; we are now concerned with what to do with our sail when tuning up and racing.

Getting Under Way for a Race. Most ocean racers have heavier canvas sails than their inshore racing sisters and this means that they dry out more slowly. In any case there may be odd wrinkles and unfairness in places as a result of the sail being stowed, not necessarily wet, but in conditions of different humidity. So get your sail up in good time before the race so that it can get stretched and fairly into place before the start. See that the batten pocket lanyards are tied with reef knots, not bows, and check your slide thimbles and seizings or grommets before they go up. Don't set the halyards and outhaul too tight at first, but check on them a couple of times and take down the slack as necessary each time, before the start. These rules still apply with Terylene sails.

If your boom gooseneck is on a slide, hoist the sail fully, that is with the headboard to its mark, which will be a black band round the mast. Under way it will be easy subsequently to bowse down on the boom, but probably impossible to hoist the sail by the halyard without luffing her up or easing the main sheet.

Halyard Loading. The weight you need on the halyard will depend on the weather, the cut of the sail, also on the type of canvas and the sort of luff rope. A flat-cut sail will need cosseting in light winds to get shape or 'flow' into the sail. Moderate halyard loading will generally help, but above all, be careful not to put too much weight on the main sheet; get the boom more amidships by pulling the lead blocks up to windward, rather than by over-hardening the sheet. Apart from a new sail, most foot outhauls should be pulled out pretty taut. I should say a general fault is to over-harden the halyard and to put too little load on the outhaul.

Battens. One of the most difficult things to cure

in a mainsail is a hard line down the forward end of the battens. It may be the result of too much roach on the sail. The trouble may be in part due to too stiff sail battens, or too long, in which case they thrust against the end of the pocket.

The best wooden sail battens are made of hickory wood. Tufnol battens are specially good in light weather. If hickory is not available, ash will serve quite well. In the case of ash, recently felled wood, unlike most timber, is to be preferred. The battens should be varnished to stop them soaking up wet and giving it out to the sails later; also to help preserve them and their spring. They may be tapered off in one or both planes, but in this case the tips may need to be canvas-covered to prevent them piercing the pockets.

In larger yachts it is often convenient to use two battens in a pocket to get the right curvature. Don't be content with any old batten. Go on trying tapers and strengths till you get a fair continuous curve through the sail.

Mast Line 'vis-à-vis' Mainsail. A sail that is too full can have some of the flow taken out of it by pulling the masthead back and putting a very slight curve in the track. The reverse action has the reverse effect, though not so happily. These things must be done with caution. While there is no great risk in putting a shade of curve in the mast above the fore triangle, it should be done only to a fractional extent below it. In a masthead rig the headsails must take priority, and bending of the mast to shape the mainsail should, as a rule, not be attempted; because the mast's principal aim will be to act as the best possible strut in compression. There is more about this subject in Chapter 17.

Mainsail Leech Shake. A fairly frequent trouble is leech shake. It is often accentuated by unnecessarily heavy leech roping, which is bad in three ways; firstly, there is the inertia of its weight, and secondly, its size prevents it drying at the same rate as the sail; also it results in extra air friction. I do not think it essential in sails up to 600 sq. ft. to have a continuous leech rope up past the reefs; tapered tails from each side of the reef cringles will be sufficient. The reef cringles are often too heavy also —unnecessarily big in diameter, and great cast bronze affairs. They should be of nylon or aluminium alloy, or if not obtainable, a good quality pressed cringle. The outhaul clew cringle, however, which gets more work, should be stouter—there is no special point in skimping this. The diameter of the reef cringles should be just big enough to pass a 'soft' (no thimble) splice of the wire reef pennant comfortably. The wire pennant can be $\frac{3}{8}$ in. in circumference for sails up to 400 sq. ft.; $\frac{1}{2}$ in. up to 800 sq. ft., and $\frac{5}{8}$ in. above that size, the limit being the weight one is likely to get in the tackle or reefing winch.

If ordinary adjustment does not cure leech shiver, lay the sail out on the loft floor and critically examine the round of the roach to ensure that it is a fair continuous curve, at least between the battens. If it has stretched in use to an unfair curve, some part of the sail will perhaps be projecting and not properly supported by its adjacent canvas. The tabling of the edge of the sail must then be removed and fair line cut. In cases of doubt, the leech curve can safely be reduced or 'straightened a little' between batten pockets. Again, tabling which has been wrongly tensioned will, in itself, cause leech shiver, so taking it off and replacing after fairing is sometimes all to the good.

A mis-shapen mainsail can sometimes be improved by removing the roping of luff and foot and re-shaping the sail, and replacing the original roping if it is in good order. If after the sailmaker has finished with it, it comes back smaller, one can adjust the black bands and have a re-measure, with a small reduction of rating. On the foot, by trying temporary lashings for the slides, with graduated amounts of drift in them, one can sometimes get a useful forecast of the effect of an alteration.

Main Boom Position. As has already been noted in connection with headsails, some close-winded boats will stand a main boom pulled in almost amidships; that is, under favourable circumstances. These will include well-cut sails in good trim and not too much sea. As soon as conditions become less favourable, one will have to sail her a bit freer and check sheets just a shade, to keep her moving. In any case this only applies to a close-winded boat. There is nothing to be gained in a heavy type cruiser by pinning her in; making her feel like a trussed hen instead of a nice freely waddling duck.

The point is that when one is close-hauled, the losses due to windage on the hull, spars and shrouds and so on, absorb a large proportion of the total useful driving power developed by the sails—shall we say about 60 per cent—so that the amount available to propel the hull is at the best 40 per cent.

Should maladjustment of the sails—or age—have reduced their efficiency by 20 per cent, which is quite possible, then since the losses are a constant amount (60 per cent of the potential best power) the previously available 40 per cent for propulsion is reduced by half, which explains why a small adjustment may make a big difference to a sail.

If one is out of trim, one has to bear away perhaps half a point to restore the total power to 100 per cent and the available to 40 per cent, so that one is travelling at the original speed, but not so close to the wind. A seaway operates in two ways; primarily it increases the boat's resistance going to windward, but also it reduces the driving efficiency of the sails owing to their movement to and fro, so that in order to keep the boat travelling at a reasonable speed one has similarly to bear away and sail a shade freer. This is discussed in more detail elsewhere.

Twist in Mainsails. The modern bermudan rigs are all tall and narrow; some are narrower than others, but all are narrow by previous standards. I started to use narrow mainsails before the Second World War and I went even narrower after the War. People seemed to think this was a mistake; but it is interesting to note that a decade later most designers now seem to agree. The reason is, of course, that experience has shown them, area for area, to be faster to windward. While this progress is to be welcomed, because it enables us to drive our boats equally fast with smaller and therefore cheaper sails, it brings in its train certain problems. In the first place it results in more 'twist' in the sail higher up; the boom close-hauled is drawn well in, nearly amidships, and as one goes up the sail, one finds it lying off progressively farther to leeward.

This twist is no bad thing in light winds because the wind at the masthead will be appreciably freer than at boom level. There will be a difference in real wind speed due to the 'wind gradient' and this difference will result in appreciable variation in the apparent direction of the wind.

The action already referred to, that of bringing the boom inboard by a shift of lead rather than by bowsing down, is in line with the question of twist; such action encourages a little twist, as well as flow, in light and moderate winds.

In stronger winds, where the boat's speed is less *relatively* to the wind, there will be less difference in the wind direction between deck and masthead. Moreover the tendency to twist will be greater with the increased wind loading, and as soon as sheets are eased for a reach, it will become excessive owing to the easing of the strong downward pull of the main sheet.

Kicking Straps. It is therefore necessary to replace this downward component. It can be done in two ways. The first motion of easing sheets should be to let the slide on the main hawse go down to leeward, rather than easing the sheet itself. The second method, which takes over when further easing of the main sheet is possible, is the use of a kicking strap. This in ocean racers is generally a purchase, taking about half-way along the boom with its standing part at deck, either by the mast foot, or out to the rail. Often the reefing purchase can be made to do the two jobs.

Except in smaller yachts one has to fall back on a purchase to haul the boom down to eyebolts, or sheet track points, near or on the rail. This is less satisfactory in as much as it has to be adjusted every time the main sheet is trimmed. But the purchase can sometimes be made to do duty as a fore guy as well. In practice very considerable loads come on this purchase and the eye in the boom must be stout and designed for pulls at various angles; or else a strop round the boom should be used. The narrower the mainsail the more the need for a kicking strap.

Forward Boom Guy. In a seaway it is essential to have a guy running forward from the main boom to hold it steady. Otherwise the boom movement in light winds will shake the wind out of the sail; and with stronger wind on the quarter you may gybe, owing to the swing of the seaway. In light airs going to windward the boom will have to be eased away from amidships and a touch of weight may have to be taken cautiously on the topping lift in light yachts as well. Too much weight on the topping lift leaves the sail in a bag; so care is needed. A strong shock-cord must be interposed.

Trim of Main Sheet on a Reach or Run. It is a little difficult to suggest specific rules for the extent to which the main sheet is to be eased for reaching. In the fresher breezes with the wind forward of the beam, it is fairly safe to ease until the sail lifts and then bring the boom aft a few inches. But one must be careful to distinguish between back-wind from the jib and a genuine lift. In light winds one generally eases a bit less than that. With the wind on or abaft the beam a rough rule is 'the angle between the boom and the beam to be at least half the angle between the apparent wind and the stern'. Naturally the boom will come on the shroud as the wind comes round, and after that the rule can't be applied, nor is it needed over that range, as the sail is more or less stalled. The wind direction should be gauged as a mean of the masthead burgee and the ribbon, or nylon-strand Irish pennants pushed well up the main shrouds, or by the pennants on the preventer backstay when the wind is

on the quarter, again pushed well up the stay. This takes care of light winds and prevents one from over-easing the sheet in those conditions.

Reefing. Passing on to the question of slab reefing, much of the 'secret' of efficient reefing lies in the gear which is described elsewhere. As to the drill, perhaps the principal advances in practice of recent years have been in the use of the boom gallows and winches. Boom gallows are simply strengthened boom crutches, sometimes left standing at sea. Generally they have three positions arranged for the boom. To reef, one lowers and hauls the boom into the leeward one.

If necessary all hands should be called on deck, having, if the circumstances allow, been given time to get togged up into oilskins. The reefing gear should be got up and everybody got to their stations; main halyard, topping lift, main sheet and fore main boom guy manned, and reefing tackle rigged on the boom. Get everything ready, carefully, deliberately. At night try and give the hands coming up a minute or two to get acclimatised to the 'light'.

All being ready, if the boom gooseneck is on a track, one eases the halyard and lets the boom down bodily until the gooseneck is at or near its lowest position, where it is secured by its catch or plunger. In larger yachts the slack has meanwhile been taken down in the topping lift so that the weight now comes on this, which helps spill the wind out of the sail. The main sheet is being hardened at the same time, and the fore (main) boom guy, which is almost always rigged at sea, is eased to suit. This keeps the boom under control, until it is somewhere near the boom crutch. Then the topping lift is eased handsomely and the boom, with all spare hands on it to steady it, is encouraged into the boom crutch slot. Here it is secured simply by heaving in on the main sheet. The operation of getting the boom well in board is much facilitated by having the main horse slide block amidships, or even to weather if found necessary by experience.

Although many people will doubt it, one can in fact, when racing without altering course, generally get the main boom in even with the wind well aft, if the gear is well arranged and you have a strong crew relative to the size of the boat, and if you lower the sail a little as you harden in. However, if it won't come in, or if the sail won't come down, one will have to luff her. Naturally the object is to do the job while remaining on the correct course.

In larger boats it is probably best to keep the first deep reef pennant rove. If it is kept down to the minimum size of wire there is not too much weight or windage. In smaller boats there is probably no difficulty in reeving a pennant even in strong winds. But as a fairly recent innovation we use 'hooks' on the sides of the boom to speed up the lacing down of a reef.

The normal system of making the standing end of a reef pennant fast to the boom, leading it up through the cringle, down the other side to a sheave, and forward, is as good as any I know.

With the boom secured in the boom crutch there is as a rule much less difficulty and delay in getting the reef neatly tied in; the boom is one with the ship. If a boom crutch is not fitted a tackle or a heavy lashing can be used from the kicking-strap shackle on the boom to the ship's side eyebolt; it is passed as the boom is coming inboard and the main sheet hardens against it. This helps to limit the movement of the boom.

Many boats have a small winch on each side of the boom to facilitate pulling down a reef. This can be used direct on the tail of a wire reef pennant, or on an all-hemp or Terylene pennant if you prefer them, in a smaller yacht; or on the fall of the reefing tackle in a larger yacht. Alternatively one of the mast winches can be used if you have a spare one; for example, you might take the turns off the main halyard winch for lowering, which offers no difficulty as a rule. With a large stiff sail I have with advantage led the reefing-tackle fall to the anchor windlass drum, at a time when, with a big heavy mainsail full of wind, we could not have pulled the sail down properly otherwise.

The next job is of course to pass the cringle lashings at clew and tack; at the same time other hands will be tying the reef points, or passing the reef lacing. The latter should be halved; start together in the middle of the sail and one work each way.

Reef points are quicker but involve some additional windage. Reef points are normally tied under the foot rope which is neatest and best. But it does not matter much if some are tied under the boom in an emergency, provided the boom is of the narrow, deep type.

There is one very simple maxim about reefing procedure, so simple that it is often neglected—'keep your special cringle lashings, lacings, reef pennants, and reefing tackle handy, placed and tallied where no one can mistake them or use them for other purposes'. I try and have a couple or more hooks in the locker with the name REEFING GEAR painted above them. In the same locker, as a rule, go the sheets, each on its own tallied hook, because often each sail requires its own length of sheet; particularly if they are wire, hemp-tailed.

If you have plenty of hands they can start hoisting the mainsail again—which will only have been lowered a few feet past the 'reefed position'—while the last few reef points are being tied, and save a valuable minute or two. The mainsail should be hoisted to its proper position *before* the main sheet is checked right out, should one be running. In large yachts the weight of the boom will now be on the topping lift, which will have been used to hoist the boom clear up above the crutch and above its working position, while the gooseneck will have been run up above its position on its slide on the mast by getting several shoulders under the boom, if necessary. If the sail won't go up, you will have to swing her momentarily towards the wind; the luff lasting only a moment, which may serve to start her up, after which she may continue going up.

As soon as the sail is up, ease the topping lift so that the main boom just bears on the sail and no more and trim the boom downhaul and the main sheet.

If you are lucky the whole job will only have taken a few minutes. Anyway, by the time the extra watch and skipper get below, let's hope there is something hot on the stove!

As to roller-reefing, there are some data about the layout in the section dealing with booms. The handling differs from that of normal reefing. In the first place one does not lower into the boom crutch, but just takes the weight on the topping lift, no more; and steadies the boom, if it be necessary owing to the motion, by using either the fore guy or the boom downhaul to a point on the rail and well forward of the horse, together with a little weight on the main sheet. To get a neat roll it is preferable to have the boom parallel to its working position and the leech within reach, so that one or more hands can pull aft on this, and keep the foot taut whilst rolling down is progressing. For this reason it is a great advantage to have a sliding gooseneck. In small yachts, no weight on the lift is needed, and they can get by without a lift.

The halyard should for preference be checked very handsomely, just a little at a time, to keep pace with the chap rolling down. Although it has many times been done with two people, to make a good quick job when racing three people are needed, excluding the helmsman; one on the halyard, one on the reef handle and one on the leech. All my recent roller reefing sails have a lanyard on their leech. They are stitched in every eight inches, loose enough to enable one to hook in a short boathook and pull the sail aft, good and hard, while rolling down.

It is a good scheme to have one deep reef in the sail in case the rolling gear sours on one. The eyes and cringles should be kept as small as is feasible. No reef points will be required, a lacing being used.

Hoisting a Trysail. Trysails should, I hold, be

Trim of a "shy" spinnaker. K.55 is correctly trimmed and has drawn away in consequence.

A Straight Luff. This picture of *Myth of Malham* racing in U.S.A. waters 1948, demonstrates the value of efficient staying and levers.

Curvature of the Mainsail Leech. An aerial view of *Myth of Malham*, with a small mainsail set, completing a Transatlantic Cruise and approaching the Devon coast.

Rani, approaching the finish to win the 1945-46 Sydney–Hobart Race. An example of the sea-going ability of a well-balanced light displacement hull.

arranged so that they can be set on the track of the mast in the same way as a mainsail. But should a defect have developed in the track, the leech is secured to the mast by collars of parrel beads, and lacing. The collars can be secured by toggles. Where the first cross-tree is well up the mast, the highest collar can be arranged to come there just below the headboard. In other cases it might be necessary to climb to the lower cross-tree, sit across this, and secure one or more collars above this as the sail is hoisted to you. If the main halyard has gone, a headsail halyard can probably be attached to the collar of the parrel beads to hoist the trysail, with or without the track, before tacking the trysail down.

Myth's 120-sq. ft. trysail was arranged so that the headboard came to the lower cross-tree when the sail was set in its lowest position. Normally the trysail was set on the mainsail track and hoisted somewhat higher than this. The two after spinnaker guys formed the port and starboard sheets. They were single parts of $1\frac{3}{4}$ in. Italian hemp, and attached with snap shackles into the clew cringle. They led to blocks on each quarter, thence to the genoa sheet winch. They were quite easy to handle as a single part, and this saves the nuisance and danger of having blocks on the clew of the trysail, which may crown one when going about or gybing, or even luffing up momentarily.

Alternatively the trysail clew can be shackled on to the mainsail outhaul on the boom for close-hauled work. It is important to get it on the outhaul if you can, so as to adjust the flow in the sail. But there is no advantage in this for reaching in gale-force winds and the boom is best left safely on its crutch. Actually a well-cut trysail is quite good on the wind without a boom, because in gale-force winds one probably does not manage to point closer than five, or even five and a half points, off the wind.

The question of the cut and material of trysails is discussed in chapter 11. It is sometimes advantageous to have a second track at the foot of the mast, with a switch point so that the trysail can be hanked on prior to the mainsail coming down, though there is often not time to avail oneself of this gadget, as by the time one has decided it is a case for the trysail, one has had to lower the mainsail. And the switch is 'one more thing to go wrong'.

Proceeding short-handed there is probably more justification for a switch than at any other time,

for then one can leave the trysail always hanked on, with the sail stowing quite neatly along the coach roof or skylights; it is generally quicker and lighter work to run up a trysail than to reef the main. You can have two complete tracks, and no switch: a good scheme.

Gaff Mainsails. There are two ways in which many existing gaff main or fore sails can be improved; by the use of vangs, and by battens. The best form of vang can only be used in a yawl or ketch. It consists of a line from the outer end of the gaff to a lead at the mizzen masthead, and thence to the deck. By adjusting this line the amount that the gaff sags off to leeward can be controlled. For this line I used nylon line of the minimum necessary strength, designed so that in a heavy gybe or a puff the line would stretch—and if necessary part—rather than damage the mizzen mast. However I had no trouble with it. The big point is that in short tacking it looks after itself.

In the case of gaff cutters the vangs port and starboard lead down to a point at or forward of the preventers at deck. They are a nuisance and add a good deal to the general clutter of gear, and are not absolutely essential if the boom is long enough to give the leech a fair slope, which can hold up the gaff. But if the boom is on the short side and a good-sized topsail is set, they are an important help in keeping the peak of the mainsail from sagging unduly to leeward.

I think it important to have the vang come off the gaff at a point, or very near to a point, where the halyard is shackled to it, to get a fair loading on the spar. In the case of yawl or ketch this means having the outer leg of the halyard moved to near the peak end.

It is desirable on a day when there is weight in the wind to peak the gaff a bit more, when vangs are to be used.

Trimming of vangs is straightforward, though one should say that there is a natural tendency to put too much weight in them. Just as a bermudan sail should have some curl or twist, so the gaff should be appreciably farther outboard than the boom.

Battens are not fashionable in a gaff sail because they are generally associated with the roached leech of a bermudan sail. All the same they are valuable to any but a perfect sail, in assisting to flatten the leech, and helping the wind to get a clean run off the sail.

13

THE HANDLING AND TRIMMING OF HEADSAILS

I propose to deal with the subject of sail handling under three headings: headsails and 'tween mastsails—mainsails, trysails, and mizzens—and spinnakers together with mizzen staysails. As regards handling, there are many ways of doing the job well, and different skippers have their own system often best adapted to the particular way in which the gear is laid out. So my remarks on handling must not be taken as anything more than either general recommendations, or at the most an indication of the particular way in which I happen to have been in the habit of doing things. The actual arrangement of the gear is a big subject; it has been covered separately in chapters 16 and 17, on running and standing rigging, and it is only referred to again here to the extent necessary to make the handling and trimming business clear.

Each heading falls naturally into three sections, setting, trimming, and handling. It is necessary to say that this division into headings is only for convenience of reference. Actually it is most important that the ship be trimmed as a whole, and that there should be no selfish sails; they must all be working in harmony with their neighbours.

Stopping up Headsails. Kicking off then with the problem of setting headsails, we have first to decide whether we are going to stop up our sails or not. The actual procedure for stopping up is referred to under the spinnaker section. Generally speaking it is an advantage in large yachts, and hardly worth while in smaller ones. In a big yacht the size of the sail increases more quickly than the strength of the manpower available for hoisting. Delay in hoisting means that the sail is flogging about; slowing the boat down and teasing the fibres and stitching of the sail. But there are many occasions when time and circumstances at sea have not permitted the stopping up of sails, so one must be prepared to deal with hoisting unstopped. Here we have a minor disadvantage of stopping; that it involves two different procedures—two different drills for the crew.

I rarely stop up the headsails in small and medium-sized boats.

Two other considerations enter into this question, to stop or not to stop. The first is the weight of wind. Clearly in light winds the necessity in large yachts is less. But since stopping up is a job which is done as a rule in advance, one will hardly know about the weight of wind. The other thing is whether one has twin stays or a single stay. Changing sails with twin stays, a stopped sail is fine; it goes up and can be hauled taut in the luff while the existing sail is still set and drawing, with much less liability to hanging up on the sail which is set, and its hanks on the other stay.

Twin versus Single Stays. A single stay has much to recommend it offshore on the grounds of weight aloft, windage, simplicity and it helps to avoid cross-hanking and snarls-up, particularly at night. If you are fitted with a single stay, your procedure will be to hank the fresh sail on to the stay below the one set, perhaps unhanking the bottom hank of the sail which is set to give you room. There should be two tack shackles, or purchases if arranged that way, so that one can get the new sail tacked down first, before one hanks on. The fresh sail will lie more closely to the deck if unstopped, should the intention be to have it in place as a standby. In this case one will secure the sail to the deck with a tier. For this purpose it is desirable to have a small centre-line rail with rounded-edged slots in it—in effect rather like a hand grip-rail. This is also a fine toe-rail when the boat is heeled. This rail can often conveniently start just clear of the mooring cleat or bollard, and subject to other deck obstructions can with advantage be run continuously or intermittently to the mast, running along the coach roof should this extend forward of the mast.

Hanking on Headsails. We have recommended in the sail design chapter that the tack of the sails should be marked with a big black spot. This will normally be the corner of the sail you will want to grab in a hurry; push it up the hatch and send it forward to be tacked down, before you hank on the rest of the sail. To hank on in a seaway, with the boat moving about, it is often handy to sit just forward of the stay, if there is room, with the stay between your legs, and facing aft. Your mate stands abaft the mast and passes the sail to you a yard at a time. Only if the second stay is clear, the sail stopped up, and if there is a man also on the spare halyard, can you hank on the head first and hoist it bit by bit as you hank the rest on.

Correct Headsail Halyard Loading. It is important when you hoist the headsail to get the correct tension in the halyard. If the sail is set flying, the halyards and luff rope are made extra heavy and it is generally necessary to set it up as taut as it will go. But this arrangement is rarely found nowadays in modern layouts, since one gets a much straighter luff by setting sail on a stay.

So let us assume we are setting sail on a stay. Here it is necessary to get the luff taut enough so that it does not sag appreciably between the hanks. But if one gets it too taut it will take the load which properly belongs to the stay, and should the wind subsequently freshen the extra weight will very likely carry away the halyard or rupture the luff of the sail. The conditions under which one is most apt to make this mistake are when setting a headsail with the wind abaft the beam. Under these conditions the forward press of the mainsail will very likely slacken the stays to some extent and if one sets up hard on the halyard, it will have all the weight when one comes on the wind.

Generally in fresh conditions there is no such risk with the wind before the beam; then one normally needs to use all the purchase one has. But in light winds with powerful winches one can easily overload the halyard. I reduce the length of mast winch handles in small yachts to minimise the risk. It also reduces the chance of these fouling the sheets.

The various arrangements for setting up halyards are discussed in detail in chapter 17. Should it be necessary to use sails set flying as in some schooners, one needs to have a really powerful rig perhaps a good winch hauling on the leg of a stout purchase. It is hardly possible to over-emphasise the importance in a breeze of getting as straight a luff as possible to one's headsails, though naturally one cannot avoid some curve in the stay or luff rope.

The straightness of the stay will depend on a variety of things; on the efficiency of the mast as a strut in compression, which in turn partly depends on the efficiency of the whole layout of the standing rigging; on the type of wire used in the stays, the object being to reduce the extension under load; on the angle at which the backstay is led and on the arrangements for tautening this.

Sheeting Positions. Having got our headsail set, we can now pass on to the important business of trimming sheets. In order to have proper control of

the sheet leads it is most desirable—almost essential —to have either slides or tracks to adjust the fore and aft position of the lead or block on deck, or to have a multiplicity of fixed positions. The alternative arrangements are described in chapter 17.

If you happen to find yourself with a boat where there has not been time to make proper arrangements to vary the position, a lot can still be done. One can provide different length strops between the sheet, the block and the deck fixture, even using a turn of stout hemp when time is short. Or, particularly in light weather where most of the difficulty occurs, by pressing into service some other fixed point on deck—freeing ports in the rail perhaps. Alternatively by adjusting the height of the sail on its stay—by adjusting the tack tackle before hardening the halyards or by putting a strop at the foot of the sail between tack and deck. One can, for light weather use, achieve much the same result as by altering the position of the sheet head. But for fresh winds where it is important to preserve the slot between the headsails, or the headsail and the main, this will not be advisable.

The old rule for the angle of the sheet to the deck is to have it in line with the gore of the headsail, that is to say, with the line where the cloths meet in their herring-bone pattern. However, in practice one needs on the average an appreciably more forward position, except in the case of long low-footed sails such as genoa jibs and genoa staysails.

Light-weather Sheeting. In light weather, both for reaching and close-hauled work, the sheet lead requires to come to deck much farther aft, compared to the breezy position. It is important to remember this. The extent of the shift aft depends on the height of the clew off the deck, since it is the angle of the sheet lead to the deck that counts. The fore and aft position should be adjusted so that the top of the sail luff lifts just before—but only just before—the remainder. This also is important.

This rule assumes a normally good cut of sail, and it is true that badly-cut or stretched sails require special treatment. But in any sail if the sheet lead is too far forward, the leech will have too much weight on it, compared to the foot, and will be too straight, instead of having a nice curve to conform with the curve of the mainsail. It is most necessary that the curve assumed by the headsail, seen in a plan view or cross-section in a horizontal plane, should correspond nicely to that of the next headsail abaft it, or the mainsail, in order that the wind slot between the sails should be of a nice shape. What one is aiming at is to pass the maximum amount of wind through the slot, as other requirements, such as an unruffled sail, allow.

How the Wind Drives Us. One derives one's driving

power from the wind by changing its speed and direction. On the wind, or with the wind on or before the beam, one is trying to change the direction of the wind from that in which it arrives so as to discharge it aft, or in a more afterly direction than that in which it was travelling when it struck one's sails.

Wind has mass and momentum, and in maintaining the balance of forces on which nature insists, if you deflect it, that is to say, change its direction from travelling at say 35 degrees on the bow to travelling away directly aft, your boat must have exerted a force on the wind 'out towards the weather quarter'. And in the process of pushing on the wind the boat itself is clearly being pushed in the opposite direction—forward and to leeward. But as the lateral plane or keel prevents its moving much sideways, it moves forward. The amount of push depends both on the *amount* of wind you can deal with and the *extent of the alteration in its direction* which you can achieve.

While changing the wind's direction you are also slowing it down—for unless you slow it down, you extract no work from the wind.

While I admit that this is an over-simplification of the problem, I believe that to think of things on these lines leads us up the right path. If one keeps this picture in mind—the wind being continually bent aft by the sails—and the aim to bend as much wind as possible over as big an angle as possible—I find it helps one with one's sail trimming for breezes which are on or anywhere forward of the beam. There is also a reaction effect, apart from the impulse effect, less easy to analyse.

Importance of a Flat Leech. The aim is as big an angle as possible, one should say, provided the leaving direction is not to weather of 'right aft'. If it does leave to weather of this, it is exerting extra leeway-making force at the expense of forward-thrusting force. This explains the unfavourable effect of a curling leech, and also why a headsail whose sheet lead is too far inboard does not work so well.

The theoretical aim also assumes an upright boat, or at least a constant angle of heel. This is not, of course, found in practice, and since an excessive angle of heel spoils the underwater shape of the boat, it is sometimes necessary to trim the sheets to limit the deflection, or bending, imparted to the wind. This explains in part why it is in general desirable to ease the sheets more in fresh winds than in light, for a given apparent wind direction.

This mental picture of the wind at work also explains why a curved sail is better than a flat one. The curve results in an orderly wind flow; an orderly change of wind direction; and therefore less eddies and a greater amount of air dealt with.

Athwartship Position of Lead. As regards the athwarships position of the lead, I mentioned just now the danger of leading a sheet too far inboard. A headsail sheet lead for close-hauled work should be as far outboard as possible, consistently with being able to sheet the sail without undue flattening. To sheet the sail means to get it hard enough to prevent it fluttering. 'Without undue flattening' is harder to define. But we all have an idea of the maximum load which should be necessary to sheet a certain size of sail, and if the load is getting unreasonably large, it may be we are over-flattening the sail. However, it is a much more common fault to find the sheet leads too far inboard.

It is very hard indeed to lay down any satisfactory formula for the athwartship position of the sheet lead, because the closer-winded the boat, the closer to the centre-line the leads need to be. And the height of the clew affects the problem too: a low-clewed sail requires a lead farther outboard. More than anything the length of the foot of the sail, or the horizontal distance of the clew from the tack is important.

The drop in actual wind speed between striking the sail and leaving it, necessary if we are to extract work from the wind, is not so noticeable on board because of the boat's own speed. The speed relative to the boat on leaving is, when on the wind or close reaching, higher than the airspeed over the water. But apart from this the air is slowed down by friction with the sails and eddying due to the interference of the mast and stays. And so it is on this account specially important to reduce the 'resistance on leaving' the headsails, since the slower moving air requires a bigger area of slot. In practice this is not always possible, but with this end in view one places one's sheet leads of one's headsail as far out as one can, and lets the leech curve outboard as far as is feasible without luff shake. Even then with overlapping sails there is such a concentration of air, such a piling up, that the front half of the mainsail lifts. In order to reduce this lifting and to increase the slot size one hardens one's mainsail sheet, and very often nowadays one takes the sheet lead from the weather end of the horse, or special slide provided to adjust the athwartship mainsheet-block position on deck. This brings one's main boom amidships; much farther inboard than one would think could pay.

Value of Overlap. The value of an overlap in a headsail is that it bends a slightly greater quantity of air than a non-overlapping sail, which would allow the passage of some air out to leeward in a comparatively 'unbent' state. Also it tidies up the flow—smooths it out and lets it away travelling nearly dead aft. Also it catches and bends some wind under the main boom which would otherwise escape without doing useful work. Even sails which are not very low-cut to the deck will with their overlap catch extra wind when the boat is heeled; and leaving the slot gives some reaction effect.

As we said the longer the foot of the headsail is the farther outboard the sheet needs to be—very appreciably farther too.

Wide-beamed boats have the advantage here when it comes to sheeting genoas with big overlaps. Similarly tumble home cuts down one's sheeting base in other boats. The leads, or the track to which the leads are attached should lie as far outboard as possible. In many of my best boats the track runs on an outboard-looking bevel of the covering board, outside the foot rail. Every inch outboard helps the genoa. In a cutter the track or alternative sheeting points should run from the mainshrouds to the counter.

Calculating the Position. For average small ocean racing boats low-clewed sails require a sheet lead placed outboard from the boat's centre-line, about 33 per cent of the lead's distance from the stay at deck. Specially close-winded boats might require it about 30 per cent, and a heavy old boat might be better 35 per cent outboard. In practice the amount one can go outboard is limited by the ship's side, since the I.Y.R.U. and the N.A.Y.R.U. both forbid the use of outriggers for sheeting to—except that in certain circumstances the headsail sheet may be led via the boom ends. Larger yachts sail faster and therefore the apparent wind comes more from ahead. To allow for this these figures should be reduced: by 1 per cent for yachts over 28 ft. water-line, 2 per cent over 33 ft., 3 per cent over 40 ft., and 4 per cent over 50 ft. on the water.

A low-clewed sail, I would describe as 'one whose clew height above the deck is not more than 20 per cent of the horizontal distance clew to tack'. For every 10 per cent or part of 10 per cent the clew is higher, subtract 1 per cent from the figures (35, 33, or 31 per cent) given in the paragraph above. The distances outboard from the centre-line are expressed as percentages because this is much easier to measure out, than angles, on board. But if you prefer angles here is a table of equivalents to the nearest half-degree:

10 degrees — $17\frac{1}{2}$ per cent
11 degrees — 19 per cent
12 degrees — 21 per cent
13 degrees — $22\frac{1}{2}$ per cent
14 degrees — 24 per cent
15 degrees — 26 per cent

16 degrees — $27\frac{1}{2}$ per cent
17 degrees — 29 per cent
18 degrees — 31 per cent
19 degrees — $32\frac{1}{2}$ per cent
20 degrees — 34 per cent
21 degrees — 36 per cent

The ordinary text book figure for the angle the 'line of sheet leads' makes with the centre-line at the tack, is 10 degrees. This is much too narrow an angle for any except high-cut jibs on fast boats, and simply encourages pinching on the wind. All this rule is approximate; so much depends on imponderables that only trials will indicate the final positions. But it is valuable and necessary to have something to start from.

In any case all long-footed sails and masthead sails will be sheeted to the ship's side, and we should have provided a track for these.

Inboard Lines of Sheet Leads. It is good practice to lay down a second track or line of leads inboard of this. The distance of this second track from the centre-line at the mast can be calculated with reference to the forestay (the inboard of the two stays in a cutter) by the 35-33-31 method. The track can then run straight through this point for 2 to 5 ft. forward of the mast and 4 to 12 ft. aft of it, according to the size of the boat and the beam, so as to run out to within 6 to 10 in. of the ship's side. A beamy boat needs it longer. The track may be 'aimed' at a point 6 in. to 1 ft. forward of the forestay according to the size of boat. The reason why this inboard track is aimed not at the stay but outboard of it, is that the small sails which are sheeted to forward positions are set in strong winds only, and the apparent wind is then freer.

In large or large beam boats a third line of leads or track is laid in a similar manner outboard and farther forward of the one described, with reference to the fore topmast stay. But with much higher cut sails setting from here, you may find in smaller yachts that the two tracks will cover your requirements, without recourse to the third.

If you want a *rough* rule, you can say that fast close-pointing boats, ex-12-metres and bigger yachts, can use 12 degrees from the stay for high-cut and 15 degrees for low-cut sails. As the boat gets slower or less weatherly these are increased, until for small cruisers the figures are 18 degrees and 21 degrees.

The great thing to remember is, however, that no lead position is sacrosanct. If it is not right, get it shifted, or put down another fresh lead.

Sheet Leads and Sails Reaching. The whole of the above applies to positions for the leads close-hauled. As soon as you ease the sheets you should consider whether the lead should not be shifted to another position farther outboard. The usual procedure is to unreeve the weather sheet and re-reeve it through the new lead, so that the change-over can be made without disturbing the sail. It is important to sheet the sail as far outboard as possible on the reach; to improve its own angle in relation to the wind and to increase the size of the slot, so as to pass more air and bend it more effectively.

On the reach the wind requires if possible to be bent through a greater angle than when close-hauled. To this end it is desirable to have more curve or flow in the sail and hence sails cut specially for reaching are extra full. Actually as soon as one eases sheets, it automatically puts more flow into a sail and I doubt whether the extra complication of changing to another sail for reaching is as a general rule justified. Quite apart from the expense, there is the extra weight to carry round and the time lost changing to and fro; and the crew's time and energy which might have been better employed perhaps.

However, I do agree that there are occasional special cases when sails can be made to serve reaching which will not stand on the wind; certain types of fisherman staysail set between the masts of schooners; sails reaching to the top of their stay, and so on.

In this connection there is one possible compromise which is worth considering—which is to use one's light-weather windward sails for reaching in moderate breezes. This has the big advantage that they can be cut longer on the luff, since, both in light weather and when reaching in moderate or moderate fresh breezes, the clearance required at the head of the sail is less. A light weather sail can also be cut a shade fuller, because on the wind it will not be sheeted so hard. However, judgment is needed as to the moment when you should change back to your normal windward sail; should it pipe up and you hang on too long to your light sail, when reaching, it will soon be out of shape. And when it pipes up, the normal weight sail, a shade smaller, will be as fast.

Sheeting to the Boom. We have agreed on the importance of having the sheet lead as far outboard as possible on the reach and under most codes of offshore rules one is permitted to sheet to the end of one's boom. But the sheet lead must be within 6 in. of the black band if penalty is to be avoided. This sheeting privilege which is not as a rule accorded to inshore racers should be exploited to the full. I keep a light sheet permanently rove through a bull's eye in the boom end. An extra cleat on the underside of the boom should be provided to make this sheet fast to; both ends will be made fast to it when stowed.

Normal practice is to put this sheet to work by bending in on to the clew as an extra sheet. However, I feel it is much better to attach to this a snatch block, or even a shackle, through which the ordinary sheet can run. Thus one can draw the sheet lead outboard a little or a lot, as conditions require, and continue to adjust the sheet in the ordinary way. Also the clew of a sail may be out of ordinary reach; but this snatch can be put on without disturbing the set of the sail.

Sails cut high in the foot are easier to sheet towards the boom end: yankee jib topsails particularly. This is quite a strong reason for not cutting a genoa too low in the foot, though even the low-cut ones can be drawn outboard a little by the boom end sheet. Sometimes when one comes on the reach it is worth easing the genoa up its stay a few feet by easing the tack tackle, or with a fixed tack putting in a short span, and taking up the slack with the halyard. This will set the sail bodily higher and make sheeting to the boom end more profitable.

Sheet Trim. As to the amount of sheet to give a headsail when reaching, up to the point where the wind is just forward of the beam, it is a pretty safe rule to ease the sheet as far as it will go without causing the sail to flutter or 'lift' on the luff. As when close-hauled, it should lift first in the upper half. This will mean that the sheet lead is well aft and giving the clew every chance to go outboard. One must impress on all hands the necessity for frequently checking the trim of the sheet when reaching.

Staysails Inside Genoa. It is often worth setting a small staysail inside the low-cut genoa on a reach with the wind about the beam. Close-reaching it will interfere with the genoa and freer it will be blanketed by the main, so it cannot be called an important sail. (This sail must not be confused with the pukka staysail set under a yankee.) It can be set flying, perhaps from the spinnaker lift, to avoid having a special halyard.

Quad Jibs. Quadrilateral jibs are permitted by the R.O.R.C. but not by the C.C.A. They are of two sorts. One is a yankee with the normal clew cut off. The object here is to avoid spoiling the mainsail by excessive back wind from the leech part of the yankee; provided the yankee 'without the clew cut-off' would have fallen within the 150 per cent overlap, this sail can be carried without penalty. We used this sail in '67 in *Monk*, successfully. The other type is a genoa, of more than 150 per cent overlap with the clew cut off; involving a small penalty. They are not always easy to set well. So few have been made that I fancy some sailmakers have never really got to terms with them, though I have had a great many set very nicely. They require of course an extra sheet. Even if you don't get it to set too well on the wind, it is quite a useful reaching sail with the upper clew sheet hauled out towards the boom end, or preventer, or pushpit or counter. A single very light upper sheet should be used; and, important, take 80 per cent of the weight on the lower.

Flattening Sail Leeches. In setting headsails the one thing to avoid is to have any part of the sail, most generally of course the leech, curling round so that it lies to weather of a fore and aft plane. All that part of the sail is doing negative work. It is bending the air past the fore and aft position and out to weather. It is probably causing eddies in the after end of the slot too. One must be continually watching one's headsails to see that this feature does not develop; continually trying to get the leech canvas to run out to a flat ending.

Too big a sail for the boat—too long on the foot, with an insufficiently wide sheeting base will give rise to these conditions in a serious form. A sheet lead placed too far inboard will do likewise.

Too much weight on the leech line will cause mild cases. Too much of a downward line to the sheet will encourage it too; sheet as far aft as is reasonable; the slot shape is improved.

But if the shape gets bad it is a matter for the sailmaker. The tabling at the leech may be too tight, if it is sewn up this way. You may be able to cure it by unstitching the seams for a couple of feet from the leech and opening them a tapered shade before restitching. This needs care; if it is carelessly done or the 'opening' is not very small and nicely graduated the last state of the sail will be worse than its first. It may flap horribly in the leech.

If the trouble develops in an otherwise nice genoa you may recut the leech line with a hollow; virtually cutting away the offending part of the sail. You are certainly much better without it, if it is lipping in, and quite a big hollow in the line of the leech, up to say 4 per cent of its length, is acceptable, should the need arise.

Battens for Headsails. Battens in the leeches of headsails can be used when sails get out of shape, or when they are nice and flat at the leech but start tremors. The ordinary wooden batten generally gets quickly broken, and Tufnol ones are better. I have used spring steel canvas coated, or hardened bronze, or even work-hardened aluminium. But they are a bit of a nuisance if there is much overlap. And so only call them into use when you actually need them, except in storm headsails where they should generally be used.

Slight leech shake does not matter, though excessive shake disturbing other sails is probably bad. It is, however, true in most cases that too slack a leech with some slight shake is far better than a too taut one, lipping up to weather.

Pulpits at the Stem. If the stay comes to the stem head, a pulpit is a help when handing sail: it consists of a frame of steel or aluminium alloy tubing running round the stem, at the height of the top life lines, to which it is attached, leaving working room between the stay and the frame. Provided they are not too high or too massive, pulpits do not look bad, and need not weigh much. But some small boats are fitted with unreasonably high and clumsy pulpits, which interfere with the foot of the sails when set.

The R.O.R.C. and the J.O.G. are apt to alter from time to time their respective mandatory requirements concerning life-lines, pulpits, and pushpits. These regulations will need to be consulted well in advance of fitting out. *See* Appendix XIII. The G.C.L. (French J.O.G.) regulations differ.

In bad weather for handing sail one crewman will sit forward of the stay facing aft with his legs either side of it, or stand with his back braced into the pulpit. He will then be well placed to pull down the sail when the halyard is eased, clear of the flogging canvas, and to unhank after the sail is lowered.

Handing Headsails. One man will be on the halyards, and one, two, three, or four men, according to the size of boat, will be ready to grasp the foot and to haul the sail down and smother it. No more men should go forward than are necessary to do the job, as it puts her head down and slows her. The replacement headsail will have been hanked on to the stay, to weather of the sail now set, if the stay is single.

If the halyard is on a winch, ease a few turns round the winch before taking the turns off the winch barrel. Otherwise it may grab your fingers. The bitter ends of the halyard fall should be made fast; I generally have a hole in the centre of its own cleat, to pass the end through and knot it. The man on the halyard can then generally let go altogether and make sure his turns are going up without snarling, and can lend a hand to smother the sail.

Practice about the sheet varies. I leave it made up in the initial stages of lowering which reduces the flogging of the sail. With a genoa it must be let go to get the clew inboard, but with staysails and yankees the whole sail can be lowered and a tier put round if necessary before the sheet is finally let go; which is very handy when the watch is alone on deck and relatively short-handed. Generally if the man on the sheet is watching from aft, he can judge when to let go. In a small boat it will often be the helmsman. In short, don't ease till it is really necessary.

If the sail is a big genoa—they are the most awkward—and a fair amount of water is slopping about in a seaway, it will be advisable to get the sail right down and the bulk hauled up to weather and secured before one starts to unhank off the stay, otherwise a bight of the sail may get full of water and haul the rest of the sail over the side. One will probably be wanting to get the sail un-hanked as quickly as possible, and so at other times one starts to unhank as the sail is coming down.

Bowsprits are another problem. I remember rather vividly times when one had to take one's oilskins off before going out to get in a big sail, hanked to the fore topmast stay. This reduced one's bulk and increased one's chance of hanging on when one was part-submerged as the bow went into a sea. Here again it is important to reduce the number of men forward, and not to go out until all is in readiness. Still in a big boat in a breeze it is generally necessary to have two men near the stem head and one at the bowsprit end, as well as a man at the halyard and one on the foredeck.

In big boats it is usual and helpful to have a net under the bowsprit. Sometimes it is triced to a horizontal wire jackstay, which runs about 2 ft. below the bowsprit to the bob stay, out to the bow-sprit shrouds. Various devices are fitted to make work easier out on the sprit. Life lines running from the top of stanchions on each bow to the sprit end are useful. Some boats have a full-blooded pulpit out at the sprit end, with life lines running from each bow.

Devices for Controlling Genoas. There are a number of devices to assist in controlling genoas, both for handing them, and also for getting a big sail with a lot of overlap about in a breeze. About the simplest is a becket sewn to the foot of the sail 'just forward of the shrouds'. This is handy to catch hold of, to haul the sail forward and so get the clew forward to the mast. Alternatively, a 'tacking line' can be attached to this point (or a little farther forward) and led through a block on the stem head; a hand heaving on this when the sheet is let go can similarly gather the sail forward. The tacking line is quite handy used in connection with the capstan, if it is an easy one to work. You have the turns on before the evolution and haul away and get all you can, which the winch will hold for you, till you need to check away. The gear is simple and worth

trying in big-sized yachts which use a genoa to windward.

Various other furling rigs have been used: bull's eyes part way up the luff rope with furling lines led from the foot, and so on. But though their owners profess great enthusiasm for them at the time, they don't seem to stick to them for long. It is something which involves extra gear which has to be hoisted and cleared with the sail.

Schooner Considerations. Passing on to the 'tween-mast sails, those of the staysail schooner can be treated very much like headsails.

Diagram 18 shows the rig we designed for the schooner *Robert Gordon*, which is a rig arranged in a way which would go well to windward, because the 'tween-mast sails and the headsail are each of good individual proportions, and in addition are arranged to work as a team, with no sail interfering unduly with any of its partners. The fisherman staysail will set close-hauled in light weather and for reaching in moderate breezes.

Although it is a convenience 'on paper' for short-handed sailing, I cannot say that I am fond of the boomed staysail. We have seen in connection with our consideration of the sheeting problems of headsails that a good deal of cosseting is needed to get the best sheet lead and set of the sail. The boom severely limits one's control over the sail, apart from which it is liable to kill the sail in light airs and a lop. For racing it is clearly non-effective; while most people when cruising use their engines in narrow channels, where otherwise, in conditions involving short tacking, the boomed staysail has a theoretical advantage.

You will hear racing men say time and again that one big sail is better than two smaller ones. This is only about a quarter true. It does not take account of the fact that with overlaps the two smaller sails often aggregate more area, and where, subject always to very careful initial design and subsequently to good trimming, the slot between sails can have a favourable reaction effect. It certainly is not true in strong winds offshore, where several smaller sails with their loading distributed, and their centre of effort nearer the deck, and with their steadying effect, due to being well spread out fore and aft, are definitely to be preferred.

14

HANDLING AND TRIMMING OF SPINNAKERS AND MIZZEN STAYSAILS

Before the handling we must settle on the gear. In the classical system for large ocean-going yachts the spinnaker boom is arranged so that it can be set up and guyed out in place before the spinnaker is hoisted; that is to say it must be provided with an outhaul to draw the tack of the sail out to the boom end, as well as a lift, and fore and aft guys. Thus one can, before hoisting sail, set the spinnaker boom firmly in place, that is to say, roughly in the position it will be in when the spinnaker is set and drawing and the boom will not, owing to the motion of the yacht, swing about and cause delays.

In small ocean racers one can spring-shackle the guys on to a light wire grommet or to a special hoop-shaped cringle at the spinnaker tack, and snap the end of a double-ended pole also into the grommet, with a spring hook which is integral with the pole. A sheet interchangeable with the after guy is used, snap-shackled into the clew. So that one can connect the other fore guy to the clew, and leave the spinnaker set when gybing; simply take the pole off the mast and pass it across, attaching the old clew to the new outer end before detaching the previous tack. The snap hook of the pole takes on an eye on the mast: or more modernly into a bell-shaped cone and trigger. In either case the fitting on the mast will be on a track.

Freewheel Gybe. Apart from the foregoing two alternatives, there are a number of new arrangements for spinnaker gear which are feasible and efficient. Perhaps the most popular is the one allowing of the 'freewheeling gybe'. This was developed in 1958 by the 12 metres working up for defence of the America's Cup. A single-ended boom has its heel well up the mast, and is controlled by a boom-end lift and a fixed boom-end inhaul. Each spinnaker-clew has two guys affixed. To gybe, the plunger release at the outboard end of the boom is operated by a lanyard, and the spinnaker is left flying while the pole is dipped under the forestay, the heel remaining in place well up the mast.

While this system is of undoubted efficiency and speed racing inshore with a well-trained crew, and not too much movement of the yacht due to the seaway, I prefer to use the two-pole system. Every skipper has his own system and drill, and while the one I now employ is not sensationally rapid for gybing it does keep the spinnaker out of trouble and there is less risk of a wrap-round the fore topmast stay.

For yachts with a rated sail area of 1,000 sq. ft. or more I fit two sheets/guys, to each clew. Thus when gybing one is always slack on the lee side and can be hooked readily into the 'new' pole end.

Poles. Two identical spinnaker poles are used. These can if desired be single-ended, which can simplify the heel fitting which should if possible be self-locking into the slide. The slider is manually slid and locked with a plunger on yachts up to about 15 tons T.M. In larger vessels it is worth having a control line and sheave at the top of each of the heel rails, and a downhaul, operated by one or two small direct-acting winches on the mast. The heel rails should be close together near the foreside of the mast and extend from about 3 ft. 6 in. above the deck or roof to a height of not less than 20 per cent of the hoist of the fore triangle (one-fifth of I in the R.O.R.C. measurement) plus 1 ft. When racing under Cruising Club of America or 'new rule' conditions a stop and black band must be placed to limit pole height to 18 per cent plus 2 ft.

I always use aluminium alloy poles; they are lighter than wood ones but, even more important perhaps, the minimum diameter is appreciably smaller and they stow more neatly on deck. For the larger yachts they can be tapered, but in the interests of economy one can normally use a plain tube, with cored aluminium castings to adapt the pole end-fittings to the tube.

The outboard end-fitting of a pole must fulfil three special needs. The attachment to a ring must be rapid; but, more important, when released the ring must not in any circumstances hang up on the fittings. It should be possible to operate the release gear locally (for attaching the spinnaker before hoisting) and also from a distance to enable the spinnaker to be released from the outboard end of the pole for gybing. Nowadays I always have a fitting under the outboard end of the pole for the foreguy, and one over the end for the topping lift.

Poles are best secured on deck in chocks accommodating the whole end-fitting: (with shock-cord lanyards) to save catching up sheets and guys on deck.

Fore-guys. At sea I always keep my fore-guys, port and starboard, rove. They run out through blocks, or nice big smooth deadeyes in the rail or bulwark, placed roughly abreast the fore-topmast stay. On the outboard ends I have snap shackles. These are snapped on to a life line forward when the guys are not in use, and in large yachts the fall inboard is wrapped round a long light cleat in the scuppers abreast the mast. If these are 14 to 28 in. long according to the size of the yacht, this will take care of the whole of the fall. In smaller yachts up to say 38 ft. water-line I lead the fore-guy falls aft to jam cleats at the fore-end of the cockpit: these perhaps on the roof. These guys serve equally well to guy out the main boom, in conjunction perhaps, with a wire pennant on the boom.

After-Guys. Apart from the plunger on the pole end it is necessary to have a means of releasing the spinnaker tack from the pole *and* its guys. This normally means that one has a snap shackle connected to the after-guy or pole end via one or two linked stainless steel rings. The ring next to the snap shackle takes into the release mechanism at the end of the pole and the fore-guy snap shackle takes into the other ring. This release gear is used only when handing the spinnaker. (For sizes and types of guy, *see* Chapter 17.)

Hoisting Spinnakers. Since spinnakers have become so full in the head I have modified my methods. I always hoist the spinnaker 'behind the jib'— whether it be stopped or not—and the moment the spinnaker halyard is belayed—with the absolute minimum of delay—the jib halyard is cast off and the jib is lowered as speedily as possible. In a small yacht the same hand will be tending the two halyards in turn. In a large yacht one will have one hand to each halyard which will save seconds, and in light weather with wind aft (when the jib will be doing nothing) the headsail can be lowered before a spinnaker in stops is full hoisted.

Tending the After-Guy. While the spinnaker is being hoisted the pole will be brought aft with the after-guy by the hand in the cockpit. If the breeze is on the beam he will put sufficient weight on the guy to bring it clear of the stay. The guy must always be on a powerful winch. The weather winch will be free at that moment for this purpose, or in a very small yacht where only a single winch is provided, the jib-sheet should be taken off the winch and made fast direct to a cleat just before the spinnaker is hoisted.

Tending the Sheet. The moment the halyard is belayed the sheet must be hauled aft with all speed. In light weather one can start to haul aft as soon as the head of the spinnaker is somewhere near the masthead. Any delay in hauling taut the sheet will not only waste time by delaying the breakout of a stopped spinnaker, but will encourage a tendency to wrap round the stay, particularly in a seaway.

Head Gap. It seems to pay to hoist the head of the spinnaker to within 2 to 5 ft., according to the size of the yacht, of the mast. The small gap probably helps to keep the spinnaker clear of the mainsail interference; excess gap would, however, have an adverse effect, causing the attitude of the sail to become less favourable, and will increase the tendency of the yacht to roll.

Use of Sail Bags. I use my spinnaker bags as 'turtles'. The underside is furnished with a stout canvas strap to which a stout lanyard is attached. With this the bag is secured to a handy point on perhaps the centre-line towing cleat, a few feet abaft the fore-topmast stay. The top of the bag has a shock-cord lanyard in the hem. The three corners of the sail can be taken out of the bag and attached, under the lee of the jib, to the halyard, guy, and sheet respectively, while the remainder of the sail remains safely in the bag till one is quite ready to hoist—straight out of the bag.

A big advantage of having two spinnaker booms, or a single-ended one, is that one can lead the lift to the boom end, reducing the risk of crippling it with excessive fore-guy loading.

Stay Wrap. In a seaway there is a distinct risk of wrapping the spinnaker round the fore topmast stay, if this is bare; particularly at the moment after hoisting, owing to the motion of the boat. So in a seaway, *directly* she is hoisted, make sure there is plenty of weight on the spinnaker sheet.

This will flatten the sail, more than it should be from the speed-trimming point of view; but this is much better than a snarl-up, which even if you do succeed in clearing it, will have meant sailing without the spinnaker for some time. The tendency to snarl-up will be worse with twin fore topmast stays than with a single one. Therefore after lowering the jib, bring the jib halyard to the mast rather than making it fast to the tacking point of the headsail. Should it still occur that she wraps around, try at once to clear it by steady pressure on the sheet and tack—the latter applied by bringing the spinnaker boom aft. If you fail to clear it, then the jib halyard is available to send someone up to clear it, if it has been brought aft.

It may seem that one is making rather a lot of this risk, but this particular sort of tangle, involving a very light sail and possibly damp conditions, can be the very deuce to deal with. More than one occasion is on record of the spinnaker having had to be cut off the stays with a jack-knife.

Forestay Anti-fouling Net. Rod Stephens and others use successfully a big mesh net which is hoisted in lieu of a sail on the fore topmast stay for the purpose of keeping the spinnaker from wrapping round the stay.

Another form of anti-fouling net, supplied by Ratsey & Lapthorne to *Cohoe III*, consists of a limited number of nylon tapes in the shape of a staysail. The luff is attached to the forestay by short tapes like reef points, which take the place of snap shackles.

A simpler alternative, suggested by Desmond Hawe, one of my crew, which works well and which I have used since 1957, is to lead the idle halyard to and fro between the fore topmast stay and the forestay, a stout lanyard being used to extend the length as necessary. In a sloop a similar arrangement can be achieved. Our later designs provide for a special 'Hawe Line'— $\frac{1}{2}$ in. wire coming from just above the upper cross-trees, which is led to and fro between the forward stay and either a vertical wire up the mast, or an inner forestay.

Spinnaker Chafe. This tautening of the foot brings it hard on to the fore topmast stay in most instances, and the motion of the boat 'saws' the foot on the stay. So it is most necessary to provide good chafing gear on the stay. Probably the best arrangement is a split plastic or wooden tube, just big enough in diameter to form a roller when lashed around the stay. It should be about 5 to 10 ft. long according to the size of the fore triangle; say about 12 per cent of the hoist. Circular grooves near the top, at the bottom, and centre will facilitate the lashing. But it is rather a bore to stow, and a piece of stout rubber tube—garden hose of good quality —split longitudinally, will answer quite well. Rubber cuts best when damped, so in splitting the tube keep a mug of water by you. The tube will need a lashing every foot or so.

Stopping up a Spinnaker. Offshore, in all yachts, particularly with modern full spinnakers in fresh winds, it is a big advantage to have the spinnaker set in stops, more particularly if the wind is out towards the beam. As the boat gets smaller, the necessity for stopping up becomes less. And in light winds one can please oneself with any boat. Inshore with a good crew well drilled, provided the sail

comes out of a well-placed, smooth-edged hatch, or out of a turtle in a small yacht, then one can safely use an unstopped spinnaker; and probably have it set and drawing quicker than a stopped sail. The big inconvenience of this for ocean racing is that it needs a specially flaked-down spinnaker under the hatch; and if there is a seaway running a stopped spinnaker is in any case less likely to get into trouble when hoisting.

There will always be occasions when it has not been possible to re-stop a spinnaker before resetting it—therefore the crew must be drilled to get it up unstopped when needs be. Also there is clearly a little risk that the top stop won't break out; the risk is greater with a spinnaker than a headsail.

The risk can be minimised by putting no stop within a fathom of the head, or one and a half fathoms in a large sail, and using light rotten-cotton. Very light cotton can be used if one progressively increases the number of turns as one goes down, until one has half a dozen at half height. The same drill applies to a headsail. In stopping up, the luff and leech should be brought together and tautened, and the sail between bunched up and tied round—not rolled up.

A good method of stopping up a spinnaker, which works nicely, is to stop the upper part normally and then to divide the bottom part into two legs, stopping each part to the luff or leech ropes, so that the finished job looks like a starfish. It assists in attaching the guys.

Having stopped up a spinnaker place it reverently in its bag. Take great care to get no turns into it; centre of the snake in first; feed the three ends in and leave them stopped together on top. I have shockcord in the hem of the bag and a stout strap handle under.

Hoisting without Stops. When one does not set the spinnaker in stops one should prepare it, in a turtle or under the fore hatch (or in larger yachts under a hatch further forward specially for this job). When one prepares a spinnaker, one wants to run down the luff or leech to see there are no turns in it. This is easier if they are taped with different colours. The finished job under the fore hatch should leave the head on top and the tack and clew showing each side, with the sail flaked down in a pile. The three corners should be secured to special points on the structure by breakable stops.

Spinnaker Trim. Turning to the problem of trimming the spinnaker once set, the basic rules can be simply stated. (1) Trim the pole at right-angles to the apparent wind—that is the wind direction one sees on the burgee. (2) Then get the sail to float up as high as it will go naturally; top up the pole lift to raise the tack of the sail and raise the heel on the mast to keep the pole horizontal. (3) The clew of the sail, controlled by the sheet, will be eased out as far as it will go without spilling the wind, and generally so that the foot of the sail floats about horizontal: clew and tack at the same level.

This refers to comparatively good conditions; as mentioned in connection with snarling up, a flatter trim is generally necessary in a big seaway.

Should the spinnaker boom heel not be provided with a track for adjusting its position, a second bracket for the cup fitting can be provided above the existing one. In small yachts where the spinnaker boom has a spring hook, three eyes at different heights are all that is needed.

For reasons explained elsewhere, the wind direction, when moderate to light, will often appear variable, and it will not as a rule be feasible to trim the pole guys to each minor momentary shift. It is generally better to have the sheet end in hand, if necessary round a winch, and draw the sheet aft a foot or two the moment the luff shows any sign of falling in, easing out again at once, inch by inch until she is eased as much as she will take. Sometimes the movement aft requires to be pretty sharp and urgent to restore a deflated spinnaker. I have a special cry for this—'tweak'.

Light Wind Trimming. In very light breezes it will often be preferable to steer on the apparent wind; that is to get your spinnaker pole set at about 60 or 70 degrees to the fore and aft line and the spinnaker drawing nicely, and then luff out as far as you can without the spinnaker falling in. In this way you will be varying your course with the shifts of apparent wind, but guarding against getting the wind too far aft and losing speed.

In light winds one wants to use a lighter sheet, not more than $\frac{3}{4}$-in. circumference in small yachts, or 1 in. or $1\frac{1}{2}$ in. in medium-sized and upwards, which will be still large enough not to cut one's hands if it breezes up a shade. This will free the sail of unnecessary weight. The whole weight of the spinnaker boom will be on the lift, again to allow the sail freedom to rise.

The reason one wants the spinnaker to float out and up in front of one's boat is threefold. Firstly, and most important, with a view to the sail bulging out beyond a triangular shape and collecting more wind; reaching out for extra unmeasured area, as it were, high up where the wind speed will, in light weather, be appreciably greater. Secondly, it allows some circulation of wind; an orderly exit at a low rate under the sail, which in turn assists the spinnaker in remaining full; it reduces its tendency to collapse from its balloon or parachute form, compared to being completely stalled. Thirdly, though not so important in displacement yachts, the pull

which the sail exerts on the hull has a greater upward component and slightly assists in offsetting the tendency of the bow to bury when running hard. A well-set spinnaker seen from abeam will have its 'forward edge' (the middle of the sail) almost vertical, as opposed to 'bulging a lot forward' halfway up the sail.

Spinnakers and Beam Winds. We have talked about the problem of sailing with the wind well aft and we must now deal with the question of spinnakers in beam breezes. If is often a problem to know just when to change from a spinnaker to a genoa and vice versa. As a rough rule, it pays to hang on to your spinnaker longer, with the wind drawing ahead, in light winds. The lighter the breeze, the farther forward the spinnaker boom can be carried with profit. In really light, steady winds it can be made to work with the apparent wind just forward of beam. Some people carry it longer, with the wind well forward of the beam, but only in specially steady winds with a good reaching spinnaker does this pay. With very light puffy winds, varying in strength, a light genoa pays better than a spinnaker which is too often falling in, specially in a seaway.

It depends a good deal what sail area rules one is sailing under, and also what one has in the way of other light canvas. If on account of a split sail, or for any other reason, one has no other light canvas, it will pay in light conditions to hang on to one's spinnaker to the bitter end.

Clearly one's spinnaker is a much bigger sail; round about 130 per cent bigger than a genoa in the case of R.O.R.C. sails. But once it starts to bury the boat, pressing her sideways, as it will in fresh breezes, then it definitely is slower than a genoa. In fresh conditions it does not, as a general rule, pay to carry a spinnaker with the wind forward of a full point abaft the beam.

Lead of the Spinnaker Sheet. It is of the utmost importance to lead the spinnaker sheet well aft when sailing with the wind broad out on the beam; in any wind strength the block should be right outboard at the aft end of the counter. If the particular rules you are racing under permit it, you can try a lead out to the main boom end. I prefer not to lead the actual sheet through a fixed block at the boom end, but to use the boom end to haul out a small snatch block; or even a shackle does quite well, which can be put over the sheet without re-reeving. This gives one a chance to adjust the amount of outhaul towards the boom end.

The reason for all this will be clear from Diagram 25. In 'A' the spinnaker is mostly pressing the boat to leeward. 'B' is much better and 'C' better still, if it is allowed.

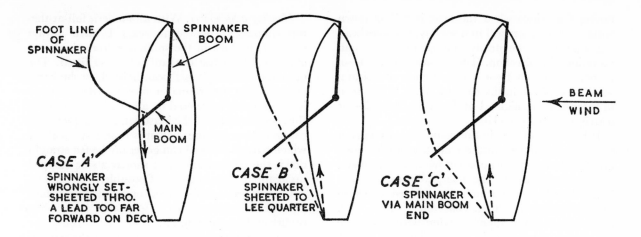

SHEETING THE SPINNAKER FOR A BEAM WIND
(THE SHEET IS SHOWN DOTTED)
Diagram 24.

One of the reasons why the spinnaker is not better with a beam wind than it is, so to speak, is because it does not get rid of the wind clearly; it allows it to flow into the back of the mainsail. A genoa imparts a better flow to the air from the point of view of the mainsail. This applies with more and more force as the wind increases, and also as the wind comes farther out on the beam where the spinnaker sheet has to be sheeted harder and harder.

The 'Steele Tweaker'. During the 1958 Bermuda Race, Tommy Steele fitted *Belmore* with a second (shock cord) spinnaker sheet; this was an instant success in providing a source of continuing tension when the weight in the sheet was relaxed due to the rolling of the yacht. It prevented the spinnaker falling in in a very light breeze and a big swell. The shock cord was bent on to the ordinary light sheet about 10 ft. away from the block in the quarter, and made fast to the top of the 'push pit'—the rail round the stern—to keep a clear lead.

Clearly a somewhat similar arrangement could be achieved in any boat. An alternative is to form a loop in the light spinnaker sheet, bridged by a shock cord.

Headsails set under Spinnakers. It is now common practice to use a 'spinnaker staysail' under the spinnaker; except when the wind is fresh and is near the beam. It is tacked down to the weather rail about 30 per cent of J (base of fore triangle) abaft the fore topmast stay. I always hoist this sail flying, on the spare spinnaker boom lift. I have the single sheet, 10 to 20 ft. in length of $\frac{1}{2}$ to $\frac{1}{8}$ in. circum-

ference Terylene, according to the yacht's size, permanently attached to the tack and bagged with the sail. This sail can be in the same canvas as the standard spinnaker. That is except in cases where it is intended also to use it under a genoa when reaching, in which case it should be in Terylene (not nylon) and 1 to 2 oz. heavier than the spinnaker. It can be extremely effective under a genoa; though only when reaching, not close hauled. I fancy it earns its money more in that role than as a genuine spinnaker staysail.

Apart from the use of a spinnaker staysail, a small genoa must be carried under a reduced area heavy weather spinnaker. The total area adds up to about the same as a full-sized spinnaker, without the spinnaker staysail. And (as nearly always) a split up sail plan gives steadier sailing. Details of the design of heavy weather spinnakers are given in the chapter on spinnaker design (11); and in the chapter on heavy weather (7).

The spinnaker staysail is valuable in light winds, wind well aft, as an indicator to warn one when the wind gets too far aft; or nearly by the lee.

Checking on Light Winds Astern. It was noted in the tactics section of the chapter on strategy that any running by the lee has a serious effect on the speed of the boat. The helmsman or sail trimmer must be continually on the look-out for a shift which will put the vessel by the lee, and must have her luffed at once to keep the wind aft, or preferably fine on the weather quarter. To assist in showing the wind direction it is desirable to have fine strands on the preventer backstays in addition to the masthead racing flag, since when the boat is rolling down wind, as is very general in a seaway, the masthead flag may never be steady enough to show small variations in direction. The 'strands' may be of nylon, teased out from a rope's end, or knitting wool, or again, thin silk ribbon. White is best seen in torch-light at night. I prefer nylon threads—or a strip of a girl's stocking.

It is worthy of note in this connection that given variations in actual wind direction result in much greater changes in the apparent wind (that is to say, the wind relative to the boat, allowing for the boat's speed), when running compared to close-hauled or close-reaching. Diagram 7 shows why. And since it is the apparent wind with which we are directly concerned in sail trimming, it follows that when running one has to watch the wind extra carefully. This effect, *viz.* the increased apparent variation for minor actual shifts in the wind when running, is much more pronounced in light than moderate breezes, and almost disappears in strong winds. A slight shift from very fine to more on the quarter has no ill results; almost as soon as the spinnaker needs trimming from this cause it will warn you by starting to fall in on its luff. But a shift from it on the quarter to just by the lee will, in light or moderate conditions, result in appreciable loss of speed.

These effects will be much more pronounced in larger faster vessels where the yacht's speed will be higher in comparison with the wind speed.

Sailing by the Lee. The reasons why sailing by the lee is so much to be avoided in light and moderate breezes are twofold. Firstly, practically no rig allows the main boom to go right forward to a right-angle, and although the upper part of the sail goes out to the rigging the lower part of the main-sail, or the mizzen, is receiving wind at a very unfavourable angle. The second and, in general, probably the more important reason is that the spinnaker, which will, or should be, lying well for-ward of the mainsail, is suffering interference; it is no longer getting a proper supply of relatively undisturbed wind.

This interference can be minimised, but not over-come, by hauling the spinnaker boom well aft. Clearly there will be no incentive to sail by the lee in fresh breezes—it will feel altogether too 'gybacious' and unsafe.

Apart from purely sail trimming considerations, such as the above, the gain in speed due to luffing out is discussed in the section on tactics.

Having followed our friend the spinnaker through the job of setting and trimming him, and dealt with most of the problems he will present us with while he is set, there comes the business of handing him.

Handing a Spinnaker. With all modern full-at-the-top spinnakers of recent years I have always released the tack of the spinnaker from the boom end; or let go the outhaul where so fitted. The or genoa has previously been hoisted, so she keeps sailing while the spinnaker flies out like a flag to leeward and is recovered by all available hands on the sheet, well abaft the mast, while being lowered cautiously, with the halyard round a cleat or winch barrel. The sail can generally be fed straight down the companion-way; shortly to be stopped up again; before bagging, if possible.

Cross-trees must be taped or padded to reduce the risk of catching up a spinnaker both when sailing and when handing.

For running under conditions when the wind is just too strong for the full-size spinnaker one can use either a small heavier weather spinnaker—'W.R.E.N.S knickers'—(details are given in chap-ter 11) or one can very well use a genoa-shaped headsail. It is set just like a spinnaker, with the tack on the spinnaker pole end.

Running Sails for Strong Winds. As to running sails for really strong winds, or for running when racing before a gale, much the best scheme is to out-haul the crew of a small or medium headsail to the spinnaker boom, the luff being left hanked on to the stay as usual. In a cutter in a gale the fore-stay should be used in preference to the fore top-mast stay. In a sloop the spinnaker pole must be guyed farther forward; or alternatively, the sail should be tacked to a point intermediate between the stay and the mast and set flying.

The second staysail in *Myth*—200 sq. ft. odd in area—works very well set this way. We used a staysail in an exactly similar way in *Thalassa*, successfully. These are drawn taut on their luff and leech, and have, when so set, a fair curve in their foot only. Under these conditions they stay put in a big sea and give no trouble. Their centre of effort is low and the foot is nicely forward, so they 'bury' the bow less than carrying the equiva-lent extra area high in the mainsail. She will run very much better under a double-reefed mainsail and a staysail set as a spinnaker, than under a single-reefed mainsail alone. The balance is much better, and the tendency to broach to is very much reduced.

Running under Gale Conditions. Or, of course, a try-sail can be set instead of the double-reefed mainsail. A further very feasible alternative under gale con-ditions is to use two headsails and have nothing set abaft the mast. Supposing you are blowing along quite happily under reefed mainsail and a big staysail outhauled to the spinnaker boom under wind Force 7 or 8, and the barometer starts dropping or there are indications of stronger blows in store. You can get up a small jib and tack it down at the base of the forestay or anywhere handy with a shackle or a stout lanyard, and make it up on deck with a sail tier until it is needed.

If the wind increases again you lower the staysail —leave it hauled out—simply drop the halyard and it is virtually self-furling, since the spinnaker boom will be well topped up. Then while you are getting ready to lower the mainsail, you can hank a few jib hanks on the stay alternating them with the staysail hanks and shackling the head of the sail to the same halyard.

As soon as the mainsail is lowered and a couple of tiers have been put round the boom, rehoist the headsails—two should go up on the same halyard without any trouble—and outhaul the second leeward headsail towards the main boom end with the boom end sheet. The boom is squared off to the rigging, topped up a little above the horizontal with the topping lift, and secured forward in the normal way with the foreguy. With a twin stay, set the headsail separately.

Or the second leeward staysail can, if you have a spare halyard, be set flying—not hanked on a stay —and sheeted to the boom end.

This leaves you with twin storm headsails and you should be as happy as a sandboy under this rig under a fresh to strong gale condition, with the boat steering comparatively easily. The wind can vary anywhere between 4 points on either quarter. You will find they are not very sensitive to extra trim; with suitable trimming of the sheets and guys you will have no gybing trouble.

There is always the odd chance of a following wave top falling on board of course; under these conditions, hang on, chaps! But the risk of being heavily pooped in deep water is not as great as people would have one believe. Where, however, one is approaching land with shelving soundings, one has to watch out.

The R.O.R.C. allow one to use twin storm spinnakers, or headsails, with a spinnaker boom, *each* side of the ship, provided the combined area does not exceed the measured sail area for rating. This means an extra pole, which as we have seen is desirable anyway. For transatlantic racing this is necessary in any case; and worth while offshore in general.

MIZZEN STAYSAILS

Mizzen staysails are sometimes treated rather casually: an old staysail is used, or something of that sort. This is quite the wrong approach, because they can be very valuable sails indeed, particularly if they are thought out as an integral part of the

sail plan. I first tried mizzen staysails in a preliminary way in *Queen Bee* when we won the Hong Kong Championship in 1928. I got down to a really sizeable sail in *Thalassa*; we must have sailed hundreds of miles with this sail set in 1934 and 1935. When I re-designed the plan of *Orion*, the 60-ton R.N.S.A. yacht, I was able to give her a 600 sq. ft. mizzen staysail, over half the mainsail area; and *Mouse of Malham*'s is more in area than the mainsail, as is the area on some later yawls and ketches.

These sails are all inboard, they are easily set and their handling is about as simple as that of any sail. The halyard block is at the mizzen masthead; the sail is set flying and tacked down to an eyebolt on the deck. It is most desirable to have the tack well to weather of the centre-line. In a ketch with a biggish mizzen hoist, the tack of the big mizzen staysail can be out on the weather rail. In a yawl it depends on the yacht's beam, the wind direction and deck layout. Several alternative tacking points are worth while: one on the cabin top, two on deck for instance. The larger mizzen staysail (if such sail is allowed: rules change) should be tacked nearer the rail than the centre-line.

A mizzen staysail is used for reaching; it can be hoisted as soon as the main boom is eased sufficiently to allow room for the sail to set to weather of it.

The R.O.R.C. allow one mizzen staysail only, and the rule is framed to discourage 'mizzen spinnakers'.

The C.C.A. after some years of allowing one mizzen staysail only returned in 1962 to allowing a second one. How long this rule will stand is any one's guess; the C.C.A. rulings being about as easy to predict as the actions of a maiden in the throes of her first love.

When this is allowed it is worth while to carry a smaller mizzen staysail, and this will be tacked nearer the mizzen mast, and perhaps $7\frac{1}{2}$ per cent of the hoist off centre-line. In any weight of breeze this sail can be carried closer to the wind than the larger sail. It can be set broad reaching in weather too heavy for the full-size mizzen staysail. Very often a small jib can be used for this purpose.

Tacking Down. The reason why a mizzen staysail works better tacked to windward can be best understood by thinking back to our old picture of bending as much wind as we can over the greatest angle possible. By tacking the mizzen staysail to weather we leave a much nicer slot between the mizzen staysail and the mainsail. Also we set the mizzen staysail itself in a better curve. The sheeting base for the sail tacked amidships would be a narrow one and we achieve almost the same effect as getting a wider sheeting base by putting the tack up to windward.

In a small yawl the mizzen staysail can be sweated up on the halyard, the halyard being then led to the weather quarter to help support the mast. With a bigger sail it is best to have a handy billy purchase between the tack of the sail and the ring bolt on deck. In the largest sizes of yacht the fall of this purchase can conveniently be led to a headsail sheet winch, which will be disengaged on the weather deck. And since the mizzen staysail will be handed before going about, the winch will be freed for its normal duty.

Sheeting to Mizzen Boom. In the case of the bigger mizzen staysail it is generally advantageous to sheet it to the mizzen boom. When the wind comes abaft the beam it may pay to lower the mizzen, particularly if it be of rather heavier canvas than it should be (which is a pretty general fault with mizzens) to give the lighter and larger staysail the best chance. Under R.O.R.C. rules the sheet lead must not be more than 6 in. abaft the black band.

Mizzen Staysail Sheet Trimming. So much for the setting of mizzen staysails, and here is a short note about trimming. Rather more than usual one needs to take account of the adjacent sails—principally the mainsail—and to adjust one's tacking position and sheets accordingly. There will often, in certain circumstances, be only just one position where the sail will set without interfering unduly with its elders and betters, although some trial may be required to find it. Once ascertained, trimming becomes simplified. On the other hand, in any

weight of wind at all, a certain amount of 'lifting' of the sail, due to wind off the mainsail, will be inevitable, and must be accepted, just like the lift of the luff of the mainsail, from the staysail or genoa; except that in the mizzen staysail's case it will be more towards the centre of the sail, and we can afford to reduce it by hardening the sheet because the sail is tacked to windward.

The straightness of the luff, while important, is not as vital as in a headsail going to windward, and will depend on the amount of weight you can put on the tack tackle. This in turn will depend on the strength of the mizzen mast and the efficiency of the mizzen preventers. The alternative arrangements for these are discussed under mizzen mast design.

Reduction of Rating. A final word concerning mizzen staysails and the rules. Under the 1962 and subsequent R.O.R.C. rulings one no longer gets a 1 per cent rebate off one's rating for not setting one, if one is a yawl or ketch. On the other hand, if there is no means of setting a mizzen staysail it is omitted from the assessment of sail area between the masts, so inform the measurer!

Mizzen masts are measured to the masthead and no black band is normally needed.

Repairs. Temporary repairs to light sails can be made with thin adhesive tape. This should preferably be applied both sides if the rent is big. 'Domestic' needles must be carried for repairing light sails, sailmaker's needles being generally too coarse. One can stitch over the tape if time allows, and the repair is much stronger than a 'cobbled' rent—simply stitched in too much of a hurry.

15

MASTING

The principles of mast design are the same for ocean racers as they are in the case of class racers. In round terms one is out to get the lightest mast with the minimum section that will have sufficient strength and rigidity to enable sail to be properly set, and stand without failure under hard racing conditions. The chief difference between designing for inshore and offshore masts is the margin of safety one allows. This will vary according to the designer's fancy, and the increase in the scantlings for offshore work may be anything from 10 per cent to 40 per cent. In general the increase in the scantlings of the mast itself will be moderate; but the fittings and the rigging will be appreciably heavier.

In practice in the past the ocean racers have sometimes had simply cruising rigs, where in the layout there has often been little effort to attain the best proportions; some portions have been only just about strong enough, while on others there has been much unnecessary weight. Apart from having an unfavourable effect on performance, this unnecessary strength and weight is often actually harmful on account of the extra inert loads which it imposes on neighbouring members.

But there are various reasons which make it necessary to have a wider margin of safety than for an inshore racer. In the first place the result of, say, the loss of a mast is clearly more serious offshore than when racing in sheltered waters. But apart from the extra stresses and risks involved it is important that the skipper and crew should have the feeling that the whole of the standing gear of the rig is unbreakable: that one could lay the yacht over on her beam ends a hundred times in a succession of squalls, without anything carrying away. To have this feeling firmly rooted in the crew is of the greatest value and nothing less should be aimed at.

There are many occasions when a decision whether to carry sail or reduce is difficult to make. It should be possible to make these decisions solely on considerations of speed without any thought or doubt as to whether she will stand the sail. You may properly consider whether the extra sail will bury her and actually result in her going to wind-

ward less effectively; but you should not have to worry about the chance of carrying away your mast, booms, or standing rigging.

I admit that one does not always achieve this state of affairs—that unexpected weaknesses turn up, and have to be put up with until they can be remedied—perhaps to the end of the season. But this does not affect the correctness of the thesis; and it is as well to have this requirement firmly in mind when one is designing or altering a rig—that is, it must be unbreakable.

To return to other considerations which require the increased factor of safety, it is clear that the average inertia loading on all parts is much greater offshore than inshore; for example the loading on the shrouds due to checking the movement of the mast when she is bucking into a sea. These loads can be considered as entirely additional to those imposed by the wind on the sails, and, being constantly reversed, are of the sort to engender fatigue.

There is one other important consideration. In a class racer at the end of a hard day's racing it is quite often necessary to adjust the rigging to line up the mast. This is after perhaps three hours of fresh breeze in sheltered or semi-sheltered waters. On a Fastnet the yacht may well have to sail in heavy weather for up to seven days, or fifty-six times as long, and is expected to hold her tune throughout.

So the standing rigging, the cross-trees, the mast fittings and their attachments to the mast, the chain plates for the shrouds, the anchorages for the backstays and forestays, and all the parts connected therewith, require to be so proportioned that not only do they remain *in situ* but retain their length and position accurately.

Compressive Loading due to Headsails. For the reasons mentioned in an earlier chapter, large fore triangles are in general use in order to exploit the headsails to the full. From this it follows that the primary function of a mast up to the point where the uppermost headsail sets, is that of a strut in compression. The headsails are, in the aggregate, of larger area than the mainsail; the compressive loading per sq. ft. on their account will be very much greater than that due to the mainsail, and

5

therefore the total loading from them very much more important. Because of the principal loading being compressive it is essential to have a hollow mast, since for a given weight of material a tube, be it in wood or in metal, is many times stronger than a solid strut. Or put in another way, it will carry a much bigger load without deflecting. Deflection in the tube will, if the loading is maintained, result in greatly increased stress, that is loading per unit area, on the tube walls. As soon as we get appreciable deflection, the distance between the point of loading and the deck is reduced, and the forestays on which the headsails are set commence to slacken, with a resulting fall of efficiency in those sails. Fortunately this in turn reduces the loading from the maximum, so that failure does not necessarily take place in an inadequate mast.

Mast Sections. Although primarily in compression, there are other forces operating on the mast, notably the pull of the mainsail luff, to which must be added the thrust of the jaws of the gaff if she is so rigged. The pull of the luff is greatest when the mainsail is strapped in hard, going to windward, and this is, of course, tending to deflect one's tube. Partly for this reason it is usual to make the section of the mast greater fore and aft than athwartships. Often it is oval; and often again pear-shaped, which gives one a good section in line with the pull of the luff on either tack. Another reason for making this section deeper fore and aft is that the mast is almost always better supported by the standing rigging athwartships than fore and aft; not only may there be more points of support, but the liability of the mast to find itself inadequately supported at moments by the backstays when going about or gybing, has to be remembered.

Finally there is the question of streamlining: getting the wind into the sail with the least disturbance of the air. The important side in my view, though others hold contrary ideas, is the windward side. One should, I hold, get the wind on to the sail with the minimum of disturbance. A pear-shaped mast will clearly have less of the section 'sticking out to windward'.

Again, going to windward in a breeze the wind arrives somewhere about $25°$ to $35°$ on the bow, according to boat size. If you examine a pear-shaped section you will see also that it offers a smaller cross-section to the wind than an oval or round mast. Diagram 25 illustrates this clearly. The mast is designed for a 450 sq. ft. sail plan for the R.N.S.A. 'Twenty-Fours'.

Rotating masts have been used, with a view to the stream-lined section being brought automatically in line with the mean pull of the mainsail luff.

Recently it has been reported that superior results have been achieved with the same mast wedged fore and aft. It may well be that this further bears out my contention that the important thing is to get unbroken wind on to the *windward* side of the sail, even at the expense of breaking up the flow in lee to some extent.

Aluminium Alloy for Masts. Which brings one to the question of materials for masts. Undoubtedly the material *par excellence* for racing and cruising hollow masts is an aluminium alloy. For the same compressive strength one can make the mast not only about 25 per cent lighter but appreciably smaller in outside section. Apart from any benefits regarding less disturbance of the flow in lee of the mainsail, the direct retarding resistance, when going to windward, of driving so much 'frontal area', is reduced. Also, apart from strength as a strut, having a more rigid modulus of elasticity the amount the mast compresses for a given weight of mast is less for aluminium alloys than wood. Thus the slacking up of the forestays in strong winds may be less. There are many different aluminium alloys and the strongest of them has not the highest resistance to corrosion.

It appears to me doubtful whether the duralumin series of alloys, magnificently strong though they are for airplane use, are really sufficiently corrosion-resistant for our purpose, and there may be difficulties in working with it at the shipyard.

At the other end of the scale the 2 per cent magnesium range alloys such as the shipyard Birmabright type of alloy, though very resistant to corrosion and in general very suitable for yacht work, is really too soft for spars. One of those which have up to date proved a good compromise between high strength, corrosion resistance, and workability, is British Standards Specification BS—AWIOC.

We have not yet enough experience to say with certainty when these spars will suffer from metal fatigue, but experience of twenty years indicates that they will have a very long life. It must be remembered that hollow wood spars do definitely deteriorate with age; that some of the failures prove on examination to be due in part to *anno domini*.

My bet is that a good aluminium alloy mast will long outlive a hollow wood mast. The aluminium alloys loses little by being unprotected, but inside a wood mast, unprotected perhaps, unseen certainly, and unventilated generally, all sorts of horrid things may be happening, which even a careful surveyor can't find out about. I have seen good looking spruce masts go to powder when they fail.

In 1948 in conjunction with Camper and Nicholson we designed aluminium masts which were fitted to five R.N.S.A. 'Twenty-Fours' and other yachts. This was perhaps the first attempt, on series, to use aluminium masts for small ocean racers, and to produce them at a reasonable price, though a few specially built up ones were used earlier. These have all as far as I know given very good service. Going back to earlier alloy masts, *Samuel Pepys*, for instance, has had fifteen seasons of hard ocean racing, with club-owned cruising between whiles. Included in her peregrinations are

several racing seasons in the Mediterranean, including winning her class in the first Giraglia Race; several Sydney–Hobart Races in Australia; two Bermuda Races, and two Trans-Atlantic Races, one of which she won; in the other she was second. Since then we have put afloat many hundreds of yachts with aluminium alloy masts.

Writing in 1969 it can be said that the aluminium alloy mast has superseded the wood mast in all but the most conservative of yachting circles.

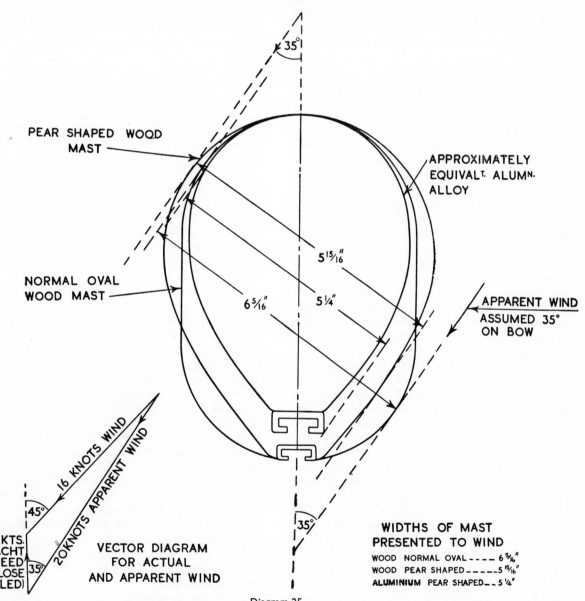

Diagram 25.
Oval, pear-shaped and aluminium pear-shaped mast sections.

Unfortunately only a few naval architects and a very few mast-builders had any extended experience of designing and building aluminium spars. As a consequence of the clear advantage of the aluminium spar a number of firms and ship-yards in many parts of Europe started manufacture with insufficient technical background and as a result there have been a number of unnecessary failures, some of which might well have endangered the yachts. (*See also* chapter 18 on mast fittings.)

Aluminium alloy masts, except in the larger sizes, are now generally made from extruded sections. These sections are from 1/16 in. to 5/16 in. in thickness according to mast size. The length of a single extrusion is limited to between 25 ft. and 40 ft., so for many masts they have to be made in more than one section, joined by sleeves or welding; or by 'iron' work. Large sizes of masts, those over 90 ft. say, are generally built up from specially formed plates joined by riveting or welding.

The choice of the best section for a particular rig is important. It will depend on the stability of the yachts, which in turn is dependent on hull form, ballast-ratio, draft and so on. The exact placing of the cross-tress, and the shroud angles, the positions of the several stays, will be important as well in this connection.

Protection of the Mast. Masts can be anodised in a special bath at a factory specially equipped for the purpose. The usual colours are either golden (rather like a new wood spar just nicely varnished) or 'natural' aluminium colour. Blue is also occasionally used. Anodising needs to be done after welding, etc., is complete and before the fittings are put on. If it is desired to paint the mast special measures are necessary. There is a note in the Construction chapter (20) about painting aluminium alloys.

Mast Winches. These from the mechanical point of view are dealt with separately. It remains to note that they need to be fastened to the mast with special care. If it is not convenient to through-bolt, then alloy bases, carefully designed for riveting are perfectly satisfactory. The sweep of the handles should be clear normally, not only of other winches, but the main boom when squared off. Here in turn the sweep of the roller-reefing gear handle must clear fixed objects on the mast.

Mast Fittings. The mast 'iron' work on aluminium alloy masts, that is to say the tangs and fittings from which shrouds, stays, halyards, and lifts take off, and on which the spreaders are mounted, are generally made either in galvanised steel or in stainless steel. These fittings are riveted or through-bolted to the mast. Riveting is achieved by one of the special methods developed by the aircraft

industry where no 'holding up' on the back is possible, and where the operation is performed by a special large scale tool in which the necessary power is provided by special leverage internal in the tool. A lot of weight aloft can be saved, with safety, by proper design of mast fittings.

In cases where it is specially desired to save weight, titanium alloy can be used in place of steel for the fittings. It is as strong as good quality steel; though its fatigue properties in practice are less satisfactory; while the weight is only 57 per cent of that of steel. The material is, however, several times more costly; its fabrication is more difficult, though with special apparatus it can be welded. Aluminium alloy fittings have been used with success in certain instances. This needs further development.

Halyards. We generally arrange for a large proportion of the halyards to be internal. This saves windage and reduces the tendency of the halyards and the other running rigging, external to the mast, to twist around one another and foul up. Masts can be lined to sound insulate them. This adds to the weight, according to the sectional area.

Aluminium alloy masts are often cursed for being noisy at moorings, in harbour. It is not generally realised that nearly all the noise is caused by wind vibrating external halyards and lifts; internal halyards not subject to the breeze, are virtually silent even when the mast is not sound insulated. Much noise can be avoided in harbour by tricing up halyards away from the mast; perhaps with shock cord.

MAGNESIUM ALLOY SPARS

Magnesium alloys are an interesting alternative to aluminium alloys for the construction of lightweight masts and spars. The material which would be used would possibly be to British Standard Specification 1356 and is likely to have an ultimate tensile strength of around 18 to 20 tons. As magnesium alloys of this type, containing about 6 per cent of aluminium, are only two-thirds of the weight of aluminium and about a quarter the weight of steel, they show to some advantage for spar making compared even to the aluminium alloys, which may be expected to have a U.T.S. of 22 tons. On the other hand the modulus of elasticity is lower than aluminium in the ratio of $6\frac{1}{2}$ to 10. In other words for a given unit loading one gets a greater compressional deflection. 'Not so stiff.' This offsets to some extent the advantage of the extra strength for weight, but some advantage will still remain. Research is needed to improve corrosion resistance; and reduce cost!

It can be gas-welded, or riveted with rivets of aluminium-magnesium alloy. It is easy to work and cut, but it has not got the same ductility as the softer forms of aluminium alloy. From a spar-making point of view this does not, however, matter too much; and its resistance to corrosion is not yet good enough to justify much use being made of it for other constructional purposes.

Riveting must receive special care on account of the nature of the substance. The distance between rivet centres is usually four rivet diameters. For $\frac{3}{32}$ in thickness, such as would be used for the smallest masts, $\frac{3}{16}$ in. diameter rivets are best. For $\frac{5}{32}$ in. such as larger ocean racers would require $\frac{1}{4}$ in rivets are suitable. The tendency to electrolytic action when in contact with any metal, other than cadmium or aluminium, is present as in the case of aluminium alloys.

The resistance to corrosion in sea air is very much less good than that of marine aluminium alloys. Moreover the difficulty of protecting it is much greater as paints do not adhere very readily. There are, however, several special ground coats and paint for use on magnesium alloys developed for aircraft. Damaged paintwork is rather awkward to make good.

For all these reasons the use of this material should, until some more resistant alloy has been developed, be confined to spars that can be lifted out and completely stripped and re-preserved after each season's use—a tiresome business and perhaps hardly a practical proposition.

Reinforcing Existing Masts. The following is mentioned particularly, because I believe it to be one of the best and easiest ways of reinforcing a wood spar. Often one finds in practice that the masthead shows signs of weakness in a particular area; or it may be a spinnaker boom which obviously is not going to stand a good blow in its present condition; or a main boom which is not man enough. In all these cases you may find it easy to get a sheet of about $\frac{1}{16}$ in. thick of corrosion-resisting aluminium alloy of the ductile type; cut it into a long strip, and work it round the spar; with very little trouble it can be worked round on the actual spar itself. But a smart yard would probably make a former to do the main bending on an old solid spar perhaps to save risk of bruising the soft spruce. It should be fixed to the wood with multiple screws, preferably short galvanised steel ones, dipped in varnish before screwing home. With the spar out of the boat the whole job can sometimes be done in an afternoon.

One of the most common troubles in converting a cruising rig into an ocean racing one is to find that if you reduce the main boom enough to get a decent aspect ratio, you are short of total area and want to set headsails to the masthead, which in-

volves strengthening the upper section of the mast. If a moderate amount of extra strength is required one can either adopt the above procedure or in the case of a round spar one can add a 'bulge' on the forward side of the section by cold water gluing on to the existing mast. I have made two hollow-glued masts with men who had never seen a hollow spar in their lives, and both masts stood up to the racket of racing offshore without trouble. So perhaps there is not so much black magic in it. If more strength than that is needed, one can cut the top section of the mast off above the cross-trees and put in a new topmast section. One can splice in with spar glue; for amateur use I think Certus cold-water glue is good. The day must be warm, or a shed heated to above 60° F. and 70° F. is better. And a real sufficiency of clamps must be used. Among the more modern glues Ciba is satisfactory and easy for the yacht yard use, where 'glue life' after mixing cannot always be controlled.

Or one can quite often get hold of an old hollow spar—a broken mast perhaps—and join it with a sleeve fishing rod joint on to your existing mast at the cap cross-trees. Light alloy sleeves are best, but a galvanised steel one built up with gas-welding does very nicely and you can hang your shrouds from tangs riveted to it if you wish.

Sleeving also makes good repairs of sprung masts at short notice, when time does not allow of a complete repair prior to a race. During the last war two destroyers came in to Scapa with their wooden topmasts completely carried away in bad weather. I had thin steel sleeves made for them, trimmed up the broken ends and inserted a distance piece, and had the repair completed in a couple of days, and the ships away again in their convoy work. As far as I could trace these repairs stood indefinitely.

Masts Stepped on Deck. As designers we have steadily developed the practice of stepping the mast on deck. Starting with smaller vessels we are now successfully using this system in Class I ocean racers of up to 50 ft. water-line. From the owner's point of view a practical feature is the greatly reduced labour of stepping and unstepping the mast for fitting out or laying up; or in case of a repair or large adjustment being needed to the mast; or when the yacht has to proceed under a bridge. Again deck leaks round the mast wedges are eliminated. Thirdly the interference of a mast in the below deck accommodation is eliminated. Fourthly, the mast is shorter and easier to transport. From a design point of view, the racking stresses on a coach-roof can be reduced; the athwartships loading is differently applied, and can be more readily taken care of. The loading on the lower shrouds is increased at the same time, but this can readily be allowed for by careful design. In general a directly loaded steel or alloy post is placed below the mast underdeck, and the usual precautions are taken to spread this loading correctly at the heel of the post through the structure of the yacht. The several cases of difficulty with masts stepped on deck have generally been due to designers or yacht builders taking insufficient care either with the details of the step on deck, or with arrangements for transmitting the thrust below the step.

Cross-tree Positioning. In laying out the design of a mast the first thing to do is to decide what sails are going to be sheeted inside and what sails outboard of the standing rigging. This problem is complicated by the fact that for a given fore triangle, the longer on the foot the sail is, or the more the overlap, the farther outboard it will set. Or put in another way, the curve of a big genoa set on the wind (viewed in plan) will lie entirely outboard of the curve taken up by a working sail, set on the same stay. Also for a given hoist, the higher the aspect ratio of the fore triangle, the farther inboard the sail will lie. This means that with a high narrow fore triangle the cross-trees must be shorter. (The allowable shortening is discussed in detail later.)

In a cutter, that is to say, a two headsail rig, on the wind the staysail or inner headsail will normally be sheeted inside the cap and topmast shrouds. The jib will probably sheet outside, except in the case of storm jibs, which will require more inboard sheeting. On a reach the staysail sheet will have to be led outside all the shrouds. In the case of a sloop-rigged vessel—that is to say one with a single headsail, and of course this applies to single headsail yawls and ketches and foremasts of schooners—endeavour should be made to set all the large headsails clear outside the standing rigging. This requirement often leads designers to shorten unduly the cross-trees. It would be better to add an extra cross-tree, than unduly to shorten. The length of the cross-tree should be proportioned to the length of the 'panel', the unsupported length of mast, between cross-trees; or from masthead to cross-tree.

Shroud Arrangement. For a given sail plan, that is to say for a given 'wind loading', the tensile loading in the shrouds is reduced by lengthening the cross-trees. By the same token the compressive loading in the mast is reduced by lengthening the cross-trees. I feel that this is most important to bear in mind. The limitation on cross-tree length is generally the sheeting problem referred to above. A good figure to aim at for important shrouds is to have the cap or upper shrouds make an angle of 14 to 15 degrees with the centre-line of the mast. Many racing boats have less angles, and get away with it. But they are cutting down

their factor of safety thereby; or are carrying a mast and shrouds of unnecessary size and weight. One can get away with 13 degrees, but in practice if one's angle is much less the adjustment will not stay put for any length of time in a seaway. This refers to all upper shrouds. The shorter lower shrouds, those running direct to the mast, not over a cross-tree, can come off at appreciably smaller angles, if need be. When converting an inshore racer to offshore work, new and lengthened cross-trees are often indicated. If it stops one from getting the genoa in quite as hard, it may also help to stop one pinching her.

The desirability of a decent shroud angle can readily be seen by drawing a simplified triangle of forces for the point at which the shroud meets the mast. At this, or any other point, the loadings in one plane must close the triangle, or quadrilateral, etc., if there are more than three loadings on that spot, to achieve conditions of equilibrium. Diagram 26 (Fig. I) shows diagrammatically the loading on the masthead carrying a jib to that point. The compressive stresses due to the halyards, etc., have been omitted as they can be conveniently considered from a graphic point of view in the fore and aft plane.

Fig. II shows the triangle of forces with a 15-degree shroud angle and Fig. III, the same sail loading of X pounds with a 10-degree shroud angle. The increase in mast and shroud loads is shown graphically by the increase in length of the lines C_2 and T_2 compared with C and T.

In general the method of obviating the bearing of the genoa on the cross-tree ends should be to place one's cross-trees closer together, and use still a decent shroud angle, rather than to reduce their length and skimp the angle. Unfortunately if one has a cutter in which one wants to set the overlapping staysail inside the shrouds, this asks for the lower cross-tree to be as high as possible. As we have said a smaller angle than 15 degrees is acceptable in the case of the lower shrouds, which lead direct from the mast to the deck. In the first place these shrouds are short and the extension (or temporary stretch) under load is small. Also they do not have to take account of the shortening of the cross-tree under compressive load. Thirdly, they may in practice be low-stressed owing to the assistance they get from the *encastré* effect of the mast in the hull. In the case of wood, the mast in way of the masthead, cross-trees and for a foot or two above the deck is always made either solid, or much thicker, to take the necessary fittings with the localised loading which is involved. For this reason most masts will comfortably stand the little bit of bending from the deck, due to being *encastré*,

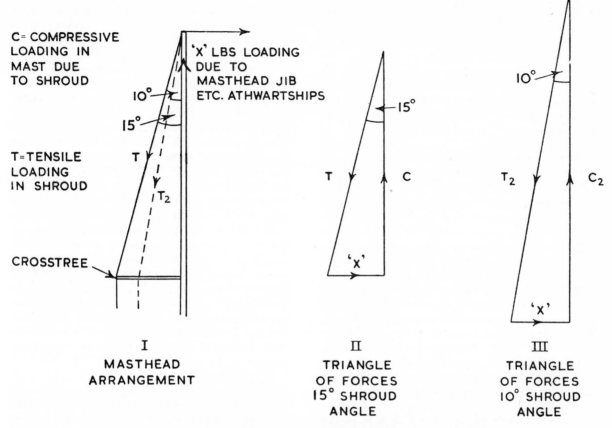

C= COMPRESSIVE LOADING IN MAST DUE TO SHROUD

'X' LBS LOADING DUE TO MASTHEAD JIB ETC. ATHWARTSHIPS

T=TENSILE LOADING IN SHROUD

CROSSTREE

I
MASTHEAD ARRANGEMENT

II
TRIANGLE OF FORCES 15° SHROUD ANGLE

III
TRIANGLE OF FORCES 10° SHROUD ANGLE

LOADING RESULTING FROM DIFFERENT SHROUD ANGLES

Diagram 26.

or stuck in the hull, and most designers welcome the support the deck, or coachroof, gives. Some pundits hold that the intention is for the mast to be perfectly straight from the heel; for it to go 'over in one piece' when the wind loading, athwartships, is applied. For this reason, among others, the mast stepped on deck must be preferred; and occasionally mast wedges are not used, and only sponge rubber and a canvas cover is fitted. On balance, I favour wedged masts, if they are to pierce the deck.

Spreader Arrangements. My general practice with bermudan rigs nowadays is to have two cross-trees below the point at which the highest headsail sets. This means two altogether for a masthead jibbed cutter. In other cases where the highest headsail terminates below the masthead, an extra cross-tree at that point will be required.

In all cases a preventer backstay is needed; a light one if no headsail is set to the masthead and

a man-sized one if headsail is set thereto. The standing backstay is an enormous comfort; it obviates the necessity for catching the preventer runners exactly on the gybe. When such manoeuvres have to be done in a seaway at night, short-handed cruising, or with one watch only on deck; the security offered to the mast is priceless.

Diamond Shrouds. Diamond shrouds, that is to say, shrouds which terminate at the mast above the deck—for example, running from a masthead over a cross-tree and back to the mast at the next cross-tree down—should never be used to support a portion of the mast on which serious headsails are to be set. The jumper struts are a form of diamond shroud, but they are often quite adequate to support the uppermost part of the mast on which only the head of a comparatively narrow mainsail will be supported.

The reason why they can't support headsails properly is that the diamond shroud never starts doing any useful work until the mast bends. In general the whole object is to prevent bends, and keep the mast straight, particularly below the point to which the highest headsail is set; any bend in a mast interferes with its efficiency as a strut.

Diamond shrouds have, however, important advantages. They clear the way for the leech of an overlapping headsail, when it is hard-sheeted for windward work. This is illustrated in Diagram 27. The dotted line is the alternative shroud run to deck. And secondly they relieve the lower part of the mast of the compressive strain which it would bear if the shroud were taken to deck. They pull up against the downward loading of the lower shrouds, and help balance these, being probably attached to the same tang, or metal fitting on the side of the mast. They reduce considerably the total length of wire necessary, compared to those coming to deck, and save windage and weight aloft thereby, but for a given shroud wind-loading and cross-tree length they increase the cross-tree or 'spreader' compressive loading (and therefore its section and weight if stresses are to be the same) compared to shrouds coming to deck. They share with linked rigging the disadvantage that one has to go aloft to adjust them, and that the rigging screws have to be aloft, with their weight and windage; unless one accepts the extra wire and leads them through a lead at the mast to deck.

The size of diamond shrouds will depend on the length of the 'unsupported' part of the mast above the spreader, and on the length of the spreader. They will be relatively light—from three-fifths to three-quarters of the circumference (or diameter) of the shroud to the top of the fore triangle.

Linked Rigging. Turning then to the question of linked rigging, by which I mean terminating the masthead shrouds (*vide* the diagram again) at the outboard end of the lower cross-trees, instead of bringing them to deck, this has the advantage that it reduces the number of shrouds and therefore the windage; since one bigger wire has less windage than two of equivalent strength. It also assists one as regards sheeting headsails; there is less chance of chafe and the sheets overhaul better round one big wire. If a staysail is to be sheeted inside the outer shrouds the reduction from two to one shroud is specially welcome.

On the other hand, quite apart from the business of having to go aloft, the adjustment of the rigging is less easy. One has not such complete control over the mast compared to the case where the shrouds all come to deck, and in consequence it is sometimes not possible to achieve such a perfectly straight mast over a range of weather and heel.

1945 Sydney–Hobart. In the light of fast cruising

it is interesting to recall that on the Christmas 1945 Hobart Race we ran for much of two days in fresh breezes with a big genoa set as a spinnaker—spinnakers were not permitted on that occasion—and had no trouble. Incidentally the second of those days was one of the nicest bits of down-wind sailing I remember. Twin headsails set as spinnakers were not barred by the rules, and having two big genoas we set one each side and ran along at about $7\frac{3}{4}$ knots in a big quartering sea in great comfort for hour after hour while we stitched away at the big mainsail, which was an old sail and had split badly earlier in the race. The boat's bard, Ray Richmond, was in good voice that day, and among many other tunes rendered a new ditty, the catch line of which went 'Roll along little *Rani*, roll along'.

In truth we did a bit of nice quiet 'Rhythmic Rolling' at times, though it never got out of hand; Rhythmic Rolling being the term I use for the down-wind roll which at times builds up into a big lurching swing and which is sometimes hard to check. I remember noting then, as on other occasions, that the less one fought the helm the better. If one resisted the temptation to correct the tendency to sheer off, up to windward, as the sea lifted one's stern, she came naturally out of the roll, and more quickly.

Mast Rake. In the early days of bermudan rigs many of us were continually experimenting with mast rake, and argument waged fast and furious between exponents of each school. My impression at that time was that it made comparatively little difference to yachts with 'long keeled' profiles. But in yachts having a short deep underwater profile the rake does have an important effect on the amount of helm carried. For example excessive weather helm can sometimes be very much reduced by reducing the amount of rake, because one is shifting the centre of effort of the sails forward. This effect is more potent in high narrow sail plans. Apart from any question of correction the principal advantage of giving extra rake is that (for a given compressive load on the mast) one's fore-topmast, and fore-stay in a cutter, is tauter. Also aerodynamically there is something to be said for the raked mast: the swept-back wing effect. But the value of this is probably slight, at the relatively low wind speeds at which yachts operate compared to aircraft. On the other hand by giving extra rake one is reducing the actual area of one's fore triangle, which is at its maximum when the mast is at right angles to the deck since the measurement is a product of perpendicular times base over two. One can argue that by raking the mast aft one gets a longer stay and more length of luff. But one is bringing the stay nearer to the mast and so the difficulty of getting the draught from the headsail clear of the mainsail is increased.

As regards the design effect of rake on the mainsail, moderation in rake is desirable; firstly, because the boom otherwise commences to droop excessively, or alternatively it is cocked up relative to the mast and loses area; the actual mainsail area is at the maximum for its rating when the boom is at right-angles to the mast; since the sail is measured as half the product of the hoist and its length on the boom. And secondly because, like a door hung on an inclined hinge, it tends always to swing into the centre-line, and this effect increases the difficulty of keeping the sail full in light airs, observing that the mainsail will be of much more weighty material than the headsail then in use.

Black Measurement Bands. At this point it may be convenient to recall that the I.Y.R.U., the new rule the R.O.R.C. and the C.C.A. all specify that there should be a black band (1 in. wide R.O.R.C.) at the point of maximum extensions; at the head of the mainsail; at the tack level with the top of boom, and round the boom where the clew may be pulled out to. Where these bands are not in place, measurements may be taken to the limit of hoist, or clew outhaul.

Cross-tree Heels. Fully hinged cross-trees can be dangerous should excessive slack temporarily develop in a shroud, *e.g.* a rigging screw slacking back. Rigidly fixed spreaders are more easily damaged at the heel; by a halyard or running backstay or by touching another rig when berthing. As a compromise I design masts with rubber between the spreader heels and the mast. In any design the heel must be bolted, or otherwise fixed, to its bracket or socket, *i.e.* not rely on the shroud tension to keep it to the mast. Likewise special care must be taken to secure the shroud to the cross-tree end positively, *e.g.* a hemp lashing to prevent it coming out of its groove is not acceptable.

Cross-tree Ends. It is of course of the utmost importance to protect the ends of cross-trees against the catch-up of halyards and spinnakers, and to reduce the fret on the genoas when sheeted home. It is such an obvious need that I hesitate to refer to it; but every year one sees accidents as a result of neglecting this precaution. I am not impressed with the efficacy of rooting discs, nor of the need for the big protective hoops one sometimes sees. If the ends are carefully bandaged, then covered with tape, and served over perhaps, with a coat of varnish to finish off, the protection should easily last the season.

With the release-and-let-flog method of handing a spinnaker, which with the modern tough nylon does not take too much out of the fabric, it is clearly

5*

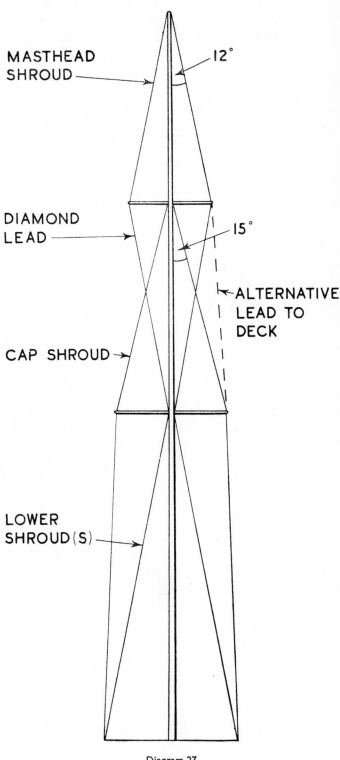

Diagram 27.
Masthead Shroud Arrangements.

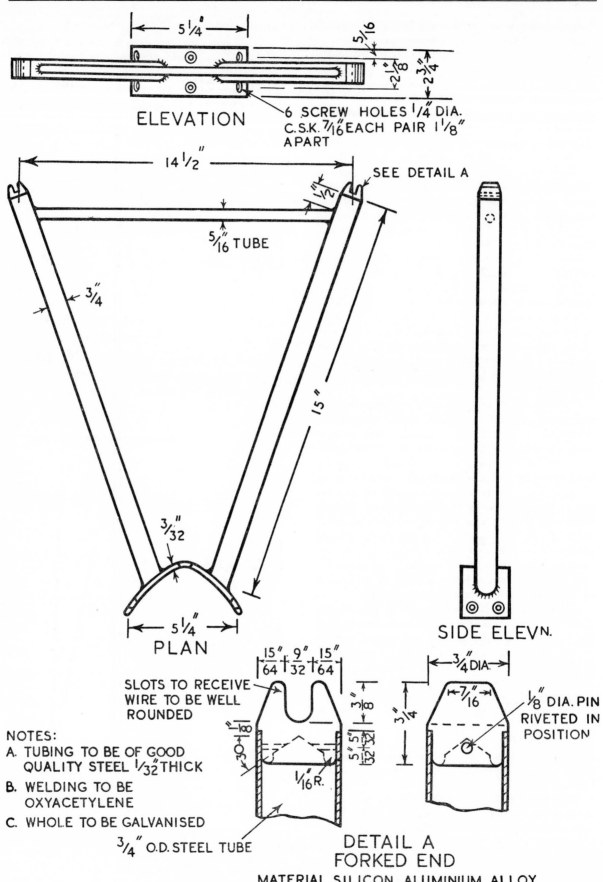

ELEVATION

6 SCREW HOLES 1/4" DIA. C.S.K. 7/16" EACH PAIR 1 1/8" APART

SEE DETAIL A

14 1/2"

5/16" TUBE

3/4"

15"

3/32"

5 1/4"

PLAN

SIDE ELEVN.

SLOTS TO RECEIVE WIRE TO BE WELL ROUNDED

NOTES:

A. TUBING TO BE OF GOOD QUALITY STEEL 1/32" THICK

B. WELDING TO BE OXYACETYLENE

C. WHOLE TO BE GALVANISED

3/4" O.D. STEEL TUBE

DETAIL A
FORKED END
MATERIAL SILICON ALUMINIUM ALLOY

1/8" DIA. PIN RIVETED IN POSITION

Diagram 28.
Rani—Jumper Struts.

very important to reduce the catch-up hazards. Moreover, with the full-topped spinnakers now (with good reason) in vogue, the spinnaker often tries, in light weather and a seaway, to catch up in the standing rigging.

The use of rigging linked at the lower cross-tree, reduces the chance of a hook-up. With unlinked direct to deck shrouds it is often worth a taut lanyard to bridge the gap between the lower cross-trees.

Bare Mastheads. Mastheads, both in wood and alloy, can be left bare of shrouds or forestays if the bare length above the shrouds is reasonably short; small that is to say, relative to the section of the mast. (This obviates the need of jumper struts, and their weight and windage; the complication and added chance of fouling sails and halyards; as well as the initial cost.) For example 6 ft. of bare mast is acceptable in a 24-ft. waterline yacht and 8 ft. in a 30-ft. waterline; in each case from top of triangle to mainsail black band. But in a 12 metre of 48-ft. waterline the 20 ft. of bare mast proved in most cases just too much and most people went to shrouds. It would certainly have been too much offshore. We can therefore say that the amount bare can be about 25 per cent of the waterline length. One can help the bare mast by running the upper shrouds to just above the top of the triangle.

16

STANDING RIGGING

As you will have guessed after reading the last chapter, the questions of mast design and standing rigging are really indivisible, since the two must be envisaged as a whole if they are to work to the best advantage. Indeed much the same can be said of most parts of the ship; that every part and member must be designed not only to fulfil its particular function, but to fulfil it with the design and efficiency of the neighbouring members in view and with the character and duty of the boat as a whole in mind.

However, the last chapter on masts had become so long that I felt it was time we paused for breath before we got from general considerations down to practical detailed ways of checking on our rig strength and layout.

Formula for Shroud Strength. It is clear that the maximum loading which comes on a rig is in the end proportional not to the sail area but to the stability of the yacht. The calculation of the load required to list a boat to 45°, under way, is a considerable one depending on the boat's ends, on which she leans, as well as on her midship section and ballast and what we need is a quick way of checking on our layout when we buy a boat, or when we come to renew our standing rigging.

Assuming a reasonable shroud angle to mast, here is a very rough rule for bermudan masthead cutters or yawls, of normal ocean racing or fast cruising types. The combined strength (breaking load) of shrouds coming to deck, other than the lower direct shrouds, should be about twice the effective weight of the ballast. In calculating effective ballast assume R.O.R.C. standard draft. Reckon inside ballast at 50 per cent; and iron ballast keels at 90 per cent unless hung specially low. Any ballast keel where the draft is less than average should figure at 90 per cent actual weight. For really shallow-draft yachts 80 per cent. Then for beamier than average boats add 10 per cent, and for specially beamy ones 20 per cent, provided they are reasonably hard bilged. For narrow boats reduce 10 per cent, for slack section reduce an additional 10 per cent. If with little or no overhangs, reduce 5 per cent again. This furnishes a comfortable safety factor for offshore work—which inshore racers will choose to reduce. Sloop shrouds

may be lighter—in proportion to triangle heights.

Lower Shroud Proportions. You may ask why I should not use the lower shrouds. The answer is that where there is an *encastré* mast, extending through the deck or coachroof to the keel, the lower shrouds get a lot of help from the mast. With a mast stepped on deck, clearly more load comes on the lower shrouds and they need to be designed accordingly, together with the associated chain plates and rigging screws. Where the more usual forward and aft lower shrouds are provided, the after one can be much lighter—speaking always of bermudan cutter rigs. Assuming the shroud angle at the mast is 3° less—say 12°—the foremost shroud should have about 0·7 of the strength of the combined upper shrouds; 0·95 if there is only one shroud, and 1·2 if the mast is stepped on deck.

In wider-beamed yachts the forward lower shroud of a cutter often interferes with the staysail and has to be eliminated, and an inner forestay substituted with the after shroud increased in strength. In sloops for different reasons—the saving of one shroud, one chain-plate and one rigging-screw, and obtaining more direct control of the lower part of the mast—a similar arrangement is attractive: *viz.* one after lower shroud each side, partnered by an inner forestay.

The amount of load which this inner forestay is called upon to carry varies widely according to the design of the upper part of the mast. With bare mast-headed sloops it is often very small; in cutters often considerable.

The way in which the loading increases as one goes down the mast can be conveniently studied at each cross-tree point in the mast by triangles of forces. Given standard shroud-to-mast angles 'the sideways thrust' of a loaded cross-tree produces the same tensile loading in the shroud running down from the point as there is in the stay running over the cross-tree. To this must of course be added the loading due to a headsail whose stay terminates at that point, plus also a share of the mainsail load, which via the track is spread over the mast.

Runner Backstays. A backstay should run aft from every point at which a headsail stay terminates. One occasionally sees a small cruiser in which jumper stays are called on to perform this duty via a standing masthead backstay. This is not good practice for offshore racing; because if enough weight is put in the standing backstay to tauten the luff of a decent-sized headsail, the jumper stays will most probably be overloaded. Alternatively or additionally you will be sailing with an inadequately taut forestay for the headsail. Not that I am decrying the standing backstay rigged in combination with jumper stays—on the contrary, I think it a most desirable fitting for a sloop or non-masthead cutter or yawl. It can be quite light—about three-fifths the circumference (or diameter) of the shroud which leads to the top of the fore triangle. But fit runners as well; even if they are not heavy ones in a very small vessel.

Apart from headsail considerations, in a seaway some more direct support is desirable on the after side of the mast.

Drift to the Runners. The runner backstays are generally led away at angles of between 15° and 25° with the mast, and thence to the ship's side. The distance between the point where they meet the deck and the main shrouds is known as the 'drift' of the stay. It is a nice problem to decide what this should be. As a start one can draw it to be the same as the base of the fore triangle of the sail with which one is dealing. The bigger the drift, the less will be the compressive load for a given horizontal component necessary to tauten the stay on which the headsail is set. This is an important consideration.

Here one must make the point that the runner will, in addition to pulling the mast backwards, also assist the shrouds in 'keeping it up sideways'. The extent to which it will help is inversely proportional to the drift. Many people hold that this 'help' to the shrouds is undesirable because it is difficult to calculate the extent of it and because it adds to the problem of adjusting the rigging. So much so that some years ago 6-metre designers in America started to move the stay inboard from the gunwale. However, I would guess that the failures they had in the runners were perhaps due to sailing with shrouds which were given insufficient initial tension.

It is a convenience to have moderate drift, because this reduces the amount of slack needed when runners are cast off for the boom to be squared off. In our many successful cutter rigs it enabled all this slack to be obtained simply with our special slotted lever without unhooking. But in sloops, and in the case of runner backstays from non-masthead jibs, when there is no such possibility it is better to go out for the reduced mast loading and get the runners well aft.

In practice the loading in the runners increases automatically, with the mast inclination *relative to the hull*. When the breeze freshens this is not unhelpful; it tautens the headsail luff automatically without the need for very high initial tensions in the runners. But it does mean that one must 'catch it' before or when going about; or better still have the necessary means, by lever or winch, to get the full loading later, should necessity arise.

With a fairly big-beamed yacht it is often possible to arrange the runners so that one can turn to windward and tack with both runners set up. I have arranged this in *Monk of Malham* and almost all my recent cutter designs.

Standing Preventer. Conversely, when there is a single standing preventer backstay amidships, on which one is relying to get one's masthead jib taut, one has to start with a high initial tension. As soon as extra compressive loading comes on a mast, due to the pull of the shrouds when one gets sailing, this shortens the mast fractionally and unless this high initial tension has been provided in the backstay it goes slack, together with the fore topmast stay and the jib luff. Alternatively one can have some means of putting on, readily, extra tension when sailing.

The difficulty here is to judge the loading accurately—to be sure that one is not overloading the stays and masthead. I attached so much importance to this in *Maid of Malham* that I designed a fearsome-looking spring-loaded screw jack, the wheel of which was operated by a wheel spanner. This enabled extra tension to be put on at any time, the exact amount being read off on a large scale 'spring balance'. There was a smaller wheel so that the spring could be locked if desired, I think the initial tension was of the order of $2\frac{1}{2}$ tons. Later we substituted twin standing masthead preventers.

Twin Standing Preventers. All this underlines the necessity for carrying the strength of the mast, when masthead working jibs are used, up to very near the masthead, which allows of two standing preventer backstays to the quarters. This arrangement has the advantage that extra tension comes on the preventer when the mast goes to leeward under sail pressure so that initial tension need not be so great. But this is achieved at the very considerable expense of the added weight aloft and windage of say 60 ft. of stay, since each backstay has to be of the same strength as the one placed on the centre-line.

I have often in the past successfully led plough steel wire round big sheaves and back to the levers directly, which saves any splices or shackles. To run plough steel round a sheave is, however, not done in the best circles and it is more usual to change over to flexible steel wire rope, when just clear of the deck, by means of two splices and thimbles and a shackle, the flexible being one size heavier to get the same strengsh.

Gear for Setting-up Runners. The four alternative methods of tautening the runners are purchases, levers, slides, and winches. In larger boats it is usual to have in addition a block on the lower end of the plough steel runner and to lead another flexible wire from a standing part on deck, through this sheave and back to deck where it is dealt with by one of the above devices, through another fixed sheave if necessary. The standing part on deck is often fitted to be unhooked from a ring bolt to assist in giving the extra slack. This block is a little apt to crown one when it is swinging about in a seaway and so should not be fitted unless it is actually needed to get the extra power. However it is better to put up with it if there is any doubt.

The slide system consists of a track along the ship's side with a slider on it carrying the runner, or the forward wire from the block. It gives good power only when the drift is small or moderate, and is suitable for all sizes of yacht. It is often used in conjunction with a lever and hook, or a winch, or a hook and purchase to get the last squeeze on. The big points about this system, when the runner comes direct to the slide, are that there is nothing to unhook off the deck and nothing swinging about between the deck and the mast, except the stay. It is remarkable, incidentally, how many people are quite content to get the runners up moderately taut and leave it at that! It must be emphasised, however, that for a runner slide to work well one must be content to have a moderate drift on the stay otherwise the mechanical advantage becomes insufficient. Quite a good plan is to have a winch each side, the leeward one sheeting a headsail and the weather one the runner slide, changing jobs at each tack. It is clearly necessary to keep the track in good condition, clean, slightly greased and free from big bulges. Occasionally the slide sticks, and in any case is less easy to cast off than most systems, though good to set up. For very small yachts one can use a horizontal plough steel wire, in lieu of a track. It should be fitted with a rigging screw or turnbuckle. The wire should be twice the diameter of the runner.

If a winch is to pull direct through a sheave on to the stay, the stay should have good drift, otherwise it is unlikely to get it up taut enough. If a winch, without a slide, is to be used in a biggish boat, it is necessary in addition to have a moving block; say for the runner stays of a cutter's stay sail. And for a sloop of any large size a purchase in addition; that is to say the standing end unhooks to give you plenty of slack to overhaul, and the two-, three- or four-fold purchase is on the other leg, plus a winch; the number of parts according to the power of the winch and size of the boat.

It is a mistake to think in such a case that simply because you have a winch you will get the power you want—don't be afraid to put extra parts in the purchase. At all costs get that runner up as taut as it needs to be.

The Use of Runner Levers. Turning to lever operation, this has, properly applied, two very considerable advantages. In the first place one gets great power combined with very quick operation. Secondly the runner comes back click, or more probably 'clunk', to the same exact setting each time one goes about. You will ask which of the systems you should use, and I would reply, on the balance, for small and medium-sized yachts, levers. It is true that the ability to give the mast a shade of fore and aft play may be of value in a seaway, with light winds, in assisting the sails to keep quiet, by lessening the shake which the hull imparts to the mast. But such easing of the runners and preventers has to be done with caution, since it is clearly in a seaway that the mast needs the support, and allowing a mast to work too much may lead in time to age fatigue.

And on occasions the mast working seems, owing to the timing of the sea synchronizing with its natural period, or I suppose a harmonic of it, suddenly to increase in the amplitude of its movement. This damps out quickly, and probably occurs again in a few moments.

So I accept the occasional disadvantage of being unable to play the rig softly down wind or on the reach, glad that I have a good powerful lever which will bring my runner back to the same taut point each time with the minimum of struggle, and will provide an insurance against those times when, perhaps wet and cold and tired, perhaps at night, one might otherwise let her sail along with something less than a full tension on the jib or forestay.

While cutters can virtually always use levers for their runners, for the larger sloops of 25 tons upwards it will be necessary to use a good general winch for the runners.

Runners in Small Yachts. A good system in small yachts is to have a short lever and a moving block on a pennant attached to the lever so as to double the amount of slack you get, thus obviating again the necessity for unhooking and at the same time avoiding the need for a long lever. The load on the lever is doubled, but in a small yacht where the headsail is half the size and the operating man is the same size, there is not much objection. One is doing the reverse of what the moving block on the bottom of runner does for a big yacht.

SMALL YACHT RUNNER ARRANGEMENT

FIRST CHECK THE AMOUNT OF SLACK BY SCALE DRAWING, REQUIRED TO ENABLE BOOM TO BE SQUARED OFF TO SHROUD. HALVE THIS AND SUBTRACT 2"— THIS WILL GIVE THE LENGTH OF LEVER REQUIRED (U.S.M.P.C. LEVERS ARE 36" LONG AND CAN BE CUT OFF TO THE REQUIRED LENGTH.)

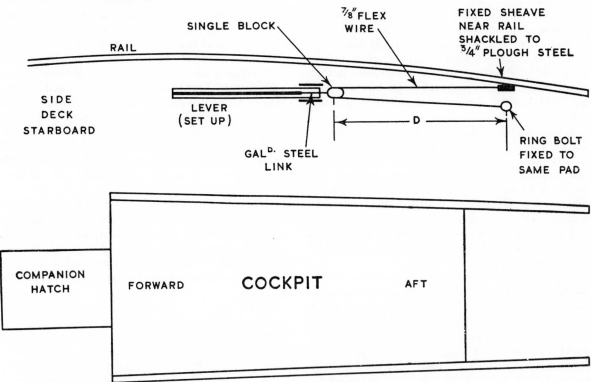

DISTANCE 'D' TO BE EQUAL TO HALF THE SLACK REQUIRED PLUS SAY 5" MARGIN FOR BLOCK ETC. NOTE —THIS ARRANGEMENT IF USED WITH MORE DRIFT TO THE RUNNER DOES NOT INCREASE THE LOAD VERY MUCH OVER THE NORMAL DIRECT ARRANGEMENT, BUT DOES AWAY WITH NECESSITY FOR UNSHACKLING OR UNLOCKING RUNNER TO GET ENOUGH SLACK.

Diagram 29.

Yet another alternative for quite small yachts is the croquet hoop type of lever with an 'overhung' post to each leg, the wire being attached to the cross bar. If one leg is considerably extended to form a handle it makes quite a good layout in conjunction with the scheme referred to in the preceding paragraph. Lever details are in chapter 18.

Forestays. The question of the inclination of the forestays is bound up with the general layout of the sail plan, and the aspect ratio of the fore triangle, and is discussed in more detail in chapter 9. But from a purely rigging standpoint, for a given mast and given runner arrangement, the smaller the angle the stay makes with the mast the tauter will be the stay, and the straighter the headsail luff when sailing.

One of the decisions to be taken is whether one should use single or twin stays. Many current designs feature twin stays to facilitate sail changes. One has twin halyards, and can sometimes set and sheet the new sail before handing the old one. Even if this is not possible one can have everything hanked on and ready to hoist, the moment the handed sail touches the deck. When the drill goes to plan one can undoubtedly make very appreciable savings in time when sail changing.

Twin Stays versus Single Stays. The cost of this is the weight and windage of twin stays. In a small Class I yacht this amounts to a length, on the fore and fore topmast stays, of about 110 ft. of $1\frac{1}{4}$ in. plus 85 ft. of $\frac{3}{4}$ in. wire and $1\frac{1}{2}$ in. hemp, staysail halyard. Being mindful of this weight and windage, in addition to the chance of a snarl-up due to complexity of gear, or the chance that hanks of one sail would hook up on a neighbouring stay, I plumped for single stays and have used them since 1949.

A minor advantage of single stays is that the loading can be arranged to come on the centre-line of the mast, obviating a twisting load. While it is true that a torque of this order in a strut under compression does not as a rule materially affect the 'principal stress' of such a system, it is mildly undesirable. Another minor consideration is that the windage and residual load on the idle stay robs the working stay of some of its otherwise rightful tension.

Some class racers have separate levers for tautening the stay on which sail is set. But owing to the inevitable sag of the working stay in a breeze, which automatically loosens the idle stay, I doubt the necessity for this. In quiet conditions only does it add much to the tautness of the working stay—that is to say when this extra load is not required.

I discovered when I took *Myth* to America in 1948 that Rod Stephens also had abandoned twin stays about that time.

An exception may be made in the case of short-handed cruisers, and must be made in the case of single-handed racers. When we re-rigged *Gypsy Moth III* we provided twin forestays and twin fore top mast stays; and somewhat similar arrangements in Alec Rose's *Lively Lady*. The object being in each case to reduce the number of sail hanking-on operations to the minimum. In *Gypsy Moth IV* we went a stage further and provided four fore topmast stays, well separated at the bottom, in addition to twin forestays.

'*Maid of Malham*' *Movable Forestays*. We had an interesting arrangement in *Maid*'s forestays. Although this is old hat now it may well be useful. They were twin and both could be set up in the normal position with the forestays parallel to the fore topmast stays. An alternative position was

provided 3 ft. farther forward on deck, to which the stays could be set up, in each case by levers, each lever port and starboard working two wire pennants running via its own bottle screw and deck sheave to a hook, which engaged the thimble at the lower end of the stay in question.

The object was to be able to move the staysail forward after shifting to a smaller jib, to keep the ship balanced and to make better use of the fore triangle. Using it this way the second jib was set at first on a tack pennant, to have it use the clear upper part of the triangle. Later we tacked it to the deck. Though it did not look so pretty on the sail plan it appeared to set equally well and being appreciably lower and farther forward it was probably more efficient, as it would result in less heeling and would help to reduce the weather helm, which turned out to be considerable in this boat, in fresh weather.

The arrangement of levers and pennants, with their screws and sheaves, between fore and aft 'foot grip' rails, all worked quite successfully, though some care was necessary to get all the four rigging screws to the same stay tension, in their various positions. Wags christened this section 'the

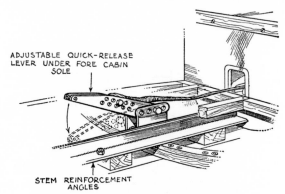

Diagram 30.
Myth of Malham—Forestay Release Lever.

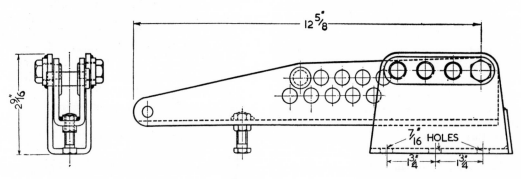

Diagram 31.
Myth of Malham—Rigging Stay Release Lever. For use with 1 in. to 1¼ in. circ. wire.

Typical yachts of the Junior Offshore Group. On the left is the author's *Wista*, 19·8 ft. water-line, which won the Championship in 1954, and on the right is *Merle of Malham*. 26 ft. 9 in. loa, 24 lwl and 8 ft. 2 in. beam. She was designed by John Illingworth & Associates for the author, and was built by C.N.M. at St Malo in 1967.

Start of Class C in the Newport-Bermuda Race. Fresh winds caused some lively spinnaker work on the line. One of *Uomie*'s crew enjoying some spinnaker uplift.

Dambuster, a light displacement Class II ocean racer designed by Illingworth and Primrose for the Royal Air Force S.A. Among her first season's successes was first in the San Sebastian-Belle Ile Race. Dimensions: *loa*: 38·3 ft.; *lwl*: 30 ft.; *beam*: 9·85 ft.; *draft*: 6·75 ft.; *sail area*: 610 sq. ft.

Blue Charm, the first of a series of similar light displacement Class III ocean racers, built in France and England. Exceptionally fast boats to windward, they have a number of successes to their credit, including a Round the Island Race Gold Bowl win in a fleet of 160 yachts.

Pherousa, second in her class in the Bermuda Race. She is a counter-sterned version of Maica but with increased ballast and sail area, and was designed by Illingworth and Primrose for Monsieur Edouard Michel.

Maica with a nice quad set: a Class III R.O.R.C. champion of 1962. She was designed by Illingworth and Primrose and in the hands of Monsieur Henri Rouault has represented France in many successful ocean races. About one hundred near sisters have been built; probably the largest class of near-one-design ocean racers built to date.

railway station'. It should be noted that alternative forestay positioning is at its best with twin stays, because in a seaway only one stay is slackened at once, and the mast is never left unsupported.

'*Myth*' *Forestay*. In the case of several of our designs the forestay is led through the deck to a sheave on the stem, and thence to a short lever under the fore cabin floor (Diagram 30). This gives it a solid anchorage and does away with usual bottle screw above the deck, which makes it difficult to stow a second staysail neatly hanked on the stay close to the deck; where it should be to reduce windage. The lever, to my design, Diagram 31, is made by Lewmar Marine, Emsworth. It provides in itself the necessary adjustment and saves the weight cost and length of a bottle screw. A shackle or hook is fitted in the forestay just clear of the deck tube, which projects above the deck to reduce leakage. A wipe of tallow has to be added to make it watertight. The shackle is cast off when it is desired to bring the stay to the mast and to use the rig as a masthead sloop for light weather.

Tie Rod Rigging. Consideration of extensions and loading brings one to the question of rod rigging. Compared to wire its primary advantage is that you can by a careful visual examination ascertain its condition and make a reasonable estimate of its life. In the case of wire rope one can only hazard an intelligent guess. In general, compared to its competitor, the normal standing wire rope rigging, and assuming an equal breaking strain, its extension under load is somewhat less, which is in its favour for some purposes. For a given weight it is a shade smaller, and also smoother with less windage than a wire rope. *Endeavour II* among many notable earlier vessels used bar rigging.

But the story does not end there, because wire rope apart from the obvious advantage of being easy to handle and join by splicing is composed of fine strands whose strength is largely imparted by drawing in manufacture, or 'cold working'. This process is only feasible in the smaller sizes; as the diameter increases the extra strength that can be given in this way becomes less.

Therefore to show to advantage bar rig must be to a high tensile formula which has nevertheless sufficient toughness to cope with fair wear and tear. Ordinary good quality mild steel for instance, reliable as it is, would never be worth while.

One of the things one has to remember about rod rigging is that it won't stand the amount of rough handling of lateral bumps—which wire will. Minor collisions with jetties of which wire would cheerfully take the shock, might put an unfair kink into a rod!

Off and on, people try stream-line rod rigging which is to be had to standard specification for yacht or airplane purposes. Now a sail boat can go almost anywhere, but one thing she cannot do is to travel head to wind. So it does seem to me that, with its high cost, stream-line rigging has not much of a future. I wrote the above for the first edition and now bring the picture up to date.

The tendency to vibration fatigue is very much greater in stream-lined or flattened oval (lenticular) sections than in round sections. This high resonance vibration is produced by the wind, and becomes serious in long lengths such as preventer backstays—where failure has occured at moorings, that is to say before sailing stresses have been added —with certain types of stainless steel. With shorter lengths of shrouds in two cross-tree rigs this risk is probably acceptable.

This type of vibration is not produced in round rod; and carbon steel, even of high U.T.S. is probably less prone to failure, though difficult to keep clean, and often marks the sails, even when protected or plated.

Particularly close-winded yachts (where the apparent wind can be $25°$ on the bow) will benefit from lenticular rigging, resistance wise. As designers we have used this in several recent special yachts, including the Class I *Oryx*.

It is, however, most important to realise that the use of rod rigging puts appreciably higher loading on many parts of the rig; compared to wire standing rigging, which has more temporary give, or spring. Parts which should be considered initially in design (and subsequently watched) include the under deck mast pillar and flanges, and its liaison with the general structure at the foot of the pillar, and the spreading of the extra compressive load in question. Then and very particularly, the mast steel work, which can suffer not only from the extra compressive load, but sometimes seriously from fatigue engendered by extra vibration. Also the chain plates (shroud plates) and stay plates must be reconsidered. The plates themselves are probably strong enough, but their attachment to the hull, again properly to spread load, needs watching. If of good mild steel they won't suffer from vibration fatigue, but, as in the case of mast fittings, certain qualities of stainless steel are less resistant to fatigue.

Incidentally, after working, after the Second War, for two years in and about Sheffield, largely on shipbuilding, but partly on steel production, I became very doubtful of the reliability of the classic fatigue testing procedure, based on the total number of stress reversals plus of course the loading factors. A few labs were paying attention to the rate of application of the reversals, but very few were equipped to carry out high resonance tests. Since then certain aircraft fuselage failures have altered things in that industry, but the results of their work have not yet fully permeated other spheres of endeavour.

One case where fatigue testing let us down was in the use of Titanium. I went very carefully into the fatigue question, as far as the testing equipment allowed, and the results were quite satisfactory. I attributed failures aloft in three important vessels —one does not use it in other yachts on account of its very great cost—to vibration caused by Terylene sail flutter.

In gale conditions this flutter can produce vibrations in the rig which are terrifying to experience, and have to be borne over long periods; by the technically minded anyway. Recent improvements in weaving and putting together of Terylene or Dacron sails have reduced the tendency. But at times it still occurs and the most careful tending of leech line and sheet won't always cure it. I am sure that many otherwise unexplained mast fitting failures have in large part been due to this. Palliatives are dealt with in the sail design sections.

Good rod rigging is available in the U.K. from South Coast Rod Rigging, 47 Stein Road, Southbourne, Emsworth, Hants. In the U.S.A. from the Macwhyte Company, Kenosha, Wisconsin; or from, more recently, the Nautical Development Company, Port Washington, N.Y.

Stainless Rigging. Stainless steel is in general an alloy of steel with chromium. The latter constituent is expensive, and the cost of the completed wire is around 75 per cent more than plough steel rigging wire. The strengths of stainless steel wire rope standing rigging of various weights, can conveniently be compared with that of plough steel wire, by reference to the tables in Appendix II. It is about equal to the special plough and a little more than normal plough steel wire. The combination of stainless steel rigging with swaged ends is generally accepted as being superior to other arrangements.

In place of splicing, a steel eye is provided with a short cylindrical shank which is cold worked on to the wire, in a way which grips the end of the wire for keeps.

Another system, which has Admiralty approval for standing rigging, is the 'Talurit' where the wire is clamped by a sleeve after being passed round a thimble. This has been used in yachts under my care for four or more seasons with success. It is much more easily applied by a yard than swaged ends. Care must be taken to use the later type of sleeves to avoid corrosion deterioration sometimes experienced. I prefer not to use this system for running rigging in yachts.

In America it is the practice during each fit-out, after polishing the swaged terminals to examine them most minutely for hair cracks, which are found to be the forerunners of failure.

From an owner's point of view, apart from the increased wire cost, the snag is that exact lengths have to be ordered from the works which specialise in the process of swaging-on the ends, which results in delay and further increased cost compared to splicing. There is also the risk that the measured length may turn out to be a little wrong. The normal practice with spliced rigging is to splice and fix the top end of the shroud or stay and leave the bottom end 'open' until the shroud is set up in its place by a temporary purchase. Stainless in larger sizes is difficult, and sometimes unreliable, when spliced.

Before ordering swaged-up rigging the rigging-plan should be drawn out to a large scale—say $\frac{3}{4}$ in. to the foot at least—an inch to the foot is better. If it is an old yacht being re-rigged, the mast and the hull should be re-measured. When we were re-rigging the Royal sailing yacht *Bloodhound* in 1962 we found that the stemhead was higher than the existing plans showed; the year before *Ortac*'s sail plan had proved to be quite approximate. Undoubtedly some hulls change in shape through the years; most generally the sheer forward increases. I normally order swaged rigging 2 in. short and if necessary insert an extra toggle between the rigging-screw and the shroud or stay.

A further alternative to the swaged terminal is one of the several systems in which the strands are splayed out beyond the terminal and secured by running in solder. This work can be done locally in the yard, but one of the dangers is that when heating up the terminal with the wire in place the temperature is allowed to rise too high and the temper of the wire strands is affected. It is probably quite safe if the rigger-turned-coppersmith is careful and in practice, but I have seen some fair circuses as a result of doing the job on board with a portable forge in the breeze.

One of the neatest of the splayed wire systems is that of Moteurs Goiot at Nantes, whose terminal is integrated at its lower end with the bottlescrew.

Having said all this, I have to confess that I normally use in my own personal yachts, galvanised standing rigging; on account of the low cost and reliability. Generally 7×7 plough, preformed wire.

LAYOUT OF MIZZEN MAST RIGGING
Mizzen mast design proceeds on exactly the same lines as for main masts, with minor exceptions. Firstly, there is no requirement for extra short crosstrees, so have your shrouds come off at 15 or 16 degrees. Secondly, arrange either a triatic stay

between mastheads of sufficient fore and aft section, or a centre-line jumper strut, to enable the mizzen to be well hardened on the wind, for there will as a rule be no forestay. When a jumper stay is fitted, light twin lower shrouds and a cross-tree from the point where the strut is positioned, makes a good layout, together with the usual topmast shroud. The triatic stay—a light one for non-

masthead rigs—can also run as an aerial. The triatic stay with insulators makes a good wireless aerial, if you have not got one up the centre of a wooden mainmast, or under the wood mast track.

For ocean racing purposes the mizzen mast should be designed primarily to stand the mizzen staysail loading, which will be greater than that

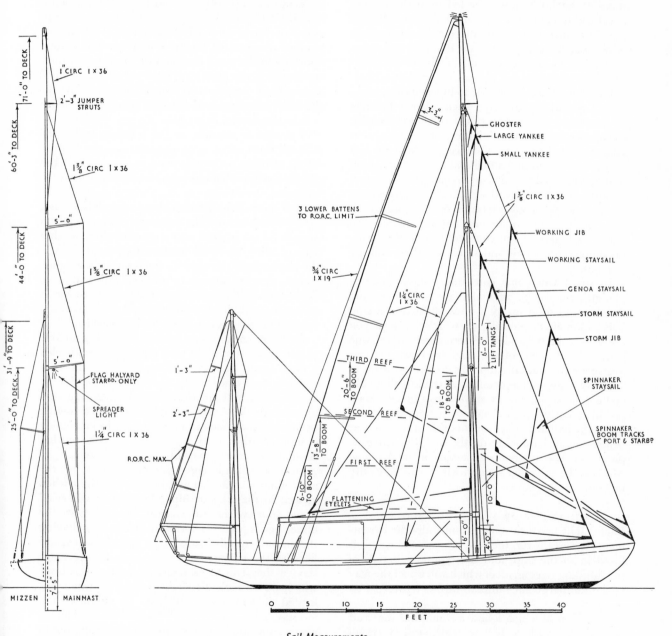

Sail Measurements

Fore triangle, 630·5 sq. ft., Mainsail 812 sq. ft., Mizzen 136 sq. ft. Total measured area, 1,578 sq. ft.
I = 60 ft. J = 21 ft. B = 25 ft. P = 65 ft. B miz = 9·8 ft. P miz = 27·75 ft.

Diagram 32.—*Bloodhound* standing rigging and sail plan as modified in 1962 for Her Majesty and the Duke of Edinburgh by Illingworth and Primrose imposed by the mizzen sail itself. The requirements will be similar to those for a masthead jib, *viz.* to carry the section of the mast well up, and have the top panel almost as good a strut as the lower ones. The loading will of course not be directly comparable with a similar-sized mainmast, as the sail will not be carried hard on the wind.

Mizzen Backstays. Whenever convenient a light standing backstay should be led from the mizzen masthead to the counter, or more likely to a bumpkin. But since one places the mizzen well aft in order to get its wind clear of the mainsail and to get a useful-sized mizzen staysail, this is not generally feasible.

Unless you have been able to fit a standing backstay, I would in any large yacht always arrange for very light mizzen preventers, solely for use with the mizzen staysail; that is if it is going to be used at all seriously. These can, if desired, be kept up and down the mast until wanted and then set up round snatch sheaves by a tiny lever on the counter. A 'croquet hoop' lever will serve for both preventers in turn, working athwartships of the counter. If this does not suit the layout, one can have small levers each side of the counter, or one can draw preventers up along slides, or set them up by purchases.

In small yawls one can simply have a single plough wire of $\frac{1}{2}$ in. circumference ending in a big thimble and set it up by a stout lanyard to a ring bolt as far aft as possible, on whichever tack you are on, on the centre-line. Alternatively where one can reach the end of the mizzen boom one can unshackle the standing topping lift and set it up to a handy billy on the counter. Alternatively again one can hoist the mizzen staysail two blocks—as a reaching sail no head clearance is necessary—and set up the halyard to the weather side of the counter before finally hardening on the tack by winch or purchase. This method was successful in *Mouse of Malham*. The weather staysail winch can generally be used.

ADJUSTMENT OF STANDING RIGGING

Each yacht needs to some extent individual treatment; to suit the rig, the type of mast, the way it is fitted in to the ship, and the type and details of the standing rigging, all of which will affect the way which the particular sail plan throws its weight on to the spars.

The remarks which follow assume that the craft is equipped with a hollow mast, and a rig of strength up to the jib and arranged in accordance with normal modern standards and practice. It should be realised that unusual arrangements of cross-trees and rigging, or spars which fall short of the ideal in strength, may well call for other, and special treatment.

The primary requirement is that, when the ship is well heeled hard on the wind, the mast should stand quite straight—or at least with the minimum of curves—between the deck and the highest point to which headsails are set. Other requirements must be subordinated to this.

To this end it will be found in a cutter, which is the difficult case (or equally with a two headsail yawl or ketch) that lying at rest with no sail set shrouds require tensioning as follows. The shroud running to the point to which the jib is set requires to be much the tautest. We assume that the rig is normally arranged, with two cross-trees below the jib head, the upper of the two being at the point where the staysail hoists to.

The shroud running to the point to which the staysail is set needs to be the next tautest. Neither of the two lower shrouds need to be very taut but the forward one should have more weight than the after one.

It is most desirable that the jib shrouds should, when lying at rest in harbour, have sufficient weight on them, port and starboard sides, so that when sailing at small angles of heel no slack is developed in the lee shroud. Such slack should only start to develop around 15° of heel. This will mean fairly high initial topmost shroud tensions, but it will not result in any increase in the maximum loading of the rigging when 'fully' heeled.

In many cases where owners have been unable to get the mast straight with the yacht well heeled I have found that the proportioning of the wire weights, cross-tree lengths, shroud angles and so on are quite faulty. I am afraid that this is most generally due to the naval architect concerned having been more interested in his hull than in his rigging design. In other cases, a perfectly good layout has been altered by the yard fitting out the yacht.

In a bermudan rigged yacht, when at rest the mast mainsail track should be quite straight when viewed in the athwartships plane. (You will need to put your eye right down near the track to see the minor bends.) This is normally achieved by having the shrouds equally loaded, port and starboard, and likewise the runner backstays; and the preventer stays if they run to each quarter. The mast head will need to look aft slightly, so that when jib-loaded it will stand straight. In addition the forestay must be correctly adjusted for length, against the fore topmast stay. A spreader should bisect the angle of the shroud supported.

The backstays generally must, in the straight harbour conditions of the mast, have considerable initial tension. In the case of the preventer, if a single stay runs to the masthead to which working headsails are set, this must have an extra high initial tension.

Check Up of Adjustment Under Way. Having got things as nicely adjusted as you can, go for a sail prior to racing, in a good breeze and calm water for preference, and try her out close-hauled well heeled —that is, sailing at her best angle for a stiff breeze. This angle varies for various boats, and is, roughly, gunwale not quite awash. In this condition with full working sail set, the mast should be quite straight to the top of the jib hoist. Put your eye down to the track when she is sailing thus, on each tack in turn, and note how the mast is standing and exactly what corrections are needed to straighten it on each tack.

For instance, if it goes over more and more in a steady outboard curve to leeward as you go higher up the mast, then the upper shrouds need more initial tension.

Come in to shelter, or run down the headsails and ease the main sheet, make the adjustments and try again. Peg away at it till the mast stands quite straight when heeled.

By reducing the mast bend at the deck we shall be keeping the whole sail plan more upright than would otherwise be the case, and therefore more efficient. By keeping the mast straight we shall be enabling it to work as a better strut in compression and this will be invaluable in keeping the luffs of our headsails taut. Finally, by eliminating the bends we shall be reducing the chance of mast failure.

In yachts where the mast is stepped below deck it is undesirable to pull the mast to an unnatural angle of rake without adjusting the position of the heel, because it puts unnecessary bending stresses in a mast which will have its principal compressive stress superimposed on this.

WIRE ROPE—GENERAL INFORMATION

Wire ropes for yacht purposes both for standing and running rigs should be laid up in construction on the 'Right hand Regular' or 'Ordinary Lay' in which the strands are twisted in one direction and the completed strands are laid up in the opposite direction. The alternative Langs Lay where they are all laid up in the same direction is liable to untwist in use, and to spin the halyard block, and foul the purchase. This undesirable feature is often encountered with continental-made wire.

A fairly recent development in wire rope construction which can be applied to nearly all types of yacht wire rope is preforming of the strands. Each individual wire is in manufacture given a helix form which approximates to the shape it will have to assume when in position in the completed laid

up wire. This results in them lying naturally in position, without a tendency to fly apart when the wire is opened. Many advantages are claimed for this system, including balanced loading on each strand and wire, and reduced internal stress, giving a longer life. It appears also that it has less extension under load. It certainly is easier to handle, and easier to splice, and has less tendency in the case of large yachts' sheets to a kink with the resultant crippling. I have had it in use for a large part of my outfits for some years and found it quite satisfactory. A good point about it is that broken small wires of running rigging lie flat on the rope.

All wire rope requires, of course, to be coated with zinc or other permanent application unless it is of stainless steel wire. It is claimed that zinc coating by electrolyte deposition is superior, owing to better adhesion and a purer coating, than the normal hot galvanising, but to date I have not been able to see much difference in results.

Standing Rigging Construction. The normal construction of wire for standing rigging is 7×7, that is to say seven strands of seven wires each. It is laid up six strands closed over the seventh as a core.

Of recent years there has been a general move towards the use of bigger individual wires in the strands, and in many cases, in spite of it being almost impossible to splice, use is often made of monitoron wire of 1×19, or for the larger sizes 1×32. In general these ropes are about 15 per cent stronger than the 7×7 and the amount of extension for a given length is reduced. Up to $1\frac{1}{4}$ in. circumference ropes go up by steps of one-eighth, or about 1 mm. in diameter. Thus it is generally feasible to use one size less with monitoron construction.

But remember three things when choosing standing rigging sizes. Firstly that quite apart from needing wire which won't fracture we need a factor of safety which will ensure that the average load is low enough for the whole rig to keep its adjustment throughout a blowy Fastnet. Secondly that a considerable proportion of the wire made the world over is less than first class and that failures do occur due to the use of wire of unknown origin. Thirdly that the straightness of a headsail luff may well demand a wire diameter larger than that needed purely for safety. Details of the strength and weight of various types of rigging are shown in Appendix II.

Checking the Rig. The masts should be inspected from truck to heel, after each hard ocean race. Preferably by the same hand each time, who will recognise any abnormality. In large yachts it is an advantage for the skipper to have a small spyglass for use in checking over things from the deck. In *Creole* I carried a monocular in my pocket when racing.

17

RUNNING RIGGING

The old ships and equally, the older yachts, had a maze of running rigging—a veritable spider's web of guys, halyards, lines, and purchases, which made sailing a business to learn, and which resulted in many operations, particularly at night, being lengthy and apt to lead to trouble.

Our aim and object in laying out more modern gear is all the time to make the equipment simpler; simpler in appearance, simpler in fact, and simpler to handle. The coming of the bermudan sail has done away with the topsail and all its attendant complications. The use of winches and levers has reduced the windage and loss of manual power occasioned by much hemp and many purchases. Hand in hand with this we are reducing the displacement of yachts for a given length, so that the necessary sails are becoming smaller.

So that we can, I feel, taking all in all, justly claim to be achieving improved efficiency. For instance in *Myth* we had only two single moving blocks; and one purchase—for the kicking strap, which needs spring. This made her very simple to handle. Last year, 1968, she completed the single-handed Trans-Atlantic Race.

When we are designing our running gear I think we should apply two tests to each item. Firstly, is this bit of equipment really necessary at all? If the answer is 'Yes', we can go on to ask ourselves, 'Is the gear as simple as we can make it, consistent with full effectiveness and giving the necessary power?'

Factors for Safety. While standing rigging must be designed to stand anything and everything that can come (by having really adequate factors of safety) an occasional failure of running gear is not dangerous and we can design running rigging with lower factors of safety and get lighter gear, which is in many cases easier to work, and in all cases relieves the boat of top weight and windage.

Many cruisers have quite sensible standing gear, but altogether unreasonably heavy running gear. It is often safer and more satisfactory to have moderate-sized running gear and renew it more often. In the case of flexible steel wire rope, laid up for running rigging, the strands are so small that it is impossible adequately to coat them when galva-

nising, without making the total weight of zinc unreasonably large. Consequently, their life is always limited, apart from age embrittlement which goes hand in hand with deterioration due to lack of protection and flexing.

Stainless Wire. The safe life of stainless steel running wire rigging is generally no longer than that of best galvanised because of the tendency of stainless wire to fatigue due to constant flexion. (A clear distinction must be made here between running and standing rigging.) There is here a hidden danger because though one renews galvanised wire after a year or two when it becomes unsightly, before the end of its useful life, stainless steel wire looks fine and bright even though it may be seriously weakened and overdue for replacement.

MAIN HALYARDS

Taking the case of main halyards: the luff rope of the sail is always in hemp or terylene and this sets the maximum loading; there is no object in having a much greater strength in the halyards. For sails up to 250 sq. ft. a $\frac{1}{2}$-in. circumference wire can be used; $\frac{5}{8}$ in. to 500; $\frac{3}{4}$ in. up to 850, and $\frac{7}{8}$ in. up to 1,200 and 1 in. to 1,600 sq. ft. with $1\frac{1}{4}$ in. above.

It is important to leave a reasonable drift between the head of the sail and the centre of the sheave to reduce the wringing loading on the part of the halyard which produces most main halyard failures. I suggest 8 in. for a $\frac{1}{2}$-in. wire, 10 in. for a $\frac{5}{8}$-in. wire, 1 ft. for $\frac{3}{4}$-in. wire and 14 in. for a 1-in. wire. The 1-in. black band painted on the mast will limit the hoist and a stop should be fitted in the sail track to correspond with this point. If the mainsail headboard halyard cringle is close to the track it will reduce the wear and tear on the wire.

Main Halyard Winches. As regards the mainsail hoisting arrangements, the maximum power needed is that required to rehoist the sail after reefing in strong winds. A reel or 'magazine' winch or a winch with top-operation—that is to say, with a handle on top of the drum—is needed, or a purchase. In the case of a purchase, small sails up to 250 sq. ft. need a single block only shackled into the end of the wire; $1\frac{1}{4}$-in. hemp is led through the block.

Getting the last few inches in the halyard with any size of sail is much easier with a sliding gooseneck so that the boom can be drawn down for the last motion, after the halyard has been secured. Above this size a second purchase is advisable in the standing leg of the hemp, to get the final swig up. A single block to this second purchase up to 500 sq. ft., and a handy billy or four-fold purchase according to size, above this.

For larger sails the halyard winch is best, and it is an asset with all sizes of sail, so that one man can hoist the mainsail without busting himself. For moderate-sized sails a $1\frac{1}{4}$-in. terylene tail can be arranged, spliced into the wire so that the wire just comes on to the drum when the sail is deep-reefed. Up to 500 sq. ft. a mechanical advantage of 6 to 1 is sufficient—a 6-in. handle on a 2-in. diameter drum or a $7\frac{1}{2}$-in. handle on a $2\frac{1}{2}$-in. drum, the length being calculated to the centre of the 'knob'. For larger sails the advantage should be increased proportionately to two-thirds of the area added. As soon as the handle gets too long, say over 12 in. on the ordinary type of winch, either a geared winch or a block should be introduced, and the winch worked on the fall of the purchase. A single block and direct winch will serve mainsails of from about 1,000 to 1,500 sq. ft. Excessive power in the winch must be avoided, or enthusiastic crew members will part your halyards.

Mainsail halyards can be accommodated complete on reel winches. These need a brake and they are in general larger, heavier, and more costly. Since the size of the drum builds up as the wire goes on, it is important to calculate your mechanical advantage allowing for this; I have sailed yachts with this arrangement where, owing to the size to which the drum builds up, one had insufficient purchase in spite of a very long handle and it was almost impossible to hoist sail after reefing in gale conditions. In general it is desirable with drum winches to introduce gearing for medium-sized and larger sails. There is always an increased risk of a jam in this type, which is more present in the case of headsails, for which use I do not favour this type.

In the equipment chapter there are details of various types of winches, and data as to the drum diameters to be used for various-sized halyard wires.

Headsail Halyards. In the case of headsail halyards there are three alternatives; tack tackles, a purchase at the mast, or the use of winches. I nowadays always use mast halyard winches, and dispense with tack tackles—it simplifies the gear on deck. One hoists the sail by hand as far as it will go, that is until it becomes too heavy, then takes three quick turns on the winch and winds her up the rest of the

way. For headsails, as mentioned earlier, I do not favour winches which wind everything on to a big drum. They are slow and heavy compared to the other method, though it is true they do stow the fall of the halyard. Also in the initial uphaul with but little weight on the halyard there is risk of getting foul turns on the drum. The steady weight of a mainsail going up gives the reel type a better chance.

It is desirable to carry a bit more of a safety margin in the headsail halyard wire than in the case of the mainsails of the same sizes. I suggest $\frac{1}{2}$-in. circumference up to 150 sq. ft. *working* headsails, $\frac{5}{8}$-in. to 350 sq. ft.; $\frac{3}{4}$-in. to 550 sq. ft.; $\frac{7}{8}$-in. to 800 sq. ft., and 1-in. to 1,100 sq. ft. and $1\frac{1}{4}$ in. over that. The steep grading up of areas from $\frac{1}{2}$ in. to $\frac{5}{8}$ in., is done purposely. In this connection I would call a working headsail one which can be carried in Force 5. If you prefer to base it on genoas to be carried only up to Force 3, add 80 per cent to the areas.

If, for very natural reasons of expense, you don't want to use halyard winches, a very good system which is simple and cheap is to have a purchase on deck; one brings the fall of the halyard, with an eye spliced in the end of the wire, to the hook of a handy billy, or a fourfold purchase, whose standing part is made fast to a ring bolt at the foot of the mast. Thus one hoists up the sail by hand till the load gets too much and then hooks on the purchase to complete the job. This obviates the necessity for a tack tackle. One has a hemp tail of about $1\frac{1}{4}$ in. bent to the wire halyard to do the hand hoisting. The wire must naturally be gauged nicely for length, and it is essential to have wire pennants at the foot and/or head of the smaller headsails, so that the halyard comes to the same position, relative to the deck, when the sail is hoisted, in all cases.

For larger yachts where mast winches are not available, a similar arrangement can be used combined with a single moving block on the fall of the halyard, the purchase being used in the standing leg of the hemp to the single block. Thus the last part of the hoist, to get the tension on the sail, is accomplished with a luff upon luff effect.

But there is no doubt that good mast winches to the headsail halyards save time and increase efficiency—up goes the sail without a pause and the halyard is hardened home directly afterwards.

The mechanical advantage recommended for mainsails will also serve for working headsails of like areas. It is undesirable to have appreciably more than this, to reduce the chance of over-tautening; the risk of carrying it away arises not at the moment of hoisting, because one cannot exert

SCHEDULE OF
MYTH OF

	ITEM		RIG		WIRE	BLOCKS	
REF.		NO. OF			CIRC.	NO.	BLOCKS L
A	B	C	D		E	F	G
B	MAIN HALYARD	1	MAST HEAD — CLEAT ON MAST — EYE PLATE AT FOOT OF MAST		$5/8"$ 51' 9"	1	
C	MAIN TACK	1	SLIDE THIMBLE — CLEAT ON MAST DECK				
D	MAIN SHEET	1					
E	MAIN OUTHAWL	1	18" THRO. BOOM — SPLICE AFTER PASSING THRO. BOOM		$1/2"$ 11'6"		
F	MAIN GUY PENANT	1	THIMBLE — THIMBLE, TH. & SHACKLE — TH. & LANYARD		$5/8"$ 11'3"	1	
G	HANDY BILLY	1					
H	REEF TACKLE (KICKING STRAP)	1					
I	REEF PENANTS	3	THIMBLE — SOFT EYE SPLICE		$1/2"$ 11' 0"	3	
K	MAIN LIFT	1	SHACKLE AT MASTHEAD (THIMBLE) — THIMBLE SPLICE AFTER FITTING TO BOOM		$1/2"$ 56'6"		
L	STAYSAIL HALYARD	1	SHACKLE TO SAIL — SPLICE AFTER PASSING THRO. BLOCK, SPECIAL BLOCK, ROPE TO WIRE SPLICE, WINCH ON MAST		$5/8"$ 38'	1	S. SH. EYE 4" SWIVEL
M	STAYSAIL TACK	2	ON SAIL, DECKLEAD $3/4"$ CLEAR DIA.				
N	STAYSL. SHEETS { PAIR LONG / PAIR SHORT }	1 / 2	THIMBLE IN EACH SHEET — ROPE WIRE SPLICES		$1/2"$ 10' 15' SHORT LONG PAIR PAIR		
P	FLAG HALYARD	1					
Q	JIB TACKS	2	WITH SAILS				
R	2ND. JIB SHEETS	2 PR.	THIMBLE IN EACH SHEET — ROPE WIRE SPLICES		$1/2"$ 41'		
S	JIB HALYARD	1	THIMBLE SPLICED AFTER PASSING SHEAVE — ROPE WIRE SPLICE, MASTHEAD SIDE SHEAVE		$3/4"$ 56'		
T	LIGHT GENOA SHEETS	1 / 1					
U	C.C.A. GENOA SHEETS	1 / 2 PR.	& SINGLE — LEAD SHS. PSS.				
V	SHEETS YANKEES	2 PR.	AS ABOVE BUT WITH WIRE SPLICED TO ROPE		$5/8"$ 35'		
W	SPKR. HALYARD	1	SPLICE WIRE TO ROPE, MASTHEAD		$5/8"$ 52'		
X	LOWER HALYARD (NOT USED IN 1948)	1	UPPER CROSS TREE — SPLICE WIRE TO ROPE		$5/8"$ 34'		
Y	GUYS FORWARD	2					
Z	GUYS AFT	2	LEAD SHEAVES P. & S.				
1	OUTHAWL	1	BOOM END				
2	SPKR. SHEET	2	SPRING SHACKLE				
3	SPKR. LIFT	1	LOWER CROSSTREES		$3/8"$ 34'	1	3"
4	RUNNER TACKLES (SEE STANDING RIGGING)				$1 1/8"$ (STANDING RIGGING)		
5	FORESAY TACKLE		DECK — LEAVE FOR SPLICING IN PLACE WITH SPARE 1FT. OF WIRE — THIMBLE		$1 1/4"$ 9'9'		

Note.—Jib halyards subsequently altered to $\frac{5}{8}$-in. diam.

RUNNING RIGGING
MALHAM

& SHEAVES WIRE		ROPE	BLOCKS & SHEAVES TO ROPE				SHACKLES			OTHER FITTINGS
SHEAVES D	TYPE	CIRC.					NO.	D PINS	NO.	
H	J	K	L	M	N	O	P	Q	R	S
$3\frac{1}{2}" \times \frac{5}{16}"$	INSET IN MAST (SEE MAST IRONWK)	$1\frac{1}{4}"$ 50'0"	1	$3\frac{1}{2}"$		SWIVEL EYE	2 1	$\frac{5}{16}"$ $\frac{1}{4}"$	1 1 1	7" CLEAT ON MAST EYEPLATE
		$1\frac{1}{4}"$ 6'0"				TH. EYE	1	$\frac{5}{16}"$	1	7" CLEAT ON MAST SLIDING GOOSENECK FITTING
		$52'^{6}$ $1\frac{1}{2}"$	1 1 2	4' 4' 4'		S.OVAL EYE TO BOLT S.OVAL & BKT. S.SH.EYE(BRONZE)	2	$\frac{5}{16}"$ $\frac{3}{8}"$	1 1	SHEET WINCH & 7" CLEAT FAIRLEAD ON BOOM HORSE & SLIDE
	INSET IN BOOM (SEE SPAR PLAN)	1" 15'		$2\frac{1}{2}"$	$1\frac{1}{2}"$	S.SH.EYE & BKT. SH. CAVE CLEAT (7)	2	$\frac{3}{16}"$	1	FAIRLEAD ON BOOM
							1	$\frac{5}{16}"$	1	EYE PLATE ON BOOM TACKLE (SEE SPKR. F. GUY)
		$1\frac{1}{4}"$ 24'	1 1	$3\frac{1}{2}"$ $3\frac{1}{2}"$		S. HOOK ON BKT. S. SH. EYE				
		$1\frac{1}{4}"$ 25'0"	1	$3\frac{1}{2}"$	2"	SHACKLE SHEAVE CLEAT } 2 BRASS BLOCKS S. SH. EYE		$\frac{5}{16}"$	1 1	RING BOLT ON MAST EYE PLATE ON BOOM 6" CLEAT
$2" \times \frac{3}{8}"$	ON BOOM						3	$\frac{1}{4}"$	3	EYEBOLT SHEAVES (SEE 6)
	INSET IN BOOM (SEE SPAR PLAN)	1" 19'	1 1	$\frac{5}{8}"$	$1\frac{1}{2}"$	BULLS EYE & BKTS. SHEAVE CLEAT (7)				SHEAVE CLEAT ONE 7"
		$1\frac{1}{4}"$ 35'					1	$\frac{5}{16}"$	1	WINCH 7" CLEAT ON MAST
							2	$\frac{5}{16}"$ SPRING	1	DECK FITTING
2"	$2\frac{1}{2}" \times \frac{3}{4}"$ SET-IN RAILS	$1\frac{1}{2}"$ 36'10"					2	$\frac{5}{16}"$ HARP	2 4 2	SHEET WINCHES HOOD FAIRLEADS S. CLEATS
		1 RND. LINE 98'				$\frac{3}{8}"$ BULL'S EYE				4" CLEAT ON MAST
							2	$\frac{3}{8}"$ SPRING		DECK FITTINGS
		$1\frac{1}{2}"$ 14' EACH LEG					2	$\frac{5}{16}"$ HARP	2 4 2 2	SHEET WINCHES HOOD FAIRLEADS (DECK) HOOD FAIRLEADS (TRACK) 8" CLEATS
	SIDE SHOW ON MAST (SEE MAST IRONWK.)	$1\frac{1}{4}"$ 51'					1	$\frac{3}{8}"$	1	WINCHES 7" CLEAT
		$1\frac{1}{8}" \times 45"$ } $\frac{3}{4}" \times 45"$ }	SINGLE SHEETS BENT ON AS REQUIRED							AS FOR JIB
$3\frac{1}{2}" \times \frac{5}{8}"$	G.M.S. SNATCH LEADS SEE (L)	65'-$1\frac{1}{2}"$ (NORMAL) EACH LEG 65'-$\frac{3}{4}"$ (LIGHT) ONE LEG $1\frac{1}{2}"$ 20' EACH LEG				MERRIMAN SELF LOCKING SNATCH BLOCKS	1	$\frac{5}{16}"$ HARP $\frac{5}{16}"$ HARP	2	WINCHES (AS JIB ABOVE) CLEATS HOOD FAIRLEADS (TRACK) LEAD BLOCKS (SEE O)
$3\frac{1}{2}" \times \frac{5}{16}"$	SET-IN MASTHD. (SEE MAST IRONWORK)	$1\frac{1}{4}"$ 50'					1	$\frac{5}{16}"$ SNAP	1	7" CLEAT
		$1\frac{1}{4}"$ 38'	1	4		SINGLE SH. EYE	1 2	$\frac{5}{16}"$ SNAP	1	7" CLEAT
		$1\frac{1}{2}"$ 39'			$2" \times \frac{3}{4}"$	FAIRLEAD SHEAVES IN RAIL AT BOW	2	$\frac{5}{16}"$ SNAP	2	8" CLEATS
		$1\frac{3}{4}"$ 52'				AS FOR YANKEES		$\frac{5}{16}"$ SNAP		
		$1\frac{1}{2}"$ 35'			$2" \times \frac{5}{8}"$	SET-IN SPKR.BOOM (SEE SPAR PLAN)	1		1	7" CLEAT ON BOOM
		$1\frac{1}{2}$-38' 1"-38'								
	SINGLE SHACKLE EYE	1" 7'					1	$\frac{1}{4}"$ SNAP	1	6" CLEAT
$4" \times \frac{1}{2}"$	DECK SHEAVES ($\frac{1}{2}"$ MIN. BRG.)						2	$\frac{1}{2}"$	2	RUNNER LEVERS ($\frac{1}{2}"$ PINS)
$4" \times \frac{1}{2}"$	FITTED UNDER FORECASTLE SOLE ($\frac{1}{2}"$ BEARING)						1	$\frac{1}{12}"$	1	SPECIAL LEVER ($\frac{1}{2}"$ PINS)

Diagram 33.

that much load, but later when the halyard may be taking on work which should properly be done by the stay.

Spinnaker Halyards. Standard practice is to have a steel wire halyard, double-ended with a shackle or snap shackle. Fore triangles of up to 350 sq. ft. can have $1\frac{1}{2}$-in.; up to 550 sq. ft., $1\frac{3}{4}$-in.; up to 800 sq. ft., $\frac{7}{8}$-in., and one inch above.

If you want a double-ended halyard, for offshore racing where the spinnaker may be set for 12 hrs. or more, I would recommend short wire tails, 3, 4, or 5 ft. long, according to the size of boat, carefully long-spliced into each end of the halyard, with the block suitably wide to pass the splice. The chafe in way of the block, with the rolling of the ship and the spinnaker swinging across the sky, pulling to and fro across a wide arc at each roll, will certainly be considerable, and the wire should take care of this. The wire can be half the hemp in circumference.

Personally, I nowadays generally use spinnaker halyards internal to the mast; one hemp leg and one wire one—a single-ended halyard—to reduce size and windage. The purpose of the hemp is only to haul it up; once up the wire is brought to a winch or to the cleat on the mast. So the hemp can be smaller; $1\frac{1}{4}$ in., $1\frac{1}{2}$ in., and $1\frac{3}{4}$ in. for all larger sizes if you are going to hoist by hand. Wire half size.

With fore triangles above 500 sq. ft., a fairly big diameter winch with a top-operated handle or gearing is a good alternative, in which case you can have an all-wire halyard and save further windage In fast yachts which draw the apparent wind ahead, spinnakers are on the average set perhaps 20 per cent of the total racing time, maybe less. So windage during the remaining 80 per cent of the time must be considered.

SPINNAKER GUYS AND SHEETS

Single after spinnaker guys require to be 110 per cent of the length of the ship, including the bowsprit, plus a length to bring them from the counter-block to the winch, with a fathom for turns and backing up added to that.

In larger yachts the wire guy with a terylene tail will be preferred to limit the stretch and enable a shy pole to be accurately adjusted. In all cases the after guy must be handled by a good winch. Normally a winch sufficient easily to sheet the largest headsail will suffice. In the yachts with a triangle of 400 sq. ft. or more it will almost invariably be a geared winch. Where an all-terylene guy is used this should preferably be plaited, again to reduce stretch and also increase the strength for a given diameter. Inability to splice most types of plaited rope should be accepted. Nylon rope is unsuitable

for after guys but is all right for fore guys and pole-lifts, where spring is an advantage.

The big strains here come when the spinnaker boom is shy—nearly right forward—in fresh conditions. The whole gear should be duplicated for quick gybing.

Most larger yachts now use snap shackles at each clew, a wire guy with a terylene tail and a separate sheet in terylene. Naturally on the lee side all this is removed and replaced by a light sheet for light weather.

Sheets and fore guys, and, if fitted, the outhaul on the spinnaker boom can be $\frac{1}{4}$ in. less than the after guy. But if the sheet is intended to serve as an after guy after gybing, it must be the same in all respects. In this case in light weather a complete light pair should be used, since it is important to relieve the spinnaker clew of unnecessary weight; or directly after gybing a light sheet should be substituted and used until just before regybing.

The foreguys, port and starboard, are in length normally twice the base of the fore triangle plus one fathom; or longer if they are to be handled from the cockpit. I keep both port and starboard fore guys always rigged both sides at sea, since the main boom often needs the services of one of them. For this purpose the main boom generally carries a wire pendant, half the diameter of the hemp, just shorter than boom length, under the boom. In larger yachts I provide long cleats for stowing the fore guys just forward of the mast near the rail. In smaller yachts I bring the fore guys to the cockpit, often to a jamming cleat; with a fixed cleat abaft it.

The guys and spinnaker sheet and spinnaker halyard—and the two spinnaker pole lifts—port and starboard for two pole gybes, may be furnished with snap shackles. The best type having the spring-loaded bolt inclined so as to assist in restraining the swinging arm from straining off. The earlier ones have the bolt at right angles. Snap shackles by Lewmar in Superston bronze are stronger than most: say 1 and 2 ton.

The method of using the spinnaker gear is fully covered in Chapter 14. The spinnaker boom lift consists of a light wire with a hemp tail spliced in, passing through a small block at the lower cross-tree. A $\frac{3}{8}$-in. wire will do for a 15-ft. boom and a $\frac{1}{2}$-in. for longer lengths. The modern two-pole system is dealt with in Chapter 14.

Headsail Sheets. Generally, the sheets are all of terylene, or of wire with terylene tails. This flexible steel wire rope goes direct to the winch, into a hemp tail of about twice the circumference of the wire, with a maximum of $1\frac{1}{4}$ in. The tail is added for convenience in handling hemp rather than wire. The length is calculated so that the necessary turns and a margin of 1 or 2 ft. come on the drum; close-hauled.

The size of wire rope sheets necessary for various sizes of working sails are as follows (if you choose to base the size on medium wind Force 3 genoas you can increase the areas by 80 per cent):

Up to 250 sq. ft. $= \frac{1}{2}$ in.; 500 sq. ft. $= \frac{5}{8}$ in.; 800 sq. ft. $= \frac{3}{4}$ in.; 1,100 sq. ft. $= \frac{7}{8}$ in.; over 1,100 sq. ft. $= 1$ in.

The reason for the steep grade of the increase in area in the smaller sizes is that in practice the $\frac{1}{2}$-in. wire galvanising deteriorates more rapidly and the strength falls off directly afterwards, owing to the heavy duty combined with the thinness of the coating which is all that can be given to those tiny strands. For all terylene, double the diameters; with a $1\frac{1}{8}$ in. minimum.

For a given strength clearly wire rope has less windage and for high-clewed sails may be preferred even in small racers. For genoa-type sails, where clews are low, all terylene is best. Plaited terylene lasts longer and generally stretches less and the difficulty of attaching the sheet may be accepted, because two bowlines on the clew make quite a decent system. (Some American plaited rope can be spliced.)

SHEETS AND SHEETING ARRANGEMENTS

Winches are universally used nowadays for sheeting headsails because they enable single part sheets to be used, and these are of value in getting the weather sheet to overhaul when putting about —specially important where there is a big overlap. In the case of a cutter's yankee, whose clew normally comes at least to the main shrouds, there will be an overlap of more than 100 per cent on the forestay. The same may apply when racing under C.C.A. rules in a sloop with a big overlapping genoa. Single part wire sheets slide around the stays and shrouds more easily, and when set they have less windage than equivalent hemp or terylene.

Sheet Stowages. If in larger yachts you use wire sheets, for the best results sheets must be individual to the sail, or at least only applied to those sails whose clews come roughly to the same position when the sail is close-hauled. Otherwise the wire will not come to the winch barrel, or too much wire will come off the winch and one will be handling a lot of wire.

Therefore there will be several pairs of sheets to stow. They will all look alike in the locker, and you will be wanting to find 'new' sheets each time you change a headsail. It is therefore imperative that every sheet should have its own clearly marked stowage position. I normally have the names painted in bold black letters over the top of each

lanyard on which the sheets are hung: YANKEE SHEETS; 2ND JIB SHEETS; 3RD JIB SHEETS; 1ST STAY-SAIL SHEET; 2ND STAYSAIL SHEET—and so on.

I like reef lacings and reefing tackles to be similarly tallied; unless you use your reefing tackle as a kicking strap tackle, which is quite good drill, if you have boom gallows (not otherwise). In this case it will be normally stowed on deck.

If you have space, similar tallies can with advantage be used for the spinnaker guys and other important or frequently used gear.

Light-weather Sheets. For very light-weather sailing for light sails special light terylene sheets are needed to relieve the sail of the weight of the sheet; $\frac{3}{4}$ in. up to 300 sq. ft.; 1 in. up to 500 sq. ft.; $1\frac{1}{8}$ in. up to 800 sq. ft., and $1\frac{1}{4}$ in. above. The sizes are set by the inability to handle thinner lines. In any case a light sheet is a safeguard against carrying the sail too long when the breeze freshens! Single sheets are often used and passed around when one goes about.

The Power of Sheet Winches. The mechanical advantage of sheet winches should be much greater than that of halyard winches. As the size of the sheets is less, this appears paradoxical, but it is accounted for partly by the necessity for a higher factor of safety in the halyard, where failure is more serious, and partly by the fact that the halyard is set up before the sail is fully sheeted and full of wind, that is to say, before the halyard is fully loaded, whereas the sheet winch must be capable of hardening in the sail at its full tension. The detailed formula for calculating the mechanical advantage required for the sheet winch of any particular sail is given in the section dealing with winches.

TYPES OF SHEET FAIRLEAD

The position of the headsail sheet lead is very important and is fully discussed in the chapter on sail trimming. It is worth while to consider for a moment the type of sheet fairlead to be used. Clearly the block with the correct size of sheave furnishes the kindest lead. However, in larger yachts, the necessity to pass the splice, between the wire and the hemp tail, through the block, results in this being pretty large and clumsy. Moreover, the lead needs frequently to alter in direction or plane of pull, according to which sail is in use, and because the block is shifted by means of a track, or otherwise, to suit conditions; as required for work close-hauled or for a reach. So the block must have considerable freedom of movement, and unless a special rig is used, is liable to fall about when the weight comes off a sheet and to cause noise and bruising. The special rigs used consist at their best of a spherical joint below the sheave, permitting universal movement, but not allowing the block to fall to the horizontal. A simpler variation where the sheave is hinged to swing in one plane often gives insufficient freedom to get fair alignment. A further scheme is to fit rubber pads to the cheeks of the ordinary block to reduce the clatter, and to shackle it in such a way that it can line itself up. Another very good and simple system is to hang the block on the lifeline by shock cord, perferably attached to the becket or crown of the block.

But on account of the size and weight and clumsiness of these arrangements in some cases it is considered preferable to use brass, bronze, or gunmetal leads without sheaves, known in England as 'Bonnets'; after the style of Kate Greenaway. It is clearly necessary to use for this and similar fittings a good quality bronze, as the loading is high, and these are discussed in Chapter 20, under the section on non-ferrous metals. Wherever possible, tracks should be used for mounting sheet leads, giving an 'infinite' variety of sheeting position. In all but the heaviest weather this enables the adjustment in position to be made directly without reeving the sheet afresh.

A cheaper system which is satisfactory and involves less maintenance than tracks is to fit a line of eye-bolts in the deck. A good deal depends on the beam and construction of the boat; and on the depth of one's pocket.

Tracks for Sheet Leads. Light alloy tracks made for use on masts and booms can also be used for sliding sheet leads. These are about one size larger than those recommended for a main sail luff. These are shown in detail under the section dealing with mast tracks. Four sizes of track are made and I suggest the following for headsail sheet leads, the sizes being working headsails which can just be carried in Force 5 breeze.

Small Track (Code Y3) sails
    area up to   100 sq. ft.
Normal Track (Code Y1) sails
    area up to   250 sq. ft.
Reinforced Track (Code Y2)
    sails area up to   400 sq. ft.
Heavy Track Side Fastened
    (Code Y2A) sails over   400 sq. ft.

Here again, when it is a genoa which can only be carried in Force 3 winds, one can increase the sail sizes allowable by 80 per cent. The tracks ordered for headsail sheets should be specified:

'With milled out gaps (*e.g.* to $\frac{5}{8}$ in. for Y1 and Y2 and Y2A); drilled for close fastenings; and drilled to suit the slider plunger.'

Fastenings should be close if the track is to develop its full strength. Intervals may depend on the construction of the yacht. For Y1, Y2, and Y3 the ideal is to have a through fastening every 4 in.

and a screw between. The fastenings should certainly not be farther apart than 3 in. The bolts and screws will have countersunk heads and must be in steel; not in brass which is strongly anodic to aluminium alloys. Stainless or galvanised steel fastenings are best; dip them in varnish before driving them into place. The sheet lead on the gunwale should be just as far outboard as you can get it, and canted a bit outboard too for preference.

The plunger holes will be drilled at intervals to suit the fastenings; probably $\frac{3}{8}$ in. or $\frac{7}{16}$ in. in diameter at 3- or 4-in. centres for small class and 5- or 6-in. centres for larger yachts. The holes should be $\frac{1}{2}$ in. deep—running down into the rail or pad on which the track is set, so that the plunger ends can have a nice radius and pass through into the plain portion to take the load. The extra depth also makes cleaning out a less frequent necessity.

Whoever is putting down these tracks must be warned that the metal is soft, and the edges once burred are very awkward to rectify in place. The heavy track Y2A, is normally supplied to suit a curved spar or pad face. With fastenings going in 'at an angle' even screws hold well.

Sliding Sheet Leads. The sliders carrying the lead or block must be of a good length to distribute the loading, say from 5 to 8 in. according to the size of the yacht. They should have aluminium alloy bodies; bronze bodies seize up in aluminium tracks. The actual fairleads should be in bronze or monel or stainless steel, insulated by hard fibre or plastic washers, or paint from the aluminium alloy. The aluminium will not stand up well as an actual lead to the sheet wire chafe. If it is necessary to have aluminium leads these should be in silicon aluminium alloy chill-cast, to harden them; this will put up the Brinell hardness by forty points odd.

The fairleads should be attached to the slider by galvanised steel plungers. Should one have to use bronze sliders, interaction with the track is likely, and they must be moved daily and when not in use, and stored separately in harbour.

As an alternative to the aluminium alloy tracks (which are lightest and cheapest) Messrs. M. S. Gibb of Warsash, near Southampton, and also Messrs. Lewmar Marine of Emsworth, Hampshire, both supply a good range of stainless steel tracks, of three sections and various lengths; with the added convenience that they can also supply, in each case, the sliders for the blocks, fitted with plungers or thumb screws. Lewmars supply a special slider for large yachts with a non tumble sheave which brings the lead close to the track and enables a genoa clew to come down close to the deck.

Other Ways of Adjusting Lead Position. If one does not have sheet lead sliders and tracks, then one must provide either a number of fixed leads at intervals, or sockets into which they can be screwed—or alternatively a series of ring bolts or pad eyes, at intervals, to which blocks can be fixed.

If you find yourself faced with a boat not fitted with multi-leads and with insufficient time to arrange these things, a good cheap alternative is to have a series of short wire strops of differing lengths, 6 in., 1 ft., 18 in., and 2 ft. perhaps, so that one can raise the block off the deck to get nearly the same effect as moving the lead aft. In light weather it leads to a good deal of banging about, and it may, unfortunately, drag the lead rather inboard, but it is better than having a wrong sheeting line.

The smaller J.O.G. ocean-racing sloops can have a series of special faired holes in their specially secured hardwood rails, like freeing ports, every 10 in., and use terylene sheets. With scrubbed teak rails this is cheap and effective.

Fore and After Guy Leads. While we are on the subject of deck leads we may deal with the guys. The pull of the fore guy will vary from being below the horizontal when on the main boom to nearly vertical when the spinnaker boom is really shy, that is to say well eased off, on or near the forestay. This must be borne in mind when arranging the lead, and is why bull's-eyes in hardwood in the rail are perhaps the best leads in small boats. In larger vessels a block can be shackled to a ring bolt on each bow. When the foremost stay on which sail is set is inboard, the leads should be abreast these. Otherwise they should be as far forward as can conveniently be arranged. The pulpit (guard rail round the bow) must be strong enough to stand some athwartship loading from the fore guy. A fore guy winch, or capstan, is needed on large yachts.

With modern spinnakers, whose pull is now more, great trouble must be taken to make the fitting on the quarter man enough to take the loading of the after guy. If sheaves are fitted in the rail they must have their axis inclined aft; the angle depending on the yacht's length relative to 'J' (base of triangle). If swivel blocks are used they must be 50 per cent stronger than your chandler recommends. And in any case blocks constrained or guided to prevent, at night, the block falling over and getting a foul lead; and almost certainly splitting sooner or later. The after guys will also serve nicely as trysail sheets, very possibly through the same quarter blocks. Each guy carries a thimble at its outboard end, and a shackle or snap shackle.

Unless you have powerful winches, with fore triangles above 600 sq. ft., a wire pendant carrying a single sheave block at its after end is generally shackled to the pole, which requires an additional

pad eye or ringbolt on the quarter for the standing end of the hemp.

With cutter rigs it is nearly always possible to use the same winch or winches for the jib and yankee sheets and the spinnaker after guy and sheet. In *Monk of Malham* (30-ft. waterline) we have a successful arrangement of one single centre line winch placed abaft the after cockpit; which is abaft the tiller. This is a Gibb type 10 c.r.; winch details in the General Equipment, chapter 22. A single winch saves weight, windage, deck clutter, and about £100 in a yacht of this size. This winch handles the after guy as well as the yankee. We have two small geared Lewmar or Gibb 6 c.r. winches for the two staysail sheets. These handle the spinnaker sheet as well, which of course has much less load on it than the guy.

Many yachts are not easily arranged for a single centre line winch and a minimum of two fully adequate winches must be provided for a sloop; four for a cutter. Class I and above sloops generally opt for four good geared winches, because for a moment when setting the spinnaker the genoa will also be in place; in smaller yachts when reaching the genoa sheet can be shifted 'by hand' on to a cleat.

STAINLESS RUNNING RIGGING

The relative strengths of stainless steel flexible wire over good quality galvanised wire can be seen in Appendix II. Stainless is a little stronger, and cost aside, it is preferred. As a material for wire it can only provide protection against corrosion, and not against fatigue failure except to the extent that this is associated with corrosion. The ordinary galvanised wire running rigging is generally discarded on account of its appearance before it has got completely tired out, but no such safeguard exists in the case of stainless wire. So although for standing rigging stainless will stand for ten seasons at least and is therefore an economy, stainless running rigging must be renewed after two good seasons' wear, and perhaps after one if it has been a specially long hard one, so that there is not so much to gain over the galvanised flexible wire, which has nearly the same strength, from the hard ocean-racer's point of view. On the other hand, if you are cruising quietly, short seasons with not many hours' hard sailing each year, the ability to resist corrosion is of more importance.

The details of runner backstays are dealt with in Chapter 16 on standing rigging, since they are in effect part of the mast rigging rather than running gear.

Details of the levers and the drawings of various types showing their method of operation, are given in Chapter 18.

CORDAGE

The cruising yachtsman is interested, as far as his running rigging and rope are concerned, primarily with durability and low initial cost. The inshore racing man is concerned much less with durability and endurance, but more with reduction of weight and windage, and with the functional efficiency characteristics.

For offshore racing we need to combine as far as may be practicable the two sets of requirements, or at least achieve a compromise, and it is from this point of view that I propose to examine the problem. Often, in point of fact, cruising yachts' gear is descended from heavy work boat equipment and is not really very handy.

Full tables as to weights, strengths, extensions of various sorts and sizes of cordages under various conditions are given in Appendix IIA.

Soft Natural Cordages. Primarily there are two types of cordage; those made from natural fibres and those whose basic thread is manufactured. Taking first the grown fibre ropes, the most sought after is the so-called Italian hemp. For yacht use this is generally lightly tarred. It is favoured on account firstly of its high strength for diameter, particularly in the smaller sizes, which means reduced windage, and because it is soft, pliable, and easily handled, being spun from slender fibres into fine yard threads. These fibres come mostly from Chile, Russia, Hungary, and Italy.

Cotton rope is also occasionally used on account of its soft pleasant nature, in smaller racing yachts, but for rigorous offshore service it has not found great favour.

The remaining groups of natural cordage are much harder and are therefore not so pleasant to use for halyard purchases and the like. The best of these is manila, produced principally in the Philippine Islands. A manila-type rope is also produced from New Zealand hemp, which is a hard fibre. In its best grade, manila is a very fine reliable rope, and for hawsers, hemp pennants, and the like, is slightly superior, weight for weight, to Italian hemp, being lighter for a given diameter. It is also in the larger sizes better wearing than the soft hemp, and as a rule appreciably cheaper. There is always to be found second-grade manila which has similar properties, but not such good strength.

Sisal. Sisal, which comes from East Africa, Java, and Mexico, makes up into a fibrous 'hairy' cordage. It has much the same strength as second-grade manila and in one respect is superior; the best quality specially treated sisal suffers less deterioration due to sharp flexion. In general it swells a lot in use, which is a bad snag, but it is a light cordage and can be used for warps, etc., if desired, with

considerable further saving in first cost. It has two special characteristics, however, apart from its tendency to swell and jam blocks and knots when wet. It has not much springiness when dry, but its elasticity when wet increases more than any other rope, and when it does break, it gives little warning; perhaps owing to the fibrous appearance of the rope the deformation is not so easily noticed.

Coir Rope. Mention may be made of coir, or 'grass' rope for hawsers. This is made of a fibre akin to coco-nut, and floats. It has rather more elasticity than any other natural cordage, and is very light for its size. Therefore, though its nominal strength is low, it is acceptable for hawsers, and cheap. But it occupies rather a lot of stowage space. Its nominal tensile strength, around the 2- and 3-in. range, is one-sixth of Italian of the same diameter and its weight is about three-fifths.

Cordage Lays. Virtually, all cordage for yacht purposes is hawser-laid, in three strands, which gives the best strength for weight. Four strand ropes give greater flexibility and may last longer on a duty where there is a good deal of working round sheaves; as opposed to haul-up-and-stay-put, which applies to halyard purchases and the like. So four-strand, sometimes known as shroud lay, is occasionally used for main sheets of large yachts, and similar jobs.

If three hawser-laid ropes are laid up together, in a direction opposite to the constituent ropes, it is known as 'cable laid'. This is only used for towing hawsers or similar duty where extra springiness is needed.

Terylene and Nylon Rope. Turning to synthetic fibre rope, although there are other small-production fibres, the principal synthetic cordages which we have are terylene, ulstron, and nylon. Speaking generally, they are greatly superior to any natural fibre rope; the only serious snag about them is their greater cost.

The early research work was commenced in 1928 and the first factory for producing nylon was opened by du Ponts in the U.S.A. in 1938. British Nylon Spinners had their factory running in 1941. It is worth noting that nylon is a generic term covering a class of new materials, and that developments within the class are still very possible, as are variations in specification. But for the time being, products being in so few hands, the qualities are uniform, the best being about 30 per cent stronger than the ordinary.

Nylon, the basic material, is a special compound of phenol (which comes from coal) and of oxygen and nitrogen from the air; and hydrogen which is obtained from water. Nylon is melted, and is hot-extruded by a pump into individual filaments.

Subsequently the filament is cold-drawn between rollers before being ready to make up into cordage. The very long uniform filaments contribute to the even performance and strength.

Synthetic Cordage Strength. Under the ordinary tensile test they are roughly twice as strong, weight for weight, as good quality natural rope; ulstron rather more than twice, as it is a light cordage. Nylon only is more elastic—the stretch for a given load is between two and three times that of hemp. This will be a disadvantage for certain services and an advantage for others. Extension does not vary much between wet and dry. (*See* table in Appendix II.) This 'spring' does, however, result in tremendous resistance to shock; for a rope of given size, nylon will stand three times the shock loading of a good hemp. Moreover, nylon or terylene will recover their original length and properties after having been highly loaded, which natural fibres do not always do because the component yarns deform under load and because slippage of the short filaments probably occurs within the rope, together with partial fracture of some threads.

The same superiority is demonstrated under endurance loading; it must be remembered that endurance figures shown in the table in Appendix II are per cent of the already much higher maximum load allotted; and even then they are remarkably better than hemp.

Cordage Deterioration. All cordage deteriorates by exposure to light and the elements. Nylon is on a par with hemp cordage in this respect—the rate of deterioration due to light and exposure is similar. But since nylon is designed to have much longer life under load it becomes necessary—in order to take advantage of this—to take special precautions to shelter it when it is not in use. On the other hand it deteriorates very much less quickly than hemp when stored in damp lockers or bilges, which is important. Natural cordage must be kept out of water and aired. Nylon is not so choosy. Terylene is less sensitive to light than nylon.

Both can be spliced without undue difficulty by an amateur, but owing to the large number of filaments in each yarn, care should be taken to avoid loss of twist, and to maintain the form and lay of yarns and strands. The usual long, short and eye splices can be made, but it is essential on account of the smoothness of the rope and the fact that its elasticity must necessarily reduce the section of fibres under load, to insert extra tucks. A short or eye splice should have four full tucks (five is better) plus half and quarter tucks. For the same reason knots must be pulled home good and tight and given an extra half turn in cases of doubt.

The resistance of both to abrasion in ordinary wear appears to be about the same as that of hemp, with the exception of one case. When nylon (but not terylene) rope is run fast over another part of nylon, heating and damage to both parts may result—more so than with hemp. The cause is not fully understood; it may be connected with the high thermal resistance of the cordage. In practice the speed necessary to give rise to these conditions would rarely be obtained in yachts.

It is clear that both have outstanding merit as a cordage and it remains for us to consider for which applications they are best suited in an offshore yacht.

Nylon Anchor Cable. I have had nylon in use for many hard seasons as an anchor warp. For instance a C.Q.R. 45-lb. anchor had three fathoms of $\frac{7}{16}$ in. chain on it and thence by $2\frac{1}{8}$ in. nylon warps. The anchor is 10 per cent larger than is nominally necessary.

From a cruising point of view there are enormous advantages. Firstly that the total weight to be carried on board is much less than with a conventional full chain cable. Weighing anchor with a small crew and a full length of chain cable in deep water is a back- and heart-breaking business. With the nylon warps the weight to be lifted is hardly perceptibly greater in deep than in shallow water. The nylon is very pleasant to handle, very much pleasanter than chain, and gathers hardly any mud. It is largely used in America, but very little in Britain as yet. The Royal Ocean Racing Club requires a certain minimum total weight of chain or equivalent to be embarked. The weight, reasonably, being related to the measured sail area.

From the holding point of view I have no criticism. The ground tackle referred to above never failed to hold, though tested in a variety of conditions and bottoms, and in some strong winds.

As the breaking strain of $2\frac{1}{8}$ in. nylon is around 4 tons, it compares with small chain cable. The extremely elastic nature of the nylon is clearly a valuable characteristic in anchor work, and appears to provide the same answer as the spring given by the weight of the chain; moreover one can afford to carry a much longer length of nylon rope than one could of chain. I do think it desirable, however, to provide a length of chain next to the anchor; even when in use as a kedge. Where a boat has no home moorings and lies always to her ground tackle, then probably all chain is advisable.

Clearly care should be taken that the fairlead at the stem, used for nylon, should be specially smooth, and kind in its lead. If it has previously been scored by wires or chain cable, it should be faired. In cases where it is intended that the yacht should lie for some days, or longer, to her nylon anchor warp, it is as well either to parcel the warp, or to bend on a short stout hemp just outboard of the lead, which would take the chafe, the nylon acting as a preventer.

I have sailed quite a bit with a nylon main sheet. I expected that its elasticity might prove a disadvantage, allowing undue extension and necessitating tautening of the sheet in a long puff of fresh wind. In practice I found no such drawback. Presumably the main sheet is not so sensitive to minor adjustment as one imagines. In this case it lasted two hard seasons and seemed to have some life in it still, though it was by no means an oversize. The good handling properties were appreciated.

Terylene is equally good and there seems no question that it is superior for services such as fore guys and kicking-strap purchases. In fact, it is difficult to imagine any duty on board the modern racer which would not, with advantage, be performed by synthetic cordage.

Plaited terylene cordage is about 15 per cent stronger than laid terylene cordage of the same diameter and shows to advantage for hard-worked services such as headsail sheets and spinnaker after guys. Even on relatively large yachts it is feasible to use all terylene plaited sheets.

In the international 12-metre *Flica III*, after we had rerigged her with a new alloy mast and so on, one pair of genoa plaited terylene sheets lasted a whole season of hard trials and racing from May to September, and still was quite serviceable. (Normally one would have used several sets of wire sheets.) But splicing is almost impossible except in the case of one or two special lays.

At this point one must issue a warning about synthetic cordages. Firstly there are two qualities of terylene fibre (and several nylon qualities). The better one is 30 per cent stronger than the other. But, quite apart from that, the manner in which the rope is made up affects the wearing properties. Some rope, particularly rope made on the Continent of Europe, is too soft and goes woolly in wear, and lasts no longer than manila. But good synthetic ropes normally have three times the life of natural fibre ropes.

STEEL WIRE ROPE FOR RUNNING RIGGING
Reference may be made to the general information about wire rope contained in the chapter on standing rigging. The strengths and weights of various types and sizes of flexible steel wire rope are shown in detail in Appendix IIB. For running rigging we have a choice of several types of wire, apart from whether or not we choose stainless steel. Different makers standardise various constructions. A typical range of available types for running rigging is: 6 × 19—flexible; 6 × 24—specially flexible; 6 ×

37—extra specially flexible. 6 × 19 means a wire rope of six strands, each strand consisting of nineteen wires. The advantage of 6 × 19 over the other two constructions mentioned is that owing to the smaller number of wires the total area of wire to be galvanised is smaller and for a given thickness of coating the weight of zinc, which adds nothing to the strength, is less. Or alternatively for a given weight of zinc a thicker coat of galvanising is deposited, and the resistance to corrosion improved.

Thickness of Zinc Coating. In the case of the very fine wires which form the running rigging of the smaller yachts and portions of the rigging of larger yachts, this is quite a big factor. For instance, the normal coating of zinc on a single wire strand ·01 in. diameter will be about ·0005 in., or half a thousandth of an inch. The high tensile property of the wire is mostly imparted by cold drawing and this wire would perhaps have a tensile value at 100 tons per sq. in., or about 18 lb., for a steel wire ·01 in. diameter ungalvanised. Supposing, as one must, that the same diameter is to be kept if galvanising is required the steel wire must be reduced to ·009 in., which reduces the strength to about 14·4 lb.

Other things being the same, therefore, the 6 × 37 is, and to a less extent that 6 × 24 is not so resistant to corrosion. This is in some measure overcome by reducing the number of fibre cords, which are considered desirable from the point of view of easing the wires' job in running round sheaves, and by drawing the small wires to a higher tensile strength. But the thinner coating of zinc cannot be overcome and in practice these wires last less well, and we have to decide where it is worth carrying this disadvantage to get the added flexibility.

Wire Rope for Sheets. The answer, as I see it, is that specially flexible wire should be fitted where the wire lead is required to be operated at full loads by a small winch. This refers in practice to the wire rope sheets and to the wire rope reef pennants where the latter are winch-operated. It does not apply to halyards, where the full load does not normally come on the halyard until after the sail has been hoisted, because sheets are normally left eased during the hoisting operation. There is no doubt that additional flexibility is a great help in handling wire rope on a sheet winch. And a broken wire rope here is not a tragedy as a halyard might be!

In yachts which have exceptionally big-barrelled winches compared with the rope size—Chapter 22 should be consulted on this subject—it would be acceptable to use 6 × 19 or some similar construction. Fortunately all except the largest yachts can now use terylene sheets.

For halyards and general use as running rigging, where reliability is a paramount consideration

6×19 is suitable. This will probably have a seventh strand consisting of a main fibre core.

Wire Rope for Runners. As to wire for runner backstays, these present rather a special problem. It is desirable to avoid a change of wire, and to run the wire continuously from the masthead to the runner level, round at least one sheave and at the same time to have as much rigidity and as little stretch as possible. So something akin to the standing rigging should be considered. The standing rigging will probably be 7×7; that is six strands of seven wires closed over a core of seven wires. For the runners 6×7 construction, the six strands closed over a single fibre core, is a good compromise, used in conjunction with generous-sized sheaves—which being at deck level will be acceptable for weight and windage. Or in small sizes you can chance using the 7×7. I have done this successfully at times. Deck sheaves should be of bronze or light alloy.

Nearly all the foregoing considerations apply generally to stainless steel wire rope with the exception of the question of the galvanising. Therefore in this case the extra-flexible construction is not open to objection. Unfortunately the range of wire ropes obtainable in stainless steel is much more limited. The pros and cons of stainless wire are discussed separately.

BLOCKS AND SHEAVES

In the matter of blocks, as in the case of so many things, the offshore racer's choice falls somewhere between that of the cruising man and the class racing owner. We cannot afford to have the largest blocks regardless of weight and windage, which the rope manufacturers would like us to choose, nor can we afford to take any chances on the insufficient strength of cut-weight fittings.

Incidentally, in arriving by patient thought and experiment, at these compromises, speaking of equipment in general, I believe that in addition to serving ourselves, we are achieving quite a lot for the yachtsman generally, including those whose interest lies in the very real delights of peaceful cruising, far from the strains and excitements of racing at sea, because nearly all the things developed are in practice a real improvement on traditional cruising gear.

In the old days blocks were made of wood, with perhaps a metal pin. More recently nearly all large blocks have been internally iron bound. The iron, or galvanised steel as it is nowadays, supplies most of the strength and the wood is largely a fairing and partly there for appearance.

For smaller blocks tufnol is the material generally chosen; with stainless steel pins. It is ideal for J.O.G. boats, cruisers, and ocean racers where reinforced by stainless steel. Tufnol and steel is sometimes used for the largest blocks with sheaves up to 5 in. in diameter, but whereas small ocean racer blocks are as cheap in tufnol and stainless as wood i.i.b., the larger ones are relatively dear.

With tufnol sheaves the crushing load needs watching. For instance it is unsuitable for use as a spherical surface of a swivel block. I am against the practice of grooving a tufnol sheave for use with wire; I find it increases the chance of splitting the sheave. For 1-in. circumference wire halyards and above I prefer to use aluminium alloy sheaves.

Messrs. Lewmar Marine (Emsworth) and Messrs. M. S. Gibb (Warsash), both in the county of Hampshire, England, make full and good ranges of tufnol/stainless reinforced blocks. Tufnol, incidentally, is a strong non-metallic fibre type substance, which well resists sea water.

6

18

MAST FITTINGS AND LEVERS

Fittings for Aluminium Masts. In the early fifties we started to make, in all sizes, aluminium alloy masts for offshore yachts at Aero Marine in Emsworth. We made masts for the J.O.G. yachts such as our *Wista* which won the Championship in 1954; *Mouse of Malham* which needed the lightest of masts owing to her special design, and won the Class III Championship that year; and *Belmore*, second once, and third once overall in the Bermuda Race. About the same time we made the 70-ft. mast for *Drumbeat*; and for many other yachts. These, and the success of the R.N.S.A. Twenty Fours masted by Camper & Nicholson, paved the way for the general use of alloy masts; a usage which has now become so nearly universal in England that first quality spruce for hollow mast making has become nearly unobtainable. Writing in 1969, spruce is, however, still used to a limited extent in Scotland, and can be had in France; notably from the Chantier Charles at Le Havre, whence we had to fetch some recently into England. Later America followed suit in the general use of aluminium masts.

At that time John Powell, with my agreement, left my staff at Aero Marine to found the Sparlight company, to make aluminium masts and other spars in Sussex. Ian Proctor Metal Masts of Duncan Road, Swanwick, Southampton, started to make very good aluminium dinghy masts, and this latter company soon also launched out into much larger spars. These two companies now make a large proportion of the offshore and 12-metre racing masts in the U.K. and Continental Europe. Marco Polo of 71 rue Fondary, Paris, make quite a lot of the smaller, and occasionally the larger masts in France. Several other firms are in production, notably the Alpa Company of Offanengo, Cremona, Italy, and their subsidiary supplier, who make very nicely-finished aluminium masts, booms, and poles. They are used in our designs of series produced glass-fibre yachts, Alpa 8, Alpa 9, and Alpa 11; the figures corresponding approximately to the overall lengths of the yachts.

With the advent of Sparlight and Ian Proctor Metal Masts almost a new era was born; the specialist mast maker who could also, when asked, design the mast; a thing which was previously left almost entirely on the plate of the yacht's architect. (An honourable exception must be made in respect of the McGruer Company at Gosport, who made very nice hollow spruce masts on the wrapped and glued principle up to the early thirties.)

I am grateful to these two companies for letting me publish here some details of their latest masts and fittings, as used on masts for sail plans designed by us. In the Appendix I give typical alloy mast sections which I have used on various successful yachts; which will be, I think, of value to owners and prospective owners.

Since we have come to rely on the good services of our aluminium specialist sparmakers, these things have in many cases passed outside the supervision of both shipyards and absent architects; and many potentially serious faults can pass into service.

In industry the best firms have an inspection department who 'report to the Managing Director' and are independent of the works management. Most of our good friends in the yachting trade have never got to that stage.

To try to help the makers I had prepared some years ago a four-page specification for every mast; apart from my normal sail and mast drawings. Anyway, with the best will in the world, errors still creep in, and some technically competent, independent chap should if feasible examine the spars with all the data available well prior to despatch; in time for full rectification.

Wood Mast Ironwork. There are many ways of attaching stays and shrouds to masts, but the old way of carrying an eye spliced in the wire, over a shoulder or chocks on the mast is now seldom used, because it does not always locate things definitely, and therefore is apt to need a little more frequent adjustment and because it cannot be used in way of a bermudan mast track.

One of the most usual systems, and a well tried one, is to have a through-mast hollow bolt and nut, supporting tangs; that is to say, straps of metal lying down each side of the mast. The arrangements illustrated in Diagram 36 are those used by Laurent Giles & Partners and are typical of good modern practice.

Care must be taken to have the tangs bear on the plain and not on the threaded portion of the through bolts. A fine thread and reduced heads should be used. These tangs are either shackled to the shrouds at their upper ends; or are in two halves each, say, an $\frac{1}{8}$ in. thick, splayed apart sufficiently to allow of the eye and thimble of the shroud to pass between, with a pin through all three. I recommend stainless steel, galvanised mild steel, or monel metal for bolts and pins. I suggest one should make these pins and any other small bolts in the system, one-third greater in diameter than the plough steel wire of the rigging which it attaches. The mild steel tangs may then be in combined thickness equal to half the diameter of the pin, provided washers are welded on round the pin holes. The diameter of the through-mast bolt depends on the mast design. If the mast is wood and not solid it will need to be larger; the critical purpose being to prevent the wood from crushing, followed by splitting. Generally in the solid part of the masts the bolts are twice the diameter of the pins and hollow, the inner diameter being that of the pin.

Shackle Sizes. Shackle pin diameters should be one-sixteenth of an inch greater than that given above, which refers to specially-made bolts. This allows for the greater width between the jaws, and the bending stress resulting, which is relatively more important in the smaller sizes unless special shackles are obtained. In any case tested shackles should be used for all standing rigging. The better type of forged shackles are tested and marked, but the average drop-forged shackle is of very variable strength—often excellent, often poor. A test is easily arranged by putting them in series, ensuring that the pull is fair and straight, and hoisting the test weight through the shackles with a chain-geared purchase of the type found in every workshop. They should be examined for distortion or cracks after test.

Chain plates, though not strictly mast fittings, can conveniently be mentioned here. They may be 30 per cent more in thickness than the thickness of the tang or combined tangs, because a greater factor of safety is generally allowable with deck fittings where weight is less critical, but where the liability to accidental damage is greater. Moreover they are generally not as wide as tangs, relatively to their thickness, since good practice is to have the bow of the shackle bearing on the chain plate which involves a radius in the aperture or, more up-to-date, the pin of a toggle.

Masthead Fittings. For wood masts or masts in aluminium alloy the masthead fitting now generally consists of a cap formed from plate with four or more tangs bent over down the sides of the mast,

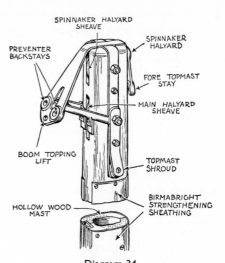

Diagram 34.
Myth of Malham—Mast Head Fittings
(Designed by Laurent Giles & Partners)

the athwartship one to the shrouds, the after one, or maybe two, to the preventer or to the two preventers if one leads to each quarter. Forward one has a tongue going to the fore topmast stay, if one is fitted, or perhaps to the jumper struts.

With a masthead rig it is very undesirable to have a big gallows to carry the standing backstay away from the mainsail headboard, because it puts a bending stress on the upper section of the mast and interferes with its work as a strut. Where a widish plate runs into a tang, to avoid either having to make this excessively thick or having high bearing stresses—crushing loads—it is good practice to weld a washer, half the thickness of the tang, on each side of the pin hole to shroud or stay.

The shroud tangs generally run a little way down the side of the mast, before bending off to their shroud line, to enable an athwartship bolt or bolts to be run through the mast. Extra tangs can run from under these bolts to take a pin through two thicknesses. One bolt can conveniently also form the axis of the masthead sheave or sheaves.

These sheaves have often to be of quite a big diameter on account of the mast depth fore and aft. Ensure that they are only the width needed—about 40 per cent more than the diameter of the wire—and are properly lightened by turning away metal between the rim and hub, and by drilling. Or better still, have them in aluminium alloy; but have the pin and cheek pieces in aluminium, not bronze. The aluminium bolt should be 40 per cent greater in diameter than a bronze bolt.

When designing the spinnaker halyard, one must remember that it will pull from anywhere between 80 degrees on one bow to 80 degrees on the other, and must do so without involving itself in chafe or putting unfair loading on its fitting, or coming off and jamming its sheaves.

Spinnaker Block. Myth's spinnaker halyards, in both her wood and alloy masts, ran round a sheave and out through the tang, which was fitted with a well-radiused copper protective bush. This ensured it being as near as possible to the masthead; to which point one is measured in any case because with masthead rig it is the point of intersection of stay and mast. It ensured also that it led clear out in front of the mast. Provision in the halyard splice 'at the top' should be made to work in a ball as a stop, to prevent the taper of the splice entering and jamming.

This orifice arrangement has the advantage of eliminating a block external to the masthead; saving windage and obviating necessity for the block, which has to swivel through 180 degrees, jamming with a foul lead and splitting. Since then I have used this arrangement in over five hundred yachts; but with a brass instead of a work-hardened copper orifice bush, as the latter used to score after a season or two, as did aluminium alloy. It is most important that the bushes have the largest feasible radius; which is aided by having a small hole barely twice the wire diameter and splicing the spinnaker halyard 'top' after the wire is in place; not forgetting to slip the small wood or tufnol ball over the wire before splicing. (The 'bottom' part of the halyard will be of terylene of about twice the wire diameter, very long spliced into the wire for ease of handling: except in the largest yachts where a reel winch is sometimes preferred.) It is also very important never to use stainless steel for the orifice bush, as mast makers like doing, because it is unkind to the wire and results in fractures.

Another common usage is to fit a swivel block, sometimes from a wee gallows forward of the stay. But the gallows needs to be pretty stoutly attached to the mast band as the athwartship loading is appreciable.

Forestay Ironwork. Forestay ironwork which I designed for a 15-ton sloop is shown in Diagram 37. The thing aimed at is, of course, low weight, and the avoidance of any tendency to cant and cut into the wood or to loosen the screws.

Halyards Internal to the Mast. Whether or not to lead halyards down the centre of a hollow mast is an oft-debated point. There is no doubt that it reduces windage, against which the occasional carry away is less easy to remedy. It also lets damp inside the mast. Snarl-ups are in practice not a serious menace. It is quite safe to lead three halyards including the main halyard, up inside and I have often, in addition, led two boom lifts and

other things internally. Among other advantages, it makes less noise in harbour.

Wireless Aerials. If one does not have internal halyards it is a good scheme to run a wireless aerial wire up the centre of a wood mast. One may also want a wire up to a masthead lamp. The lamp is very handy for signalling in a larger yacht and still more useful for shining on a masthead burgee, being either kept alight continuously or used occasionally with a push key. If used continuously the R.O.R.C. require a shield to obviate the risk of the light being mistaken for the masthead light of a vessel under power. Alternatively the insulated aerial can be run up or near the mainsail track. Aluminium is a fair conductor of electricity, and the track itself can be made to serve. Alternatively the triatic stay, between mastheads, can be used in conjunction with insulators. Insulators in other standing rigging offer windage and added weight and are not always completely reliable, so they should if possible be avoided except in non-masthead sloop preventers. Generally speaking they are necessary only for transmitting (*e.g.* a radio telephone) or receiving from distances of over 1,500 miles.

A common insulated wire can be taped up to a back stay if desired, and is quite O.K. for ordinary receiving.

Tang Details. On the outer side of the mast tangs welded-on sockets are often mounted for the heel of the cross-trees. I have the tangs well 'drawn down' by forging at the upper ends, to about half their full thickness, extended a little farther up the mast than most designs, and secured to the mast by multiple wood screws or rivets if the mast is in alloy. Unless this is done tangs are apt to work loose, and to fret the bolt owing to the variable loading coming wholly first on, say, the forward lower shroud, when going to windward, then on the after lower shroud when running.

Another way of forming the tangs is to make them from standard steel angles. Your steel stockist can get for you steel which costs only a little more than mild steel—the quantity is in any case very small—which has much improved qualities. The necessity for welding must, however, be studied; maybe where welding is required mild steel will be preferred.

The angles are run in pairs down the side of the mast, flanges 'back to back' but $\frac{3}{8}$ in. to $\frac{3}{4}$ in. (according to the size of boat) apart. These flanges standing out from the mast can be used to attach shrouds to, the thimble or the swaged fitting being passed between the flanges, and pins passed through to attach them. The part of the outstanding flange not required is cut away, leaving flat tangs which are worked to suit the mast, by forging. The attachment of the tangs must, however, be by wood screws or small solid through bolts, so the tangs must be run well up the mast. The heel of the cross-tree is formed into a steel fitting to stop, like the thimbles, between the flanges, and attach similarly through a pin. This system of tangs is particularly attractive with light alloy masts, where set screw or rivets are used to attach the tangs.

Mast Bands. A popular alternative to the tangs is to have a mast band running right round the mast underneath the mainsail track. This is convenient where a forestay has to be taken off, as it can be shackled or directly bolted through the flanges, facing forward, with the spinnaker block shackled to a bolt above and the staysail halyard to a block shackled to a bolt below, in the same flange, which should be reinforced to twice the thickness of the band itself. The band should be wide; about the same width as the mast's mean diameter and with strategically placed lightening holes.

The edges of the mast band should be very slightly belled to prevent it cutting into the wood. The through bolt is generally retained as well as multiple wood screws to guard against the band settling, but the bolt is generally lighter. The track must be fastened through in way of the band.

Alloys for Yacht Fittings. First-class bronze alloys such as Tungum or Everdur have the same tensile strength as good mild steel, but the hollow through bolts have to be watched if they are in bronze, as they are apt to be crushed after a season or two. Quite a bit of trouble was experienced in American boats in this way. High tensile stainless steel is, I suppose, the best of all materials for these through bolts and pins; but monel metal, which is a natural alloy roughly two-thirds copper and one-third nickel, runs them close, for long life offshore, because, though not so strong, it is considerably more resistant to sea-water corrosion than even high chromium stainless steel. Its strength and resistance to fatigue is the same as those of best mild steel, but it does not machine so freely. In general it has better resistance to fatigue than high tensile stainless steel. At this point I think I should sound a word of warning about brass alloys for bottle screws, and other highly stressed fittings. Great care should be taken to use a really high-grade alloy such as the Everdur or Tungum, or Superston. Many well-known alloys such as manganese bronze, sometimes known as high tensile brass, which have quite good all-round figures, are entirely unreliable in use, being specially liable to failure due to stress concentrations at sharpish corners. They are also liable to de-zincify if constantly immersed in sea water.

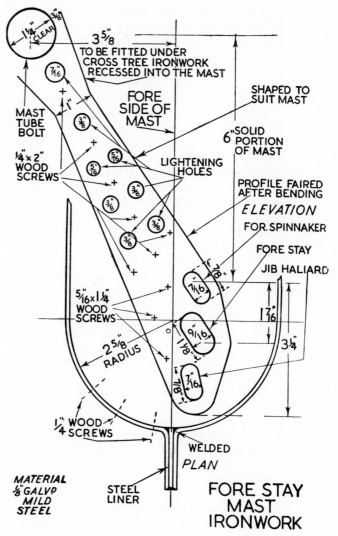

Diagram 35.

For the man of moderate means galvanised steel —steel of one of the standard ranges—takes a lot of beating.

Welding in the lighter sizes of plating, $\frac{1}{8}$ in. and below, is best done, for mast fittings, by oxy-acetylene. Monel metal welds very nicely by the same process. The strengths of various materials are tabulated in the Appendices for ready reference.

Cross-trees. As a material for cross-trees or shroud spreaders there is not much to choose between wood and aluminium alloy tubes. Solid wood cross-trees can be shaped with their larger portions in the centre, tapering to each end, a thing difficult to arrange in metal, but nevertheless desirable for a strut in pure compression. It is most desirable to have a ferrule over the ends of wood cross-trees, to prevent splitting. It is essential to lash the cross-tree to the shroud at its outer end to prevent any chance of the shroud jumping out of its groove and to obviate any up-and-down movement of the cross-tree on the shroud, on the lee side.

Aluminium alloy tubes as spreaders are a little smaller in average cross-section than an equivalent wood cross-tree, and offer less windage. The outer end fittings are turned out of aluminium alloy bar.

A higher tensile material than the ordinary shipyard standard tube should be used. A.W. 10 is a good British Standard Specification for tubes. The heels of the cross-trees must be wood-plugged deeper than the sockets. I always specify hard rubber sleeves between the cross-trees and the sockets, when sockets are fitted, to reduce the chance of damage to cross-tree heels when adjacent yachts foul one another in harbour; or when runners get caught round a spreader.

Mast Tracks and Slides. If aluminium alloy fittings are used and aluminium alloy fastenings are impracticable, they should be associated with cadmium plated or galvanised mild steel, for bolts, pins, and fastenings, rather than a brass alloy. The natural difference in potential in an electrolyte is less, and the risk of interaction is correspondingly reduced. This goes for the fastenings in mast tracks; though trouble here may not develop since the sea water drains away and is washed down by rain when at anchor. When similar track is used in a horizontal position, such as on a boom, or for a deck track for adjustable sheet leads or sheet horse or runner slides, then it becomes imperative to avoid brass fastenings.

Birmabright and similar alloys are extremely resistant to sea water provided they are, as indicated above, suitably fastened. They are not the strongest of the aluminium alloys; the duralumin series, for instance, are stronger, but for general ship work less easily worked, and requiring more protection against corrosion. Birmabright type is very ductile and easily worked for bending the tracks. For mast tracks it is the obvious choice. For deck tracks it is liable to damage, being softer. However it can fairly readily be recessed into a rail protected by tapered battens.

Fastening for Tracks. Special care is needed in fastening aluminium alloy tracks: they are very easily damaged in the process, and even small grooves and dents internal to the track may leave a legacy of trouble, and are very difficult indeed completely to cure. The joints between the sections of track should be on a slight bevel, *viz*, not at right angles to the track, to reduce the possibility of the slide jamming.

Some years ago I arranged tests to destruction of aluminium alloy mast tracks and slides. The most important thing that came to light was that the standard distance apart of fastenings was far too great. In order to develop the full strength of the track it was necessary to fasten it every 2 in. I like fastenings slightly off line or 'staggered' in wood masts. A saving in weight was found possible without loss of strength by reducing the width of the lips of the track; or in other words increasing the gap.

As to the slides, the shape was modified to give a little more strength where the loop meets the slide part. This small alteration increased the strength by 100 per cent per slide. The present slides by Gibbons incorporate this.

Attachments of Slide to Sails. It is important too, that the method of attachment of the sail to the slide should allow plenty of freedom, and also be immune from chafe. We have used aluminium alloy shackles. Larger boats can use galvanised steel shackles. I think thimbles round the eye of the slide and attached to the sail by a spliced grommet, a whipping being used to close the grommet to the eye, are just as good. More recently terylene tape has been successfully used to connect thimbles to the eyelets in the sail. In an emergency several turns of soft iron galvanised or stainless wire turned up so as to allow plenty of movement between the wire and the slide, serve well. The sail should be bound with tape under the wire.

Laurent Giles & Partners designed for Gibbons to manufacture a slide illustrated in Diagram 36.

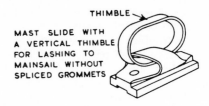

Diagram 36.
Laurent Giles Slide.

The thimble can be lashed directly to the mainsail without the need for a grommet which is a very awkward little chap to splice. The lashing must go right round the groove of the thimble.

The Americans sometimes use a very simple device designed I believe by Herreshoff. A shorter length of say $\frac{3}{16}$ in. wire with two eyes worked into the two ends (by brazing or drop-forging) is passed through the slide and bent round so that the eyes are the same distance apart as the diameter of the luff rope, which is then passed between the eyes in the end of the wire, which are lashed to one another through the sail, or sewn through for smaller sails direct on to the luff rope. Simply to lash the slides with marline to the sail is to invite trouble offshore due to chafe.

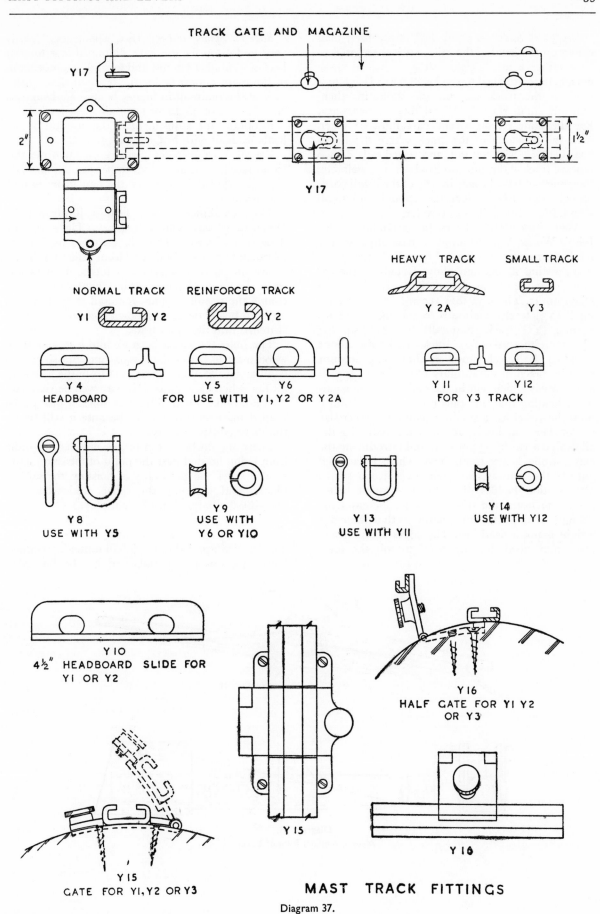

TRACK GATE AND MAGAZINE

Y17

2"

1½"

Y17

HEAVY TRACK   SMALL TRACK

Y2A   Y3

NORMAL TRACK   REINFORCED TRACK

Y1   Y2   Y2

Y4   Y11   Y12
HEADBOARD   FOR USE WITH Y1, Y2 OR Y2A   FOR Y3 TRACK

Y4   Y5   Y6

Y8   Y9   Y13   Y14
USE WITH Y5   USE WITH   USE WITH Y11   USE WITH Y12
              Y6 OR Y10

Y10
4½" HEADBOARD SLIDE FOR
Y1 OR Y2

Y16
HALF GATE FOR Y1 Y2
OR Y3

Y15

Y18

Y15
GATE FOR Y1, Y2 OR Y3

MAST TRACK FITTINGS

Diagram 37.

Headboard Slides. A good deal of localised load comes on the head of the sail, and it is essential to have either a much bigger slide or two or three normal ones attached to the headboard. If a gate is used in the track, to run the slides in, then, multiple small slides will probably be necessary. For the same reason special care must be taken with the fastening of the track where the headboard comes, with full sail, and reefed sails. If two types of track of the same internal size are available, then one can have bronze in way of the headboard, though lately I have given this up and gone to all aluminium without ill results so far.

Mast Track Maker. Messrs. James Gibbons of St. John's Works, Wolverhampton, have supplied the tracks for many of the masts I have had, in a corrosion-resisting aluminium alloy. Details of the fittings they supply as alternatives are shown in Diagram 37. The sizes they recommend are: $\frac{7}{8}$ in. small (Y3) track—mainsails to 400 sq. ft.; $1\frac{1}{4}$ in. normal (Y1) track—mainsails to 1,200 sq. ft.; $1\frac{1}{4}$ in. reinforced (Y2) track—mainsails above 1,200 sq. ft. I feel, however, that some account must be taken of the stability of the vessel as well as the areas which will in the end settle the maximum loading that one puts on spars and fittings. So if the vessel has a smallish mainsail for her size or for her stability I recommend reducing the allowable areas by 25 per cent and introducing the extra strong heavy track, Y2a, which is fastened outside the runway, for areas over 1,000 sq. ft. This section besides giving one a much better chance to fasten the track securely, increases the strength of the mast appreciably so that the extra weight is not a dead loss. The edges of the heavy track may need 'turning over' to suit the mast shape.

Slide for Spinnaker Boom Heel. This track, Y2a, is very useful too for use with sliding fittings for the heel of spinnaker booms, and for sliding goosenecks of the main boom; or for the outhaul slide of the tack of the mainsail in bigger boats. (*See* Diagram 40.) The use of tracks for headsail sheet lead slides —to obtain fine adjustment in the position of the lead—is dealt with in Chapter 17.

For all these purposes it is necessary to order the closer spacing for fastenings to be specially drilled. It is also desirable to order the gap to be milled out specially.

The remainder of the fittings illustrated in Diagram 39 are self-explanatory. These are to designs by Laurent Giles & Partners or Robert Clark and are also obtainable from James Gibbons, as are the *fin de siècle* switch points and magazine track shown in Diagram 23 in Chapter 10. These enable the trysail or spare mainsail to be brought up from below decks on its own piece of track and switched into the main track.

The mast track can be sunk into a groove in a wood mast to better the stream-line. But since the wind arrives at about 28 degrees from the fore and aft line when close-hauled, it may well be that this does not make much difference unless a nice pear-shaped mast section is used, because it will be in the dirty eddies anyway.

There should be a stop to prevent the top slide from being hoisted past the point of measurement. It also saves the possibility of hoisting the sail to blocks, and jamming the splice, and worse, of allowing the halyard insufficient play.

STAY LEVERS

The lever as applied to the job of tautening runner backstays, was first popularised by the late Mr.

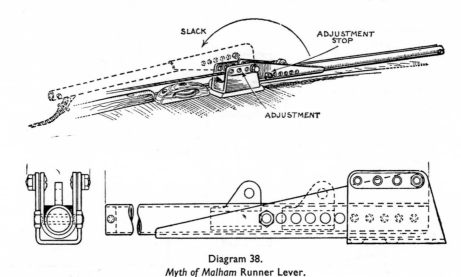

Diagram 38.
Myth of Malham Runner Lever.

Highfield. The essence of his design is a flat-sided U-section lever, on two pivots entering the lever from the outside, with the wire to be tautened running down the centre of the U, to a point about two-thirds of the way up the lever, where a bolt through the sides of the lever locates the thimble of the wire. By arranging the pivots a little above the horizontal line of the wire in its tautened position, the lever is self-locking. These levers are widely used and successful for small and moderate-sized boats.

The Highfield. Several alternative positions were provided for the bolt in the lever which gives one a coarse adjustment to the length of the wire, but in operation the thimble in the wire is fixed relatively to the lever. Consequently the amount of slack which it gives is limited to twice the distance between pivot and bolt. This means that one hardly has enough slack for the lee runner close-hauled, and has to unhook the runner from the lever. Moreover the power is limited, and at times when one can't get it set up quick enough, before weight comes on the stay, it may, in any except the smallest boats, be impossible to set up the lever.

For use in *Thalassa* in 1935 I designed a new lever. The wire thimble was carried on a trunnion which slid in grooves in the lever, so that when the lever was put over to the slack position the trunnion ran away from its stop up to the end of the lever. This was designed to give sufficient slack to enable one to turn to windward without releasing the wire from the lever. When squaring the boom off before the wind, the wire with its trunnion was released from the lever by a spring-loaded catch.

The first levers I had made to this design were fabricated, the runway being formed by welding strips of steel to a standard U section, to form the trim lever; this being to save weight when compared to a casting. However the strips distorted a shade in the welding and the trunnion did not run as freely as I hoped, when tested ashore, so the levers were not fitted on board. Minor alterations to the catches and other details were made and bronze castings were substituted for fabricated portions, but these were not ready until we built *Maid of Malham* the following autumn. They were successful, though fairly heavy.

Tubular Levers. In 1938 for *Mite of Malham* I used a slotted tube to replace the casting. The boat being small I overhung the lever pivot from one side which simplifies the construction. The slot runs down one side of the tube—the free side, naturally. The pivot needs to be good and strong; and flanged. This type is light, simple, and effective in small sizes.

In *Myth* I carried the use of the slotted tube a stage farther; this forms the basis of a lever pivoted on both sides of the wire, and is not too heavy so that one can make it good and long and obtain all the slack one needs without unhooking. This design of lever, which the Lewmar Company make (commercially available) at their works in Emsworth, seems about as simple a job as one can get. By having alternative pivot positions and an adjustable stop bolt one does away with the need for a bottle screw. They are shown in detail in Diagram 38. They are available in $1\frac{1}{4}$ and $1\frac{1}{2}$ in. diameters.

Laurent Giles & Partners have a good lever which uses an 'I' section bar instead of a tube and achieves the same result, the slide being replaced by two rollers, one each side of the bar, which pivot on the ends of a big link to which the wire is attached through an adjustable screw fitting. This is illustrated in Diagram 39.

The alternative layouts or rigs for operating the runner backstays are dealt with in the chapter on masting and standing rigging.

Diagram 39.
Laurent Giles Lever

6*

19

HULL DESIGN

It is outside the scope of this book to go in great detail into the question of hull lines. We shall therefore consider the question in general terms, and study the features and proportions which the owner can look for when he buys a boat. We will first discuss the question from a sea-going point of view, and then consider the way in which the rating affects the design.

Light Displacement Tendency. The modern tendency has sometimes been towards light displacement for a given length, and I believe that this has in part come to stay; since for a given amount of material one gets more boat, and a faster boat, by going light. And the size of the rig needed is roughly in proportion to the displacement, so in this respect too the lighter boat is easier to work, costs less to build, and much less to maintain, since replacements of rigging and sails are smaller.

But if we are to get boats of roomy, light displacement we must have a good freeboard amidships which to some eyes gives the boat an unusual appearance. This good freeboard is also clearly desirable from a general sea-going point of view in keel boats, for the obvious reason that it makes the boat drier. This is borne out in practice; in bad weather very much less water comes on board. From a racing point of view you may take the purist stand that the amount of water coming on board should not affect the issue, since one has presumably everything on deck watertight and a watertight cockpit. However there does in practice seem to be a limit to the amount which even the toughest crews will stand, and after which a reduction of sail is made. In a high freeboard boat you can virtually never put your rail under.

Light displacement boats have had in the past a mixed reputation as sea boats. This is probably because in general they have been associated either with very long ends, or with excessively rounded forward sections; or both. I have had ten light displacement personal boats, that is to say, boats with a displacement of not more than those of the international metre class boats for their respective length. They had varying overhangs and sections and were all of quite different designs; five built to rating rules of one sort or another and five to no

rule at all. I am satisfied that a moderate displacement boat with short ends can be entirely sea-worthy, and sea-kindly into the bargain.

It may be remarked in passing that though of late years it has become fashionable to decry the 6-, 8-, and 12-metres as being heavy boats, and though they are heavier than some other inshore day-racing classes, they are still light in displacement compared with average cruising and ocean-racing yachts of the same length.

History of Existing Forms. Because light displacement boats have in the past been almost entirely inshore racing boats which have gone in for long overhangs to get the most out of the then existing rules, we have got used to this combination: light boats and long ends. Meanwhile pilot cutters and many fishing boats, and the cruising yachts that were evolved from them, had straight stems and relatively heavy displacement.

The work boats were originally designed in many cases as much to heave-to as to sail, and had low freeboard in the waist or quarters for launching pulling boats or working nets. As they were fine stout craft, many cruising men took advantage not only of the well-tried designs but of the fact that long usage enabled these types of boats to be produced in their native yards relatively inexpensively.

The net result—though there are naturally a great many exceptions—was that the heavy boats had as a rule the short ends.

Now this seems to me wrong. It is the heavy boats which should have the long ends, to match their displacement and to enable them to have the buoyancy to keep the boat dry, and to help the designer to draw out their lines to a logical conclusion. It also gives them appreciable extra stability to help them carry the big area of canvas they will need to drive them. Those long ends will, on the other hand, not be so necessary to the light boat and moreover may throw a light boat about; they may make her motion excessively quick.

Behaviour of Light Boats. Mite, Rani, and *Myth* were all boats of quite light displacement with quite short ends; with their overhangs forward and aft only totalling between one-seventh and one-ninth of their full length. Little *Mite of Malham* designed by Todor Foretic, who had studied naval architecture in America, was built in Yugoslavia in 1938. *Rani* was designed by A. C. Barber of Pitt Street, Sydney, in 1935. *Myth of Malham* was designed by Laurent Giles & Partners in 1946. So we have a wide field and the lines are naturally fairly different. It is interesting to record that all were good boats at sea; reasonably dry, quick but not too violent in their motion, and easily handled in all weathers. So also were *Wista, Blue Charm, Mouse of Malham* and their many sisters, short-ended light displacement boats designed by us at Emsworth.

You often hear it said that the heavy boats will come into their own in dirty weather. But in practice this is sometimes a fallacy. Among boats of a size—that is to say of the same length—the good heavy boats do well as a rule in the light stuff. The reason is that the amount of 'wetted area' of the underwater portion of the hull in a heavy boat will be perhaps only 10 to 20 per cent more than that of a light displacement hull of the same length—perhaps less. And the sail area may well be 30 to 60 per cent more. At the low speeds the resistance is more a function of the wetted area than the displacement.

'Rani'. It is with great pleasure that I am able to print, with Mr. Barber's permission, the lines of *Rani*, because these lines represent a brilliant design; a very easily driven hull that was fast and sea-kindly under all conditions. Her designed freeboard was about 3 ft. 6 in. forward and 2 ft. 6 in. aft. The draft is 5 ft. 8 in. and the overall length just under 35 ft. The designed displacement was around 6·4 tons with a waterline length of 29 ft. 9 in. and a beam of 9 ft. Diagram 61 shows the profile waterlines, and sections. She was floating rather lower with a biggish engine and so on, when I had her. She was designed without any reference to the R.O.R.C. rule, but her ends were kept short because the famous Australian Sydney Amateurs' Club sets a limit on the overall length of a boat at 35 ft. So by chance, because the R.O.R.C. rule was at that time almost an overall length measurement, she fits very snugly into the rule with a 22-ft. rating.

Tumble-home. The hull has quite a bit of tumble-home. This reduces windage on the weather side when heeled. Also in a light displacement boat which is well heeled over, it reduces the extent to which the hull rises out of the water, and thus possibly loses keel grip. In certain cases it also helps to avoid excessive bulk in the quarters and thus assist hull balance. But tumble-home has the serious disadvantage that it reduces the sheeting base for genoas—particularly serious in relatively

narrow boats with big fore triangles. However the genoa in the case of cutters is only an auxiliary sail; her serious sails are the yankees or high-cut jibs and the staysails that set under it. So as regards tumble-home, it is a case of balancing up one thing against the other.

Rani as you can see from her plans has not a very hard section and so she heels a fair amount in sailing in moderate breezes. She is only moderately stiff in a blow having a ballast keel of 2·6 tons; that is to say a ballast ratio of 40 per cent. It is slung rather too high up in the hull to get maximum stability, but this cuts wetted area and improves her performance in light weather; so, like most other things in design, it is a compromise.

'Myth of Malham' to windward. Myth of Malham on the other hand has her 50 per cent ballast slung extraordinarily low, which increases her wetted area and puts her at a slight disadvantage in light and moderate reaching weather. But it is worth a great deal to her on the wind; she is immensely stiff for a narrow boat, and partly to this she owes her rather special ability to go to windward in fresh conditions. Her sections are a shade fuller in the ends than *Rani*'s and just occasionally the bow will slam when going to windward; not a regular pounding, but just now and then it will really bump.

The 1948 Santander–Belle Isle was an interesting race, because we were turning to windward right across the Bay for 236 miles in breezes Force 3 to 6. *Myth* was in her best form and we finished ahead of the fleet, which included open division yachts of nearly twice her rating. Going at that speed hard on the wind any boat of that size is going to take a bit of a beating, but I am bound to say that we had some specially jerky patches; quite a bit more of a slam than I had ever known before in her. I was aftwards interested to hear that almost every skipper when he got in said that his back teeth were a bit loose; and there was a deal of paint missing off most bows too.

The point of the story is that this goes to show how careful one must be, in judging the sea behaviour of the boat one is sailing, to allow in one's mind for the speed and exact sea conditions at that time.

Incidentally, had we in *Myth* reduced to a small jib and no staysail, as we would have done cruising, there is little doubt that we should have been quite comfortable, and still gone to windward faster than most cruisers. I put in this bit in fairness to the ocean racer; and in case one might otherwise get the impression that they are fierce jobs. This is far from being the case; they are mostly very easy boats to cruise in. In fact, if I were setting out to cruise two-handed round the world, I would consider building something very like *Myth*, but with a little less cut away in her profile forward and a little less rake on her rudder foot aft. This would would make her less quick on the helm and more able to get along on her own. As it is, during the Fastnet Race she sailed herself to windward for periods of up to 10 min. quite perfectly, with no one at the helm. The helm is left free and moves a little to and fro as if a phantom helmsman was at work. The speedometer rises too, though we are hard on the wind; the phantom does better than the man! And down wind with twin staysails also, she will almost steer herself, provided the sea is moderate. To get back to our muttons.

Extreme Light Displacement. As an example in light displacement, though not the latest still very interesting is the design of *Ea*, completed in 1953. She represents a serious attempt by one of Italy's leading designers to build a relatively large and really light displacement ocean racer. On a $46\frac{1}{2}$-ft. waterline she displaces only 18·6 tons. The conception of this design is not unlike that underlying *Gulvain*, built in aluminium alloy at Shoreham in 1948/49, of Laurent Giles & Partners design.

I raced against *Ea* in 1953 in a race of 180 miles in *Giraglia*. There is no doubt that she is fast and steady on the reach; there was no important windward work on that occasion. Later in the season she won the big race to Spain, and in 1954 she distinguished herself again. She is very well finished and nicely equipped. The modest depth and relatively small beam still provides plenty of excellent accommodation when one gets up to a boat of this size, and with a roof is lighter and more easily ventilated than a deeper hull—important in the Mediterranean. Her exceptional light displacement has resulted in rather an expensive form of construction, and this offsets part of the normal advantage of light displacement.

But in the modest sail plan she still takes up savings. In designing this the aspect ratio both of the mainsail and of the fore triangle have been sacrificed in order to reduce the mast length—the height above deck is less than the overall length of the yacht. This also reduces the attendant loadings on a light hull. Moreover she will fit the C.C.A. rating better, should that club in the future, as I hope, allow light displacement vessels to race.

In as long a boat as this, fully fitted and with a powerful engine, the weight remaining for allocation to ballast, in this case 7 tons, is bound to be small relative to the vessel's size, and a low sail plan matches this. Much of the stability is of course in the topsides and ends of the boat; but a smaller engine and equivalently increased ballast would be an improvement, I fancy.

She is triple mahogany skinned, two diagonal, and the outer fore and aft. Inside the bent acacia timbers (used in place of unobtainable rock elm and equally good) are multiple longitudinal members of oregon. The deck beams are laminated mahogany and there are several strength bulkheads of beech ply. The floors, mast step, and engine beds are light fabricated steel in a careful combined layout. The deck is in two strakes, the under one mahogany diagonally laid with teak on top. The rudder is in bronze, and separated from the main fin; a layout which is becoming almost standard practice with light construction because the rudder head comes out conveniently farther aft and because the splitting up of the reduced area of lateral resistance (reduced to match the sail area) tends to steadier performance in strong winds and a seaway. The 50 h.p. diesel 3,000 r.p.m. Scripps engine (2:1 gear) gives 8·5 knots under power. It goes neatly under the saloon sole. The galley is forward, next the hands' quarters. A small sea-going galley opposite the lavatory aft would be an advantage for Atlantic conditions. *Ea* incidentally is the Latin for 'She'.

Nearly ten years later Cass Bruynzeel gave designers a chance with *Stormvogel* to do another serious large and very light displacement yacht. Jack Laurent Giles, Van de Stadt, and I with Angus Primrose, jointly did this yacht. We each did two sets of hull lines which were modelled and tank tested. It was interesting, and curious, to see how very little difference there was in the results between the three best ones; one from each board. Brunzeel very generously gave each of the designers a share in the final boat. Hull lines by Van de Stadt; sail plan, deck, and accommodation by Illingworth & Primrose; construction details and general pulling together of the drawings very capably done by Jack Giles and his staff. Since then she has won line honours in the Bermuda Race, the Buenos Aires–Rio, the Sydney–Hobart, the China Sea, and the Trans-Pacific Race. She was built in South Africa.

Heavier Displacement. Having dealt fairly fully with light displacement we must, to keep the perspective right, turn to medium and medium-heavy displacement yachts. We have seen that the principle virtue of the light yacht is its low cost for a given length and speed; cheaper to buy, and cheaper to maintain its rig and sails. A secondary important advantage in the medium and larger sizes of yacht is the reduced amount of work in handling the reduced sail area: in smaller yachts the difference in area is less important, work wise.

Turning to the heavier yacht, for a given measured, or effective length, the speed at sea will

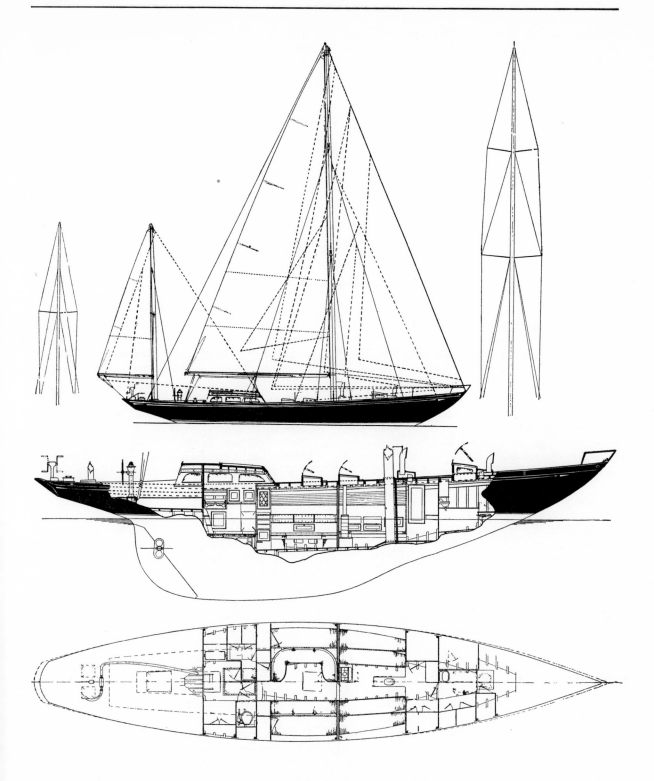

Diagram 40.

Circe, designed by Sparkman & Stephens for Mr. Carl Hardeberg and built in Sweden by Neglinge-Varvet. Dimensions:—
L.O.A.: 56 ft. $9\frac{1}{2}$ in.; *L.W.L.*: 39 ft.; *Beam*: 11 ft. $8\frac{3}{4}$ in.; *Draft*: 8 ft.; *Sail Area:* mainsail 617 sq. ft., storm trysail 143 sq. ft., mizzen 111 sq. ft., mizzen staysail 365 sq. ft., storm forestaysail 91 sq. ft., balloon forestaysail 322 sq. ft., genoa 835 sq. ft., small genoa 720 sq. ft., No. 2 jib 284 sq. ft., working jib 505 sq. ft., balloon jib 800 sq. ft., light genoa jib 835 sq. ft.

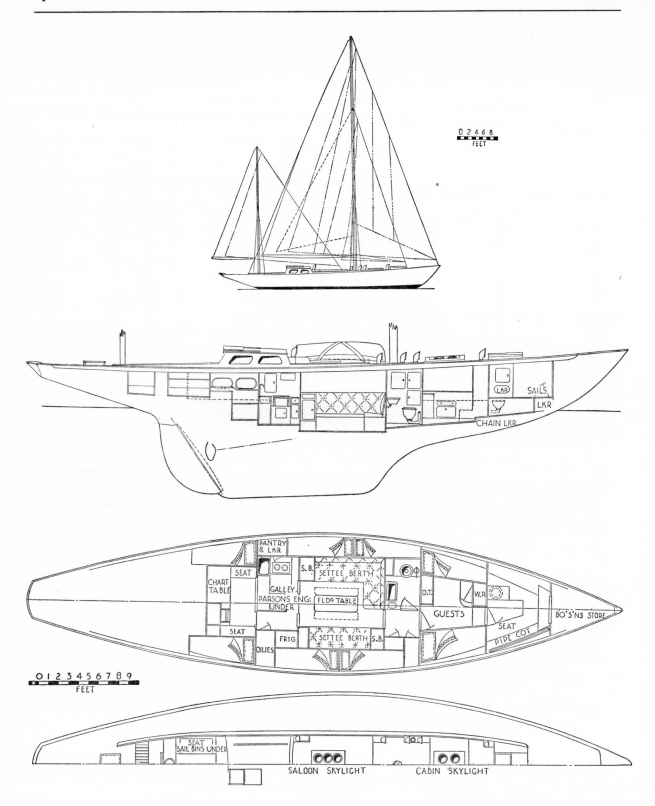

Diagram 41.

Lutine. **Lloyd's Yacht Club's Class I** Ocean Racer. Designed by Laurent Giles & Partners. **Dimensions:**—*Length O.A.*: 59 ft. 9 in.; *L.W.L.*: 41 ft. 6 in.; *Beam:* 13 ft. 7 in.; *Draft:* 8 ft. 4 in.

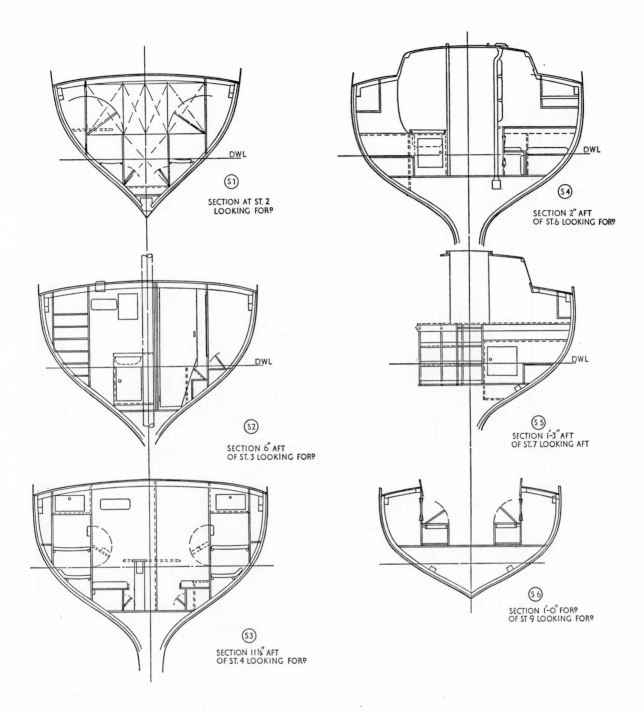

Diagram 42.
Sections of *Quiver IV*. See diagram 45 on page 150 for correlation.

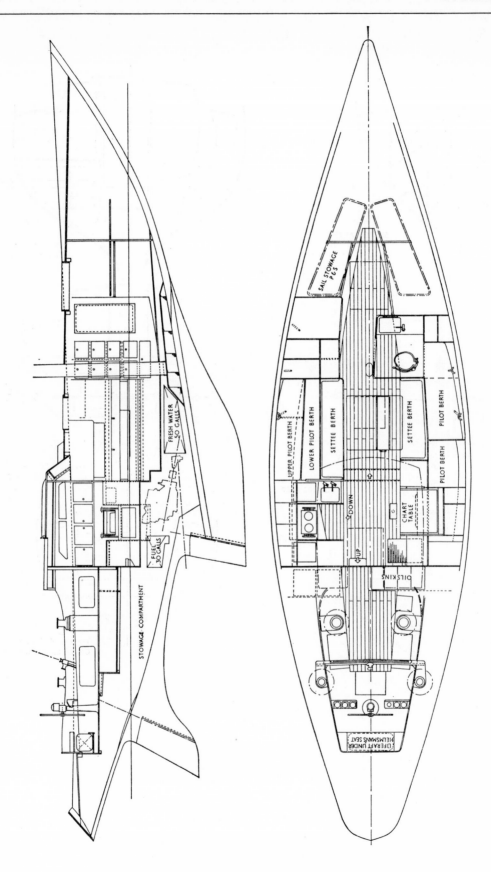

Diagram 43.

Phantom, designed and built by Camper and Nicholson in 1968 for Mr. G. Pattison. Dimensions:—L.O.A.: 51 ft. 6 in.; L.W.L.: 36 ft.; beam: 13 ft. 6 in.; draft: 7 ft. 9 in.

Quiver III. Class II points champion 1961, Class II winner and second overall in the Fastnet Race 1962. Designed by Camper and Nicholson for Mr. S. H. R. Clarke, Dimensions: *loa*: 44 ft. 6 in.; *lwl*: 33 ft.; *beam*: 11 ft.; *draft*: 6 ft. 9 in.; *sail area*: 946 sq. ft.

Quiver IV. Built for R. E. Clarke, Esq., by Camper and Nicholson in 1965 and whose drawings are reproduced on page 150. A very successful Class 1 boat.

Quiver V. Owner Rendall Clarke. Builders and designers (1969) Camper and Nicholson. Dimensions: *loa:* 50 ft. 8 in.; *lwl:* 36 ft.; *beam:* 13 ft. 10 in.; *draught:* 7 ft. 9 in. R.O.R.C. rating: 30 ft. Sloop rig. This yacht, with a separated rudder and built in wood is typical of a good modern small Class 1 ocean racer.

La Meloria. A 1967 Camper and Nicholson boat whose drawings are reproduced on page 152. A brilliant boat in light weather, she was built for the Two Ton Cup, although not quite up to the limit of rating.

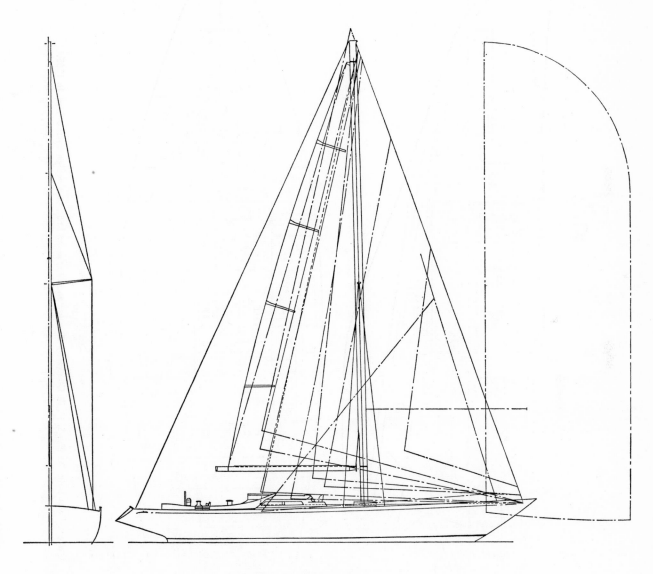

Diagram 44.
Phantom—sail plan. Total sail area of this attractive light-displacement yacht is 956 sq. ft.

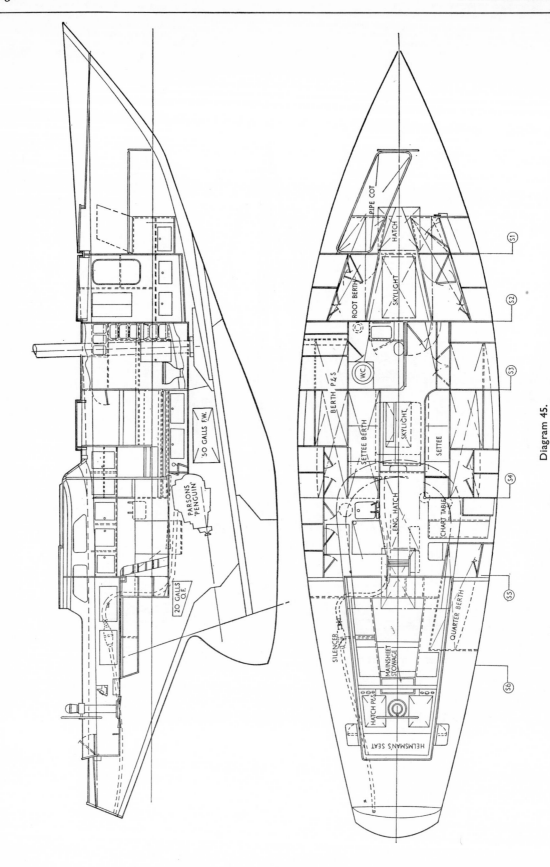

Diagram 45.

Quiver IV was built for Mr. S. H. R. Clarke by Camper and Nicholson Ltd., to a design by the firm, in 1965.
Dimensions:—L.O.A.: 48 ft. 1 in.; L.W.L.: 35 ft.; beam: 12 ft.; draft: 7 ft. 6 in.

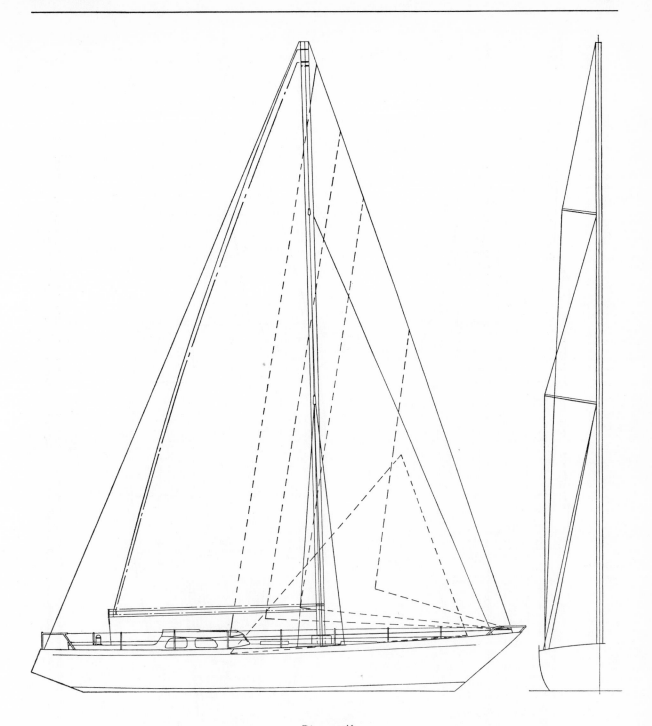

Diagram 46.
Quiver IV. Total sail area of the auxiliary sloop is 1,183 sq. ft.

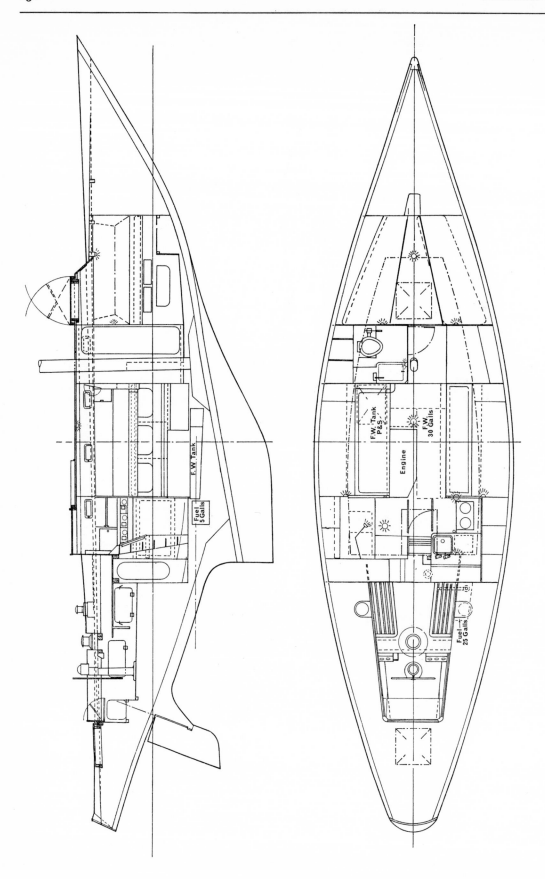

Diagram 47.

La Meloria, another Camper and Nicholson designed and built yacht. She was completed in 1967 for Captain G. B. Pera. Dimensions:—L.O.A.: 44 ft. 4 in.; L.W.L.: 31 ft.; beam: 11 ft. 9 in.; draft: 6 ft. 10 in.

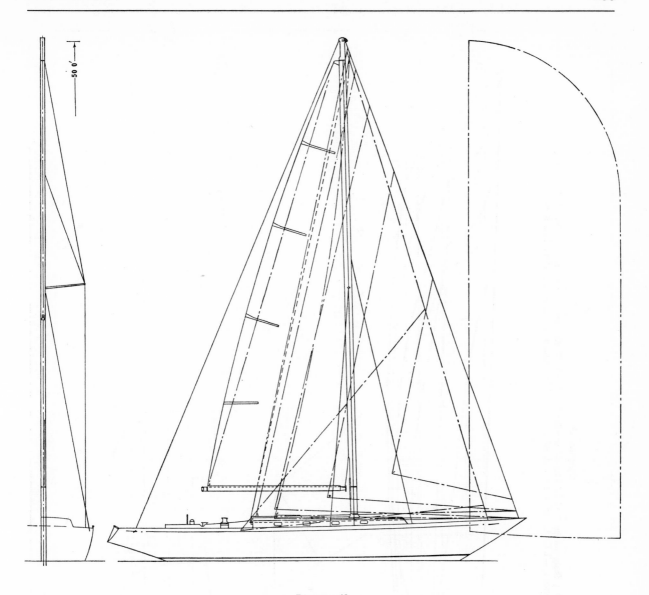

Diagram 48.
La Meloria—sail plan. Total sail area is 793 sq. ft.

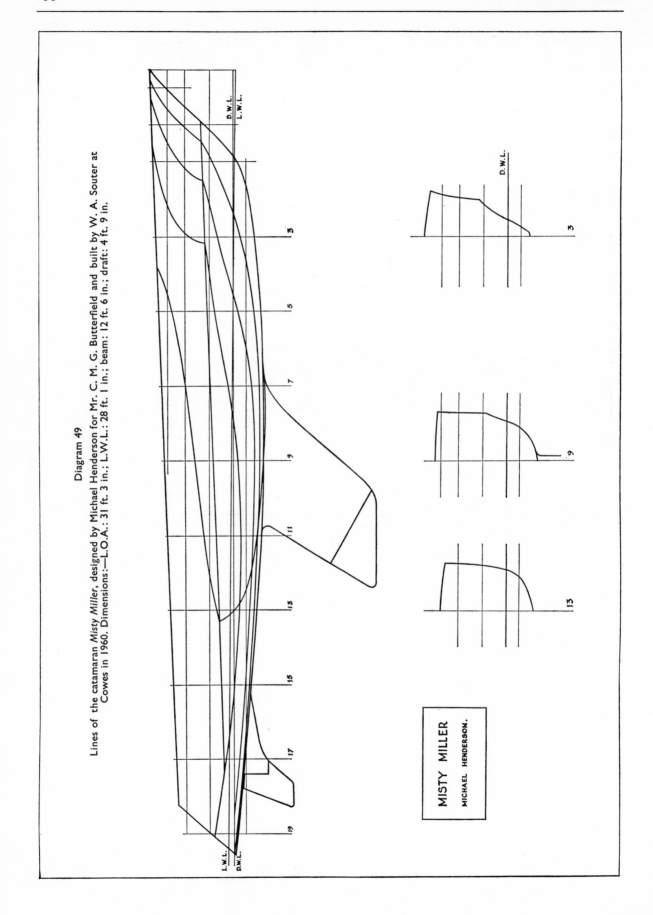

Diagram 49

Lines of the catamaran *Misty Miller*, designed by Michael Henderson for Mr. C. M. G. Butterfield and built by W. A. Souter at Cowes in 1960. Dimensions:—L.O.A.: 31 ft. 3 in.; L.W.L.: 28 ft. 1 in.; beam: 12 ft. 6 in.; draft: 4 ft. 9 in.

MISTY MILLER

MICHAEL HENDERSON.

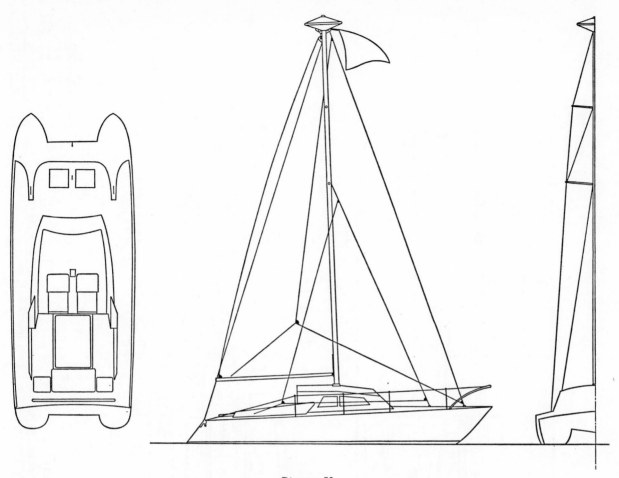

Diagram 50
Sail plan of the cutter-rigged *Misty Miller*. Total sail area is 720 sq. ft.

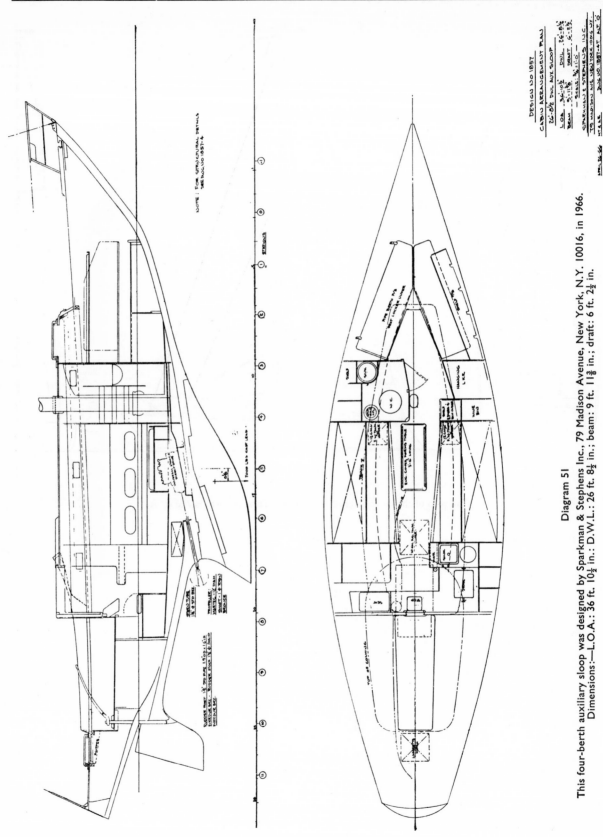

Diagram 51

This four-berth auxiliary sloop was designed by Sparkman & Stephens Inc., 79 Madison Avenue, New York, N.Y. 10016, in 1966.
Dimensions:—L.O.A.: 36 ft. $10\frac{1}{4}$ in.: D.W.L.: 26 ft. $8\frac{1}{2}$ in.; beam: 9 ft. $11\frac{3}{8}$ in.; draft: 6 ft. $2\frac{1}{2}$ in.

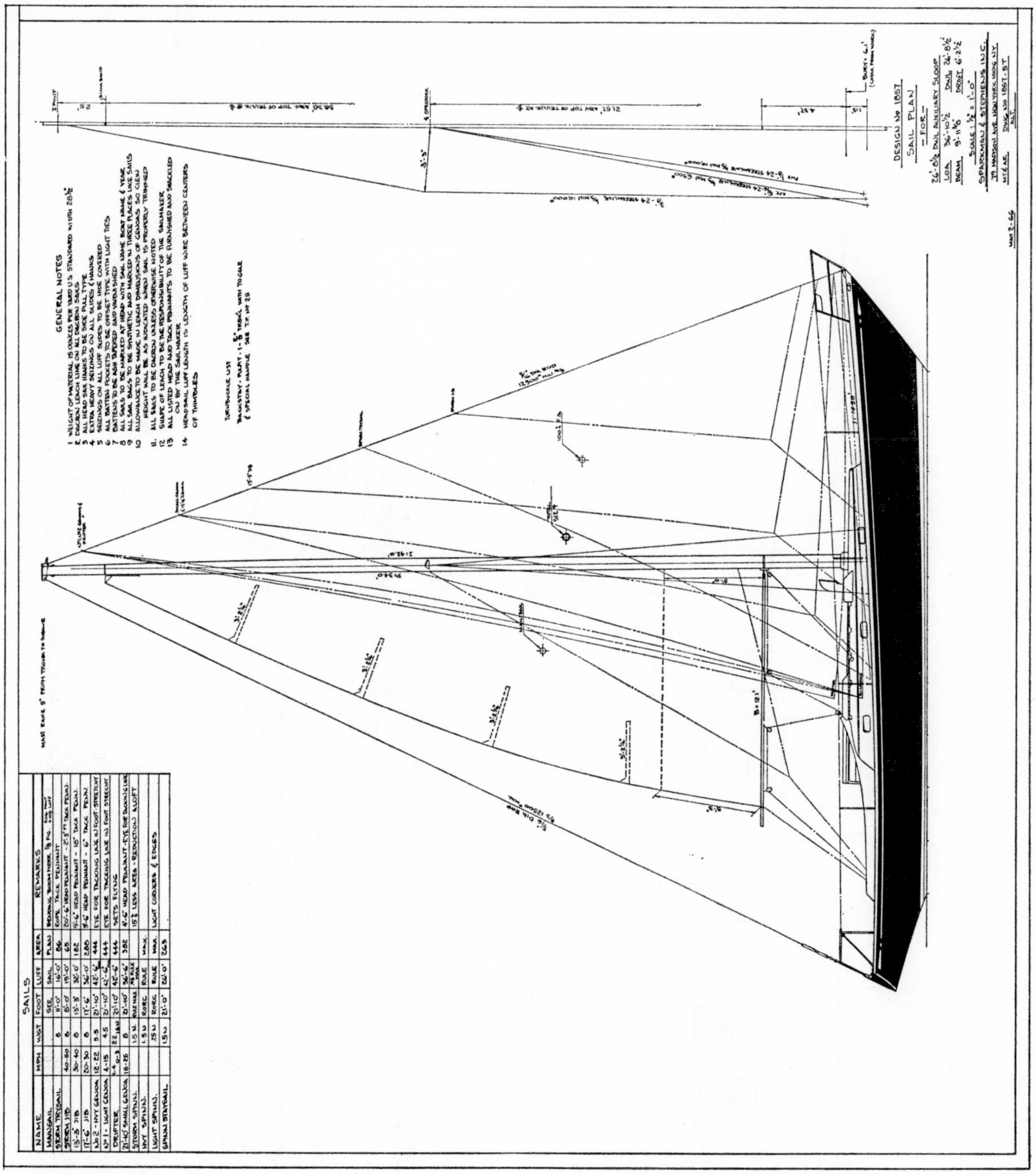

Diagram 52.

Sail plan of the 26 ft. 8½ in. waterline auxiliary sloop illustrated on the previous page. Note the rod rigging.

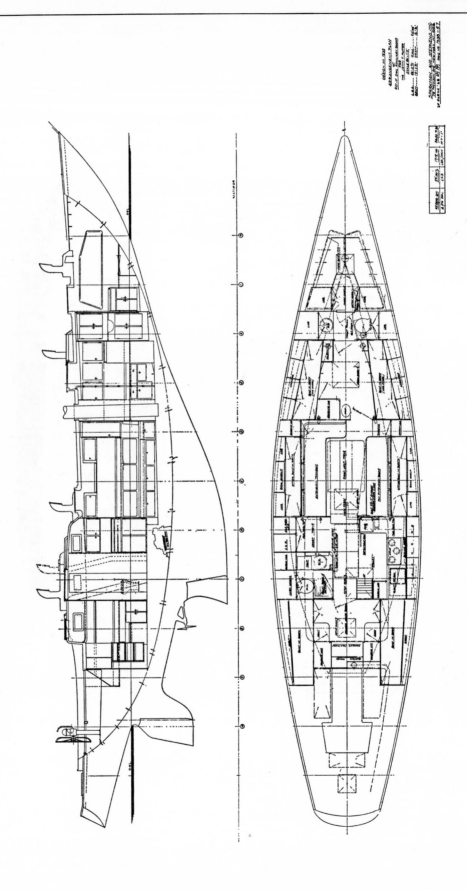

Diagram 53.

A medium-displacement auxiliary sloop designed in 1968 by Sparkman & Stephens Inc. for Mr. John T. Poiter.
Dimensions:—L.O.A.: 55 ft. 8¾ in.; D.W.L.: 40 ft.; beam: 12 ft. 4¼ in; draft.: 8 ft. 1¼ in.

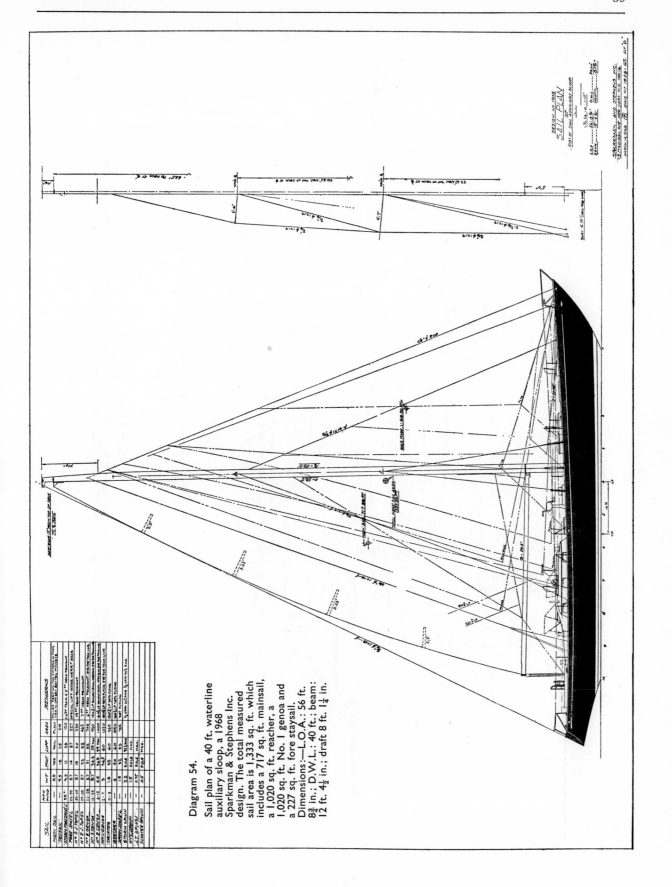

Diagram 54.

Sail plan of a 40 ft. waterline auxiliary sloop, a 1968 Sparkman & Stephens Inc. design. The total measured sail area is 1,333 sq. ft. which includes a 717 sq. ft. mainsail, a 1,020 sq. ft. reacher, a 1,020 sq. ft. No. 1 genoa and a 227 sq. ft. fore staysail. Dimensions:—L.O.A.: 56 ft. $8\frac{3}{4}$ in.; D.W.L.: 40 ft.; beam: 12 ft. $4\frac{1}{2}$ in.; draft 8 ft. $1\frac{1}{4}$ in.

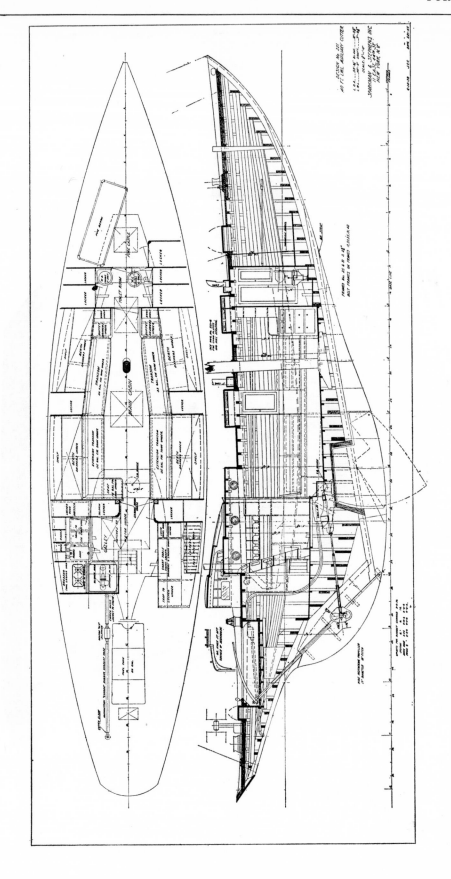

Diagram 55.

A 40 ft. waterline auxiliary cutter of medium displacement designed by Sparkman & Stephens Inc. Power comes from a Gray 4-22 Dimensions:—L.O.A.: 55 ft. $9\frac{1}{4}$ in.; L.W.L.: 40 ft.; beam: 12 ft. $5\frac{5}{8}$ in.; draft: 7 ft. $8\frac{7}{8}$ in.

Diagram 56.
Sail plan of a Sparkman & Stephens 40ft. waterline auxiliary cutter designed for Mr. R. J. Reynolds. (See also Diagram 55.)
Mainsail area is 660 sq. ft.

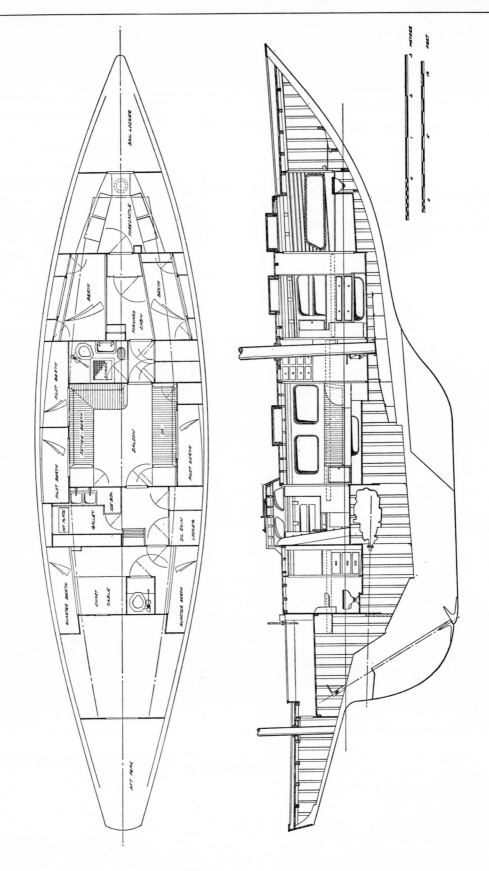

Diagram 57.

Susanna II, an auxiliary yawl designed by Laurent Giles & Partners Ltd. for Mr. C. Brainovitch. Dimensions:—L.O.A.: 63 ft. 6 in.; L.W.L.: 45 ft. 3 in.; beam: 14 ft. $5\frac{1}{2}$ in.; draft: 9 ft. 3 in.

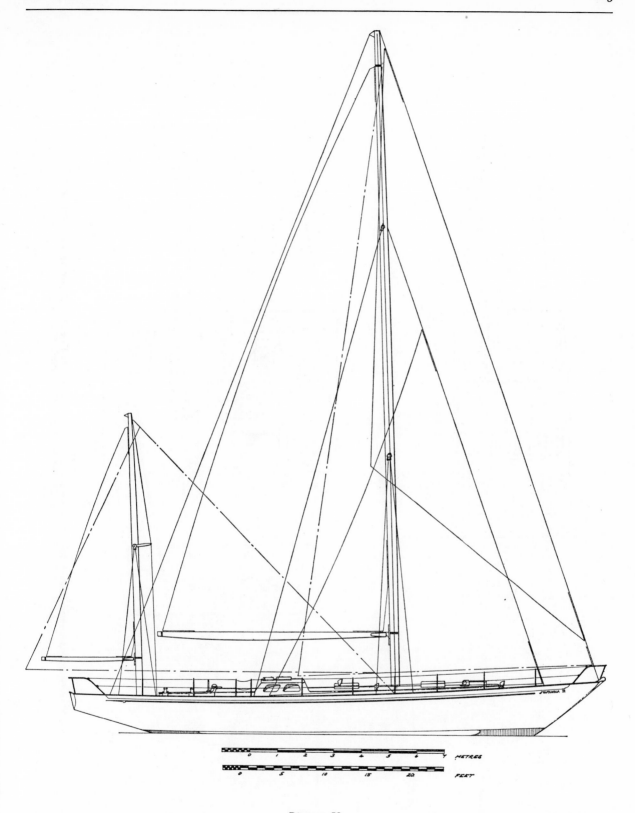

Diagram 58.
Sail plan of *Susanna II*. Total sail area is 1,850 sq. ft. The boat was built in 1963 by Cantieri Sangermani of Lavagna, Italy.

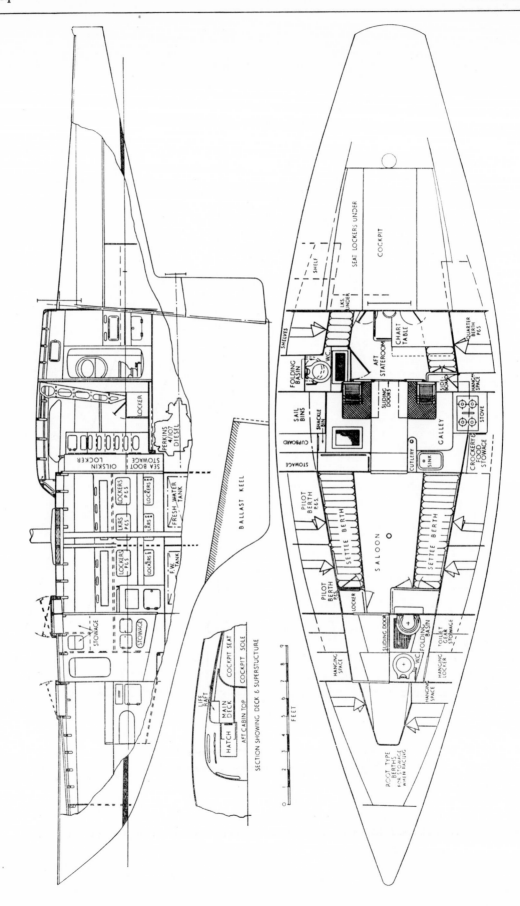

Diagram 59.
Outlaw, light displacement Class I ocean racer owned by Hon. Max Aitken, designed by Illingworth and Primrose.
L.O.A.: 48 ft. 6 in.; L.W.L.: 39 ft. 9 in.; Beam: 13 ft.; Draft: 8 ft. $2\frac{1}{2}$ ins

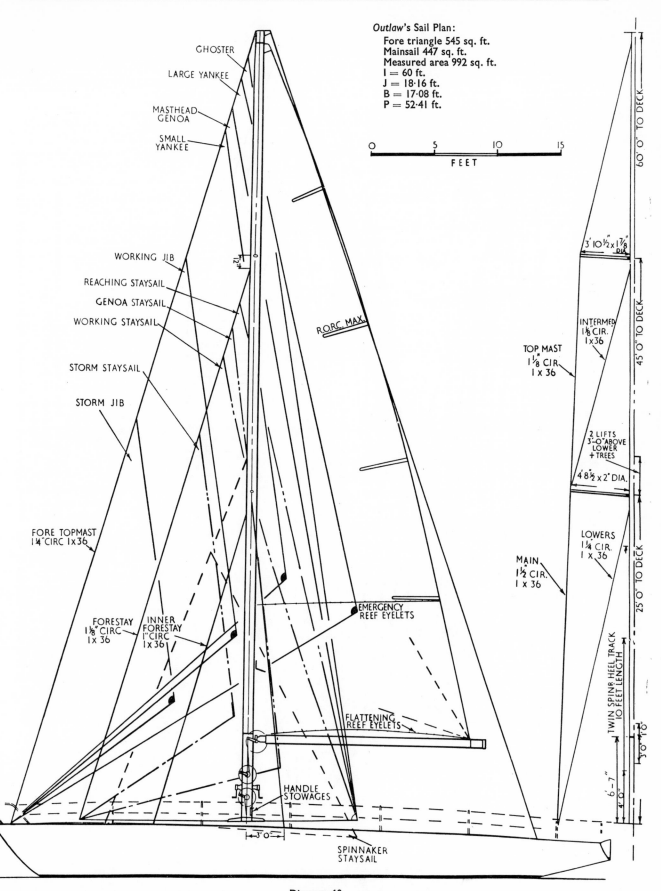

Outlaw's Sail Plan:
Fore triangle 545 sq. ft.
Mainsail 447 sq. ft.
Measured area 992 sq. ft.
I = 60 ft.
J = 18·16 ft.
B = 17·08 ft.
P = 52·41 ft.

Diagram 60.
Sail plan of *Outlaw*, a successful ocean-racer built by W. A. Souter of Cowes in 1963. Total measured sail area is 992 sq. ft.

7

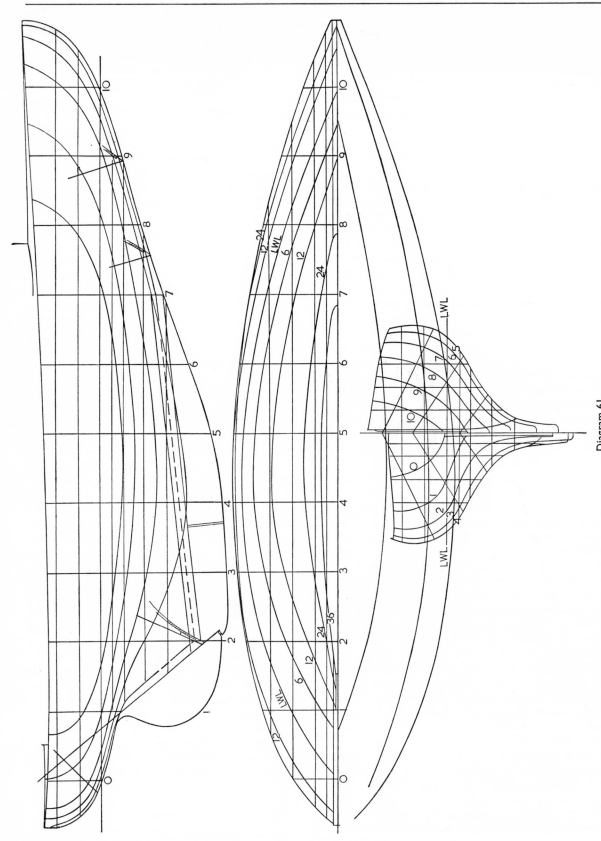

Diagram 61.

The lines of *Rani* designed by A. C. Barber, show a very easily driven hull, fast and sea-kindly under all conditions.

in general be about the same; but requiring a larger sail area. The beam and the headroom will be greater; there will be more accommodation space and comfort on board for that same length. And sometimes the beamier boat will sail more upright. But other things, such as quality and finish being the same, she will cost appreciably more to build.

Writing in 1969 I should mention that I have, in recent years, owned two good heavy yachts: *Monk of Malham* 30 ft. water line for the Admiral's Cup and similar races; and *Merle of Malham*, 21 ft. water line, a Quarter-Ton Cup yacht.

Transom Sterns. I have been very satisfied with a series of five transom-sterned designs which we have done at Emsworth of heavy and medium-heavy displacement. Though they are very different in size, varying between 3·2 and 8·3 tons weight, corresponding to waterline lengths of between 21 and 27 ft., they all have the same good feel at sea; a confidence-breeding feel, because they deal with more or less any seaway without fuss or worry, and are steady on the helm. They have an easy motion and don't knock themselves about; and above all they really get to windward, even in bad conditions. In any of these, even the smallest, I would be happy to set off across the Atlantic without any special preparations other than embarking a few extra jerricans of water; and perhaps a bottle of whisky to celebrate the halfway-across day.

I have had the fairly rare chances of sailing many transom-stern yachts which were of our same basic design as the counter-stern versions of *Maica* type. In all we have built nearly a hundred of these. Naturally the aft lines are altered for the transom version, but basically they are exactly the same boat, with the same displacement. I have done Fastnets and Bermudas, among many other races, in these yachts. Both types are good all round yachts, in terms of speed and seaworthiness. The counter-stern version is fractionally faster on the reach, and on the run too, provided there is not too much of a following sea. In the latter conditions transom-stern comes again into its own, because it is pushed around less by its (non-existing) counter, and has therefore better directional stability. The reason that the transom-stern design is less easily applied to light displacement is simply that with an outboard rudder one cannot easily cut the underwater area down to the amount that equates to a small sail area. In a number of boats I have managed a compromise by not carrying the rudder blade to the full draft, and cutting the area of the fin at the 'lower back end'.

Underwater Areas. Pressure on ocean racing designers as the years went on obliged them pro-

gressively to cut down the fin area, in many cases to an unhealthy extent. All of us have felt these pressures and some of the resulting yachts are by no means easy in fresh reaching conditions, and really shockers to hold in fresh following winds. Some of the recent yachts in the Mediterranean begin to get quite wild with only Force 4 astern.

One has tried hard to resist the temptation to over-do the fin area cutting; particularly with owners who are unlikely to cope in difficult conditions; one has to sacrifice knowingly some speed in light conditions in aid of producing a seaworthy yacht with reasonable directional stability. But clearly, the rule makers are going to have to come to the aid of the owners and protect them against the more enterprising designers.

As an aid to directional stability I have used in a number of designs dagger boards or drop keels in the counter. These were successfully used in the Class I racers *Outlaw* and *Oryx*; and in the Class II *Monk of Malham*, *Yanica*, and *Gentilhomme de Fortune*; and in some of the lighter Class III yachts. But to be any good these have to be arranged very carefully with reference to the main fin and rudder.

Stability and Windward Work. I would like to enlarge a bit on the question of stability and windward work. The ability in a ship to stand up reasonably to her canvas is of supreme importance and the few minutes gained here and there in other ways will be of no avail if you can't get her to windward in a breeze. Under these conditions if she won't stand up reasonably you will be losing hours, not minutes, in an offshore race.

This does not mean that they must sail nearly upright; take for instance the famous Nicholson designed trio, *Foxhound, Bloodhound,* and *Stiarna*—near sisters. They are all wonderful boats to windward, but they have fairly slack sections and they take up a fair initial angle of heel.

Hanging the Ballast Low. One can get one's stability of course in a variety of ways—hard bilge, big beam, or relatively big ballast ratios, and hanging the ballast low; and one can help out with the sail plan to a certain extent. A schooner or a ketch, and a yawl to a limited extent, will have a lower centre of effort to its sails than a cutter or a sloop. Comparing a masthead cutter with a sloop or 'low triangle' cutter, the masthead rig has a lower centre of effort provided the aspect ratios are constant. If one had a hull which was not too stiff, one would keep the boom a shade lower than usual and keep one's mainsail aspect ratio around 2·6 rather than 3 : 1.

Light versus Heavy Construction. This necessity for stability does not mean, however, that one has to go to unduly light scantlings—that is to say unduly light constructional members—because there is an allowance under the R.O.R.C. rating and the 'new rule' to compensate for the weight of construction, which takes care of this question.

The C.C.A. in 1962 introduced a stability test which was in effect an inclining experiment, to take the place of the previous ballast ratio factor. The latter had been in part evaded by heavy structural members. It also unduly encouraged very wide boats which could afford to have a small ballast ratio. This stability test is found again in the new rating rule; though whether it will survive the test of time seems doubtful.

The Fastnet Race is rarely sailed without a decent bit of windward work. In 1947, 1955 and again in 1956 which were nominally light-weather races, there were spells of windward work when it was only just possible to carry full sail; and in 1947 a further 24 hrs. with a nice breeze, just less than whole sail.

In the case of the smallest size of ocean racer and particularly in J.O.G. racing, the ability to get to windward becomes of such paramount importance that in this special case one can hardly afford to compromise as to stability. So in a boat under say 26-ft. waterline one way or another she must be pretty stiff to succeed.

Ratio of Sail Area to Displacement. There is in this connection one thing to avoid, and that is cutting the sail area unduly in a less stiff boat. One may be tempted to do so, saying that it is no good having a big rig one can't carry. While this is, of course, a perfectly good truism, it must be remembered that the area normally used under the R.O.R.C. new rule of rating (there is no scale laid down—it is entirely at the owner's option) is even now quite moderate; far less for the size of boat than under the international metre class rating rules for instance. Any further appreciable cut completely spoils the boat's light-weather performance. And as we have noted, elsewhere, since most races are sailed, in whatever part of the world, in the summer season, the depressions and blows rarely last the whole race out, so that it is normal to have at least a proportion of light weather in every race.

Tai Mo Shan was a typical example, in the original racing rig, of this difficulty. She was of easy section and had a moderate beam and a ballast ratio around 38 per cent, so she was not a great sail carrier, and did not do much in a blow. And in spite of a low rating she was no real good in light weather, because in deference to her sail-carrying power, she had been given a very small rig.

Eventually ballast was added as well as sail area, and she was a much improved racer and with her big freeboard she was still the fine ocean cruiser she had always been.

The rigs given to the two yachts designed by Laurent Giles & Partners and referred to earlier in the chapter, form an interesting comparison. The light displacement boat is around 640 sq. ft. The other, which the architects call their 'Biscay' design, has 870 sq. ft., being of course a more imposing vessel, as befits the Vice-Commodore of an important club. They should both rate a little over 32 ft.

Beam. I am sometimes asked which is best for ocean racers, a small beam or a big beam. The only answer one can give in brief is that there are good narrow boats and good broad boats; and so again you can take your choice.

The Americans have always, since the beginning of yachting, favoured bigger beamed boats than the Europeans. The models of the America's Cup challengers and defenders in the New York Yacht Club's model room show clearly the very great difference in beam, maintained through the years. The same difference can be noticed today in ocean racing craft on the two sides of the Atlantic. It is said that the basic reason is that the narrow boat is more suited to our short steep Channel seas and to North Sea conditions. I am more inclined to believe that chance and local work boats together have set different fashions, which have simply been maintained in their own home waters.

When, however, we come to light displacement boats—boats that are very light for their length— there does appear to be something special to be said for keeping the beam moderate to get a sea-kindly type.

The American C.C.A. rating rule, being framed naturally with typical American boats in mind, does tend to encourage the beamy boat. But this is a less important effect than at first appears because the boats with the lesser beam are allowed a stronger ballast ratio—quite a sensible provision.

C.C.A. Rule Effect on Design. The C.C.A. rule as it stands in 1969, allows basic sail area on a displacement basis which is slightly in favour of a fairly ample displacement for length. This in conjunction with biggish beams and a waterline measured at a distance of about 1 to 2 ft. above the load waterline, according to size, has gradually produced a characteristic type, which with the help of the good sense and skill of the American designers is a generally healthy one. But it shows less variation than is seen in Europe. As there is no penalty on girth measurement, the rule encourages fairly full powerful end sections and it is well to bear this in mind in building to it.

Up until 1961 the C.C.A. rule had a heavy penalty on stability via ballast ratio; which led to the use of ridiculously heavy bronze floors by some famous American designers; expensively camouflaged ballast. And of very heavily-built water tanks, low-slung over-size electric accumulators, and the like. Things were getting out of hand and so they changed the rule to include an inclining experiment as a measure of stability. But the angle to which the vessel was inclined was so small (to make it easy to apply in practice) that this part of the rule is likely to come in for revision by the high-powered committee, which is gallantly, at the time of writing, trying to sort out a new international rule.

The measurement in America of length on a plane well above the waterline has resulted in tucking up the counters and in straightening out of the ends above that plane. The necessity to tuck away displacement with a big beam and with a minimum wetted area has led to filling in the garboard turn, and to slackening off of the bilgeline, so that, rather as in the much narrower international classes, the waistline seems in some cases to have slipped a bit. However, so nicely are the lines drawn that these boats go like smoke in spite of their displacement, more particularly when reaching. Unfortunately many healthy light-displacement boats are excluded from the Bermuda Race. Though one sympathises with the rule-makers' fear that crazy plywood skiffs might some day predominate, one hopes that a way round may found. In the case of occasional more or less distin-guished visiting yachts our kind American hosts have turned a blind eye to the displacement limits. But this is fundamentally an unsatisfactory state of affairs, for potential owners and designers alike.

Quarter Beam Depth and the R.O.R.C. Rule. British offshore yacht designers who up to then had had no special reason to choose a particular section, have under recent rules been set a somewhat similar problem in designing around the immersed quarter beam depth, or near measurements which are the standard point on which depth, as a part substitute for displacement, is gauged.

The R.O.R.C. rule was formulated originally more with a view to measuring existing cruising boats than to guiding the design. The early pundits were necessarily and rightly impressed with the requirement to give the straight-stemmers a decent chance against the out-and-out racing types. Moreover, boats had to be measured afloat. The rule bases its length measurement on the distance between girth stations, which encourages short ends. Nevertheless it has succeeded over the years in bringing together a great variety of yachts and in giving them fine racing with everyone feeling that they had a sporting chance of winning.

The R.O.R.C. rule measures the depth *below the water* at a quarter of the beam out from the centre-line. Depth is measured from the inside of the skin.

Some Recent English Designs. Special shortening of the bow overhang has paid and may still pay, although the 'new', 1957–68 R.O.R.C. rule treats bow overhang more favourably than in the past. The fashion was led by *Mindy* and followed by *Myth of Malham.* More recently, a number of potent racers have had the same feature, which in lightish boats is not necessarily at all bad. *Uomie* is a good one from Arthur Robb's board and *Phizz* by Frederick Parker. Among the amateur designers Guy Thomson is outstanding with his *Calliopes.*

Charles Nicholson, Jnr., has been very successful with the fairly big-beamed boats and these are short-ended in some cases; *Griffin II*, ex *Alitia*, ex *Yeoman*, winner of the 1951 Fastnet, by the same designer had these features less pronouncedly. He has also shown his versatility in the design of *Cohoe II* and *Cohoe III*, both 26-ft. waterline but widely different in type; and more recently with the similar sized *Jolinas.*

Among the medium-sized yachts, *Quiver III* 33-ft. waterline has gone very well indeed in fresh weather conditions. The designer has chosen in this case to gamble on a small sail area and a low rating and in a good number of races in 1961 and 1962 this gamble paid off. Since then Peter Nicholson, now the leader of the great firm, has put out many fine and successful designs.

More recently but with the same object in view, Angus Primrose and I at Emsworth put forward in 1960 two new designs: the *Maica* and *Blue Charm* types, both 'New Twenty-Four-Footers'. These are of special interest because they are contemporary designs, out of the same stable, and of the same waterline length—the R.O.R.C. minimum—but of completely different type. *Maica* of 5·3 tons displacement was designed to be an all-rounder: fast but with an easy motion; to have no tricks and be as easy to sail as possible. Her construction is normal, and economy is to be achieved by series production. She can sleep seven. *Blue Charm* is a light boat designed as a flat-out ocean racer, which, owing to its small displacement—3·45 tons—can be produced economically. Her sail area is only two-thirds that of *Maica*, and so, apart from the obvious economy in hull material, there will be a *pro rata* saving in mast, rigging, and sail costs. In fact the final costs of the boats come out very closely in proportion to their weights. The *Blue Charms* have five berths.

In the first big race in which these two types were matched—210 miles in 1961 to Harwich—they finished first and second on corrected time separated only by a couple of minutes. *Maica* was the winner over *Alcina*, but later in the season *Blue Charm* (the first of her class) had her revenge in the Woodbine Trophy, *Maica* being second and *Alcina* third—among a hundred-odd starters, incidentally. The point of the story is that under the R.O.R.C. rule of rating both heavy and light boats can have roughly equal chances of success.

About one hundred of the *Maicas*—some with counters and some transom-sterned—have been built at the time of writing. They have been described by the Press as 'Baby Belmores'. This is, however, inaccurate; *Belmore* was designed to the C.C.A. rule as it was in 1958, and has in consequence a heavy displacement of 8·3 tons on a 26·5-ft. waterline. *Maica*'s were a completely new set of lines drawn in 1959.

We can continue the interesting comparison between light and medium displacement performances in a larger size of boat in events of 1962, when Illingworth & Primrose had two new designs put afloat, both of about 6½ tons displacement; *Brigantine* of 26·5-ft. waterline and *Dambuster*—30 ft. on the water. Each won a good R.O.R.C. Class race during the season, so that comparison can be considered fair; as between good boats of the same vintage. Both will sail well up to their ratings to windward in any weight of breeze. In fresh windward work the lighter boat may have the edge, and *vice versa*; a thing which may surprise some people, but which is explained by considerations dealt with elsewhere in this book.

As to the recent work of Laurent Giles & Partners, the interest in sea-going light displacement sailing yachts which followed in the train of *Myth* resulted in a number of yachts on more or less similar lines. It was also inevitable that in the course of his designing, Giles should have continued a parallel output of conventional yachts. Of the 250 or so boats built to their drawings since the *Myth* about 10 per cent have in fact followed that line. But there have been many lying between the extremes of light and heavy. Giles himself was an enthusiast for the lights; suitably dealt with. He was equally enthusiastic for the modern interpretation of the intermediate displacement type. On the light displacement side we have *Sopranino* (Diagram 86); the successful *Miranda IV* in the Mediterranean; and then the latest of them *Gypsella*. Among the heavier boats we have *Lutine*; though she failed when quite new in American seas she has since settled down to do really well in European waters. And also *Nina V* in the Mediterranean. *Lutine*'s plans are shown in Diagram 41.

Sparkman & Stephens continue to design lovely yachts and I am glad to have their permission to publish their plans. The maximum speeds of their designs are in general high for their length, in spite of ample beam, and a displacement which has not been unduly reduced. This is perhaps a legacy of their experience in the model towing tanks, together with their experience of the bonus which the C.C.A. rule confers on displacement.

Future Rule Tendencies. It is always difficult to prophesy which way the rules of rating will be altered because new tendencies may become evident in yacht design which need special treatment.

The new rating rule together with the present rule of the Royal Ocean Racing Club is given in Appendices VII and VIII. Some notes are provided on the practical effect of this 'new't-rule, commonly called, although it is now quite long established. Since the last edition was published a change has been made in the sizes of yachts eligible for the R.O.R.C. Classes. Owing to present-day costs few yachts had been added in recent years to Classes I and II whereas Class III was growing out of proportion. To achieve a better distribution of yachts in each class the Class I consists of yachts from 30 ft. to 70 ft. rating. Class II has been split into IIA 25 ft. to under 29 ft. and IIB 22·5 ft. to under 25 ft; Class IIIA into 21 ft. to under 22·5 ft. and Class IIIB 19 ft. to under 21 ft.

At the time of going to press a high-powered international committee has, as previously mentioned, drafted a new international rule of rating. This is roughly based on the R.O.R.C. hull measurement but allowing rather more generous buttocks, in part substituting an inclining experiment for the scantling allowance, slightly more generous sail plan overlaps and stiffer aspect ratio penalties. Details of the rule are given in Appendix VII.

It is hoped by the rule makers that this rule of measurement will be acceptable world wide to replace the R.O.R.C. and C.C.A. measurement and rating rules. Broadly speaking, at present the R.O.R.C. system is in use throughout Europe, Asia, and Australia, and the C.C.A. rule in North and South America. One of the big difficulties is that the R.O.R.C. can measure almost any vessel afloat, while the C.C.A. generally call for architects' drawings which are often not available in older vessels.

It is very possible that an attempt will be made later to tax very small fins; or to give a bonus to yachts with a fair amount of underwater wetted area. The rule makers have not during the present new rule been brave enough to wear this thorny crown, but there is no doubt that the recent tendency to build 'rule fitting' yachts with very small keel fins, very big beams, and very low ballast ratios, has produced a crop of less healthy yachts of which purchasers of second-hand vessels need to beware.

You may say at this point that you just want a good boat and no attention paid to rating. And that is certainly the way you should start your design. However, it is as well to study the impact of the rule on a boat, because it is against her rating that a boat's performance is judged by others, and probably in time, by yourself. However fair a rule tries to be, and however cunningly it is devised, there are bound to be some features which it favours more than others. The best way is to know your rule and what it likes, and then to compromise a little at certain points to meet it, which can generally be done without real sacrifice of the design.

Hull Balance. The balance of a hull is achieved by having matching ends or rather halves of a boat, not necessarily the same at both ends, but in bulk and line such that when the ship is heeled she does not tend to run up into the wind or dive away from it. This is of course the job of the architect and is a big part of his problem. The curves of areas for the hull heeled at 25 or 30 degrees for an easy bilged boat, should lie roughly parallel to the curve of areas upright, and fairness of diagonals is important.

One of the most interesting methods of checking on balance is the late Rear-Admiral Turner's Metacentric Shelf method, which furnishes one with a draughtsman's ready method of finding out how any design of hull will behave in respect of balance. This method is extraordinarily accurate and useful for this purpose; but there is a danger. If the amateur designer takes this system as a foundation for his lines he will very likely end up with a boat which is very much the same at both ends—and though it will probably balance, it will lack power in its quarters. In other words it should be used only as a semi-final check after which small adjustments only need be made, perhaps to the keel, perhaps to the body; and should not be used as a foundation of design. The art of the thing is to get a fast and powerful hull that will still balance.

The other point to have clear in mind is that although naturally one arranges the position of the sail plan carefully so that its centre of effort is in the correct place, balance is fundamentally a thing of the hull. Although you may improve the balance, perhaps by moving the mast forward to reduce a tendency to gripe, you will not make a really well-balanced boat of her. On the other hand a boat like *Myth* or *Monk of Malham* which are really well-balanced, will sail quite well under any two, or all three sails; or under staysail alone.

It is important to distinguish between *weight* on the tiller and helm *angle*. If a yacht has a good big rudder which enables one to steer with minimum helm—important—and a shortish tiller (to which the designer has perhaps been driven by an owner demanding a lot of accommodation leaving little cockpit length) a yacht may be heavy to steer, still without carrying any excess helm; that is to say being a well balanced and good-steering hull. The answer is probably in that case to have wheel steering, which takes up much less cockpit length than a tiller.

Just another word about the balance of the ends. Tests have shown that at low and moderate speeds —within the range of the speeds we can expect from *small* hulls—that the shape of the fore body is more important to speed than the shape of the run. This enables the designer of a small yacht to place the maximum bulk of his boat aft of the centre of the waterline and to have kinder entries in his waterlines. Fortunately also this often makes a boat, other things being the same, easier in a seaway, and easier to balance.

Rails and Bulwarks. Bulwarks are favoured chiefly because they look nice in a boat; they are 'shippy'. On straight-sheered decks they can be curved to simulate a more normal sheer line. They also give one a feeling of security when moving about the deck at sea. This is probably partly illusory, because a good toe rail with the life-line (which one must have anyway) will provide nearly all the safety that is to be had. In low-freeboard boats they do defer the moment when the rail goes under and they keep some of the sea in its place. But they involve appreciable weight and windage and collect quite a weight of water in the lee scuppers, which has a negative effect on stability, and so hardly pay their way from a racing point of view. One gets a minute allowance under R.O.R.C. rules which is now incorporated in the scantling component of the stability allowance. The C.C.A. allowance is greater, and more commensurate with their cost to speed.

Sheer Line. The origin of the curved sheer line is partly to do with the shape of the work craft, from whaling to surf boats, from which yachts are descended; and perhaps partly because the sailing ships had high fo'c'sles and poops with lower levels between in way of the hatches.

At any rate we have become accustomed to a curved sheer line which is fundamentally unsuited to the small and moderate-sized yacht, and becomes particularly tiresome in a light displacement design, because it either robs you of your space in the hull in her middle length, where you most need it, or alternatively, if you give yourself the depth you need here, it pushes the ends of the boat up unreasonably. So for better or for worse in small yachts the flat or reverse sheer deck has come to stay.

Freeboards and Rating. There is no doubt that extra freeboard means extra weight—which might otherwise be put into the keel without changing the scantling allowance—and some appreciable extra windage going to windward. Therefore there is an allowance for freeboard and depth in the R.O.R.C. rule and the new international rule. Under the old rule the freeboard allowance was really intended to compensate for the extra measured length which you get owing to the girth station being pushed out by the extra freeboard. The depth allowance should compensate for the cost-to-speed of the freeboard, which depth you need to get the desirable amount of room in your hull in the middle length. Under the 1957 and subsequent rules the freeboard allowance is amalgamated with the scantling allowance. (*See* Appendices VII and VIII.)

In the C.C.A. rule where girth stations do not affect length the freeboard is measured at the waterline endings, and a bonus awarded on this. There is no additional allowance for depth of freeboard at middle length.

Although the C.C.A. freeboard bonus decreases if you are measured in a heavy condition, the displacement—in calculating this, allowance is made for trim—will increase by about enough to compensate for this. So in practice there is no need to off-load a lot of stores and so on before measurement.

Stern Shapes. People often ask me which sort of stern is most seaworthy, and generally go on to suggest that a canoe stern is likely to part the overtaking seas and prevent them breaking on board. Personally I have failed to detect any difference in the manner in which the various shapes react to overtaking waves. One of the worst poops I remember was entering Hong Kong Harbour in a strong breeze at the end of a short offshore race in 1928. I had then a nice Albert Strange designed yawl *Queen Bee* in which we managed that year to lift the championship. She had a canoe stern, but when the sea decided to come aboard over the stern, it just came.

Conversely when we crossed the Atlantic to the eastward in *Myth* in 1948, the wind and sea were for a lot of the time strong or fresh and occasionally gale force on our quarter or astern; the prevailing winds being westerly. We never took any sea water over the stern, although *Myth* has a big square cut-off transom. The only casual wave which really intruded in a big way came over the quarter abreast the helmsman—which no shape of stern would have avoided.

I do think a little bit of buoyancy in the stern section does help, and there is no doubt that good freeboard here does assist too, in keeping the sea from slopping over into the cockpit: it helps protect one from those casual undisciplined wave tops which comes across from time to time. In her original trim the *Maid of Malham* had not much freeboard aft, for her length, and the water used to topple in from the lee side as well as the weather side when she was heeled. She has since been retrimmed with advantage.

Now and then friends, talking about long offshore passages, generally having not done any, shudder at the thought of a transom stern: 'One is so unprotected in a following sea.' Other things being equal they are in fact steadier running, because the counter, when struck by an overtaking sea, often slews the yacht slightly off course. I have built two class designs of different sizes, both identical except for counter and transom versions; and myself tried and seen this thing. Among the notable transom-sterners we may note old *Landfall*, 60-ft. waterline. Our *Belmore* has crossed many oceans, including a direct passage from Rio de Janeiro to Portsmouth, England.

Some years ago there was a well-marked tendency among British designers of ocean racers to draw out long thin counters, sometimes with very modest freeboard, in order to get the best sailing length in between the measurer's girth chains. This fashion is now less popular and the stern is either chopped off or tucked up; in the latter case sometimes to an extent where the counter is in effect more like a canoe stern. But the possibility of obtaining extra length aft should always be borne in mind; and the long counter used where it pays. Provided it is not too wide it has no ill effect on seaworthiness, and it may ease her motion going to windward.

Cost and Displacement. I have indicated the advantages of light displacement and must add a word as to the degree to which one should go. A good seagoing form can be evolved with extremely light displacement and this in itself does not indicate a low limit. I would say that the economical limit of low displacement is that at which the construction can still be simple and the ballast ratio still adequate. At this point the boat should be good value; cheaper to build and with appreciably less sail area and rigging to maintain than a heavy displacement boat of the same length. But when one has to have triple skins and multi-stringers and so on the economy may disappear; though it must be said that it depends mostly on the technique to which the yard is accustomed.

However it is a fallacy that light displacement yachts must necessarily cost more because the men have to put in more careful work. Men in a particular yard get used to working to a particular standard which in round terms they will maintain whatever the type of boat. But conversely it is clearly the case that some light displacement designs are unsuited to those accustomed only to build, say, large fishing craft. Small fishing boats on the other hand often demand, and get, nice work.

In 1955 we completed the design of a 33-ft. waterline yawl *Artica II*, for the Italian Naval Sailing Association. She has a main mast 49-ft. deck to truck, and beam of 10 ft. Fitted with aluminium alloy frames, beams, and floors, she represents at $5\frac{1}{2}$ tons somewhere near the present low limit of practicable displacement. Writing in 1969 it is satisfactory to record that she is still winning good races.

7*

20

CONSTRUCTION

This is not a draughtsman's manual and no attempt has been made to cover completely this vast subject. All that we shall try and do is to say a few things about the special requirements of offshore racing, and a little about new developments in construction.

When building a cruiser one generally is not very particular as to the weight of the scantlings. One can use Lloyd's, or go a bit above as fancy takes one, or copy fishing boat practice if we are using that sort of a building yard. If we are doing a one-design boat the drawings are detailed. If it is to be built to an International rule the scantlings are laid down neatly in advance. But when we come to designing our ocean racer we have a completely free hand. We can build it anyhow we please—which is one of the reasons why the problem of designing such a craft is so fascinating.

We noted in the design chapter that the problem sometimes boils itself down to getting the lightest hull we can, subject to the over-riding consideration that it must be fully strong enough to cope with all conditions at sea. The scantling component dead-line of the R.O.R.C. rule makes it advisable not to go appreciably below Lloyd's old R class scantlings or thereabouts, and these give us a good rough guide to our minimum sizes, though we are not in any way bound to them.

Loading at Sea. The primary difference between the stresses found inshore and offshore in yacht racing is that while inshore the loading is comparatively static, at sea, owing to the motion, it is alternating, which not only results in reversals of loading at each roll or pitch, but increases appreciably the maximum loading, due firstly to the inertia effects of the masses to be dealt with and secondly to the blows and strains, which the sea deals out to the hull.

There is another difference in loading, due to rig fashion. For reasons discussed in the chapter on rigs, it is usual in offshore racers to allow a much bigger proportion of the total sail area in the fore triangle which appreciably increases the compressive loading in the mast, and the thrust of the mast on the step. This loading, in combination with the upward pull of the shrouds, tends firstly to open the garboard seams and secondly to straighten the ship's side between the gunwale and the keel in way of the mast.

The ballast keel will represent somewhere between 30 and 60 per cent of the total displacement and in a seaway the resulting bending loads on the structure are severe, principally just above the wood keel. And so broadly, the ocean racer's special problems of construction centre mainly around the floors, for both sets of loads have their seat thereabouts.

I will deal firstly with wood construction because the majority of specially-built yachts, to the owners' own requirements, are so built.

Floor Arrangement. In many larger yachts one deals with this problem by providing deep steel plate floors extending from the cabin sole to the keel. There are steel angles welded or riveted on to these at the top and bottom to stiffen them and to take the keel bolts; and they are bolted through to the frames or to the strength bulkheads. In addition there is a longitudinal steel central member between the steel floors. The mast steps on to this steel network.

Owing perhaps to the facilities available at the building yard, using all wood floors, the yard often prefer the wood keelson which runs over the top of the wood floors and is checked not too deeply into them. The keel bolts then run up through this keelson. The keelson is deepened in way of the mast to form a step, tapering away forward and aft in depth. It is most important to have ample washers, plates really, of similar material under the keel bolt heads (or nuts) on this keelson. Obvious, but still a matter which often receives insufficient attention. This construction has the snag that it takes up rather a lot of space under the sole, and reduces stowage space which is required for water tanks, anchors, chain, stores, and electric batteries. However, tanks and batteries can be divided, and food tins and water containers can be stowed farther forward, and passed in under the keelson. The point where the ballast keel or deadwood ends forward is potentially weak, particularly with the ballast concentrated. Either the stem here must be deep, or reinforced.

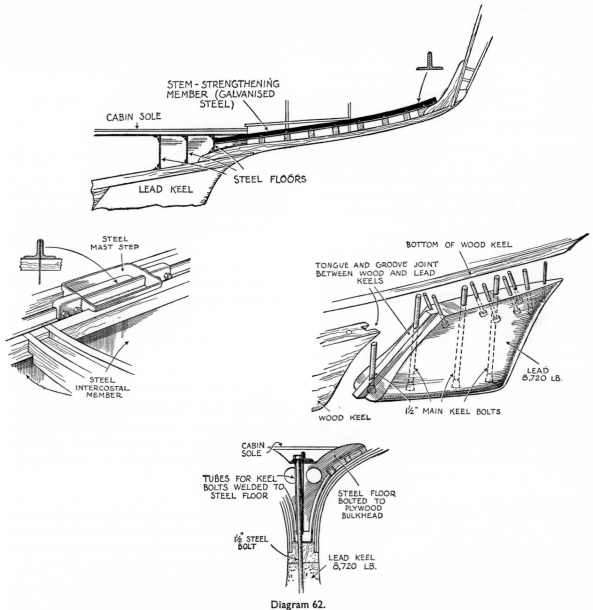

Diagram 62.
Myth of Malham—Composite Stem Construction, Steel Floors, Keel and Mast-step

Laminated Members. Much more recently (1962–9) we have used in many dozens of boats a different system. The centre-line framing: stem, wood keel, stern post, and hog, are made up in one continuous lamination from stem head to transom. This requires a biggish mould, but once this is made the centre line of a big yacht can be made up very quickly and cheaply. As 'grown crooks' are now a rarity this system is all the more desirable, since apart from avoiding scarphed joints between stem and keel and so on, it keeps the grain following truly the curved members. Very many years ago in

a new yacht of mine, owing to the builders inability to get grown crooks, they used a stem of which part had relatively short grain. The stem split at sea; in bad weather the vessel and all of us could easily have been lost.

In conjunction with this laminated centre line I generally use important main laminated wood floors; wide enough to pass the keel bolt through, without undue reduction of section. These look like leaf springs, tapering away as they get further from the centre line. I believe these are an almost ideal way of gradually transferring the loading imposed by the ballast keel to the structure generally, and probably better in general than less flexible steel floors. In the way of the mast I often put in several virtually all-round-the-ship laminated members; carried through the coachroof where necessary by important hanging knees. They may join or overlap the laminated floors. Unfortunately the R.O.R.C. scantling allowance is not kind as a rule to long floors and special members.

In larger yachts it is still desirable to have a steel centre line fabricated member to distribute the thrust of the mast heel; and towards the end of a boat the conventional forged mild steel (or if the owner is rich enough in stainless steel) can be useful; as can the occasional use of plate floors where the bilge is narrow; right aft perhaps. Wherever possible I like to run the steamed timber in one length, laminated if necessary, from gunwale to gunwale; and secured to the wood keel by one, two, or three bolts.

Deck Beams. All main deck beams should be laminated. Once the former is made, and using the same mould throughout, making them up out of strips of spruce (or mahogany, much cheaper and glues equally well) is a simple job for the apprentices. The reasoning is the same. These laminated members, floors, knees, beams, or what will you, not only have the grain running the right way but the penetration of a 'permanent' modern glue into the relatively thin laminates further increases the strength. And finally when properly designed, they have in practice no tendency to distort, or straighten out like purely steamed members.

Timbers. By the same token I virtually never use grown timbers (frames), but nearly always use the ply bulkheads as strength and shape-keeping members. The use of grown timbers in old traditional construction, generally between each or each two steamed, was dictated by a wish to assist in keeping shape, for which it was held the steamed alone were insufficient. But stressed ply bulkheads were then a rarity; or, earlier, unknown. And the long deep laminated floors or all round the hull laminated members had not been thought of; partly because glue was much less good.

We owe the rapid progress of glues largely to the now dying wooden aircraft industry. There are several first-class products but care must be taken to use a glue which has a long pot life after mixing and is not, at the time of application, too temperature conscious; one which will operate well over the range of temperatures likely to be encountered in the yard in question. Normally, glueing should be discontinued in all but specially-heated sheds in frosty or near frosty conditions. I have had consistently good results from Aerodux type 185; CIBA

Ltd., Cambridge, England; and from Leicester Lovell & Co., North Baddesley, Southampton, Hampshire. These are recorcinol formaldehyde glues.

Side Planking. As regards the skin, the lightest construction is cold moulded. The yacht's lines need to be made up complete in mould form and placed up-side-down. A groove is cut to take the centre line members, stem, keel, and so on. Then thin strips of knife-cut wood, generally mahogany of 3 or 4 mm. thick, are bent cold and run diagonally from the centre line members to 'above' the gunwale. The next skins are glued on, opposite diagonally again, until nearly the required total thickness is achieved. Then the outermost skin is put on, generally fore and aft, which makes painting easier. If the yacht is to be varnished, specially cut uniform mahogany (preferably Honduras) is specified for the outer skin.

Multi-Stringers. I sometimes run the rabbet line down and out at the bottom of the stem so that in way of the ballast the skin comes to the bottom of the wood keel, and gets a much better hold of the centre line. Where objection is taken to the cost of a complete mould one can, as an alternative, make conventional vertical moulds straight off the laying-down floor, but at rather closer spacing than usual, and then put in small multi-stringers at very close spacing, notched into the centre-line framing at each end. On these one can then glue the first skin. This system we used successfully on the Class I racer *Glenan* and other yachts. But I prefer the full moulded hull, which when turned over is timbered out and fitted with the leaf spring floors and so on.

There is a tendency among those using both cold and hot (enclave dried) moulded hulls unduly to decrease the size and increase the spacing of the timbers because the skin is so strong and homogeneous. In estuary cruisers one gets away with it, but for really serious offshore sailing one can easily over-play this one, and later need to add timbers and refasten where movement is apparent.

Nearly all that I have said about the constructional members applies equally to yachts conventionally planked. Clearly in the planked vessels one chooses closer timbers and a greater thickness of planking; planks carefully weathered after rough sawing. I always try and arrange for glued and splined top and bottom sides, provided weathered timber is available. Carefully done this not only makes for a stronger hull, but saves a deal of paint upkeep, once afloat, and through the years.

Choice of Timber. Selected good African mahogany is today a reasonably priced boat building timber which can be used for nearly every part of a yacht; in the context of the wood constructional systems

I have outlined. Where money allows, a conventionally planked yacht will obviously be planked in teak, but the material cost will be at least three times as great, and the labour time appreciably increased. New glues do cope with teak splines. I don't use teak, unless specially asked, for anything except skin, deck, soles, and deck trim. While in so many ways the king of woods for these jobs, it is when short grained not so strong, as well as being heavy, and expensive to buy and work.

There are many African sources of mahogany; little comes now from the West Indies. The lightest good mahogany is generally from the Grand Bassam, but it is generally a little less strong than some other sources. I like to weather it naturally; but skilfully kiln-dried mahogany can be useful.

Modern paints are more resistant to worm attack and the need and wish to have an all teak boat, with teak centre-line framing, is less today than of old. Much of the prejudice against mahogany as a skin-planking wood stems from 'nail sickness'; deterioration around the fastenings. This is generally in way of iron or steel floors and if you adopt my modern right-round timbers, and laminated wood floors you won't, I guess, suffer this thing. In yachts with steel floors I try and plank up to the top of the floors with other than mahogany: teak or pitch pine for preference; or if the money does not permit, iroko, or larch. Iroko is good also for deadwood; less easily attacked by worm; cheap and fairly easily worked. It takes glue less well than mahogany; but with modern glues, acceptably.

Strength in Way of Mast. I mentioned the tendency of the sides to straighten out under the mast and shroud loading and our modern answers. This has in the past generally been countered by the use of two or three over-size grown frames, in way of the mast. Something similar happens at the runner backstays. Steamed timbers whose grain runs with the wood all the way are very much stronger for their weight than grown timber. Moreover they can be run round in one piece, whereas grown timbers have as a rule to be built up in several sections, if they are to conform to modern midship sections. Anyway a grown timber is not ideal for the extent of the stiffening needed in way of the mast. It is better to use laminated bent timbers rather than to try to bend excessively large frames which tend to straighten subsequently. The floor of course takes care of the stiffness or shape up as far as the cabin sole. We should take firmly on to these with either strengthened timbers or a frame of steel or aluminium alloy, or alternatively with a strength bulkhead. We can have the rods from the neighbourhood of the chain plates to the steel floors. But these are not much good unless

they are initially stressed, preferably by a turnbuckle, or bottle-screw, with the usual right and left-hand threads. Of course one can get the necessary rigidity by simply making everything half as heavy again as it needs to be. But I am assuming that the object of the operation is to make things as light as possible consistent with getting the necessary enduring strength and the enduring accuracy of form.

Loading Due to Runners. With the use of levers we now get out running backstays, on the average, much tauter than we used to and when the boat is heeled and the mast goes over bodily, slightly to leeward, the runners, in addition to holding the mast back, will also assist the shrouds a great deal. This, within limits, is no bad thing as it tautens up the forestay by a like amount, but it does result in greatly increased loading at the point of attachment of the runners, and specific arrangements are needed to counter this. While designers arrange terrific chain plates to the shrouds, running way down into the bilge, they are often content simply to bolt the runners through the shelf. I have seen a modern gunwale lifted so that one saw daylight under it. Incidentally I notice that some American 6's have moved their runners in from the ship's side, feeling that these have been doing too much work.

Shrouds to the Mast Heel. There is quite a lot to be said for running the shrouds through the deck to the steel floors. This is done on some 'class' boats and reduces the tendency of the hull to straighten out—which is unfortunately the natural thing for bent timbers and bent planking to do—and replaces this with a smaller opposite tendency and transfers the shroud loading to a point close to where the mast-step load arrives.

However this has to be schemed out in advance of the accommodation into which it cuts a good bit; this method can cut into the bunks. One would have to use the space abreast the shrouds for stowages that could be arranged between the run of the shrouds. It is doubtful whether any gland will keep out all the drips all the time. Heavy grease with soft packing will help a lot. Very positive location of the guides at deck level must be provided, and these must lead the shroud kindly round a big radius bend. If this is done plough steel wire, that is, the stiffer standing rigging, will function without trouble round this point. Two subsidiary advantages are that the windage of the rigging screws is eliminated and their weight is lowered. Implicit in the primary advantage is the reduction in the weight of the necessary special bracing to the timbers in way of the mast, but the compressive athwartship stress on the deck level, tending to close in the ship's side towards one another is still there and slightly increased, so the necessity to fit bracing to the coachroof, if one's mast passes through this, is still present.

Stepping a Mast on Deck. Then there is the important alternative scheme of stepping the mast on deck which I have used in over six hundred yachts. The two principal advantages of this are that one does away with or reduces mast obstruction below decks—important in small yachts—and that one does away with possible deck leaks here. In the bermuda rig, as we have observed in the chapter on masting and rigging, the mast is primarily a strut in pure compression. However if it starts its life as an *encastré* beam—a stalk planted in the hull—it is bound to bend. And its function as a straight strut is interfered with, if the mast is allowed to go over much. In practice this interference appears to be not too great, and the shrouds are appreciably relieved by the extent of the loading necessary to bend the mast. So the *encastré* effect will be a positive assistance if the extent to which the mast goes over bodily can be reduced to a negligible amount. This incidentally is strong argument in favour of high initial shroud tensions. A subsidiary advantage of the scheme of stepping the mast on deck is that re-stepping when fitting out is much facilitated; and the same for canal passages.

Stepping of the mast on deck is feasible with an all-round framing of steel or aluminium alloy, or with a similar type of bulkhead with doors or openings in it. A version of this used in our *Maica*-type yachts, to allow a free gangway on the centre line. Another scheme without undue complication, is to have a steel tubular pillar either side of the mast, on a bulkhead. These, wood dressed, are not visible. Athwartships, the span between the pillar tops is bridged on deck by a steel mast step. Or alternatively again an aluminium or steel tube can be fitted, in way of the mast, underdeck. The all-round frame can be combined with the floor and additional local longitudinals if necessary. When it is used, the distance between the lower cross-trees and the deck will need reconsideration, since this distance is normally increased and the shroud angle decreased, partly on account of the support which the lower part of the mast gets from the deck or from the cabin roof. This won't suit the cutters whose staysails sheet inside the main span of the shrouds.

Plywood Decks. Turning to the question of decks, there are clear advantages in marine plywood; particularly in the absence of teak and many of the other good decking woods. Its merit lies in its lack of seams and in its uniform strength in all directions; also it is very appreciably cheaper to lay than

narrow deck planking—since these planks must be narrow to minimise distortion under changes of moisture and temperature. Thickness for thickness it is not light—contrary to popular idea—and saving in weight must come from using a lesser thickness and a lesser number of fastenings, which strength for strength, is feasible, while still saving weight.

I am not yet sure that ply will be a long-term success for ships' sides, where bruising may have unfortunate results. But clearly it is first-class for decks of all sized yachts. It must in any case be heavily painted and/or be covered in good canvas carefully put on, on top of wet paint or special compound. Provided the paint above is looked after it will last twenty years at least. The smaller the yacht, the greater the advantage appears to be, since the difficulties of deck laying are greater and it is relatively more costly than in large yachts. But I have used, very successfully ply decks in yachts of up to 100 feet in length. And for coach-roofs, I think it is tops: it can be very much lighter and tighter and cheaper than many alternative constructions, though honourable mention must be made of pressed woods, such as tempered masonite, for the same duty. Canvas for decks should be (basically from the mill) untreated to assist paint adherence.

But a word of warning should be sounded concerning ply. There are umpteen qualities. The highest quality which allows of practically no faults in the layers, is as scarce as hen's teeth, and generally is only found in aircraft construction. It is many per cent stronger than the ordinary good plywood. The next grades are still quite suitable for marine construction. The bonding material, however, is important and the general term 'waterproof' covers a multitude of plywood sins, and should not be trusted. Double phenolic bonded is satisfactory; though there are a number of other bonding specifications developed for airplane use which are also good. In any case the ends of the ply grain after cutting and before erection should be treated with a preservative, such as cuprinol, provided aluminium alloy is not bedded thereon. The plywood BS 1088 is all right for yachts.

There are, of course, many other places where plywood can be used with advantage such as in constructing the bottom and sides of the cockpit where it saves the great weight of the lead sheet metal trays used in old-time standard practice to ensure watertightness. For bulkheads, including sides and the ends of deck erections, it is fine, and far stronger than slabs of mahogany or tongued and grooved board. But the whole of the plywood in the bilges must be coated with preservative.

Another wood which has not enjoyed all the popularity it deserves is western red cedar. This is available in fair quantity from Commonwealth sources—Canada as a rule. It has the outstanding merits of being exceptionally proof against warping and shrinking and is very resistant to rot. It is very light—generally around 25 lb. per cu. ft., which is 4 lb. less than Sitka spruce—though not so strong under bending. Naturally, as with very light woods, it is soft. For internal joinery work generally it has no peer, and saves pounds over the use of 'common deal'; and it does not warp.

Aluminium for Ship Work. As to aluminium alloys for framing and similar duties I am sure there is a bright future for these materials provided the correct alloys are used, and provided the necessary care is taken with the fastenings and painting. The whole of the structure (except skin and deck) of *Artica II* is in aluminium alloy. We used this in this yacht because of the prime need to save weight, while maintaining the strength required of an ocean racer. She displaces only 5·4 tons on a 33-ft. waterline. But after ten years some renewals of alloy were needed.

Aluminium alloy for use in small craft generally comes roughly into two categories; that required to be worked for general use about the ship, and that needed for spars. The resistance to corrosion of the types varies, but is in any case fundamentally better than that of steel; other than stainless steel, which on account of its cost is not in very general use. It does, however, suffer from the special disability that it is apt to corrode if in direct contact with many other metals. This arises from electrolytic action—'corrosion currents'—between aluminium alloys and other metals when in contact with one another in sea-moistened air, or in sea water. The rate of corrosion is much greater in sea water than in the air. The degree of corrosion depends on the natural differences in electrical potential between the metals. Any material which is rich in copper or nickel such as brass, bronze, or monel metal, is therefore not suitable for fastenings. Stainless steel and lead are also very slightly anodic to aluminium though not nearly so strongly as copper and brass.

Contact with other Metals. Iron and mild steel are slightly anodic, but very much less so than brass. Cadmium has approximately the same electrolytic potential as aluminium and is therefore very suitable from this point of view as a coating for steel in contact with aluminium alloy. Unfortunately, it does not in general stand up to sea air and wear quite as well as zinc coating—such as galvanising.

Zinc is cathodic to aluminium and therefore any action should be in the zinc and not in the aluminium. In practice it is a satisfactory coating for steel fastenings used for securing aluminium, in cases where cadmium is not available. A few woods are said to affect aluminium alloys adversely, but I have so far been able to explain this by some definite reason such as the use of a wrong alloy, in all instances which have come to my notice.

Mercury is 'very anodic' and care must in consequence be taken that no mercury anti-fouling paint is used on aluminium alloys.

Insulating Gaskets. To avoid electrolytic effects the aluminium alloys should be insulated from metals other than cadmium or zinc. Fibre sheeting of a water-resisting type of tufnol; or rubber sheet or a plastic liner, according to the position, are all good. A good dollop of bituminous paint is pretty effective and easier of application in cases where aluminium sections come up against steel structures. Zinc oxide paste is recommended, alternatively.

Paints for Light Alloys. In cases where the parts in contact are not going to be regularly and constantly immersed, such as steel fittings well up in aluminium alloy masts, zinc oxide, or zinc chromate paints are probably sufficient, provided the paint is rich enough in those constituents. Lead base paints are unsuitable. Care must be taken that protective paints containing sulphate of copper are not used on wood or canvas adjacent to light alloys.

The alloys referred to below have excellent resistance to corrosion and don't in general need painting as a protection against the sea. But when they require painting for the purpose referred to in the preceding paragraph, or for decorative purposes, they may need special cleaning. If they are greasy, thorough degreasing with a solvent such as trichlorethylene should be carried out; alkalis can be used for degreasing, but it is inadvisable as all alkalis will attack aluminium, and are deadly enemies of almost all paints, so that the merest trace remaining on the surface or in a crack may prove dangerous. The paints referred to above are good for first coats, and will adhere well. Many fittings and sections come from the makers in a protected condition. Anodising is the best known, but there are forms of pickling, and other patent processes. These do not, as a rule, need to be painted over.

Talking of aluminium alloys for general ship use as frames, channels, stiffening angles, and so on, the easiest range of alloys readily available are those containing round about 2 per cent of magnesium. These may also contain some manganese and chromium, in small doses. A typical British Standard Specification is A.W.4. This range of alloy work hardens only to a moderate degree and in so doing there is a gain in strength. It is of the utmost importance to have corrosion resisting rivets also.

Light Alloys—Bending and Forging. Alloys in this group can be cold bent, extruded and joined with facility. In fact, it is remarkable through what acute bends heavy sections can be worked. Panel beating to get bends in two planes is easy. It is worth remembering that when heavy sheets are to be bent the edges should first be trimmed fair of shearing ridges. Hot forging is not so straight forward. A shipyard tradesman can however soon learn to cope with frame bending, provided he has an electric furnace. A.W.5 or A.W.6 may be preferred for hot bending. A.W.4 for cold work.

The welding of structural aluminium members by torch is feasible. B.O.C. No. 35 covered wire rods are often used with magnesium aluminium alloys.

For rough calculations of *ultimate* strength you can assume that this material is half the strength of mild steel and one-third the weight. In practice for frames, etc., of small craft, it can be used with only 50 per cent increase dimensions compared to steel.

For castings such as fairleads, cleats, and bollards, aluminium silicon alloys—12 per cent silicon, Specification A.C.6—has excellent resistance to corrosion. But they are all relatively soft compared to steel and no complete cure has yet been found for the scoring which wire rope causes in aluminium alloy fairleads and drums of winches. Some appreciable improvement in hardness can, however, be achieved by chill coating. This material as cast is as strong as good cast iron; and stronger than much indifferent ordinary cast iron!

In Chapter 15 there are notes on the use of light alloys for spars.

While I do not suggest that these alloys are a panacea for many ills, I do believe that they are far superior to grown frames where strength for weight is sought. In Britain they are an indigenous product, which is advantageous. They should represent an appreciable saving in weight in larger yachts when compared to steel frames, and the labour of shaping should, where the technique is developed, prove to be much reduced. And they are non-magnetic—an advantage we cannot forget for racing offshore. Although we can arrange perfect compensation for the compass errors while swinging round a buoy, we can never be absolutely sure that some heeling error may not be lurking, nor that a severe pounding in a seaway may not change the natural magnetism of a steel, or composite steel, vessel.

The all-aluminium hull is proved and entirely feasible. As a start dozens of such life-boats were put into service in the finest of our liners. Small waviness between frames and dents in the plating,

which do not affect the watertightness and would be of little consequence in a work boat, prove troublesome in the racing yacht. But shipyards who have experience of alluminium alloy construction learn to overcome this difficulty, which arrives particularly in all welded constructions. Some still prefer, with reason, to use riveting between the angled frames and the skin; though more costly than welded-on strip frames.

In Britain amongst the good and reasonable yards for alloy building up to 60 ft. are Camper and Nicholson and Freezer & Co., Hayling Island. A.C.N.A.M. at Chateau du Loire in France have built two very fine yawls for me recently in aluminium alloy; they have an extensive experience of working only in this material. Chantier de la Perrière in Lorient, France, traditionally steel builders, have made brave attempts to break into the alloy construction market in all sizes of vessel.

It is still an expensive form of construction. In my view its principal field should be in large motor cruisers where light weight with strength are of primary importance; in enabling one to use lower powered engines to reach the target performance. But many successful sailing yachts have recently been so built; mostly from America and mostly in cases where cost was unimportant. Huey Long's two famous world-girdling ocean racers are outstanding examples.

R.O.R.C. Scantling Component. At this point I must explain how the new International rule and the R.O.R.C. scantling component work. Since this can produce one's rating in the case of a heavily-built boat or increase it in an extra-light one, it is an important affair. It is designed to equalise the chances of the light, and the heavy yacht.

The scantling component under the 1968 R.O.R.C. rule is an important factor in the calculation of the stability allowance. It is based on the average weight 'W' per sq. ft. of the topsides, together with the average weight of frames per superficial foot, to which is added the weight of 1 sq. ft. of the deck and the average weight of deck beams per superficial foot. It does not include the extra heavy timbers in way of the mast nor the stiffening bulkhead's weight. W is then corrected for freeboard, bulwarks, or raised deck bonus if any, as show in Appendix VII.

The formula for calculating the scantling component

$$= \frac{66\ W\ \text{corrected}}{L + B + 1 \cdot 5D} - 10$$

Where: L = length, B = beam, and D = depth, all in accordance with rules of measuring these factors. The stability allowance is determined by the scantling component and other components if

Oryx: a Class I racer which has had three brilliant seasons, in 1966, 1967 and 1968. Her principle dimensions are loa 49 ft., lwl 38 ft., beam 12 ft. 8 in., draft 8 ft. I in. She was designed by Illingworth and Primrose and built by Labbe at St Malo for M François Bouygyes, winner in 1968 of both the Cowes-Dinard and Channel Race.

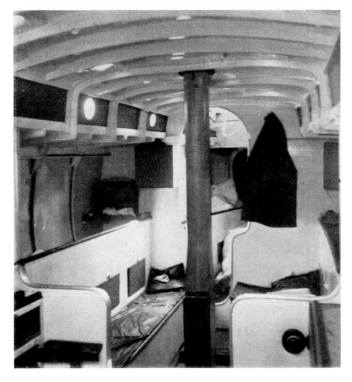
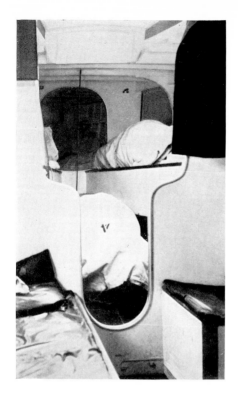

The interior of *Myth of Malham*. Photograph of the saloon looking forward into the fore cabin taken the morning after she finished at Plymouth to win the 1947 Fastnet. The deep bunk outboard of the settees can clearly be seen. A good idea of the light interior is also had. The panels of the bunks are apple green. The cushions are dark red, the mahogany is wax finished. On the right is a peep into the forecastle, where the sail bags have been moved in order to expose the sail locker in the stem.

Inside *Oryx*, looking aft from inside the fore cabin right through to the cockpit. The large service hatch from the galley can be seen in the port bulkhead. The saloon layout, similar to *Monk of Malham*'s, is efficient and comfortable.

Oryx. The navigator's spacious department. With all instruments to hand, he is separated from the mainstream of activity but still in ready contact with the helmsman. Note the retaining belt hanging from the chart table.

The self-contained galley in *Oryx*. The U shape grants the cook immediate access to food, sinks, plates, etc., without encroaching on passage-way space. A retaining belt is fitted, as on the navigator's desk.

Oryx. Note the up-and-down companionways and the bending boom.

Stormvogel. Mr. C. Bruynzeel's great ocean racer, representing the joint work of three designers: Van de Stadt, Laurent Giles and Partners, and Illingworth and Primrose. 'She broke the record for the fastest time for a R.O.R.C. race when she completed the 1963 220-mile Hook race in under 24 hours.' Her dimensions are: *loa:* 73 ft.; *lwl:* 59 ft.; *beam:* 16 ft.; *draft:* 9·1 ft.; *sail area:* 2,277 sq. ft.

applicable: + shallow draft + iron ballast + weight of engine — light alloy mast. In the new rule the scantling allowance has less weight—rating wise—being partly replaced by the inclining test.

In connection with this component I want to make an important point. Under the R.O.R.C. rule this allowance in addition to levelling the chances between similar boats of heavy and light construction did also give in effect an allowance to the boat of heavy displacement as compared with one of light displacement, because the total surface area of a heavy displacement boat is little, if any, more than that of a light one. Take your light displacement boat and fill in the midship section under water to make it a heavy displacement one and you have a smaller area in contact with the water. But at the same time you probably increase your beam a little which just about compensates for this. So for given scantlings, that is to say, for given dimensions of constructional members, the scantling allowance was the same for both types, although relatively to the amount of ballast one would carry, the heavy displacement boat is really more lightly built. Or to put it the other way round, if you wanted to get the same ballast ratio in a light as in a heavy displacement boat, say about the normal 46 per cent, you have to put up with a much smaller scantling allowance.

As from the 1962 season the C.C.A. rule of measurement employs an inclining experiment as a substitute for the previously used direct tax on ballast ratio, which had been widely evaded by the use of heavy metal fittings in the bottom of the boat, and which encouraged unduly beamy (less sea kindly) hulls. For the inclining experiment, at the time of measurement all tanks must be 'pressed-up' full.

Cockpit Details. We shall start the next chapter by estimating the amount of space we were going to need there and we will now think about some of the constructional details. The old-fashioned cockpit has its seats at deck level and this is still suitable in a bigger boat or with high coamings. But in smaller boats particularly those with high freeboards, the seats can with advantage be as much as 10 in. below deck level, so that the sitting crew get the extra shelter and reduce the windage they would occasion by sitting higher.

I like cockpit coamings to slope outboard at the top. With the modern long coachroof much more water comes aft than previously and it may be advisable in these cases to increase the height of the cockpit coaming a little. Fortunately higher freeboards have largely offset this disability.

All the same I think a 7-in. coaming for even small boats is not too high. A broad beading which projects outward will further assist in keeping the water out of the cockpit when heeled, without increasing the normal silhouette. These broad cappings are also good for sitting on, cruising in light or astern breezes. Care should be taken that the winch chocks do not cause an obstruction which results in the water which is running down the side decks being cascaded into the cockpit. I use brass or aluminium alloy ones which are 'hollow' frames.

I don't like lockers under the side decks with access from a door above the seats. They fill up with water from the cockpit seats and remain full till one goes about, the stuff in there getting nicely pulped in time, while you are carrying extra water on the lee side.

Seat lockers and doors for access to sail bins, or better still for access to sheet and guy stowage, are a necessary evil. All seats should have drains at their outboard edges, to return water to the cockpit bottom (or to an overboard drain) when heeled. The two forms of drain I alternatively use are either a diagonal pipe from the forward outboard end of the seat; or a near horizontal pipe from the same point straight over the side. Apart from this, one makes on the lids as good a joint as possible and any leakage into the bilge is accepted. The C.C.A. require catches to lids.

Tiller heads which finish just above the cockpit floor save weight and space. Remember that the leverage you get depends not on the length of the tiller but on the distance your hand on the tiller is away from the nearest point on the rudder stock; that is to say, a tiller coming off at right angles to the stock can be very much shorter than one lying parallel to the deck.

ACCOMMODATION

It is every owner's privilege to design or rearrange his own accommodation according to his particular fancy. The cynic will say 'to make his own mistakes his own way', but this is not the whole truth, for in nearly every boat, however small, one can pick up one or two useful ideas—the fruit of practical experience from cruising and racing. While I am against the owner interfering with the lines and fundamental construction put forward by the naval architect, there is no doubt that one gets the greatest fun from laying out one's boat on deck and below. And so I shall not attempt to interfere with your pleasure by suggesting anything too hard and fast in the way of accommodation plans, but only put forward a few ideas, to leaven the loaf, as it were.

Before one can decide how much room one has to play with below, the cockpit must be laid out. The crews employed racing will be larger than in an equivalent boat cruising, and space allowance must be made accordingly. However the C.C.A. and the Junior Offshore Group (J.O.G.) lays down a maximum cockpit volume which must be studied in the design stage. In a small craft, or in a medium-sized racer of light displacement, it is most desirable to have the cockpit placed not too far aft, so that when a couple of extra hands come

up from below it does not put her down by the stern too much.

For this reason I am not very keen on the popular 'bridge deck' (between the cockpit and the main companionway) which results in the hands sitting farther aft in the cockpit than would otherwise be the case. It makes access to the cabin through the companionway less easy, and it helps to guide the tops of the waves into the accommodation. In a small boat it makes it impossible in bad weather to shelter up against the doghouse or coachroof ending. I admit it provides a good perch for the compass and the main sheet, but the latter can equally well, or better, be landed on the coachroof, or doghouse forward bulkhead which carries it nicely clear of the life-lines. Diagram 63 shows a compass mounting which is between twin companionways. But if one accepts a bridge deck one might as well take advantage of it to locate an owner's cabin under it, as I did in *Monk of Malham*, launched in 1965.

Fundamental Accommodation Needs. I would say, from the start, think about the boat under way; visualise her at sea, and fit in your harbour requirements afterwards. What one must set out to provide are: The best possible sleeping berths; first-class chart working space; practical cooking arrangements; simple seating clear of the bunks; accessible sail stowage; adequate ventilation; the minimum of deck openings, properly watertight; a W.C. convenient to use under way; adequate oilskin stowage.

Most people who have tried open accommodation, with the minimum of doors and bulkheads, are very much in its favour. Doors are really quite heavy in the aggregate, and when you think of the banging to and fro, apart from their finger-pinching propensities and the necessity to wrestle with them in bad weather, together with the space they occupy when they are open, you will class them as public enemy number four at sea in small yachts.

To Divide or not to Divide. In the majority of the small-sized yachts which we have designed, we have only one partition bulkhead, apart from the 'partial' strength bulkheads which form the sides to the galley and chart table and so on; this one

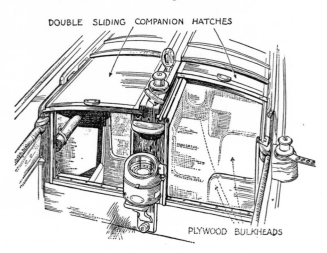

Diagram 63.
Myth of Malham—Companionways and Compass.

bulkhead being between the fore cabin and the saloon. It is of ply and is intended to help the hull keep shape near the mast; if you have a partition bulkhead, you might just as well make it do a real job. This may or may not have a door, but only a moderate-sized opening in it; perhaps with a lightweight waterproofed curtain; and even when cruising in mixed company, this arrangement has proved to provide reasonable privacy. The resulting sense of spaciousness and the resulting convenience in working and living below are very real. And the boat gets less fuggy at sea in bad weather.

In a larger yacht doors are less in the way, and weight is of less moment. In some cases they may well justify their place in the boat by providing a quiet place for sleeping, for with a big crew the difficulty of finding quiet is, of course, greatly increased. Since I, in 1946, removed a quarter of a ton of teak doors in *Latifa*, now by rule, doors must not be removed prior to a Bermuda race.

Freeboard. I mentioned in an earlier chapter that it was necessary for light displacement boats to have a good freeboard in order to get a proper amount of room in them. Though designed a long time ago we may still instance *Myth*, which has a 4-ft freeboard forward and 3 ft. aft. We have over 6-ft. headroom in the centre of the ship, and not much less throughout the length of the coachroof, which runs well into the forward cabin. There are six full-sized, roomy, permanent berths; clear of the settees, on which extra sleeping accommodation can be arranged. There is a good galley over 3 ft. long in the centre of the ship, and a permanent chart table 3 ft. 2 in. by 2 ft. 4 in. There is tank stowage for 94 gallons of water and a really ample

lockerage for sails and ship's gear—with room to spare. All this on a displacement, in R.O.R.C. measurement trim, of under 8 tons. Diagrams 64 and 65 show her accommodation.

With the help of reverse sheer in a more recent design, the 1962 *Dambuster*, we have achieved the same accommodation—six ex settees or eight berths total—and from 5 ft. to 6 ft. 1in. headroom in the saloon, with only 6·3 tons displacement on a 30-ft. waterline. Thus we have a fast yacht giving first-class racing fun to a large crew at the minimum cost.

In *Maica* we planned the same arrangement, on a smaller scale. On a displacement of $5\frac{1}{4}$ tons we have two settees and five other berths, a decent chart table (a fixed one) and a proper galley aft 3 ft. 8 in., fore and aft. And here in the after end of the saloon we have 6 ft. of headroom. Her arrangement appears in Diagram 1.

In both boats these things would be manifestly impossible without good freeboard. But once we have got used to the 'new look' in freeboards, and have realised that this same freeboard helps to keep the sea in its place, then we can have this amount of space, and also increased comfort per ton of displacement.

The most valuable part of the accommodation below decks is the after half, because the motion there is much less than forward, and so in framing the general layout we must carefully consider what equipment has the best claim to be located there.

Taking the small size of boat first, say a 24-ft to 26-ft. waterliner, let us assume a crew of five or six. The first thing to realise is that racing offshore in a very small boat does not really call for a saloon,

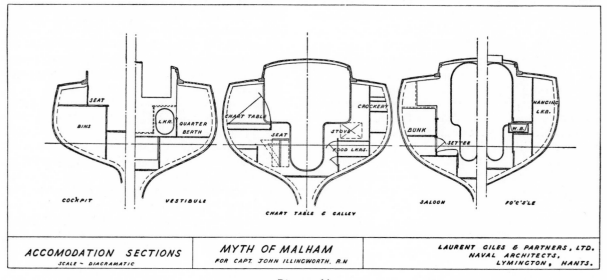

Diagram 64.
Myth of Malham—accommodation sections.

There will never be more than four people eating below at a time, and meals will be taken out of a bowl and a mug, sitting below.

Hands will do very little lounging below. They will be either eating, cooking, working on the chart table, or resting in their bunks. So what we need in a yacht of this size is a chart table and a galley, and bunks for the skipper, navigator, and the two hands off watch. One also requires seats for three or four persons independent of the bunks; it is inconvenient to have to fold up a bunk in order to sit down and pull on a sea-boot, or have a cup of soup. These seats need only be 10 or 12 in. deep—a plain board, perferably one slightly sloped down from the front, will do. This requirement is simple but important, and often forgotten. The seats can be flap-up if one so desires. All this to be as far aft as can be managed.

While dealing with accommodation I make no apology in this new book for referring to older yachts which have proved their worth on every sea and ocean. In my own boat, *Minx*, I have made a number of changes. I have reduced the size of the companionway because the galley needs some protection, otherwise the primus, or calor gas stove may have trouble in doing its stuff in the draught. So in *Myth* and *Minx* it is sheltered as far as is feasible. The alternative of providing a 'pram' hood over the companionway is always attractive, particularly in a small boat where important functions are necessarily concentrated under the companionway, and more particularly where there is no doghouse.

Forward of this galley space are the two crew berths, one watch consisting of two chaps. The standard fo'c'sle has an extra berth and locker for harbour use, and the headspan. So in harbour one would furl the two midship berths and make a saloon of it. As you will see, *Minx* has two berths forward, the standing one forming the sail rack at sea. So that all five of a crew can sleep in comfort in harbour. Though truth be told, a spare Dunlopillo or air mattress on the cabin sole is no great hardship—if six clear feet can be found.

An alternative layout would be to have two quarter berths, with the chart table lying over the bunk farthest from an offset hatch. Then next forward, a well-protected galley; not too far forward facing the third berth. This gives one a little more length of ship to dispose of on the galley side, because the second quarter berth economises in ship length by tucking its feet behind the cockpit.

When one comes to the next bigger size, one can consider a layout on the lines of *Myth*, where one has two deep quarter berths, with next forward a chart table and galley, in the widest part of the ship, opposite one another. In this size with a 9 ft. 4 in. beam the cook and navigator can work in the same section of the ship—and clear of the draught and drip of the companionway.

The Blue Charms. The *Maicas* of which about a hundred have been built were designed as an improvement on the R.N.S.A. 'Twenty-Fours', after ten honourable years of sailing. The *Maicas* accommodate two more people (when needs be), have more headroom, heel less, go faster and rate lower than the R.N.S.A. 'Twenty-Fours', all on the same displacement. (Accommodation Diagram 1.) But with the rising costs of building there was need of something to give the same racing speed at less cost. The *Blue Charms*, of which ten have been built at the time of writing, displace only $3\frac{1}{2}$ tons and cost about two-thirds as much.

The accommodation provides two quarter berths; galley opposite the fixed chart-table in the middle of the boat's length; two outboard berths forward of that; but with folding wood leeboards to allow of narrow settees inboard of the bunks.

Monk of Malham. I designed and built in 1965 a 30-ft. waterline ocean racer for myself. Although I still felt no need to go away from the *Myth* layout for the simplest pure ocean racers, twenty years later I had a yen to have a layout which though still practical for racing offshore, would provide a higher degree of owner comfort. On the same overall length, using nearly 2 ft. more beam enabled one to have the companionway ladder between the chart-table and the galley; and with a four-cylinder Perkins diesel engine under that sole.

The space abaft this makes a good owner's cabin in the steady part of the ship; accessible from the chart-room and thus not used as a passage to anywhere, and furnished with a folding wash basin. The penalty for this otherwise excellent arrangement is that the companionway is not so easily accessible from the cockpit. The top step, incidentally, is enclosed by wings and inclined so as to drain to the bilge; this in conjunction with a special three-coamings hinged hatch keeps the sea out even in the worst weather. It eliminates, apart from the probability of leaks; the risk of a jammed sliding companion hatch after a collision; which is always a nasty thought.

The bigger beam enables one to have in the saloon four berths clear of the settees. The two berths each side are at different levels, with the head of the upper berth further forward and the feet in a tunnel behind the W.C., or the hanging locker opposite.

I feel that this layout is a sophisticated one for medium size ocean racers. The working portion of

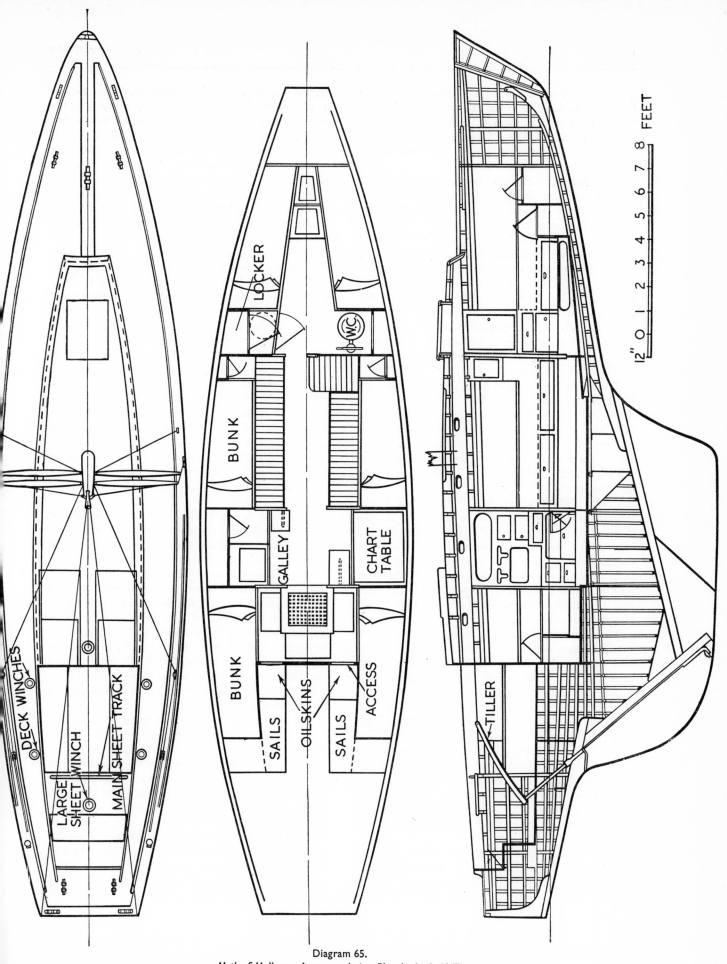

Diagram 65.

Myth of Malham—Accommodation Plan (as built 1947)

Principal Dimensions:—*Length O.A.:* 37 ft. 9 in.; *L.W.L.:* 33 ft. 6 in.; *Beam:* 9 ft. 4 in.; *Draft:* 7 ft.; *Thames Tonnage:* 12.

accommodation, galley and chart-table, where lights are liable to be in use at any time during the night, plus a certain amount of noise day and night, is centrally placed. The off-watch boys are not too far forward for comfort, have very good berths isolated from the working area.

The third part of the accommodation; the owner's cabin in harbour and probably berths for skipper and navigator—non-watch keepers—is completely separate but accessible to the cockpit for consultation via two opening ports (which also provide splash-proof ventilation in all ordinary conditions).

Continuing with the ventilation problem with this accommodation layout, the galley has an exhaust mushroom in the after bulkhead of the small moulded doghouse. There are two pairs of rubber cowls over dorade-type boxes, near the centre line further forward, between the low coamings so that they do not protrude above the general profile.

Monk was very nicely built by Constructions Navales Malouines at St. Malo in France and two sister ships by W. A. Souter & Son at Cowes, Isle of Wight. *Monk* has in general the same speed and performance as *Myth*; with a rating 5 ft. lower, which is a measure of the progress in design which we have been able to achieve in the intervening eighteen years.

Quarter Berth Protection. At this juncture I should perhaps say that quarter berths must have splash-proof canvas curtains—or other ways of keeping the big dollops that must occasionally get down the companionway. In 1969 I fitted a zip-curtain, to fulfil the same purpose, in *Oryx*. The *Myth* curtains let down from a roll into a deep groove at the after end, to seal off the bunk. They are perfectly simple roll-up canvas screens.

The next consideration is to ventilate the bunk space, because one has to seal oneself off in there in bad weather. Ventilation can as a rule readily be provided from forward into the main part of the boat. The skipper and navigator of *Myth* in 1947 registered occasional fat heads through not having a 'CO_2 drain' to let off the used air from their nicely protected bunks in the quarters. For 1948, holes were cut in the partial bulkheads at the bunk heads. The *Myth* quarter berths are, incidentally, thanks to her good freeboard, deep enough to provide good hanging space at the after end, and room for railway racks for stowing odd clothes as well. One can sit up in them, and they are almost like little cabins.

Large Yachts—Hands' Bunks. As soon as one gets to the bigger boats (Diagram 67) accommodation problems should ease, but I am strongly of the opinion that no chance of making use of the after

half of the ship must be missed. In *Latifa*, for our 1946 all-amateur crew, I made extra bunks in the sail locker under the cockpit—crawl-in billets, but in the steady part of the ship. *Orion*, the R.N.S.A. yacht, had very similar arrangements, and jolly comfortable they could be. Between the owner's sleeping cabin, which was abaft the main companion, and forward of the after sail locker, is another hatch to a compartment with less than full headroom, abreast the cockpit, fitted for two bunks, a lavatory, and a charging plant.

These places are excellent for younger crew members, or paid hands, if one is lucky enough to have them. It is quite important to provide seagoing accommodation for paid hands other than in the fo'c'sle. If one provides berths in the quarter, they can bring their blankets aft and get real sleep at sea, which is quite often nearly impossible in the fo'c'sle, partly owing to sail changing, but chiefly because of the motion. As one will normally divide paid hands, who will be best acquainted with the bosun's store, between the two watches, one berth will suffice for two hands, or two berths for four hands. This scheme has the considerable extra advantage that the whole of the fo'c'sle is available at sea as a sail room, and part of a bunk can be utilised for each of the regularly used sails, with a prominent label on the bulkhead behind and above it.

Designing a big yacht, of 50-ft. waterline or more I always ask the owner to consider having bunks permanently aft, where many bigger yachts have only their sail locker or their engine.

In any size of boat anyone—such as the skipper, navigator, or cook—who it may have been decided is not to stand a watch, should have his own bunk. Otherwise being out of a watch does not mean much. The remaining crew members should sleep in turns, on the 'hot bunk' principle, in the most suitable remaining bunks, which will generally be the after ones; though in fine weather considerations of quiet may dictate the use of a bunk placed farther forward in the ship.

The settee berths should be fitted with flap-up leeboards or leeboards formed by a stout flat batten and canvas side. Alternatively, a canvas leeboard may be used, preferably triangular or trapeze shape with eyelets at its apex, and is most effective. From the eyelets lanyards runs upwards. It is simple, inexpensive, and stows under the cushion in harbour.

Bunk Details. While on the subject of bunks, I must emphasise that it is of the utmost importance to have really adequate leeboards. If one has a sort of feeling that one might fall out, one instinctively braces oneself and sleeps with half an eye aware of

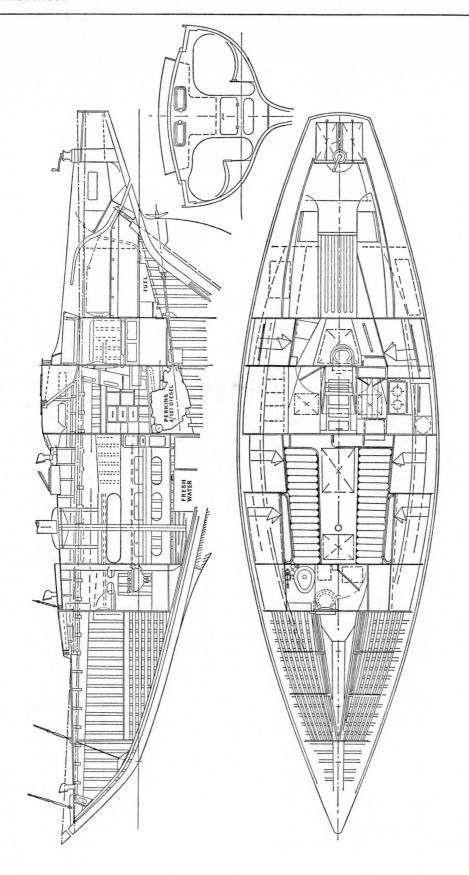

Diagram 66.

Monk of Malham is an Illingworth and Primrose design of 1965. She was built at St. Malo by C.N.M. Dimensions:—L.O.A.: 39 ft.; L.W.L.: 30 ft.; beam: 11 ft. $1\frac{1}{4}$ in.; draft: 6 ft. 9 in.

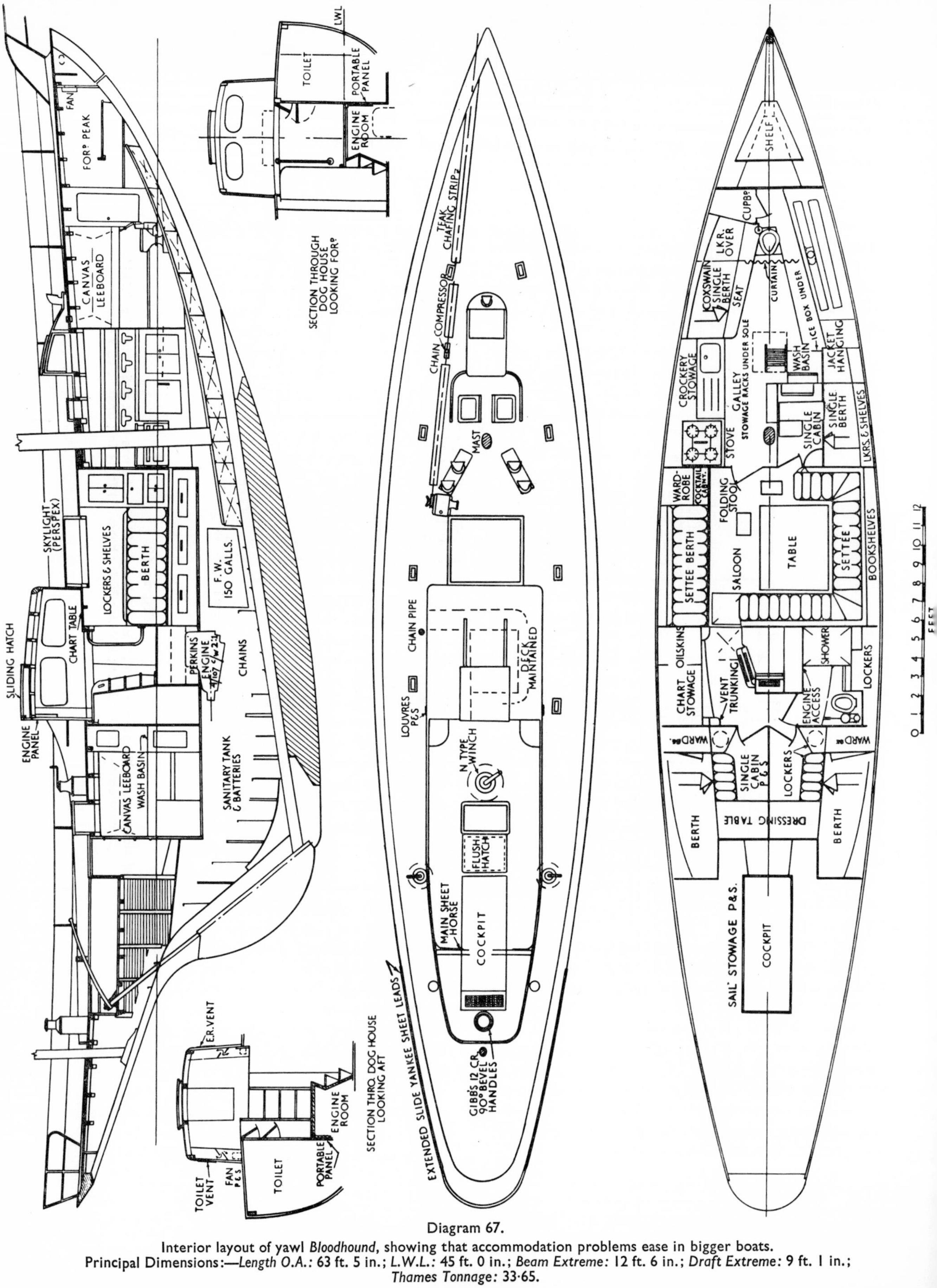

Diagram 67.
Interior layout of yawl *Bloodhound*, showing that accommodation problems ease in bigger boats.
Principal Dimensions:—*Length O.A.*: 63 ft. 5 in.; *L.W.L.*: 45 ft. 0 in.; *Beam Extreme*: 12 ft. 6 in.; *Draft Extreme*: 9 ft. 1 in.;
Thames Tonnage: 33·65.

the danger. One should be able to climb into one's bunk and sink down behind the leeboard, secure and chocked off for a 3-hr. caulk.

The wood leeboard should be 10 in. above the mattress level. It may be portable if you wish, but solid enough to give one confidence. In the *Myth* there are canvas bunk bottoms, which are light and take up a slight curve. On top of these we have, 1-in. thick only, a mattress, 50 per cent wider than the bunk's nominal width. This then rides up round the sides of the bunk. The mattress is in Resilotex, a textile equivalent to sponge rubber. Various other light foams are available. The rubber will do equally well, though it is heavier. These small thicknesses on top of canvas give real comfort.

A fixed leeboard can be much lighter and simpler than folding one of equivalent strength. Personally, where the general layout permits, I like fixed bunks. They help keep the ship tidy at sea, and one can have narrow settees inboard of them which, in practice, are quite adequate, particularly if they are sloped down outboard. The fixed leeboard of the bunk behind one is a good back rest. A 9-ft. beam is the minimum in which this arrangement can be used with two settees. An 8-ft. beam can do one 12-in. settee in front of a fixed bunk, with a settee berth opposite; or two narrow settees and folding leeboards to form the settee backs. Again, the settee berths must have really good leeboards of one sort or another. We often use trapeze-shaped terylene cloths with lanyards at each corner, which fold under the cushion when not in use.

For sea-going purposes a wide bunk is not necessary; it is, beyond a certain point, almost a disadvantage. If there is plenty of space a 2-ft. wide berth is fine. If space is limited, 22 in. at the head, tapering to 13 in. at the foot is acceptable, and much good sleeping has been done in narrower berths than this, such as 20-in. tapering to 14 in. In such cases, however, particularly if there are several such berths, the bunk should, if at all possible, be 6 ft. 5 in. long, as the occasional tall occupant will not be able to curl up in a narrow bunk.

Root Berths. Sometimes root cots are useful. They are canvas berths (Diagram 68) stretched between the ship's side, or some fixed part of the bulkhead or structure, on one side, and a tube running through the hem of the canvas on the other. This tube can as a rule be located in three alternative positions, giving a flat level harbour berth, a trough-like one, and a deeper narrow trough, with the tube higher than the edge of the canvas on the ship's side, for bad weather or turning to windward. In addition, there will be a housed position for the

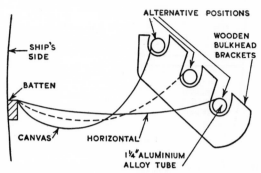

ROOT BERTH

NOTE: IF TAPERED HEAD TO FOOT THE SLOPE OF BRACKETS SHOULD BE GREATER AT THE WIDER END

ALTERNATIVE POSITIONS

WOODEN BULKHEAD BRACKETS

SHIP'S SIDE

BATTEN

CANVAS

HORIZONTAL

1¼" ALUMINIUM ALLOY TUBE

Diagram 68.

tube, which may be simply rolled up with the canvas against the ship's side, or rolled up and dropped out of sight in a well. Or again by rolling up so as to contain the bedding it may serve as a back rest. We had two in *Maid*.

Although perfectly practicable, I don't think the root cots are quite as comfortable as *Myth*'s berths described above; the tube catches one's shoulder with line pressure at times. But they are very light and can be fitted by an amateur. Where a folding bunk is wanted for a small yacht, they are much less heavy and less expensive than a pullman berth. Sometimes they are very handy as an extra berth for racing which can be completely removed and stowed in the fo'c'sle, or after peak, when cruising or in harbour with a smaller crew. For this use they have a tube in a hem each side. In any case they should be easily detachable so that they can be removed to be scrubbed or dry cleaned at the end of the season. In 'converting' a cruiser to an ocean racer they are an easy way of adding bunks in the part of the ship you want them in; for instance, over the fixed bunk, or inboard of a fixed bunk.

Shelf Berths. In *Thalassa* I fitted a very simple extra berth by having a hinged board which, when folded, lay on top of a 6-ft. long shelf above the settee in the saloon. This is shown in Diagram 69. When in use as a bunk the board is hinged inboard and hung from two or three chains; the length of the chain can be varied by hooking into any link, thus increasing the height of the inboard edge. With an overwidth sponge rubber mattress, it was quite comfortable.

Talking of sponge rubber, one can now get non-proprietary slabs 6 ft. × 3 ft., 1 in. thick, at a much more reasonable price than the more fancy ones made up with special cellular matrix and so on.

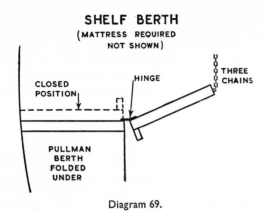

SHELF BERTH
(MATTRESS REQUIRED NOT SHOWN)

Diagram 69.

Another comfortable mattress which takes up little room and is not too heavy is that made up by short horse hairs dipped in latex (liquid rubber). Quilted Terylene sleeping bags on a canvas-bottomed bunk are light, inexpensive and comfortable enough. Spring mattresses take up rather an undue amount of space, which is usually required for lockers.

Chart Tables and Seats. Chart tables from the pilot's point of view are discussed in more detail in Chapter 8, on navigation, but some details are included here too for the sake of completing our talk on accommodation. The first point is to determine the size. Unfortunately, there is no fixed width to Admiralty charts which are of all shapes and sizes—some are as much as 4 ft. north and south. However, French charts are more or less standard, and can lie flat with a little to spare on a table 41 in. × 31 in. One useful size to remember is that British charts are all folded when new so as to go into a drawer or well, 21 in. × 29 in. This corresponds roughly to the absolute minimum practicable size of a chart table. If there is room, I should have it 2 ft. × 3 ft., and more than that both ways is an advantage.

The chart stowage should be very adjacent to the chart table, so that there is no excuse for not putting away a chart directly after use, thus keeping it in decent condition and saving any amount of unnecessary wear and tear and confusion. A locker under the chart table, or a well, disclosed by lifting the table top, are suitable alternatives. Three inches in depth for a chart locker is enough for a small yacht, and 5 in. for a larger one when longer cruises and races are in mind, and say $1\frac{1}{2}$ in. depth for a J.O.G. racer.

Make sure the table top is made of seasoned wood which will not warp. Ply on a western red cedar frame is good. If you have to fit up a chart table at short notice—for instance, if you ship as navigator and find no chart table in the yacht—

you can generally buy or borrow a drawing-board and three stout hinges and so fix up a decent folding chart table over your bunk or in the W.C.— even if the navigator cannot claim unrestricted tenancy of this salubrious spot, he will find a ready-made seat there.

This brings me rather naturally to the question of seats. Though not essential, I certainly regard them as very desirable in connection with the chart table. It depends, of course, on the height of the table above the cabin sole; if circumstances necessitate a high one, it is not so essential. For one thing, the seats chock the navigator off nicely, and if he can get his knees up under the table drawer, he is pretty well fixed and can have two hands free for the work, even in a seaway. Apart from this, quite appreciable periods are put in at the chart table for working out sights, and some sort of seating is desirable. *Myth* has a flap-up seat which seems very efficient, although it is nearly always in position, and could equally well be fixed and made stronger for its weight. As an alternative *Dyarchy* has a wood rail across in front of the table which is know as the Altar Rail, and which is highly spoken of as a strong simple form of bottom support.

A navigator's retaining belt of 6 in. wide webbing, or of triple thickness 12 oz. terylene cloth cross stitched to stiffen it, should also be provided inboard of the table between carefully chosen strong points; pad eyes or similar. A stout eye should be provided at each end, one with a stout lanyard and adjustment at one end and a hook or clip at the other.

Some chart tables have a slot in the 'front edge' with a radius and/or a roller to pass charts through when they are rather long from north to south; when one is working on the top of the chart one passes them through. I like a small beading, rounded at the edges to avoid cutting the chart, which will also stop pencils, books, and so on from glissading off with the ship heeled. In order to prevent sliding, there should be fore and aft ribs on the cabin sole, about $1\frac{1}{2}$ in. high in front of the table.

Hand grips or rails are most useful internal fittings, in larger yachts. They need careful positioning, after the accommodation is mainly complete, and should run the length of the roof at least; and vertically near bulkhead openings and companionways. If necessary extra grips should be fitted to enable one to hoist oneself into a bunk: readily, even on the weather side when heeled.

Navigation Extras. Needless to say, a book rack is required, in which Pilots (sailing directions) and so on can be stowed. Also a rack, preferably with vertical holes in it, for dividers, of which at least two pairs should be provided in case of accidents, and pencils; also a wee hole or rack for the ever-elusive india-rubbers. A proper stowage should also be provided for the sextant, the deck watch, and the hand bearing compass; these must be very handy, for a headland or light may come up for a moment through the haze, or the sun may appear for an instant and be gone again. In these cases one must be able to reach out and take a bearing or a sight with the minimum of delay.

Protected stowages (rings) should be arranged also for 3 to 8 electric torches, according to the yacht's size—casualties to torches are frequent—and for one or two 'steamer scarers' (extra powerful torches) and a soft-lined trough for the binoculars.

Galley Arrangements. Cooking equipment is dealt with in the food section. We have already re-marked on the need to locate the stove reasonably clear of hatch draughts. I think the cook should, if at all possible, have a seat from which to tend the galley, in which he can wedge himself, like the navigator at his table. Fore and aft strips on the galley sole (floor) are needed too, particularly as it may get greasy. If the boat is arranged 'open' with few doors, the cook works in better conditions, with better ventilation. Drawers should, if being built in, be of the self-locking type, illustrated in Diagram 77. Failing a seat one may provide a 'band, canvas, cook retaining'. Detail as for the navigator's belt; but, and this is important, if possible arranged so that the cook can lean on it either way with his or her tummy or bottom; according to the tack.

Sail Stowage. Sail stowage when racing at sea can, and often must, be quite different from that which is used in harbour, when sail bags can be stuffed into the fore peak and other recesses. At sea they must be as far as possible out of the ends of the ship,

in common with any other odd weights, in order to make the boat a 'smaller pendulum' fore and aft so that she may follow the motion of the seas more readily. Again, they must all be easily accessible. A permanent slatted bin for each sail is ideal, as they are less likely to get mildewed when left wet in bins than in bags. And it is easy to return them to store after use, if you have bins.

When the engine is under the sole, spinnakers and storm sails can well be stowed under the cock-pit, perhaps with a hinged companionway ladder.

However, there is often not room for special sail bins in accessible positions. The next best thing is to have fixed berths in the fo'c'sle or forward cabin; to which there will preferably be direct access by a hatch to the deck. Note that these should be deep fixed berths in preference to pipe cots, if they are to be used as sail stowages at sea. If leeboards are not fitted the bags can be hooked up (by the under-bag handles for preference) to big hooks fitted to the shelf. But the hooks must 'go round' 80 degrees at least to get a secure hold of a bag. The mattresses should also have a sea stowage; if they are of thin sponge rubber or similar substance they can be laid out 'additional' into bunks farther aft, since wet sails will occupy the bunks forward, at times. In any case, arrangements must be made so that sails are not left sculling about on the fo'c'sle floor after a sail change—a state of affairs which quickly leads to confusion, as well as to dirty sails.

If sails are not binned at sea they will have to be returned to their bags in most cases, and as a wet sail takes up a lot more room than a dry one, I always order my sail bags to be 50 per cent over-size in dimensions. It is important for each sail to have a number, and for this number to be marked prominently on both sides of the sail at each of the

MYTH OF MALHAM'S SAIL LIST

No.	Sail	Area	Material	
1.	Mainsail	446 sq. ft.	12 oz. terylene	
2.	Light yankee	496 sq. ft.	8 oz. terylene	If no genoa is carried 6 oz. terylene to be used.
3.	Heavy yankee	316 sq. ft.	10 oz. terylene	5 ft. pennant at head.
4.	Working jib	237 sq. ft.	11 oz. terylene	17 ft. 6 in. pennant at head.
5.	Storm jib	121 sq. ft.	13 oz. cotton	27 ft. pennant at head and three battens in leach 12, 15, 15 in.
6.	Light staysail (A)	358 sq. ft.	7 oz. terylene	Hollow in leech of sail 14 in. 17 ft. from top.
7.	Light staysail (B)	326 sq. ft.	7 oz. terylene	Hollow in leech of sail 14 in. 17 ft. from top. 1 ft. 8 in. foot pennant.
8.	Working staysail	228 sq. ft.	11 oz. terylene	
10.	Storm staysail	112 sq. ft.	13 oz. cotton	{ 11 ft. pennant at head. Three battens in leach 12, 15, and 15 in. { 1 ft. 6 in. foot pennant.
11.	(spare)			
12.	Trysail	144 sq. ft.		Headboard as for mainsail to R.O.R.C. limits. Diagonal from clew to leach 11 ft.
13.	Genoa	646 sq. ft.	5 oz. terylene	
14.	Light spinnaker	To R.O.R.C. limits	1 oz. terylene	Horizontally cut or chevron cut.
15.	Spinnaker	To R.O.R.C. limits	3 oz. nylon	Vertically cut.
16.	Storm spinnaker luff and leech 29 ft. width 24 ft. at foot and 19 ft. at half height.		5 oz. nylon	Vertically cut

three corners. This number should also appear in a dozen places in a really big size on the sail bag. I also have the tack of headsails marked with a big black spot for ease of recognition at night, since the tack is the first thing one wants to find before starting to hank on a sail to the stay.

The patent 'Magic Marker' or (less easily) Indian ink can be used to paint on numbers if the sailmaker's types are not available. A thick blue pencil is the last resort. Incidentally Indian ink is handy for emergency black measurement bands on the spars. The varnish should be removed with knife or rasp first.

Sail Lists. A sail list is necessary showing the leading particulars and the identification numbers. If the sails are stowed in different parts of the ship, then this should be shown as well. The sail list should be posted in a dry but accessible place— over the chart table or in the deck house perhaps. In addition a copy should be posted in each sail room. The lettering of the list must be prominent; typing the whole table in capitals is about the minimum size for clarity.

Myth's list is shown on the previous page, simply as a specimen of the type of list I have in mind. We use no number nine, not on account of any grudge against the medical officer, but it confuses when down-side up.

VENTILATING ARRANGEMENTS

Adequate ventilation arrangements need more care in a boat used for ocean racing than in a cruising yacht, because one will be pushing her much harder, and the decks, particularly to windward, will in consequence be wetter. More and heavier spray will be coming over and the forehatch will of necessity be closed for longer periods. The larger crew required for racing has a bearing on this, in that not only do they need more individual air, but far more cooking has to be done. For instance, for a large crew, the whole breakfast can hardly ever be got on the stove at once.

So the object is to devise methods of keeping up a current of air in the boat without admitting the sea, and with the minimum waste of space, weight, windage, and deck obstruction. There is scope for a great deal of useful ingenuity here, since each boat's problem differs in detail according to the layout. The great thing is to realise that it is a problem, and when building or taking over a boat, thought should be given to planning the method which will suit the particular boat best.

It is better to have a small ventilator that can be left open permanently than a big one which has to be shut down in bad weather, when it is really needed most. It is extraordinary what a difference

a constant trickle of fresh air will make to the atmosphere of a boat, and if this is absent, how fat the heads of the watch below can become. And thus more prone to seasickness too.

One is generally told that the flow of air in a boat is from aft to forward; this is often true when the fore-hatch is open, but when nothing is open there is no flow. Consequently, by putting in a supply ventilator forward, one is, in theory, trying to reverse the natural order of things. Actually, most vents work sometimes as supplies and sometimes as exhausts, according to conditions. It does not matter too much, as long as there is flow in and out of the boat. If a difference of pressure exists at the bow between the atmosphere outside and inside the boat, all that is wanted is a baffled hole and no large cowls are really needed in practice at sea. I think it important that one ventilator be placed as near the stem head as possible to get a real flow of air right through the boat. Here again, the more open the boat the better; the cutting up of the boat into small compartments makes the problem of ventilation more difficult.

Hatch Modification. To get down to brass tacks, here are some alternative methods of ventilation. Firstly, the fore-hatch should have 'wings' or wedge-shaped sides on hinges, tapering to a point forward. They may be hinged to the hatch cover, which in passing, one might remark, should itself invariably be stoutly hinged to the ship and never a loose removable cover. Otherwise, sooner or later it will go over the side and leave one in at least temporary trouble. Alternatively, but less desirable, because of their projections and the vulnerability of light sails, the wings may be hinged to the top of the coaming of the hatch. When these wings are erected the sides of the hatch are splash-proof and there is a slot open along the after edge for ventilation. Clearly this can be left open long after the hatch itself has had to be closed. A fore-hatch can have canvas over the forward edge to help seal it when the wings are in place.

Dorade Ventilator. I am told this is a very old dodge, but at any rate, Rod and Olin Stephens developed it in a very practical way in their famous yawl *Dorade*, in which they won two Fastnets and a Transatlantic race, and it has generally been called by this name ever since. It is illustrated in Diagram 70. In its essentials it consists of a 'capacity' or space fitted with small water drain holes. Air is fed in by a cowl with a downward extension into the space, and the leadaway for the air is from a pipe standing well up towards the top of the space.

This space in *Dorade* was a box on deck, but many other spaces can be used. If the box is

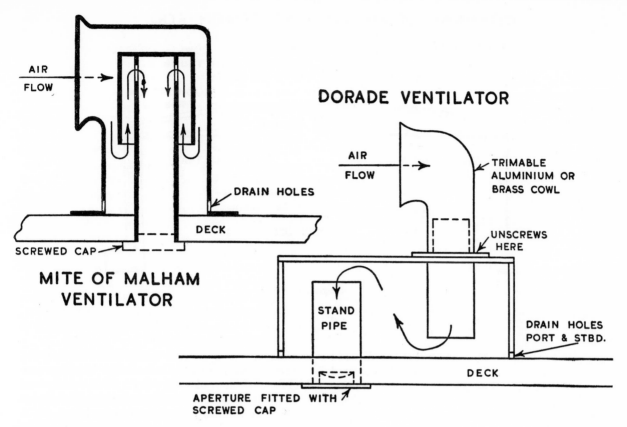

DORADE VENTILATOR

AIR FLOW

TRIMABLE ALUMINIUM OR BRASS COWL

DRAIN HOLES

UNSCREWS HERE

DECK

SCREWED CAP

MITE OF MALHAM VENTILATOR

STAND PIPE

DRAIN HOLES PORT & STBD.

DECK

APERTURE FITTED WITH SCREWED CAP

Diagram 70.

rectangular in plan the long axis is best placed fore and aft. Often, however, this is not convenient. The ventilator box can be built into the forward end of a hatch box or coachroof, in any place where it can be drained on to the deck. The cowl is sometimes a nuisance, as a sheet will occasionally get a turn round it and maybe lifts it over the side, or at any rate gets foul. An alternative is to have openings, in the side of a box placed up from the deck, in the fore end of the coachroof perhaps.

A design of this sort I have worked out in Diagram 71. The side-light boards are made to do the double job, forming also an air scoop. On the wind one or another will always be collecting wind, and the other one probably acting as an exhaust. If the dinghy fits between, one is incurring no extra windage. A similar arrangement could be had at the forward end of the coachroof, abreast the other end of the dinghy, but the side-lights are more likely to be obscured by sails in that position. The maximum feasible volume should be provided for the vent box.

Each boat requires its own treatment, and this scheme is simply to illustrate the sort of way of dealing with the matter, rather than to suggest a specific layout. The great thing is to have as big a box, compared to the openings, as is possible.

It is always as well to have the screwed plug handy, preferably on a lanyard in the cabin or saloon, or in small vents a big cork or rubber plug. Engineering firms sometimes keep a good line in rubber plugs, rather longer than the average bath plug, and with a good taper, for sealing up boiler tubes in a state of preservation. Or plumbers' suppliers will sell you an expanding plug, rubber jointed.

There are nearly always certain conditions which are too much for the best ventilator. During *Latifa*'s east to west Atlantic crossing for the 1946 Bermuda Race, she took a couple of quick seas across her foredeck; the first one filled her Dorade-type ventilator box and the second one delivered not only a nice dollop of water into the galley, but a live and kicking fish about the size of a sprat. This was preserved by the doctor in a bottle of spirit, and was later formally presented to Rod 'In Memoriam Ventilatoris Doradumsis'.

Another version, with which I have been shipmates, is shown in Diagram 71.

'Myth's' Bow Vent. In *Myth* (Diagram 72) I

INTERNAL VENTILATOR TO COACH ROOF

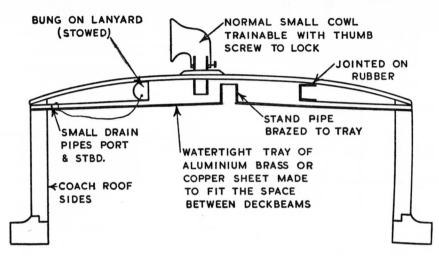

Diagram 71.

used the whole of the bow, forward of the 'forward transom', as a draining space. Air is admitted through slots in the forward half of a short stumpy stanchion, at which the life-lines terminate. Holes are drilled through the transom very near the top, to let air into the boat. The drain holes are less than a foot above the water, and undoubtedly some water finds its way in there as she sticks her nose into it. This drains off in two long streams, as the bow rises. I have used similar arrangements in very many yachts since, of all sizes. The drain is preferably higher. A bulkhead is fitted on a frame about 2 ft. from the stem. Often air is admitted through two 'false hawse pipes'. Under some conditions air

exhausts out of here. A small alteration in wind direction seems to affect this change. We have only twice seen any water coming into the hull; and then not much. I once stopped by it and studied it going to windward at over 6 knots into quite a popple of sea in the Channel Race in 1947, with a wind of Force 6 or 7.

More Bow Vents. Many long-bowed boats keep their noses comparatively dry in a seaway, and use can be made of this by fixing a tiny cowl up there. Nothing much is, or should be, stowed right in the eyes, so one can let the odd drips drain quietly into the bilge from there. This is about as simple a solution as one could want. Or if you don't like this idea you can make a little Dorade box of the space between the foremost ends of the rails, where they meet, simply decking over a small triangular area. The space is divided in half by a fore and aft partition. An oval hole in the rail on each bow, which looks like a hawse-pipe, can then admit the air, and a couple of small stand pipes transmit it below. This is the arrangement for *Minx of Malham. Wista's* aluminium tubular mast acts similarly, but the intake is at the masthead.

Quarter Berths. With canvas fronts these need ventilation and a carbon dioxide 'drain'. About the best way to get fresh air in is to connect a light alloy tube or hose to the foot of the bunk from under an open bridge deck, or some other sheltered corner of the cockpit.

I think I have said enough to do what I intended; to show that there are a hundred ways of providing ventilation with the minimum of leakage.

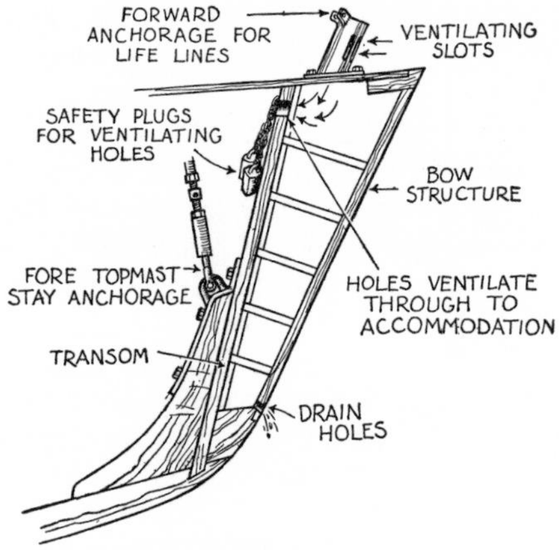

Diagram 72.
Myth of Malham—Bow Vent.

VENTILATORS CUM LIGHTBOARDS

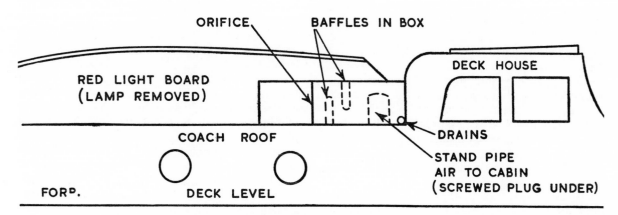

ELEVATION

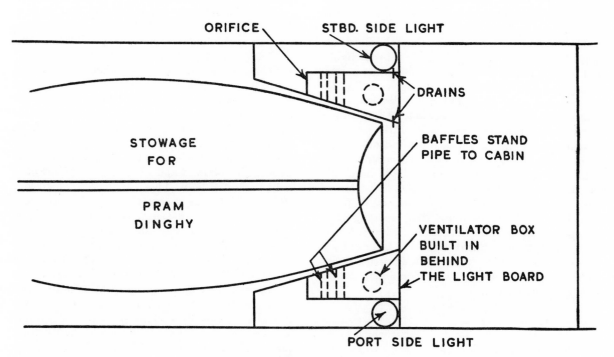

PLAN

Diagram 73.
A design for ventilators *cum* lightboards

SHIP'S LAVATORY

In a very small-class ocean-racing yacht I am not much in favour of making a separate compartment to the 'head' or lavatory. If so arranged, it is bound to be minute, and probably badly ventilated, so that there will be further disinclination on the part of the potentially seasick crew man to wrestle with a most necessary daily function. And so the last stage of that man will be worse than the first.

I fancy that the disposal of this homely engine in the fo'c'sle, or fore cabin, as it is fashionable to call it now, which will probably be used only as a sail room at sea, is best in boats of 25-ft. waterline and under. Here it will be just part of the furniture and take up less of the precious boat length than if it were in a caboose of its own. A partial bulkhead can be used to screen the user, or a canvas curtain.

Many head seats are mounted too high, which results in a precarious perch in a seaway—11 to 13 in. off the deck is sufficient. Apart from it being easier to steady oneself, the resulting posture is favourable to functional success, and the weight of the machine is lowered in the boat. If one is facing athwartships, which is slightly to be preferred, unless there is a locker opposite to get one's toe against, one should have a strategically placed foot bar on the cabin sole. The minimum complete headroom over the seat is 3 ft., and 3 ft. 2 in. is better.

Unnecessary weight is sometimes lavished on head fittings. The piping should be in reasonably light plastic tubing. However, in spite of the weight and maintenance involved, I would have in the ship's side shut-off cocks to the pan discharge and water inlet, since one can never absolutely guarantee against a fractured pipe.[1] By a little judicious machine work the weight of these and other skin fittings can be appreciably reduced compared to the rough castings with which one is normally faced. The discharge overboard should be on or near the waterline, where the tendency to flood back is reduced, and the water drag resulting from an opening in the ship's side is less. Messrs. Blake of Gosport make a Birmabright W.C., originally for flying boats, which is very light. They also make to my design a tilting W.C. which on a tack can be kept roughly upright.

ILLUMINATION, STOWAGE, AND OTHER DETAILS

Just a few words about light. A yacht which looks and feels light inside is easier to keep clean and more habitable, and therefore as a racer, more efficient. The advent of the coachroof has made the problem of admitting light more easy in temperate climes, such as Scotland and the English Channel.

I like plenty of fixed lights in the side of the coach-roof. Fixed lights don't leak; don't project into the cabin for you to bump your head on, cost less, and weigh less than opening ports. If necessary, one can put them in the deck of the coachroof, but they are devilish slippery things, and are likely to be partly blanked by the dinghy. So they need careful positioning. Alternatively, or additionally in bigger boats, you can have glass trianglar-sectioned deck lights. If need by, one can arrange fixed ports, fitted flush with the ship's side. But they either weaken the structure or involve a lot of compensatory stiffening and weight, and they are a danger in case of minor collisions. So taken all in all, one is better off if one can manage without them. In small yachts of light displacement, perspex lights in place of glass save a lot of weight. They are splinter-proof and I believe as safe as armour plate glass. But they scratch in time and the scratches take a good bit of getting out. Metal polish can be used.

The problem of getting sufficient light into a boat will, of course, be very much simplified if one paints in light shades below decks. One can afford a certain amount of light varnished or waxed mahogany if it is otherwise a really light-painted boat. But if she is inclined to be dark, it is better to paint it all in light colours.

This said, it needs also to be said that ways of preventing too much daylight, from getting to the sleepers in the bunks, needs to be provided; simple dark curtains or perhaps deadlights of ply.

Placing of Lamps. As to the artificial lighting, I think it important to place this where it will not dazzle those in the cockpit when they look into the doghouse, or into the accommodation through the companionway. With a little care the lights can be placed shining forward or downward on to the chart table or galley. Many odd parts, partial bulkheads, the mast and so on, can be called in to help baffle the light. Those bulkheads which face the companionway closely must be painted darker, or dulled, so as not to reflect the light.

I have not seen anything better than 12 volt accumulators for small boats, or 24 volts for larger ones, with the battery under the cabin sole; with ventilation, but as low as possible—if necessary, in a wooden watertight well. We had two 45 amp.-hour 12-volt batteries in *Myth* for crossing the Atlantic, and hardly used the second one. Naturally we were careful with the lights, and had modest powered bulbs except over the chart table. If you have an engine to charge your batteries, so much the better, but with care, and two batteries, so that one can be away charging, one manages very well without the charging engine.

[1] A plastic pipe insulates the lightweight aluminium alloy from a bronze hull valve.

Wet Clothing Stowage. Apart from the main requirements which have been outlined, there are minor things which one should provide. The first is a stowage space for hopelessly wet clothes. Obviously, they cannot be put back in one's locker, and they should not be left sculling about. They soon get smelly. I shall never forget the stench of wet clothes in the bin in the head of *Thalassa* in the 1935 Fastnet. So the place chosen should be well vented or away from the accommodation. A locker, or bin, or corner of a sail locker under the cockpit may serve.

It is generally possible to put up a couple of rods or wires, or taut nylon lines for drying clothes or airing sails. Wires and rods should be rustless and lines untarred to avoid staining one's clothes—though I can hear you say that *your* clothes at sea are not the sort that mind. One may need different lines at sea from those used in harbour. The forward cabin or fo'c'sle at sea should generally be given up to sails and the lines can probably be run along over the bunks near the ship's side. These would not be practicable in harbour with bunks in use. Really soaked clothes can never be dried in this way, but the lines will be useful for airing 'dampies'. In big boats the galley can sometimes be used, particularly if you have allowed yourself the weight and luxury of a coal stove.

Which reminds me of the 1931 Fastnet in *Viking*. We were the limit boat, and going out to the Rock we just caught the westerly gale which was blowing the early birds home. Her 24 hours' time allowance, which the rating of her big beam and depth and her short ends earned for her, on this occasion turned out to be not nearly enough, and we bucked into the gale for a couple of days, and hove-to at times. The one thing she could do was to heave-to nicely. With a close-reefed mainsail and with the main sheet eased and a boom guy rigged to keep the great boom at rest, and the staysail backed to weather, she lay as quietly as could be; we knew by then, from the wireless, that the greyhounds of the fleet were home and that we might as well take it easily. In fact, she was so quiet that at the height of the blow I climbed on to the cross-trees to pass the time, and watch the big seas rolling by. My height of eye was over 30 ft. up, I suppose, but I could not see over the wave crests.

All of which is rather missing the point, which was the coal stove. In this boat, where the displacement was big, the weight was not so critical. The stove cooked us fine meals and dried our clothes, thanks to the valiant efforts of the ex-naval cookie, who wrestled ceaselessly in the little galley, with smoke and oaths pouring forth in equal proportions.

Actually, the difficulty of gimballing such a stove, together with the business of getting rid of the

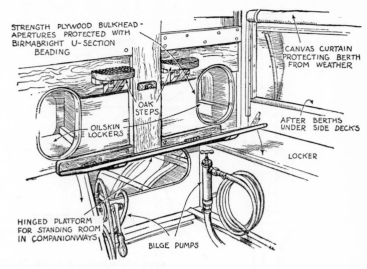

Diagram 74.
Myth of Malham—Oilskin Lockers, Quarter Berths, etc.

fumes, make it hardly a proposition compared with a good gas range.

Oilskin Stowages. The stowages one finds in yachts for 'skins vary between nothing at all and those that take far more than their fair share of the best of the ship. It is clear that one must have a reasonable stowage, preferably near the companionway, otherwise the gear will be littered all over the boat, will get damaged, and apart from the wet-nuisance aspect, will not be readily found by their owners in an emergency.

I normally use and recommend short coats and trousers. Aside from their greater efficiency, the hanging space required is much less. If they are hung in an open lobby, it is as well to have a rail round their lower parts, otherwise they swing out when the ship is heeled and get in the way and are clutched at when the ship lurches.

In a small boat the problem is much more acute, because the space available is decreasing much more quickly than the number of the crew. In *Myth* I used the space under the cockpit seats, with access from forward, inside the boat, through oval holes in the bulkhead—Diagram 69. They simply hung in to the bilge. This was quite successful for short coats and trousers and used space that would have been otherwise more or less wasted. Doing her again, I would give the lockers another 6 in. fore and aft. There was one to port and one to starboard; one for each watch.

In general, I would say the oilskin locker need not have a door—this saves weight and makes access easier. It may be cased in at the lower end to contain its burden and have access through a big oval aperture which does not look unsightly. The

8

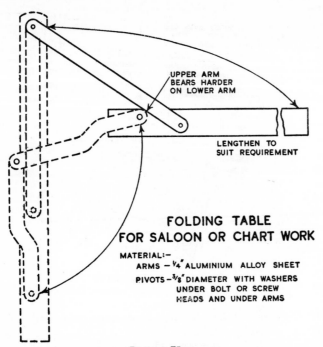

UPPER ARM
BEARS HARDER
ON LOWER ARM

LENGTHEN TO
SUIT REQUIREMENT

FOLDING TABLE
FOR SALOON OR CHART WORK

MATERIAL:—
ARMS — $\frac{1}{4}$" ALUMINIUM ALLOY SHEET
PIVOTS — $\frac{3}{8}$" DIAMETER WITH WASHERS
UNDER BOLT OR SCREW
HEADS AND UNDER ARMS

Diagram 75.
Design for a general-purpose folding table.

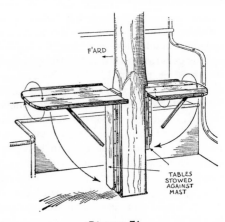

F'ARD

TABLES
STOWED
AGAINST
MAST

Diagram 76.
Myth's Folding Saloon Table.

extra air in a doorless locker reduces the tendency of the oilskins to stick. Fortunately the latest oilskins don't stick much, which enables one to use pigeon hole stowages. In *Oryx* I put numbered pigeon holes for each crewman's 'skins, with his adjusted safety harness in there as well. All these are close to the two companionways.

Saloon Tables. If the table is gimballed it must be fairly narrow. Otherwise the angle it takes up raises or lowers its edges to an extent that makes it unusable in a seaway. The pendulum may be under the cabin sole, connected by a long link; the weight is lowered and the chance of the pendulum fouling one's legs is reduced.

The pillars of any table must be at least 50 per cent stronger than usual. If they are run up in a form of aluminium alloy tubes from sole to deck above, not much weight is involved, and the pillars are useful to steady oneself on.

In small yachts at sea I find saloon tables are an unmitigated nuisance. They buy up a lot of space and can rarely be used for meals, which have in any case to be taken in a bowl off one's knees, or held in the hand. For *Rani* I designed folding tables of the type illustrated in Diagram 76. These I used again in *Myth* and *Minx of Malham*. An alternative design of folding table is that shown in Diagram 75; this is suitable for folding against a bulkhead and is self locking in its horizontal position. The *Rani* type which folds against the mast is best held up by a

light alloy clip, over the three leaves at its end away from the hinge, and a chain to the deck above. These are ready for use in harbour and out of the way at sea. Guards should be provided in the sea position.

Cabin Sole Floorboards. There is little doubt that teak is the best wood for these, because it does not swell and because it is so easy to wipe over and always looks tidy. They can be made as little as $\frac{1}{2}$ in. thick provided they are adequately stiffened underneath with strips of western red cedar which are fixed to the boards and run across into the main bearers or teak-faced ply.

Elm takes a nice white appearance when scrubbed, but warps more. Of the soft woods western red is best because it virtually hardly swells and does not warp and therefore does not jam the board. But it is so soft that the surface is soon impregnated with dirt. If you do not mind the appearance these boards can be covered with $\frac{3}{32}$ in. thickness of pressed wood or synthetic covering—if, as may well be, you can't get teak.

The fore and aft non-skid strips should be quite shallow and well rounded. Otherwise they will be painful to the bare feet—which are some of the best sea-going footwear.

A multiplicity of hatches or lifting floor-boards should be provided, because a whole mass of stuff can with advantage be stowed under here—tinned food, bunches of spare galvanised shackles, and so on;

one is always getting the weight as low as is feasible.

Draining the Corners. Adequate drainage should be provided to the *corners* of every space within reach of a hatch or opening scuttles. One often sees tiddley gratings only near the centre-line and nice water traps at the side where water may lie for hours if one is heeled on a tack. Gratings are not essential; just a sizeable hole at the extreme corners port and starboard.

Fore and aft seats also need drainage if they are under a companion hatch. And for the same reason broken seats in a cockpit are preferred; or a short length of tube from the corner into the well, if it is self-draining or watertight. Otherwise a drain to the bilge.

Lightweight Aluminium Fittings. Much development has been done for aircraft, and some of these fittings can be very useful in yachts where weight and space have to be saved. Messrs. L. A. Rumbold, Kingsgate, Kilburn, London, N.W.6, are specialists in light fittings and will make lightweight furniture and hardware to suit particular needs. Vickers Armstrong, Weybridge, Surrey, make folding tables, folding wash basins, clothes racks, toilets.

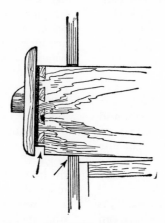

Diagram 77 —Self-locking drawer.

22

GENERAL EQUIPMENT

In this chapter, which deals with miscellaneous equipment for offshore yachts, I am describing what are really quite separate subjects. For convenience the chapter is divided into the following parts: wind tell-tales, compasses, winches, boom gallows, repair equipment, and deck equipment.

WIND TELL-TALES

The requirement as regards a racing flag is to provide something which will indicate faithfully the breezes' direction with the minimum of weight and windage. I find a flag which is not too long in comparison with its breath flies out best in light airs and last longer too, and so can be made of the lightest stuff, silk or nylon for preference. I generally have mine made in the radio of 4 : 5. The breadth I make 2 in. for every 10 ft. of mast height. This seems to provide about the minimum which can be seen clearly at night. White in the flag is best seen at night and a darker colour by day, so horizontal stripes of white and another colour are practical.

As regards the burgee-stick, an aluminium alloy tube of $\frac{7}{16}$ in. diameter is suitable for masts up to say 60 ft. and $\frac{1}{2}$ in. above this. The length, using the normal burgee halyard arrangement, should be four times the breadth of the flag. It is clearly essential to have an arrangement whereby the flag rotates freely on the stick. I have found the normal arrangement of a wire rotating round a screw fixed in a hardwood plug at the top, and at its lower end looped round the tube, to work quite adequately, with the flag sewn to the wire. A more ormolu arrangement is to have a very light alloy tube sewn into the flag.

Some people use a tiny nylon wind-sock permanently at the masthead. But a racing flag must be carried as well in Great Britain, which is double windage. In some other countries this is not compulsory and the sock can be left up there and obviates the necessity for halyards. And there is no doubt that it gives one a very true wind indication. As to the halyards, very fine wire has less windage and obviates the necessity for continually tautening up the hemp or nylon fishing line.

In addition to whatever one has at the masthead,

one must have a supply of very light pennants for use on the shrouds and the backstays. I personally use a few fine strands of nylon cord. One odd length of half a fathom stranded up will last you a season or more or strips of nylon stocking; if you are lucky enough still to have your girl friend or wife in spite of the yacht. When these strands are finely fluffed out they will react to the merest rumour of a breeze. Those on the backstay are invaluable when reaching and running in light airs, and those in the shrouds, which should be 8 or 10 ft. from the deck, invaluable on the wind. Pennants on the runner backstays are not much use, being too much affected by the flow of the mainsail. Those on the lee shrouds will be useful in indicating the flow in lee of the mainsail.

If nylon is not available a couple of feet of knitting wool of a dark fluffy type will be good value and more easily seen than nylon, which may require a hand to sit below it and report changes in the wind. Some people use light silk ribbons; I prefer the other alternatives.

COMPASSES

It is strange that one seldom comes across a really decent, well-mounted compass. Presumably this is principally because the average yachtsman and even the average ocean-racing man is prepared to put up with an indifferent arrangement, and though he will spend a great deal of time and money on his other equipment, he sometimes gets the cheapest thing in compasses that comes his way. Very often this turns out to be a big, clumsy, inaccurate, ship's life-boat compass, such as is found in most ship-chandler's stock. Some compass makers are not much wiser, for they allow the yachtsman to buy unsuitable instruments.

Compass Positions. When one lays out the deck of a small or moderate-sized ocean racer one thinks primarily of two things—firstly how to place the dinghy where it will be least in the way and offer least windage, and secondly how to arrange the helmsman and his compass to the best advantage.

It is of real importance to get the compass mounted where it can be seen with the minimum eye-strain and where the eye falls naturally on it.

In this respect wheel steering has an enormous advantage because one can sit neatly and almost directly behind the compass. But make sure your steering gear is all non-ferrous.

With tiller steering, if there is a bridge deck ahead of the helmsman, it may be worth fitting the compass on an aluminium slide—these can be obtained standard large sail-track size—so that it can be slid across opposite the helmsman according to the tack he is on. This avoids parallax error in viewing the compass from one side. I have very successfully used two compasses one each side. There is some risk of magnetic interference of the one with the other, if they are too close; 3 ft. is generally safe. One can test for interference in harbour, by removing each in turn on various positions of the ship's head. With a tiller one of the great difficulties is to get the compass high enough, so that the crews knees do not obscure and so that one does not have to look down too much. In *Myth* we overcame the difficulty by having twin companion hatches and mounting the compass between, on the after side of the coachroof. With a single companionway the same height can be achieved with one compass on each side of the companionway; or with a bracket on each side, to which the compass can be shifted when one goes about—though this arrangement has its obvious dangers.

The bridge deck next abaft the companion hatch is a nuisance in many ways, as it cuts down one's cockpit space or alternatively robs one of the shelter of the coachroof at sea. And it is awkward to step over when going below in a small boat. But it does furnish one with a decent place to park the compass; or better, as in *Monk of Malham*, two compasses three feet apart.

Needless to say if she is a big boat with plenty of pit, one can build a special bridge or a proper stand from the cockpit floor. But often cockpit space does not allow of this, and one has to suffer with the compass mounted between one's knees or too far away, or off centre where it is really only visible on one tack.

Design of the Compass Bowl. Turning to the instrument itself, there are in my view a number of requirements which, though straightforward, are hardly ever found together. There is a lot to be said for the grid compass, the grid being two parallel lines or bars mounted on a 'second face' which can be rotated and set to a course read off the graduations on the bezel. To steer, the single line or bar mounted on the card is simply kept parallel to the grid. Of necessity the grid must be a long way from the card to allow room for the card to tilt within the bowl. I have found that many people take

some time to get used to this arrangement and meanwhile steer very badly! And I still think careful steersmen are more accurate using an ordinary type. Moreover the under face sometimes collects mist and water which is not easy to be rid of, and so I am still inclined to the use of a lubber's line, if the face is well designed.

I suggest the requirements are firstly that the card shall be as damped and as dead-beat as is possible consistently with providing enough ring to allow of really clear figures, and secondly that the lubber line shall be situated close to the card to avoid a type of parallax error which arises from the necessity to view the compass sitting at the tiller when one is well off the centre-line of the ship, and maybe some distance away also. I like a lubber line consisting of wire curved to follow the swing of the card.

Then as to the gradation of the card. Many still favour the use of 0 to 90 degrees either side of north and south. The less figures one has, the clearer they are to read, which is in favour of the 0 to 90 degree figuring as opposed to the 0 to 360 degrees. On the other hand there is the risk of mixing the figures on either side of north and south. Recently in attempts to enable a steering compass to be used for taking bearings with an azimuth ring, two sets of 360 degree figures have been used around the card, one being downside up, which further increases the chance of error. I prefer to be without the points and quarter points if the degree figures are clear. It is important that the 10 degree marks be distinctive as against the 5 degree intermediates; white figures on a black card. Tired helmsmen, sometimes wearing wet glasses, desperately need a good clear compass if they are to steer a proper race-worthy course.

In most small and medium yachts the steering compass is 'wooded' on many bearings, particularly when heeled. Moreover when the navigator attempts to use it for taking bearings of shore objects, he has generally to disturb the helmsman. All of which goes to show that one should use a separate compass for taking bearings, most probably a hand bearing compass. In larger yachts it is occasionally feasible to mount a second compass way up on top of a deck house where a good all-round bearing can be had, except for the sails, and where it forms a ready check on the steering compass.

An alternative is a bearing plate similarly mounted when occasion demands, from which one reads the bearing of the object relative to the ship's head, shouting on to the helmsman who reads the ship's head at the same moment. Such a plate requires to be gimballed or pivoted with axis fore and aft, and is certainly a 'second best' arrangement.

If you use the flat top type compass bowl, I believe that provided the card has a fair swing within its bowl, it should be able to dip not less than 20 degrees, only athwartships gimballing is necessary. That is to say the axis of the single gimbals should be fore and aft. This simplified mounting seems to cut out the mad dance which the bowl does on occasions in a seaway when it is double gimballed. The fast motor boat compasses are mostly without gimbals and appear satisfactory for the angles they work at, with the exception of occasional steep turns in a seaway. They have about 28 degrees of movement from the horizontal within the bowl. The elimination of a gimbal reduces the size of the compass binnacle—an important advantage in some cases—and also its weight and cost.

Compass Lighting. The lighting of the bowl is important. It is not feasible as a rule to use the hooded cover with a light placed in the side, because the light is either non-effective on one tack or shines in one's face when steering. Also the extra window increases the difficulty of vision. Moreover the cover is a beast to stow below. A watertight electric light fitting under the bowl, which allows the bowl to tilt to 50 degrees on the roll, and which lights the card through a large, ground glass window in the bottom of the bowl, appears to be the best arrangement. But the window must be large. A simple shutter over the light is an advantage to adjust the intensity of the illumination so that one can get the necessary minimum of light, which will not engender night blindness.

As a stand-by one can carry a pedal cycle self-contained red rear light with a prepared bracket. The Ever Ready Company (Holloway, London, N.7) market one with an internal switch which is splash-proof. Test first, however, that it has no magnetic effect on your own compass.

The bowl should have fore and aft line scribed by the makers clearly on the outside of the rim, to assist in lining up the compass in the fore and aft line of the ship.

In addition to the shutter on the light the upper walls of the binnacle should be painted matt black to avoid dazzling the eye. It will generally be advisable to blank out some of the ground glass under the bowl by a mask; a dark piece of paper stuck over with waterproof glue. Sufficient light is generaly furnished by a large half-moon aperture directing light towards the foremost part of the rim of the card, by an athwartships, or alternatively again use red light. Permanently reddened bulbs are hard to come by, but ladies' nail vanish, which

can be had in many deepening tones, answers excellently and dries at once.

Practical Tests. Some of the most accurate compasses, made for big ships' use, are for yacht use not sufficiently damped or dead-beat. The airplane types on the other hand are sometimes insufficiently accurate, though very dead-beat and lightly damped. Once disturbed the big ship compass is too slow in settling again. For this purpose we require standard figures to work to and the test I use is to deflect the card artificially $45°$ away from its correct reading, steady it there and release it, recording the time it takes to steady again within I degree of the true reading. This should be not more than $\frac{1}{2}$ min. and between 20 and 25 secs. is the time for the better types. The first swing past the true reading should also be noted, and should not be more than 12 degrees for an average good instrument. The artificial deflection is best created with a magnet.

Commercial Type Compasses. You may well at this point remark that these are nice generalisations but where do I go to get the compass I need. For twenty years I have used the American Danforth White (earlier called Kelvin and White) domed top 'Constellation' compass. This is a very fine job indeed. The lighting is on the dome which works satisfactorily: but should be protected by a three-pronged brass hoop. In other respects it meets all requirements. It is available in five sizes and several types of mounting and the smaller 'Corsair' may be used where space is restricted; in J.O.G. yachts perhaps.

Henry Browne manufacture a domed top 'Sestrel' compass which is used on many ocean racers, they come in two sizes 'Major' and 'Minor'; with bulkhead or flange mounting. They have also produced the 'Sestrel-Moore' type in a perspex bowl, which can be read in the vertical position as well as from above, and has a magnified card.

Compass Card Magnification. Most magnifying prisms over the bowl are not suitable for use in a racing boat where one is constantly shifting one's position in relation to the wheel or tiller, particularly as they increase the weight and cost and the liability to get foul of sheets. The American Kelvin & White Constellation compass, however, has a domed bowl which does all that is wanted, and is valuable because the compass position becomes less critical when it can be mounted farther fron the helmsman.

Turning again to the question of taking bearings. The hand bearing compass has come to be a usual fitting in most small racers. It enables the navigator to get bearings from any part of the ship shifting his position according to the relative bearing of the object and the sails which are set. This may be important, particularly since with the ship moving about it is not enough to have a peep-hole between two sails; one requires to have unimpaired vision over quite an arc, both vertically and horizontally, in the general direction of the distant object.

Hand Bearing Compasses. A hand bearing compass consists as a rule of a vertical handle with the small bowl, perhaps 3 in. in diameter at the top. A sight fitted with a magnifying prism is used to view the object, in conjunction with the card, when the compass is brought up to eye level. The principal difficulty in its use is to steady oneself in bad weather whilst taking a bearing. In steel yachts one should stand as far from magnetism as possible, perhaps on a skylight.

There is, or should be, a torch fitted in the stem to illuminate the card from underneath. Nearly always this is too bright 'as made'. I normally keep well-used torch batteries and fit one in place of the two dry cells, and generally use a red light. A light which first comes up in the far distance faintly, can then be seen, and a bearing can be taken without feeling dazzled. A further difficulty arises here, with long-sighted people who have to hold the compass well away to focus on the figures, that the faint light then illuminates hardly enough. It is therefore important to choose a card with bold figures. There is today, in 1969, a crying need for a better dead-beat easily read hand bearer.

With good prisms one just about manages; I suppose improved magnification is required, but I must admit that I have not completely solved this one yet. Anyway, a good deal of practice is needed to get consistently reliable and accurate bearings with a hand compass. One should at first get someone to work with one and check every bearing till one finds that both are consistently getting the same answer.

The question of compass adjustment is dealt with in Chapter 8.

WINCHES

The deck winch or mast winch is a modern substitute for a purchase. It is a means of obtaining mechanical advantage; of increasing the load which one or two crew members can apply to a rope; most generally a sheet or a halyard. It has a higher mechanical efficiency than a purchase; that is to say there is less loss of power due to friction.

If the drum of a direct-acting winch is 4 in. in diameter, that is 2 in. in radius, and you operate it with a handle which projects so that your hand grasps it at a mean distance of 16 in. from the centre of the drum, you get a mechanical advantage of 8 : 1. A purchase to give you a similar advantage

would be a cumbersome thing. It would have to be 'luff upon luff', or two purchases in series. The friction losses would be high; and it would be very slow to overhaul, which is annoying, and very wasteful of time and labour in the case of sheets, where the ability to use single parts is of great value. This is particularly so when overlapping sails have to be sheeted. The single part overhauls, round the shrouds and so on, very much more readily.

Calculation of Winch Power. My formula for the minimum mechanical advantage necessary in a headsail sheet winch is as follows. This is the minimum and when in doubt provide more.

$$\frac{A\,U\,F\sqrt{\dfrac{L}{D}}}{175H} - 1$$

Where A is the area of the sail.
  U is the maximum wind force Beaufort scale in which the sail will be carried on the wind.
  L is length of luff.
  D is diagonal of sail; luff to clew.
  H 'hand factor'.
  F is the friction factor.

Operating single-handed involves one's right hand on the winch and the left on the fall of the sheet coming off the barrel. Allowing for the comparatively unfavourable operating position the hand factor is 1. In big yachts where one has a second man on the fall of the sheets, and where one can normally achieve a suitable position to get both left and right hands fairly on a nice big handle, the hand factor will be 1·6.

In the biggest yachts where there are two cranks to the winch, on each of which a man works a ratchet lever with both his hands, the factor can be 3·2. But where an all-round action is necessary, *i.e.* where there is no ratchet, the hand factor should be decreased by one-eighth. This will refer to the mechanical advantage required of one crank; in its low gear if two speeds are fitted.

The factor $\sqrt{\dfrac{L}{D}}$ needs a little explanation. It is a measure of the aspect ratio of the sail and is necessary because sails with a higher aspect ratio have to be sheeted appreciably flatter, and require appreciably more sheet load *for a given area.*

F, the friction factor, is unity for a good direct acting winch, 1·25 for a very good geared winch in good oily condition and up to 2 in. more primitive geared winches less well maintained. These figures are based on bench trials lifting test weights.

One would naturally apply this formula to the

sail which one thought or knew from experience required the most sheeting; in cases of doubt one would work it out for each sail. If our largest working headsail (Force 5) is 300 sq. ft., our light weather Force 2 genoa will perhaps be 600 sq. ft., and can, of course, be sheeted on the same winch, as far as power is concerned. A 400-sq. ft. yankee which could only be carried in Force 3 could equally well be sheeted.

Naturally a formula of this sort cannot give exact results. There are so many minor factors such as the mechanical efficiency of the sheet leads. But I believe it will form a valuable guide, and that its application will in many cases help to obviate the all too common fault of fitting winches which cannot properly control the sheets in fresh breezes. This trouble results in resort to luffing up to get the sheets hard in, or to sailing with sheets not properly sheeted home; or more commonly to a bit of each, with other periods where sheet trimming is not sufficiently indulged because of the shocking struggle necessary to get things home. The answer it gives is a minimum. A greater advantage does no harm, but anything greatly in excess will be slow and waste time in getting the sail sheeted home; unless it has 'two speeds'.

Working out a few examples in conjunction with the minimum drum sizes will quickly make it clear how necessary it is to have gearing in one's winches, in a yacht of any size.

But when in doubt it is wise to over winch rather than the reverse. Particularly so in family boats, where the crew is likely to include from time to time the old, the very young and the ladies. Many boats suffer from too small, insufficiently powerful, winches with tiny barrels. The modern winch with aluminium alloy drums weighs very little. However, some types of very cumbersome winches are still on the market and so it is wise to make sure of the weight when one is ordering.

Direct-acting Winches. Winches for small yachts are for the most part direct-acting, the handle working on the same spindle as the drum. We will for the moment consider the most usual type, in which one catches two or more turns round the drum before hauling in on sheet or halyard, tending the fall with one hand and operating the lever with the other. There will normally be two sets of ratchets, one between the drum and the fixed winch base, and the other between the handle and the drum. The former will allow the drum to rotate in one direction only; clockwise as a rule. By 'free-wheeling' in this direction it allows slack to be wound down by pulling on the fall of the sheet or halyard, the slack running freely off the drum, until sufficient weight comes on the sheet to require

the drum to be turned by the handle. A typical example is shown in Diagram 78. It is suitable for genoas up to 250 sq. ft. A stop must be placed to prevent the handle flying right round. The exact curve on the drum face is critical to each design of winch.

Other good direct-acting winches include Gibb type and for very small and for small J.O.G. boats; and Gibb type for larger J.O.G. For small Class III yachts type 7 C.R. These are all direct acting, or nearly so in the case of the 7 C.R. and viable where a reasonably-priced sheet winch is sought.

Halyard Winches. For headsails, most people use only top handle types for halyard winches, but for small Class III and J.O.G. yachts where headsails can be hoisted by hand up to the point of hardening I much prefer bottom operation. The handles can be left always in place, the turns can be more quickly caught on the drum, and the winch will be lighter and cheaper. This applies also to staysails of small cutters. Thus Gibb 585 can be used up a 32-ft. hoist, type 587 up to 50 ft. Above that geared winches will be needed, such as Lewmar No. 922. It is however most important that over-powered winches should not be used on halyards; since in practice it is easy to overload initially a halyard, so that when the adjacent stay stretches the extra load causes failure. For mainsails and spinnakers the same winches can be used up to a 58-ft. mast. Above that a geared winch is preferable. Many will prefer, particularly for short-handed cruising, reel (magazine) winches. We use

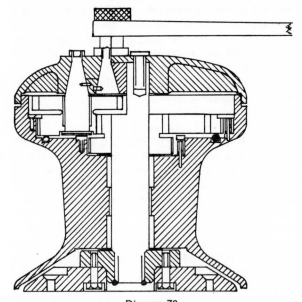

Diagram 78.
A typical 'free-wheeling' winch.

Goiot for J.O.G. or Class III; Goiot for larger Class III and Class II yachts; and the Australian Barlow for Class I yachts. But reel winches are necessarily more expensive and bulky; and once in a way either get the wire jammed up in the drum; or their brake fails and causes an accident. The handle may be located on top of the drum, which is convenient for a halyard winch mounted on the mast (with its spindle horizontal) where it is necessary to have an all-round motion to the handle to speed up hoisting of the sail.

In the case of the smaller ocean racers with working headsail areas up to 500 sq. ft. the usual practice is to have headsail sheet winches mounted on frames or chocks on the deck, or on the cockpit coamings.

The Siting of Winches on Deck. A third system for sheet winches is to have the handle mounted on a 'downwards extension' of the spindle, under the side deck or bridge deck. This is in regular use for day racing boats where the access to the underside of the side decks is not restricted by watertight cockpit sides, and where a second crew member is available to wind in under deck while one man catches the turns and tends the fall.

It is clearly not as a rule convenient for small ocean racers, where the arrangement must permit of the sail being sheeted by one man. This type of winch can, however, be used with the spindle horizontal, passing through and mounted on a stout coaming. The drum is on the out-board and the handle on the in-board side of the coaming. The slight disadvantage here is that there is only a very limited arc of direction from which the sheet can lead to the winch, whereas if the spindle is mounted vertically, one can get an almost all-round lead to the drum, provided only that the lead to the drum is slightly 'up to the drum'.

It is important to remember this when siting one's sheet winches; with a vertical drum axis one must arrange for the drum centre to be a little higher than the block or fairlead from which the lead comes to the winch. Otherwise the turns will ride up the winch barrel, and sometimes override and jam. One can incline the spindle if one knows exactly whence the lead is coming, but in practice with different sized sails sheeting at various points this is not always feasible.

When laying out sheet winches, bear in mind the possibility of placing a single powerful winch amidships, taking the lead to it by a snatch block each side where necessary. This saves the initial cost and weight of one winch, compared to the normal practice of one each side.

There are other calls on the sheet winches too, besides the sheet duty, such as to set up the braces

8*

or guys of the spinnaker pole. To save the weight and cost of a capstan one can use a sheet winch to break out the anchor, provided this can subsequently be man-handled. It also frees the space on the foredeck normally occupied by a capstan.

Calculation of Drum Diameters. It is necessary to increase the size of drum to suit the size of wire sheet; thicker wire will not grip on a small diameter drum without an excessive number of turns, and these will result in loss of time and power. The drum diameter for good operation of a halyard winch I take at $3\frac{1}{2}$ times the wire circumference. For sheets with nylon or with terylene around $2\frac{1}{2}$ times the circumference; and either with whelps (strips or corrugations on the barrel) or with knurling (mechanical roughening).

These drum diameters are the minimum. It is not as a rule convenient to put them up, in the case of halyard winches; and as a sail is not hard sheeted when one is hoisting, less strain relative to the wire size comes on them at that moment. But in the case of sheet winches it is very desirable to increase the drum diameter beyond those given as a minimum so as to reduce the number of turns necessary and/or the weight on the fall for handling, where this can conveniently be done.

So the order of things is this. Having decided your sail plan in detail and worked the areas to each sail, estimate carefully the maximum wind strength in which they will be carried to windward. Determine the sheet sizes from the table in Chapter 17. Calculate from this your minimum drum diameter; then from the formula given earlier in this chapter the necessary mechanical advantage. You are then ready to choose your winches.

The trouble here is that the bigger the drum, the smaller is the mechanical advantage given by the same lever length; and there is a limit to the length of lever which can conveniently be wielded. Therefore the modern method is to use geared winches, to combine big drum diameters with the necessary mechanical advantage and a handy lever length.

Geared Winches. Apart from cost and the obvious needs of correct mechanical advantage and of reliability, the things in order of importance to be looked for are:

(*a*) A very free running drum (unless the drum is very free one cannot get down the maximum of slack sheet; and very much more time and labour is expended in winching in after going about. It is almost essential that the drum spins free from the gearing, *viz* that the ratchet is arranged so that the gearing is stationary during the preliminary spinning of the drum).

(b) An adequate drum; diameter and design (a question dealt with separately) and an easily shipped handle.

(c) A winch which is as quiet as possible (noisy winches which keep the crew awake at night are a menace to sleep, rest, and winning races).

(d) Ease of maintenance (oiling after every day's racing should be painless, and monthly dismantling easy by a ham-fisted crewman).

(e) When under full hand power the friction should be as low as possible and not increase unduly when maintenance has not been possible. (More expensive winches have needle roller bearings. But most of the lost power is due to the design in which the cages and bearings are not rigid enough to keep gearing alignment, and or from badly-cut gears.)

(f) The winch should be as light as possible, consistent with the other qualities sought.

Types of Geared Winch. A typical example of good modern practice is the winch illustrated in Diagram 79, which is suitable for working headsails up to 300 sq. ft. It has a 6 : 1 gear ratio and an all-round motion to the handle mounted on an extension spindle. The handle has a ratchet in it for sweating up the last part of the load. The construction is in corrosion-resisting aluminium and the winch weighs only about 5 lb. These are made to Sparkman & Stephens designs and marketed by us at Emsworth.

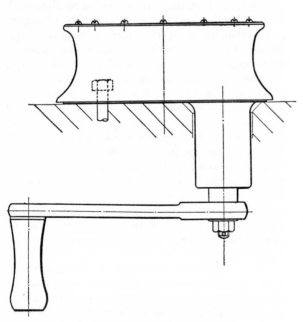

Diagram 79.

Geared Winch for under deck operation (can also be used with the axis horizontal through a coaming). Made by U.S. M.P. Company Ltd., Bradford, England. Under licence from Sparkman & Stephens.

Other good winches, but all of which we have used ourselves at sea include the following (double the sail area for light sails):

Type	Maximum mechanical advantage	Weight	For working sail area up to say:
Gibb 6CR	17 : 1	15 lb.	400 sq. ft.
Gibb 9CR (2 speed)	36 : 1	21 lb.	700 sq. ft.
Gibb 10CR (2 speed)	50 : 1	24 lb.	900 sq. ft.
Lewmar 830 (single speed)	22 : 1	Alloy 16 lb. / Bronze 24 lb.	450 sq. ft.
Lewmar 816 (single speed)	28·75 : 1	20 lb.	600 sq. ft.
Lewmar 840	37·3 : 1	40 lb.	750 sq. ft.

The American Barient winches operate beautifully, but their cost excludes them from use by European owners. The Australian Barlow winches, near cousins to the Barient, are good and less expensive, though still very dear; and heavy. The Gibb are among the cheapest range of really good winches.

The Goiot range of geared winches are carefully made, light, and well finished. They are in the three available sizes suitable approximately for working areas of 250, 300, and 350 sq. ft. (the latter using a long handle) and a larger two-speed winch. But they suffer from the disadvantage that they are stiff on the overrun and don't free-wheel well enough, owing only partly to the water-excluding seals.

Another special fitting, used on *Myth of Malham* on the 1968 Single Handed Trans-Atlantic Race and designed by Max Gunning is a wire main sheet, with self-reeling winch. The drum of this winch is fitted with coarse thread onto the spindle. The pawl-wheel is free, but is pressed against a ferodo ring by the drum moving a short distance on the thread just mentioned. When the sheet is reeled in, the spindle, pawl-wheel and drum are pressed together, and form one solid unit. When, however, the handle is turned back the drum moves on the spindle away from the pawl-wheel and the latter is free to slip. The drum can now be turned by the pull on the wire, just as far as the handle is turned, after which it again fetches up against the pawl-wheel and is locked. In practice this movement is continuous, and the sheet can be reeled in or out just as far as required, without taking it off a cleat, and making it up afterwards. I personally prefer a hemp or terylene sheet, but this wire one does really seem to work well.

BOOM GALLOWS

The old idea of a main boom crutch was something which was got out in harbour to hold the boom in place when the sail was lowered for stowage. Nowadays it is usual and desirable to make the crutch sufficiently strong and convenient to enable it to support the boom while reefing is going on, with the sail still set, or alternatively to hold the boom securely for as long as is necessary in gale conditions when the trysail is set. They are provided with three boom positions, one amidships and one each side for reefing. In any event the two wing slots should be reasonably deep to ensure that once in place for reefing, the boom does not jump out.

In larger yachts it is quite a good scheme to leave this crutch standing throughout the yacht's life. In this way it can be made lighter in construction. It is also useful to grasp when moving about the deck. In this case special care should be taken that the corners where the cross member meets the upright are well rounded, so as to reduce the chance of the main sheet fouling.

In smaller racers the windage is relatively more important, and the problem of providing a housing gear of sufficient strength is not so difficult. In *Myth* I arranged gallows as shown in Diagram 60. The construction is light but strong. The cross-bar is in western red cedar with aluminium alloy facing at the ends. The pillars are alloy tubes $1\frac{1}{8}$ in. in diameter. The cross-bracing wires are $\frac{1}{2}$ in. When not in use the gallows are lowered to the bridge deck. The wires are self-housing as very small weights are attached to them inside the side lockers.

An alternative scheme was used successfully in *Maid* where there was a little more room in the side decks aft. The boom crutch was of galvanised steel tube hinged at its lower ends, where they met

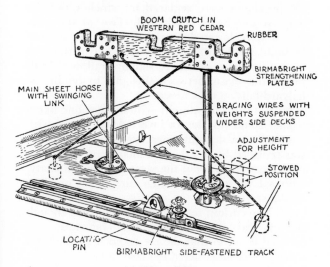

Diagram 80.
Myth of Malham—Boom Crutch and Main Sheet Horse.

the deck. Housed, it lay like a hoop flat on deck round the after end of the cockpit. Laurent Giles & Partners designed a neat hinge which allowed the bottom of the upright tubes to drop into a socket, after reaching the vertical working position.

REPAIR EQUIPMENT

When the regatta racing boat splits a mainsail or springs a spar, she is not far from a repair yard. If similar trouble befalls the cruising man he may if he chooses put away the sail and drop the spar on deck. He can proceed on his comparatively unhurried way on his trysail. Or if it is a big auxiliary yacht he can turn on his engine to help complete his passage, and seek solace in his champagne and with his blondes.

No such course is open to the ocean racer who must make good his defects to the best of his ability and continue meanwhile to press on with the race. At the same time he cannot afford to carry weighty repair equipment, and so the choice of tools and gear requires to be carefully considered. To this end a list of tools and repair material appropriate to a small and moderate-sized ocean racer are shown in Appendix XIV together with a short list of supplementary equipment which it is suggested should be carried in the larger racers; shall we say those over 40-ft. waterline, where the extra weight is relatively unimportant.

At the same time as you prepare your tools and stow them, go through the miscellaneous stuff on board or in your store and throw out anything that is not needed. In a recent case I went through the tool lockers of a small racer with a designed displacement of 7 tons, and dispensed with over 3 cwt. of entirely superfluous stuff including such items as old engine propellers which had been buying up useful space and displacement for months. From *Latifa* before the Bermuda Race of 1946 we landed about $3\frac{1}{2}$ tons of unwanted gear!

In small racers, for the stowage of the tools try to find a dry drawer or locker low down in the ship. The best preservative for tools is lanolin grease; it resists rust and throws off water better than mineral grease, though its lubricating value for heavily loaded bearings is less than that of mineral oils.

Sail Repair Outfit. This grease is specially valuable for preserving sail needles, which can be stowed in a piece of canvas impregnated with it, or in a small tube or box lined with grease. Care should be taken to include several fine needles in the outfit for light sail repairs; these will be the sails most subject to tearing. A supply of large pins should be carried for securing a patch in place while it is being sewn. They are handier than spare needles, and although professional sailmakers may not need them, they are valuable to the amateur.

Quite passable temporary repairs can be made to sails with special sticky tape, particularly light sails. The tape must be thin and fresh, about $1\frac{1}{2}$ in. wide. It should be put on both sides of the sail in way of the gash and carefully pressed on to the canvas. Medical tape in good big widths can be used on small tears and small holes in mainsails, again as a temporary measure, and if time allows stitched over.

The same thin sticky tape is very handy for repairing chafed servings; or for covering up the odd strand of a wire splice which might otherwise cut one's hands. At a pinch ordinary insulating tape will do the trick, very temporarily.

Binding Wire. Special mention may be made of the desirability of carrying binding wire—soft galvanised iron **or** stainless steel wire—for repair purposes. This should not be confused with serving wire. Stainless steel wire is the most useful emergency repair material available for a great variety of purposes. Here are four typical instances of its use: (1) Spliced grommet at mainsail headboard needs emergency replacement: sail taped over to reduce chafe and stainless wire used. (It was still perfect at end of the season.) (2) Special twisted shackle for mainsail tack mislaid; stainless steel wire used in lieu (*Myth of Malham*). (3) Crewman fell off the coachroof during a race on to the tiller and broke it off 1 ft. from the rudder stock. Complete repair made in a few minutes by binding with stainless steel wire over multiple spare hacksaw blades laid around the fracture. Ship kept sailing meanwhile playing the main sheet. Race continued without appreciable delay (*Maid of Malham*, 1937). (4) Cross-tree socket wrenched off mast—lashed into place (*Myth*, Fastnet 1949).

DECK EQUIPMENT AND WINDAGE

Life-line Stanchions. The R.O.R.C. in 1963 made it compulsory to carry 'double' life-lines round the boat; upper life-lines should be at a height of 24 in.

The best stanchions are corrosion-resisting aluminium alloy of the Birmabright, Noral, or Seabright type, which can readily be straightened if they get bent; when berthing for instance, $1\frac{1}{8}$ in. diameter is a good size tube for average yachts, with $1\frac{1}{4}$ in. for bigger yachts of over 45-ft. waterline. J.O.G. yachts with 20 in. stanchions can get away with 1 in. diameter of stout gauge.

These stanchions need no painting, and no bushing of the holes where the wire passes. But galvanised steel tube stanchions do, to prevent them cutting the wire; failure to provide a soft bush may lead to a dangerous carry away of the wire. A short

length of copper tube pushed into the hole and belled over at the ends is an easy way out.

They can be rigged into sockets or over stubs of length twice the tube diameter, made of galvanised steel or better, galvanised iron which rusts less quickly when the zinc gets chipped. I like to turn the flanges of these sockets up at one side and get a fastening into the rail or bulwarks. Nearly all sockets are insufficiently fastened to the deck, and special care should be taken to get if possible one through fastening at the inboard side, which with a horizontal one into the rail and one screw forward and one aft will generally hold. Messrs. Lewmar Marine supply an excellent range of stainless steel stanchions and sockets. But specify long-toed sockets.

Windage. We have dealt with the question of reducing the windage of masts and standing and running rigging in the various chapters dealing with those matters (15, 16 and 17). In addition to those obvious causes of windage, we should survey our deck and see whether there are any further ways in which we can reduce our air resistance. Here is a list of matters which I found required attention in a yawl. The list is not exhaustive, but simply indicates the type of action one can take. The improvement from each source is small, but in the aggregate must be appreciable:

(*a*) Two lifebuoys previously stowed on mizzen shrouds. New stowage position arranged on deck.

(*b*) There were five halyard purchases, there being no winches. They were attached to the mast some 1 to 2 ft. above deck with cleats at shoulder height. The falls were habitually made up and hung from these cleats. The bottom 6 ft. of the mast was in consequence a real Christmas tree. Two of the purchases were replaced by winches and the halyard purchases eliminated. Two of the purchases were lowered nearer the deck by shifting eyebolts and lengthening the wire halyards which were due for renewal. A shallow rail was built round the masts between skylights to retain the halyard falls on deck at sea.

(*c*) A 10-ft. long dinghy with a sheer line like a whaler stood up like an inverted half moon with one end on a skylight when stowed on deck. This was replaced by a 7 ft. 6 in. long pram with 6 in. more beam and about the same carrying capacity, with a level gunwale, which stowed flat on deck over a skylight.

(*d*) The cockpit seats were at deck level, though the pit was quite a deep one. The seats were lowered 6 in., so that the crew and helmsman got more shelter and offered less resistance.

(*e*) A large meat and vegetable safe was stowed on deck abaft the mizzen mast. The contents got very bedraggled after a heavy passage at sea. The safe was put ashore giving welcome deck space and a reduction in top weight and windage, and the vegetables and meat stowed in zinc racks in the counter.

(*f*) The light boards were big enough for a tramp steamer and attached to the main shrouds. Huge oil lamps were shipped here, which never kept alight on the leeside in a seaway owing to the slack shrouds shaking them. Moreover they were covered by the staysail in fine weather. These were replaced by much smaller electric lamps in smaller light boards mounted above a skylight where they could generally be seen under the sails.

Spray Hoods. Carefully designed canvas spray hoods over the hatches are a valuable aid to ventilating the boat while keeping the sea out of the accommodation. These should be capable of folding in position. The hems should be secured to the coamings of the hatch by some special method, such as a drawstring in the hem, lying in a groove, or below a prominent beading. Spray hoods are particularly worth while for racing in warm climates, where in all but the smallest yachts the windage should be accepted.

Shock Cord. Shock cord (thick, springy elastic) is a valuable asset in rigging. A supply of it in two or three sizes should be available when fitting out, and subsequently kept on board, just as one keeps a supply of hambro line, 2-lb. line, and cod line. Typical uses are:

(*a*) Between runner backstays and the heels of the lower cross-trees (to prevent the leeward slack runner getting round the end of the spreader).

(*b*) Port and starboard in combination with hooks to secure the slackened leeward runner forward towards the shrouds.

(*c*) Laid taut across the top of a coachroof or on deck—most useful for securing odd coiled lines, falls of halyards, or for holding a torch in a horizontal position shining over the foredeck during a night sail change.

(*d*) In combination with hooks or eyes to secure a variety of objects below—as an improvement on lanyards.

(*e*) To keep flag halyards taut. In my latest design of mast I have nylon fishing line flag halyards—which are 100 lb. strength, slide freely in the eye at the masthead, do not easily rot, and have less windage and stretch than the usual hemp line—to a cleat which slides in a short vertical track, and is held down by shock cord.

(*f*) Across a bight of the topping lift to keep the excess slack under control.

(*j*) In the topping lift, to take main boom weight in calms.

SPECTACLES—OFFSHORE

Many of us in later life, although our long sight is still good, need spectacles for chart work and in order to see the compass properly. I have found it necessary to have two pairs; one pair giving specially good close-up magnification for chart work (particularly necessary when one is tired towards the end of a long passage) and another pair arranged for best vision at a distance of about 40 in. for use when steering by compass. The latter are particularly useful at night.

In each case the lower half of the lens only is fitted (with no frame over) so that one's distant sight for lookout purposes is at once available. Over the ears I have full flexible 'hooks' to ensure that they don't fall or blow off in a breeze or when the ship is bumping.

These specs are made up specially for me by Messrs. Gould, Opticians, Norfolk Street, Sheffield, who are prepared to supply other yachtsmen. When one is ordering, in addition to sending the optical formula of one's reading spectacles, one should state whether one has a low, normal, or high bridge to one's nose; since the position of the line of the top of the lens with reference to the pupil of the eye is important.

Some sailing men use plastic lenses, which have the advantage that they do not break or splinter if a blow is received, say from a slack runner, or a wire halyard if astray.

SAFETY BELTS

The R.O.R.C. rule now makes the provision of safety belts or harness for every member of the crew compulsory, and the rule states that they should be used in heavy weather by anyone on deck or in the cockpit. They are awkward things to put on and restrict quick movement, but they can be life-savers, and the skipper will have to decide for himself what constitutes 'heavy weather'. The best-known safety harness is the Haward Safety Belt which can be supplied in canvas or terylene. Several other makes have recently come on the market, including one which combines a lightweight life-jacket with the harness, by Offshore Clothing, Salcombe, Devon (no relation to this book).

Wheel Steering. On a small or medium-sized yacht about one and a half turns hard over to hard over is right to give 38 degrees of helm. If you have more turns she may be difficult to control going fast in a seaway down wind. Good wire and quadrant steering is okay, and under half the price of mechanical steering. The lead of the wires over large special sheaves must be very carefully arranged. Goiot (address: 28 Rue du Frère Louis, 44 —Nantes) have complete wire steering gear in several sizes: they supply the pedastal, self-aligning sheaves, and quadrants for mounting on the rudder stock.

Mechanically-geared steering is often preferred; and the ratio turns hard over to hard over can be very gradually increased in yachts displacing more than 25 tons to keep the effort down to a reasonable one. I prefer larger steering wheels, rather than excessive ratios; it enables one not only better to control the vessel but to steer while sitting well out from the centre line and be better able to see the sails when one is going to windward. The wheel diameters I suggest are from 24 in. on a 24-ft. waterliner up to 42 in. on larger yachts. I always use smooth rimmed wheels, rather than spoked ones.

In Britain most of the mechanical gears are made by either Messrs. Mathaway (c/o British Polar, Helen Street, Glasgow) or by Messrs. Whitlock (Langley Terrace, Latimer Road, Luton, Bedfordshire).

23

AUXILIARY ENGINES AND ELECTRICS

The new international rule, the Royal Ocean Racing Club, and also the C.C.A. rules, make allowance in the rating rule for auxiliary engines. These vary according to the type of propellers, and their position as well. The R.O.R.C. has a weight of engine component which is a plus in calculating the Stability Allowance. (*See* Appendix VIII.)

These allowances are framed to compensate for the moderate loss in performance, under sail, due to a well-arranged auxiliary power unit. Clearly no more could be allowed. It therefore behoves us to install our engine, if we feel we need one, or to modify our existing power unit, to ensure that we waste no more sailing power than we need to.

Rating Allowance for Propellers. This allowance is granted under each of the three rules. The detail is indicated in the relative Appendix.

The American arrangements concerning propeller allowances are too long to be explained and condensed into a paragraph; they are shown in full in Appendix XII. The allowances, on the whole, run to about the same average as the British, though the depth of immersion of the propeller forms an extra variant in the C.C.A. rule.

Propellers in the Deadwood and Rudder. The only position in which a large propeller is almost intolerable is in a bad aperture wholly in the rudder. In this position if the aperture is large it normally results in one having to use about twice as much helm for a given result. The drag is great and the boat is, as a rule, much less pleasant to steer. A moderate-sized and properly streamlined aperture, in the deadwood, fitted with a two-bladed fixed propeller which can be set vertically when sailing, is a good proposition, from a sailing point of view. The streamlining of the aperture is desirable, not only to reduce the drag, but to get the water reasonably 'clean' to the propeller under power. A two-bladed propeller often gives rise to considerable vibration under power, as both blades enter comparatively dead water in way of the stern post at the same moment, which results in pulsing torque. However this may, with a small engine and a well-faired aperture, be moderate and acceptable for

auxiliary use, but for cruising a three-bladed propeller will be much quieter.

A folding propeller out through the quarter—it should be on the port side for a clockwise turning, or 'right handed wheel'—undoubtedly offers very little resistance, and is attractive in very light displacement boats where the propeller allowances probably do not compensate for the drag. In heavier displacement yachts with larger sail plans a fixed propeller off centre is thought by some experts to be properly covered by the allowance; provided it is only just over the 5 per cent of beam off centre which is required to earn the increased allowance. Great care is necessary to get the propeller out of the hull without use of a clumsy shaft bracket and bearing. It is generally possible instead to arrange a tube outside the projecting propeller shaft, not exceeding the propeller boss diameter, which is carried on (welded to) a flange which is at the suitable angle to be recessed at least partly in the skin planking; which will at this point have been reinforced by the inside shaft log.

Propeller Drag. Some years ago I spent part of a very cold winter week-end anchored in a dinghy in the strongest spring tideway we could find, armed with an assortment of propellers, brackets, outriggers, and spring balances, to measure the relative drag of various arrangements. It seems agreed that at the higher speeds propeller drag is a minor factor, and this tideway provided water speeds up to 3 knots. We did the tests several times over and obtained very good repeat figures. The resistances, on folding, free-rotating, and fixed propellers (of the same power) were at 3 knots in the ratio of $3\frac{1}{4}$, 5, 7. This included the slim shaft bracket.

The advantage of the folding clam-shell propeller became somewhat more marked at slower speeds, under 2 knots. The fixed-bladed propeller used was a good one from the sailing point of view with a biggish pitch and moderate-sized blades for the power. In practice of course no propeller is as free-rotating as this one; there is some gland friction. A folding propeller arranged over the rudder and as near as possible to the centre line, offers, one supposes, the least drag of all. The C.C.A. rule at one time paid it the compliment of making no propeller allowance in this case, though this decision may have been partly dictated by a wish to discourage an arrangement which gives as a rule very little immersion to the propeller. Apart from this, the C.C.A. rule has quite a potent little factor increasing the propeller allowance with the immersion, on the grounds that its drag is increased, and again, one imagines, to discourage, shallow shafts.

Small Power Units. It is remarkable what can be achieved by a small-powered unit with proper stern gear and in a decently designed hull. The 8 h.p. Stuart Turner drove the 35-ft. waterline *Maid* with a sea-going displacement of 15 tons at 4·1 knots. In 1937, after the racing season was over and when we were on our way from Brittany, we encountered one of those rare persistent calms, so we motored all the way to Portland—about 48 hrs. on the engine—averaging our 4 knots through the water on less than full throttle. It lived under the cabin sole and had a centrifugal clutch, so there was no gear-box weight or control complication.

Battery Charging. One of the principal jobs for which the engine is wanted between races or cruises is charging the battery, which we will need for lighting inside the boat, for the side-lights, and for lighting the compass bowl. The problem is to get this charge done without churning round the engine at high revs., in neutral. A separate charging unit is a waste of space and weight, and out of place in anything except a large yacht. An alternator can now be fitted, in place of a dynamo, which gives a high charge at low main engine speed; little above tick-over revs. Where the engine maker is uncooperative about this it may be necessary to take the drive off some other shaft. A 20 amp alternator is no problem but a very large alternator may make starting less easy, unless a clutch is provided. In any case a switch in the alternator circuit should be provided and 'broken' for starting.

The batteries can generally be placed in a plywood well (leave the slings in place) under the cabin sole where they act as ballast. A wooden splash-proof lid should be placed over their box. The placing of the electric lights is discussed in the accommodation chapter. For wiring, I use ordinary good 'cab tyre' rubber-covered flex.

In specifying the wiring arrangements I divide the port and starboard lights up so that the blowing of one fuse does not plunge a compartment into complete darkness. I think it important for the bow (red and green) lights to have their own private use as they are so often in trouble due to water.

Then there should be a separate fuse for the mast lights and another for the compass and stern light. For deck lighting I use Avica flood lights; one mounted on the fore side of each mast does not dazzle the helmsman and I think a neater arrangement than having spreader lights. Under the lower forestay it is clear of lifts and halyards. Opinions vary, but I like to floodlight the deck for sail changes; and for setting or handing a spinnaker at night.

It is in any case well worth while to have isolating switches to each battery. With diesel engines, which as a rule cannot be hand started, I always have two separate batteries and disconnect one when I stop the engine (after charging both batteries). Or in larger yachts keep a separate engine starting battery as well. The R.O.R.C. require a shaft brake to be fitted if charging is to be indulged in during a race. This is cheaply done by having two base hinged pieces of hard wood which can be screwed towards one another by a big fly nut and are held apart between whiles by a coil spring.

Engine Weights. The rating rules make a rating allowance for your bare engine weight. Engine makers tell fibs sometimes about their weights; like the ladies they like to think they weigh very little. So before putting the engine aboard get it weighed and get a certificate from the weighing authority as to its net dry weight.

Reduction gear and starter and dynamo or alternator can be included; but not the shafting. In designing many fail to make insufficient allowance for the extra weights; engine bearers, piping and valves, filters, tanks and fuel, water in circulation, exhaust and silencer, as well as shafting, stern tube and propeller, which can easily more than double the normal engine weight, which is one of the reasons why so many yachts are by the stern. I always try and fit welded aluminium tanks, to reduce weight.

Clearly one must be specially careful about the real total engine weight in light displacement yachts and realise, for a given waterline, effectively what one is sacrificing in ballast weight. On the other hand provided one designs a yacht from the start with a certain engine in view one can have plenty of power without affecting the sailing performance too much and without sacrifice of offshore racing potential.

In very many Class I and II yachts which we have designed we have fitted diesel engines; Perkins 4/107, 38 h.p., or a similar Indenor-Peugeot for instance, under the sole. Either under the saloon, or under the galley/chart room. Thus located they are more accessible and less dripped

A good shot of the foredeck activity aboard *Maryca* during her One Ton Cup race in Denmark.

Maryca under spinnaker taking part in the One Ton Cup in Danish Waters. She was subsequently campaigned with success in several offshore races by the Lecouteur family.

Series production of offshore racers to Illingworth and Primrose designs by Constructions Mecaniques de Normandie at Cherbourg

Belmore. Owned by R. Steele and built by Aero Marine, Emsworth, to the author's designs. *Loa:* 36 ft. 4 in.; *lwl:* 26 ft. 6 in.; *beam:* 9 ft. 6 in.; *draft:* 5 ft. $11\frac{1}{2}$ in. Third overall in Bermuda Race 1958; second overall 1960. A yacht that is still winning first-class races.

on than under the cockpit or the companionway steps. The weight is much lower, helping stability, and apart from that more in the centre of the yacht, which is advantageous for reasons explained in another chapter. At the time of writing I am finishing the building of a 32-ft. waterline sailing yacht with a 60-h.p. diesel which goes neatly under the sole and which should give her over 8 knots under power. A direct drive Perkins or Peugeot run at 65 per cent power gives around $6\frac{1}{4}$ knots; with a reduction gear and run at 80 per cent power about a knot more.

People seem scared about the smell of a diesel engine. I am sure that this is a misconception; that in practice it is far less objectionable than a petrol engine, the smell of which often makes one feel queasy. Petrol engine protagonists assure me that I am prejudiced and that it is only because ten years in submarines have inoculated me to diesel smells. But in most of our yachts, where the installation has been well done, I defy anyone to detect the faintest trace of diesel odour.

In smaller Class III yachts the problem of fitting a diesel is less easy. Good small diesels which we have used are made by Arona and Technimotori in Italy, and Volvo in Sweden. The Technimotori is the neatest and smallest. But all make a lot of noise. We have successfully used in several yachts the small English Listers; very reliable but rather a noisy and heavy piece of ironmongery. All yachtsmen await a three or four cylinder small diesel which need not be thermally efficient but which is more liveable-with, noise and vibration-wise.

Exhaust Pipe Precautions. Having placed the engine low it becomes specially important to keep the exhaust pipe dry, and I, personally, am not content in a serious offshore boat with anything less than a stop-cock in the exhaust pipe. Or, alternatively, a screw cap, or even a good old-fashioned bung, in the ship's side exhaust orifices. In each case a drain cock should be fitted to the lowest point and opened as soon as the engine stops when the fuel tap is shut off, in the case of petrol engines.

Folding Propellers. The folding propeller, in which the blades fall back and lie together, must not be confused with the feathering propeller. The latter is so much less efficient from a sailing point of view that it earns a higher allowance under the R.O.R.C. rule. In America the folding propeller, sometimes called, aptly, a clam-shell propeller, was, I believe, like so many other good things in sailing, introduced by Nat Herreshoff. In England, Stuart Turner and the Bergius Companies, among others, make good folding propellers. The Bergius one can be 'locked open' by an internal rod up the shaft-centre.

In *Maica* we used to dive down and put thick rubber bands round the propeller to make sure they remained closed when sailing—on a 40° angle of heel, it is not at all certain they would do so otherwise. In *Rani*, I drilled a wee hole in each blade and wired them together with fine copper wire. This could be broken out only by giving the engine a good rev. up.

Reducing Engine Drag. A good deal can be done in many cases to improve existing installations. A more suitable propeller is the first line of attack. If the engine hardly develops the revolutions promised by its makers, a smaller or altered wheel should be adopted. It is perfectly feasible to cut something off the tips of the blades and still have good propulsion. Often this also enables one to reduce the size of the aperture or—very beneficially—to bring a propeller fitted through the quarter closer in to the ship's side by shortening the shaft.

The streamlining of the existing aperture is often not only possible but fairly easy. In the case of projecting stern tubes these can perhaps be fitted with fairing pieces.

On the other hand if the engine is really oversize for the boat no allowance will compensate for the damage it does to your sailing performance. There is only one thing to do—bite on the bullet, and chuck it out. Then either do without, or get a boy's-size one for a boy's job—and you will be charmed by the amount of extra space you have. Make sure you get a complete new set of boy's-size stern gear to match the new engine.

24

WIND AND WEATHER

Before the season, if it be your first visit in that part of the world, it is well worth studying the sections dealing with weather, which you will find in the British Admiralty Sailing Directions or Pilots. There are only a few such pages to each Pilot, and they give you a measured and dispassionate account of the average course of the weather in that part of the world. The average wind direction and strength for each month of the year, with the proportion of the time for which the winds blow from each direction, are shown on British and American Special Wind Charts with multiple wind roses, and are well worth having in the case of races or passages which are going to take you well off shore. The broadcast forecasts condensed into five minutes or less of report, and covering a wide area can never hope to tell you the whole story. Moreover you probably only get them twice a day and they are made up some little while before they go on the air, so that it is small wonder that they are not always accurate for your particular case.

However I always get all the broadcast weather reports I can and if possible the *current* weather map. Most of those published in the daily morning papers are compiled early in the evening before and are therefore rather *vieux jeux* by the time they reach the yacht, if the start is late in the day. Do not necessarily treat the weather reports as gospel, but taking them into consideration in conjunction with the barometer readings which you have been taking and logging hourly, and in conjunction with the look of the weather on the spot, make your own personal over-all forecast.

Try and get an idea of the degree of accuracy of the reports and over the area in question. For instance the weather in the Gulf Stream area of the Bermuda Race is partly unpredictable and in general the weather between the Gulf Stream and Bermuda in light or moderate conditions cannot be very accurately reported because of local variations which are clearly outside the scope of such reports. But they give you a sort of general picture of the fresher winds which are likely.

British Weather Reports. In British waters, the reports concerning marked depressions coming up from the south-west are normally very accurate because these follow a fairly regular pattern, and no large land areas are likely to intervene and upset the forecasters' calculations.

On the other hand light easterly weather will result in many less complete forecasts as far as wind is concerned, even though the general type of weather, which is of course the thing which interests most people ashore, is foretold with sufficient accuracy.

The British weather reports go out at differing times on Sundays; and the times vary from year to year so take a good look at your current *Reed's Almanac*. It is useful to know exactly which areas the reports are talking about and these are shown in Diagrams 81 and 82. Where three areas meet at a point where one might be during a Fastnet race this map is worth having, because one will be making a note of the weather in the three areas concerned and realising that any of the three, should they differ, may be applicable. An alarm clock is a useful reminder to switch on.

Tinting as a Weather Indicator. Before we get down to the more detailed consideration of weather there are one or two minor generalisations which are of interest. One of the first things is to disabuse our minds of the idea that a colour in the sky in itself indicates the weather to be expected. For instance that green tints mean storms, or that red in the morning is the sailor's warning. It can be shown that the optical processes involved have no direct relevance to good or bad weather. What we can say instead is that colour *combined* with the general configuration of the sky is of value. It is not easy to describe just what one means, but one can get near it by saying that tints which merge softly into one another—they may be vivid in themselves—hold no menace. Conversely, hard outlines, ragged, gaudy, or as it is called 'angry' sky tints hold promise of bad or at least changeable weather.

Some account must be taken of local conditions according to the part of the world in question, but this as a generalisation is a fairly universal one.

High, dark red cloud at dawn is a bad weather sign, but possibly only means rain rather than wind. Low, soft red clouds in the morning are not ominous.

It is often said that a low sunset with the sun going down on the horizon with a bank of cloud over it, is a good sign, that conversely a high sunset with sun setting into a bank of cloud instead of the horizon is a bad portent. Personally I don't reckon much of this rule, nor of similar things about high and low dawns, which are often due to temporary night clouds, with no great significance.

But there are some skies which warn one definitely. On the La Rochelle Race of 1947 I was lying in my quarter berth after a short caulk. We were sailing quietly along on a reach. As I awoke, a lifted corner of the canvas bunk-curtain disclosed through one of the companionways a gaudy green jagged little corner of sky the sight of which jacked me out of my berth in a brace of shakes. We called all hands and we got the yankee off her and were hanking on a small jib when the wind hit us. A moment later we handed the mainsail, and left her tearing along at over 8 knots under big staysail only. The wind backed through 180° in a few minutes, and back again; shortly afterwards it eased to Force 6 and down came the rain and the thunder. The mainsail and a small spinnaker were set in turn.

General Outlines of Clouds. The things which one naturally needs to distinguish between are heavy black clouds which at a casual glance look threatening, and really hard wicked skies which indicate approach of bad weather. It can of course blow very hard out of a clear blue sky; but that is beside my present point which is simply that heavy black clouds don't necessarily indicate strong winds. You may say that this is obvious, but I have so often come across people at sea who made wrong estimates on this account that I make no apology for emphasising this thing.

One must not for instance be scared by large quantities of heavy night cloud at dawn, which often disappear as the sun gets up.

Barometers. Many barometers in yachts are insufficiently sensitive. They should if possible be so sensitive that you can see the needle moving as the boat swings in a seaway; owing to the pressure differences created inside the ship as a result of her motion; the companionway's angle and position relative to the wind is constantly altering, causing some 'pumping'. The barometer should also be fitted to correct itself for temperature. It is desirable

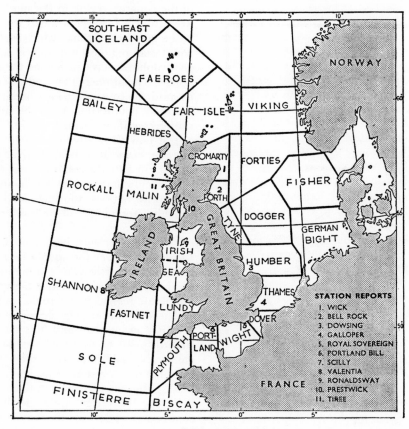

Diagram 81.
Areas specified in British weather reports.

to avoid big index errors; comparison with a known accurate barometer in the same port being the easiest check, of course. The average English barometer reading is about 1,015 millibars; a little lower in Scotland.

The barometer should be read and logged hourly; and more frequently, say every half-hour, when the approach of bad weather is expected, these extra notations being made in the remarks column of the deck log.

BASIC WINDS

To get down to more detailed study of our subject, the 'Met.' men will tell you that there are three sorts of wind—gradient wind, which is the result of differences in barometric pressure, the wind tending simply to flow from areas of high to areas of low pressure—geostrophic wind, due to the rotation of the earth, the earth tending to spin round under the air layer; since you and your boat are on the earth, or rather the sea, this tendency is noticeable to you —and the cyclostrophic force wind or the result of the centrifugal force which works on your air because of its motion in a circular path.

The geostrophic and cyclostrophic effects operate

Diagram 82.

Gale Warning Points Stations in the British Isles. These points are used by the B.B.C. weather forecasts to describe gale areas.

horizontally, but since there may be temperature differences between the surface air and the upper air resulting in pressure differences—the higher the temperature the higher the pressure, other things being the same—there may well be movement of air in a vertical direction as well.

In addition to these primary effects, the surface of the sea has a frictional or retarding effect on the wind. If there is any land in the neighbourhood this effect will be accentuated.

Resultant Wind. So the wind we feel on board will be a resultant of all these things, to which must be added the natural turbulence of flowing air, which gives rise to the local and momentary variations which we know so well.

For our purposes we can generally neglect the cyclostrophic effect. The geostrophic wind is, however, important and results in the air of our wind following a curved path, instead of flowing directly into an area of low pressure.

Planetary Wind System. The important factor controlling air flow is temperature which in turn controls pressure, and produces gradient wind. The average temperature, speaking in a very general way of the oceans, is clearly highest in the region of the equator, owing to the sun being more overhead, and it is lower towards the poles. Thus the basic gradient surface wind *might* be from the equatorial regions. But this is acted on by the geostrophic effects which bend the direction. In the northern hemisphere the wind is bent to the right of its gradient (pressure wind) path. Moreover some eventual equilibrium must be achieved, so this simple condition does not obtain.

Just how these effects work out is complex and includes reversal of wind flow at certain heights. But at any rate the result is that belts of high pressure accumulate to the north and south of the equatorial regions, the belts having their centres roughly around 35° of latitude, north, and 35°, south.

Wide low-pressure belts tend to form between these, that is over the equatorial regions, and also north of the northern belt of high and south of the southern belt of high, that is to say centring in the temperate regions in 55° to 60° of latitude.

The weak pressure grades which obtain roughly but not exactly around the equator—they are slightly more to the north—cause windless areas called the doldrums. Into these the winds blow from the high pressure belts, being deflected in the process by the earth's rotational movement, to form the north-east trades in the northern and south-east trades in the southern hemisphere. These effects operate regularly in the Atlantic and Pacific Oceans.

In the northern hemisphere there are fairly well defined belts of light variable winds running around the high pressure area centring in about 32° of latitude. These are known as the 'horse latitudes'. A similar effect is present in the southern latitudes but over somewhat wider areas.

North of the horse latitudes we come to the areas of westerlies, which blow most of the year round, but not as steadily as the trade winds because they are subject to a succession of depressions—moderate ones in summer and deeper ones in the winter—

which move in irregular series, also to the westward.

In the southern latitudes there are similar westerlies but stronger because there is less land interference. They are known as the Roaring Forties and function in rather higher latitudes.

The Monsoons. These are the general oceanic winds, but the land masses have pronounced effects. Over Asia in summer a very large low pressure system reigns, while in winter a pronounced high or anticyclonic region develops. These effects overcome the general world winds and instead of the

WORLD WINDS IN NORTHERN HEMISPHERE—WINTER

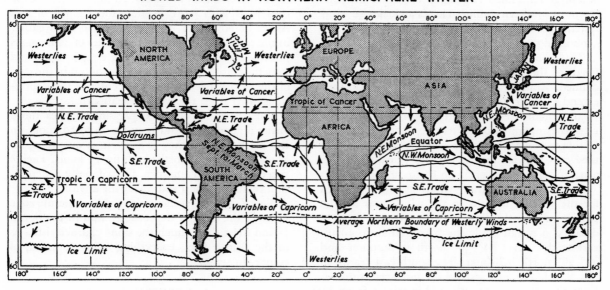

WORLD WINDS IN NORTHERN HEMISPHERE—SUMMER

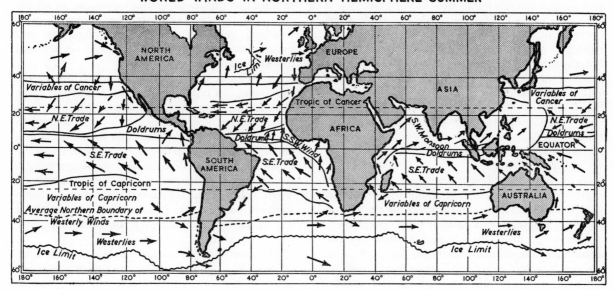

Diagrams 83 and 84.

trades one has in the Indian Ocean and the China Seas a north-east monsoon in winter, and a south-west monsoon most of the summer, in sympathy with the high anticyclonic clockwise, and the low cyclonic or anticlockwise systems.

In addition to these winds, a north-west prevailing wind sometimes known as a north-west monsoon blows in the southern hemisphere in summer, south of the equator in the Indian Ocean, and over much of the Dutch East Indies, down to the north coast of Australia and over 'the Islands' to the north-east.

Australia furnishes another example of the effect of a large land mass. A general 'low' over the continent in southern summer causes a clockwise wind system, speaking generally, round the coasts. A general high causes the reverse in winter.

The Doldrums. The official Doldrums are all to the north of the equator. Their area is not very well defined. Roughly in summer in the Atlantic they extend $5°$ to $10°$ and in winter from $0°$ to $2\frac{1}{2}°$ north. In the Pacific in winter, off the central American coast they operate from $4°$ to $9°$, reducing to $3°$ to $7°$ farther west. In the summer west of Central America they cover a wide area north of $6°$; farther west in a narrower area tapering to $8°$ to $12°$ and less.

Trade Winds. The trade winds should be studied for the various months in the wind roses for the particular month; they vary in strength a good deal. As a rough guide the North Atlantic north-east trades cover $11°$–$30°$ north in summer and $2\frac{1}{2}°$–$26°$ north in winter. The south-east trades in the South Atlantic extend in northern summer from $5°$ north to $25°$ south, and in winter from the equator to $25°$; or $30°$ towards the African shores, and though not extending close to the land.

In the North Pacific the north-east trade wind operates in summer from $12°$–$29°$ north, and in winter $8°$–$25°$, or $28°$ north as the American coast is approached. The South Pacific south-east trades limits in summer are $8°$ north—$20°$ or $25°$ south. In winter they are from $4°$ north to $35°$ south, off South America, but not so far south elsewhere.

The Indian Ocean south-east trade wind functions in northern summer over $5°$–$25°$ south. Occasionally it blows farther north than this. In winter $10°$ south to $29°$ south.

Trade Wind Strength. The average strength of the north-east Atlantic trades is about 10 knots from January to June and about 7 knots for the rest of the year. The south-east Atlantic trades are fresher; averaging 12 knots to July and 14 knots in the autumn. As these are averages over the whole belt, on many whole days, or weeks, they will be stronger, and generally stronger in the middle rather than the edge of the belts.

Westerlies. In northern summer the westerly wind belts are $35°$ to about $65°$ north and in the south $36°$–$65°$ south. In northern winter still $36°$–$65°$ north and about $40°$–$65°$ south. They are stronger in their respective winters, and, as already mentioned, stronger still in the southern band. Their actual direction is variable from north-west to south-west. Next to these belts nearer the equator, that is to say between them and the trade wind areas, are the variables of Cancer and Capricorn, in the northern and southern hemispheres. Here one gets light winds, generally high pressures and not much rain. The westerlies dip down as far as the Mediterranean in winter. In the North Atlantic they blow with more average force north of $45°$. As we noted earlier, the variations in the weather in the westerlies belt is due to a series of depressions passing through the areas from west to east, and sometimes from south-west to north-east in the case of the British Isles, where the centre of the depressions often skirts the western seaboards.

The speed at which depression centres move varies a good deal, and may be up to 50 knots. In the North Pacific they are given as averaging 20 knots and in the North Atlantic 15 knots. Pacific speeds are less in summer. Occasionally a depression remains almost stationary for a while.

New Zealand is sufficiently in the temperate zone to be in the path of depressions, and in the South Island these show much the same characteristics as in the British Isles, everything being reversed, of course, in sense.

DEPRESSIONS

Barometric Indication of Wind to Come. There are very small daily variations in the barometer in all except the coldest climates, unconnected with weather; generally a rise in the forenoon and middle watches and falls in the dogs or first and morning watches.

In Atlantic and English Channel waters the barometer is a reliable indication of increase to be expected in wind from the south, south-east, or west. The barometer does not seem so helpful in foretelling rising winds from other directions, and is particularly unhelpful on occasions when northerly winds are in store. What is probably happening is that there are changes of pressure occurring on either side of you which are sufficient to cause strong winds but they by chance have not caused any variation in pressure at the particular point where you are.

The amount of warning one gets is very variable. A long slow fall indicates generally deteriorating weather. But for many of the summer gales in European and Atlantic waters the fall only shortly precedes the short-lived gale. The normal course of a gale which is caused by depressions moving across the Atlantic from the westward is for the wind to back, that is to say change in direction anticlockwise as the barometer falls. If the gale is to be violent and the storm centre is to pass north of you, the extent of the backing will be greater and may go temporarily round to the east of south. The wind will then veer back to south-west and eventually to north of west, probably on a rising barometer. If the rise is sudden, the strongest puffs of the gale are likely to follow immediately after.

Changes of Wind Felt in a Depression. If the centre of the depression is to pass to the south of you, the wind will back from perhaps south through east and north and steady at north-west or west.

If the centre of the depression passes near one's boat the wind falls light and varies, then comes strong out of the north-west instead of backing right round steadily.

The size of depressions vary very much—they may be anything from 100 to 2,000 miles in diameter. The normal life of a depression in its course is four to five days; but occasionally it may be much longer.

Other things being the same, the nearer the centre of the depression is passing, the quicker will be the barometric rise and fall, and the sharper will be the changes in wind force and direction. But other things may affect the problem. For instance the difference between travelling 8 knots towards or away from a depression centre is 16 knots and will have a marked effect. I mention 8 knots as this will be quite usual speed for moderate-sized yachts racing in fresh winds. If you are going towards an advancing depression the glass will fall more rapidly.

Gales in summer months, which are the months with which we are most concerned, on an average blow rather more than one day per month, in waters round the British Isles. So one should get in the habit of mind of thinking of a moderate gale not as something fearsome, but as part of the weather we are likely to meet.

The backing of a wind which is blowing anywhere from north to WSW is, as we have noted, generally in Atlantic and British coastal waters, a sign of a change of weather and increase of wind. It must be remembered that the backing of a wind which is coming from other directions, say from the eastwards, should not be taken as necessarily an indication of increase in wind strength.

Wind Direction Relative to Depression Centre. In the case of a depression north of the equator the surface wind direction is almost along the isobars but inclining 15–20 degrees inwards towards the centre;

isobars being the lines of equal pressure or 'contours' which one sees on the weather map. Therefore the wind is travelling anticlockwise in a spiral direction, with reducing radius. When a weather map is available one can forecast the wind strength according to the closeness of the isobars which ring a depression; the closer the isobars, the greater is the difference in barometric reading or pressure over that area and the stronger will be the wind.

Conversely, the wind direction round an area of high pressure follows generally, but less definitely round the isobars in a clockwise direction; but inclined in an outward direction from the centre. The distance apart of the isobars will always be greater and the wind strength much less. The area centre will be less well defined and travelling often more slowly than a depression; it may well be stationary. The directions are reversed in the southern hemispheres.

As we said earlier, areas of low pressure, 'depressions', are moving regularly around a great deal of the temperate parts of the earth, in general to the eastward. In the case of the Atlantic they move often in winter, and less often in summer, mostly in an ENE direction. Thus they often pass up the coasts of the British Isles, or to one side of them, more often the northward. But although this is a fairly usual course for the centre of a low to take, one can never be sure of this; their track may switch off and curl and bend all over the place at times.

Between adjacent moving lows there may be ridges, rather than circular areas, of high pressure, particularly when the depressions are near to-together; that is, when not more than 48 hrs. apart.

These spells between depressions often produce clear skies, and north-west winds of no great weight.

Cold Fronts. In mid-Atlantic dry cold air from the north may, as it comes eastward, meet moister warmer air from the south and semi-tropical waters. These two moving areas of air do not at once mix; they travel along together with an approximare dividing line between them. The speed of the advancing cold area being often greater, it traps an inclusion or wedge of warmer air of southerly origin. This patch or area travels along with the system generally, and at the line where the cold air temporarily gives way to less dense southerly air is known as a 'warm front'; at the point where the area passes over and the cold dense air resumes is the 'cold front' again.

Warm Front. This area of trapped southerly air may be 'bulgy' or of other shapes, but is mostly wedge-shaped. Then the cold front begins overtaking the warm air, and gradually rolls this area upwards, and infiltrates underneath, and meets other cold air. This front is then said to be 'occluded'. These warm fronts and conditions proceed from the west accompanied by a falling barometer and freshening but variable breeze from the south or SSW or even SW, which will probably veer as the area passes over and resumes a cold front. In summer these winds are fresh, and occasionally strong but not often of gale force.

The warm sector or wedge will perhaps be 8°–12° warmer, with dull sky and low cloud, and perhaps mist. Normally after the cold front resumes charge, the breeze will continue to veer towards north. Later, the barometer rises slowly, and clearer and less squally weather returns.

Secondary Depressions. The secondary depression is a small low on the outskirts of a main low pressure area. It will circulate (anticlockwise in the northern, clockwise in the southern hemisphere) part way round the main low, as well as advancing along with the whole system. And since it generally develops in lower latitude than the main, it follows that the secondary will travel pretty fast, and come on you quickly. Partly for this reason they appear quite intense at times, with strong winds; the sequence of their change will probably be rapid and the duration will be shorter than that of a main depression.

OTHER WINDS

Onshore and Offshore Winds. Then there is the question of onshore and offshore winds; onshore in the forenoon and perhaps early afternoon when the land is heating up, and offshore in the first watch while the land is cooling down with relatively little change in sea temperature.

The problem for the skipper in this connection will be to gauge how far offshore these breezes will blow on a particular occasion. These breezes are light in European waters, mostly around Force 1 or 2–3 at a maximum. And clearly when there are fresh or strong breezes blowing due to other causes, the effects in question will be negligible. On the other hand in a day of light airs and calms they may furnish the best breezes of the day.

Since the effects are directly dependent on the sun's action, we must expect very modified breezes when the weather is or has been overcast over the land, and hope for good shore breezes in hot clear weather. The distance they reach offshore is very variable since it may be affected by barometric changes due to other causes and for this reason can never, in European waters, be relied on absolutely. In other parts of the world, where local knowledge must be sought, they are sometimes as regular as a clock. In English waters the general distance off-

shore is up to about 10 miles, though occasionally it is greater, owing to the configuration of the coast, and naturally the breeze fails short of this on many occasions.

Off the coasts of Spain and in the Mediterranean the effects extend somewhat farther. When there are high cliffs the offshore breeze may skip (at the sea's surface) a strip near the land, and only come into effect farther offshore. A similar effect may be noticed occasionally where there are warm shallow or tideless waters near the shore, which seems to form a sort of no man's land, over which the offshore breeze travels before striking down to a height where our sails can reach. The onshore breeze during the day is in general more useful than offshore breeze at night.

Shaping of a Course in Light-weather Coastal Work. The amount of deviation from one's direct course which is to be made to suit onshore and offshore breezes will have to be gauged accordingly. The occasions on which one has a comparatively free choice are when one is turning to windward along the coast in very light weather, and then it is almost invariably better to be within 8 miles of the mean coastline, that is allowing for irregularities, rather than, shall we say, in the middle of the English Channel. But remember this applies only to light weather. For instance if you have a nice steady breeze offshore in the Bay of Biscay it would be madness to go looking for offshore and inshore breezes down the coast of France; even if you did not sail farther these breezes would be interfering with your steady breeze, rather than helping you. Moreover owing to outlying dangers, you might not be able to get conveniently into the areas.

The Beaufort Wind Scale. The wind scale which has been in general use for more than a hundred years is the Beaufort scale. This was initiated by Admiral Sir Francis Beaufort about the time of the Battle of Trafalgar. The scale has been several times revised. It includes in its criteria the effect on fishing vessels, useful when larger sailing ships went out of general use, and the effect of the breeze in raising waves.

More recently with increased use of aircraft one hears the speed of the wind quoted simply in land miles per hour. But yachtsmen generally stick to the Beaufort scale; which is perhaps right and natural since the scale was designed for sailing ships.

The scale is given in Appendix I. The height of the waves must be taken as very approximate, since this will depend on their fetch from the nearest land, and the length of time the wind has been blowing in just that direction. The equivalent land mile wind speeds have been added as well as the speed in knots or nautical miles per hour.

Wind Variation with Height. The wind speed is less at the surface of the sea than at a height. The higher one goes up to about 2,000 ft., the stronger the wind blows, and the more it is veered in the northern hemisphere compared to the surface wind. In cloudy weather the difference between surface wind speed and speed of the wind high up is considerable. It is less on clear sunny days, when the heating of the air at the surface by the sun is appreciable.

This difference in speed and direction is due partly to the friction effect of the earth's surface. The reason the heating effect reduces this difference is that it causes vertical movement and turbulence of air, and a greater admixture of the upper and lower air belts.

The difference in direction between winds at the surface and winds higher up, at about 2,000 ft., varies over the land from about 10°–40°. Much the same applies to sea areas where the wind is coming off the land. At sea the difference is less; about 5°–25°.

In fine weather, that is to say, with a steady barometer and no great pressure differences over the area to cause wind, the comparative lack of interchange of high and low air over the land at night results in a calm at night on many occasions. If a fine warm sunny day follows, as the sun comes into action and causes air movement in a vertical plane, any existing upper wind starts to drag the surface air with it and causes an appreciable breeze at the surface, which will rise through the forenoon to a maximum in the afternoon watch. These are known as diurnal winds. The effects are felt less at sea than over the land, but if your boat is in the neighbourhood of the land you may expect them. They will be additional to, or superimposed on, the onshore and offshore winds, which were referred to earlier.

Thus if you are fairly close to the land in a calm at dawn and see some clouds moving steadily across the sky at between 2,000 and 3,000 ft., you will expect that the resulting breeze when the sun comes up will be backed a little in direction from this when it first starts to get up. But this breeze will in turn be distorted by a direct inshore effect. So by taking the mean of these you can often form a fair guess at the wind direction to be expected. The handings referred to are reversed in the southern hemisphere.

Winds in Medium and Higher Atmosphere. Variations in winds in the high air, above about 10,000 ft., depend on the temperature variations, which are often present. Thus as a generalisation there will be changes of wind speed and of wind direction, with increasing altitude, in the high air. But since there is a very general temperature (and therefore pressure) gradient from the equator to the polar regions and as these effects increase with height, they in conjunction with the earth's rotation tend to cause general westerly winds at increasing heights in both hemispheres.

Easterly winds on the other hand are generally the child of factors which are stronger near the surface of the sea, and these winds in consequence get less powerful higher up. Thus with easterly winds you will often see very high clouds going the opposite way. But with surface westerlies the high clouds are normally travelling in the same direction.

From the foregoing we see that it is quite unsafe to deduce anything concerning the surface winds to come—which are things which interest us as yachtsmen—from the movement of very high cloud. However, the movement of clouds around 3,000 ft. indicates an air movement which may well translate itself, as we have previously seen, into surface wind of nearly the same direction.

CLOUDS

Clouds are made of tiny particles of water, snow, or ice in suspension. The cloud takes shape when water vapour is cooled below the air's dew point. If the process takes place near the sea, the cloud is called fog. A cubic yard of cloud may carry up to 4 grams of water. Its power to support water varies a lot according to conditions; when it becomes overloaded, rain, sleet, hail, or snow falls.

We can divide the clouds roughly into three types: High Cloud—20,000 ft. and above—cirrus or with a name prefixed by 'cirro'; Medium Cloud—20,000—7,000 ft.—with names prefixed by 'alto'; Low Cloud—below 7,000 ft.

Clouds are classified by appearance. Some clouds fit exactly into a particular type, but on the other hand there are many borderline cases. Students seem always to be finding new names for special sorts of clouds partly for this reason. Moreover the height divisions are not completely accurate; for instance in very cold weather cirrus may come well down below its 20,000 ft. At any rate here are some of the principal types.

Cirrus. High delicate white clouds which cast no shadows, often fibrous and silky looking. The actual form is varied; separate fine tufts; lines of delicate cloud against a blue background sky; feather-like formations; often very wispy; in fact wispy is perhaps the best adjective. Cirrus clouds consist mostly of the ice crystals and the sun can be clearly seen through them. 'Mares' tails' are one sort of cirrus.

Fast-moving, long, wispy cirrus—wispy and long as opposed to foamy—if (and only if) followed later by a sheet or veil of high cirro-stratus transparent cloud, or sometimes alto-stratus in heavy array, is often the forerunner of a depression. Often when these depression front conditions arise there will be low clouds as well, but these will generally break up and disperse and disappear about the same time.

The next stage after the veil of cirro-stratus, with the sun showing with a halo, is perhaps a thicker veil of medium-height cloud; alto-stratus. The sun becomes dull and hardly seen; then is obscured. Then nimbo-stratus low rain clouds and wind, not necessarily very strong, arrive. The speed of change will depend on the speed of advance of the depression.

Cirro-cumulus. Another form of very high cloud. An area or patch of tiny white flaky clouds, the flakes being rounded in form. Normally arranged in close lines giving a fan-like appearance. Sometimes likened to ripples. It is a delicately figured cloud and sometimes called mackerel sky.

Cirro-stratus. A high-floating, thin, milky veil. Sun or moon has a halo when showing through. Sometimes show some structure with indistinct disarranged filaments.

Alto-cumulus. Often spectacular medium-height clouds. Globe-like, fleecy elements composing a regular pattern of lines perhaps in two directions; or waves of cloudlets shaded away. The light shading is characteristic, compared to cirro-cumulus. Clear sky generally shows through in irregular lines. Occasionally has a special turret-shaped outline to the cloud tops, which may forecast thunder to come.

Alto-stratus. A level sheet of intermediate height cloud; grey to grey-blue in colour as a rule. Similar to cirro-stratus but greyer, and lower; the sun can be seen perhaps dimly through, but does not cause halos. Sometimes of varying thickness, but often covers most of a watery-looking sky and may be associated with rain.

Strato-cumulus. Often large patches or layers of lowish cloud, soft dull and grey, or darker. Largish lumps of grey cloud, joining together. The shadows in the cloud are heavier than in alto-cumulus. The cloudlets sometimes are in waves or different bands, or in big rolls; but sometimes have no special arrangement. Typical height 2,000–4,000 ft. Night cloud, which answers to this description, is often present extensively at sunrise, and disappears with the day.

True Cumulus. Large, thick, towering clouds with a definite base at 2,000–6,000 ft. They are caused by a rising column of air in which condensation is going on. Dome-shaped top with irregular edge. White and strongly shaded, or blackish with a

silvery edge, according to how they are lighted. Edges are often hard. May cause rain showers.

Fracto-cumulus. Generally similar but more ragged and changeable in form, again with pronounced white and shade effects.

Fair Weather Cumulus. Roughly similar, but smaller, whiter, separated clouds; more stable than fracto-cumulus. Often forms over land on fine warm sunny days. Is sometimes a valuable guide to the direction of a distant island on which one may be making a landfall. These fair weather cumulus clouds are almost invariably flat and longer compared to their depth (as well as smaller) than true cumulus which is a deep cloud vertically. These clouds may disperse in the evening giving way to alto-cumulus or strato-cumulus; but this does not mean that the fine weather is breaking.

Stratus. A regular soft grey layer of low cloud, like fog but not reaching to the sea. Often hangs over adjacent hills on the shore close to the sea. Scotch mist. Typical height 500–1,500 ft.

Fracto-stratus. Drifting dark ragged masses of low cloud.

Nimbo-stratus (or Nimbus). A shapeless racing layer of dull to dark grey cloud. Typical height 1,000–2,000 ft. Often causes steady rain. Ragged low scudding clouds sometimes travel with it in windy weather.

Cumulo-nimbus. A heavy mass of cloud rising from 2,000 or 4,000 ft. to considerable heights. The tops show various shapes; towers, mountains, or spreading out with a flat top; or feathery edges, which are the frozen particles being dispersed by high-level wind currents. The base has sometimes, but not always, low ragged cloud edges with it. These nimbus clouds come with heavy showers. In its heavy grey form sometimes part of a thundery sky.

Cumulo-nimbus is also nearly always present in the rear of a depression. As the weather starts to clear, with clear bright patches and probably gusts and squalls, these clouds are seen; but mixed with true cumulus and fracto-cumulus. So the typical silhouette of the cumulo-nimbus may not be seen. But clouds in rear of a depression are often seen against a spreading deep blue sky with good visibility by day, followed perhaps by mists at night.

Lenticularis. Lozenge-shaped clouds noted at varying heights, often with warm winds. Sometimes shaded lightly, but again often pearly white. It is a form of alto-cumulus.

THUNDER, SQUALLS, AND STORMS

It is useful sometimes to be able to distinguish the type of sky which precedes thundery conditions, partly to distinguish it from the cirrus which goes before the depression. The pre-thundery sky is essentially a dense layer of cirrus with soft merging outlines, combined sometimes with a veil of cirro-stratus which may cover only a part of the sky. There may also be medium-height alto-cumulus clouds, some of these having dome-like tops. There will be light to very light wind.

The actual thunder clouds and gusts may or may not follow later; this depends on what else in the way of weather is knocking about.

In heat thunder storms there is almost always a change of wind when the actual storm hits one. There may be an additional shift of wind just before the storm gets to you; not so violent. These storms are generally found in coastal regions and soon clear.

Cold Fronts and Thunder. On the other hand thunder may come with the front of a depression, generally a cold front. The same temporary sudden change of wind and gusts or squalls arise; but this storm is simply part of the depression and endeav-our should be made to distinguish it from thundery fine weather.

Line Squalls. One particular form of the approach of a cold front is a line squall. A line or roll or wedge of low black cloud comes up steadily. The existing wind falls calm and when the cloud line reaches one, the new wind, generally coming from roughly the same direction as the cloud roll, comes in strongly. There is a quick drop in temperature and a rise in the barometer as the wind arrives. Sometimes there is thunder, and generally heavy rain or hail.

In European waters the typical sequence starts with a light southerly wind. The storm arrives from the west, west-nor'-west, or north-west; the long roll of cloud against a background of light or medium grey sky. The south wind dies away, and as the cloud reaches one it comes up strong from the nor'-nor'-west. Rain probably follows and the wind then eases a little but continues to blow from somewhere around west or nor'-west.

The 'Southerly Buster' off the New South Wales coast of Australia is a similar affair. Here the north-easter will die away to be replaced by a strong southerly, which will blow for 12 to 30 hrs. before veering and easing off.

You will hear people talking about seeing a line squall on the water. While there is no doubt one can see a genuine cold front squall, the thing to which people generally refer is just a patch of wind approaching across the sea, and to keep referring to these as line squalls is alarmism.

Clouds in Tropical Areas. The foregoing data con-cerning clouds apply primarily to temperate zones, where most of our cruising and racing will be done. The basic types of cloud are the same in tropical

places but their disposition is different, and they sometimes have different meanings. There are few if any regular depressions, with their special cloud systems. Instead, special cloud formations are associated with a particular season, or some parts of the day of a particular season, or even with particular neighbourhoods. Forecasting from the sky is therefore a different job and often specialised to the region.

Cumulus which is reckoned in temperate zones as a medium-height cloud, rises under the tropical conditions to enormous heights, with tremendous vertical cloud development.

Trade Wind Cloud. In trade wind areas strato-cumulus is normal; often with occasional pieces of real cumulus below it, which are sometimes called trade wind cumulus.

Tropical Storms. Hurricanes, cyclones, or ty-phoons, as they are variously called in their native parts, will not often come the way of the ocean racer or cruiser, because one takes care to keep out of the tropical regions during the months when they are current. Occasionally however one may come across one which has not been playing the game. And there are parts of the North Pacific and the China Seas where no month is completely clear, though from February to April they are less likely.

They are in essence similar to depressions in the temperate regions, being circular storms in which the circulation of wind is anticlockwise in the northern and clockwise in the southern hemisphere. But they cover much smaller areas and the drop in pressure across them is much 'steeper'. The winds are in consequence very much stronger.

The angle of convergence of the wind or 'in-draft' is around 130°. If one faces the wind the centre of a tropical storm of this nature will be about $10\frac{1}{2}$ points, or 120°, on one's right-hand side, in the northern, or left-hand in the southern hemisphere.

Their track almost always bends or curves con-tinuously to the right in the northern and to the left in the southern hemisphere. The speed of advance of the storm centre is generally, but by no means always, between 10 and 20 knots. The centre area of the storm where winds are light and varied, and the cloud and rain will probably lift, may be from 5 to 50 miles across. In this area the seas may be confused and occasionally dangerous. Directly away from the centre the winds are very high and squally and the shifts in direction are naturally very rapid.

A typical storm would have winds of hurricane force at 20 to 40 miles from the centre; that is to say, winds of over 65 knots; they may be anything up to twice that figure. 50 and 60 miles from the centre there would be an appreciable drop to perhaps full gale winds of 55 knots, Force 10 to 11, while at 150 miles away one might be down to merely strong breeze; Force 6 conditions of say 25 knots. Very heavy rain is usual in the storm area, which helps to keep the sea down, and the sky is densely overcast.

Tropical Storm Signs. Apart from any wireless warning, the first indication will probably be the arrival of a swell. Swell will extend hundreds of miles ahead of the storm, but since the waves take time to spread, the amount of warning varies very much according to the speed of the storm centre. The spread of waves is discussed at more length in the chapter on waves. The direction from which the swell is coming will tell you the direction in which the centre was—but at the time the wave left it. The *change* in direction may thus be interesting in indicating the side to which the depression is to pass.

But of course swell can emanate from storms other than hurricanes. The diurnal or regular daily movements of the barometer must be allowed for before deciding on the likelihood of a barometric movement portending a storm.

Its diurnal range in the tropics will be up to $2\frac{1}{2}$ millibars of movement, the highs being at 0400 and 1600 hrs. and the lows at 2400 and 0800 hrs.

Often before the barometer starts to fall, or any other sign is seen, a slight high cirrus haze is seen to cover the sky. But this alone is not a sufficient indication. It causes halos round the sun and moon and lurid tints at sundown. The wind may drop light and the air is often sultry. The cirrus cloud then changes as a rule from haze to the more characteristic strips. It is said that the point where these strips appear to converge is near the distant storm centre. The next stage is a thickening into cirro-stratus; then alto-cumulus; then banks of low black cloud come up and gather into a great mass, with the storm proper.

Meanwhile the barometer has been slowly dropping. With the arrival of the edge of the storm there is quickened and irregular falling. Should one be going to pass through the centre there will be a last quick drop; as the hangman would term it. The total drop may be 60 millibars or more.

Ship Handling in Storm Conditions. As to what action to take in the vicinity of a storm, in the northern hemisphere the quadrant of the storm circle to the right of the track looking in the direction of the storm's advance is the 'bad' quadrant which may tend to push you towards the storm centre.

The side on the left is the 'safe' quadrant.

First get on the starboard tack in the northern hemisphere (port tack in southern hemisphere) and reach along while you are reducing sail.

Using the rule previously given (*viz.* face the wind and the storm centre is $10\frac{1}{2}$ points on your right—left in southern hemisphere), you can get a rough idea of where it is at that moment. LOG THE BEARING OF THE CENTRE at frequent intervals. Taking your own speed into consideration you can with luck estimate roughly the track of the storm and whether it is going to pass one side or the other of you. If there is no change in the wind direction you are somewhere near the track of the storm.

Subject to having sea room, if you decide you are in the safe quadrant or in the track of the storm run with the wind on the starboard quarter (port quarter in southern hemisphere). If you decide you are in the bad quarter proceed close-hauled in the starboard tack as long as conditions permit, then heave-to on the starboard tack (port tack in southern hemisphere).

This action will carry you away from the storm centre and the storm track. If you don't manage to get clear it will probably be a case of getting all sail off just before the worst of it. When the centre or trough line of the storm is past, the barometer will start to rise.

25

WAVES

A study of the behaviour of waves is interesting to us for three reasons. In the first place a knowledge of the manner in which water moves in a wave helps us in considering the behaviour of a hull in a seaway. Secondly, observations of wave and swell can sometimes help us to forecast approaching changes in the weather. Finally, a knowledge of the ocean-wide habits of the wave can help us to estimate the surface drift which we have suffered, and the extent to which it has affected our dead-reckoning position.

Basic Motion of Water Particles. Neglecting for the moment surface drift—and it is negligible in semi-sheltered waters—the actual movement of water on the surface over which the waves are moving is *forward* as the wave crest passes and *backwards* as the trough comes abreast it. It is important to remember this. The amplitude or extent of this movement is about equal to the wave height. One can verify this by watching floating driftwood. There is of course a vertical component to the movement as well, the cycle being said to constitute full rotary motion for each particle, but for the moment it is the horizontal part in which we are interested. This movement, constantly to and fro, round and round, takes place below the surface as well, the extent of the motion becoming gradually less until it virtually disappears at a depth which calculation, verified by experiment, shows to be about half a wave length. As well as this regular movement there is a surface boil caused by wind friction or drag, and when one comes to consider the extent to which the surface water is agitated it is possible to visualise why in a seaway a deep-draft vessel works better to windward, since for every foot one goes down, movement of the water becomes less. The desirability of getting one's rudder and fin into relatively undisturbed water is rather similar to the requirements of a propeller, which works best in like conditions. This partly explains why the bigger boats show to so much greater advantage over the small ones in the open sea, than in sheltered water, a thing about which, on the average, there can be doubt. So much so that the R.O.R.C. rule when applied to inshore racing has to use a different time scale in which the allowances are smaller.

The Value of Draft. Apart from the effectiveness of the fin in a general sense, there are two other considerations. The first is the obvious one, of surface drift which is less as one goes deeper. The second one is the question of the effect of lateral displacement, due to the 'to and fro' motion of the seas on the hull and in turn on the sails. It is pretty clear that to have the boat moved bodily towards and away from the wind at each sea is likely to have an adverse effect on the performance of the sails. The deeper we can go with our fin the more we can check this tendency. The fact that the depth to which the movement takes place is a function of the length of the wave explains, if you think about it and watch the sea at work, why certain wave lengths are much wetter for the boat to work in than others.

If you think back through the small boats you know, you will, I fancy, find that those which have struck you by their ability to get windward, in a seaway, are generally pretty deep-footed.

One can't have it all ways, and this deeper draft steadying one's mean course is going to result in more relative motion between the wave tops and your topsides, and will make the boat a shade wetter. You can't make an omelette without breaking eggs, and you can't get to windward in a seaway in a hurry and keep dry.

Wave Speed. However to get back to our waves. By the speed of a wave, we mean the rate at which the crest travels along, which of course must not be confused with motion of a particle of water which we have just been talking about; the speed of a wave in knots is approximately equal to the square root of the distance in feet between wave crests, plus 35 per cent. The length and speed of the waves in deep water depends on three factors: the strength of the wind, the length of time it has been blowing and the size of the area or sea over which these conditions obtain—the longer the distance the faster the waves. If the wind blows for some time in open water the wave speed gets to be the same as that of the wind. Though this appears strange, after a prolonged steady blow, the wave speed will in the end appreciably exceed the speed of the wind then ruling. I have on several occasions seen these conditions in the Indian Ocean during the monsoon season.

These 'fast waves' even in much less than monsoon conditions have one important effect on the wind, which is of interest to us in our sail boat. Research shows that they result in the surface wind speed being the same as the wind speed higher up. Thus after a wind, which is constant in speed at masthead height, has been blowing for some time the mean speed of the wind, as felt by the sails, will gradually increase. The knowledge that this is happening may be of assistance in gauging the sequence of a storm, or in making sail changes.

Planing. Turning to the question of downwind sailing, these wave speeds explain why it is difficult to get a yacht to plane in open water. Planing as the yachtsman understands it, is getting one's boat to go appreciably faster than its theoretical maximum speed, down wind. This theoretical maximum is said to be $1\cdot4 \sqrt{L}$ where L is the effective sailing length, including useful overhang. Beyond this speed, further increases are difficult because the bow wave and stern wave, which one raises, form a trough in which the boat runs. It is convenient to divide the ways of planing into three, though a combination of two must often be in operation. Firstly there is the possibility of the boat 'climbing up and over' her own bow wave. This is confined to light-displacement types, with suitable bow forms; most classes of small open racing boat will do this to some extent. The increase in speed is moderate. Then we have stage two, when the boat gets properly 'on the step' very like a planing power-boat. The moment this happens there is an increase of anything from 50–200 per cent in speed due to the rise out of the water reducing wetted surface and particularly the wave-making; the track or wake flattens. This phenomenon is confined to dinghy types which appear to plane off their counter. It is seen to the best advantage in classes with unrestricted sail area such as the Australian 12-, 16-, and 18-ft. classes; or less frequently in the international 14-footers and the like. The third way is what I call wave riding; and it is this which is most likely to interest us offshore. Our shape and displacement will normally prevent us from planing, as the dinghy knows it, and owing to our relatively small sail area, compared with our displacement, our wave riding is likely to be confined to stronger winds.

For good planing conditions the wind speed requires to be, I suppose, about three times the wave speed, the object being to remain on the front of the top of a wave crest, which is manifestly impossible when one's propulsive wind power is only

about keeping up with one's wave, conditions which obtain in a long blow. So one's best chances of planing are at the start of a blow, or in waters, such as the Irish Sea, where the area is sufficiently confined to prevent very long seas.

Of course only racers of light and moderate displacement will plane—*Tre Sang* and *Mouse of Malham* plane quite often—*Myth of Malham*, being of greater displacement for her length, occasionally and for short spells.

As we observed previously that the amplitude of the movement of a particle of surface water is dependent on the height of the wave; and it follows that the surface speed of water is proportional to the height and inversely proportional to the time of passage between crests. And as we have already noted that the speed of a crest is proportional to the square root of the length of a wave, the time must vary in the same way.

Wave Riding. Wave-ride-planing is possible, chiefly, through being able to exploit the forward movement of surface water on wave crests. If the boat is shallow-bodied and can lie pretty well on the surface she can remain for a few moments poised in the forward running crest.

The surface water speed is greatest, we can now see, when waves are high and short and as these short waves will be moving slower themselves, it is easier to remain on them. So these are the best conditions, subject to the consideration that a wave must be big enough to carry the boat. A dinghy will plane on quite a small crest, but *Tre Sang*'s $2\frac{3}{4}$ tons requires a bigger body of moving water, while to get *Myth* to plane one needs the conditions just right: the waves to be just big enough; if they get a shade bigger and longer one can't keep up with them.

I am bound to admit that when, racing offshore in *Mouse*, the wind got up just that extra bit to enable one to wave-ride regularly, the thrill of the extra 3 or 4 knots, which the others did not have, was worth a lot.

Supposing one managed to find a sea with 80-ft. waves 7 ft. high, the wave speed would be just 12 knots and the forward surface water speed at the crests $3\frac{1}{2}$ knots. So that if one's displacement yacht was doing $8\frac{3}{4}$ knots in her own right, the sea might well lift her along the extra bit to get her up to 12 knots for a while. One must remember that some of her is deeper and dragging. The increase may not sound spectacular on paper, but it feels quite jolly and appreciable in practice and is probably about as much as one is likely to get on a displacement boat, unless she is exceptionally light and shallow. Taking an extremely optimistic case of an odd high wave, for its length, let us say we have 100-ft.

length and a height of 11 ft. This gives you a surface speed of 4·7 knots and a wave and planing speed of 13·6 knots. Quite different considerations, of course, come into it with dinghies once they 'get on the step'. They generally get the best speed with wind on the quarter, that is to say under conditions when they don't leave the wind behind—and lose driving power too seriously on beginning to plane. They are probably functioning in more moderate breezes than we are considering offshore.

Ask yourself what is the ratio between length and height before a wave gets so high that it starts to break. I may mention that one nearly always underestimates the *length* of a sea.

Anyway skilled observers tell me that the figure is 9:1; when a wave increases in height more than one-ninth of its length, it topples over, so that roughly this is its maximum height. A sea of 150 ft. length could in open water be raised from a flat calm in about 3 hrs. by a 45-m.p.h. breeze. This illustrates the point that these planing conditions will only last for a little while. Though the rate of increase of wave length is found to be more gradual as times goes on, very soon the waves will lengthen beyond our 'planing band' of say, 80–100 ft.

So by today's standards this type of down-wind sailing is of limited value to the offshore racer, and one generally still concentrates on windward performance. But as we get to learn more about light displacement boats, designing them with a view to incorporating their natural life and fire with a reasonable modicum of comfort, watertightness, and sea-worthiness—as we progress it may well be that big wave riding will become a regular part of the racing offshore.

Swell as a Forecaster. We will pass to a brief consideration of the information which can be obtained from swell when we are at sea.

We may define swell as wave motion resulting from distant winds, as opposed to the more usual seaway, which results more or less from present winds.

The waves produced by wind, in general, get higher and longer with (1) the increase of the distance over which the wind is blowing; (2) the length of time the wind has been blowing; (3) the wind strength. And it has already been seen that the speed of the individual wave crests increases as the square root of the wave length.

But where the storm is violent and/or its speed of advance is limited, as in the case of tropical storms, and occasionally summer storms in more temperate areas, then advance warning is often given by the arrival of a swell.

The arrival of a swell advancing into comparative calm water is normally quick—as most of us have noticed at sea. One minute it is calm; a

minute or two later there is a long regular swell. It has been suggested that the rate at which a swell penetrates a calm area is half the wave speed; but I cannot vouch for this. The suddenness of its arrival is not in fact any indication of the nature of the disturbance which has caused the swell. Moreover since the length of the swell is a function of the three factors (1), (2), and (3) operating in the storm or disturbance area, it is not possible as a rule to accurately deduce the wind speed. However this may be known approximately from radio weather reports, or perhaps guessed from knowledge of the storms typical to the area and time of year.

It is, however, important that while a swell wave sent out from a storm area into areas of comparative calm retains a roughly constant speed of advance and length, its height decreases as it gets farther away from the edge of the storm or disturbance area. Conversely this means that if a long, low swell of regular length builds up in height fairly quickly, the edge of the storm is approaching you fairly quickly. That is to say the rate of build-up of height is a guide to the rate of approach of the disturbance. As a further check, as the storm area approaches the crests of the swell waves get shorter in lateral length. Should there be little or no build-up in height it may be that the storm is going to pass you by. In this case the direction from which the swell is coming will alter slowly, veering if the centre is passing to the north of you, and backing if to the south.

Tropical Storms. In the case of a tropical storm of limited area which is travelling directly towards one, if, in the northern hemisphere, one faces the direction of the swell, arriving over comparative calm areas, then the storm centre is a little to the right of where you are facing. As the storm approaches closely the swell direction will back slightly. In the southern hemisphere for 'right' read left for 'back' read veer. As soon as one is within the area of a severe circular storm, the sea will, of course, be confused.

Supposing you are in the area but off track of the centre. In the northern hemisphere the highest seas and strongest winds will be encountered when, as you face the line of approach of the centre, it passes you on your starboard side. Should it pass on your port side as you face it, then the wind strength (and sea height) will be less. In other words the worst of a moving tropical storm is, in the northern hemisphere, on its right hand of the path of the centre, the left hand in the southern hemisphere. This is largely of academic interest because one can't often choose one's side, but there is some more about ship handling in tropical storms in the wind and weather chapter.

As we noted earlier the height and length of waves require time and sea space to build up. So if a storm area travels across land to a comparatively calm sea area, at first there will be no waves and no swell will be sent out. Thus little or no warning swell can be expected ahead from a tropical storm coming off the land, or when it has only a small sea space to cover after leaving the land and before reaching you.

A moving storm covering a bigger area will take longer to build up the sea. A circular moving storm of full gale force with a 20-mile radius might build up its full sea in 5 hrs. One with a 200-mile radius might take 24 hrs.; but the seas will be bigger.

But it must be said again that the speed of advance of storm centres and 'fronts' varies and that it is sometimes the case that, even with tropical storms, the storm front travels as fast as the swell it is sending out, so that no great reliance can be placed on getting 'swell warning'.

26

THE BERMUDA AND RIO RACES

Elsewhere we have discussed the implications of the two principal forms of international measurement, and this discussion should first be studied and digested before proceeding to detailed consideration of the conditions and requirements of the Bermuda Race. The C.C.A. rule is given in full in Appendix XII.

We will endeavour to take questions in the order in which they will require to be settled; choice of the yacht to be entered; preparations at home; shipment and custom formalities; final preparations and finally race tactics and navigation.

The Bermuda Race is nowadays run biennially, over a course of 635 miles from Brenton Reef, off Newport, Rhode Island, to the island of Bermuda. The race is sponsored by the Cruising Club of America. The C.C.A. has no club house, and the secretary's address is therefore not permanent, but the club secretary can always be reached care of the New York Yacht Club in 37 West 44th Street. The race generally takes place between June 13 and June 28, with entries closing one month earlier.

Yachts Eligible. Of recent years entry has been by invitation, but any reputable large enough European yacht is likely, on application, to receive an invitation. Regarding the choice of a yacht, this will to the individual naturally be limited; just the same the possibility of exchanging use of yachts with another owner for the season can be borne in mind, and when the purchase of a yacht is in prospect for use at home, it may be as well to bear the requirements of the Bermuda Race in mind. To be eligible in 1968 yachts had to comply as follows:

(a) Ballast ratio may not exceed 48 per cent, except in the case of metal boats where it may not exceed 50 per cent.

(b) A plus correction for light displacement may not exceed 12 per cent of 'L'.

(c) L.O.A. may not exceed 73 ft.

(d) (1) 'L' shall not be less than 27·5 ft.
    (2) The rating, calculated exclusive of any 'S' correction, shall not be less than 24·5 ft.
    (3) Average freeboard to top of covering board at ends of L.W.L. shall be at least 2·5 ft.

(e) Combined overhangs may not exceed 35 per cent of L.O.A.

(f) The cockpit shall have a volume, measured to the lowest point in the coaming over which water can escape, not exceeding 6 per cent of 'L' × measured beam × freeboard aft— all from your measurement certificate.

Length overall is laid down as being 'from the aftermost part of the counter or traffrail to the intersection of the forward side of the stem, and the top of the covering board, or the extension of either, or both, if necessary'.

Ballast is computed as being the sum of the fixed ballast (inside and out) plus the weight of any movable gear stored below the line of the cabin floor, other than a normal quantity of consumable stores. Thus anchor cable stored under the floor would be so counted.

The ballast ratio limit now 48 per cent was originally imposed with a view to excluding the yacht of purely racing type. However there is a fairly heavy penalty, included in the C.C.A. rating rule, on ballast ratio, and there is therefore no great incentive to use an unduly high ratio. No doubt with this in mind, the committee made some exceptions regarding the strict enforcement of the former 46 per cent top limit; when for instance the ballast ratio of the yacht with the displacement measured in cruising trim comes to about 46 per cent.

The Trophies. The Bermuda Trophy, today the most coveted yachting trophy in the world, is awarded to the yacht making the best corrected time regardless of class. Owing to the large entry— and to the high quality of a portion of the entry, the chances of an individual entry succeeding in bringing home the premier honour at the first attempt is small and it will be as well to take account of the other trophies and in the first instance set one's hat on one of these.

The race is divided into six or more classes, according to rating, the top part of the fleet forming class A. A normal fast-type cutter or yawl of medium size generally rates 3 or 4 ft. or so more than her waterline length, the larger boats having rather a greater and the smallest rather less difference.

Recently designers by exploiting big beam and using small ballast ratios have achieved potent racers with ratings below their waterline lengths. In *Belmore* by careful figuring out of all the factors we got a 26-ft. rating on a $26\frac{1}{2}$-ft. waterline with a good ballast ratio of 42 per cent and 668 sq. ft. of sail.

In addition there is a trophy for the best corrected time by a yacht measuring not more than 40 ft. overall—so it is better to be just under rather than just over 40 ft. There is another trophy for the best performance on corrected time by a yacht built prior to 1934. There are normally special 'outright' prizes: for the first yacht to finish, the best performance on corrected time by a schooner, and the best corrected time by a foreign entrant. Prizes for the best corrected time by a cutter, and another for yawls and ketches, generally go to the class prize winners.

Time Allowances. The time allowance scale—which is of course independent of the rating rule—is shown in Appendix XII. It is based directly on rating and distance, and produces therefore a fixed time allowance for each boat regardless of the elapsed time of the race. This scale is framed to cover races offshore and inshore, and in consequence it tends, when used for ocean races, slightly to favour the medium to large boats, whose performance is not so much reduced by a seaway. This advantage, of course, becomes more marked when there is much turning to windward, because the course is virtually lengthened while the time allowance is fixed. An adjustment is made, however, in favour of the smaller yachts, by assuming a longer course than the direct rhumb line course. It may be noted in passing that prior to the adoption of the time correction factor, or 'time-on-time' system of allowances by the R.O.R.C. this club had an 'inshore' and an 'offshore' time scale, the latter allowances being appreciably larger.

Until 1954, when the yawl *Malay* won the Bermuda Trophy, none of the modern series of Bermuda Races had been won by a yacht small by American standards. But *Finisterre*, a beamy centreboard yawl of Sparkman and Stephens design, $27\frac{1}{2}$-ft. waterline won in 1956, 1958, and 1960. In 1958 she was followed home by *Golliwog*, a slightly larger near sister (both rate a little below their waterline length) and *Belmore*. *Belmore* was second to *Finisterre*, overall among 130 entrants in 1960.

Best Size of Yacht. Probably the best sizes of yacht, should one be building specially, lie between 40- and 43-ft. waterline, though there is no doubt that any good boat has a chance. When building, don't forget to incorporate lifting eyes to the keel inside in the bilges, to facilitate lifting the yacht by a crane or derrick onto and off a cradle; this in connection with shipment.

It is necessary while still considering the type of boat one is going to enter, to say something about prevailing conditions. Forty per cent of races are sailed primarily either to windward or on a fairly close fetch; in the other 60 per cent reaching predominates. Winds of Force 3–6 are common. Very light conditions sometimes cover a proportion—occasionally a large proportion—and most often the last half of the course. Winds of gale force are only rarely met in these particular latitudes at this time of the year. There, in a nutshell, is a précis of what you may expect.

Although at times there has been much hard reaching in the Bermuda Race, there has only rarely been any significant running under spinnakers. In 1948 we all had longish periods under spinnaker, mostly in moderate wind conditions, and in 1958 we had two days of sometimes hard spinnaker work. 1960 had the rare gale. 1962, in which I sailed *Pherousa*, was virtually all reaching, and very properly was won by the grand old schooner *Nina*.

One needs primarily to bear in mind reaching with the wind just before the beam. One should go through one's sail list with this in mind, and these conditions may govern one's choice of the sails to be renewed, or of sails to be added. For instance since reaching with sheets just eased is a likely condition, yawls must make sure that they have a good mizzen staysail in the locker.

If one is making a serious bid for Trophy honours, to avoid shocks and disappointments it is as well, should one have time, to work out carefully one's C.C.A. rating, preferably while one is considering one's entry. For this purpose the work sheet or rating blank should be obtained from the club, or copied from Appendix XII in this book. To avoid mistakes it is as well to have this done, or checked by a naval architect familiar with the rule. In any case an independent check is most desirable in the case of a long calculation of this kind. It can best be worked out from the drawings. The displacement will require to be known, or calculated.

Sail Area and Rating. The masthead rig, often a masthead sloop or single headsail yawl has become a firm favourite in the U.S.A. recently. This is probably due to the efficiency of this rig down wind in light airs (often racing on the east coast of the States is light and in the Sound specially) when a modern 'spherical' spinnaker gets wind 'both sides' of the head of the main. With this rig a moderate aspect ratio main appears desirable. A sloop with a higher aspect ratio is still a potent combination for racing to Bermuda.

It should be remembered that although in theory the C.C.A. and the R.O.R.C. rule are equally hard on sail area and the American yachts on the average carry appreciably more area than equivalent European offshore racers, it is always difficult to estimate exactly how much area pays under a rule; and American practice has settled on a slightly more generous allowance of canvas, possibly on account of the average East Coast inshore conditions, rather than exact rule conditions. Anyway because there is so much reaching—on the average—and also because in three out of four races there is an appreciable amount of light weather it is most necessary to have a good big sail plan for the Bermuda Race. About 10 per cent more than the optimum under R.O.R.C. rating appears desirable, assuming the 'existing' aspect ratios are maintained. If not, then the increase must be larger unless the yacht is tender—*e.g.* one has sacrificed ballast to get the rating down—I still favour a mainsail aspect ratio of between 2·5 and 2·8—even at the expense of incurring the C.C.A. penalty—for sloops.

As an instance, I have just seen the drawings of a new American ocean racer of 34-ft. waterline by a famous naval architect. She displaces 13·8 tons and has a rated sail area of 1,160 sq. ft., C.C.A. measurement, or about 1,110 sq. ft. by British sail measurement rules. The normal English practice for such a boat—she has a pretty cut-away profile and a very moderate wetted under-water area—would be round 960 sq. ft.

Race Preparations. Turning to the question of preparation, labour costs in the U.S.A. are and have always been appreciably higher than elsewhere and moreover seem likely to remain so. In many cases they will be double those prevailing in other countries. It therefore behoves one, if expense is an important consideration, to go out with everything as complete as possible. If one sails from Europe to the U.S.A. for the race it may well be that the cost of refit on arrival will equal the cost of shipping out, unless one has with one a goodly stock of spare running rigging, and unless the crew do a reasonable proportion of the work.

Compulsory Equipment. The list of compulsory equipment varies only a little from year to year; but this should be checked in advance for the year in question. The last list was as follows:

Necessary charts and navigating equipment; two compasses, one of which must be strongly mounted; set of International Code flags and code book; radar reflector; rigid dinghy, supplemented by additional dinghy or rafts of any type desired, so that entire crew can be carried in rough water with safety (*Note*: inflatable rafts or boats should be tested before the race); two bilge pumps; fog horn; fixed bow pulpit and wire lifelines with stanchions; shutters for large deckhouse windows; all hatches and skylights must be secured to prevent loss overboard (suitable hinges or lanyards are required); small storm trysail and storm jib designed for vessel; two coastguard-approved portable fire extinguishers, accessibly located in different parts of the vessel; Coast Guard-approved life jacket for each member of the crew, carried where readily accessible; two life rings, each equipped with a water light, a whistle and dye marker (the life rings must be located handy to the helmsman. It is recommended that they be of the horseshoe type—yellow, orange, or red in colour and have a drogue attached); flag float (ballasted float with pole and flag); first-aid kit, including instruction book and sufficient supplies to cover all contingencies on an emergency basis; twelve red parachute-type distress signals readily accessible; two white flares for signalling; safety belts for each member of crew; rigging cutter; the name of yacht must be clearly painted on such equipment as dinghy, oars, life ring, rafts, life jackets, ballasted pole with flag, etc.; two anchors with cables; 10 gallons of water per man, reasonably divided among two or more separate tanks (with separate shut-off cocks) or containers; stores sufficient for the crew for a period of three weeks; two powerful water-resistant flashlights; seacocks on all underwater openings (must not be frozen) except on deck scuppers where outlets are close to the waterline; if vessel steers with tiller a spare tiller is required; if vessel steers with a wheel, emergency tiller and spare cable are required; all life line stanchion sockets must be through-bolted.

In addition to the equipment required above, it is strongly recommended that every yacht carry emergency repair equipment—spare turnbuckles, wire, shackles, blocks, winch handles, soft wood plugs to fit underwater hull openings, etc. Also, each yacht should carry some form of radio transmitter for emergency use. (Beware of war surplus Gibson Girls, etc., which may no longer be operative.) As to the type of raft to be carried, authorities recommend the canopy type as by far the safest. Emergency water, food, and compass should be packed in raft and raft secured by line to yacht to prevent loss in emergency.

The following are not allowed to be used in the race:

Engines for propelling; radar; radio transmitters; loran; radio telephones; double-clewed jibs; loose-footed light-weight mainsails; double-luffed mainsails; bent spars (whether permanently or mechanically bent); twin spinnakers exceeding total rated sail area; automatic steering and similar electronic equipment other than radio receiver, direction-finding, and sounding equipment.

Allowable Headsail Sheet Leads. The rules regarding the sheeting of headsails and spinnakers have been varied from time to time. One should get the current rules for the year and try and sort them out in advance, because it affects the design of the sails intended primarily for reaching.

What has always been the case in recent years, and what one can more or less rely on, is that headsails can be sheeted to the main boom, and mizzen staysails to the mizzen boom.

The largest alteration at present needed to a British yacht with R.O.R.C. race sails going out to race under C.C.A. conditions is of course to the headsails. The 1962 minimum headsail—for which the rating will 'charge' you anyway—is 150 per cent base of triangle measured clew to luff; at right angles. This comes out about 158 per cent, J, genoa foot length, against 150 per cent J, R.O.R.C. normal. The spinnaker permitted is now the same. These differences are dealt with in more detail elsewhere in this book.

Spinnakers. The R.O.R.C. spinnakers, 180 per cent J in width, need no alteration. The hard-weather spinnakers also will normally not require to be altered.

As regards the headsails, it usually amounts to providing at least one new genoa of the biggest size that can profitably be carried. The designing of such a sail is fully discussed in Chapter 10.

Shipment. Turning to the question of getting one's boat from one's home port to Newport, Rhode Island—be it from South America, the East Coast of America, or Europe or Australia—the first job maybe is a cradle. Diagram 85 shows in perspective, but dimensioned, the cradle used for transporting the *Myth* to America. These scantlings are very ample and would suffice for any boat of up to 35-ft. waterline, the details of the hangers, etc., being altered, *bien entendu*, to suit the keel profile. Only the lifting rods and the eyes need stepping up in proportion to the displacement of the yacht, *Myth*'s being designed for a 10-ton lift. Be sure the eye flanges are big enough—not less than four times the bolt diameter. The wire slings should be as long as the derrick lift allows: not less than 150 per cent of the distance between the fore and aft bolts. They should be of the same diameter as the rods, which are weakened by the cutting of screw threads.

The next problem is getting the boat into and out of the cradle. One can build the cradle round her and launch her in it, towing her to the ship and hoisting her on board still in the cradle. If

before hoisting her out again the cradle is ballasted to make it just negatively buoyant, the cradle can be drawn away from the yacht when she is afloat; and hoisted back again into the ship, on to the quay, or a lighter, by derrick or crane. Otherwise one might have to re-slip to get the yacht out. *Myth*'s cradle in Oregon pine needed 1,200 lb. of ballast.

Alternatively one can build the cradle around the yacht on the slip, dismantle it and re-erect it on board the ship, lifting the yacht separately into the cradle. If one is building a new yacht one can probably incorporate lifting eyes to the top of the keel bolts; provided this is thought of early in the design of a big boat. Owing to the smaller number of keel bolts in a small yacht there is generally less difficulty here in incorporating the arrangements later.

Alternatively she can be lifted with slings or gripes placed round the boat. But be very sure that the slingers use good stretchers between the slings (a stout spar above the yacht's deck to hold the slings apart). I have seen some nasty crushing take place when this has not been properly attended to —when the slingers have slipped in a few sacks to pack the slings out from the yacht's side and assumed this would be good enough.

If she is to be carried between decks, under hatches, it is possible to shore her up carefully in place and thus save the considerable expense of a cradle. In this case see that the keel is firmly located in all directions and try to get steadying shores on the topstrake in three places each side. This is much less likely to strain her than bilge shores, unless these can take on a strength bulkhead through a big shaped pad. If one can get shores down from the deck above on to big wood pads on deck near the covering board each side, so much the better.

I have seen small yachts travel quite safely cradled only in a cargo hold of potato sacks and bales. I have even seen them arrive in good order laid on their sides on a certain amount of soft packing; old canvas and the like; but I would not recommend this.

Import and Customs Regulation. There is a heavy import duty on yachts going into the U.S.A. and visiting yachts normally have to get a bond, signed by someone acceptable to the customs, for the amount of the duty, the bond being forfeitable if the yacht is not re-exported or sailed away.

If one can get some kind friend in the States to 'do the necessary' in advance, filling the several forms out and giving the bond, then things will be eased, and delays avoided. He would require to know the value of your yacht. If one arrives in

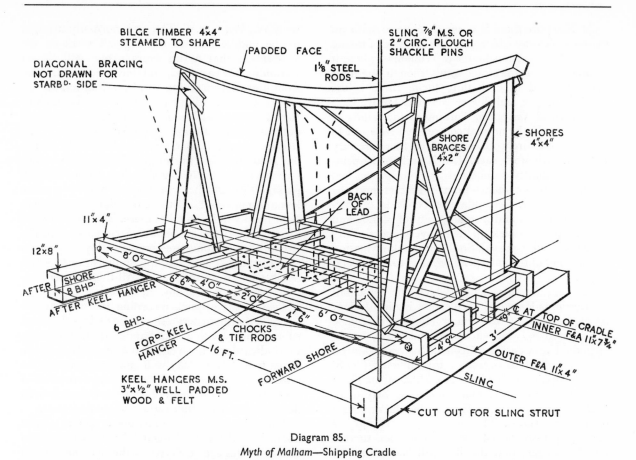

Diagram 85.
Myth of Malham—Shipping Cradle

Diagonally braced, rectangular, strong back-spreader is fitted above the deck for the steel rods. Wood pads landing firmly on four points on covering board. Whole secured by nuts above the strong back. Slings take off this.

New York without preparations, then practically the only way of getting the matter expeditiously dealt with is to employ a customs agent; any shipping office will put you on to one. He knows the ropes, will arrange the bond and straighten out the forms so that you are free to proceed in a few hours, provided you can get the customs officer to visit your craft to clear it. Campbell and Gardner, 15 Whitehall Street, New York 4, are good people.

But it is an expensive job—the customs agent charged 100 dollars for his two hours' help in clearing *Myth* in 1948. In a smaller port one can dispense with the agent's services if you have someone to sign the bond. At the port from which one leaves the U.S.A. customs clearance is required, and the customs agent normally will want to clear his bond at this time. All this is a tiresome business and it is worth making application ahead to the Bureau of Customs at Washington to ask for the import bond to be waived in the particular case of a yacht coming specifically to race and remaining for a limited period. One should give the particulars of the yacht and the ports one plans to

visit, with approximate dates of arrival and departure. I understand that in many cases this is granted. In any case it is clear that it is much simpler to make one's entry and departure at a port like Newport, Rhode Island, rather than New York. If asked in advance the C.C.A. can generally (and very kindly) get a cruising warrant for a visiting yacht which eases customs formalities, and the need for a bond disappears.

Needless to say, once over there, one gets every assistance from American yachtsmen, but they cannot help the ruling labour charges. With the American standard of living and average wage rather higher than anywhere else in the world, it stands to reason the repairs will cost about three times as much as in Europe. Therefore it pays to go well equipped with replacement running gear, or alternatively to tuck one's own splices, and to have a really complete tool and sail repair kit on board. With these precautions taken there is no reason why the Bermuda Race should be a specially expensive enterprise. Paint, hemp, and so on, are no dearer there than elsewhere.

At Newport there is a small shipyard with an excellent slipway which can take any size of racing yacht—Messrs. Manchester & Williams—where it is handy to get a pre-race scrub, though one must book in good time. Failing them, there is the excellent larger and dearer Newport Shipyard.

Tactics and Navigation. Turning to the sailing of the race itself, the normal course from Newport to Bermuda is entirely offshore and it is therefore very much a navigator's race. This is perhaps its principal peculiarity compared to the other two premier offshore races—*i.e.* the Fastnet and the Sydney–Hobart. Bermuda itself consists of low-lying coral reefs and a small group of islands and may be hard to pick up; it has very occasionally been completely missed. So the celestial navigation department of the enterprise requires to be in good order.

The only ocean chart on which one could sail the Bermuda Race had a scale allowing insufficient room for plotting the minor changes of course necessitated by wind variations and so on, but in 1956 the U.S. Coast and Geodetic Survey produced a special chart to overcome this difficulty: U.S. Hydrographic Office Chart No. H.O. 1650. Title: 'Cape Cod to Cape Romaine including Bermuda.'

One can also usefully draw in the direct course on plotting sheets. The 'true' course is 149° or about south-south-east by compass. But therein lurks a danger: that this line will become sacrosanct. Remember that the rhumb line is only the direct course from Newport. If for reasons of weather, by steering off to gain speed, or by faulty steering or because of a faulty sight, or for any other reason you get off the original rhumb line then it should cease to be your guide. By all means draw a fresh one from your present position to Bermuda; this new rhumb line is the only one which, from then onwards, should interest you. In other words the problem in a sense starts afresh from your present position regardless of what courses you happen to have steered from Newport.

Having I hope dethroned King Rhumb Line, and signed him on as a useful A.B. instead, we can proceed with more detailed consideration of the course.

Allowance for Gulf Stream Set. The principal difficulty in the pilotage is of course the Gulf Stream. This runs in a generally east-north-easterly direction. It normally operates over a band 160 miles wide which one enters about 120 miles after leaving the start off Newport. The total extent one is set during the crossing is very variable, and of course depends on the speed of one's boat as well as the direction and speed of the current. The current may set anything from 5–45 miles in 24 hours, and may be N.W., W., or S.W. The set is normally stronger in the middle than at the edges. I work on the assumption that as an average one will be set 25 miles to the eastward, and that one should, apart from guesses concerning wind possibilities, lay off one's course accordingly. That is to say, lay it off so that if one's guess has been correct, one will come out 'on the rhumb line' at the *southern* edge of the stream. In a small boat, say, round the 28-ft. rating, one could increase this to 30 miles. If the weather forecast indicates the likelihood of a fast reaching passage through the area one can make it 5 miles less and conversely, if there are signs of probable light head winds, 10 miles more. The Woods Hole Oceanic Institute has made yearly surveys of the stream and the condensed report with yearly tracks of the stream—with varying sinuous curves—can be obtained from the C.C.A. All theses considerations are in respect of current alone.

Two sensitive quick recording thermometers—*e.g.* milk thermometers—should be on board. Also a rubber bucket with a stout handle. If one is turning to windward and has a choice of courses, the change of sea temperature may well enable you to opt for crossing the stream at a point where there is a south-going component. The report describes in detail how to play that rather fascinating game.

The point is that one must make up one's mind about it at the start. In general the weather forecasting in this area covered by the race, appears to be somewhat unreliable, the vagaries probably being due partly to the effects of the Gulf Stream. So unless you are a keen gambler I would not advocate hanging your hat on the wireless reports. Even the U.S. Navy and the Coast Guard appear unable at times to agree about the weather forecast.

Prevailing Winds. There is no doubt that a lot of the wind in the race area in June comes from between the south and the south-south-west, and the tendency is for it to be more southerly on the south side of the stream. So should this be the forecast, in general, it undoubtedly pays to get rather to the west than the east of the rhumb line. For some years prior to 1948 those who were to the west had been specially lucky, and by 1948 it had become almost an obsession among some of the pundits—I called it the 'westward fixation'. It is almost worse than rhumb-line-phobia. As a result during the 1948 race quite a lot of the best skippers overplayed this particular suit.

Very often one can tell when the Gulf Stream is entered by a change in water colour to a more distinct blue and on occasions by a visible tide line, also by the presence of long lines of weed. This weed is also found clear to the south but not much to the north of the stream. While in the stream one may have short, moderate squalls of Force 5 or 6 or so, coming along for no particular reason. Typical Gulf Stream weather in June is fine with small white fleecy clouds about. Light squalls are often very local and can be seen on the water. We were in *Latifa* in 1946, sailing, I suppose, only just out of sight of *Baruna* in quite light conditions, when she had the clew of her genoa blown out. If convenient, one should steer towards the squalls, since in light windward work one often gets a nice lift out of them. When one leaves the Gulf Stream proper one sometimes encounters a strong west-going set for a little while, and sometimes a continuation of the east-going current. In fact all the way to Bermuda, the sets though not likely to be very large, are quite unpredictable.

Naturally after leaving the Gulf Stream one takes every opportunity of getting a sight, since one never knows when the visibility may close down, and which sight may be the last.

There is now a well-powered radio beacon on the island. Fortunately real fogs are almost unknown in June, but low visibility often prevails.

Many submerged coral reefs lie off the west and north of the island, running in places up to 9 miles out from the islands, so care is necessary in making one's landfall. Gibbs Hill near the centre of the Islands has a fine powerful light, the loom of which can be seen up to 25 miles away in fine weather only. The loom of the air field light near the north end of the islands is usually to be seen, even when Gibbs Hill cannot be. The reefs seen from well up (from a cross-tree shall we say) look by day quite green in colour; provided that there is not too much sea running.

The finish can sometimes be approached from either side, leaving the island either to port or to starboard. Normally it is to starboard, but the alternative may be valuable if one finds oneself turning to windward, and well off to the westward in the final stages of the race. But in 1954 the finish had to be approached from the north.

THE RIO RACE

Though of relatively recent origin, this 1,200-mile event is gaining in stature. The course is from Buenos Aires to Rio de Janiero, and the races have been held triennially, in 1947, 1950, 1953, 1956, 1959, 1962, 1965, and 1968. It is generally held in early February, to finish in the Brazilian capital in time for Carnival.

The C.C.A. rule of measurement and the C.C.A. time scale, based on distance, are used. Both these are shown in Appendix XII. Since all Argentine boats are normally measured in nearly fresh water, all visiting boats naturally have to be remeasured in like conditions. The range of yachts eligible is virtually the same as for the Bermuda Race.

Horses for Courses. It is fairly clear that over a long average, yachts of some 40–45-ft. waterline will be more favoured than in the Bermuda Race because the winds are largely ahead. However, smaller prospective entries must not be discouraged because the 1953 race results brought all Class III up with fair winds to take all the premier honours.

Expected Weather. Continuing to consider the choice of a boat to enter, we find a baffling selection of weathers may face us. In 1947 the winds were moderate to slack. In 1950, when Great Britain was represented by Colonel Scholfield in *Blue Disa*, they started in strong headwinds; then a fresh following breeze for the first 200 miles of open sea; a long series of blows and moderate gales from ahead; a spell of light variables, and finally a short moderate gale astern with heavy rain which blew them nearly to the finish.

In 1953 the American *White Mist* reported being on the wind for nine of the twelve days. Of these nine days 36 hrs. were occupied by a blow from ahead, the wind being up to Force 7. For the remaining seven windward days the Force did not rise above 4. For two days they encountered very light winds. Others, however, had a higher proportion of fair winds.

Though on occasions south-east winds are found towards the finish, Rio bestrides the Tropic of Capricorn, and so the south-easterly Trades are not encountered.

The very helpful Argentine Club is sometimes able to make special arrangements to assist with shipping for visiting yachts. In transit, on this passage, keep your yacht sides and decks protected from a blistering sun; or serious top-side leaks may result.

The First Legs. Turning to the race itself, the long starting leg is in the River Plate. Here there are hardly any orthodox tides; the current and the height of the water depend more on the wind and weather. This unpredictable rise and fall may be as much as 15 ft., and it behoves one not to get ashore with the wind turning suddenly westerly—the 'dirty' pampero arriving with a cloud of dust from the Pampas. But some distance can be saved by going across the Ortry Bank at the north side of the river mouth, when there is water there.

Once offshore there are no important constant current sets. It is said to be good strategy to keep offshore after passing Cabo Polonio which is about 100 miles north-east of Punta del Est, the northern side of the mouth of the River Plate. North of

Polonio for the next 500 miles to Cabo de Santa Maria there is apt to be a definite shoreward set in strong easterlies. As a result, three of the 1953 competitors found some unwanted land in contact with their keels; and this set was noted by others.

To Windward up the Coast. North of Santa Maria is the island of Santa Catarina, and thence the shore curves away to the west of the direct course. One school of thought favours, in head winds, closing the shore for land and sea breezes, but in 1953 and 1956, and again in 1962, this did not pay any particular dividend, nor did the long tacks offshore. The relatively short tacks up the rhumb line seemed as good as anything, with a slight bias towards the easterly side of it. But in 1968 a long leg offshore paid off handsomely.

In the first two races they had, finishing up the big harbour at Rio, to contend with the strong unfavourable currents which run therein. In later races the finish was outside.

Navigation. Radio reception is best near dawn or at dusk! The visibility is variable. Evening star-sights may be good; the days are often overcast. There are two good radio beacons at Rio, one of which may be picked up as much as 100 miles away. The broadcasted weather reports—special arrangements are made—are, owing to the difficult met. conditions, not generally reliable. Much the same applies in the Bermuda Race. Neither is baro-metric movement necessarily a very good guide.

But what does it matter when one is sailing along quietly at night with the stars overhead in their millions, and the temperature so salubrious that one is still dressed only in shorts and a shirt!

27

OFFSHORE RACING AND LIVING AFLOAT IN THE MEDITERRANEAN

The tideless Mediterranean has long furnished happy hunting grounds for cruising yachtsmen, but offshore racing has not until recently been so much in the limelight. A start had, however, been made in a small way in 1925. A small committee met in France and organised a race from Marseilles round Giraglia, off the north of Corsica and back to Marseilles. The following year the executive was enlarged by the inclusion of yachtsmen from Spain and Italy and took the title of Comité International des Courses—Croisières de la Mediterranée. Presidents were in turn elected from each of the nations.

From 1926, until the outbreak of the Spanish Civil War in 1935, a race was organised each year. The start was somewhere in the south of France; the finish was variously in the Balearics, Barcelona, Algiers, or Ajaccio.

In 1938 a fresh beginning was made. René Levanville, President of the French Union National des Croiseurs, and to whom offshore racing in Europe owes so much, in conjunction with the Societé Nautique de Marseilles organised a race from the island of Porquerolles to Monte Carlo. Fifteen yachts including four Italian were entered; a goodly muster and a good instance of how yachtsmen can help in international relations, because at the end of the Spanish Civil War the political atmosphere in general was far from friendly.

The following year under the same auspices the race was staged from Marseilles round Porquerolles and back to Marseilles. But with the world war clouds already gathering fast, there were only seven in the fleet.

After the War. Once more in 1947 a new series was launched, again by the U.N.C. In 1949, still with René Levanville in the van of organisers, ably supported by Beppe Croce for Italy and Sans Mora for Spain, the thing got going on a firm basis.

The R.O.R.C. rating rule was adopted, also the three R.O.R.C. classes according to rating. Eighteen raced from Cannes to Porto Ferraio in Elba, and then to Portofino in Italy. In 1950 a great fleet including five 100-tonners met at St.

Tropez. They raced to Ajaccio, capital of Corsica, and then to the lovely port of Ischia in Italy. In the latter event the Italian Navy made the best performance of the fleet with an Italian built Laurent Giles designed R.N.S.A. 'Twenty-Four', *Orsa Minore*, skippered by that most skilful ship driver Giani Pera.

More New Yachts. In 1951 again from St. Tropez they raced to Barcelona and then to Palma de Majorca and finally Ibiza. New stars were rising, and honours were divided between the lovely new Class I 'Forty'-rater Laurent Giles designed *Miranda IV* owned by Carlo Ciampi, and a new Italian naval yacht, the cutter *Chiar di Luna*, again with Giani Pera in charge. *Miranda* was interesting in that she was of very light displacement and had a rudder on a skeg separated from the ballast keel. *Chiar* in Class III is a clever design, some $27\frac{1}{2}$ ft. on the water but rating only some $21\frac{1}{2}$ ft.; below the R.N.S.A. 'Twenty-Four's'.

Bigger Fleets. Though I had raced and cruised in the Mediterranean under sail in the past, it was not until 1952 that I had the chance to take part in the new offshore races. In that year we raced 330 miles from Cannes to Cagliari the port at the southern end of Sardinia; then in the second race 240 miles from Cagliari to Palermo. Twenty-four yachts started, ranging from a 150-ton schooner to ours the smallest entry; and including five Italians, of whom three were newly built for ocean racing; one Spaniard, one German, and one American. The latter was the very smart Stephens yawl *Berna*. The remainder were French, headed by the Commodore's beautifully kept 86-ton ketch *Aile Blanche*.

From Cannes a mistral blew us down to the western side of Sardinia. This leg of the course, about 180 miles, is dead straight and well offshore. The mistral freshened up to about 40 knots for several hours, and we covered $166\frac{1}{2}$ miles in the first 24 hrs. from the start to our first shore fix. It is, incidentally, the best day's run I have recorded in a 24-ft. waterline boat. *Angela* was a pre-war Rasmussen-built boat with, for nowadays, a low

9*

freeboard; she is just below the R.O.R.C. minimum standard freeboard and carries a small penalty. On deck with a quartering sea we were as wet as a half-tide rock, and appreciated the warmth of the Mediterranean summer conditions; what would have been in the North Sea a rather cold hard sail in a wet boat was in fact a really jolly one.

'Angela'. This yacht had a small sail area even for her length, of some 320 sq. ft., set in a sloop rig. In the strongest of the blow we only had to roll down four and a half rolls of main, say between 6 and 7 ft., and substitute a working jib for a genoa. She was a nicely-balanced boat with fair ends, and ran well in strong conditions, giving us very little trouble with the steering, though we had to hang on to prevent ourselves being washed out of the shallow cockpit. Pera in *Chiar di Luna* was a close second to us in Class III. *Mait*, a new Class I moderate displacement Baglietto designed and built Italian cutter, took premier honours of the fleet from *Angela* by 18 min.

Racing to Palermo. The second race, to Palermo, was sailed virtually all to windward, in winds principally Force 1-3 and occasionally 4, with only short calm patches between. Three-quarters of the race is clear offshore, and sights were used on the second day. The last 60 miles are along the north Sicilian shores, really magnificent scenery with rugged hills, sometimes of over 3,000 ft., close to the coast.

Here we encountered conditions which are often met round Sicily, really strong but very variable winds coming from all directions in turn. For more than an hour we were on the wind, Force 6 reefed. Then half an hour's calm with full sail; and then some knock down gusts, alternating with a few minutes of calm. The winds seemed to come down the valley and sweep round the cliffs, blowing parallel to the shore at times; then the fresh onshore breeze of the day will supervene for a time.

On arrival we found we had beaten *Chiar di Luna* by the narrow margin of $9\frac{1}{2}$ min. for premier honours, and to win the championship cup of the year for the combined results of the two races. We had been very lucky to have had practically no light-weather reaching and running in either race, a thing that would have unstitched us, compared with *Chiar* at least.

Le Petit Fastnet. For 1953 the R.O.R.C. measurement for rating was retained, but combined with a time on distance scale, as the committee had felt that the occasional long calms made the time on time too favourable to the smaller yachts.

The face of the fleet was changing—with many fine new yachts there at the start for their first race.

The big event of the year was from Cannes round a lighthouse-surmounted rock, off the north of Corsica, the Giraglia, to San Remo in Italy. Mostly in reaching conditions Jacques Barbou's 44 ft. cutter *Jalina* made the best corrected time of the fleet and took Class II. M. Ferdinand Belou's new *Enchanteur II* from Marseilles won Class I, and ourselves in *Samuel Pepys*, the R.N.S.A. 'Twenty-Four', Class III.

It was an interesting race for us because we in Class III were in sight of one another throughout, darkness apart, and at the finish there was only 38 secs. between us and the new Italian *Swallow*, Gianni Pera in charge.

Later they raced from Marseilles to S'Agaro and thence to Formentor in Majorca. In the latter, big black *Ea* beat the band, in a reaching race. She was built in 1953 by Cantieri Bagliettoi; a most interesting boat.

Giraglia. Since then, writing in 1969, the Giraglia has become the big Mediterranean offshore race. Raced annually, the course is fixed, but reversible—generally Toulon–Giraglia–San Remo in the odd years and San Remo–Giraglia–Toulon in the even years. The start is usually on 14 July. The longer leg, between Toulon and the Giraglia Island, is traditionally down wind in the odd years and up wind in the even years. Wind strengths vary; often the race is a mixture of light winds with perhaps 12 hrs. of brisk breezes, sometimes reaching and holding Force 7. The lucky boats generally finish the race in 30 to 40 hrs.

Apart from the Giraglia there are every year at least one (sometimes two) international races. The course is varied sometimes from a French to a Balearic island port.

The R.O.R.C. rule is used to determine rating and used with a time on distance scale. R.O.R.C. safety rules are in general applied, but dinghy requirements sometimes differ. To date the new rule has not been accepted and the R.O.R.C. rating is being continued. Entries and detailed information are handled from either: Secretary U.N.C., 82 Boulevard Haussman, Paris; or Yachts Club Italiano, Porticciolo Duca degli Abruzzi, Genova, Italy.

Mediterranean Racing Conditions. I mentioned the Palermo Race conditions in a little detail because they are to be found on occasions, though by no means always, when hot weather is encountered in combination with close-by high land, cliffs, and valleys. The higher and closer they are, and the hotter the weather, the stronger are the gusts likely to be.

Another typical type of weather which is much in evidence at times is the thunder squall. This is met more frequently and on the average in more violent form than on the Atlantic seaboards. The thunder clouds can generally be seen in good time as they gather, often associated with cumulus over the land. The difficult thing is that though thunder may be about, and appear fairly close all day, the squalls may not reach the area where you are, and you may carry on sailing on the prevailing wind.

It is therefore important to plan your sail reductions but not to execute them until it is clear that the squall is actually coming your way.

Apart from these winds and the land and sea breezes, the prevailing summer wind over the Western Mediterranean is between W.N.W. and N.N.W. This is a fairly marked prevalence to the west of Sardinia and between there and Malta.

In the area between Sardinia and Italy the winds are variable; gale strength wind, apart from local gusting, is virtually never met in the summer months. In the Gulf of Lyons and again off the North African coast more strong wind is encountered; and occasionally of moderate gale force in summer.

Land and Sea Breezes. The land and sea breezes are much more marked than in the Atlantic racing areas. The onshore breeze is pretty generally the stronger. Off the North African coast the onshore breeze often blows in the afternoon and 'dogs' at Force 4–5 up to 10 or more miles out to sea. Elsewhere it is from Force 2 to 4, depending on the massif of the land and on the heat of the day. The offshore breeze will not as a rule come up until after midnight, and may blow until just after dawn. But it is much less reliable and as a rule weaker. When working ashore it is well worth remembering that both breezes tend to some extent to be canalised up or down the valleys and the bays which extend from them.

We have talked about the breezes, and to put the whole thing in perspective we must now talk about the calms, of which there is a far higher proportion than in the Atlantic. In general at sea the nights are quite likely to be calm, that is, in the absence of some general wind system. After nightfall and shortly after dawn are often specially flat spots. And one may, at sea, away from the land breezes, get several days in succession with only paltry breezes.

Use of the Barometer. In summer in the Mediterranean the common barometer is of little if any help in foretelling the weather. So much so that I did not include one in the equipment of *Angela*. The only hope is to use a barograph instrument or to make a half-hourly plot, or graph, from the common barometer. With such records one can with care differentiate between the diurnal movements

and others. I would say, in large yachts carry a barograph. Otherwise, don't bother with a barometer at all.

Mediterranean Requirements. It is against the weather background that we must consider what special measures and alterations are desirable to make the most of Mediterranean conditions. We have firstly more than the usual ration of calms, and secondly more frequent, and often more sudden, changes of wind. On deck and inside the ship we have to cope with relatively high temperatures.

Light Sails. As to making the best of really light weather we shall clearly need to spend even more time, money, and trouble than is usual in boats equipped for the Atlantic, on light-weather sails and light sheets. The recommended weights of canvas for ghosting sails are laid out in Appendix IV and it will be important to see that these weights are not exceeded. I like to have a single light-weight headsail sheet to each of the ghosting sails. This saves the drag of the weather sheet on a sail which is trying to set and keep full in light airs in spite of the motion of the ship. With good drill in light airs very little is lost in passing the single sheet round, when going about.

Apart from the headsails it is desirable that the mainsail canvas shall not be greater in weight than the figures quoted in Appendix IV. You could go 1 oz. lighter should you be prepared to sacrifice a little sail life. But not more, because of the squalls which abound.

Sail Plan Design. So much for existing sail plans. If one is designing a new sail plan for either a new or an existing boat there are three things which need special consideration.

Firstly the total sail area. There is a formula in Chapter 9 on page 59 which can be used for calculating the area required for racing under the R.O.R.C. rating rule in the Atlantic. The R.O.R.C. rating rule is used in the Mediterranean races, but with the lighter average conditions it will pay under the rule to have more sail area. I would add 8 per cent to the figure which the formula gives one. For light-weather sailing offshore it is important to have a fair proportion of the sail area in either headsails or 'tween mast staysails.

The tactics and practices of light-weather sailing are fully covered in Chapter 6, and there is no need to repeat them here, but only perhaps to emphasise the need to study these aspects.

Reefing. The second requirement stated, to cope with more frequent changes of sail, can be met in a number of ways. Roller reefing will have an added appeal. The pros and cons were discussed earlier in the book, but there will be an extra pro for the quickly changing conditions to be met.

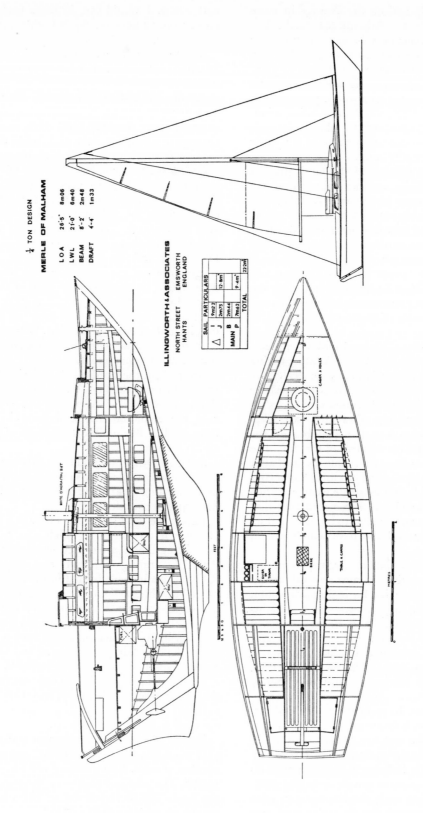

¼ TON DESIGN

MERLE OF MALHAM

LOA	26'5"	8m06
LWL	21'0"	6m40
BEAM	8'-2'	2m48
DRAFT	4'-4'	1m33

ILLINGWORTH & ASSOCIATES

NORTH STREET   EMSWORTH
HANTS   ENGLAND

SAIL PARTICULARS

△	I	9m02	
	J	2m75	12·8m²
MAIN	B	2m144	
	P	7m62	9·4m²
	TOTAL		22·2m²

Diagram 86.

Merle of Malham—a 26 ft. 5 in. ¼-ton design. Total sail area is 237 sq. ft.

On the other hand if one has a cutter rig the matter is solved in another way, because one hardly ever reefs the main, but shifts headsails.

There will be an added incentive to use duplicate stays for setting headsails; a thing which on the balance I recommended against for Atlantic use, on the score of weight, windage, and snarling propensities.

Stays and Headsails. One is not permitted, fortunately, to change to light-weather mainsails. But if, in variable weather, one has a cutter rig with normal and ghosting canvas hanked on to alternative stays, one can change the weight of two-thirds of the total canvas in a jiffy. The fashion in the Mediterranean at present is all for masthead genoas. While these are undoubtedly potent sails, I still think that a cutter setting two sails all the time can do as well if not better in light airs. The ghosting yankee and ghosting staysail can be and will be, if the table in the Appendix is followed, appreciably lighter than the genoa. And it is a more flexible rig for sail changing.

Special Hull Measures. Turning to the hull, we come first to the protection of the decks and coachroofs. If the decks are laid in a single skin, unless they are of teak or ply and in first-class order it is desirable to cover them. Otherwise it is very difficult indeed, under the constant sun, to keep them anything like watertight. Canvassing is a good normal answer. As an alternative I used successfully some years ago corticine covering, laid on the maker's patent hot compound. This corticine is about $\frac{1}{4}$ in. thick; the weight is compensated for in rating and it certainly did reduce the temperature of the deck; we had a bridge deck uncovered and had a ready comparison. It needs non-skid painting over to prevent it getting too slippery. It must be declared as part of the deck weight for scantlings. In the case of coachroofs, the decking will be thinner, its insulation value smaller. I recommend lining the inside, under the deck beams with thin ply or thin hard board such as Masonite; the latter by special order can be obtained $\frac{3}{32}$ in. in thickness. This forms an air space with valuable insulating properties. Purists would remove this during the laid-up period, but the chances of dry rot setting up here seem small.

Single-skin yachts' sides almost all open up when lying in harbour, unless glued splines are fitted between each plank. When the boat is not occupied I have a canvas curtain hung either right round, or on the south side if moored east and west. This is laced to the bulwarks or toe rail and hangs down to the waterline. When one is living on board it is desirable to swill the decks down at frequent intervals. This helps keep the boat cool and keeps

the ship's sides from getting too dry. White paint is cooler than colours. Red paint seems to stand better than blue.

Ventilation. Clearly ventilation must command extra attention. A windsail for harbour use is worthwhile. It need not be very long, say 5–10 ft. according to the yacht size. It can hang from the forestay and discharge down the hatch. Some form of vent which can be left open when going to windward in a wet seaway is of even more importance than normally. While normally one designs this of a size merely to keep a small flow of air to freshen things up, in the Mediterranean one wants a bigger flow to help cool down a space where several are sleeping and cooking. If there is no space on deck for the necessary size of baffle box, one can consider leading the inboard discharge to a point where any water coming in will drain direct to the bilge. For example the vent pipe from a cowl can be led down to just above a grating in the cabin sole, or just above the stem in the forward part of the fo'c'sle.

Slipping Intervals. Marine growth in warm sea waters is in general much faster than in more temperate climes, and one's plans therefore must include far more frequent slippings; particularly as with no tide, one cannot dry out alongside a wall for a scrub.

Gangplanks. One of the delightful features of Mediterranean yachting is that in harbours one can almost always anchor just off and draw the yacht's stern towards the jetty. Smaller yachts can draw their sterns in when necessary to step ashore, but larger yachts, say from 35-ft waterline and upwards generally carry a light folding gangplank. One end has a pair of small wheels and the other end is secured to the jetty or yacht, whichever is the higher. The length is from 7 to 11 ft. according to the size of the yacht. For lightness, the strength is in the relatively deep sectioned side members, which can be built up box section like a hollow spar; plugged for 6 in. at the ends. The two halves can hinge in the middle and be secured together when extended by 1-ft. long aluminium or galvanised steel straps running along the outside of each member at the join.

In another design the side members are continuous and joined together by slats a few inches apart. Each slat is attached to the side member by a single bolt and washer so that it can pivot. To fold, the side members are brought together, the slats swinging to an acute angle, like a parallel rule (when erected a portable block or frame is bolted between the ends of each side member). One then has a long thin affair to stow instead of a broad one. This design appears suited to aluminium alloy construction.

In some cases portable wire bracing is arranged under the gangway to enable this to be more lightly constructed. A strut is erected under the centre of each side member and functions like a jumper strut on a mast. In practice these appear to be somewhat of a problem, fouling the jetty or ship's side unless distance is very well kept, and I do not recommend these.

Two portable stanchions and a cotton rope finish the job off. These, on one side of the gangplank only, seem to me adequate, and this arrangement facilitates carrying gear and stores over the gangway, compared with a line each side of the plank.

An awning for the Mediterranean is a 'must' for harbour use. All that is needed is a rectangular strip of canvas laid fore and aft over the main boom, the boom slightly topped up in the case of a small yacht. If the boat is a small one, then it is an advantage to have the gooseneck on a slide. At each end of the awning is an aluminium tube in the hem as a stretcher, and it is drawn quite taut by hemp guys from each end of the tubes running forward and aft to deck level. If there is accommodation forward of the mast, another smaller awning can be triced to the forestay, with a hole in it for the windsail if necessary. These awnings roll up into a very small space. The width should be the beam of the boat, and the awning can be canted to 'face the south' as necessary.

Mediterranean Sun. Finally a word about clothing. Whereas wet and cold are the public enemies number two and three in the North Atlantic, so is old Sol in the Mediterranean. Even if crewmen are hardened, sun has a tiring sapping effect on crews. So when the sun is beating down, good shady hats, covered bodies, and sun glasses should be the order of the day.

A tanin-containing anti-sun lotion is generally most effective, preferably rubbed in beforehand. And don't forget that sun burns through light clothing.

Diet. In the Mediterranean summer cooking heats up the boat, particularly if it is a small one, and I never cook except in bad weather or in the cool of the late evening or early morning. In spite of its weight an ice-box is worth its place in the boat as a morale-raiser. A small ice-box will keep the butter from liquefying, keep salads appetising, and cold meats edible. If you can trust the source of the ice it is more economical of weight to break up bits of ice to put in the drinking water rather than to attempt to keep bottles of water cold. Ice can be obtained virtually everywhere, even in quite small ports. Very small yachts can use several large Thermos jars.

Refrigerators. Refrigerators of the absorption type (Electrolux, etc.) will only work if they are placed in a draughty place—very difficult to find below unless it is in a gangway. And they must be gimballed if they are to work at sea. In really hot weather the temperature will be marginal for this type, and one rarely has the amps to run a compressor type. If it is paraffin-fired the difficulty of keeping it sufficiently clean will beat you some of the time anyway. Bottled gas firing is more efficient.

Fuels. Bottled gas is readily obtainable in Italy or France, Algeria, and Malta, subject of course to the inevitable complication of differing types of bottles. It is much less easy in Spain and Greece and some other places. Paraffin (kerosine) is generally obtainable but often dirty and of poor quality. It can be improved for use in stoves and engines by well mixing in a small proportion—5 to 20 per cent as necessary—of petrol. Petrol is readily obtainable; is reasonable in price at Gibraltar and Malta and dear in most other places. Diesel oil is generally easily had also, but variable in cleanliness. (Make sure you get the light sort—'gas oil'—rather than the heavy dark oil, which is used in motor ships.) An additional fine filter should be fitted in the supply line; in addition to that supplied by the engine makers.

28

JUNIOR OFFSHORE GROUP RACING

In the early years of the Royal Ocean Racing Club the low limit of size of yachts eligible was varied according to the length and difficulty of the course. For many years the low limit of the Fastnet was 35-ft. waterline and for shorter races 24 or 25 ft. During the thirties as ocean racer design developed, the craft naturally became more expensive. Then the cost of labour and materials rose sharply as a result of the Second World War, and it became clear to me that if the sport were to prosper and expand we had to exploit the smaller and less expensive craft.

The Trend of the Small Racer. After the Second World War the low limit of the Fastnet Race was reduced to $27\frac{1}{2}$ ft. of rating, that is to say a boat of between 29- and 35-ft. waterline, according to type. In 1950 we staged a Trans-Atlantic race for boats of 24-ft. waterline and above. Three of the five entrants were in fact between 24 and 26 ft. in the water; but for the lowering of the limit there probably would have been no race. In the event, it was a great tussle. The three small boats covered the course from Bermuda to Plymouth in twenty-one days, arriving within 3 hrs. of one another, to take the first three places on corrected time. The winner was Adlard Coles in the Reimers designed canoe-sterned sloop *Cohoe I*. It is interesting to note that all these three boats were less on the waterline than the *beam* of the 1905 Trans-Atlantic winner.

It was not until 1953 that the Fastnet was thrown open to Class III, that is to say, to boats of 19-ft. rating. And as it happened in that year it was won by *Favona*, a new 24-ft. waterliner, of $21\frac{1}{2}$ ft. rating. This boat had just been completed by Aero Marine of Emsworth to designs by Robert Clark, for Sir Michael Newton. The design is, incidentally, an interesting example of the logical development of what has come to be thought of as the normal type of ocean racer.

And so with the march of time we find ourselves doing much the same races in smaller and smaller boats, reduction in size being matched by the steady development in design of hull, rig and equipment.

Formation of the Junior Offshore Group. Meanwhile in 1950 we had formed the J.O.G. to develop smaller fast cruisers and to race offshore yachts of between 16- and 20-ft. waterline. At that time it was expected that the Royal Ocean Racing Club would initiate a class for boats of over 20 ft. and under 24 ft. on the water. Later, when this did not occur, this range of racers also was taken under the group's wing and named 'J.O.G. Class IV', while the original boats of between 16 and 20 ft. were called 'J.O.G. Class V'. These numbers follow in sequence from the R.O.R.C. Classes I, II, and III which cover ocean racers of from 70 to 19 ft. rating, subject to a minimum waterline of 24 ft.

A few years later the M.O.R.C. (Midget Ocean Racing Club) was formed in the U.S.A. It operates almost exactly on J.O.G. lines, on both the east and west coasts of the United States.

The races given by the J.O.G., seven, eight, or nine a year, vary in length from 40 to 230 miles. The programme is specially designed so that every race, except the August Holiday races, can be achieved between Friday evening office closing and 09.00 Monday office opening. The starts are mostly out of Portsmouth. Then towards the end of Cowes Week the J.O.G. fleet heads west. The principal event, is sometimes round the Eddystone—a famous lighthouse well offshore near Plymouth—but more generally from the Solent to Dartmouth, via the Cherbourg mark; followed later by a race to the Channel Islands. In 1964 the Scottish branch of the J.O.G. was formed and since then has operated successfully out of the Clyde.

Safety Rules. J.O.G.'s first business as a club was to lay down a code of special safety limitations for Class V. These are shown in full in Appendix XIII. The principal requirement for Class V is that a minimum stability figure should be achieved. The factors in the stability formula include beam to length ratio, the freeboard, the draught, and the ballast ratio. The second rule calls for minimum buoyancy in the yacht. The third rule, again an important one, lays down the maximum allowable volume of the watertight cockpit, which is related to the approximate volume of the hull above water. Finally the area of the companionway is limited to 3 sq. ft. and this opening must be 3 in. above deck level. These 'rules' were subsequently modified to become 'recommendations'.

There are other requirements, which a normally well-built boat will automatically meet. A list of the compulsory equipment is included in the Appendix.

The rule of measurement for rating now follows that of the R.O.R.C. Spinnakers are now used; or any bona fide headsail properly tacked down may be boomed out to weather by a spar of any length desired. There are also bonuses for carrying a 'hard' (non-collapsible) dinghy.

The 'office' of the J.O.G. is effectively Richard Hood's residence at Bursledon, near Southampton. The latest information and branch secretary's addresses (which change) can be verified by Richard Hood, the J.O.G.'s Secretary.

Historical. In the autumn of 1949 Patrick Ellam had sent me particulars of his big open canoe *Theta* together with the chart of the passages he had made during that summer—these included several crossings of the English Channel—proposing to me the formation of a club to race such canoes offshore. I replied that I was very keen in principle to encourage the racing of smaller boats offshore but that I envisaged the use of a different type of craft. I suggested some preliminary 'staff requirements' for such boats. I felt they should be capable of being hard sailed without being 'sat out'; that is, naturally stable; that they should be fitted with weather-proof accommodation capable of housing the crew; that the deck, cockpit, and hatches should be sea-tight. I felt that the cabin should enable simple hot meals to be cooked and have a small chart board or table suitable for plotting.

THE BUILDING OF *SOPRANINO*

Nothing daunted, Patrick commissioned Laurent Giles & Partners to design him a boat which would fulfil these requirements but still as far as possible retain canoe characteristics. Thus was *Sopranino* born, a remarkable boat with a very talented skipper. Only 17 ft. 6 in. waterline and 19 ft. 8 in. overall and displacing a little over $\frac{1}{2}$ ton, she felt like an overgrown dinghy to sail. With her small beam of 5 ft. 4 in. and a relatively large sail area she sailed with a big angle of heel. I had in the design stage advised a little more beam, but very naturally with the *Theta* background in mind, Patrick was keen to retain something of the charm of the canoe, and there is no doubt that his faith in her was not misplaced.

Soon after completion in 1950 she sailed, *hors concours*, with the racers from Plymouth for Santander in Spain. We had rather a beastly little turn to windward in a stiff lop to Ushant and I in *Myth* remember saying that it must put paid to Patrick's chances of making a good passage, and what rotten luck. However, less than 24 hrs. after the last of the ocean racing fleet had tied up in Santander *Sopranino* came in. And within a few minutes Patrick emerged from his dog kennel-sized cabin clad in immaculate *tenue de yachting*, with nicely creased white flannels; and wearing a monocle to boot.

The story of her splendid voyages, totalling some 10,000 miles and ending in New York, is very well told in detail by Patrick Ellam and Colin Mudie in their book *Sopranino*, published in England by Rupert Hart-Davis and in America by W. W. Norton.

Details of 'Sopranino'. Sopranino is clinker built, of only $\frac{3}{8}$ in. mahogany, with small steamed oak frames at 4-in. centres, strengthened by ply bulkheads. A mild steel fin carries the lead bulb of ballast, these together weighing 600 lb. The bare hull weighs 430 lb. The separate rudder is mounted on a skeg.

She is probably too narrow to accommodate quarter berths; at any rate the two bunks are forward. A chart table and galley opposite are abreast the companionway hatch, which as might be expected is the only place below where there is just sitting headroom for one person. Ozanote blocks were used to make the boat unsinkable, stowed in all available spare spaces.

Her drawings are shown in Diagram 87.

The racing rig is a tall masthead cutter, of miniature *Myth* type, involving a 27-ft. mast. For her Atlantic passage she had a 21-ft. stick with a single spreader and a sloop sail plan. The cruising mainsail was cut with a gore, like our trysail in the *Myth*; the gore resembling that of a headsail. Twin jibs, cut high in the foot, were set on twin forestays as running sails.

Self-steering Gear. The twin booms were pivoted 6 ft. up the mast, the after guys being led in the usual way to the tiller for self-steering. The booms were set between 5° and 10° forward. The single fore-guy runs from one boom end to the other through a block at the stem head, and then down the second boom to a cleat near the heel. A line limited the tiller travel. In addition a running line round some cleats, connected to the tiller by stout shock (elastic) cords, acted as a damper.

Braine gear was fitted for self steering on the reach. The pull of the main sheet, on a quadrant fitted abaft the rudder head, balances the weather

Phantom. Camper and Nicholson's Class 1 ocean racer; a yacht that proved very successful in the earlier races of 1968.

Sir Francis Chichester's arrival in Sydney. Wearing her full suit of sails in a fair breeze, Gipsy Moth IV beats up the coast of New South Wales at $7\frac{1}{2}$ knots.

The modified Chinese balance lug rig of Galway Blazer II.

Pacha. This very advanced Class I ocean racer was designed and launched by Camper and Nicholson from its Southampton yard in April 1969 for Monsieur Francois Bouygues. Dimensions: *loa:* 54 ft. 5 in.; *lwl:* 40 ft.; *beam:* 14 ft. 5 in.; *draught:* 8 ft. 5 in.; displacement about $13\frac{1}{2}$ tons. Sloop rig. R.O.R.C. rating: $35\frac{1}{2}$ ft. This very light displacement aluminium built racer is extremely cut away in underwater profile, having a very small central keel well separated from the rudder which is well aft. Her accommodation is almost a replica of *Oryx*'s except that owing to the light displacement the engine is in the middle of the saloon and the case can be used as a table.

Crusade. Built by W. A. Souter at Cowes, to design by Alan Gurney, she was launched in May 1969 for Sir Max Aitken. Dimensions: *loa:* 62 ft.; *lwl:* 47 ft. 1 in.; *beam:* 15 ft. 4 in.; *draught:* 8 ft. 6 in.; displacement about $18\frac{1}{2}$ tons. The cutter rig is reminiscent of the rig which we gave Sir Max's previous Class 1 yacht *Outlaw*, in 1963; except that she has a removable forestay in case she is used as a sloop. The construction is generally similar to that of *Outlaw* with laminated centre line, beams and principal timbers and cold moulded skin.

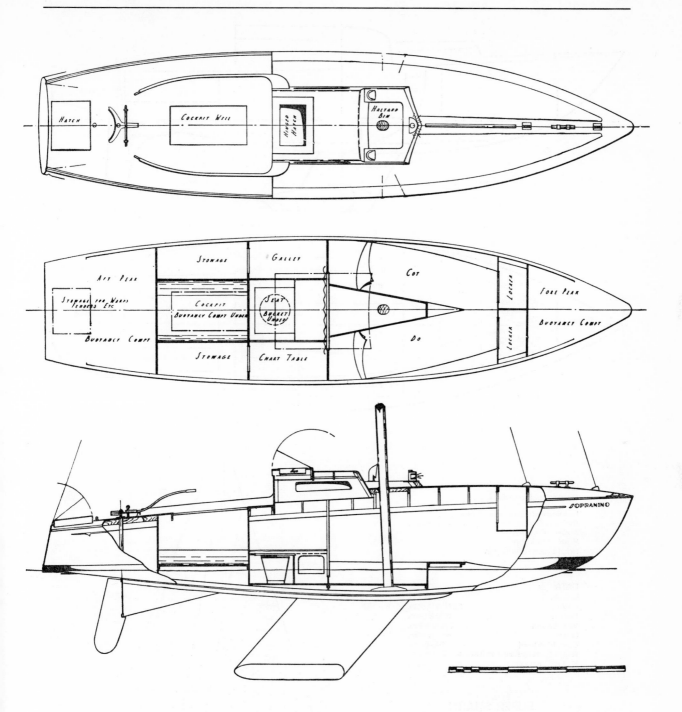

Diagram 87.

Sopranino, the forerunner of the Junior Offshore Group; made the crossing of the Atlantic in 1952. She was designed by Laurent Giles and Partners for Patrick Ellam, and was built by Wootten's at Cookham Dean. Dimensions:—*L.O.A.*: 19 ft. 8 in.; *L.W.L.*: 17 ft. 6 in.; *Beam*: 5 ft. 4 in.; *Draft*: 3 ft. 8½ in.

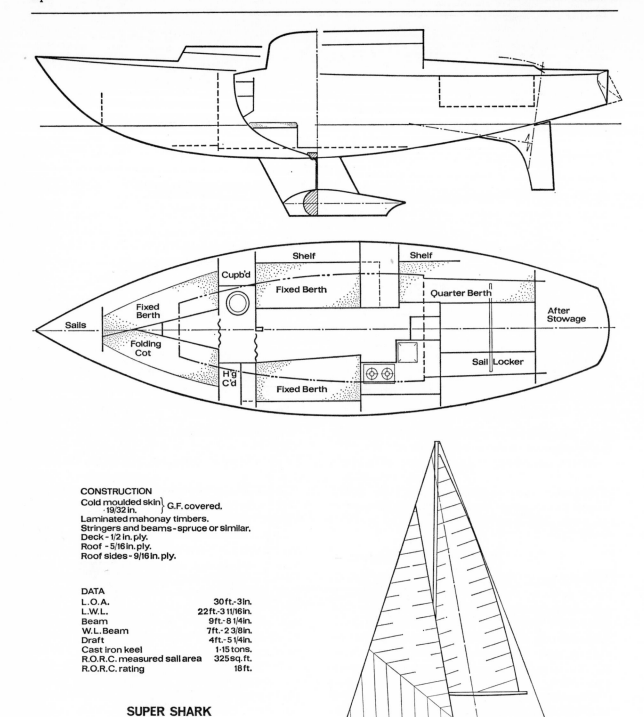

CONSTRUCTION
Cold moulded skin ⎫ G.F. covered.
·19/32 in. ⎭
Laminated mahonay timbers.
Stringers and beams - spruce or similar.
Deck - 1/2 in. ply.
Roof - 5/16 in. ply.
Roof sides - 9/16 in. ply.

DATA
L.O.A.   30 ft.-3 in.
L.W.L.   22 ft.-3 11/16 in.
Beam   9 ft.- 8 1/4 in.
W.L. Beam   7 ft.- 2 3/8 in.
Draft   4 ft.- 5 1/4 in.
Cast iron keel   1·15 tons.
R.O.R.C. measured sail area   325 sq. ft.
R.O.R.C. rating   18 ft.

SUPER SHARK

Design by Francois Sergent
64 Rue St. Sabin
Paris (II)

Diagram 88.

Super Shark—a modern very light-displacement French design.
Dimensions:—*L.O.A.*: 30 ft. 3 in.; *L.W.L.*: 22 ft. $3\frac{1}{16}$ in.; *Beam*: 2 ft. $8\frac{1}{4}$ in.; *Draft*: 4 ft. $5\frac{1}{4}$ in.

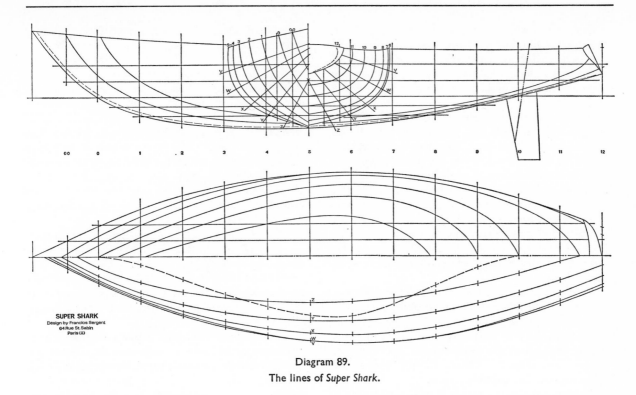

SUPER SHARK
Design by Francios Sergent
64 Rue St.Sabin
Paris (II)

Diagram 89.
The lines of *Super Shark*.

helm. The position of attachment on the quadrant can be adjusted. A damper is also fitted.

What a fascinating subject this must have been; more or less suddenly to be faced with the problem of designing and building an ocean racer-cruiser several times smaller than any built previously!

LARGER CLASS V BOATS

Sopranino represents the minimum size of J.O.G. racer. Although experience proved her to be fully adequate to the stresses and strains at sea, her light build made her somewhat vulnerable in harbour. And strangely enough, it was in harbour once again that the space below, with room for only one to sit up, proved somewhat less than most would accept, even among the enthusiasts.

The extra space and comfort that can be achieved in a slightly larger boat of say 7 ft. in the beam and 20 ft. on the water, is enormous. She involves about double the amount of material, but since approximately the same number of operations have to be gone through in building, the extra cost is less than might be expected. Class V boats have settled down to somewhere near these dimensions. In such a boat five people can be seated below; one can get in and out of the bunks without undue gymnastics, and access to stores and stored sails is easy.

'*Wista*'. The drawings in Diagram 92 show *Wista*, a boat designed by us and built to these dimensions by Aero Marine, Emsworth, Hants, for Mr. Nevill Tuffnel.

She is a boat of moderate displacement, with a 'level' wood keel; and a cast-iron ballast keel forming the whole of the centre 'skeg'. The rudder is mounted on a separate skeg, some way abaft this. We reckon that this layout enables one to produce a better boat for the money; a longer boat and a faster boat for the money than if she had the more conventional construction with a keel sloping down to the heel. But it is, as I see it, important not to confuse the issue by giving such a boat racing dinghy-like lines, because the latter are designed to be sailed upright; really upright.

She has a mahogany skin and a ply deck—I am sure that ply decks are much the strongest and best deck for small and moderate-sized craft. In fact in a few years, I am inclined to bet that the laid deck will be as dead as the dodo for this size of yacht if not for most. There are three berths. At sea the forward bunk will not be needed and over the head of this is the chart table, incidentally a good big one, which is stowed forward in harbour.

The W.C. is of the bucket and Elsan type with a flap over the seat which forms the central perch for the navigator-cook. This boat is designed to be raced by a crew of three.

Probably most people would prefer a sloop rig on the score of simplicity. In this case the owner had chosen a cutter, which would probably have an advantage in light weather, carrying as it does the principal headsail higher up, though a sloop of the same area may be faster in a breeze and rate lower.

'Wista' at Sea. I chartered Wista from the owner for the 1954 season, and in her we did all the J.O.G. races of that year. However much trouble one takes with a design some are much happier in the result than others, and Wista was one of the happy ones. She carries her canvas very well, and gets to windward in a purposeful manner in almost any weather. For instance in winds Force 6–7 with a well rolled down main and two little headsails, jib, and staysail, each of 25 sq. ft., she will be quite fast to windward in a typical fresh south-westerly in the Channel.

That autumn we cruised among the Channel Islands and the adjacent French islands, and found that one had for cruising too all the essentials; and many were the jolly parties we had in her diminutive cabin. Later she was bought by Mrs. P. Balogh and won the Cowes–Dinard and many other races in her capable hands.

Thus I was able to satisfy myself concerning a thesis which I had propounded some time before; that provided one was prepared for some austerity at times one could have a proper season's ocean racing and cruising, and just as much fun as in a bigger boat, in a J.O.G. racer costing far less.

'Top Hat'. One of our contributions to the J.O.G. fleet was the design of the Top Hat— with (for a Labour member) a sports version The Cloth Cap. This is a 21-ft. waterline J.O.G. racer with four berths, in moulded ply construction, with a 50 per cent ballast ratio and 285 sq. ft. of sail.

Every few years I get a new urge to make myself a really small ocean racer. So in 1967 we designed and built Merle of Malham for the quarter ton cup— the 15-ft. R.O.R.C. rating cup. Her drawings are produced in Diagram 86. I perhaps overplayed the waterline length; to 21 ft. for a 15 ft. of rating. Anyway, transom sterned, with a displacement of 3 tons, she was a very fine little yacht in which one would be quite prepared to set off across the Atlantic without any special preparation. (This is one of the questions I ask myself when I do the sketch designs of a new small yacht.) In the capable hands of David Colquhoun she won two good races late in the season of 1967.

Turning to the more general questions in connection with the layout of J.O.G. Class V racers, it can be said that most of the points made elsewhere in connection with the design of the larger ocean racers still apply. But one or two fresh problems arise which are peculiar to the smaller craft.

SPECIAL REQUIREMENTS

Bearing-out Spars. A bearing-out spar is allowed for use to weather with the headsails, and no limit is set to the length. To boom out effectively a large genoa (50 per cent overlap) set on a stay, the spar needs to be 160 per cent of the length of the foot of the fore-triangle. Wista has a folding spar to facilitate stowage. No guys are needed; the weather sheet forms an afterbrace and the lee sheet, led round the mooring cleat or bits on the foredeck, steadies the spar in seaway.

Crew Weight and Trim. Then there is the problem of crew weight, which in J.O.G. racing is much larger in proportion to the displacement. The object here, as I see it, should be to lay out the boat so that whether the crew are mostly turned in or mostly in the cockpit the trim shall not be largely disturbed.

Taking Wista, because her plans are shown here, with a crew of three we will sometimes have one on deck and occasionally three. By having the cockpit fairly well into the boat, a thing which is facilitated by the layout shown, and the only sleeping billets at sea in the quarter berths, it does not alter the trim much when a man leaves his bunk for the deck. In these berths the weather berth man is further outboard than someone sitting on the weather side deck. On a long leg on the wind the watch below, if one hand only is involved, must be turned in on that side. Particularly so as the third man will probably be mostly in the companion hatch. Even a hand seated on the throne is well abaft the mast.

Windage on deck becomes important in smaller craft, and in Wista the cockpit seats are below the deck level.

Reverse Sheer. For J.O.G. boats reverse sheer has become very popular; deservedly so, because it gives that bit extra of headroom over the bunks and over the chart table and galley. And also because it helps keep the boat dry going to windward. A further advantage is that it generally produces a much stronger boat in those cases where it enables the coachroof to be shortened, because of the extra room generally, in the hull.

Fore Hatches and Ventilators. In English waters I think a J.O.G. boat should not need a fore hatch. A waterproof ventilator forward is in any case compulsory. In Tiger V, 20-ft. waterline and in Tiger IV, 22 ft. 3 in. on the water, also in the R.N.S.A. 'Twenty-Fours' the 'false hawse pipes' admit the air. These do not look unsightly and the extra windage and deck clutter of a box is eliminated. The lack of a forehatch reduces building cost, eliminates a source of leakage, and the foredeck is clearer for working and stronger. For hotter climates, a hatch forward may be desirable.

Accommodation. If the accommodation is fitted out in best yacht style, with a full complement of lockers, drawers, cupboards, sideboards, and the like, the cost of this equipment will be out of proportion to the rest of the boat. Though these fittings are smaller than in, say, a R.O.R.C. racer, the labour of making them may well be as great, and in certain cases greater where access is awkward.

As one of the main reasons for the existence of the Junior Offshore Group is to reduce the overall costs, I shall frame my remarks concerning accommodation on the assumption that we are planning to provide for all essential requirements at the minimum of expense, and to some extent regardless of any need to provide an interior with a stereotyped appearance. For those who are prepared to spend a little more, it is always easy to add to the minimum, either in the design stage or later.

Berths and Upholstery. I would say first arrange for decent berths. For J.O.G. boats I prefer canvas bottomed bunks, over which a really thin mattress is adequate—$\frac{3}{4}$ in. of sponge rubber is very comfortable and saves a lot of height (sitting head room), weight, and expense—compared to the normal rubber foam mattress on a hard bunk bottom.

At a pinch an extra folded army blanket serves quite well in place of a mattress and costs only a few shillings. In the case of bunks which will be used at sea, I use triangular canvas lee boards, which trice up to the deck above. These need only be long enough fore and aft to take one's shoulder and thigh. The canvas must be doubled in way of the eye at the apex of the triangle, and the cleat above must be accessible from inside the bunk. Roll-up curtains over the quarter berths keep out the drops, and these can be made in plastic material, which looks fresh and nice in a cabin, the after lower corner being secured taut by a lanyard when the curtain is down.

Any form of fixed upholstery is expensive. It is better to have four or five loose cushions covered in some gay-coloured material; for choice a single colour and not a patterned job. These look homely in harbour and can be used as pillows at night or at sea.

Bilge Stringers and Bulkheads. I suggest every endeavour in the earliest design stage should be made to locate hull members so that they can serve a dual purpose; as regards accommodation as well as their primary purpose of contributing to the strength of the structure, or vice versa. A bilge stringer can often be run at the correct height for lacing the bunk bottoms direct on to this, the edges being eased to avoid cutting the lanyards. In addition the basic accommodation members, even if not strength members, should be thought out in advance. For instance by making the width of the cockpit well the same as the width between the bunks, and between the chart table and galley, it is often possible to run two fore and aft members right the length of the middle half of the boat. These will be about 2 ft. apart, in the centre, and perhaps turning towards one another at each end of the craft. If these are put in first with the partial bulkheads or necessary bearers or struts, the rest of the accommodation is quickly built up.

Quite a slight ply bulkhead on one side of a galley, or perhaps forming a hanging space, will contribute to the stiffness of the section if it is battened and well fastened to a timber. Multiple wood screws are allowable for this purpose; but keep them quite small to avoid weakening the timber.

Chart Table. Next the chart table, or more accurately the plotting board. If the top is made of $\frac{1}{2}$-in. ply and forms a box only 1 or $1\frac{1}{2}$ in. deep, open at one edge, then spare charts can be nicely stowed. On the bulkhead battens can hold the parallel rule and the few books that are needed. Some vertical holes in a wood chock are all that is required to house the pencils, divider and so on.

Stowage of Personal Gear. For the stowage of clothes I recommend a rack over the extreme foot of each berth for a kit bag. In the case of quarter berths, all that is needed are three or four slats about 13 in. clear of the bunk or a little more if room above allows. In addition I would provide, nearer the heads of the bunks, nets on the ship's side, the lower edge secured to battens on the timbers, and the upper edge and sides supported by a light shock cord, secured at its ends, and hooking up in the middle if necessary. Light laths may be fitted behind the nets, horizontally across the timbers, to keep sweaters and caps and so on off the ship's side. Alternatively smaller nets can be set up on an extendable spring curtain rail.

If one does not like the look of nets set up in this way, one can have the top edge on a rail; an aluminium tube will do nicely, running to standard ironmonger's plated brackets. Shore-going clothes are probably best put in one or two small suitcases in the fore peak or after peak. Often it is feasible to share a case. The cases can be put in light rubber or plastic bags. The lightest and cheapest form of plastic bag can be obtained from Translantic Plastics, 53 Fulham High Street, London, s.w.6, who make them in many sizes.

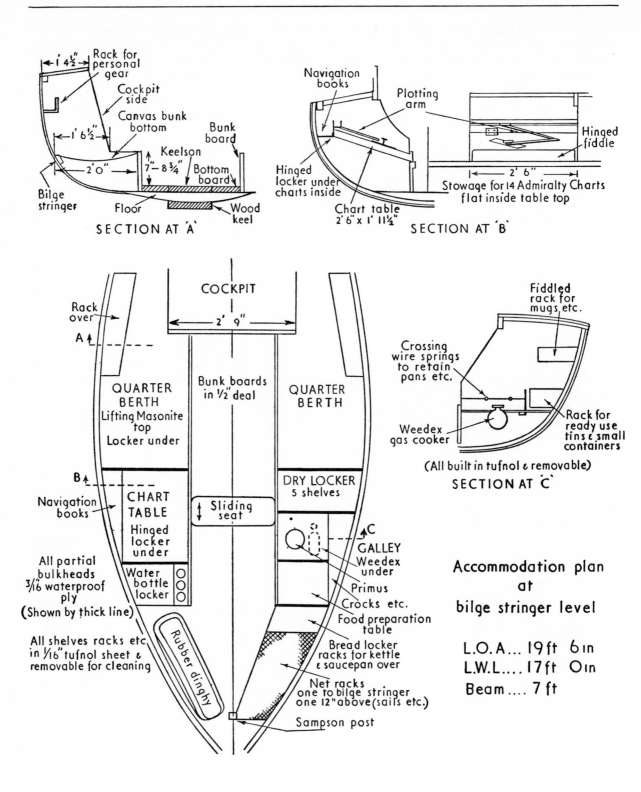

SECTION AT 'A'

Rack for personal gear
Cockpit side
Canvas bunk bottom
Bunk board
Keelson
Bottom board
Bilge stringer
Floor
Wood keel
$1'4\frac{1}{2}''$
$1'6\frac{1}{2}''$
$2'0''$
$7''-8\frac{3}{4}''$

SECTION AT 'B'

Navigation books
Plotting arm
Hinged fiddle
Hinged locker under charts inside
Chart table $2'6'' \times 1'11\frac{1}{2}''$
$2'6''$
Stowage for 14 Admiralty Charts flat inside table top

COCKPIT
$2'9''$
Rack over
Bunk boards in $\frac{1}{2}''$ deal
QUARTER BERTH
Lifting Masonite top Locker under
QUARTER BERTH
DRY LOCKER 5 shelves
Navigation books
CHART TABLE
Hinged locker under
Sliding seat
GALLEY
Weedex under
Primus
Crocks etc.
Food preparation table
Water bottle locker
Bread locker racks for kettle & saucepan over
All partial bulkheads $\frac{3}{16}$ waterproof ply (Shown by thick line)
Rubber dinghy
Net racks one to bilge stringer one 12" above (sails etc.)
All shelves racks etc. in $\frac{1}{16}''$ tufnol sheet & removable for cleaning
Sampson post

Fiddled rack for mugs, etc.
Crossing wire springs to retain pans etc.
Weedex gas cooker
Rack for ready use tins & small containers
(All built in tufnol & removable)
SECTION AT 'C'

Accommodation plan at bilge stringer level

L.O.A... 19ft 6in
L.W.L.... 17ft 0in
Beam.... 7 ft

Diagram 90.
The layout of a 17 ft. L.W.L. J.O.G. racer *Paso Doble* built by Aero Marine for Mr. George Tuck and Mr. Desmond Hanon. Fittings designed by the owners.

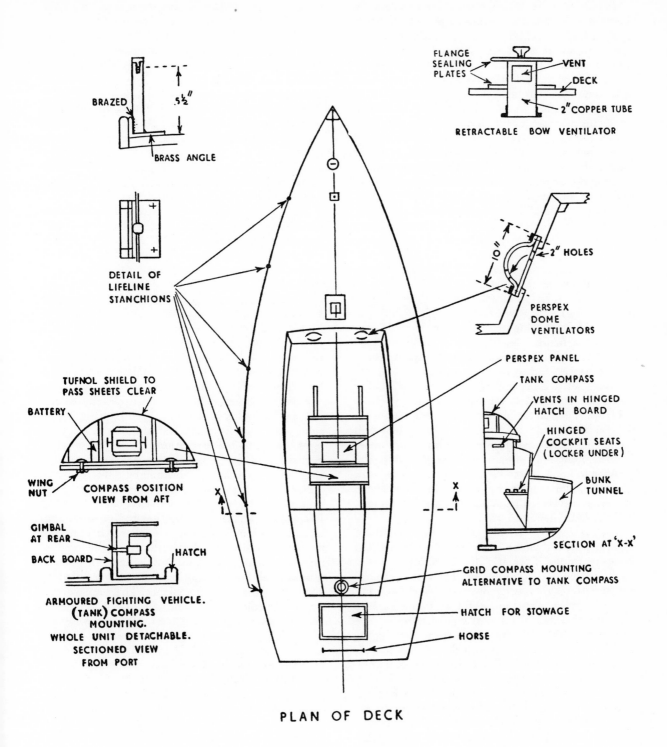

Diagram 91.
Plan of deck of J.O.G. racer *Paso Doble*, and details of compass fitments and bow ventilator.

Oilskin Stowage. When one comes to Class IV boats it is sometimes feasible to provide hanging spaces, both for oilskins and separately for shore-going clothes. It is not necessary to have a door to the cuboard. A dry space between two light ply or plastic board and a few hooks will serve well, with a batten to prevent them swinging inboard.

In the smallest boats it is necessary to have a sea-going stowage for oilskins. Generally they cannot be hung up, but must be stuffed into some small space, perhaps under the quarter berths, or better under the cockpit, on a light rack to keep them clear of the bilge. Fortunately modern plastic 'skins do not go so tacky.

Galleys for Small Cruisers. The J.O.G. rules require that a galley capable of being operated at sea shall be provided. With so little space available, before laying out the galley, it is advisable to purchase the plates, mugs, kettle, containers, and pans, so that the racks can be made to suit.

Water Stowage. In small yachts where two or three comprise the whole crew, there is a good deal to be said for stowing one's water in portable containers, particularly in the case of shallow bilged boats. The containers can readily be taken ashore to the nearest tap to be filled and they generally produce better water than a fixed water tank, being easier to clean and to ventilate when the yacht is laid up. They avoid the need for manufacturing special tanks, and for fitting a pipe system and pump. *Sopranino* carried 100 quart aluminium water bottles, filling only as many as were needed for the passage in hand. These measured 1 ft. long by 4 in. diameter, and so were easy to stow in odd corners. An alternative used in *Wista* is plastic containers, equally light and clean.

Internal Lighting. In the case of lighting, if an engine with a dynamo is not fitted we can again simplify things if we use dry batteries in place of the more usual accumulator. The cost of replacing batteries is not much more than that of charging a wet battery, and the weight and first cost of wiring and triennial renewal cost of batteries are eliminated. The chart table needs the most light, and in *Wista* we use two 6 volt dry battery lamps. The batteries are $2\frac{1}{2} \times 2\frac{1}{2} \times 4\frac{1}{4}$ in.; they are manufactured by Messrs. Ever Ready, Ltd., Holloway, London, N.7. The lamps were made up in neat wood containers with proper tumbler switches. For cabin lighting of lower power, and for use over a bunk head or galley, Messrs. Pifco of Watling Street, Manchester 4, market a reasonably priced good-looking self-contained light. A wood base should be fitted to make it sea-water drip proof.

For lighting odd corners such as the forepeak, one can use an ordinary pedal cycle battery lamp on a bracket, costing five bob complete. The Ever Ready type is more drip proof than most.

Where everything is close together and the helmsman is not far from the companionway it is particularly important to fit the lights where they will not dazzle him. That is to say in general they should shine forward, and surfaces which face him should not be too light in colour, if the lamp light falls directly on them. Even though lamps below will only intermittently be used, the night blindness engendered may last some time. A dry battery navigation light on the stem head—a combined lantern—is convenient and eliminates a fruitful source of wiring or fuse-blowing trouble.

Small Sail Plans. Almost everything I have written elsewhere concerning the design of rigs and sails appears to apply equally to J.O.G. boats, in fact remarkably so. There are, however, two points to note; that when it starts to blow the reduction in sail area will generally have to be relatively larger and made sooner. This partly because in small boats the ratio of sail area to displacement is much higher, and needs to be because of the higher ratio of wetted surface to displacement. But stability on the other hand bears a closer relation to displacement. And partly also because small yachts rarely have as powerful a ballast ratio.

Levers and Winches. Now as to deck equipment, Messrs. Reynolds of Tyseley, Birmingham, make some very nice little tapered aluminium alloy or light steel life-line stanchions. Small reasonably priced levers for Class V boats are marketed by Brookes & Adams Ltd., Birmingham 19.

For Class IV sloops the best levers are the $1\frac{1}{4}$ in. type made by the Lewmar Co. of Emsworth, Hampshire. For the smallest headsails a snubbing winch, that is a drum with a single ratchet and no handle, is indicated. They are also useful on the mast for sweating up a sail single handed, though not essential. For working headsails of over 80 sq. ft. a handled winch is a convenience. There are a great number on the market. The U.S.M.P. Company's E type, though not the cheapest, has the advantage of multiple pawls and reduced lost motion. Messrs. Simpson and Lawrence's Dragon size roller reefing gear is good. But nick the brass at the slots of the ring nuts, at the end of the worm, to secure them.

Hull Types. It is not possible in one chapter to cover fully the many types of yachts which have been drawn for J.O.G. racing, but a most interesting collection of designs was forthcoming as a result of the *Yachting World* 1952 J.O.G. design competition, and reproductions of the folders are available from that journal.

Handling. In boats of *Top Hat*'s and of *Wista*'s size and type where there is reasonable stability the

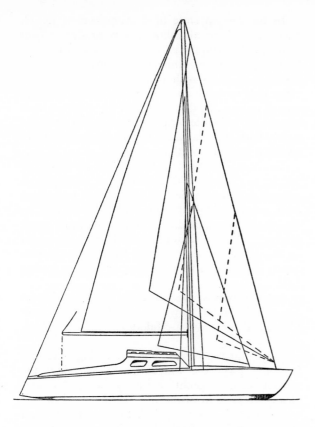

Diagram 92.

Tiger V *Wista*, designed and built at Emsworth by Aero Marine for Mr. Nevill Tuffnel. Dimensions:—*L.O.A.*: 24 ft.; *L.W L.*: 20 ft.; *Beam*: 7 ft.; *Sail Area*: mainsail 112·5 sq. ft., yankee 116 sq. ft., staysail 47 sq. ft.

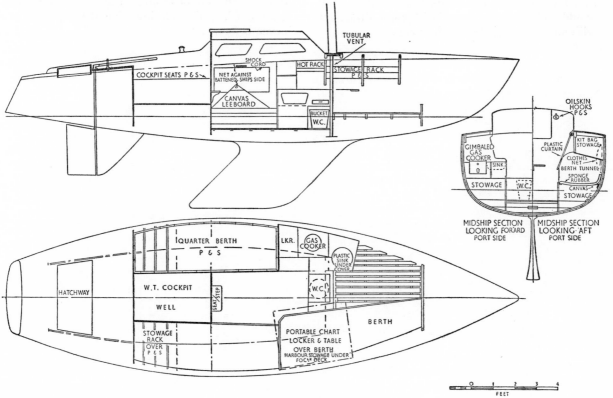

handling follows very much along the lines which we have indicated elsewhere in this book for larger craft. In fact in re-reading these chapters in the light of J.O.G. requirements, I came across no important differences.

In J.O.G. yachts which have less stability—though still enough for safety—an important difference may arise regarding sail changing. For perfect handling such boats will sometimes need a great number of sail changes and this may well prove too great a strain on a crew, particularly on a crew of two. According to the strength and endurance of your crew at the moment you will have to decide whether to undertake the particular sail change in question. Often slight decreases in wind strength cannot be ideally followed by an immediate increase in sail.

By the same token you may decide, on handing a sail, to leave it hanked on to its stay, with another sail set above it perhaps, and lashed down to the deck with sail tiers. These should normally be in place round a middle line mooring cleat, or handgrip, always ready for use. One puts up with the extra windage, so that it may be ready to hoist again, with the minimum of effort.

In other ways, it will be possible to save the crew; the man below, for instance. Often one can stand on, on the same tack, to save turning out the hand into the other weather berth, rather longer than would ordinarily be considered good drill, but without major prejudice to the result.

In the present state of development of J.O.G. racers I think the aim should be to produce a boat with simple equipment; to try to avoid numerous gadgets which sometimes breed unreliability and result in troubles with which small crews cannot cope, and in any case increase the initial cost and cost of upkeep. In this branch of the sport we have something valuable and we must guard it like a newly-born child against certain ailments, one of which is over-elaboration.

To those who plan to build their own craft, I would say consider the alternative of buying a proven design of basic hull (which can be had on hire purchase for half the completed cost) and do the deck; accommodation and equipment work yourself. Much disappointment can be saved in this way. And don't forget that a boat intelligently shared can be more fun, as well as costing half.

Top Hat bare or decked hulls can be had from Souter's Yard at Cowes, and Merle hulls from Construction Navals Malouines at St. Malo, France.

So we find the Junior Offshore racing—perhaps in some ways the toughest, and certainly the newest form of yacht racing—making slow and steady progress in Britain.

And what is quite certain is that as a result of all this the smallest of tabloid cruisers are getting a 'new look', and such intensive development as never before.

29

THE LATEST R.O.R.C. SAIL RULINGS

THE 'TON' CLASSES

A big gap was left in yacht racing when the international six metres, eights, and twelve metre classes died. Since the war the gap has been partly filled by R.O.R.C. rated yachts, racing on handicap, or more properly on time allowance, round the inshore courses. But there was a need for classes which could again race without time allowance; which would be equally suitable for R.O.R.C. or J.O.G. racing and real cruising. That would ensure not only a greater appeal for the classes and more building to them, but would mean that the yachts would command good second-hand prices. This in sharp contrast to the old metre classes where a year-old boat would often be sold for a third of its original cost or less.

THE CRUISER/RACERS

Shortly after the Second World War the International Yacht Racing Union made a gallant effort to fill exactly this gap with their 'Cruiser Racer' classes. This resulted in a successful class of cruiser racer eight metres on the Clyde, and very limited use in Scandinavia and France. Elsewhere the classes did not catch on at all. This was primarily because they did not do well enough in R.O.R.C. rating races, which by then included all the principal races in Cowes Week and other inshore regattas, as well as offshore events. A few, including two French Cruiser Racer Twelves are however still racing with the R.O.R.C. fleets.

When the famous One Ton Cup, previously for six metres, came up for reallocation a few years ago, the Commodore of the Cercle de la Voile de Paris (X.V.P.), Jean Peytel, consulted me. I plumped strongly for a series of one-rating races under a R.O.R.C. limit of 22 ft. and against some opposition we held to this. Three years of One Ton Cup racing has provided us with very keen competition and some advanced new boats. I urged at that time very strongly that the rules for cabin fittings and the like be tightened. The '8 Cruiser Racer' code was used but much more will need to be done in the future if useful boats are to survive the intense competition; that is to say preserve their ability to be practical and durable fast cruisers.

THE HALF TON

A year later, in the winter 1965–6 in consultation with yachtsmen from La Rochelle, we got the 'Half Ton' Class off the ground; for racing under an 18-ft. R.O.R.C. rating limit. As for the One Ton, the Coupe International was for a mixture of inshore and offshore racing. The first series were attended mostly by French entrants but at the time of writing Half Tonners are building in several countries, including Britain, where the Junior Offshore Group are in charge of selection. The J.O.G. have a special sub-committee to look after the interests of the Half Tonners and Quarter Tonners.

The Half Tonners are 'large J.O.G. boats' and a very good size of general purpose yacht; to race offshore in Class IV. They can be built for about half the cost of One Tonners and sleep up to five people. Cabin fittings and headroom are controlled.

TWO TONNERS

About the same time I managed to sell the one-rating idea to the Yacht Club Italiano in Genoa, and with the able help of Beppe Croce, the President of that hospitable club, they put on the first series of races for yachts of 28-ft. rating in September 1967. This rating enables one to build a yacht of 32- to 34-ft. waterline, which will accommodate a paid hand; or two at a pinch; a thing important to Mediterranean owners.

Chin Blu III, the first yacht to be built with this rating limit in mind was to our design for Pierre Fabre, and constructed in the excellent yard of Sangermani at Lavagna.

QUARTER TON

The latest development of one-rating yachts is a class to race under a 15-ft. R.O.R.C. limit. That is to say in J.O.G. Class V. The rules will follow the pattern of the other 'classes': minimum headroom over a minimum area and other interior rules to keep the yachts habitable and useful; compliance with J.O.G. standard safety rules; and the races a mixture of inshore and offshore events.

The class was stimulated by a very successful design competition put on by the French Yachting Journal, *Cahiers du Yachting*.

I had for some time felt that Class V of J.O.G.—originally the strongest end of the J.O.G. racing—was being overshadowed by the larger Class IV yachts. So I decided to build a Quarter Tonner, *Merle of Malham*, which could be used also as a J.O.G. club yacht. Her plans are reproduced in Diagram 86 on page 240. At the time of writing she has completed very satisfactory trials and two sister ships are well advanced. They have four really good berths, a good galley, and a very good chart table.

THREE TONNERS

I have in hand a project for a 35-ft. rating class; to race in the Mediterranean in the first instance. If this comes to fruition we shall have a tidy pattern of classes; 35, 28, 22, 18, and 15 ft. in rating. You will notice that the gaps in rating come progressively less as the size decreases. The object is to cater for a good range of racing yachts without creating too great a multiplicity of classes; and remembering always that every yacht can be a potential offshore racer in R.O.R.C. or J.O.G. apart from any class racing which she may do.

We shall, however, need to watch much more carefully in the future the question of minimum equipment and cabin fittings. The classes based in the northern waters and the Atlantic have proved fairly ready to accede to this most necessary discipline, but things are less easy at present in the Mediterranean. But unless full codes are brought quickly into use the classes risk developing into skinned out freaks, and falling from grace as worthwhile long-term offshore yachts.

ONE TON CLASS YACHT AND R.O.R.C. DESIGN

Twenty-four yachts from eight nations were entered for the One Ton Cup races held in Denmark in 1966; only the second series of races held under the new conditions of 22-ft. R.O.R.C. rating. This was a very adequate tribute to the popularity of the underlying idea.

Already the design pattern for that series is beginning to emerge. The original series in 1965 brought together yachts of from 24- to 26-ft.

waterline. The second year they were mostly of between 26- and 27½-ft. waterline; with big beams and often heavier scantlings to permit the larger yachts to have enough sail area. In 1967 they are up to 30-ft. waterline!

Most of the rigs were masthead sloops. These proved useful when close tacking in avoiding the use of runner levers or tackles; this in spite of the larger area of headsail to be sheeted. When the R.O.R.C. rule is next rewritten mainsail area will have to be slightly less taxed (or fore triangle more taxed) to keep a proper balance; but the alteration must be modest to ensure that main masts are kept well into the boats. This is partly because of recent developments in spinnaker cutting and techniques, which have given fore triangle area extra importance.

As the R.O.R.C. rule is the one in question naturally these remarks refer in general to yachts built under this rule of measurement. It is simply the case that the rule has come under heaviest pressure in connection with the One Ton Cup races.

NEW MINOR SAIL CONSIDERATIONS

In 1967 R.O.R.C. mainsails fitted with shorter Cruising Club of America battens have an allowance of 2½ per cent added 'free' area or allowance. This is a sensible rule, avoiding the need to have different battens for the Bermuda and Buenos Aires–Rio Races, to those in regular R.O.R.C. use.

Masthead black bands could previously be 4 per cent of hoist of triangle plus 1 ft. below the masthead in a masthead rig. To come into line with the C.C.A. the 'plus 1 ft.' is now deleted; except under a slight penalty, to permit of the use of existing mainsails.

The existing light penalties on overlaps larger than 50 per cent 'J' allow the use of the modern C.C.A. sails, who's 'base' is measured at right angles to the stay and not horizontally. That is to say the U.S.A. headsails generally have an overlap of between 60 and 65 per cent, and the tax on this is very light. In fact sometimes I opt to use such overlaps in R.O.R.C. racing in the Mediterranean.

30

SINGLE-HANDED OFFSHORE RACING

The Vessel. Dealing first with single-hulled vessels, the fundamental requirements of a single-handed long-distance offshore yacht, which is to race without time allowance are, as I see them:

(*a*) She must have enough length and 'class' to give her the basic speed needed nowadays, to put her in the possibly-winning bracket.

(*b*) The fin, or ballast keel plus deadwood (plus skeg and rudder if so fitted) must not be too great in area (not to slow her in light weather) but must give her just sufficient directional stability to ensure steady steering under vane, under bad sea conditions.

(*c*) The displacement must be modest to enable her to be driven by a reasonable total sail area.

(*d*) This means that to get a good ballast ratio she requires very careful light construction; of minimum weight for sufficient strength.

(*e*) The hull lines should be specially drawn for ease of motion at sea; requiring that excess beam relative to displacement be avoided.

(*f*) The sail plan should be really special, firstly to ensure that no sail is too large for 'him' to have to delay unduly in rehoisting sail, secondly, arranged so that most conditions can be coped with, without unhanking sail, thirdly, that efficient large running sails are provided which the single man can readily handle.

Other desirable design features include:

(*g*) A dog house or observation post whence the situation can be assessed without going on deck.

(*h*) Very much more powerful sheet (and halyard) winches than would normally be fitted for the size of sail; the latter very carefully positioned in a smallish, well-protected cockpit.

(*i*) A main deck which is flush for ease of working and strength, with minimum weight and windage, and a very easy access main companionway hatch with good protection.

(*j*) More than usual care devoted to safe and easy access to the self-steering gear, and more than usual care to its controls, and the anti-chafe and anti-snarl arrangements.

(*k*) The whole of the single-handers accommodation, including the W.C., to be carefully design-ed and concentrated right aft, and every detail specially designed for easiest working by a near-exhausted man.

(*l*) A horizontal jack stay, or two in a larger yacht, with perhaps an extra one aft, to enable the crew to go the length of the deck with the minimum of unhooking of his safety harness.

(*m*) Specially powerful all round mast head light or lights, designed to indicate that the yacht, if not out of control, is unable to manoeuvre, no one being on deck. This in turn requiring powerful electric batteries and a reliable charging plant which will operate with the vessel occasionally heeled to at least 40 degrees.

Size of Yacht. Commenting in a little more detail on the 'requirements' which I have suggested, we come first to size. Maybe some day the principal prizes will be given for results on time allowance, based on the R.O.R.C. or a new international rule of rating. But in the case of the first three quadrennial Trans-Atlantic solo races the principal prize, the Observer Trophy; and the prizes for the placed yachts, have been open; first home wins without any time allowance. In 1964 and 1968 special prizes have been put up for smaller yachts on handicap. Thus in each race the largest, longest yacht has won. Writing early in 1968, before this year's race, there are likely to be at least six yachts with an overall length of around 55 ft.; four specially built and two close to standard hulls.

Single Hulls. Single hulls, among these yachts must be the favourites; and it may well be that we have not yet seen the limit of size for the solo races; that the next race may see larger vessels such as *Stormvogel* and converted 12-metres competing. On the other hand special conditions, extreme either way, could favour slightly smaller yachts, of between say 30- and 34-ft. waterline. A 30-ft. waterline with a large sail plan could win in predominantly light weather against larger vessels with roughly the same total sail area. Or a vessel of say 33-ft. waterline could possibly beat the big ones in very variable and squally, to bad weather; thanks to easier handling; with less tiring and frequent sail changes.

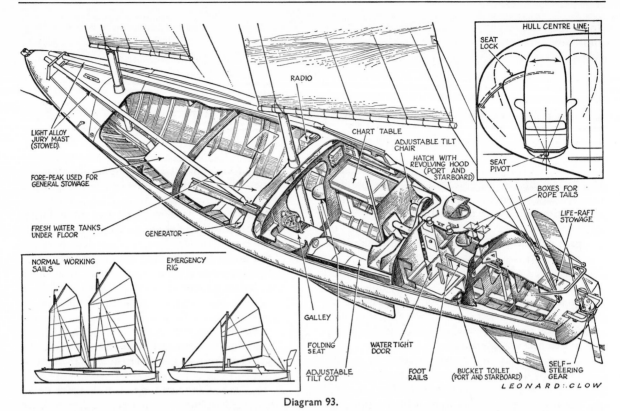

Diagram 93.

The junk-rigged *Galway Blazer II*, a very interesting boat, designed by Angus Primrose for Commander Bill King. The schooner, built by W. A. Souter in 1968, carries 522 sq. ft. of sail
Dimensions:—*L.O.A.*: 42 ft.; *L.W.L.*: 32 ft.; *Beam*: 10 ft. 6 in.; *Draft*: 6 ft.

Sail Plans. Enlarging on the item (*f*) above, we may note that the third condition, the provision of efficient large running sails presents perhaps the least easily solved problem. This is particularly so in the larger vessels; a large yacht will go quite fast to windward in moderate conditions in spite of being at the time appreciably under canvassed; but this is not the case down wind. This aspect should therefore have priority treatment.

The factor of safety of standing rigging, and particularly of mast fittings, needs special consideration. A newish ocean racing aluminium mast with standard type fittings is certainly okay for a Trans-Atlantic race; though clearly one has a critical survey when fitting out. However, if real world-girdling is in question then I like very much to increase the factors of safety; in effect to design specially, rather than to take, off the shelf, the excellent normal fittings made by our good aluminium spar makers. In some cases going one size up is sufficient. But a very hard look at the whole rig detail is desirable.

Gipsy Moth IV's rig after her 30,000-mile passage gets virtually a clean bill of health; everything was specially considered for world-girdling. *Lively Lady*'s mainmast, designed under economy con-ditions for the return Trans-Atlantic and general sailing, gave trouble on the round-the-world voyage. It had not been back to the makers for revision of the fittings in the light of the new task, and the complete renewal of the rigging.

The Ideal Rig for Single-handed Racing. For big ('maximum') yachts I tend to prefer the staysail schooner rig to any others for this purpose. I recommended this to Francis Chichester, but probably following on Eric Tabarly's success he went firm on a ketch rig. By a twist of fate Eric Tabarly asked me, after his first Trans-Atlantic win, what I preferred, and I told him a schooner, which indeed he chose for his next *Pen Duick*; which won him a Fastnet and a R.O.R.C. Championship; while Francis reverted to a ketch! Evidently the ketch is a perfectly good rig, and when one is converting a big single-masted vessel to a single-hander, this is an obvious choice. But one of the disadvantages of a ketch rig is that if one is to get a decent-sized worthwhile mizzen together with a biggish gap between the mizzen mast and the leech of the mainsail, one needs to have a fairly long counter which in some respects is less favourable to the fitting of self-steering gear.

For medium sized single-handed vessels which

can be driven by a sail area not requiring so much subdivision, I much prefer the cutter, rigged without runners like *Gipsy Moth III*, and provided with two tracks on the after side of the mast to enable a trysail to be kept always ready and hanked on.

Myth of Malham by chance fits pretty neatly into the requirements of a single-hander. She has a small displacement ($7 \cdot 6$ tons), on a fairly long waterline of $33\frac{1}{2}$ ft. She is relatively long on her ballast keel and deadwood, making her fundamentally a steady boat. She is nicely balanced on the helm which is important if the boat is to steer well under a vane. She has a very short overhang aft and a strong vertical transom, which makes for an ideal mounting for the self-steering gear. She has very little windage above deck, but quite sufficient accommodation, laid out, again by chance, almost ideally for a single-hander, with a well protected pilot berth, and just forward of that a good chart table one side and good galley on the other. She was conceived and built long before Blondie Hasler and a few other dedicated enthusiasts founded the modern sport of single-handed ocean racing. And therefore it is, as I say, largely a matter of chance that she fits so neatly into the frame. The reason was, partly, that being very short of money at the time I built her, I had to go in for a light boat in order to get the length and speed I was looking for. The Laurent Giles hull lines of 1946 are still today a pleasure to the eye.

'*Lively Lady*'. Although by no means, on paper, the ideal single-handed ocean racer, on account of her notable fast non-stop passage to Melbourne in 1967, and her subsequent successful rounding of the Horn, she is worthy of mention. Following work on her in 1962 she was further modified by us to a yawl/ketch in 1965.

Trans-Atlantic Races. At the time of writing we are coming up to within a few weeks of the start of the third single-handed Trans-Atlantic Race. As might be expected, the first race, in 1960, was patronised by a small fleet of widely varying type and size. It was won fairly comfortably by Francis Chichester in the Robert Clark designed *Gipsy Moth III*; a fairly heavy displacement boat of about 27-ft. waterline, which had been built for Francis Chichester by Messrs. Tyrrell of Arklow, Eire. She was rigged at this time as a conventional 80 per cent sloop. Colonel 'Blondie' Hasler came a very creditable second, considering the small size of his vessel; a modified Folkboat named *Jester*, and characterised by the junk rig.

There was no handicap in the Observer Trophy in 1960, and the order in which the first finished was:

Gipsy Moth III	Francis Chichester	40 days 12 hrs.
Jester	Blondie Hasler	48 days 12 hrs.
Cardinal Virtue	David Lewis	55 days 1 hr.
Eira	Val Howells	62 days 6 hrs.

Shortly after this race I rerigged *Gipsy Moth III* giving her a masthead cutter rig with low hoist staysail, having no runners. Francis found the yacht considerably improved for the special purpose of single-handed sailing; carrying less helm, having a small mainsail, and a more easily adjusted set of headsails; and giving the facility which the cutter rig affords in being able to drop one of the two sails and not to be bare headed when changing jibs. Between the 1960 and 1964 races Francis very enterprisingly sailed across the Atlantic on a solo cruise to New York, beating his previous time quite handsomely; in order, he said, to keep his hand in and to thoroughly test out the new rig.

The 1964 Race. When the fleet came to the line for the next single-handed Trans-Atlantic Race in Plymouth harbour, and heading this time not for New York, but for Newport, Rhode Island, the look of the fleet had already considerably changed. Still the principal prize was without handicap and clearly the larger boats were going to have the best of it. Short prices in the betting were being given obviously on Francis Chichester with his very superior bank balance of experience on his side, and on Eric Tabarly who had the new *Pen Duick II*, a yacht about 35-ft. waterline, of light displacement and ketch rigged. Built by the Chantier Navale Costantini at La Trinitè-sur-Mer, of plywood, she was a hard chined boat. Much the largest of the entries, and skippered by a younger and stronger man, she was really an obvious favourite. However, Eric Tabarly told me himself that he was nervous about his celestial navigation, and unsure of his self-steering gear. Francis Chichester was once again trusting to the slightly improved form of 'Miranda' steering. This was in effect a small reefable mizzen sail which lay head to wind and directly actuated the rudder. Having no servo effect it was not very sensitive. I sailed on board and noted that in practice the yacht steered a relatively zig-zag course. But as in previous passages it stuck the course and got the yacht across the Atlantic. Eric Tabarly was using what was virtually his own self-steering gear based, of course, once more on a vane. This gave him trouble and eventually broke down about two-thirds of the way across the Atlantic, which resulted in his having to steer the boat for as much of the time as possible from that moment onwards. The remarkably fast time which he made he attributed partly to having done this, and having succeeded in sticking out that part of the passage with the minimum of time below, to win by a handsome margin from Francis Chichester. He also took the handicap prize; finishing in the very fast actual time of 21 days 23 hrs.

Third home was Val Howells in *Akka*.

Fourth home was a newcomer to offshore racing in the person of Alec Rose in *Lively Lady*. He had bought her off the mud in Yarmouth, Isle of Wight. We altered the accommodation, built a dog house to be suitable for single-handed sailing and completely rerigged her for him with an aluminium mast incorporating the special whisker poles (bearing out spars for the big jibs); although different in detail on the same principal to those used in the rerigged *Gipsy Moth III*.

The later finishers in the order of their completing the course were:

Pen Duick II	Eric Tabarly	21 days 23 hrs.
Gipsy Moth III	Francis Chichester	22 days 18 hrs.
Akka	Val Howells	24 days 7 hrs.
Lively Lady	Alec Rose	25 days 4 hrs.
Jester	Blondie Hasler	27 days 9 hrs.

Rereading what I have written above at the proof stage, after the now famous 1968 race, I think my views and remarks have proved to be valid. The results of this great race were as follows:

1. *Sir Thomas Lipton*
2. *Voortrekker*
3. *Cheers*.
4. *Spirit of Cutty Sark*
5. *Golden Cockerel*
6. *Opus*
7. *Gancia Girl*
8. *Myth of Malham*
9. *Maxine*
10. *Maguelonne*

Commenting on the race one can only say that to the great amount of trouble and grief suffered by the multi-hulls there is the notable exception of the small boat *Cheers*. This was a magnificent feat by a relatively small vessel with a remarkable jockey aboard, who, by his own admission was lucky not to have been struck by any particularly vicious weather. I do not think it in any way invalidated the general conclusions that we have drawn.

PARTICULARS OF *GIPSY MOTH IV*

I am devoting quite a bit of this chapter to *Gipsy Moth IV* because she is one of the few British yachts designed completely and specially for single-handed racing; and of near maximum size. Several other fine yachts of near the same size are being entered for the present single-handed race, but most of them even the newly-built ones are slight adaptations of a standard hull, or of a standard ocean racing hull;

or again of a vessel designed as a compromise between an ocean racer and a single-handed racer. One's other excuse for devoting space to this yacht is that she made a very successful record-round-the-world single-handed passage.

The leading particulars of *Gipsy Moth IV* are as follows:

Designers: Illingworth & Primrose, North Street, Emsworth, Hampshire.

Builders: Camper & Nicholson Ltd., Gosport, Hampshire.

Length overall: 54 ft. Length waterline: 38 ft. 5 in.

Maximum beam: 10·5 ft. Draft: 7·75 ft.

Design displacement: 10·4 tons. Lead ballast: 3·75 tons.

Measured sail area per R.O.R.C. measurement: 854 sq. ft. plus 250 sq. ft. of mizzen staysail.

Area of special large genoas (running sails): 450 sq. ft. each.

Thames measurement: 18·5 tons.

The Design of 'Gipsy Moth IV'. The design of a single-handed ocean racer must, like any other ocean racer, be something of a compromise between the fastest boat possible of the size in question, and the most comfortable and easiest to handle boat of the same size. Clearly the whole design must in practice revolve around this very nicely balance compromise. I had hoped that I had made this point clear when I started the design of *Gipsy Moth IV*, to Francis Chichester, but reading his account of the voyage round the world it does seem clear that he had never really hoisted in the necessity for the compromise. Put in another way, it was obvious that unless we designed him a very fast boat of great length and without unnecessary wetted surface, it could never have the fundamental speed required to give it a good chance of achieving the passage target of 100 days from Plymouth to Sydney, New South Wales. It would have been very easy for us to have designed him a yacht with a very much longer keel and greater wetted surface and with more beam and more displacement which would have sailed more upright but would have been once again a much slower craft.

Designing the first large single-handed world-girdling racer was a matter of very great interest because one had no prototype to start from. In many ways the task was quite different to that of designing the ordinary ocean racer because ocean racers in general, be they built to the C.C.A. rating rule, or the R.O.R.C. rating rule, must be fast relative to their rating rather than fundamentally fast regardless of their rating. As we shall see, this in practice completely alters one's method of design procedure which of course was additionally complicated by the need to make the yacht suitable for single-crew operation.

We had done a sketch design of a light displacement yacht of shorter waterline length, which it would be possible to build fairly economically at Souter's shipyard in Cowes. This sketch design was made under a cover of the code name 'The New York Express', although at that time the round-the-world voyage was already under active consideration. But before this boat got beyond sketch design and rough quotation stage we were given instructions to proceed with a more ambitious project comprising a longer boat to a high specification for building by Camper & Nicholson. Our design programme went roughly this way. Francis Chichester decided that the mainsail should not exceed the size of that which he had successfully used in *Gipsy Moth III* when we rerigged her as a cutter, with the aluminium Sparlight mast. This area was 289 sq. ft. Starting from this basic mainsail area we designed the largest decent ketch rig possible. This had two headsails, cutter fashion. With a good hoist on the staysail it was found impossible, or at least very difficult, to do without runners, but the point of attachment of the running backstays to the deck was kept so close to the mast so that except with the mainsail eased right off it was not necessary to slack off the levers. Four foremast headstays were provided just abaft the stemhead. The two foremost ones were designed to carry only the running sails on their own side of the ship, *viz.* very large light genoas which could be boomed out on the very long whisker poles (bearing-out spars) which were carried up and down the mast. On the after pair of forestays were carried a large working jib and a storm jib. Francis Chichester did not like this arrangement and altered it. But I do not know why.

Twin forestays, running up to the upper crosstree were provided; on these a small staysail and a considerably larger overlapping staysail were hanked on. The object of all this was to provide six permanently hanked on headsails which should obviate the need for almost all changes of sail involving hanking on. The mizzen was a useful sized sail, as big as we felt was reasonable without projecting beyond the limits set by a fixed-standing backstay, and the need to provide plenty of gap between the after end of the mainsail and the mizzen mast. This gap allows for a really useful mizzen staysail to be set; and guards against excessive back winding of the mizzen by the flow off the main when close-hauled.

The Hull Design. This sail plan having been established, we then proceeded to consider what was the largest hull which could properly be driven by this limited sail plan. We settled for a design waterline length of 38 ft. With the addition of useful overhangs she would have a practical waterline length of well over 42 ft. The point which needs to be emphasised about the need for a long vessel, is that although very high speeds are occasionally developed by smaller ocean racers, these high speeds demand that the yacht shall be very hard driven, which is a thing in practice that the single-hander, especially someone of limited strength and of considerable age, will not normally be able to achieve. So it is essential if very long passages are to be made without risk to the boat and gear and without unduly tiring the lone navigator, that the natural speed of the yacht be really high, without the need of hard driving. This can only be achieved by having a fast type of yacht with a long waterline potential.

The problem of designing and building a yacht of around 10 tons displacement of 54 ft. length with sufficient strength to stand up to the Roaring Forties and all the other vicissitudes round-the-world voyaging entails, driven at high speed, was an interesting and not a straightforward one. It was of course required, from a design point of view, to accommodate on board without unduly decreasing the freeboard, the permanent weights which had to be carried. These included a powerful transmitter wireless set with very large special batteries to suit; and to ensure that the powerful, all round mast head lights, etc., could be kept burning over long periods when charging was not convenient. The four-cylinder Perkins diesel engine, Type 4/107, had been fitted with a very large alternator to enable the batteries to be charged in the minimum running time. A very special, large, pneumatic dinghy had been provided, fitted with a small sailing rig. (In a special large trough in the counter of the yacht.) A paraffin heating stove of the incandescent burner type was fitted in the navigator's compartment. The exhaust from this was led through a baffled system to the after end of the dog house, *viz.* into the cockpit, where it would have the best chance of neither being flooded nor blown back.

The Self-steering Gear. At our request Colonel 'Blondie' Hasler very kindly designed a new larger and much stronger self-steering gear of the servo type. The standard Hasler gear had been conceived for and used successfully in much smaller boats for long passages; originally in *Jester*, and later in slightly larger yachts such as *Lively Lady*, about 27-ft. waterline. But these were much slower vessels than *Gipsy Moth IV*, and it is clear that the loading imposed on the self-steering gear increases very much with the size and speed of

10

the yacht. The loading directly due to the speed probably increases as the square of the speed. Apart from this, having to mount the gear on the end of a long counter which must necessarily swing through a wide arc of the water in a big following seaway, will once again add to the loading. Apart from the ability to stick the stresses engendered, vastly greater than in the slower boats, there was need to provide for a greater torque to cope with the larger vessel. All this I was quite unable to get across to Francis Chichester, and after his voyage he reiterates in his book that the smaller lighter Hasler gear would have been better. *Gipsy Moth* was a well-balanced yacht in the sense that she carried very little angle of helm, but, especially with a modest length of tiller, she naturally required a fairly large steering effort when steered by hand. As the yacht was designed for 98 per cent self-steering use, this slightly additional effort was in practice not likely to be an important disadvantage, and we specified a portable tiller extension for use, which we call 'the donkey', should long periods of hand-steering be needed. I don't know whether in fact Francis took this tube extension with him on his voyage. If anyone doubts that the steering efforts on a yacht go up with size and speed, they have only to try on the tiller of various sizes of yachts. Moreover no designer would think of giving the ordinary rudder gear the same size fittings for all sizes of yachts. (Appendix XIX gives data concerning several types of self-steering gear.)

Continuing with our thoughts about the weights to be carried, the considerable tankage needed included not only a lot of fresh water, and of diesel fuel for daily battery charging, but also paraffin; and an electric capstan to assist in handling the warps streamed astern. Apart from the liquids, the tankage itself was an appreciable weight, although aluminium alloy was used wherever feasible.

The yacht's diesel tanks were nearly full when the yacht was launched and in spite of this she floated almost exactly on her marks. In other words she was overall a little lighter than her design.

Hull Details. With such a modest displacement, and so many weights to carry, designing a hull to be strong enough, that is to say never to have a chance of failing, even in the worst weather, and to include a reasonable amount of ballast, was an interesting and a difficult problem. Camper & Nicholsons had never before built a large sail boat with virtually completely laminated members and with cold moulded skin. We had magnificent co-operation from them in achieving exactly our design and in carrying out what to them, in many cases, were partly new techniques. Among the principal features of the general construction were a

completely laminated centre line; in one lamination from steamhead through the keel, stern post, and on to the horn timber of the counter. Mahogany strips (in a 53-ft. boat they are almost wide enough to be called planks) about $\frac{7}{16}$ in. thick, are bent round inside a special former and glued to one another one at a time, until the centre line of the vessel is built up into effectively a single member. This permits a reduction of the overall thicknesses of the members while still keeping up the strength. One avoids the discontinuity which arises with normal construction at the points where the upper part of the stem is joined to the main part of the stem, and where this in turn is scarphed into the wooden keel, and so on throughout the boat. The weight of the mahogany with the glue is often also appreciably less than the conventional oak or equivalent centre line members.

As is normal with a cold-moulded hull, this yacht was built upside down on a soft wood mould. It is the making of this mould, together with strip planking on top of the mould, which adds to the expense of a one-off boat of this type. The skins are laid up one at a time and glued and stapled to one another and fastened to the laminated centre line, which will have been placed in the mould prior to starting to plank up.

When all the skins are in place the hull is turned over and timbered out and the laminated wooden floors are put in place. Care and special skill are required at each stage to ensure that the yacht's shape is carefully kept. The deck beams, since she was primarily a flush-decked ship, except for the short dog house, were laminated in spruce.

Displacement and Ballast. On the whole, through the design and building, we had managed to agree with Francis Chichester on all the major points, and to meet his wishes in so far as we felt them to be reasonable, and only occasionally when we were insistent we had finally got Francis to agree, on all except one point, that of the displacement. Having persuaded him that a certain minimum length of boat was necessary to achieve the speed to do the passage in the target time set, we could not get him to agree to give us a free hand as to the displacement which in the general interests we should naturally have kept as low as was feasible. Thus, due to his having stuck to an unreasonably low maximum displacement, we found ourselves unable to provide the ballast ratio which we wanted. After trials I was able to persuade him that the yacht would be faster in all but the lightest airs with more ballast, and that the sail area we had provided was in fact quite adequate for the very slightly added wetted surface which would result in adding the 1 ton of ballast which I proposed, and which was in fact fitted. The tons per inch immersion of *Gipsy Moth* were about 0·51 and thus the amount of additional wetted surface in sinking the vessel by that number of inches was very small compared to the additional stability; and this helped not only the speed, but the ease in living aboard at a smaller angle of heel.

The whole problem of stability had been slightly complicated because Francis Chichester had asked that good headroom be achieved under the flush deck, just forward and just aft of the main mast. He wished, very reasonably, that the boat should be a good family cruiser after she had completed the round-the-world voyage. It seemed to the Chichesters that such an expensive vessel should finish its life usefully. I agreed and did everything I could to make the yacht comfortable for subsequent use, but inevitably this demanded a little more freeboard and the raising of the deck weights, compared, for instance, to Tabarly's *Pen Duicks*, which were conceived with the single idea of race-winning. However, with the extra ballast referred to above the yacht was very adequately stable, and the high freeboard made her drier.

Francis has reproached me with making the boat narrow. The truth of the matter is that within the confines of the displacement of say $10\frac{1}{2}$ tons, on a waterline length of 38 ft., if one gives her a big beam, one gets a set of lines which have hard turns in them and are certainly likely to be much less seakindly in the sense that the motion of the boat would be likely to be more violent.

Deck Layout. To give more room round the forestays the yacht was given a bit of flare in the topsides and particularly in the bulwarks. This was a good idea of Angus Primrose's, making not only for a more roomy platform, but tending to throw the spray off; and with no R.O.R.C. rule contra. Continuing aft down the deck one comes on the starboard side to the electric Smallwood capstan which was designed to be able under full control with only one man available, to check away and recover a long warp for towing aft and steadying the running of the vessel. There is a lot of weight on the warp with a fast vessel. The deck itself was made of relatively thin plywood which was carefully reinforced in the way of all the items involving heavy loading. A great amount of weight was saved here in a way which is not easy in the ordinary ocean racer because in the R.O.R.C. rule one gets no allowances for reinforcements, but only for the thickness of the main deck. As we went along we had to stiffen up certain items. For instance, we made a new fore hatch cover, but this is the only way to go about saving weight, to start with the lightest thing that you think will serve and then if

necessary to modify it. If you start patent-safety-heavy you will hardly ever get around to lightening things. The main saloon skylights were designed with Goiot hatches which I have found to be not only light, but strong enough, and watertight. The frames are of aluminium alloy.

One of our major preoccupations was to make the doghouse strong enough, and yet keep it light. Francis was very properly concerned with those cases of conventional superstructures which had carried away in the Roaring Forties. *Gipsy Moth IV's* roof was cold moulded in, effectively, one continuous curve. The fixed lights in perspex were specially hot moulded to the curve of the doghouse. All this was necessarily special and expensive work, but provided a doghouse which stood up to knockdowns and bad weather round the Horn, and so on, without being in any way excessive in weight. On top of the companionway hatch box was fixed the special Lewmar X shaped main sheet track which, itself being cambered, added rather than detracted from the general strength. Going aft again, the mizzen mast was stepped on a specially formed member over the top of the tiller. This enabled us to step the mizzen mast exactly where wanted, and to continue the general body of the fin well aft, and without too much wetted surface, and thus we helped to steady the boat. The rudder post was extended to above the main deck where a quadrant was fitted, and on this quadrant the Hasler steering gear operated. Immediately abaft that quadrant there was a good sized hatch into a lazarette for general stowage of cordage and so on. To the single-handed navigator this is often a much better place for stowing things than the forecastle. Then abaft that there was a specially built large semi-sunk deck locker in which was stowed the special dinghy. The whole of the decking of the transom was thickened up to take the racking strain of the the big self-steering gear.

As far as the accommodation is concerned, the lone navigator need only use, in effect, the after 8 ft. of the accommodation which provides his own berth and W.C., a very large chart table with the wireless outboard of it, the very large galley, and a swinging table to eat off.

The galley was designed by Lady Chichester, and the after loo was a small affair chosen by Francis Chichester at the Boat Show. I gather that in practice he preferred to go further forward and use the Blake toilet in Sheila Chichester's powder room.

As far as I know, apart from self-steering gear trouble shortly before reaching Sydney, nothing in the way of gear or rigging failed on passage. Considering the amount of trouble which even the best ocean racers may expect to experience in 25,000 miles of ocean racing, we felt proud of *Gipsy Moth IV* and her splendid skipper. The only modification of moment made during Francis Chichester's stop at Sydney was one which had been originally discussed in the design stage, *viz.* that of filling in the small cut away part of the deadwood just forward of the rudder. I felt that on the way to Sydney speed was the essence of the requirements with the 100 days target passage in mind, but that after that the emphasis would be rather on surviving the Roaring Forties without any very special speed target, apart from making, as the yacht did, the fastest single-handed passage round the world: and by far.

Rig. A lot of the detail work on the rig was very capably done by Sir David Mackworth, who was at that time working for me. He put in an enormous amount of time, care and trouble, and the almost completely trouble-free ride it gave Sir Francis is a credit to him, and to Messrs. Ian Proctor who made the spars. A lot of the detailing of the hull was done by various members of my staff, but principally by Angus Primrose and John Sharp. In a vessel as special as this one, and with such exacting requirements, both as regards weight saving and reliability, the amount of design work required is tremendous; practically every item is a one-off special.

'Gipsy Moth' Today. Naturally everyone had hoped *Gipsy Moth* would lead a long and useful life and possibly take part in the 1968 single-handed Trans-Atlantic race. Unfortunately this was not to be. She was presented by Lord Dulverton to the Cutty Sark Foundation, and is now fitted into a concrete dock close to *Cutty Sark* at Greenwich, where she is open for public view to anyone; and is well worth a visit by anyone interested technically in the study of single-handers.

MULTIHULLED SINGLE-HANDERS

Dealing first with multihulled vessels generally; apart from their obvious and great speed potential, their displacement, owing to being unballasted, can be very light and they can, speaking in general terms, be driven by a very small sail area—clearly advantageous to the lone navigator. The craft will sail much more upright than a single-hulled craft; thus, other things being equal, making work on board easier. Work includes sail shifting and trimming, cooking, and navigation; apart from a great number of other tasks such as filling and charging batteries, sending shore telephone messages, and making minor repairs.

So far so good. But just about there the advantages stop pretty short. I said that other things being the same the advantage of being upright is considerable. Unfortunately they are not likely to be the same. In general in bad weather, and specially to windward, a multihull hard driven is apt to have a rather special and difficult motion which can often be more difficult to cope with than the motion of a less upright single-hulled vessel.

Leaving aside the often present anxiety that the normal good liaison between the hulls may prove to be insufficiently good in prolonged very bad weather and big seas (a thing which technical progress should in time resolve), the fundamental drawback of the multihulled vessels is the doubt about their ability to survive a knock-down. In contrast, we know that all good single-hulled ocean going vessels will survive repeated knock-downs, with rarely any damage. On several occasions I have looked over the main or mizzen masthead into the trough of the seas; and when perhaps sundry stores landed into the roof; and whence we have sailed on.

The two-handed Round Britain Race was brilliantly won by a trimaran, and multihull enthusiasts will with reason point to a number of other long voyages successfully achieved; some of them short-handed. But in many cases the vessel has been either madly short of sail area (which annuls their fundamental speed advantage) or carefully sailed by good, and lucky, crews.

Michael Henderson made a very determined and thorough attempt to combine the speed of the catamaran with near single-hulled safety, and I am glad to be able to publish the plans of the last of his famous ballasted offshore cats, *Misty Miller*; which got round the Fastnet course, and across the Atlantic later on.

When one equates the total number of people lost offshore in recent years in multihull vessels with those lost in single-hull vessels, and taking into consideration the infinitely greater number of single-hulled vessels sailing, it is difficult to avoid the conclusion that development of multihull offshore craft has, safetywise, a long way to go.

LIST OF APPENDICES

APPENDIX I

BEAUFORT WIND SCALE

Beaufort Number	Speed Knots	Land m.p.h.	Description	Height of Waves (ft.)	Effect on Fishing Smacks
0	0	0	Calm.	—	
1	2	2·3	Light air. Ruffles with the appearance of scales are formed.		Sufficient to give steerage way, wind free.
2	5	5·8	Light breeze. Small wavelets still short but more pronounced. Crests do not break.	$\frac{1}{2}$	With light canvas and topsails full and bye make 2 knots.
3	9	10·3	Gentle breeze. Large wavelets' crests begin to break. Perhaps scattered white horses.	2	Begin to heel over slightly under topsails; up to 3 knots full and bye.
4	13	15	Moderate breeze. Small waves becoming longer. Frequent white horses.	4	Good working breeze. Smacks heel considerably on a wind with all sail.
5	18	20·7	Fresh breeze. Moderate waves take a more pronounced long form. Many white horses.	6	Shorten sail.
6	24	27·6	Strong breeze. Larger waves form; foam crests more extensive (probably some spray).	9	Double reef gaff mainsails.
7	30	34·5	Moderate gale. Sea heaps up; white foam from breaking waves begins to be blown with wind. Spindrift seen.	13	Remains in harbour or lie to at sea.
8	37	42·6	Fresh gale. Moderate high waves; edges of crests break into spindrift. Foam blown into well marked streaks. Spray reduces visibility.	18	Take shelter.
9	44	50·6	Strong gale. High waves. Dense streaks of foam. Spray affects visibility.	23	
10	51	58·7	Whole gale. Very high waves with long overhanging crests. Dense white foam streaks. Whole surface of sea takes white appearance.	30	
11	60	69	Storm, exceptionally high waves (small ships lost to view behind waves). Sea completely covered with long white patches of foam. Everywhere the edges of wave crests are blown into froth. Visibility poor.	40 or more	
12	—	—	Hurricane. Air filled with foam and spray. Sea completely white with spray. Visibility very seriously affected.	40 or more	

APPENDIX II

WEIGHTS AND STRENGTHS OF CORDAGE AND WIRE ROPE
(in lbs. unless otherwise stated as tons)

A. TENSILE STRENGTH OF CORDAGE

Circumference in inches	Nylon	Terylene (High Tenacity)	Terylene (Plied Heavy Denier)	Terylene (Pre-stretched)	Ulstron	Italian Hemp	Best Grade Manila	Sisal
$\frac{1}{2}$	700(0·70)	650(0·98)	—	650(0·98)	550(0·63)	480(1·5)	220(0·9)	250(0·9)
$\frac{3}{4}$	1,650(1·67)	1,250(1·95)	—	1,250(1·95)	1,100(1·3)	1,010(3·13)	500(1·9)	560(1·9)
1	2,980(2·85)	2,240(3·5)	—	2,240(3·5)	2,000(2·3)	1,340(3·9)	1,200(3·6)	1,060(3·6)
$1\frac{1}{4}$	4,590(4·38)	3,500(5·5)	—	3,500(5·5)	3,000(3·5)	1,680(5·1)	1,570(4·7)	1,400(4·7)
$1\frac{1}{2}$	6,610(6·4)	5,000(7·8)	—	5,000(7·8)	4,250(5)	2,350(8·3)	2,350(7·2)	2,100(7·2)
	tons	tons	tons	tons	tons			
2	5·2(11·3)	4(13·8)	—	—	3·25(8·9)	4,140(13·4)	4,480(13)	3,970(13)
3	11·8(25·3)	9(31)	8(31)	—	7·5(20)	9,410(30)	10,080(29)	8,960(29)
4	19·6(44·8)	15·5(55)	13·5(55)	—	12·5(35·5)	16,240(52)	17,192(51)	15,288(51)

The figures in brackets are the approximate weights of the rope per 100 ft. in lb. For coir ropes of these sizes divide strength figures by 6 and multiply the weight figures by 0·6 from the Italian Hemp column. It should be pointed out that Italian Hemp is now almost unobtainable. Nylon is the strongest synthetic rope made, ideal for anchor warps and suitable for mooring lines. It stretches and has excellent shock-absorbing characteristics. Terylene is good for most purposes. Marlow Ropes' High Tenacity Terylene is a lustrous white, ideal for sheets and mooring lines. P.H.D. Terylene is a dull, creamier white, tough and less expensive than High Tenacity Terylene. Terylene has better resistance to strong acids and alkalis than Nylon. Pre-stretched Terylene is for halyards and can replace steel wire in some applications. It is flexible but less so than standard Terylene. Ulstron is a lightweight, green rope, pleasant to handle and it floats. Good for applications where there is little abrasion. Ideal for spinnaker sheets and can be used for mooring lines.

WEIGHT STRENGTH RATIOS

Tensile strength in lb.
Divided by Weight per 100 ft.

$$\left\{ \begin{array}{llllll} \text{Nylon} & .. & .. & .. & .. & 682 \\ \text{Manila (Best)} & .. & .. & .. & 335 \\ \text{Italian Hemp} & .. & .. & .. & 316 \\ \text{Sisal} & .. & .. & .. & .. & 296 \end{array} \right.$$

EXTENSION UNDER LOAD
OF VARIOUS CORDAGES EACH $1\frac{1}{4}$ in. CIRC.

Cordage	Percentage Extension		
Load	·2 tons	·4 tons	·7 tons
Nylon dry	18	26	32
Nylon wet	17	24	30
Italian dry	5	7	9
Italian wet	7	10	12
Manila dry	8	11	12
Manila wet	10	13	15
Sisal dry	4	7	13
Sisal wet	9	12	18

ENDURANCE STRENGTH
OF VARIOUS SMALL CORDAGES

Cordage	Tensile Strength	Sustained Load Tests	
	(Normal Test)	75% Load	50% Load
Nylon	950 lb.	10 days*	Indefinitely
Italian	720 lb.	2 min.	20 hrs.
Manila	520 lb.	5 min.	$3\frac{1}{2}$ hrs.
Sisal	554 lb.	4 min.	$\frac{3}{4}$ hr.

Notes.—(i)   * Broke at splice on Test.
     (ii)   At 25 per cent full load all cordages stood indefinitely.
    (iii)   The figures refer to $\frac{5}{8}$ in. circ. cordage.

IMPACT STRENGTH
OF VARIOUS CORDAGES
(Breaking strength of $1\frac{1}{4}$ in. circ. rope loaded by dropping weight attached to a 5-ft. length)

Cordage	Weight lb.
Nylon dry	490
Nylon wet	400
Italian dry	160
Italian wet	120
Manila dry	110
Manila wet	70
Sisal dry	120
Sisal wet	80

LOSS OF STRENGTH
OF CORDAGES WHEN FROZEN
(Effect on Tensile Strength per cent Original)

Nylon	−10%
Waterproofed Manila	−21%
Normal Italian	−50%
Waterproofed Italian	−29%
Sisal	−36%

B. STEEL WIRE ROPE WEIGHTS AND STRENGTHS

Circumference	Diameter (approx.)		Weight per 100 ft. 7/7	Stainless Steel 7/7 (Standing)	Special Galvd. Standing Rigging 7/7	Standard Galvd. Standing Rigging 7/7	Stainless Steel Running Rigging 6/19 One Main Fibre Core	Weight per 100 ft. 6/19 One Main Fibre Core	Galvd. Running Rigging 6/19 One Main Fibre Core	Galvd. Running Rigging 6/24 Seven Fibre Cores	Weight per 100 ft. 6/24 Seven Fibre Cores	Galvd. Running Extra Special Flexible 6/37 One Main Fibre Core	Weight per 100 ft. 6/37 One Main Fibre Core	Galvd. Rigging 6/7 One Main Fibre Core	Galvd. Rigging 6/7 One Main Fibre Core Weight per 100 ft.
in.	in.	mm.	lb.	tons	tons	tons	tons	lb.	tons	tons	lb.	tons	lb.	tons	lb.
$\frac{3}{8}$	$\frac{1}{8}$	3	3·2	·58		·5	·54	2·9	·51					·42	2·2
$\frac{1}{2}$	$\frac{5}{32}$	4	4·5	1·0	1·15	·9	·8	4·0	·72	·68	3·7			·73	4·0
$\frac{5}{8}$	$\frac{3}{16}$	5	7·0	1·52	1·70	1·4	1·2	6·3	1·1	1·0	5·6			1·2	6·3
$\frac{3}{4}$	$\frac{1}{4}$	6	10·0	2·39	2·38	2·0	1·7	9·0	1·6	1·5	8·1			1·6	9·0
$\frac{7}{8}$	$\frac{9}{32}$	7	13·4	3·19	3·37	3·0	2·3	12·0	2·1	2·1	12·0			2·4	12·0
1	$\frac{5}{16}$	8	20·0	4·9	4·91	4·0	3·06	18	2·9	2·6	16	3·0	18	3·2	18
$1\frac{1}{4}$	$\frac{7}{16}$	10	27·9	6·7	6·74	6·0	4·75	25	4·5	4·4	24	4·4	25	4·8	25
$1\frac{1}{2}$	$\frac{1}{2}$	12	40·0	9·7	9·79	8·7		36	6·4	6·1	33	6·3	36	6·9	36
$1\frac{3}{4}$	$\frac{9}{16}$	14	55·6	13·3	13·39	11·8		50	8·6	8·2	47	8·5	50	9·4	50
2	$\frac{5}{8}$	16	73·4	17·4	17·57	15·7		66	11·7	11·2	60	11·3	66	12·5	66

APPENDIX III

WEIGHTS AND STRENGTHS OF MATERIALS USED IN YACHT CONSTRUCTION

Material	Ultimate Tensile Strength Tons sq. in.	Elongation per cent	Remarks
Mild steel ordinary	24	30	
Mild steel best quality ..	30	30	
Medium carbon steel ..	40	18	·3 per cent carbon
Wrought iron	19	25	
Naval brass bars	26	20	
Manganese brass ..	33	25	Known as high tensile brass
Phosphor bronze bars ..	30	20	
Monel metal.. ..	34	30	Standard quality
'K' monel metal ..	60	30	Hardened
Copper bar and sheet ..	14	35	
Aluminium bronze ..	32	20	
Stainless steel	35	27	Specification S61
Stainless steel 'Staybrite' ..	37	27	Specification S62
Stainless steel	46	13	
Magnesium alloy bars, etc. ..	18	10–14	B.S. Specification 1354 or 1356
Magnesium cast alloy ..	15	8	
Aluminium alloy bars, etc. ..	14	19	Specification AW4 and AW5
Aluminium for spars ..	22	10	Specification AW100
Aluminium alloy castings ..	11	6	Specification AC6
Common cast iron	10–12	0	
Special cast iron	14	0	
Malleable cast iron	18	5	
Cast steel	30	15	
Gunmetal (cast)	16	10	
Cast high tensile bronze (say)	28	15	

Material	Weight of a sq. ft. $\frac{1}{8}$ in. thick lb.	Weight of a cu. ft. lb.	Specific Gravity
Wrought iron	5	485	7·8
Steel	5·1	490	7·82
Cast iron	4·4	450	7·1
Copper	5·7	550	8·9
Gunmetal } (say) .. Bronze	5·6	545	8·6
Brass	5·5	530	8·4
Lead	7·4	711	11·4
Aluminium alloys (say) ..	1·8	169	2·7
Monel metal.. ..	5·8	558	8·9
Magnesium alloys (say) ..	1·2	113	1·8

Note.—Recognised weights of timbers are given at the end of **Appendix VIII**

APPENDIX IV

RECOMMENDED WEIGHTS OF SAIL CLOTH FOR OCEAN RACERS
(Ounces per Standard Yard of English Cloth)

Area of Sail in Question—sq. ft.	60	100	150	210	280	370	490	650	860	1,140	1,520	2,000
Mainsails and mizzens	6	7	8	10	11	12	13	14	16	18	20	22
Storm sails, trysails, and jibs	9	11	13	14	15	17	18					
Working headsails for wind Force 5–6	7	8	10	11	12	13	14	15	17	19		
Moderate breeze sails genoas, yankees overlap staysails for wind Force 3–4	4	5	6	7	8	9	10	11	12	13	$13\frac{1}{2}$	14
Light-weather headsails for wind Force 1–2, cotton	$2\frac{1}{2}$	3	$3\frac{1}{2}$	4	$4\frac{1}{2}$	5	$5\frac{1}{2}$	6	$6\frac{1}{2}$	7	8	$8\frac{1}{2}$
Light-weather headsails for wind Force 1–2, dacron	2	$2\frac{1}{2}$	3	$3\frac{1}{2}$	$3\frac{1}{2}$	4	$4\frac{1}{2}$	5	$5\frac{1}{2}$	6	$6\frac{1}{2}$	7
Spinnaker nylon, dacron (or terylene)		$1\frac{1}{2}$	$1\frac{1}{2}$	$1\frac{1}{2}$	$1\frac{1}{2}$	$1\frac{3}{4}$	$1\frac{3}{4}$	2	2	$2\frac{1}{2}$	3	3
Spinnaker cotton best quality		2	2	2	$2\frac{1}{2}$	$2\frac{1}{2}$	$2\frac{1}{2}$	3	3	$3\frac{1}{2}$	4	4

Note—(1) The weights apply to cotton or dacron or terylene except where otherwise indicated.

(2) For spinnakers the area shown in the area of the fore triangle in which they are to be set, *i.e.* $\dfrac{I \times J}{2}$

(3) For heavy-weather spinnakers use 2 oz. more.

(4) For use in America where the standard width of cloth is $28\frac{1}{2}$ in. the cloth weights in the table should be decreased by 14 per cent. To convert to grammes per square metre multiply figures in the table by 34.

(5) If nylon or dacron (terylene) is used for storm sails on account of its resistance to mildew use 15 per cent less weight than cotton.

(6) Heavier canvas is usually graded by numbers instead of ounces on the following conversion scale:

00–37 oz.	3–27.5 oz.	7–20 oz.	12–12.5 oz.
0–34 oz.	4–25.5 oz.	8–18 oz.	14–10.5 oz.
1–31 oz.	5–23.5 oz.	9–16.5 oz.	16– 8.5 oz.
2–29 oz.	6–22.5 oz.	10–15 oz.	

(7) Where a particular sail is designed for use over an intermediate range of wind, interpolate, *e.g.* a yankee 280 sq. ft. designed to stand in wind Force 5 (but not 6) weight is 10 oz.

(8) Mizzen staysails should normally be made to the scale of weights applicable to light-weather sails, since, although they will be set in winds stronger than 2, they will not be used on the wind. Small mizzen staysails, *i.e.* those less than full size, should be 1 oz. heavier.

APPENDIX V

PHYSICAL PROPERTIES OF TEXTILE FIBRES

Property	'Terylene'		Nylon		Viscose Rayon	Acetate Rayon	Cotton	Silk	Wool
	'M' type	'F' type	Medium	Best					
Specific gravity	1·38	1·38	1·14	1·14	1·52	1·33	1·52	1·35	1·32
Dry tenacity (q.p.d.)	4·5–5·5	6–7	4·5–5·5	6–7	2·1	1·3	3·5	4·9	1·4
Extension at break %	25–15	12·5–7·5	25–20	19–15	21·0	29·0	7·3	26·0	38·0
Ratio *wet tenacity* % dry tenacity	100	100	85–90	85–90	44–54	60–65	110–130	75–95	76–97
Moisture regain %	about 0·4	about 0·4	4·2	4·2	11·0	6·0	8·5	11·0	16·0
Modulus of elasticity q.p.d.	100	120	24·0	45·0	65·0	31·0	55·0	85·0	28·0
Sectional shape	Circular		Circular		Serrated	Trefoil	Bean-shaped	Tri-angular	Circular

(With acknowledgements to the Imperial Chemical Company of Great Britain)

NOTE

Ulstron has approximately 94 per cent of the strength of average terylene of the same circumference. As its weight is only 65 per cent of terylene rope of the same circumference its strength for weight is much higher.

APPENDIX VI
CREW INSTRUCTION SHEET

DEAR ————,

This is to confirm that I have booked you in for the *Monk of Malham* for the following races:

(1) *Race*.................... *Starting Date*..............

 Time and Place.......... ....

 ....

(2) Suggested you bring:—(*a*) Short oilskin coat, smock and hood, or so'wester. NOTE.—Trousers are essential. Important that the coat be good fitting, if possible double-breasted, flapped, or otherwise secured at front. Trousers, lanyards or rubber bands at bottoms. (*b*) Three neck scarves, or strips of towelling in lieu. (*c*) .. changes of clothing (one on and ... spare). (Each to consist of trousers, shirt, two sweaters, socks or stockings, thick vest and long pants [or equivalent].) (*d*) Your favourite brand of liver pill and some glucose and barley sugar if you like it. Razor and washing gear. (*e*) Safety harness. (*f*) Torch, and spare battery. (*g*) Knife. (*h*) Magister shoes, or short sea boots. (Sea boots to be capable of being kicked off easily.) (*i*) Mae West or Gieve's waistcoat. (*j*) Soft kit bag (there is a locker for each crew member).

(3) Please do not bring (there is no storage for them) suitcases. Shore-going clothes to be confined to one yachting jacket, one white shirt and club tie and one pair of tidy trousers. (There is stowage for these; which are necessary for functions at the receiving club at the finish.)

(4) In acknowledging this please furnish your address and phone No. to which any last-minute messages can be sent.

Yours sincerely,
J. H. ILLINGWORTH.

APPENDIX VII

INTERNATIONAL OFFSHORE RULE (I.O.R.) MARK 1 MEASUREMENT RULE FOR OFFSHORE RACING

Effective as determined by local authority and with time scales at the discretion of the organizing authority for the race concerned

PART ONE

101. *Introduction and Rating Formula*
It is not possible for the rule to cover every eventuality and the Committee therefore reserves the right to modify the rule at any time or to deal with any peculiarity of design and to give such rating as they consider equitable.

Changes in the rule requiring new or altered measurements or the remeasurement of existing yachts shall be made with due care so as to minimize the need for new measurements of the yacht. Designers and owners of new yachts incorporating features intended to exploit provisions of the rule should consult the Committee or its local representative before undertaking questionable details or forms and the Committee shall interpret this rule so as not to discourage developments tending to increase the speed of yachts, but to minimize the incorporation of features tending by unusual methods to reduce the rating.

102. *Rating Certificates*
No yacht shall have more than one valid rating certificate at any one time. The rating certificate issued under this rule shall except as mentioned below, be valid for four years from the date of measurement unless a change is made in any of the rule parameters or there is a change of ownership of the yacht in which case the change shall be notified to the measurer or rating authority and the existing rating certificate cancelled automatically. It may be convenient for rating authorities to allow the validity to exceed the four years to the end of the yachting season following the date of measurement or re-measurement provided that this extension does not exceed one year. In the case of re-measurement which gives the full four years extension of validity the re-measurement must include complete sail area and freeboards and an inclining test if necessary. A smaller re-measurement or re-calculation shall not extend the former date of expiry in any way.

The authority having custody of rating certificates shall supply a copy of any rating certificate to any person on payment of a copying charge.

103. *Measurements*
Dimensions of sails shall be taken in feet to one place of decimals. All other measurements including headboards and battens shall be in feet to two places of decimals. Measurements shall be taken from the yacht whenever practicable. Where this is unduly difficult, the measurer shall have the option of using the plans, or such other sources of information as he considers reliable.

Measurements in the metric system shall be in meters to three places of decimals except that measurements of sails shall be to two places. Sail areas shall be given in square meters to two decimal places. Constants or other dimensions given in the text or formulas are to be read as feet and converted to meters by dividing by 3·281.

Percentages including CGF and EPF shall be taken to the nearest fourth decimal place.

Final ratings in feet shall be given to the nearest single decimal place and in meters to the nearest second place. The intermediate step MR shall be calculated to the nearest third place in feet and fourth place in meters.

Rated sail area shall be rounded to one decimal place in square feet and two decimal places in square meters.

Draft correction and Freeboard correction shall be used in the formula to third place in feet and fourth place in meters.

L, B and D in the formula shall be used to the nearest third place in feet and fourth place in meters.

Where hollows or projections or other deviations from the fair surface of the hull occur in the way of a point of measurement the measurer shall adjust the measurement by relating it to the fair surface of the hull.

Pounds (lbs) shall be converted to kilos by dividing by 2·205.

104. *Formula*

$$MR = \frac{0 \cdot 13 L \sqrt{S}}{\sqrt{BD}} + 0 \cdot 25 L + 0 \cdot 20 \sqrt{S} + DC + FC$$

$$R = MR \times EPF \times CGF$$

105. *Owner's Responsibility After Measurement*
Owners of boats measured under this Rule should study the Rule carefully, to be thoroughly familiar with the numerous factors that affect rating. Subsequent to measurement, owners must conscientiously avoid making any changes which would affect the rating as such changes, if made without remeasurement would disqualify them for competition. A few typical examples are listed below:

.1 Sails may not be replaced or altered, in a manner to increase their size beyond the measured limits on which the rating certicate is based, without being remeasured.

.2 Measurement Bands, Stoppers and Halyard Markers: These must be maintained accurately in place and, regardless of the circumstances, a boat is not entitled to exceed these limitations without remeasurement. It is at

10*

all times the owner's responsibility to keep all sails within the measurement limits.

.3 *Trimming of Headsails and Spinnakers:* The restrictions to sheeting are clearly outlined in paras. 858, 860, and 861. It is important that these restrictions be adhered to, particular attention being called to the requirements that mainsail be set when trimming to the main boom.

.4 *Propellers:* These may not be changed after measurement to smaller diameter or less blade width, or in type without remeasurement.

.5 The selection of sails where there is a restriction as to the number or type which can be used: for example, the selection between a loose-footed or secured foot mainsail, etc.

.6 Ballast of any type and heavy deck gear, which affects the trim or stability of the boat must be on board and in place when stability measurements are made and must not be changed in amount or location without remeasurement.

PART TWO

Preparation for Hull and Rig Measurement

201. *General Measurement Procedure:* To secure an accurate and fair measurement, it is necessary to have close cooperation between owner and measurer. It is desirable that the owner should be familiar with all parts of the measurement rule.

202. *Hull Measuring Procedure:* The principal hull measurements may be taken either in or out of the water. Measurement ashore with the yacht approximately level is preferred and is sometimes essential. Inclined stability, waterline beam and freeboard must be taken with the yacht afloat, and with stores and equipment located exactly as further detailed below.

The owner or his responsible agent must be present and available at the time of measurement. The yacht to be measured must be afloat and ready, in the following condition, for the measurer:

.1 Completely rigged and ready to sail.

.2 All sails must be abaft the foremost mast. The mainsail and the schooner foresail shall be in place furled. Booms shall be secured at the low points of P, PY, H or HY, as the case may be.

All sails except mainsail and schooner foresail shall be stowed below decks on the cabin sole and not forward of the main mast. In the event it is necessary to pile the sails, they shall be distributed aft of the mast over the length of the main cabin or its equivalent, with the heavier sails on the cabin sole and lighter sails piled over them, but no higher than necessary. Further requirements for measurement include the following:

A. All water tanks will be empty.

B. Fuel tanks, if small, aft of amidships and low in the hull may be full (pressed up); otherwise they shall be empty.

C. The mainsail will be bent in its furled position as will the mizzen of a yawl or ketch. Sails between masts in schooners if normally bent to mast and spars when furled will also be similarly treated.

D. All bedding will be stowed in its normal bunks; all navigational and cooking appliances will be in their normal positions for racing, together with all tools and gear necessary for offshore sailing. No portable gear or equipment, unless clearly stated in other paragraphs of this rule, shall be stowed forward of the forewardmost mast in the measurement condition.

E. If an outboard motor is carried when racing, it will be stowed in the position normally assigned to it at that time.

F. No clothing, food or stores will be on board.

G. The yacht's dinghy will not be on board, but the life raft or rafts will be on board, stowed in the position used when racing.

H. The yacht's head will not be depressed through lying to a mooring.

I. Inside ballast, anchor chains and anchor, also sea anchor if carried, will be stowed in the positions used for them when racing. The anchor chain will invariably be stowed in its locker. The positions will be recorded in the Rating Certificate.

J. All sump tanks shall be empty and bilges must be pumped dry.

K. No personnel shall be on board while flotation measurements are being taken, except as may be required by the measurer during inclining measurements.

L. Centreboard(s), if any, must be fully raised.

M. Measurement point bands on masts and booms must be in place.

N. If the above conditions are not all fulfilled, MEASUREMENT WILL BE REFUSED.

203. *Sail Measuring Procedure:* Certain sails must be measured as explained in Part VIII, i.e., spinnakers, jibs, mizzen staysails, overlapping sails, gaff sails and topsails. These sails must be made available to the measurer for measuring or for checking marked dimensions. Measurements of all sails required to be measured must be measured with normal tension between measurement points and free of wrinkles across line of measurement and must include the fabric length between measurement points. Measuring point at corner of a sail shall be the intersection of the adjacent outside edges projected. All other measurement points shall be at the extreme outside of rope, wire or fabric of the sail's edge.

The instructions to measurers will provide further detail.

204. *Measurement Bands:* Measurements may not be taken to locations defined by black or other contrasting painted bands unless these bands, with accompanying stoppers or halyard markings, are in place at the time of measurements. If measurements are taken to such bands, their location cannot be changed without invalidating the rating certificate.

PART THREE—HULL MEASUREMENTS

301. Symbols used to determine hull measurements are noted below for reference and described, with methods of application in the following paragraphs:

AGO	After Girth Overhang. See 312.5C.
AGS	After Girth Station. See 312.2A.
AIGS	After Inner Girth Station. See 312..B.
AOC	After Overhang Component. See 319.
ASBD	After Stations Beam Difference. See 313.6.
ASFD	After Stations Freeboard Difference. See 315.6.
ASVD	After Stations Vertical Height Difference. See 314.
B	Rated Beam. See 310.
BA	Beam Aft. See 313.4.
BAI	Beam Aft Inner. See 313.6.
BF	Beam Forward. See 313.1.
BFI	Beam Forward, Inner. See 313.2.
BMAX	Maximum Beam. See 310.
D	Rated Depth. See 324.
FA	Freeboard Aft. See 315.4.
FAI	Freeboard Aft, Inner. See 315.5.
FD	Forward Depth. See 322.1.
FDI	Forward Depth, Immersed. See 323.
FF	Freeboard Forward. See 315.1.
FFD	Freeboard at Forward Depth. See 323.
FFI	Freeboard Forward Inner. See 315.2.
FGO	Forward Girth Overhang. See 312.5A.
FGS	Forward Girth Station. See 312.1A.
FIGS	Forward Inner Girth Stations. See 312.1B.
FMD	Freeboard at Midship Depth. See 323.
FOC	Forward Overhang Component. See 317.
FSBD	Forward Stations Beam Difference. See 213C.
FSFD	Forward Stations Freeboard Difference. See 313.3.
GD	Girth Difference. See 312.4.
GSDA	Girth Station Difference Aft. See 312.5D.
GSDF	Girth Station Difference Forward. See 312.5B.
L	Rated Length. See 316.
LBG	Length Between Girth Stations. See 312.5E.
LBGC	Length Between Girth Stations, Corrected. See 318.
LLA	Normal Limit of Length Aft. See 320.
LOA	Length Overall. See 311.
MD	Midship Depth. See 322.2.
MDI	Midship Depth Immersed. See 322.2.
VHA	Vertical Height Aft. See 314.
VHAI	Vertical Height Aft, Inner. See 314.
Y	Normal Limit of Length Aft, Special. See 320.

302. *Top of Covering Board:* The top of the covering board is, in a yacht of traditional wooden build, the line of intersection of the deck and the topsides. This definition applies also to other forms of construction where the deck and the topsides are clearly defined and meet in a sharp line. Other variations likely to be met are described in Paras. 303 and 304 below.

303. *Sheer Line:* For the purpose of determining freeboards at FGS, FIGS and FD, MD, AIGS and AGS, the sheer line shall be defined as follows:

.1 In the conventional case, the sheer line shall be the line formed by the intersection of the top of the covering board and the topsides of the yacht. In the normal case this will show as a fair continuous curve. Regardless of the nature of the deck edge, the sheer line for purposes of measurement shall always lie on the surface of the hull or bulwark, if used, and may not be projected into space. Where the sheer line is not a continuous sharp intersection between topsides and deck on the surface of the hull, the position of the sheer line shall be determined by one of the following rules:

A. Where the deck and topsides are joined by a radius the sheer line shall be located along the line where tangents of 45° to the horizontal touch the surface.

B. Where the sheer line as defined above is more than 5% B inboard of a vertical tangent to the hull, the sheer line shall be taken along the line of the points 5% of B inboard of the vertical tangent.

304. *Raised Decks and Discontinuous Sheer Lines:* Raised decks and discontinuous sheer lines may result in artificial ratings for one or more of the following reasons, in which case alternate methods of measurement shall be used as described.

.1 As unusual freeboard at either end could result in a distorted value of "L", the fair extension of the conventional sheer line shall be used to determine girths, and a raised deck at either end shall not be used in the determination of girths unless it extends over at least 25% LOA.

.2 Unusual freeboard or sheer at the point of B measurement may artificially increase B. If this occurs, the provisions of para. 310.2 shall apply.

.3 Unusual freeboard at the mast may shorten the length of "I", or related dimensions. If this condition exists, the low point of measurement of "I" shall not be taken higher than the level of the deck or its fair extension at the inner face of the stem.

.4 Unusual freeboard at either end may increase the freeboard correction. In this case, no such increase shall be recorded unless the length of the raised section at either end exceeds 25% of the overall length of the yacht.

.5 The adjustments described above shall be used when, as in the case of wood construction, there are clear distinctions between the raised deck and the main deck levels. When this condition is blurred, as in the case of a yacht with a continuous but unusual sheer line which may approximate the result of a raised deck as described above but without providing a clear distinction between the separate deck levels, the measurer shall arbitrarily assign a sheer line as nearly as possible averaging the deck levels but having a fair continuous curve without double inflection. All freeboard, girth and rig height measurements shall be taken to this line, as shall the BMAX provided the established line is concave upward. In case the establishment of this special sheer line is considered necessary, the measurer shall advise the national authority so as to assure identical measurement of similar boats.

305. *Girths*

.1 Girths of a yacht are taken round the canoe body of the yacht from top of covering board on one side to top of covering board on the other. The points on the covering board and on the lowest part of the girth (normally on the centreline of the yacht) must lie in the same vertical athwartships plane; in between these points the girth may take the shortest course and all hollows except as mentioned in sub-para (3) below may be bridged.

.2 No girth may be placed so that any part of it cuts or crosses the edge of a transom.

.3 If a girth has to be placed where the canoe body of the yacht is extended downwards in the form of a skeg, deadwood, keel or other similar extension the girth should not be carried fully round the extension but the following rules should be adhered to:

A. If the extension downwards is a section with parallel or nearly parallel sides, not more than 8% of the rated beam in width, and the section of the canoe body meets it at an angle not steeper than 45° to the horizontal, then the girth is taken from top of covering board to the points where, on each side, the canoe body meets the extension plus an addition, as if the canoe body continued at its former angle on each side, to meet an apex on the centreline of the yacht.

B. If the extension downwards is married into the canoe body of the yacht in a reverse curve, the girth is taken from top of covering board to the points on each side of the yacht where the total width of the extension is 8% of the rated beam, provided that the section of the canoe body is not steeper than 45° to the horizontal at this point plus an addition, as if the canoe body continued at its former angle on each side, to meet at an apex on the centreline of the yacht.

C. If the section of the canoe body makes an angle steeper than 45° to the horizontal at a point where the width of the extension downwards is greater than 8% of B, or where it meets an extension downwards with parallel or nearly parallel sides as in para. 304.3(A), then the girth is taken from top of covering board to the points on each side of the yacht where the section of the hull makes an angle of 45° to the horizontal: plus an addition, as if the canoe body continued at an angle of 45° on each side, to meet at an apex on the centreline of the yacht.

D. If, for some exceptional reason, a girth cannot possibly be measured in accordance with the principles given in the three sub-paras. above, it may be taken at a different place, its length measured, and the correct position of the corrected girth calculated by interpolation or extrapolation.

306. *Transom sterns.* A yacht shall be deemed as having a transom stern only when ALL the following conditions are fulfilled:

.1 The after side of the sternpost, on which the rudder must be hung, and the transom board at the centreline of the yacht must be in the same plane.

.2 The sternpost must be joined to the main keel of the yacht by deadwood of not less depth than the sternpost (i.e. a separate skeg does not qualify).

.3 In a fixed keel yacht the bottom of the sternpost must have at least 85% of the maximum draft of the yacht.

.4 In a centreboard yacht the bottom of the sternpost must have at least 85% of the maximum draft of the yacht when the centreboard is raised and at least 35% of the maximum draft of the yacht when the centreboard is lowered.

307. *Vertical heights*

.1 Vertical heights are measured at such sections as may be necessary, towards the ends of the yacht. A vertical height is the vertical distance between the top of covering board and the lowest part of the canoe body of the yacht at the same section, normally though not necessarily on the centreline.

.2 Should the section be in way of a skeg, deadwood, keel or other extension as described in para. 305.3 (A, B and C) the lowest part of the canoe body of the yacht shall be taken as the lowest point of the girth projected to the centreline, as described in the above para.

.3 If it is impossible to obtain a girth position (see para. 305.3 (D) in the correct place the vertical height for the girth in the correct place must also be obtained by interpolation or extrapolation.

308. *Beam forward and aft* Beams forward and aft, measured at a girth station, shall be the maximum beam of the hull excluding any bulwark or rubbing strake at that station.

309. *Freeboards*
.1 These will be measured at given stations when the yacht is in standard measurement trim. At any station they will be measured on each side of the yacht and the mean taken. The freeboard shall be the vertical distance between the top of covering board as defined and the waterline, with the yacht in full measurement trim.
.2 Standard measurement trim is defined in para. 202.

310. *Beam*
.1 The position of the maximum beam of the yacht will be found, and its position relative to the length of the yacht will be recorded. The maximum beam, which will not include any extraneous features such as rubbing strakes, etc., will be measured and recorded BMAX. In a flush decked yacht having straight or concave sheer the rated beam (B) shall be the maximum beam of the hull proper, measured at the same section as BMAX at a height not above points one-sixth of BMAX below top of covering board.
.2 If the yacht has a raised deck extending to the side in way of the BMAX position, or a reverse sheer, the amount by which height of top of covering board at BMAX position exceeds the height (at the same section) of an imaginary straight line joining the centreline of deck at the fore and after ends of the yacht, shall be measured and recorded. When measuring B, this figure must be added to one-sixth of BMAX, in order to find the distance below the covering board above which B may not be measured.

311. *Length overall* (LOA). The length overall of a yacht will be measured to include the whole hull, but not spars or projections fixed to the hull such as bowsprits, bumpkins, pulpits, etc.; it will be measured between:
.1 A point forward being the forwardmost of the following points:
A. The stem of the yacht, whether carried above deck level or not.
B. The bulwarks of the yacht if extended to the stem.
C. When the bulwarks are broken at the extreme bow to allow for a fitting for forestay or for an anchor fairlead/roller, or for a pulpit leg, the point taken will be on the fitting where the fair extension of the bulwark meets the fair extension of the stem, or if this point lies outside the fitting, to the foremost point on the fitting bounded by the above two extensions, to
.2 A point aft, being the extreme after end of the hull and bulwarks or taffrail of the yacht whether at, above, or below deck level. Rubbing strakes at the stern will be included. If rudder and/or push-pit extend abaft this point, neither one nor the other will be included.

312. *Girths:* Girths, as defined in para. 305.1, will be measured:
.1 Forward, the measurements will be at two places:
A. At the forward girth station, FGS, where the girth is equal to one-half of B.
B. At the forward inner girth station, FIGS, where the girth is equal to three-quarters of B.
.2 Aft, the measurements will be at two places, unless the yacht has a transom stern:
A. At the after girth station, AGS, where the girth is equal to three-quarters of B.
B. At the after inner girth station, AIGS, where the girth is equal to seven-eighths of B.
.3 If the yacht has a transom stern, as defined in para. 306, no girth will be taken but the after girth station AGS shall be placed as defined in para. 321 below.
.4 If an after girth three-quarters of B in length cannot be placed on the yacht or is found to cut the transom, a girth will be taken as far aft as possible and its position recorded as AGS. The length of the girth will be measured and the difference between its length and $\frac{3}{4}$B will be

recorded as girth difference (GD) the inner girth station AIGS will then be measured with a girth length of $\frac{7}{8}$B+GD.
On yachts where a GD is not required, it will be recorded as zero.
.5 The following horizontal distances will be taken and recorded:
A. The distance between forward end of LOA and FGS, recorded as forward girth overhang (FGO).
B. The distance between FGS and FIGS, recorded as girth station difference forward (GSDF).
C. The distance between after end of LOA and AGS, recorded as after girth overhang (AGO).
D. The distance between AGS and AIGS, recorded as girth station difference aft (GSDA). In transom stern yachts GSDA will be zero.
E. The distance between FGS and AGS, recorded as length between girth stations (LBG). By definition LBG= LOA — (FGO + AGO).

313. *Beam Forward and Aft.* The maximum beam of the hull at each of the girth stations will be measured as defined in para. 303 and recorded.
.1 The beam at FGS shall be beam forward (BF). See below, 7.
.2 The beam at FIGS shall be beam forward, inner (BFI).
.3 BFI — BF = FSBD (forward stations beam difference). If this is negative it will be taken as zero.
.4 The beam at AGS shall be beam aft (BA). See 8 below.
.5 The beam at AIGS shall be beam aft, inner (BAI).
.6 BAI — BA = ASBD (after stations beam difference). If this is negative, it will be taken as zero.
.7 If BF is greater than BFI, the figure for BFI will be substituted for BF.
.8 If BA is greater than BAI, the figure for BAI will be substituted for BA.

314. *Vertical Heights.* The vertical height (see para. 307) will be measured and recorded at AGS and AIGS, as vertical height aft (VHA) and as vertical height aft inner (VHAI). VHAI — VHA = ASVD (after stations vertical height difference).

315. *Freeboards forward and aft.* Freeboards at each of the girth stations will be measured as defined in para. 309.1 and recorded.
.1 The freeboard at FGS shall be freeboard forward (FF).
.2 The freeboard at FIGS shall be freeboard forward inner (FFI).
.3 FF — FFI = FSFD (forward stations freeboard difference) and can either be positive or negative.
.4 The freeboard at AGS shall be freeboard aft (FA).
.5 The freeboard at AIGS shall be freeboard aft inner (FAI).
.6 FA — FAI = ASFD (after stations freeboard difference) and can be either positive or negative.

316. *Formula for rated length* (L)
$$L = LBG — FOC — AOCC$$
FOC (forward overhang component) is the amount by which the forward end of L lies abaft FGS. If it lies forward of FGS, FOC will be negative and consequently will be an addition to LBG.
AOCC (after overhang component corrected) is the amount by which the after end of L lies forward of AGS. If it lies abaft of AGS, AOCC will be negative and consequently will be an addition to LBG.

317. *Formula for forward overhang component* (FOC)
$$FOC = GSDF \left(\frac{FF — 0\cdot3B + 0\cdot15BF}{0\cdot125B + FSFD — 0\cdot15FSBD} \right)$$
FOC will never be taken as greater than $1\cdot5 \times$ GSDF.

318. *Formula for LBG corrected* (LBGC)
$$LBGC = LBG + \frac{GD \times GSDA}{0\cdot125B}$$

319. *Formula for after overhang component* (AOC)
$$AOC = GSDA \left[0\cdot4 \left(\frac{FA — VHA — 0\cdot024LBGC}{ASFD + ASVD} \right) + 0\cdot6 \left(\frac{FA — 0\cdot375B — 0\cdot5GD + 0\cdot2BA}{0\cdot0625B + ASFD — 0\cdot2ASBD} \right) \right]$$

320. *Formula for after overhang corrected* (AOCC)
If AOC is positive AOCC shall be equal to AOC or 1.25 GSDA whichever is the smaller.

If AOC is negative, the calculated after end of L may lie well abaft the "useful" hull of the yacht. For this reason a point known as limit of length aft is established for each yacht measured (except for yachts with transom sterns). The distance of LLA *abaft* AGS shall be called Y and will be recorded. The position of LLA is as follows:

LLA lies at the aftermost point of the hull except:

In a yacht with a counter cut off with a transom sloping forward from the deck, LLA lies at the aftermost point of the transom at a height, from lowest point of transom, equal to one-half of the total height of the transom measured from the lowest point, to the highest point at deck level.

If the negative AOC is numerically greater than Y:
$$AOCC = 0.4AOC - 0.65Y$$
If the negative AOC is numerically less than Y:
$$AOCC = AOC$$

321. *Transom sterns*. In a transom stern yacht there is one position of AGS only and this is also the after end of L. AOC and Y are therefore zero. An arbitrary position for the "bottom" of the transom is fixed where its overall width is 10% of B the rated beam. The "top" of the transom is taken as the highest point on its surface at deck level. Then, if the transom is vertical or slopes forward from the deck, the position of AGS lies at the aftermost point of the transom at 40% of the total height of the transom from "bottom" to "top". If the transom slopes aft from the deck, the position of AGS lies at the "bottom" of the transom as defined.

322. *Depth*
Forward and midship depth. Depth is measured in two positions:
.1 Forward depth (FD) at a distance abaft FGS of one-quarter of LBG. FD is measured vertically from the level of top of the covering board to a point on the outside of the planking or skin of the yacht at the same section, offset one-tenth of B from the centreline of the yacht.
.2 *Midship depth* (MD) at a distance abaft FGS of one-half of LBG. MD is measured vertically from level of top of covering board to a point on the outside of the planking or skin of the yacht, at the same section, offset one-quarter of B from the centreline of the yacht.

323. *Immersed depths*. The freeboards at the FD and MD stations are measured and recorded as FFD (freeboard at forward depth) and FMD (freeboard at midship depth) respectively. The immersed depths at FD and MD positions are known as FDI (forward depth immersed) and MDI (midship depth immersed) respectively, and:
$$FDI = FD - FFD$$
$$MDI = MD - FMD$$

324. Formula for D (rated depth)
$$D = 1.15MDI + 0.9FDI + 0.055 (3FOC - AOCC) + \frac{L + 10}{30}$$

PART FOUR—FREEBOARD CORRECTION (FC)
401. *Symbols*
FB   Base Freeboard. See 402.
FM   Measured Freeboard. See 403.
FC   Freeboard Correction. See 404.
FF   Freeboard at forward girth station. (Hull measurement. See 315.1)
FA   Freeboard at after girth station. (Hull measurement, See 315.4)

402. *Base Freeboard* (FB)
$$FB = 0.057L + 1.20 \text{ ft.}$$

403. *Measured Freeboard* (FM)
$$FM = \frac{1.2FF + 0.8FA}{2}$$

404. *Freeboard Correction* (FC)
.1 If measured freeboard exceeds base freeboard then

$FC = 0.15$ (FM–FB) and will be subtracted from the measured rating.
.2 If Measured freeboard is less than base freeboard then $FC = 0.25$ (FB — FM) and will be added to the measured rating.

PART FIVE—DRAFT CORRECTION DC
501. Symbols to determine draft adjustments are noted below for reference and described, with methods of application, in the following paragraphs:
CD   Centreboard extension. See 508.
CF   Centreboard factor. See 509.
DD   Draft difference for keel yachts. See 504.
DDC   Draft difference for centreboard yachts. See 510.
DM   Hull draft. See 503 and 507.
DB   Base draft for keel yachts See 502.
DCB   Base draft for centreboard yachts. See 506.
DMX   Draft correction for keel yachts. See 505.
DMXC   Draft correction for centreboard yachts. See 511.
DC   Draft correction, either DMX or DMXC

Keel Yachts
502. *Base draft for keel yachts* (DB)
$$DB = 0.145L + 2.0 \text{ ft.}$$

503. Hull Draft, DM, shall be taken to the deepest part of the fixed keel or other fixed appendage, from the flotation line in the measurement condition. DM may apply to either keel or centreboard yachts.

504. Draft difference for keel yachts, DD = DM — DB and may be either positive or negative.

505. Draft correction for keel yachts, DMX, is correction to rating obtained from the appropriate formula as below:
.1 Where DD is negative, $DMX = 0.10DB\left(\dfrac{3}{3-DD} - 1.0\right)$ ft.
.2 Where DD is positive, and not more than 1.0 ft. $DMX = 0.85DD$
.3 Where DD is more than 1.0 ft. $DMX = DD - 0.15$ ft.

Centreboard Yachts
506. *Base draft for centreboard yachts* (DCB)
$$DCB = 0.45L + 2.0 \text{ ft.}$$

507. Hull draft, DM, as defined above (in 503).

508. Centreboard Extension, CD, shall be the maximum extension of the centreboard, vertically below the deepest part of the fixed keel if the board lies in the centreplane of the yacht, or if not in the centreplane, the maximum extension from the adjacent hull surface in the plane of the board. When there is more than one board, the greatest extension shall be used.

If the draft with boards extended does not exceed the draft of the fixed keel the yacht shall be treated as a fixed keel yacht.

509. Centreboard factor, CF, shall be obtained from the appropriate formula, as below:
.1 in the case of a single centreboard $CF = \dfrac{CD^2}{0.5L + 1.5}$ ft.
.2 Where two or more centreboards are installed,
$$CF = \frac{CD^2}{0.45L + 1.5} \text{ ft.}$$

510. Draft difference for centreboard yachts, DDC = DM + CF — DCB, which may be either positive or negative.

511. Draft correction for centreboard yachts, DMXC, shall be determined according to the appropriate formula, as follows:
.1 When DDC is negative, $DMXC = 0.10DCB\left(\dfrac{3}{3-DDC} - 1\right)$ ft.
.2 When DDC is positive and not more than 1.0 ft. $DMXC = 0.85$ DDC.
.3 When DDC is more than 1.0 ft. $DMXC = DDC - 0.15$ ft.

PART SIX—ENGINE AND PROPELLER ALLOWANCE

901. Symbols used in the definition and calculation of engine and propeller allowances are listed below for reference and described, with methods of application in the following paragraphs.

EPF   Engine and propeller factor. See 602.
EW   Engine weight. See 603.
EWD   Engine weight distance. See 604.
EM   Engine moment. See 605.
PS   Propeller size. See 609.
EMF   Engine moment factor. See 606.
DF   Propeller drag factor. See 608.
PF   Propeller factor. See 607.
PD   Propeller depth. See 607. 2.
BD   Base draft. See 502.
L   Length. See 316.

602. Engine and propeller factor, EPF, results from the application of the following formula:

$$\text{EPF} = 1 - \left(\frac{\text{EMF} + \text{DF}}{100} \right)$$

EPF shall not be taken as less than 0·9600.
The engine and propeller factor shall apply only if:

.1 The racing propeller can be demonstrated to be capable of driving the yacht in calm water at a speed of at least $0.75 \sqrt{\text{L}}$ knots.

.2 The propeller is at all times ready for use and shall not be retracted, housed, shielded or faired except by a conventional strut or aperture.

.3 The propeller is locked or otherwise secured in an easily releasable manner to prevent rotation while racing.

603. Engine dry weight, EW, shall be the engine dry weight in pounds taken from the manufacturer's catalogue. Reverse and reduction gear, if installed, and engine mounted dynamo and/or selfstarter shall be included in the engine weight.

604. Engine weight distance, EWD, shall be the horizontal distance in feet between the centre of the cylinder block of the engine and the mid point of LBG.

605. Engine moment, EM, is the product of EW and EWD; that is EM = EW × EWD.

606. Engine moment factor, EMF, shall be determined according to the formula:

$$\text{EMF} = \frac{0 \cdot 1 \ \text{EM}}{\text{L}^2 \times \text{B} \times \text{D}}$$

EMF shall not be taken as more than 1·0.

607. *Propeller.*

.1 Propeller Factor, PF, in the formula in para. 608 is taken from the following table as applicable:

Type of Propeller	Types of Installation		
	In Aperture	Out of Aperture	
		With exposed Shaft	Other
Folding	·95	·85	·35
Feathering	·95	1·05	·55
Solid	1·05	2·05	1·55

To qualify for full "In Aperture" propeller factor, an aperture must have a height of not less than $112\frac{1}{2}\%$ of the propeller diameter and a fore and aft opening of not less than 40% of the propeller diameter at distances of one third the diameter above and below the centre of the shaft line. If the aperture is smaller than these minimum dimensions, the propeller factor shall be taken as one-half of the "In Aperture" propeller factors tabulated.

To qualify for "With Exposed Shaft" propeller factor, the distance from the centre of the propeller (as determined by the intersection of the blade axis and shaft) to the point at which the shaft line emerges from the hull or appendage must not be less than 150% propeller diameter; propeller blade tip clearance must not be more than 25% of the propeller diameter.

Any out of aperture installation not qualifying as "With Exposed Shaft" is to be classified as "Other".

.2 Propeller Depth, PD, is measured from the centre of the propeller hub to the LWL plane.

.3 Propeller size, PS, is the diameter of the propeller or four times the greatest width of the blades, whichever is less. If the propeller blades are not of normal elliptical or near rectangular shape, the average blade width instead of the greatest width shall be used to determine propeller size. Widths shall be measured across the driving face of the blade on a chord at right angles to the radius of the blade.

608. Propeller drag factor, DF, shall be calculated from the following formula:

$$\text{DF} = 1 - \left(\text{PF} \times \sqrt{\frac{\text{PD}}{\text{BD}}} \times \frac{\text{PS}}{\text{L}} \right)$$

609. Propeller size, PS, shall be the diameter of the propeller, or four times the greatest width of the blade, whichever is less. Provided the propeller is of normal, elliptical, assymetric elliptical or near rectangular shape, its greatest width shall be measured across the surface of the blade at right angles to the radius. If the blade is of any other shape its average width shall be used instead of its greatest width to determine propeller size.

PART SEVEN—CENTRE OF GRAVITY FACTOR

701. *Symbols*
BWL   Waterline Beam. See 704.
CGF   Centre of Gravity Factor. See 705.
L   Rated Length. See 314.
RM   Righting Moment. See 702.
TR   Tenderness Ratio. See 703.

702. To obtain the righting moment at one degree heel—RM—the yacht shall be inclined as covered by separate instructions to measurers. The appropriate CCA booklet may be considered applicable subject to the preparation of the yacht as covered in para. 202 of these rules. Note that the heel angle for stability measurement is not limited to 1°, but that the measured stability shall be corrected to 1° of heel for use in the formula for TR (Tenderness Ratio). See 703.

In the case of a yacht fitted with any form of centreboard, lee board or drop keel the inclining tests will be carried out with the board or keel fully raised. The weight of each board or keel shall be assessed and the vertical distance by which the centre of gravity of these can be lowered shall be measured. To the measured righting moment at 1° of heel must be added:

"Weight of board or drop keel × vertical drop of CG × 0·0175.

703. *Tenderness Ratio*—TR—is determined from the following formula:

$$\text{TR} = \frac{0 \cdot 97\text{L} \times (\text{BWL})^3}{\text{RM}}$$

704. *Waterline Beam*—BWL—is the waterline beam measured in the same vertical station as BMAX.

705. *Centre of Gravity Factor*—CGF—is determined from the following formula:

$$\text{CGF} = \frac{1 \cdot 4}{\text{TR} - 6 \cdot 1} + 0 \cdot 9350$$

PART EIGHT
RIG AND SAIL AREA MEASUREMENTS

801. Symbols used to determine the dimensions for sail area are noted below for reference. They are further described in subsequent paragraphs.

Dimensions Requiring Measurements

BAD — Height of Mainsail Tack above Deck. (Lower termination of P.) See 813.1B.

BADS — Height of Foresail Tack in Schooner. (Lower termination of PS.) See 838.

BADX — Height of Lower Termination of IS above Deck See 840.

BADY — Height of Mizzen Tack above the Deck. (Lower termination of PY.) See 823.1A.

BAL — Distance between outer measurement of E and bale on boom end. See 812.1.

BALF — The same for Foresails of Schooner. See 841.3.

BALY — The same for Mizzens. See 821.

BL, 2— Length of Mainsail Battens numbered from the top. See 846.

BYI, 2— Length of Mizzen Battens numbered from the top. See 846.

BSL, 2— Length of Schooner Foresail Battens numbered from the top. See 846.1, 2, 3, and 4.

BLP — Batten Leach Penalty. See 846.1.

E — Length of the Foot of the Mainsail. See 812.

EC — Length of the Foot of the Mainsail, corrected. See 812.2.

EB — Distance between Masts in Two-Masted Rigs. See 832 and 836.

EBC — Distance between Masts in Two-Masted Rigs, corrected. See 837.

EF — Length of the Foot of the Foresail in Schooners. See 841.3.

EY — Length of the Foot of the Mizzen. See 820.

EYC — Length of the Foot of the Mizzen, corrected. See 822.

G — Length of Head of Gaff Mainsail along Gaff. See 816.

GF — Length of Head of Gaff Foresail along Gaff. See 841.3.

GY — Length of Head of Gaff Mizzen along Gaff. See 828.

H — Length of Hoist Gaff Mainsail. See 814.

HC — Length of Hoist of Gaff Mainsail, corrected. See 815.

HF — Length of Hoist Gaff Foresail. See 841.3.

HY — Length of Hoist Gaff Mizzen. See 826.

HB — Width of Headboard of Mainsail. See 845.1.

HBF — Width of Headboard of Foresail. See 841.3.

HBS — Width of Headboard of Spinnaker. See 845.3.

HBY — Width of Headboard of Mizzen. See 845.2.

I — Length of Foretriangle Hoist. See 809.

IC — Length of Foretriangle Hoist, corrected. See 809.3.

IS — Length of Hoist on Foreside of Schooner Mainmast. See 840.

LY — Length of Hoist on Foreside Mizzen Mast. See 825.

J — Length of Foretriangle Base. See 806.

JC — Length of Foretriangle Base, corrected. See 806.1.

LP — Least Perpendicular of Jibs as derived. See 810.1.

LPG — Least Perpendicular of Genoas set on Forestay. See 810.1A.

LPIS — Least Perpendicular of Staysails set on Inner Tack Point. See 810.1C.

MSAT — Measured Sail Area of Topsail. See 817.

OF — Greatest Overlap of Foresails abaft Mainmast in Schooners. See 837.

P — Length of Mainsail Hoist. See 813.1.

PC — Length of Mainsail Hoist, corrected. See 813.2.

PS — Length of Foresail Hoist in Schooners. See 838.

PSC — Length of Foresail Hoist in Schooners, corrected. See 839.

PY — Length of Mizzen Hoist. See 823.

PYC — Length of Mizzen Hoist, corrected. See 824.

SF — Spinnaker Foot Length. See 808.

SL — Spinnaker Luff Leach Length. See 808.

SMG — Spinnaker Midgirth Length. See 808.

SMW — Spinnaker Maximum Width. See 808.

SPH — Maximum Height of Spinnaker Pole above Deck. See 851.

SPL — Spinnaker Pole Length. See 807.

YSD — Mizzen Staysail Depth. See 830.

YSF — Mizzen Staysail Foot Length. See 829.

YSMG — Mizzen Staysail Midgirth Length. See 831.

Dimensions and Areas derived from Calculations

LP — Least Perpendicular in Foretriangle. See 810.1.

MSA — Measured Sail Area derived from Simple Triangulation. See 802.

MSAT — Measured Sail Area of Gaff Topsail. 817.

RSA — Rated Sail Area derived by Appropriate Formula. See 803.

RSAB — Rated Sail Area between Masts Unrestricted. See 841.1.

RSAC — Combined RSA between and abaft Masts. See 843.

RSAD — Rated Sail Area between Masts and Staysails. See 841.2.

RSAF — Rated Sail Area Foretriangle. See 811.

RSAG — Rated Sail Area between Masts Foresail only. See 841.4.

RSAK — Rated Sail Area of Mizzen Staysail. See 834.

RSAM — Rated Sail Area of Mainsail. See 818 and 819.

RSAT — Total Rated Sail Area. See 804 and 844.

RSAY — Rated Sail Area of Mizzen. See 835.

$\sqrt{S}$ — Square root of RSAT. See 104.

YSAC — Combined Area of Mizzen and Mizzen Staysail. See 835.

CALCULATION OF SAIL AREA

802. Determination of MSA: MSA is the measured sail area determined by applying triangulation to the uncorrected measurements of a single element of the rig.

803. Determination of RSA: RSA shall be the rated sail area of any part of the rig determined by applying the corrected dimensions in the formulae as further defined.

804. Determination of RSAT: The RSAT to be used for each rig is the sum of the RSA for each sail or part of the rig as defined below:

A. For Cat Rig—Mainsail only. (RSAM) (Section 818).

B. For Sloop or Cutter—Mainsail and Fore triangle (RSAM and RSAF) (Sections 818 and 811).

C. For Yawl or Ketch—Foretriangle and combined Rated sail area between and abaft the masts (RSAF and RSAC) (Sections 811, 843.1 and 844). A Yawl or Ketch is a two-masted rig in which the height of the after mast (IY) is less than the height of the forward mast (the greater of I or P + BAD). No distinction between a yawl or ketch is required by these rules.

D. For Schooner (two-masted) Foretriangle and combined Rated sail area between and abaft the masts (RSAF and RSAC) (Sections 811, 843.2, and 844). A Schooner is a two-masted yacht in which the height of the after, or mainmast (IS) is equal to or greater than the height of the foremast (the greater of I or PS).

E. For other rigs—a study of details for measurement of the rigs specifically covered above should point the way to appropriate measurement of other rigs.

In these rules the word headsail is defined as a sail set in the foretriangle. It can be either a spinnaker or a jib. Paragraph 850 defines the proportions and limitations of jibs and spinnakers. (See also 848 and 852.)

805. *Height of Deck*
The height of deck used as a datum for sail area measurements shall be taken at 4% of B above the covering board abreast the mast. For raised or stepped decks see 302, 303 and 304, also instructions to measurers.

FORETRIANGLE

806. *Base of Foretriangle*
Determination of J: J is the actual foretriangle base taken from the foreside of the mast at the deck to the centreline of the foremost stay on which headsails are set (the centreline of the luff if the foremast headsail is set flying) extended if necessary to intersect the top of the rail, including rail cap or its extension or bowsprit if used, or to the centreline of the deck, should this be above the rail or rail cap.

.1 Determination of JC: JC shall be the corrected base of the foretriangle taken as the greatest of the three measurements, J, SPL, or SMW divided by 1.80. (See 852.1B.)

807. *Spinnaker Pole*
Determination of SPL: SPL is the length of the spinnaker pole when in its fitting on the mast and set in a horizontal position athwartships, measured from the centreline of the yacht to the extreme outboard end of the pole and any fittings used when a spinnaker is set. (See 806.1.)

808. *Spinnaker (for definition see Para. 850 and 852)*
Determination of SMW: SMW shall be spinnaker maximum width, whether at the foot or across the body of the sail, measured between points on the luff and leach equidistant from the head. (See 852.1B.)
Determination of Spinnaker luff or leach: SL shall be the greatest length of spinnaker luff and leach. (See 852.1A.)
Determination of Spinnaker Foot Length: SF shall be the distance from tack to clew measured in the shortest path on the surface of the sail. (See para. 852.1F.)
Determination of Spinnaker midgirth length: SMG shall be the distance between the midpoints of luff and leech measured in the shortest path on the surface of the sail. (See paras. 852.1E and F.)

809. *Height of Foretriangle*
Determination of I: I is the foretriangle height measured along the foreside of the mast from the main deck (as defined in 805) (see 302, 303 and 304) to either:
.1 The highest of the following three points:
  A. The intersection of the centreline of the highest stay used for headsails, with the fair line of the foreside of the mast or topmast (projected if necessary).
  B. The centre of the highest eye bolt or eye used for headsail or spinnaker halyard block. A spinnaker halyard block may be set forward enough to permit a clear lead, without measurement penalty.
  C. To intersection of the foreside of the mast or topmast with the highest strop used for headsail or spinnaker halyard.
.2 As determined under the 1957 R.O.R.C. Rule, Section V, para. (11), as reprinted in 1968. This method may at the owner's option be applied to yachts holding R.O.R.C. Rule certificates valid during any part of 1969 or earlier.
.3 Determination of IC: IC is the corrected foretriangle height determined by increasing "I" according to any of the requirements of these rules. (See 851 and 852.1A.)

810. *Headsail Overlap*
.1 Determination of LP: LP is least perpendicular, taken as the greatest of:
  A. LPG the greatest dimension of any jib carried, measured on the perpendicular from luff to clew.
  B. 1.5JC: or
  C. LPIS the greatest distance between the clew of any headsail and the foremost jib stay measured perpendicular to the stay (or to the position of the luff of the foremast jib if set flying) which occurs because of tacking such headsail inside another headsail and abaft the foremost tack position. (Owners and crew members must note) (See 848).

811. Foretriangle Rated Sail Area RSAF shall be calculated according to the following formula:

$$RSAF = \frac{IC \times JC}{6} + \frac{IC \times LP}{3} + 0.2JC\,(IC - 2JC)$$

The quantity $0.2JC\,(IC - 2JC)$ shall be discarded if negative.

MAINSAIL

812. *Foot of Mainsails*
Determination of E: E is the length, measured along the boom, of the foot of the mainsail taken from the after side of mast (or the fair extension of track, if used) to extreme aftermost position to which the sail can be extended. If this latter point is inside of boom end, it shall be located by the inner edge of a 1-inch measurement band around the boom.
  .1 Determination of BAL: BAL is the distance from the outer measurement point of E, to any bale on the boom provided for the lead of any headsail sheet.
  2. Determination of EC: EC is the corrected length of the

foot of the mainsail obtained by adding to E any amount by which BAL exceeds 0.25 ft.
  A. For staysail ketch, see 842A.
  B. For loose footed mainsail, see para. 842C.

813. *Jib headed mainsails*
.1 Determination of P: P is the measured length of the hoist of a jib headed mainsail. It is the distance along the afterside of the mainmast from the highest level to which the head of the sail may be set to the lowest position of the tack. The highest point shall be taken as the top of the highest sheave used for the main halyard, or to the lower edge of a 1-inch black band (but see sub-paragraph below), provided either a fixed stop or an accurate halyard mark will indicate exactly when the highest part of the sail is at the level of the lower edge of the band. The lowest position of the foot shall normally be the fair extension of the top of the boom track or boom if there is no track.
  A. If a sliding gooseneck is used, measurement is to be made with the boom at the extreme bottom of the slide unless the lowest sailing position of the foot of the sail (boom or boom track) is marked by the upper edge of a 1-inch black band around the mast. The top of the boom (or track) shall not be carried below this point when the mainsail is set, except when actually putting in or shaking out a reef in the mainsail.
  B. BAD shall be the distance between the low point used in the determination of P, and the main deck at the mast. This shall not without penalty be taken as more than $0.05P + 4.0$ ft. Any excess shall be added to PC.
  C. In the event that the tack of the sail is carried below the boom, its lowest position shall be marked by the upper edge of 1-inch measurement band around the mast from which the low point of P shall be measured.
  D. If rake of mast exceeds 15%, P shall be taken as the vertical height. Per cent of rake shall be determined by taking the horizontal distance on deck between plumb-bob or equivalent suspended freely from masthead, and dividing this distance by the height of masthead from deck measured along after side of mast.
  E. Mainsail head. The head of the jib headed mainsail shall not without penalty be located so that the upper point for measuring P is more than 0.041 below the upper point of I, or in the case of schooner, 0.04 IS below the upper point of IS. In the event that the head of the sail is so located the difference shall be included in PC.
.2 Determination of PC: PC is the corrected length of P. P shall be increased as required by any of the provisions of these rules, such as height, headboard size or batten length, or position of the head or foot.

814. *Gaff Mainsail*
Determination of H: H is the measured length of the hoist for a gaff mainsail. It shall be the distance along the after side of the mast from the lower edge of 1-inch black band around the mast, above which mark the upper inner edge of the throat cringle of the mainsail shall not be hoisted, to the upper side of the boom or measurement band, denoting the lowest point of the tack, as defined in 813.1A, B and C. BAD for gaff mainsails shall not without penalty exceed $0.05\,(H + 6G) + 4.0$ ft. any excess shall be added to HC.

815. Determination of HC: HC shall be the corrected length of the hoist of a gaff headed mainsail. H shall be increased as required by any of the provisions of these rules and entered into the RSA formula as HC.

816. Determination of G: G is the measured length of the head of the mainsail along the gaff. It is the distance from the afterside of mast to outboard point of gaff, determined in a manner similar to that for outboard end of main boom in 812 above.

817. *Topsail*
Determination of MSAT: MSAT shall be the area of the topsail calculated from the measurement of the three sides. Taking the height from the upper point of the mainsail hoist to the highest point to which the topsail may be set, including sprit if any; the length of gaff (G) to which it is sheeted, plus extension of club if any; and the length of leach measured from the sail when stretched taut.

818. *Determination of* RSAM: mainsail rated sail area shall be calculated according to the applicable formula:
.1 For jib headed mainsail: $RSAM = 0.35EC \times PC + 0.2E$ $(PC - 2E)$.
A. The quantity $0.2E (PC - 2E)$ shall be discarded if negative, or
.2 For gaff headed mainsail:
$$RSAM = 0.35 (HC \times EC) + 0.35G\sqrt{HC^2 + E^2} + 0.2E (HC - 2E) + 0.6MSAT$$
A. the quantity $0.2E (HC - 2E)$ shall be discarded if negative.

819. A yacht must be rated with a mainsail. If RSAM calculated as above is less than $0.094(IC)^2$, RSAM shall be taken as $0.094(IC)^2$. In schooners the limits for main are $0.094(IS)^2$.

MIZZENS (YAWL AND KETCH) INCLUDING MIZZEN
STAYSAILS (SPINNAKERS)
820. *Foot of Mizzen*
Determination of EY: EY is the measured length of the foot of the mizzen sail. The method by which this is measured shall follow that used for the foot of the mainsail.
821. Determination of BALY: BALY is the distance from the outer measurement point of EY to any bale on the mizzen-boom provided for the lead of any mizzen staysail sheet.

822. Determination of EYC: EYC is the corrected length of the foot of the mizzen sail. This shall be the greater of EY or $0.85\frac{E}{P} \times PY$ plus any amount by which BALY exceeds 0.25 ft.

823. *Jib headed Mizzen*
.1 Determination of PY: PY is the measured length of the hoist of a jib headed mizzen sail. The method by which this is measured shall follow that used for the hoist of the mainsail (para. 813).
A. The height of the lower point of PY, BADY, shall not without penalty be taken as more than $0.05PY + 4.0$ ft. Any excess shall be added to PYC.
B. The head of a jib headed mizzen shall not without penalty be located so that the upper point of PY is more than $0.041Y$ below the upper point of IY (see 825).

824. Determination of PYC: PYC is the corrected length of the hoist of the jib headed mizzen sail, determined by increasing P as required by any of the provisions of these rules such as headboard size or batten length, and in this case any increment required by the position of the top of mizzen staysail halyard sheave or the point of attachment of the block.

825. Determination of IY: IY is the height measured along the foreside of the mizzen mast from the deck as defined in para. 805 to the higher of:
A. The centre of the highest eyebolt or eye used for a mizzen staysail, or
B. The intersection of the foreside of the mast with the highest strop used for the halyard of a mizzen staysail.

826. *Gaff Mizzen*
Determination of HY: HY is the measured length of the hoist of a gaff mizzen sail. The method by which this is determined shall follow that used for a gaff mainsail (para. 814). BADY shall not without penalty be taken as more than 0.05 $(HY + 0.6GY) + 4.0$ ft. Any excess shall be added to HY.

827. Determination of HYC: HYC is the corrected length of the hoist of a gaff mizzen sail, determined by increasing HY according to any of the provisions of these rules including but not limited to the following:
Any excess in batten length (para. 846).

828. Determination of GY: GY is the measured length of the mizzen sail along the gaff from the mast to the furthest point of extension determined as in the case of the main boom covered in Section (812).

829. *Mizzen Staysail*
Determination of YSF: YSF is the distance measured along the edge of the foot of the mizzen staysail from tack to clew.

830. Determination of YSD: YSD is the shortest distance that can be measured across the mizzen staysail from head to foot.

831. Determination of mizzen staysail mid girth YSMG: YSMG is the distance measured on the surface of the sail from the mid point of the luff to the mid point of the leach.

832. Determination of EB: EB is the distance at deck level between the after side of the mainmast or fair projection of track to the foreside of the mizzen mast.

833. Mizzen Rated Sail Area (Yawls and Ketches) RSAY— Mizzen rated sail area shall be calculated according to the following formula, providing simple triangular area:

For jib headed mizzens: $RSAY = \dfrac{EYC \times PYC}{2}$

For gaff headed mizzens:
$$RSAY = 0.5 (HYC \times EY) + 0.5 \sqrt{HYC^2 + EY^2}$$

834. Mizzen Staysail Rated Area RSAK — Mizzen staysail rated area shall be determined by the formula
$$RSAK = YSD \times \left(\frac{YSF + YSMG}{3}\right) \times 0.30\frac{EB}{E}$$

835. Determination of YSAC: YSAC is the combined area of the Mizzen and Mizzen Staysail found by the formula:
$$YSAC = \frac{RSAY + RSAK}{2}$$

This YSAC and RSAM shall be further combined to become RSAC (see para. 843).

SCHOONERS AND STAYSAIL KETCHES
(AREA BETWEEN MASTS)
836. Determination of EB (2-masted schooners)—EB is the distance measured at the deck from the foreside of the main-mast to the afterside of the foremast (or fair extension of tack if used).

837. Determination of EBC: EBC is the corrected distance between the masts of a 2-masted schooner, determined by increasing EB to include any overlap (OF) of the foresail or lower main staysail beyond the main mast (see 855).

838. Determination of PS: PS is the distance measured along the after side of the foremast used in the determination of area between the masts.
.1 The upper measurement point shall be the higher of the following, used for sails aft of the mast:
A. The top of the highest sheave, in the mast, or
B. The highest eyebolt (centre of eye) or pennant of a halyard block.
.2 The lower measurement point shall be lowest position of the foot of the foresail or main staysail or other sail set between the masts, taken as described under para. 813B.
When a jib headed foresail is used between the masts of a schooner PS shall be measured as for the luff of a jib headed mainsail. (See 841.3 and 813.1.)

839. Determination of PSC: PSC is the corrected value of PS taking into account the provisions of rules 813B and 813E and any penalty due to battens or headboards.

840. Determination of IS: IS is the distance measured along the foreside of the mainmast used in the determination of area between the masts.
  .1 The upper measurement point shall be the higher of the following used for sails forward of the mast:
    A. The top of the highest sheave, in the mast, or
    B. The highest eyebolt (centre of eye) or pennant of a halyard block.
  .2 The height of the lower point of measurement, BADX, shall be taken at the same height above the deck as the lower point of measurement of PS.

841. Rated Sail Area between the masts (2-masted schooners and staysail ketches) shall be calculated as follows:
  .1 Yachts using an unrestricted list of topmast staysails between the masts shall have RSAB calculated by the formula:
$$RSAB = 0\cdot5EBC\ (PS + IS)$$
  .2 For gaff or jib headed foresail schooners carrying not more than two topmast staysails and following the limitations of para. 866.1A:
$$RSAD = 0\cdot4EBC\ (PS + IS)$$
  .3 For gaff or jib headed foresail schooners carrying only such sails plus topsail, if measured, but no staysails between the masts, measurement shall be according to the mainsail formula where EF is the foot of the foresail, HF is the hoist of the gaff foresail and GF the length of gaff.
$$RSAG = 0\cdot35\ (EF \times PSC) + 0\cdot2EF\ (PSC - 2EF)$$
or
For gaff headed foresail
$$RSAG = 0\cdot35\ (HC \times EF) + 0\cdot35G\sqrt{HC^2 + EF^2} + 0.2EF(HC - 2EF) + 0\cdot6MSAT$$

842. *Rating of unusual sails*
  A. Mainsail RSA of Staysail Ketch. This shall be treated as a schooner under para. 841.1. Any overlap of a lower mizzen staysail shall be added to EBC.
  B. Rated area of quadrilateral mainsail (other than gaff sail) or other unusual mainsail to be $0\cdot75MSA + 0\cdot2E$ (P–2E).
      The aspect ratio correction above shall not be taken as a minus quantity.
  C. Mainsails, mizzens or foresails in para. 841 without booms—where these are used, the E, EY or EF measurement is the maximum measurement (at right angles to the luff) of the sail when new. The measurer shall sign the sail and mark the dimensions.
  D. Main backstay sails (Mules) as used on jib headed yawls and ketches shall have 50% of their MSA as determined by measurement of the sail when new added to the mainsail RSA to arrive at the final RSAM for the rig. Mizzen staysail may not be carried in addition.
  E. Gaff mainsails—if the length of the gaff is less than $0\cdot6E$ or peaks higher than $70°$ above the horizontal, mainsail RSA will be calculated as a jib headed mainsail (para. 818.1), using $P = HC + G$.

843. Combined Rated Sail Area between and abaft the masts RSAC: RSAC shall represent the combined rated sail area exclusive of the foretriangle in any yacht having two masts. The following elements shall be included according to rig:
  RSAM   Mainsail rated area—yawl, ketch or schooner. See 818 and 819.
  YSAC   combined area of mizzen and mizzen staysail—yawl or ketch. See 835.
  RSAB   Rated area between the masts of schooners and staysail ketch. See 841.1.
  RSAD   Rated area between masts of schooner with two topmast staysails. See 841.2.
  RSAG   Rated area between masts of schooner with foresail only. See 841.3.
The appropriate elements are to be combined with the mainsail by the following formulae:

  .1 For yawls or ketches
$$RSAC = RSAM + \frac{(YSAC)^2}{RSAM + YSAC} + RSAK = RSAY$$
Where RSAK = RSAY is positive; if RSAK = RSAY is negative use formula $RSAC = RSAM + \dfrac{(YSAC)^2}{RSAM + YSAC}$
  .2 For schooners and staysail ketches
$$RSAC = RSAM + \frac{(RSAB)^2}{RSAM + RSAB}$$
In the above formula, RSAD or RSAG may be substituted for RSAB as appropriate.

844. RSAT *two-masted rigs*
The total rated sail area for all two-masted rigs shall be found from the formula:
$$RSAT = RSAC + RSAF$$

MISCELLANEOUS LIMITATIONS AND CORRECTIVE ADJUSTMENTS

845. *Headboards*
  .1 Headboards in jib headed mainsails shall not without penalty exceed 3% of E but shall not be required to be less than $4\frac{1}{2}$in. Any excess width shall be multiplied by $\frac{P}{E}$ and added to PC in computing mainsail rated area.
  .2 Headboards in jib headed mizzens shall not without penalty exceed 3% of EY but shall not be required to be less than $4\frac{1}{2}$in. Any excess width shall be multiplied by $\frac{PY}{EY}$ and added to PYC in computing RSAY.
  .3 Headboards' width in spinnakers shall not without penalty exceed 5% of SPL. Any excess width shall be multiplied by $\frac{1\cdot8 \times SL}{SMWS}$ and added to IC.
  .4 Headboards may not be used in jibs.

846. *Battens*
  .1 The number of battens in any mainsail, mizzen or foresail in a schooner shall without penalty be limited to four, except that, when the foot of the sail exceeds 40 ft., five battens may be used. Batten spacing shall be approximately even between head and clew. In addition the distance between the top batten measured from the centre line of the pocket, and the head of the sail (junction of leach and headboard) shall not without penalty be less than 20% of the length of the leach measured along the seam (17% in the case of 5 battens). Should it be less, the deficit (BLP) shall be added to the length of the top batten.
  .2 The length of the battens shall not without penalty exceed:
      for upper and lower battens — $0\cdot10E + 1$ ft.
      for intermediate battens   — $0\cdot12E + 1$ ft.
      In the case of any excess length, the whole length of the top batten excess plus $\frac{1}{6}$ of the total excess length of the remaining battens shall be multiplied by $\frac{P}{E}$ and added to P in computing the RSA of jib headed sails.
  .3 In the event of the number of battens being in excess of those allowed in (A) above, the total length of the longest excess intermediate battens shall be multiplied by $\frac{P}{E}$ and added to P in computing the RSA of jib headed sails.
  .4 For gaff sails, $\frac{1}{6}$ of the total excess of all battens shall be added to H in computing RSA.
  .5 Battens may be used in jibs and forestay sails only if:
    A. their length is not more than $0\cdot08J$, and
    B. their forward end is forward of the centreline of the mast supporting their halyard.
    C. the number of battens is limited to four, which must be arranged with approximately equal spacing between head and clew.
  .6 Battens may not be used in spinnakers.

847. *Boom depth*
If the maximum depth of the boom exceeds 5% of E (EY in the case of mizzens) the excess shall be added to P (PY in the case of mizzens). Excess boom depths on between mast sails for schooners shall be similarly treated.

848. *Staysails*
No staysail or jib may be set inside another headsail and tacked in such a position that its clew if trimmed flat along the centre line of the yacht would fall abaft a line parallel to the foremost headstay or luff of headsail set flying and separated from it by the dimension of LP declared for rating. This provision shall not be interpreted to prevent the use of any sail for which a yacht has been measured with an appropriate LP but rather to establish control of the dimensions and fore and aft positions of sails providing a double head rig. Such sails may be tacked athwartships as desired.

849. *Clewboards*
No clewboards may be used in jibs or staysails.

850. *Distinction between spinnakers and jibs*
A sail shall not be measured as a spinnaker unless the mid girth is 75% or more of the foot length and is symmetrical about a line joining the head to the centre of the foot. No jib may have a mid girth measured between the mid points of luff and leach more than 50% of the foot length. Thus head sails with midgirths between 50% and 75% shall not be allowed.

851. *Height of spinnaker track* (SPM)
The arrangement to support the inboard end of the spinnaker pole on the mast shall be made so that the height of the inboard end of the pole is controlled. It shall not without penalty be capable of being set higher than 0·25I above the deck. When this limit is exceeded, such amount shall be added to I, in computing IC.

852. *Spinnaker*
.1 The spinnaker shall be subject to the following limitations:
A. Luff and leach, shall be of equal length, which shall not without penalty exceed $\cdot 95\sqrt{(I^2 + JC^2)}$. When this length is exceeded twice the excess shall be added to I, in computing IC.
B. Maximum width shall not without penalty exceed 1·8J or 1·8SPL. When width is greater, JC will be correspondingly increased (para. 806.1).
C. Headboard to be limited as covered under para. 845.3.
D. Spinnakers shall be symmetrical about a line joining head to the centre of the foot.
E. Mid girth shall be not less than 75% of foot length.
F. Spinnakers shall be measured with such tension as will in the opinion of the measurer produce an approximation of the size when set, running in a suitable breeze. The measurer shall sign the sail indicating the date of measurement, and the maximum length of luff and leach and maximum width, and his approval with respect to all other requirements. These measurements shall apply during the unaltered life of the sail.
G. Notwithstanding any failure to meet the above limitations, any bona fide headsail, otherwise permitted and for which the yacht has been measured, may be used as a spare spinnaker. Such a sail may be tacked to or sheeted to the spinnaker pole when the spinnaker is not set.
H. Struts, spools or similar devices used solely for the purpose of keeping the spinnaker guy away from the windward main or foremost shrouds are permitted but are not to be used for any other purpose.
I. Spinnaker Pole. When the mainsail is set the outboard end of the spinnaker pole may be used only on the windward side of the yacht (i.e., that opposite to the main boom). A spinnaker pole may only be used with its inboard end attached to the mast (foremast if more than one mast).

853. *Squaresail*
A yacht may carry a squaresail, square topsail, raffee or a twin spinnaker rig, instead of a spinnaker. The actual area of such sails may not exceed the rated foretriangle area (RSAF), nor may the total length of their boom or booms exceed SPL.

854. *Running Sails*
When mainsail is not set two spinnaker poles, or one spinnaker pole and main boom, may be simultaneously used without violating para. 861B or the first sentence of para. 852I and two jibs may be set, neither of which may exceed the area of the biggest jib for which the boat is measured.

855. *Foresails of Schooners*
Jib headed, gaff headed or quadrilateral foresails or lower main staysails shall not overlap the mainmast unless measured accordingly. The maximum such overlap shall be added to EB in the determination of EBC.

856. *Miscellaneous Restrictions*
Double luffed sails (those with thick or wrap-around luffs, not spinnakers or squaresails) rotating masts, mechanically or permanently bent spars or similar contrivances, are excluded for yachts measured under the rule. Mainsails, schooner foresails and mizzens may be reefed at the foot only. Roach, slab or flattening reefs are permitted along the foot only.

SPECIAL LIMITATIONS ON SAILS AND SAIL TRIMMING
857. *General*
As sails must be set and trimmed in a manner consistent with the way they are measured, conflicts will exist between these rules and those of the I.Y.R.U. and National Authorities. In such cases, the I.O.R. rules will govern but when not in conflict, the rules of the I.Y.R.U. or the appropriate National Authority shall be observed.

858. *Trimming to Spars*
Sheets of spinnakers, headsails, mizzen staysails, loose-footed sails may not be trimmed to spars, outside the measurement points, except that such sheets may be trimmed to the usual bale or fitting on the after end of a main or mizzen boom. (See paras. 812.1, 812.2 and 821.)

859. *Mainsails*
A. Loose-footed Mainsails. These are permitted only when they are the regular mainsail normally used for the boat in question. Under these conditions, when a loose-footed mainsail is used, it is not permissible to carry on board a second mainsail that is not loose-footed, nor is it permissible to shift back and forth between a loose-footed and a secured foot mainsail for various races; rather the selection must be made regarding mainsail type at the time the measurement certificate is issued.
B. Light-weight Mainsails. These are not permitted to be carried on board with the expectation of improved performance, as for varying weather conditions or points of sailing, but rather a second mainsail can only be carried on board as a bona fide spare for emergency replacement.
C. Storm Trysails. These, as distinguished from loose-footed mainsails, must be materially smaller than a normal close reefed mainsail and of a strength consistent with their intended purpose, viz. use in extremely severe weather.

860. *Headsails*
A. Headsails may be sheeted from only one point on the sail (thus excluding quadrilateral or similar sails).
B. Headsails may be sheeted to any part of the rail or deck (or to the main boom so long as the mainsail is set) and to spinnaker pole when pole is set on opposite side from main boom but may not be sheeted to any other spar or outrigger.
C. No combination of jib and tack pennant will be permitted, whether hanked on to a stay or set flying, the combined luff of which cannot be fully stretched when hoisted on the highest genoa halyard and tacked at the fore end of J.
D. No sail shall be set to fly out kitewise and over mainsail and/or spinnaker by sheeting over main boom or by any

other means. This provision does not apply to the spin-naker sheet when the sail is properly set as required under para. B of this section.

861. *Spinnaker*
A. Spinnakers may be sheeted from only one point on the sail.
B. Spinnakers may be sheeted to any part of the rail or deck or to the main boom so long as the mainsail is set, but to no other spar or outrigger.
C. A bona fide jib used as a spinnaker as permitted under para. 854 may be tacked to or sheeted to the spinnaker pole when the spinnaker is not set.
D. The spinnaker tack must be carried close to the spinnaker pole on the side opposite the main boom. The spinnaker shall not be carried without the spinnaker pole except when gybing.
E. Spinnaker strut is permitted. 852H.

862. *Mizzen Staysail on Yawl or Ketch*
A. Sheet Leads—Mizzen staysails may be sheeted to the rail or hull, and to the mizzen boom (whether or not the mizzen is set) but they may not be sheeted to any other spar or outrigger.
B. Mizzen staysails must be three-cornered (head, tack and clew). The tack or tack pennant must be secured abaft the point of intersection of the after side of the mainmast with the main deck and also must be secured directly to and no higher than the rail cap, deck or cabin top (includes dog house top).
C. There are no restrictions on the number of mizzen stay-sails on board but not more than one may be set at the same time.
D. No mizzen staysail may be carried on a yawl or ketch whose mizzen is set on a permanent backstay in lieu of a mizzen mast.

863. *Sails between the Masts in Schooners*
A. Sails set between the masts may be trimmed to any part of the rail or the deck, or to the main boom. However, when the mainsail is not set, the area of any sail set between the masts must not exceed the total measured areas of the mainsail and of the area between the masts.
B. Double clewed sails are not permitted.
C. No sail set between the masts may extend below the lower points used in the measurement of PS and IS.

864. *Foresails*
.1 Foresails are subject to restrictions governing mainsails as described in paras. 860A, B and C. Restrictions in regard to the use of topmast staysails must also be observed as follows:
A. When the area between the masts is measured according to para. 841.2 not more than two top-mast staysails may be carried, one of which must be a bona fide Fisherman staysail, while the other must be materially larger and suitable for down-wind work. When the smaller staysail is used, the regular foresail must be set but the foresail may or may not be set when the larger staysail is being used. With the exception of yachts rated for a fore topsail, which may then be carried, no other sails may be used in the space between the masts.
B. When the area between the masts is rated as in para. 841.3 the foresail and topsail, if any, as declared at the time of measurement, are the only sails that may be carried between the masts.

865. *Staysails*
Restrictions on the tack location of staysails are needed for their correct measurement and use. Accordingly attention is called to Section 848 and 810.1C.

866. *Summary of Permissible Sails*
.1 Sails which exceed the confines of the measurement points, whether by means of spars or outriggers or otherwise, are prohibited unless clearly permitted by the rules. Following is a brief summary of sails which are permitted:
A. Cat Rig—mainsail or storm trysail and main topsail if rated for same.
B. Sloop or Cutter—cat rig plus jibs; plus spinnakers or equivalent.
C. Yawl or Ketch—a sloop or cutter rig plus mizzen or mizzen storm trysail and mizzen topsail if rated for same, plus mizzen staysail.
D. Two-masted schooner—a sloop or cutter rig plus sails between the masts as declared for measurement.
E. Miscellaneous—a cat rig may not carry a spinnaker unless accepting this as a basis for fore triangle measurement, in which case classification and measurement would be as for a sloop or cutter. Conversely, a schooner, yawl or ketch which carries neither headsails nor spinnakers may be rated with-out fore triangle measurement by following the normal procedures outlined in the foregoing but using zero for the fore triangle rated area.

Part 9 is overleaf

PART TEN—METRIC EQUIVALENTS

1001. *Metric equivalents as applicable.* All measurements except dimension of sails shall be in metres to three places of decimals. Weights shall be in kilograms to the nearest half unit. Constants and formulae tabulated below shall be used in place of these in the body of the rule when metric measurement is used.

Paragraph

324. Formula for D—For $\dfrac{L + 10}{30}$ use $\dfrac{L + 3 \cdot 048}{30}$

402. Formula for FB—For 1·20 ft. use 0·366 m.

502. and 506. Formula for DB and DCB—For 2·0 ft. use 0·610 m.

505. and 511. Formula for DMX and DMXC use

$$0 \cdot 1 DB \times \left(\frac{\cdot 915}{\cdot 915 - DD} - 1 \right) \text{m.}$$

.2 For 1·0 ft. use 0·305 m.
.3 For 1·0 ft. use 0·305 m. for 0·15 ft. use 0·046 m.

602. For $0 \cdot 75 \sqrt{L}$ 1 m. use $0 \cdot 414 \sqrt{L}$ 1 m.

606. Formula for EMF—use $EMF = \dfrac{\cdot 006243 \, EM}{L^2 \times B \times D}$

703. Formula for TR—use $TR = 16 \cdot 018 \left(\dfrac{0 \cdot 97 \, L \times (BWL)^3}{RM} \right)$

Sail Areas

812. .2 For 0·25 ft. use 0·076 m.
813. .1B For 4·0 ft. use 1·219 m.
814. For 4·0 ft. use 1·219 m.
822. For 0·25 ft. use 0·076 m.
823. .1A For 4·0 ft. use 1·219 m.
826. For 4·0 ft. use 1·219 m.
845. .1 and .2 For 4½ in. use 0·114 m.
846. .2 For 0·10 E + 1 ft. use 0·10 E + 0·305 m.
       For 0·12 E + 1 ft. use 0·12 E + 0·305 m.

Part Nine — Plates

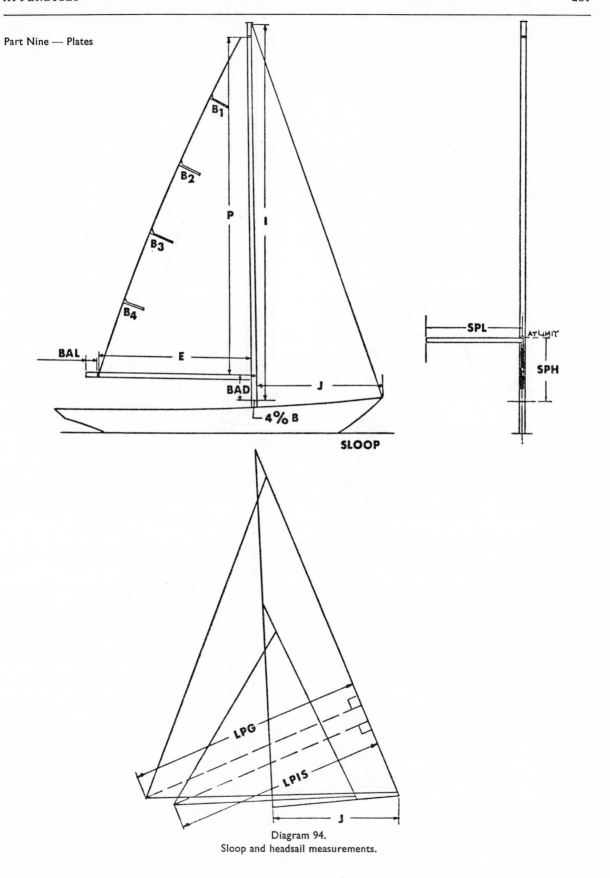

Diagram 94.
Sloop and headsail measurements.

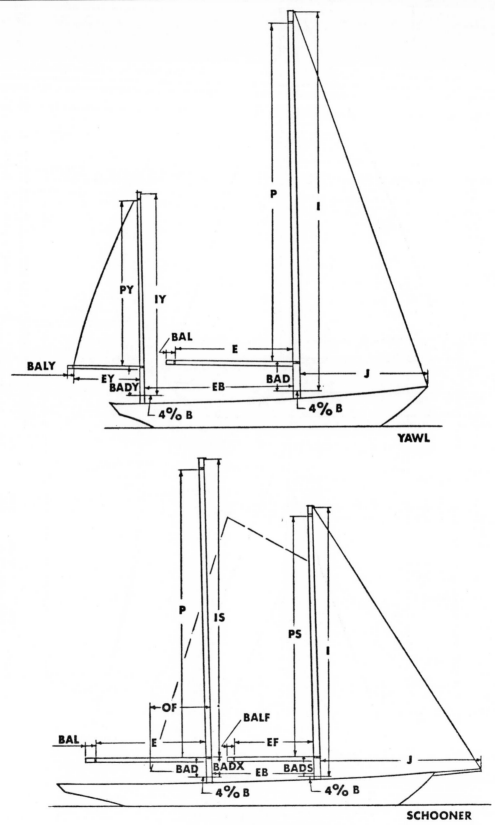

Diagram 95.
Yawl and schooner sail measurements.

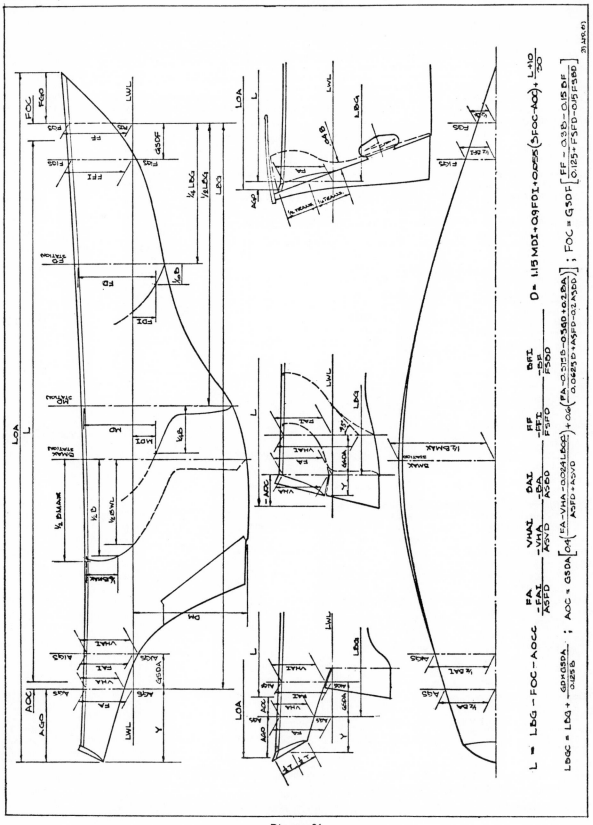

Diagram 96.
Hull measurements.

APPENDIX VIII

THE R.O.R.C. RULE OF MEASUREMENT AND RATING, 1957 AS AMENDED 1967
INTRODUCTION

The object of the Rule of Measurement and Rating is to bring together by time allowance when racing together in open water, yachts of the widest possible range of type and size.

The intention is to assist in promoting Rule 2(b) of the R.O.R.C. by encouraging the design and building of yachts in which speed and seaworthiness are combined, without favouring any particular type.

It is not possible for the Rule to cover every eventuality and the Committee, therefore, reserve the right to modify the Rule at any time, or to deal with any peculiarity of design which does not conform to the spirit of the Rule, and to give such rating as they consiser equitable.

SCANTLING COMPONENT
EXAMPLE OF CALCULATION OF W

Main frames of steel. Thickness $\frac{1}{8}$ in. Sizes of angle 2×2 in. Spacing 24 in.
    Material weight   490

$$\frac{\text{Weight of material} \times \text{thickness} \times (\text{sum of flanges—thickness})}{12 \times \text{Spacing}} = \frac{490}{12} \times \frac{1}{8} \times \frac{31}{8} \times \frac{1}{24} = \cdot82 \qquad W = \cdot82$$

Intermediate frames of Oak. Scantlings $1\frac{1}{4} \times 1\frac{1}{8}$ in. No. between frames 2. $W = \cdot49$
    Material weight   50

$$\frac{\text{Weight of material}}{12} \times \frac{\text{Moulding} \times \text{Siding} \times \text{No. between frames}}{\text{Spacing of main frames}} = \frac{50}{12} \times \frac{5}{4} \times \frac{9}{8} \times \frac{2}{24} = \cdot49$$

Deck beams of Pine. Scantlings $3\frac{1}{2} \times 2\frac{1}{2}$ in. Spacing 15 in. $W = 1\cdot75$
    Material weight   36

$$\frac{\text{Weight of material}}{12} \times \frac{\text{moulding} \times \text{siding}}{\text{Spacing}} = \frac{36}{12} \times \frac{7}{2} \times \frac{5}{2} \times \frac{1}{15} = 1\cdot75$$

Topsides of Mahogany. Thickness $1\frac{1}{8}$ in. $W = 3\cdot37$
    Material weight   36

$$\frac{\text{Weight of material}}{12} \times \text{thickness} = \frac{36}{12} \times \frac{9}{8} = 3\cdot37$$

Deck of Pine. Thickness $\frac{7}{8}$ in. $W = 2\cdot63$
    Material weight   36

$$\frac{\text{Weight of material}}{12} \times \text{thickness} = \frac{36}{12} \times \frac{7}{8} = 2\cdot63$$

Deck canvassed (add $\cdot25$) $W = \cdot25$
                             Total $\overline{W = 9\cdot31}$

SCANTLING COMPONENT
(Metric Measurement)
EXAMPLE OF CALCULATION OF W

Main frames of steel. Thickness 3 mm. Sizes of angles 50×50 mm. $W = 0\cdot238$
    Spacing 600 mm. Material weight   490

$$\frac{\text{Weight of material} \times \text{thickness} \times (\text{sum of flanges—thickness})}{1000 \times \text{Spacing}} = \frac{490}{1000} \times 3 \times 97 \times \frac{1}{600} = 0\cdot238$$

Intermediate frames of Oak. Scantlings 32×28 mm. No. between frames 2. $W = 0\cdot149$
    Material weight   50

$$\frac{\text{Weight of material}}{1000} \times \frac{\text{Moulding} \times \text{Siding} \times \text{No. between frames}}{\text{Spacing of main frames}} = \frac{50}{1000} \times 32 \times 28 \times \frac{2}{600} = 0\cdot149$$

Deck beams of Pine. Scantlings 85×60 mm. Spacing 375 mm. $W = 0\cdot490$
    Material weight   36

$$\frac{\text{Weight of material}}{1000} \times \frac{\text{moulding} \times \text{siding}}{\text{Spacing}} = \frac{36}{1000} \times \frac{85 \times 60}{375} = 0\cdot490$$

Topsides of Mahogany. Thickness 28 mm. $W = 1\cdot008$
    Material weight   36

$$\frac{\text{Weight of material} \times \text{thickness}}{1000} = \frac{36}{1000} \times 28 = 1\cdot008$$

Deck of Pine. Thickness 22 mm. $W = 0\cdot792$
    Material weight   36

$$\frac{\text{Weight of material} \times \text{thickness}}{1000} = \frac{36}{1000} \times 22 = 0\cdot792$$

Deck canvassed (add $\cdot076$) $W = 0\cdot076$
                             Total $\overline{W = 2\cdot753}$

Additional example of non-canvas deck coverings, weight 0·15 lbs./sq. ft. as weighed.

$$\frac{\text{Weight of material per square foot}}{3\cdot28} = \frac{0\cdot15}{3\cdot28} = 0\cdot046 \qquad W = 0\cdot046$$

If this covering had been used in the above example instead of canvas, total W would have been 2·723.

I. RATING FORMULA

I (1). Measured Rating,

$$MR = \cdot 15 \frac{L\sqrt{S}}{\sqrt{BD}} + \cdot 2(L + \sqrt{S})$$

Where L = Length.
   B = Beam.
   D = Depth.
   S = Rated Sail Area.

I (2). Rating, R = MR ± Stability Allowance (cor.) — Propeller Allowance + Draft Penalty.

I (3). All measurements, except dimensions of sails and scantling details, shall be in feet to two places of decimals. Dimensions of sails and spars for calculation of sail area shall be taken in feet to one decimal place, except battens, headboards and boom depth which shall be taken in feet to two decimal places. Sail areas shall be given in square feet to one decimal place. Scantling details shall be measured in inches and fractions or decimals of inches. Percentages shall be taken to one decimal place.

II. BEAM

II. Beam, B, shall be the greatest Breadth, measured to the outside of normal planking at a height not exceeding half the freeboard height at this position.

III. LENGTH

III (1). Length, L, shall be found as follows:—

$$L = LBG - (FOC + AOC)$$

LBG = Horizontal length between FGS and AGS (see Rule III (2)) or AGS cor. (see Rule III (9)).
FOC = Forward Overhang Component (see Rule III (7)).
AOC = After Overhang Component (see Rules III (8), (9) and (10)).

It is intended that L shall approximate to the distance between a point forward where the freeboard and the half-girth (see Rule III (3)) are equal, and a point aft where the freeboard and the half-girth less one-eighth B are equal. Any case where L does not so approximate may be treated as a peculiarity of design under paragraph 3 of the Introduction to the Rule and, if the Committee so direct, alternative measurements shall be taken.

III (2). Girth stations, except in special cases dealt with under rules III (8), (9) and (10), shall be found as follows:—
FGS, Forward Girth Station, where the girth equals $\frac{1}{2}$B.
FIGS, Forward Inner Girth Station, where the girth equals $\frac{3}{4}$B.
AGS, After Girth Station, where the girth equals $\frac{3}{4}$B.
AIGS, After Inner Girth Station, where the girth equals $\frac{7}{8}$B.
GSDf = Horizontal distance between FGS and FIGS.
GSDa = Horizontal distance between AGS and AIGS.

III (3). Girths shall be chain girth measurements and, except in cases dealt with under Rule III (5), shall be taken from covering board to covering board, and the points on the covering board and the forward or after profile through which they pass shall be in the same vertical athwartships plane.

III (4). Covering board shall be taken as the point where the extension of the curve of the top of the deck intersects with the curve of the side.

III (5). In a yacht where tumble-home exceeds 5 per cent of B at each side, girth stations, freeboards and depths shall be based on the points where the tumble-home is not more than 5 per cent of B.

III (6). (i) Freeboard shall be measured to the covering board, except as provided in Rule III (5), at each girth station on each side of the yacht, and shall be measured in normal racing trim with full equipment but without consumable stores, petrol, water, dinghy or crew aboard.

(ii) If it is necessary to measure the freeboards with water, consumable stores, etc. aboard, the weight of such stores shall be estimated and the following allowance in feet added to each freeboard measurement:—

$$\frac{\text{Weight of Stores in lbs.}}{40 \times LWL \times B}$$

(iii)   FF = Freeboard at FGS
     FSFD = FF − Freeboard at FIGS
       FA = Freeboard at AGS
     ASFD = FA − Freeboard at AIGS

III (7). $$FOC = \frac{FF - B/4}{B/8 + FSFD} \times GSDf$$

FOC may be positive or negative and shall be entered with the appropriate sign in computing Length under Rule III (1).

III (8). $$AOC = \frac{FA - B/4}{B/16 + ASFD} \times GSDa$$

If AOC is positive it shall be entered as such in computing Length under Rule III (1).
If AOC is negative, the lesser, numerically, of the following shall be taken:—
(a) negative AOC
(b) $\dfrac{\text{negative AOC} + 3y}{4}$

y shall be found as follows:—
(i) Transom board sloping aft from the deck—
Horizontal distance between AGS (or AGS cor.) and extreme after end of hull.
(ii) Transom board vertical or sloping forward from deck—
Horizontal distance between AGS (or AGS cor.) and the point on the centre line of the transom board $\frac{3}{4}$ of distance from the intersection of the deck and transom board to the inter-section of the transom board with the under side of the hull planking, or the waterline if the lower part of the transom board is submerged.

III (9). CUT-OFF COUNTERS
Where the counter is cut-off inside one or both of the normal after girth stations, AGS cor. and AIGS cor. shall be found. A girth shall be taken as far aft as possible without cutting the transom. The girth, AGS cor. shall be measured, and the difference between its length and $\frac{3}{4}$B shall be the Girth Difference, GD. AIGS cor. shall be taken with a girth wire of length equal to $\frac{7}{8}$B + GD. FA, ASFD and GSDa shall be found using AGS cor. and AIGS cor.

$$AOC = \frac{FA - GD/2 - B/4}{B/16 + ASFD} \times GSDa$$

LBG is the length between FGS and AGS cor.

III (10). TRANSOM STERNS
(i) A yacht shall be deemed as having a normal transom stern when all the following conditions are fulfilled:—
(a) The after side of the sternpost, on which the rudder must be hung, and the transom board are in the same plane.
(b) The sternpost is joined to the main keel of the yacht by deadwood (i.e. a separate skeg does not qualify).
(c) In a fixed keel yacht the bottom of the sternpost must have at least 85 per cent of the maximum draft of the yacht.
(d) In a centreboard yacht the bottom of the sternpost must have at least 85 per cent of the maximum draft of the yacht when the centreboard is raised and at least 35 per cent of the maximum draft of the yacht when the centreboard is lowered.

(ii) The after end of L in a yacht with a normal transom stern as defined above shall be at a point one-quarter of the horizontal distance between the after end of the water-line and a perpendicular from the junction of the top of the deck or deck extended and the after face of the transom on the centre line.
AOC is zero and LBG shall be the length between FGS and the after end of L.

(iii) If the stern is not a normal transom as defined in (i), the girths shall be taken round the canoe body of the hull and shall not enclose deadwood or skeg.
Note:—In the case of some yachts with cut-off counters it may only be possible to take the after girths when the yacht is slipped.

IV. DEPTH

IV (1).

$$D = QBDI + FDI + \frac{3FOC - AOC}{16} + \frac{L + 10}{30} + \frac{B}{20}$$

   QBD = Quarter Beam Depth
  QBDI = Quarter Beam Depth Immersed
    FD = Forward Depth
   FDI = Forward Depth Immersed
   FFD = Freeboard at Forward Depth
   FMD = Freeboard at Mid Depth
     t = Thickness of Deck

In the above formula, if AOC is negative and has been corrected under Rule III (8), AOC cor. shall be substituted for AOC.

IV (2). (i) FD shall be taken one-quarter of LBG abaft FGS and shall be measured vertically from a straight line joining the underside of the deck at the sides of the vessel to a point on the inside of the wood planking one-tenth of B out from the centre line.

(ii) QBD shall be taken at Mid Depth, one-half of LBG abaft FGS, and shall be measured vertically from a straight line joining the underside of the deck at the sides of the vessel to a point on the inside of the wood planking one-quarter of B out from the centre line.

(iii) When taking FD and QBD in a steel or light alloy vessel, each shall have deducted ·003 (LBG − 5).

(iv) In a yacht with a plywood or plastic hull, both FD and QBD shall have deducted ·004 (LBG − 5) − 1·3t_1, where t_1 expressed in feet is the thickness of the hull at the positions where the measurements are taken. This rule shall not apply to yachts built and first commissioned before 1960.

IV (3). Freeboards, FFD and FMD shall be measured and corrected if necessary (Rule III (6) (ii)).

IV (4). QBDI = QBD + t − FMD.

IV (5). (i) FDI = FD + t − FFD.

(ii) FDI shall be corrected to compensate for variations due to length of overhangs by adding into D:—
$$\frac{3FOC - AOC}{16}$$

V. SAIL AREA

V (1).   S = Rated Sail Area

MA = Measured Area

MSA = Measured Sail Area, and is the sum of all MA for which the yacht has been measured

BPA = Bowsprit Allowance

ARA = Aspect Ratio Allowance

V (2). BLACK BANDS

Black bands at least 1 in. in width may be used on spars. The inner edge of black band shall indicate the limit to which the sail may be stretched. In the case of the head, upper inner edge of cringle or upper edge of headboard; in the case of tack, upper side of boom; in the case of the clew, the point where the leech and the foot, extended if necessary, meet.

When black bands are used, a chock or stop shall be fitted so that the head of the sail cannot be stretched above the lower edge of black band.

V (3). BERMUDA SAILS—MAIN

(i) b = Length measured along the boom from the after side of mast to the outhaul, pin of slide, at its full extension aft, or to black band.

(ii) p = Height measured along the after side of the mast, from the underside of the upper black band if fitted, or if not from the highest of the following points:—The top of the highest sheave in the mast or topmast, or the highest juncture of the mast or topmast with the eyebolts (centre of eye) or pennant of a halyard block used for sails aft of the mast; to the upper side of the boom when in its lowest position, or to black band.

(iii) In yachts which carry the upper halyard block on a pennant, the upper point of measurement shall be the point at which the pennant is fastened to the mast.

(iv) If the highest point of p is more than 4 per cent of I below the highest point of I, half the excess shall be added to p.

(v) If the black band at the lowest point of p is higher than 5 per cent of p as measured, plus 4 ft. above the main deck (see Rule V (19) (ix)) half the excess shall be added to p.

$$MA \text{ for inclusion in } MSA = \frac{b \times p}{2}$$

V (4). BERMUDA SAIL—WITH BENT MAST

p. To be measured from the highest sheave, in a line parallel to the after side of the straight part of the mast, to the upper side of the boom.

b_3. Is the distance from the point on the boom to which p is measured to the after side of the mast.

MA for inclusion in MSA=
$$\frac{p(b - b_3)}{2} + p \times b_3$$

V (5). GAFF SAILS—MAIN OR MIZZEN

b. Length of boom taken as for Bermuda sails.

g. Length of gaff when lying on the top of the boom measured from the after side of the mast to the outer end of head when fully extended.

h. To be measured along the afterside of the mast from the upper side of the boom when in its lowest position, or from black band, to the highest position to which the throat cringle of the mainsail can be hoisted, or to the lower edge of a black band above which mark the upper inner edge of the throat cringle of the mainsail shall not be hoisted.

d. Diagonal distance from outboard end of boom to throat cringle shall not be measured, but shall be calculated from the following formula:—
$$d = ·96\sqrt{b^2 + h^2}$$
MA for inclusion in MSA:—
$$\frac{(b \times h) + (g \times d)}{2}$$

V (6). TOPSAILS—MAIN OR MIZZEN

p. To be measured as for Bermuda sails.

h. To be measured as for gaff mainsails.

I. The shortest distance measured across the topsail from the sheet cringle to the luff rope.

MA for inclusion in MSA:—
$$\frac{I(p - h)}{2}$$

V (7). YAWLS AND KETCHES—THE MIZZEN

(i) b miz., p miz., h miz., g miz., and d miz. shall be taken as for mainsails.

(ii) If the lowest point of p miz. is higher than 5 per cent of p miz. as measured, plus 4 ft. above the main deck (see Rule V (19) (ix)) half the excess shall be added to p miz.

(iii) If the highest point of p miz. is more than 4 per cent of p_3 below the highest point of p_3, half the excess shall be added to p miz.

(iv) p_3 shall be measured along the foreside of the mizzen mast from the point of attachment of the mizzen staysail halyard block or top of sheave (which may be hung sufficiently forward of the mast to provide a clear lead for the halyard without requiring the height measurement to be obtained by extending the line through the point of support, providing the mizzen staysail halyard block is no further from the mast than necessary for clearance) to the level of the main deck at its junction with the mizzen mast.

(v) b_1 shall be the distance measured at deck level between the forward side of the mizzen mast and the after side of the main mast.

V (8). YAWLS AND KETCHES—MIZZEN MEASURED AREA

MA of mizzen for inclusion in MSA:—
$$m \left(1 - \frac{3b}{4b_1} \right) + ·04(p_3 \times b_1)$$

Where m = area of mizzen, or mizzen plus mizzen topsail, measured and calculated as described in Rules V (3) to V (6).

V (9). FORESAIL SCHOONERS

In a schooner that sets a gaff, or jib-headed foresail abaft the foremast this sail shall be measured as for mainsails under Rule V (3) or (5). Where the foresail is a quadrilateral sail using a wishbone or similar device, the area shall be calculated as for gaff mainsail and topsail in Rule V (5) and (6).

MA of Foresail and Mainsail for inclusion in MSA:—

Foresail MA +
$$\text{Mainsail MA} \left(\frac{\text{Mainsail MA}}{\text{Mainsail MA} + \text{Foresail MA}} \right)$$

Limitations:—

(i) Where the MA of 'Mainsail' is less than 50 per cent of the MA of the Foresail the rig shall be rated as a Yawl or Ketch.

(ii) If the Foresail overlaps abaft the foreside of the main-mast the yacht shall be measured on the area between masts as in Rule V (10).

V (10). STAYSAIL SCHOONERS AND WISHBONE KETCHES

There shall be no limit to the number or shape of sails set between the masts, but should any sails overlap abaft the foreside of the aftermost mast the largest overlap shall be added to b_1 in calculating the area between the masts.

(i) b_1 shall be the distance measured at the deck level between the foreside of the mainmast and the afterside of the foremast.

(ii) p_1 to be measured along the afterside of the foremast from the higher of the following points:—the top of the highest sheave in the mast or topmast, or the highest juncture of the mast or topmast with the eye-bolt (centre of eye) or pennant of a halyard block, whether such sheave, block or pennant be used for sails forward or aft of the mast, to the main deck.

(iii) p_3 to be measured along the foreside of the mainmast from the highest of the following points:—the top of the highest sheave in the mast or topmast or the highest juncture of the mast or topmast with the eye-bolt (centre of eye) or pennant of a halyard block used for sails forward or aft of the mast, to the main deck.

(iv) MA between masts:—

$$\frac{9b_1 (p_1 + p_3)}{20}$$

(v) MA of sail on aftermost mast will be calculated as in Rule V (3) or (5).

(vi) MA for inclusion in MSA Schooners:—
MA between masts +

$$\text{Mainsail MA} \left(\frac{\text{Mainsail MA}}{\text{Mainsail MA} + \text{MA between masts}} \right)$$

(vii) MA for inclusion in MSA Ketches:—
MA between masts +

$$\text{Mizzen MA} \left(\frac{\text{Mizzen MA}}{\text{Mizzen MA} + \text{MA between masts}} \right)$$

Limitations:—

(i) If p_3 as measured is less than $\cdot 6p_1$ then p_3 for MA shall be $\cdot 6p_3$.

(ii) If p_1 as measured is less than $\cdot 6p_3$ then p_1 for MA shall be $\cdot 6p_3$.

V (11). FORETRIANGLE

(i) I in the foretriangle to be measured along the foreside of the foremost mast from the main deck centre line, (see Rule V (19) (ix)), to the top of the highest sheave used for headsails or spinnaker, whether fitted in the mast or supported by the mast on a pennant, strut or outrigger, provided such support shall not be arranged to raise unduly the effective point of attachment to the mast, or otherwise enlarge the foretriangle, except that the normal spinnaker halyard blocks may be set forward enough to produce a clear lead without penalty.

(ii) J. The base J to be measured from the foreside of the mast (foremast in the case of a schooner) at the deck to the point where the centre line of the stay (or luff of the foremost headsail if this is set flying), extended if necessary, cuts the top of the bowsprit, or, if no bowsprit is fitted, to where it cuts the top of the fair line of the bulwark, including cap if fitted, or to where it cuts the centre line of the deck, if this is above the level of the top of the bulwark as defined.

(iii) If the following limitation of the spinnaker boom, spinnaker or headsails is exceeded, an addition will be made as follows to the measurement of I and/or J, which will become I cor. and/or J cor.

V (12). SPINNAKER BOOM

If the length of any spinnaker boom, measured when in position and at right angles to the centre line of the yacht, from its extreme outboard end to the centre line of yacht, exceeds the base J, the excess shall be added to J.

If the inboard end of the spinnaker boom is mounted further forward of the foreside of the mast than half the diameter of the mast measured at deck level, any excess shall be added to the length of spinnaker boom.

V (13). SPINNAKER

(i) If the length of the luff or leech of any spinnaker exceeds $\cdot 95\sqrt{I^2 + (J + \text{Pen. spin.})^2}$ the excess shall be added to the height of I. Pen. spin. indicates the greater of the penalties incurred by the length of spinnaker boom, Rule V (12) or width of spinnaker under Sub-para. (ii) below.

(ii) If the foot and/or widest part of the sail, measured between points on the luff and leech equidistant from the head, exceeds 180 per cent of the base of the foretriangle J, five-ninths of the excess shall be added to J.

(iii) Any spinnaker in which the widest part exceeds 150 per cent J, must be symmetrical about a line joining the head with the centre of the foot, and the width of the sail at half the distance between the head and centre of a straight line joining

tack and clew must not be less than 75 per cent of the width between tack and clew. If either or both of these conditions are not fulfilled, the spinnaker shall be measured as a headsail under Rule V (14) (iii).

V (14). HEADSAILS

(i) Headsails shall be measured as though in new condition and as in position when hoisted and stretched aft along the centre line of the yacht. The horizontal distance shall be measured between the foremost part of the tack and a perpendicular dropped from the aftermost part of the clew (of the aftermost clew if more than one).

(ii) If a headsail is tacked down abaft the foremost point of J, the distance between the point where it is tacked down and the foremost point of J shall be added to the measurement of the headsail taken as in paragraph (i).

(iii) If the measurement of the largest headsail taken as in (i), (iii) and (iv) exceeds $1\cdot 5J$ (or $1\cdot 5J$ corrected under Rules V (12) and (13)) but does not exceed $1\cdot 8J$, J (or J corrected) shall be increased by $0\cdot 4$ times the excess. If the largest headsail exceeds $1\cdot 8J$ the whole of the excess over $1\cdot 8J$ shall also be added to J corrected.

(iv) A headsail with a leech which is extended aft of a straight line from head to clew (lowest clew) by a second sheet or other device shall be measured, as follows:—

'A' is measured as in V (14) (i). 'B' is the length of a perpendicular, in the case of a quadrilateral sail, from the upper clew, in the case of a sail with convex leech, from the point on the leech where the roach is greatest, to the straight line from head to clew (lowest clew).

'A' + 'B' shall be the measurement of the headsail for the purposes of Rule V (14) (iii).

(v) When a spinnaker is set, a headsail may be tacked down anywhere within the foretriangle, but unless it is set in its normal position and conforms with Rules V (14) (i), (ii), (iii) and (iv) this headsail must not exceed $1\cdot 5$ per cent J from tack to clew, or $0\cdot 6$ I from head to clew, nor must the tack of the sail be set more than 2 feet above the main deck.

V (15). FORETRIANGLE CORRECTIONS

When more than one of the corrections under Rules V (12) and V (13) are measured, the greatest only shall be applied. Any further correction under Rule V (14) will be applied in addition.

V (16). AREA OF FORETRIANGLE

MA of foretriangle for inclusion in MSA shall cover all headsails and spinnakers, and shall be found after correcting values of I and J.

$$\text{Foretriangle MA} = \frac{\text{I cor.} \times \text{J cor.}}{2}$$

V (17). BOWSPRIT ALLOWANCE

This rule shall not apply to any yacht which has been built since 1940 or fitted with a bowsprit since that date.

Jb = Length of bowsprit from the outer side of the stem to the forward end of J, as defined in Rule V (ii).

$$\text{Bowsprit Allowance, BPA} = \frac{\text{Jb} - \cdot 1\text{J}}{2}$$

If negative, BPA to be disregarded. If BPA is positive, the area of foretriangle to be included in MSA =

$$\frac{\text{I cor.} \times (\text{J cor.} - \text{BPA})}{2}$$

V (18). SQUARESAIL

If a yacht carries a squaresail, square topsail or raffee (together or separately) instead of a spinnaker, the actual area of these shall be computed; and if their area exceeds the product of I and J, the excess shall be added to the total area.

V (19). MISCELLANEOUS LIMITS AND CORRECTIONS

(i) Bermuda Headboards: If the effective horizontal extension of headboard of a Bermuda sail exceeds 3 per cent of b for that sail the excess shall be added to b.

(ii) Spinnaker Headboard: If the greatest width of headboard of a spinnaker exceeds 5 per cent of the length of the spinnaker boom, 5 times the excess shall be added to the spinnaker boom.

(iii) Boom: If the maximum depth of a boom exceeds 4 per cent of b, (or b miz. in the case of a mizzen boom), the excess shall be added to p (or to p miz. in the case of a mizzen boom).

(iv) (a) Battens, if fitted, shall divide the leech into approximately equal parts and shall not exceed five in number without penalty. The maximum length of the longest batten shall not, without penalty, exceed 14 per cent of b plus 1·5 feet, if four or fewer battens are fitted, or 12 per cent of b plus 1 foot if five battens are fitted. If any batten exceeds the above limits, one-quarter of the excess of each batten shall be added to b, but the total addition shall not exceed ·8b. If more than five battens are fitted, the penalty to b shall be ·8b.

(b) If mainsail, (or mizzen), battens do not exceed the limits in paragraph (c) below, MA of mainsail shall be reduced by 2·5 per cent for the purpose of calculating sail area.

(c) Battens shall divide the leech into approximately equal parts and shall not exceed five in number if b is 40 ft. or more, or four in number if b is less than 40 ft.

The maximum length of top and bottom battens shall not exceed 10 per cent of b plus one foot, the maximum length of intermediate battens shall not exceed 12 per cent of b plus one foot.

(d) Rules (a), (b) and (c) shall apply in similar manner to mizzens and mizzen battens.

(v) Headsails, spinnakers and between-masts sails may be sheeted to main, fore, or mizzen boom, but if the point of attachment is more than 6 inches outside the limit of b, the excess shall be added to b.

(vi) If a rotating mast is fitted, double the greatest diameter of mast shall be added to b. If a double mainsail is fitted, the area shall be double that for a single mainsail.

(vii) Any mizzen staysail set must be triangular in shape, and the width measured from a point halfway up the leech to a point halfway up the luff must not exceed 55 per cent of the length of the foot.

The tack or tack pennant must be secured abaft the point of intersection of the after side of the main mast with the main deck, and also must be secured directly to and no higher than the rail-cap, deck or cabin top. The length of the luff including tack pennant when tacked down shall not exceed:—

$$\sqrt{b_1{}^2 + p_3{}^2}$$

(viii) The inboard end of the spinnaker boom must be carried on the mast and the centre point of the boom fitting may not be set higher than ·18 I + 2 feet above the deck, (see Rule V (19) (ix)), without penalty. If this height is exceeded the excess shall be added to I, (or to I cor. if there is already a penalty on account of spinnaker luff/leech). A penalty incurred by height of spinnaker boom will not give an increased luff/leech limit.

(ix) Measurement of the height of any part of the sail plan shall normally be taken from the centreline of the deck, but if this measurement is reduced by the camber or shape of deck, or cabin top, the height of main deck shall be taken as not higher than 4 per cent of measured beam, B, above the covering board in way of the mast.

If a raised deck in way of the mast does not extend over the whole base of the foretriangle, the height of raised deck above the normal sheerline at mast position must be added to the height of foretriangle as determined in the first paragraph.

V (20).   ASPECT RATIO ALLOWANCE
ARA shall be a percentage determined as follows:—
Cutters, sloops and schooners:—
$$ARA = \frac{20(J + b)}{I + p}$$
Yawls and ketches:—
$$ARA = \frac{20(J + b + ·25\, b\ miz.)}{I + p + ·25\, p\ miz.}$$
Wishbone ketches:—
$$ARA = \frac{20(J + b_1 + ·25\, b\ miz.)}{I + p_1 + ·25\, p\ miz.}$$
Gaff sail without topsail, instead of p use h + 0·9 g.
J, b or b miz. shall never be entered in ARA exceeding I, p or p miz., respectively.
Note:—In calculating ARA use J, I and b, *not* J cor., I cor. and b cor. (b cor. = b + penalties to b).

V (21).   RATED SAIL AREA
(i) Yacht with Bermudian mainsail:—
$$S = \frac{MSA(90 - ARA)}{100}$$
(ii) Yacht with Gaff mainsail:—
$$S = \frac{MSA(84 - ARA)}{100}$$
A yacht newly gaff rigged after 31st December, 1967, will normally be given rig allowance as for bermudian rig.

V (22).   PROHIBITIONS
(i) The spinnaker shall not have a foot stick, or more than one sheet, or any contrivance for extending the sail to other than a three-cornered shape.
(ii) Special light-weather mainsails shall not be allowed.
(iii) Not more than one size and weight of mizzen staysail may be carried on board.

VI. RAISED DECKS

VI.   A yacht whose deck, extending out to the topsides, is subdivided into portions at different levels, shall be classified as of 'Raised Deck Type'.

The normal sheer line of the yacht, i.e. what would have been the sheer line had the deck followed an unbroken curve from bow to stern, shall be determined, and several equally spaced vertical measurements shall be taken between the normal sheer line and the raised portion of the deck. The mean height of the raised deck shall be found from these measure-measurements.

Raised Deck Bonus shall be determined as follows:—
$$RDB = Mean\ height \times \frac{Length\ of\ Raised\ Deck}{Length\ overall}$$

VII. STABILITY ALLOWANCE

VII (1).   Stability Allowance, STA = ± Scantling Component + Shallow Draft Component + Iron Ballast Component + Weight of Engine Component — Light Alloy Mast Component.

VII (2).   STABILITY ALLOWANCE CORRECTION
(i) If STA is negative it shall be taken as a percentage of MR without correction and added to MR.
(ii) In yachts built after 31st December, 1929, if STA is positive it shall be corrected as follows, and the corrected STA expressed as a percentage of MR and deducted from MR:—
$$STA\ cor. = \frac{STA}{·05\ STA + 1}\ per\ cent$$
(iii) In yachts built and fitted out before 1st January, 1930, if STA is positive it shall be taken as a percentage of MR without correction and deducted from MR, but in no case shall the deduction exceed 20 per cent.
(iv) In yachts built and fitted out before 1st January, 1915, a positive component of 2 per cent shall be added to STA. In no case shall the deduction, including this additional bonus, exceed 22 per cent.

VII (3).   SCANTLINGS
W. The weight of one square foot of the topsides, together with the average weight of frames per superficial foot, shall be added to the weight of one square foot of the deck and the average weight of deck beams per superficial foot. Certain other exceptional components of the hull above the waterline may be included at the discretion of the Committee.
Measurements for Scantlings to be made as follows:—
(i) Mouldings and sidings at head of:—
(a) Grown frames.
(b) Bent timbers.
(ii) Scantlings of steel frames, and reverse frames if carried to the head of frames.
(iii) Number of bent timbers between grown or steel frames.
(iv) Spacing of grown or steel frames and reverse frames centre to centre.
(v) Mouldings and sidings of ordinary deck beams taken midway between the centre line and side of vessel, and spacing centre to centre.
(vi) Stringers above the waterline—moulding, sidings, length, and spacing centre to centre.
(vii) Thickness of topside planking and deck.
(viii) Description of material from which frames, deck beams, stringers, planking and deck are constructed.

(ix) In the case of steel vessels the minimum thickness of shell plating shall be taken.

(x) If the deck is covered, the weight of one square foot of the covering material shall be added to W. When canvas is the covering material the figure of ·25 lbs. shall be used.

Certified information as to dimensions and materials may be supplied by designers or yacht yards.

Owners of yachts in which special materials, including plywood, have been used, must supply certified weights of these materials, or samples from which the weight can be ascertained.

Where the scantlings or internal fittings of a yacht do not conform to standard practice, scantling allowances may be modified at the discretion of the Committee.

See Appendix for standard weights of materials.

VII (4). W shall be corrected as follows:—
$T = FF + FMD + FA + ·5\ Bk + 3$ (Raised Deck Bonus).
Bk = Height of Bulwark measured vertically from the top of the rail to the covering board at FMD.

$$W\ \text{cor.} = W \left(\frac{10T}{3L + 72} + 0·5 \right)$$

Note:—When the yacht has a raised deck the figures for FF, FMD and FA used in calculating T will be the freeboards to the main deck (NOT to the raised deck) level, irrespective of whether these expressions are measured to the raised deck level elsewhere in the calculation of rating.

VII (5). SCANTLING COMPONENT
$$ScC = \frac{66\ W\ \text{cor.}}{L + B + 1·5D} - 10$$

VII (6). SHALLOW DRAFT COMPONENT
The owner of a yacht which has not more than 80 per cent (iron keel 82 per cent) of the maximum draft permitted for the waterline length (16 per cent LWL + 2 ft.) may claim a bonus if he can provide reasonable facilities for measurement of the draft.

If the draft taken to the bottom of the fixed keel with full cruising equipment, but without consumable stores, petrol, water, dinghy or crew aboard, is over 66 per cent (iron keel 68 per cent), but does not exceed 80 per cent (iron keel 82 per cent) of the maximum draft limit, a component of 2 shall be included in Stability Allowance. If the draft is 66 per cent (iron keel 68 per cent) of the maximum draft limit, or less, component of 4 shall be included in Stability Allowance. If the yacht is fitted with a centreplate, the component in each case shall be halved.

VII (7). IRON BALLAST COMPONENT
An iron ballast component of 2 shall be included in Stability Allowance, provided:—

(a) not less than 75 per cent of the total weight of ballast is of iron, or material of lower specific gravity, and

(b) the weight of lead, if any, carried below the level of the wood keel is not more than $12\frac{1}{2}$ per cent of the total weight of ballast.

VII (8). WEIGHT OF ENGINE COMPONENT
Engine Component is based upon the weight of engine including electric starter, dynamo and gears, but not propeller-shaft, piping, tanks or battery. See also Rule VII (10).
$$\frac{5 \times \text{weight of engine in lbs.}}{L \times B \times D}$$

VII (9). LIGHT ALLOY MAST COMPONENT
If the yacht has a light alloy mast or one of equivalent weight or less she shall have a negative component of 1·0. If the mast is of fibreglass the negative component shall be Zero.

VII (10). ENGINE AND PROPELLER ALLOWANCES
Weight of engine component and propeller allowance are only included in the Rating Rule to permit yachts which have auxiliary engines for cruising purposes to compete in races without disadvantage: they are not intended as artificial means to improve ratings.

Where weight of engine component is allowed the yacht must race with the engine, and all the equipment therefor, efficiently installed for it to be in full working order and, unless temporarily out of service, capable of propelling the yacht at a speed of not less than $0·8\sqrt{L}$ knots in calm water.

The pitch of a solid propeller must not exceed the diameter or it will be counted as a feathering propeller. Reversing, (but not feathering), variable pitch propellers must also observe the above limit.

VIII. PROPELLER ALLOWANCE
Rule VII (10) must be complied with.
VIII. Propeller Allowance shall be a percentage of MR corrected for STA, the percentage to be:—

$$4 \times \frac{\text{Prop. Size}}{\sqrt{BD}} \times \text{Prop. factor}$$

PROPELLER SIZE shall be the diameter of the propeller, or four times the greatest width of the blade, whichever is less. Provided the propeller blade is of normal, elliptical, asymmetric elliptical or near rectangular shape, its greatest width shall be measured across the surface of the blade at right angles to the radius. If the blade is any other shape, its average width will be used instead of its greatest width to determine propeller size.

PROPELLER FACTOR		PROPELLER TYPE AND INSTALLATION
(a)	0·5	Folding on centre *not* in aperture.
(b)	2·0	Folding off centre.
(c)	0·75	Feathering 2-blade on centre *not* in aperture.
(d)	1·0	Feathering 2-blade on centre in aperture.
(e)	3·0	Feathering 2-blade off centre.
(f)	1·0	Feathering 3-blade on centre *not* in aperture.
(g)	1·5	Feathering 3-blade on centre in aperture.
(h)	4·0	Feathering 3-blade off centre.
(i)	2·0	Solid 2-blade on centre *not* in aperture.
(j)	3·0	Solid 2-blade on centre in aperture.
(k)	5·25	Solid 2-blade off centre.
(l)	3·0	Solid 3-blade on centre *not* in aperture.
(m)	4·5	Solid 3-blade on centre in aperture.
(n)	6·0	Solid 3-blade off centre.

If four or more blades are fitted, the propeller factor shall be as for a three-bladed propeller of similar type.

'Off centre'. The propeller hub must be not less than 5 per cent of B off centre.

The owner must supply certified information as to the diameter of the propeller, the width of the blades and pitch. In the absence of information on any of these dimensions a temporary allowance may be given, the percentage of MR corrected for STA to be:—
$$\frac{\text{Prop. Factor}}{2}$$

IX. DRAFT
IX (1). Draft, taken with full cruising equipment but without consumable stores, petrol, water, dinghy, or crew aboard, shall not without penalty exceed 16 per cent of the length on waterline, plus two feet. One-and-a-half times any excess shall be added to the rating. This does not apply to yachts built before December, 1939.

IX (2). The draft of a yacht fitted with centreboard shall be taken at a point three-quarters of the distance between the bottom of the fixed keel and the bottom of the centreboard in its lowest position.

X. TIME CORRECTION
X. Time Correction Factor, $TCF = \dfrac{\sqrt{R} + 3}{10}$

TCF shall be calculated to four places of decimals.

A yacht's Elapsed Time in a race of any length shall be multiplied by her TCF to find her Corrected Time.

Age allowance—Yachts built before 1st January 1963 and any one design or yacht with an absolutely standard hull of which the first of the series was completed before that date, will be given an allowance of 1 per cent deducted from her Time Correction Factor. The rating will not be changed.

Note:—For purposes of the R.Y.A. Time on Distance Handicap System, Basic Speed Figure, BSF is found as follows:—

$$BSF = \frac{514·3}{TCF} \text{ secs. per nautical mile.}$$

BSF is the theoretical time which the yacht should take to sail one nautical mile of the course.

APPENDIX

METRIC EQUIVALENTS

I (3). All measurements, except dimensions of sails and scantling details, shall be in metres to three places of decimals. Dimensions of sails and spars for calculation of sail area shall be taken in metres to two decimal places, except battens, headboards and boom depth which shall be taken in metres to three decimal places. Sail areas shall be given in square metres to two decimal places. Scantling details shall be measured in millimetres and fractions or decimals of millimetres. Percentages shall be taken to one decimal place.

III (6).

For $\dfrac{\text{Weight of stores in lbs.}}{40 \times \text{LWL} \times \text{B}}$ use $\dfrac{\text{Weight of stores in Kilos}}{640 \times \text{LWL} \times \text{B}}$

IV (1)   Depth—For $\dfrac{L + 10}{30}$ ft. use $\dfrac{L + 3.049}{30}$ m.

IV (2).   (iii) For $.003 (LBG - 5)$ use $.003 (LBG - 1.524)$.
          (iv) For $.004 (LBG) - 5) - 1.3t_1$ use $.004 (LBG) - 1.524) - 1.3t_1$.

V (3).   (v) For $0.05 p + 4$ ft. use $0.05 p + 1.22$.

V (7).   (i) 2nd Para. For $.05 p$ miz. $+ 4.0$ read $.05 p$ miz. $+ 1.22$.

V (19). Sail Area—Miscellaneous Limits and Corrections.
         (iv) Battens—For 1.5 ft. use 0.46 m., and for 1 ft. use 0.30 m.
         (viii) Height of spinnaker boom—for $.18 I + 2$ ft. use $.18 I + 0.61$ m.

VII (3).   Calculation of W shall be undertaken in the same way as for British measurements, but using measurements of scantlings in metres together with the standard weights of materials in lbs. per cubic foot as in the Appendix. See example.

VII (3).   (x) For $.25$ lbs. use $.076$.

VII (4).   W cor.—For $3L + 72$ use $3L + 21.95$.

VII (6).   Shallow Draft Component:—
For 16 per cent LWL $+ 2$ ft. use 16 per cent LWL $+ 0.610$ m.

VII (8).   Weight of engine component:—
For $\dfrac{5 \times \text{wt. of Engine in lbs.}}{L \times B \times D \text{ feet}}$
use $\dfrac{0.312 \times \text{wt. of Engine in Kilos.}}{L \times B \times D \text{ metres}}$

IX (1). Draft—For 16 per cent of length on waterline, plus 2 ft. use 16 per cent of length on waterline, plus 0.610 metres.

RATING expressed in metres shall be multiplied by 3.28 to give Rating in feet.

STANDARD WEIGHTS OF MATERIALS

The following standard weights in lbs. per cubic foot must be used in computing 'W':—

WOOD WEIGHTS

Acacia	44	Mahogany 36
Afrormosia	50	Makore 45
Ash, British	46	Niangon 42
Beech	45	Oak 50
Birch, British	45	Parana Pine 36
Cedar, red or white	30	Pine, pitch, American 42
Cedar, Port Orford	32	Pine, pitch, Caribbean 45
Chestnut	34	Pine, yellow and white 32
Cypress	40	Pine, others and fir 36
Elm, English	40	Serayah, white 33
Elm, rock	45	Spruce 30
Greenheart	62	Teak 50
Iron Bark	72	Utile 41
Iroko	40	Yeng 55
Jarrah	68	Yacal 60
Larch, British	33	
STEEL	490	

LIGHT ALLOYS

Aluminium alloys—170 lbs. per cubic foot.
Magnesium alloys—113 lbs. per cubic foot.

APPENDIX IX

ROYAL OCEAN RACING CLUB SPECIAL REGULATIONS

Vertical line indicates an alteration in 1969

Ocean racing yachts inevitably sail at times out of sight of one another, and the person in charge may be the sole judge of fair play. When signing his declaration he must either be entirely satisfied that the race has been sailed in complete obedience to all the rules for that race or he must qualify his declaration suitably.

RACING REGULATIONS

1. R.O.R.C. racing regulations vary certain details of the I.Y.R.U. racing rules and R.Y.A. prescriptions. The variations of any rule apply only to those details mentioned, and in every other respect I.Y.R.U. racing rules and R.Y.A. prescriptions remain valid and must be observed.

2. RACE COMMITTEE (*Affecting Rule 1*). The race committee shall be the committee of the R.O.R.C. or the club(s) organising the race. The senior officer of the organising club(s) present at a race, or in the absence of an officer, the senior members of the committee of the organising club(s) present at a race or, in the absence of an officer, the senior member of the committee of the organising club(s) or R.O.R.C., may call a race sub-committee of not more than five nor less than three in number. The sub-committee shall be chosen from officers, members of the committee or senior members of the R.O.R.C., the organising club(s) or other yacht clubs. The sub-committee will be included in the term "race committee" wherever it is used.

3. SAILING RULES (*Affecting Rules 3.2 (k) and 36–43*). Races will be started and sailed under I.Y.R.U. racing rules subject to the R.Y.A. prescriptions and R.O.R.C. special regulations but, between the times specified in sailing instructions, I.Y.R.U. Rules 36 to 43 inclusive will cease to be applicable and will be replaced by Part D (Steering and Sailing Rules) of International Regulations for Preventing Collisions at Sea.

4. RULE INFRINGEMENTS (*Affecting Rules 72, 73, 74*).
   (a) If the race committee considers that a breach of the rules has been committed, it may impose a time penalty by increasing the yacht's T.C.F. for that race by either 5 per cent or 10 per cent, disqualify the yacht or recommend the R.O.R.C. committee to refer the matter to the R.Y.A. for action under I.Y.R.U. racing rule 74.
   (b) If a yacht incurs a time penalty under this regulation and subsequently might qualify for a prize based on elapsed times, her elapsed time shall be increased by 5 per cent before deciding whether she has won that prize.

5. RATING (*Affecting Rule 19*). A yacht must have a valid R.O.R.C. rating. The ratings and T.C.F.s of all competitors will be posted with sailing instructions on the notice board of the headquarters from which the race is started. The T.C.F. so posted at the time of the start shall be final for that race, subject only to any penalty imposed under Special Regulation 4.

6. SAIL NUMBERS (*Affecting Rule 25*). Sail numbers allotted by a national authority must be carried on the mainsail and spinnaker and must be displayed by alternative means if neither mainsail nor spinnaker is set. Numbers must contrast sharply in colour with the sail.

The sail number of not less size than specified must be displayed in the lifelines on the side of the yacht which faces the race committee at the start, and similarly when crossing the finishing line.

For sails made after 31st March 1966, R.O.R.C. numbers must not be smaller than the dimensions given below:—

Mainsail foot "b"	Height	Width	Thickness	Space between
15 ft. and under	18″	12″	3″	4
Over 15 ft.	21″	14″	3″	4″

7. SAILING INSTRUCTIONS (*Affecting Rule* 3). As far as possible names and ratings of competitors will be included in sailing instructions supplied to yachts, but these may not be complete or exact. Recall numbers will not be included, nor will the time and place at which protests will be heard. In the event of a protest, the time and place for the hearing will be arranged and notified to those concerned as soon as possible.

8. RECALLS (*Affecting Rules* 8 *and* 51.1). Recall numbers will not be displayed. When a yacht starts prematurely, a gun will be fired or suitable sound signal made as soon as possible after her starting signal, and numeral pennant O will be broken out. A premature starter shall return in accordance with I.Y.R.U. racing rule 51.1, but the race committee will not inform her that she has wholly returned to the right side of the starting line.

9. BOARDING, LEAVING AND GOING ASHORE WHILST RACING (*Affecting Rules* 56, 57 *and* 59). Crew may board their yacht by any means up to two hours after her starting signal and may leave by any means to take no further part in the race, but otherwise crew, gear or stores may be taken to or from the shore only in her dinghy propelled by oars.

10. NAVIGATION LIGHTS (*Affecting Rule* 53). Competitors must show port, starboard and stern navigation lights from sunset to sunrise. Such lights and any other lights shown must comply with the requirements of International Regulations for Preventing Collisions at Sea No. 1 (b), and navigation lights must be mounted so that they will not be masked by sails.

11. ELECTRONIC AIDS, RADIO TRANSMISSION AND RECEPTION. No electronic aid other than the following may be used in a R.O.R.C. race:
  (a) Speedometer and log;
  (b) Depth sounder;
  (c) Wind speed and direction indicator;
  (d) Radio receiver;
  (e) Radio direction finder;
  (f) Radio transmitter if used for private business or emergency purposes only.
These devices may not be linked to each other in any way except that the radio receiver and direction finder may be combined.
Radar, hyperbolic navigational aids and prearranged radio transmissions for the use of individual competitors are prohibited.

12. CARRYING, SETTING AND SHEETING SAILS (*Affecting Rule* 54).
  (a) Sails shall be set only in those areas which have been declared for inclusion in the sail area and must not exceed the limits specified.
  (b) Sails may be sheeted to the main, fore or mizzen boom, but the point of attachment of the sheet lead to the boom may not without penalty be more than 6 inches outside the after black band or, if there is no black band, the clew outhaul sheave.
  (c) Only one size and weight of mizzen sail may be carried on board.
  (d) A device for keeping the spinnaker boom clear of the shrouds shall not be regarded as a second spinnaker boom.
  (e) Special light-weather mainsails are prohibited.

13. HARD-WEATHER RUNNING SAILS (*Affecting Rule* 54). Two hard-weather running sails may be carried, set on spinnaker booms forward of the mast, provided:—
  (a) The sum of the area of the two sails does not exceed 100 per cent of measured sail area.
  (b) The mainsail is not set at the same time as the leeward running sail, except when shifting sail.
  (c) Neither spinnaker boom is longer, nor mounted further forward, than is permitted by the rule of measurement for the yacht's rating.

14. AUTOMATIC, mechanical and wind-vane devices for steering are prohibited.

15. USE OF ENGINE AND POWER PUMP (*Affecting Rules* 60, 62 *and* 64).
  (a) An engine or power pump may not be used except for charging batteries, pumping bilges, or supplying power for weighing anchor or hauling off, and if the main engine is used a part of the shaft between the gear box and stern tube must be held stationary.
  (b) If an engine is used to recover a man overboard, to render assistance, or in any other grave emergency, full details must be reported on the declaration.

16. DECLARATION. A completed declaration shall be lodged with the race committee as soon as practicable after a yacht has finished. Delay in lodging her declaration may result in a yacht being penalised or disqualified. Any contravention of any rule to which she is subject, as well as any mark of the course which is not sighted, must be reported on the declaration.

17. OWNERSHIP OF YACHTS (*Affecting Rule* 20.2). The race committee may at its discretion take no action under I.Y.R.U. rule 20.2.

18. OWNER STEERING ANOTHER YACHT (*Affecting Rule* 55). The race committee may at its discretion take no action under I.Y.R.U. rule 55.

19. CANCELLATION OR POSTPONEMENT OF RACES (*Affecting Rules* 5, 12 *and* 13). No race shall be resailed or declared void except at the discretion of the R.O.R.C. committee.

SAFETY REGULATIONS

The safety of a yacht and her crew entered for a R.O.R.C. race is the sole and inescapable responsibility of the owner, who must do his best to ensure that the yacht is fully found, thoroughly seaworthy and manned by an experienced crew who are physically fit to face bad weather.

He should be satisfied as to the soundess of hull, caulking, spars, standing and running rigging, storm sails and all other gear. Safety equipment should be properly maintained and stowed, and the crew should know where it is kept and how it should be used.

Protection should be provided for ports and deck openings, and provision made to cover them if broken, the propellor shaft secured so that it cannot withdraw, and any opening in the hull should be accessible, with suitable means provided to seal it off.

The person in charge during the race is responsible for ensuring that the yacht is sailed with proper precaution. He must anticipate spending long periods at sea with no shelter within easy reach and no means of obtaining assistance.

R.O.R.C. safety regulations specify certain compulsory equipment. There are many other items which are essential or desirable in a well-found yacht, and a list of these will be provided by the secretary, if requested.

It is emphasized that the R.O.R.C. accepts no responsibility or liability for loss of life or injury to members or others, or for the loss of, or damage to any vessel.

20. INSPECTION. A yacht may be inspected at any time. If she does not comply with safety regulations her entry may be rejected under I.Y.R.U. racing rule 1.4, or she will be liable to disqualification or the time penalty in special regulation 4.

21. RESPONSIBILITY FOR RACING. Under I.Y.R.U. racing rule 1.3 it is the sole responsibility of each yacht to decide whether or not to start or to continue to race.

22. COMPULSORY EQUIPMENT. The following equipment must be carried and must be of a kind adequate for the size of the yacht when off-shore racing or cruising:—
  (a) STORM SAIL(s) capable of sailing to windward in heavy weather.
  (b) LIFELINES, of wire rope or metal tube, must be fitted continuously round the hull at a minimum height of 24 inches from deck level and no further inboard from the edge of the deck than 5 per cent of maximum beam, or 6 inches, whichever is the greater, and the bow pulpit must pass outside the forestay and the luff of the headsail. This last provision is not compulsory in a yacht built before 1950 if the forestay is attached to a bowsprit.

If the vertical gap between rail cap and lifeline exceeds 18 inches, a second lifeline must be fitted and must also go right round the yacht, including the forestay, while the yacht is racing, but this may be removable forward of the after upright of the bow pulpit. Lifelines must be supported at intervals not exceeding 7 feet. The head of a stanchion must not be angled outwards from the point of its attachment to the hull at more than 10 degrees from vertical.

(c) LIFEBUOYS. Two lifebuoys. One with self-igniting light must be rigged within reach of the helmsman.

(d) LIFEJACKETS. One for each crew member.

(e) SAFETY HARNESS. One for each crew member.

(f) LIFERAFTS. A liferaft (or liferafts), which is stable and capable of carrying the whole crew of the yacht with one compartment deflated must be carried on deck (not under a dinghy), or in a special stowage opening immediately to the deck and containing the liferafts only.

Every liferaft must comply with the following minimum requirements:—

(i) It must be specially designed for, and solely for the use of saving life at sea.

(ii) It must have at least two separate buoyancy compartments, each of which must be automatically inflatable.

(iii) It must have a canopy to cover the occupants, and this must be automatically inflatable in liferafts made after 1st January, 1964.

(iv) It must have in its pack at least:—

1 sea anchor or drogue	1 baler
1 bellows for hand inflation	1 repair kit
1 signalling torch	2 paddles
3 B.O.T. approved hand flares	1 safety knife
2 parachute flares	1 rescue quoit and line

(v) Each liferaft must have a valid annual certificate.

(vi) Liferafts purchased after 31st December 1965 must comply with Merchant Shipping (Life-Saving Appliances) Rules 1965:—

Rule 25—Annual Survey
Rule 35—As for Class XII (Equipment of Liferafts)
Schedule 9, Part I—As for Class XII

(g) DINGHY (1) of any type suitable for kedging or for use as the yacht's tender.

(h) DISTRESS SIGNALS. Red night-signals (6) including 2 parachute signals.

(i) FOG SIGNAL (1).

(j) BILGE PUMPS (2). To be operated independently.

(k) FIRST AID equipment, with provisions for burns.

(l) FIRE EXTINGUISHERS (2), chemical type.

(m) ANCHORS (2) and CHAIN. A yacht must carry a minimum weight of chain or an equivalent weight (or the deficit if the chain is too light) of internal ballast forward of the mast. This minimum weight is based on measured sail area (M.S.A.) as shown in the R.O.R.C. rating certificate, as follows:—

Measured Sail Areas	Minimum Weight	Length and size corresponding to Minimum Weight
Up to 300 sq. ft.	85 lbs.	25 fath. of $\frac{1}{4}$ inch dia.
301– 400 ,,	105 ,,	30 ,, $\frac{1}{4}$,, ,,
401– 600 ,,	135 ,,	25 ,, $\frac{5}{16}$,, ,,
601– 800 ,,	160 ,,	30 ,, $\frac{5}{16}$,, ,,
801–1,100 ,,	240 ,,	30 ,, $\frac{3}{8}$,, ,,
1,101–1,300 ,,	280 ,,	35 ,, $\frac{3}{8}$,, ,,
1,301–1,600 ,,	360 ,,	45 ,, $\frac{3}{8}$,, ,,
1,601–1,900 ,,	495 ,,	45 ,, $\frac{7}{16}$,, ,,
1,901–2,300 ,,	635 ,,	45 ,, $\frac{1}{2}$,, ,,
Over 2,300 ,,	845 ,,	60 ,, $\frac{1}{2}$,, ,,

(n) EMERGENCY STEERING. Every yacht must be capable of being steered directly from the rudder stock. Yachts with wooden tillers must carry a spare tiller.

(o) RADAR REFLECTOR (1).

(p) DRINKING WATER. In addition to the main supply of drinking water, two gallons must be carried in a separate independent container as an emergency supply.

(q) PORTABLE SAIL NUMBER.

(r) RACING FLAG.

(s) CLASS FLAG.

APPENDIX X

TYPICAL R.O.R.C. PROGRAMME (1969)

Race	Miles	Date
1. Bassurelle Race, start and finish at Southsea	220	Friday, 2nd May
2. Ryde to Harwich	210	Friday, 16th May
3. Harwich to Hook of Holland	220	Friday, 23rd May
4. Owers—CH 1, start and finish at Southsea	220	Saturday, 24th May
5. Owers—Shambles—CH 1, start and finish at Southsea	210	Friday, 6th June
6. Morgan Cup Race, start and finish at Southsea ..	205	Friday, 20th June
7. Holyhead to Dun Laoghaire	215	Saturday, 21st June
8. Round Gotland	340	Sunday, 29th June
9. West Mersea to Ostend	215	Friday, 11th July
10. Cherbourg, Eddystone, Solent	240	Sunday, 13th July
11. Skaw Race from Skagen	290	Wednesday, 16th July
12. Cowes to Dinard	180	Friday, 18th July
13. Skagen to Solent	650	Monday, 21st July
14. Channel Race, start and finish at Southsea	240	Friday, 1st August
15. Fastnet Race	605	Saturday, 9th August
16. Plymouth to La Rochelle	350	Sunday, 17th August
17. La Rochelle to Benodet	205	Friday, 22nd August
18. Middle Sea Race, start and finish at Malta, G.C. ..	604	Saturday, 1st November

SOME OTHER OPEN WATER RACES

Name of Yacht Club   *Name of Race, Course, etc.*   *Approx. Distance*

EAST COAST AND NORTH SEA

Name of Yacht Club	Name of Race, Course, etc.	Approx. Distance
Noordzeeclub	Hook to Harwich. Finish at Cork L.V.	105
R. Corinthian Y.C.	Thames Estuary Race	95
Crouch Y.C.	Cork and Sunk Race for the Houghton Cup	90
Noordzeeclub	Ijmuiden to Harwich	125
Noordzeeclub	Hook to Ostend	70

ENGLISH CHANNEL

Name of Yacht Club	Name of Race, Course, etc.	Approx. Distance
R. Lymington Y.C.	Lymington, round the Wight and return	52
Island S.C.	Cowes to Cherbourg	80
R. Lymington Y.C.	Lymington to Guernsey	100
R. London Y.C.	Cowes to Guernsey	110
Island S.C.	Round the Isle of Wight	52
	Race for yachts 5–25 tons T.M. for Gold Roman Challenge Bowl	
	Race for yachts over 25 tons T.M. for Crankshaw Challenge Bowl	
Island Sailing Club	Cowes to Ouistreham	100
R. Lymington Y.C.	Lymington, round the Wight and return, by night	52

WEST COAST, IRISH SEA, AND CLYDE

Name of Yacht Club	Name of Race, Course, etc.	Approx. Distance
R. Mersey Y.C.	Rock Ferry to Holyhead	80
Irish Cruising Club.	Dun Laoghaire to Holyhead	54
R. Anglesey and R. Dee Y.C.'s	Beaumaris to Holyhead	31
R. Anglesey and R. Dee Y.C.'s	Holyhead to Dun Laoghaire	54
Tranmere S.C.	Rock Ferry, Morecambe Bay, Bar L.V.	62
Clyde Cruising Club	Clyde to Dun Laoghaire	175
Tranmere S.C.	Midnight Race, Rock Ferry to Douglas, I.o.M.	72
Irish Cruising Club	Dun Laoghaire to Clyde, direct	175
Clyde Cruising Club	From Largs round Ailsa Craig and Arran to Hunters Quay	—
R. Welsh Y.C.	Round Anglesey	46
Clyde Cruising Club	Ailsa Craig Trophy	—

APPENDIX XI

NOTES CONCERNING THE 1968 R.O.R.C. RULE OF MEASUREMENT AND RATING

The present R.O.R.C. rating rule shown in Appendix VIII was first made available in the summer of 1956.

The following notes comparing the present Rule with the former one may be of interest.

The basic Rating Formula itself (Section I) has not been altered but the method of arriving at some of the component parts, length, depth, and rated sail area, are very much altered. 'Beam' is unaltered, being measured at a height not exceeding half the freeboard height.

In measuring length 'Inner Girth Stations' are now used as well as the old girth stations. Thus the two forward stations are where the girth is half beam and three-quarters beam, and aft where the girth is three-quarters and seven-eighths beam. Previously the girth stations were so far outboard that it encouraged snubbed or much shortened

overhangs. The exact method of calculating the 'length' for the Formula from these girth stations and from the freeboard at these girth stations is complex but it will suffice to say that in the upshot it allows the designer to lengthen his forward overhang appreciably without incurring much penalty.

A penalty for counters which have been cut off short is still in effect retained. The measured overhang in the case of transom sterns is slightly reduced; this seems fair because the old Rule which measured the length to a point well outboard of any possible waterline ending was hard on a type which makes for economical building.

The method of calculating depth is complex. Suffice to say that 'Quarter Beam Depth Immersed' and the 'Forward Depth Immersed' are the powerful factors in the Formula, and that depth of the hull above the water has now no influence. This is not illogical provided freeboard is sufficiently encouraged elsewhere in the Formula. Forward Depth Immersed is measured at quarter length one-tenth of the beam out from the centre line.

There are several innovations to the method of sail area measurement. There is a mild bonus on low aspect ratios; that is to say where the hoist of the sails is low compared to the foot-length in the case of mainsail and mizzens, or the triangle base in the case of headsails. This is a logical step as a 'special measurer' because the high aspect ratio provides on the average a faster rig for a given area. However, rightly, this bonus is light and so far has not led to a general return to the old-fashioned inefficient low aspect ratios. The schooner rig is now rated more realistically with limitation on masthead relationships and between mast area.

The fore triangle is now measured at 100 per cent of its area, instead of 85 per cent. Previously it was unquestionably too lightly taxed, bearing in mind the larger wider spinnakers which were introduced in 1949. However, in comparing the rated area of the mainsail it must not be forgotten that the roach may add 10 per cent to the rated area, and much of it high up where it will be most valuable in both light and moderate conditions. Incidentally should anyone now wish to produce a gaff mainsail in 1969, it will be treated and measured as a normal bermudian mainsail.

Offshore it is desirable to have a large proportion of one's area in the fore triangle to ensure a sufficient area of light ghosting canvas, since the wind will be shaken out of a mainsail by the motion in a seaway. Thus my guess is that there will not be any strong temptation to move masts forward unduly in genuine ocean racers, though some in dual purpose yachts which are largely aimed at inshore regatta racing on the R.O.R.C. Formula.

In spite of the inclusion of freeboard in the stability allowance the Rule does not give any temptation to increasing the freeboard beyond a reasonable minimum, and there may be a return to the practice of achieving one's headroom by careful exploitation of the maximum of coach roofs; provided that one's main deck camber does not exceed 4 per cent of a yacht's beam, as any excess above this would increase the "I" measurement of the foretriangle. However, it is clear that any attempt to build an unduly low freeboard boat will meet with special penalty action under the powers conferred on the R.O.R.C. Committee in connection with peculiarities of design.

Under this new Rule the bonus on a good beam is still considerable though less than that afforded by the old rule which (though designers were slow to recognise it) was very strong.

The penalties on a yawl with a mizzen set well clear of the mainsail are likely to be sufficient to ensure a general return to the always popular cutter rig traditional to British yachting.

The stability allowance now includes and in effect supersedes, a pure scantling allowance. The effect of the scantlings which was very strong is now rightly, in my view, reduced. (With particular consideration being given to glass fibre yachts, which have now had the 15 per cent penalty on scantlings cancelled.) Also rightly the freeboard bonus is amalgamated with the scantling allowance as is the bulwark allowance, and the allowance for a raised deck if fitted. But the effect of the freeboard allowance is not strong. A 1 per cent T.C.F. will also be allowed on yachts built before 1963 and subsequent class yachts built to a design prior to that date.

Other component parts of the stability allowance are the bonuses on iron ballast, shallow draft, and engine weight, and the penalty on aluminium masts. These seem fairly equitable.

The propeller allowance has been more thoroughly covered than before, various diameters and positions being given different allowances; with the proviso that the auxiliary installation should be efficient in calm water, to propel a yacht at not less than $.8\sqrt{w.l.}$ in knots.

APPENDIX XII

CRUISING CLUB OF AMERICA

AMENDED TO 1967

MEASUREMENT RULE FOR RACING

INTRODUCTION AND RATING FORMULA

The fundamental purpose of the Measurement Rule of the Cruising Club of America is to provide a method of rating yachts of varying lengths, types, rigs and hull designs in order that they may compete with each other on an equitable basis. Manifestly, it is difficult to develop a rule which meets every condition, and impossible to devise one that will anticipate each new innovation of tomorrow. The policy of the Cruising Club of America, therefore, has been to seek constant improvement in the rule to keep pace with advances in the design of yachts and in the use of new materials. Changes in the rule are made only after careful consideration so that evolution of the rule can be accomplished gradually on the basis of proven experience and with a minimum of hardship to existing yachts.

The C.C.A. Rule, as well as the time allowance tables that customarily are used in conjunction with it, is based upon the assumption that a triangular course will be sailed with approximately equal legs of close hauled, running and reaching conditions. If the courses actually sailed vary significantly from this assumed norm, it is desirable, particularly in long-distance races, to provide some means of adjusting handicaps to assure fair competition. The larger or higher rated yachts are favoured if courses are predominantly to windward; whereas the smaller or lower rated yachts have the advantage in downwind races. One method frequently employed to compensate for such departures from the assumed norm is to adjust the distance used in calculating handicaps; thus, in a race principally to windward, the length of the course, for purposes of computing time allowances, is assumed to be longer than the actual distance; and conversely, in a downwind race the course is assumed to be shorter than it actually is.

As there are other, simpler rules in current use, which provide reasonably accurate comparative ratings, the question is frequently asked if there is any real need for the detailed specifications called for by the C.C.A. Rule. The answer lies in the fact that the simpler the rule, the greater is the opportunity for the ingenuity of designers and owners to find loopholes, thereby creating inequitable advantages. The Cruising Club of America welcomes innovation within the Spirit of the Rule, because new ideas may well be the forerunners of significant beneficial changes in ocean racing. Accordingly, new ideas may require changes in the rule, if equitable ratings are to be maintained, and over a period of time such changes will lead to a more complicated and detailed measurement rule. The long-term efficacy of the C.C.A. Rule is attested to by the fact that most racing-cruising boats in American waters, as well as substantial numbers in other countries, are designed for performance under this rule rather than under any of the simpler rules.

The equitable rating of yachts of widely varying dimensions and types is a complicated procedure; nevertheless, the basic principles of the C.C.A. Rule are reasonably simple and not only can, but should, be understood by all owners of yachts rated under it. The underlying concepts which determine potential speed require neither a familiarity with higher mathematics nor a scientific training. The following discussion of the formula of the rule endeavours to explain in simple terms these basic concepts of the rule. For those seeking greater refinement, a careful study of the provisions of the rule itself is recommended.

THE RATING FORMULA

The time honoured theory is that a yacht's speed is related to the square root of its waterline length. The time allowance tables contained herein, as well as those used by the North American Yacht Racing Union, the New York Yacht Club and other organizations, are founded on this basic premise. To use such tables, however, it is first necessary that each yacht have a 'Rating', for, as will be observed from examination of the tables, time allowances are correlated to Ratings.

The C.C.A. Rule provides the method for rating a yacht. However, in arriving at the rating, the rule takes into account not only waterline length, but also other factors which influence a yacht's speed. The C.C.A. Rating Formula is:—

$R = (L \pm Bm. \pm Dra. \pm Displ. \pm S) \times Stab. F. \times Prop.$

The abbreviations used in the formula represent the following:

$R = $ Rating, or as it is sometimes called, Rated Length. This is the end result of the measurement of the yacht. Under this rule it is stated in feet and tenths of a foot. It is this figure that is used to enter the time allowance tables.

$L = $ Measured Length, which is determined from a weighted average of the waterline length and the length of a plane parallel to and 4 per cent above the waterline (4 per cent WL) plus, where necessary, a Transom Correction (Tc). A Transom Correction is required where the 4 per cent WL intersects the stern transom. The combination of these figures, it is believed, gives a more accurate appraisal of a yacht's speed potential than waterline length alone (see paragraphs 301 to 307, inclusive). L is also used as the basis for determining the standards for many of the other factors in the formula.

$Bm = $ Beam Correction. Since, generally, an increase in beam increases resistance, the rule provides for a credit (i.e., a reduction in rating) where a yacht's beam is in excess of the standard established by the rule, and conversely a penalty (or an increase in rating) where the actual beam is less than the standard (see paragraphs 308 to 310, inclusive).

Dra. = Draft Correction. Deep draft is regarded as providing a more effective lateral plane for better performance to windward. The calculations affecting draft also take into account centreboards. Where a yacht's draft exceeds the standard she takes a penalty; where it is less, she receives a credit (see paragraphs 602 to 606, inclusive).

Disp. = Displacement Correction. Displacement or the weight of the yacht offers resistance to hull movement through water and therefore the rule gives a credit where actual displacement is greater than the standard or base displacement and imposes a penalty when it is less (see paragraphs 607 to 609, inclusive).

$S = $ Sail Area Correction. Sails provide the force to drive a yacht through the water. The larger the sail area or the more efficient the sail plan, the greater, generally, is the potential for increased speed. The rule, therefore, corrects for variations both in sail area and sail plan from the standard, by giving credits for smaller and/or less efficient sail plans. The importance of sails is evidence by the number, scope and detail of the sail measurement provisions of the rule (see paragraphs 401 to 415, inclusive; 501 to 511, inclusive; and 701 to 709, inclusive).

After corrections for Beam, Draft, Displacement and Sail Area are made to L, the result, called 'Corrected L', is then further adjusted by two multipliers, as follows:

Stab. F = Stability Factor. A yacht's ability to carry sail depends to a very important degree upon its stability characteristics. To determine these, the rule requires actual measurement of the righting moment by inclining the yacht. From this, the actual relative stability is calculated and a Stability Factor is derived for use in the rating formula (see paragraph 610). The more stability the yacht has, the higher its rating will be and vice versa.

Prop. = Propeller Factor. The amount of resistance, or drag, caused by propellers varies with the size, type, location and installation. The rule evaluates each such variable, and the combination thereof results in a factor for use in the rating formula (see paragraph 611).

From the foregoing it can be seen that the Measurement Rule is confined to a determination of and correction for design differences between competing yachts, and does not in any way reduce the challenge to the crew to demonstrate their ability in the art of sailing or to obtain the most efficient performance, or to exercise continually good seamanship, strategy and judgment in competitive racing with different types and sizes of yachts. Further, the rule does not undertake to usurp the function of the Race Committee as to the conditions of the race, matters of safety, or the like. It is important in this regard, however, that the owner recognize that the validity of his measurement certificate depends upon his compliance with this Measurement Rule.

PART I
GENERAL

101. PURPOSE OF RULE. This rule is intended to provide an equitable method of predicting the potential speed of normal sailing yachts which differ in their dimensions and proportions, producing ratings from which time allowances may be assigned in accordance with N.A.Y.R.U. time allowance tables, or other suitable handicapping basis. The form of the rule permits the independent adjustment of the various factors and it is intended that these may be revised by the Measurement Rule Committee of the C.A.A. from time to time as necessary in order to maintain the most accurate relationship between rating and potential speed.

102. ELIGIBILITY OF YACHTS. Limitations regarding maximum and minimum dimensions, ballast ratio, watertight cockpits, et cetera, are not considered part of the Measurement Rule but rather should be determined by the governing body controlling any given race. Such limitations should be clearly covered in the printed instructions for the race.

103. RELATIONSHIP TO RACING RULES. Where the Cruising Club of America Measurement Rule is at variance with the Racing Rules of the N.A.Y.R.U., the former will govern. There is no conflict between the N.A.Y.R.U. Right of Way Rules and the C.C.A. Measurement Rule.

104. PLANS NOT AVAILABLE. If plans are not available, measurements must be taken off the boat and lines must either be taken off, or the boat must be weighed, to arrive at displacement.

105. POWERS OF MEASUREMENT RULE COMMITTEE. Inasmuch as it is impossible at the time of drawing any measurement rule to foresee all of the peculiarities of design or construction which might affect the relationship between rating and speed, it is hereby provided that if because of any peculiarity of form, construction, or rig, a yacht does not appear to be fairly rated by this Rule, *the measurer shall report such peculiarity to the C.C.A. Measurement Rule Committee* which shall award a certificate of rating as it may consider suitable. Any type of construction or rig which accomplishes the essential purposes, or provides the essential advantages, of any construction or rig which is either prohibited, or for which penalties are provided in the Rule, will be prohibited or will take the same penalties, as though it were specifically mentioned in the Rule. This power of the Measurement Rule Committee shall include the proper rating of unusual scantlings, tankage, or other arrangements which could unfairly affect the Rating of a Yacht.

106. ELIGIBILITY AND DUTIES OF MEASURERS. Measurers must be designated by a recognized yachting association and certified by the Cruising Club of America. Measurers shall not measure yachts in which they have participated in the design, construction or alteration; or yachts designed, built or altered by a firm in which they have a business interest; or yachts of which they themselves are the owners or part owners, or regular crew members.

The Measurement Rule imposes responsibility for compliance on both owners and measurers. It shall be the duty of a measurer to verify that the owner has complied with matters relating to owner's responsibility under Part II hereof.

Note.—A list of items to be checked and verified by the measurer is part of the data sheet submitted and certified by the measurer.

107. FORM MEASUREMENT CERTIFICATE. A form certificate set up to facilitate recording measurements under the Rule is available and may be obtained from the Secretary of The Cruising Club of America.

108. ACCURACY OF MEASUREMENTS AND CALCULATIONS. Measurements are to be made in feet with decimals to the nearest hundredth. Displacement is to be stated in cubic feet to nearest tenth.

PART II
OWNER'S PREPARATION FOR HULL AND RIG MEASUREMENT

201. GENERAL MEASUREMENT PROCEDURE. To secure an accurate and fair measurement it is necessary to have close co-operation between owner, designer, and measurer. It is essential that the owner should be familiar with all parts of the measurement rule.

First, the owner must make the boat available to the measurer afloat and in suitable trim and with required equipment on board and in place.

Second, on completion of measurements of hull and rig, and based on the flotation at measurement times, the measurer must obtain from the designer additional information.

202. HULL MEASURING PROCEDURE. The principal hull measurements enumerated in Part III are dependent on accurate determination of the load waterline or plane of floatation. The measuring must be done in a location which will provide extremely smooth water and quiet wind conditions. A skiff should be available from which to take the overboard measurements.

The owner or his responsible agent must be present and available at the time of measurement. The yacht to be measured must be afloat and ready in the following condition for the measurer:—

(1) Completely rigged and ready to sail.

(2) All working sails must be in place and furled. Where sails have booms, the booms must be secured at the low point of P, P_{miz}, H, or H_{miz}, as the case may be.

The working jib or roller furling jib (or staysail and jib in the case of a double head rig) shall be bagged and located on deck on centreline halfway between its mast and jib stay.

In case the mainsail, mizzen or foresail or any other sail are roller furling along the mast or stay, they shall be bagged and placed on deck on the fore and aft centreline halfway between normal positions of tack and clew of that sail.

(3) All sails to be used when racing are to be on board, and all sails, except as required in (2) above, are to be stowed below decks in the locations used for stowage of sails when racing.

(4) All working equipment and stores shall be in place occupied while racing, and shall include 2 anchors of normal size and weight, each with chain or warp, spinnaker pole(s), blocks and running rigging.

Dinghy and/or life raft(s) if on board at time of measurement must always be carried and in the same locations when racing.

(5) All normal navigating, galley, electrical, fire extinguishing, life saving, medical, engine and other equipment must be on board and in appropriate locations which must be maintained when racing.

(6) All inside ballast shall be in position to stay for the duration of the rating certificate for which the yacht is being measured.

(7) Water and fuel tanks shall be full or empty in accordance with the following provisions:

(a) The owner may certify to the measurer which tanks are not used when racing and those tanks must be and remain empty during weighing, measuring and racing.

(b) Any tank not certified to be empty while racing shall be either full and pressed up to avoid free surface or empty, depending upon which condition maximizes the rating. Generally, this will require that tanks wholly below the lowest cabin sole must be full; those wholly or partially above it must be empty. Wherever doubt exists, measurements shall be taken in both conditions and those which yield the maximum rating shall be used. In case of further question, the measurer shall submit a full report to the Measurement Rule Committee for a ruling.

(c) The term 'tanks' includes all containers, whether or not permanently installed. All containers not permanently installed shall be stowed at time of weighing and measurement in the locations where they are to be carried while racing.

(8) All sump tanks shall be empty and bilges must be pumped dry.

(9) No personnel shall be on board while hull or weighing measurements are being taken, except as may be required by the measurer during inclining measurements.

(10) Consumable stores aboard shall not exceed 20 pounds weight per man of crew. The number of crew will be determined by 3 plus the total Rated Sail Area, taken from the rating certificate, divided by 250. Any excess over a whole number in RSA/250 will be taken as a whole number.

Consumable stores shall include food, beverages, ice, stove fuel, bottled water, crews' sea bags, sleeping bags, magazines, books, etc.

(11) The yacht must be level during the taking of all hull measurements and during inclining. Any yacht with a bow down trim with no one on board will not be acceptable for measurement. Proper trim may be obtained for measuring by moving gear aft.

(12) Centreboard(s), if any, must be fully raised.

(13) Measurement point bands on masts and booms must be in place (see 204).

(14) The owner must be sure that the yacht will be inclined and weighed in the same condition as for hull measurements.

203. SAIL MEASURING PROCEDURE. Certain sails must be measured as explained in Parts IV and V, i.e., spinnakers, jibs, mizzen staysails, overlapping sails, gaff sails and topsails. These sails must be made available to the measurer for measuring or for checking marked dimensions and for determining the maximum LP or other basic dimensions as described in Part V. Measurements of all sails required to be measured, such as LP of jibs, mizzen staysail and spinnaker dimensions, must be measured with normal tension between measurement points and free of wrinkles across line of measurement and must include the fabric length between measurement points. Measuring point at corner of a sail shall be the intersection of the adjacent outside edges projected. All other measurement points shall be at the extreme outside of rope, wire or fabric of the sail's edge.

204. BLACK BANDS. Measurements may not be taken to locations defined by black bands unless these bands, with accompanying stoppers or halyard markings, are in place at the time of measurements. If measurements are taken to black bands the location of bands cannot be changed without invalidating the rating certificate.

PART III

HULL MEASUREMENTS TO BE MADE AFLOAT

301. LOA (LENGTH OVER ALL) shall be the length from the aftermost part of the hull or taffrail to the intersection of the forward side of the stem and the top of the covering board, or the fair extension of either, or both, if necessary.

302. OHF (OVERHANG FORWARD) shall be the horizontal measurement from the forward point determining LOA and the intersection of the face of the stem with the plane of flotation.

303. OHA (OVERHANG AFT) shall be the horizontal measurement from the aftermost point determining LOA to the intersection of the stern profile with the plane of flotation.

304. LWL (LOAD WATER LINE) shall be the length of the load water line determined by subtracting from the LOA the forward and after overhangs.

305. 4% WL (4% WATER LINE LENGTH). The length measured in a plane parallel to the LWL and 4% of the LWL above same. This 4% length may not be measured as less than the LWL, nor may its measured length be reduced by local jogs, notches or unfair hollows, any of which if present shall be bridged in measuring in a manner to produce a normal 4% WL length measurement.

306. TC (TRANSOM CORRECTION). Should the 4% WL plane intersect the stern transom, then one-quarter of the horizontal transverse measurement along the transom, from the edge at the point of intersection to the centre line, shall be entered in the L formula as a plus quantity.

307. L (MEASURED LENGTH):—
$$L = \cdot 3 \text{ LWL} + \cdot 7 \text{ of the } 4\% \text{ WL} + \text{Tc}$$

308. MEAS. BM (MEASURED BEAM):—
$$\text{Meas. Bm} = \frac{\text{Max LWL Beam} + 4\% \text{ WL Beam}}{2}$$
4% WL Beam to be measured at same station as Max LWL Beam.

309. BASE BM (BASE BEAM) $= \cdot 187 \text{ L} + 3 \cdot 2$

310. BM (BEAM CORRECTION):—
$$\text{Bm} = \text{K (Base Beam} - \text{Meas. Beam)}$$
If Base Beam is greater than Meas. Beam use $\text{K} = \cdot 5$ and insert Bm as a plus correction.
If Base Beam is less than Meas. Beam use $\text{K} = \cdot 25$ and insert Bm as a minus correction.

PART IV

RIG AND SAIL MEASUREMENTS

401. GENERAL. For most of the measurements described in this section, detailed procedures are given whereby they may be determined on a fair basis under ordinary circumstances. However, if these procedures are found not to cover completely in individual cases, the measurer will decide how best to get a reliable figure for the measurement in question. For instance, where masts enter through cabin trunk tops the theoretical intersection of the centreline of the main deck with the masts can be determined by utilizing a standard camber of $\frac{1}{2}$ in. per foot of beam to calculate the distance from accessible point of measurement to the theoretical intersection point, or in the case of raised deck or reverse sheer construction where the cabin top is the main deck, the intersection point should be at the cabin top, or the measurer may obtain the intersection point by certification from the designer if it cannot be ascertained directly by inspection and auxiliary measurements.

402. B (DETERMINATION OF B). B is the measured length of the foot of the mainsail taken from the after side of mast at the fair extension of track if used, to extreme aftermost position to which the sail can be extended. If this latter point is inside of boom end, it must be located by inner edge of 1 in. black band around boom.

(a) For staysail ketch, B = distance between masts (see 506 (4) (a)).

(b) For batten correction, see 506 (3) (c).

403. P (DETERMINATION OF P). P is the measured length of the hoist of a jib headed mainsail. It shall be the distance along afterside of mainmast from the top of boom, projected fairly, or boom track if used, projected fairly, to the top of the highest sheave used for the main halyard; or to the underside of 1 in. black band, provided either a fixed stopper or accurate halyard marking will indicate exactly when highest part of sail reaches underside of band.

(a) If sliding gooseneck is used, measurement is to be made with boom at extreme bottom of travel unless this point is determined by a removable stopper or the upper edge of 1 in. black band around mast. Top of boom (or track) may not be carried below this measurement point when mainsail is set, except when actually putting in or shaking out a reef in the mainsail.

(b) The low point used in determination of P may not be taken higher than $\cdot 05 \text{ P} + 4 \cdot 0$ feet above main deck.

(c) If boom gooseneck is above tack of sail, maximum distance from gooseneck to tack must be added to P dimension as otherwise measured. (See 506 (4) (a) excepting stays'l ketch.)

(d) If rake of mast exceeds 15 per cent, P shall be taken as the vertical height. Percent of rake shall be determined by taking the horizontal distance on deck between plumb bob or equivalent suspended freely from masthead, and dividing this distance by the height of masthead from deck measured along after side of mast.

(e) If head board width exceeds 3 per cent of B, see 506 (1) for correction to P.

404. H (DETERMINATION OF H). H is the measured length of the hoist for a gaff mainsail. It shall be the distance along the after side of the mast from the lower edge of 1 in. black band around the mast, above which mark the upper inner edge of the throat cringle of the mainsail shall not be hoisted, to the upper side of the boom or black band, the location of which is not higher than $\cdot 05$ (H + $\cdot 6$G) + $4 \cdot 0$ ft. above main deck.

405. G (DETERMINATION OF G). G is the measured length of the head of the mainsail along the gaff. It is the distance from the afterside of mast to outboard point of gaff, determined in a manner similar to that for outboard end of main boom in 402 above.

406. B_2 (DETERMINATION OF B_2). B_2 is the measured length of the base used in calculating the area of the Fore Triangle and must be whichever is the *greatest* of the following:

(a) J (ACTUAL FORE TRIANGLE BASE), which is the distance from the foreside of the mast at the deck to the centre-line of the foremost stay on which headsails are set (the centreline of the luff if the foremost headsail is set flying), extended if necessary, to intersect the top of the bow sprit, or if no bow sprit, the top of the rail, including cap if used, and extended if necessary, or to the centreline of the deck, if same is above the rail or rail cap. (See 401 above.)

(b) SPINNAKER POLE LENGTH. Spinnaker pole is measured when set horizontal on the mast and at right angles to the centreline of the yacht, measurement being from the centreline to the extreme outboard end of the pole, including all fixed fittings.

(c) Spinnaker width divided by $1 \cdot 8$.

407. P_2 (DETERMINATION OF P_2). P_2 is the Fore Triangle height measured along the fore side of the mast from the intersection of the main deck centreline (projected if necessary) to which-ever is highest of the following:

(1) The intersection of the centreline of the highest stay used for headsails, with the fair line of the foreside of the mast or topmast (projected if necessary).

(2) The centre of the highest eye bolt or eye used for head-sail or spinnaker halyard block. A spinnaker halyard block may be set forward enough to permit a clear lead, without measurement penalty.

(3) To intersection of the foreside of the mast or topmast (projected if necessary) with the highest strop used for headsail or spinnaker halyard.

408. B_{miz} (DETERMINATION OF B_{miz}). B_{mzi} is the measured length of the foot of the mizzen sail. The method used in cal-culating B_{miz} for yawls and ketches is identical to that used for determining B in Par. 402, except that, in calculating *rated sail area*,

B_{miz} may not be less than $0 \cdot 85 \dfrac{B}{P} \times P_{miz}$.

409. P_{miz} (DETERMINATION OF P_{miz}). P_{miz} is the measured length of the hoist of a jib headed mizzen sail. The method used in calculating P_{miz} for yawls and ketches is identical to that used for determining P in 403, except that

(a) The upper point of measurement for the P_{miz} cannot be taken below the attachment of mizzen staysail halyard block or top of sheave. Block may be hung sufficiently forward of the mast to provide clear lead for halyard without requiring the point of measurement to be obtained by extending a line through the point of sup-port, providing mizzen staysail halyard block is no farther from the mast than necessary for clearance.

(b) Lower point of measurement for P_{miz} must not be taken higher than $\cdot 05$ P_{miz} + $4 \cdot 0$ ft. above main deck at mizzen mast.

410. H_{miz} (DETERMINATION OF H_{miz}). H_{miz} is the measured length of the hoist of a gaff mizzen sail. It is determined in a manner similar to that used in determining H (404 above) except that the upper limit may not be taken as less than 80 per cent from the lower limit to the mizzen staysail halyard block, and the lower limit shall not be higher than $\cdot 05$ (H_{miz} + $\cdot 6$ G_{miz}) + $4 \cdot 0$ ft. above main deck at mizzen mast.

411. G_{miz} (DETERMINATION OF G_{miz}). G_{miz} is the measured length of the head of the mizzen sail along the gaff. It is determined in a manner similar to that used in determining G (405 above).

412. B_1 (DETERMINATION OF B_1 (2-MASTED SCHOONERS)). B_1 is the distance measured at the deck from the foreside of the mainmast to the afterside of the foremast (or fair extension of track if used).

(Note that if there is any overlap of the foresail or lower main staysail beyond the foreside of the mainmast, this over-lap must be added to the distance between the masts in determining B_1.)

413. P_1 (DETERMINATION OF P_1 (2-MASTED SCHOONERS)). P_1 is the distance measured along the afterside of the foremast from (1) the higher of the following points: (a) the top of the highest sheave in the mast, or (b) the highest juncture of the mast with the eyebolt (centre of eye) or pennant of a halyard block, used for sails *aft* of the mast, to (2) the upper side of the boom or track, (a) when resting against the lower part of the gooseneck or (b) when resting on the saddle, or (c) to a black band if no boom is carried; such lower points to be no higher above the deck than the corresponding point on the mainmast or the limits of 403 (b) or 404. Exception: Peak Halyard Blocks are to be disregarded in taking this measurement.

Note.—If sliding gooseneck is used, measurement is to be made with boom at extreme bottom of travel unless this point is determined by a removable stopper or the upper edge of 1 in. black band around mast. Top of boom (or track) may not be carried below this measurement point when foresail is set.

414. P_3 (DETERMINATION OF P_3 (2-MASTED SCHOONERS)). P_3 is the distance measured along the foreside of the mainmast from (1) the higher of the following points: (a) the top of the highest sheave in the mast, or (b) the highest juncture of the mast with the eyebolt (centre of eye) or pennant of a halyard block, used for sails *forward* of the mast, to (2) (a) the exten-sion of the upper side of the boom or track of the foresail, or (b) the lower main staysail when resting parallel to the deck against the lower part of the gooseneck, or (c) when resting on the saddle, or (d) to a point the same height above the deck as the tack of the foresail or lower main staysail if no boom is carried.

Note.—If sliding gooseneck is used, measurement is to be made with boom at extreme bottom of travel unless this point is determined by a removable stopper or the upper edge of 1 in. black band around mast. Top of boom (or track) may not be carried below this measurement point when foresail is set.

415. SPINNAKER MEASUREMENTS AND LIMITATIONS. All meas-urements are to be taken with such tension in the sail as will produce, as nearly as possible, an approximation of the size when set running before a moderate breeze. Head of sails measured under this Rule are to be signed and marked by the measurer with the maximum length of the luff or the leach (whichever is greater) and with the maximum width that can be found in the sail, measuring between points on the luff and leach equidistant from the head. These marked dimensions can be used as long as the sail is used without alteration. Headboard shall not be longer than one-twentieth of the length of the spinnaker pole. No footyard or other con-trivance for extending the sail shall be used.

(a) Spinnaker Maximum Length: Luff and leach *may not exceed* $\cdot 95 \sqrt{P_2{}^2 + B_2{}^2}$.

(b) Spinnaker Maximum Width: Spinnaker width *may not exceed* 180 per cent of J without incurring the penalty of increasing B_2 (see 406).

PART V

CALCULATION OF MEASURED, RATED AND BASE SAIL AREAS

501. MEASURED SAIL AREA (MSA) is the actual square footage of area as calculated when using the dimensions described in Part IV or as determined in 505, 506 and 509.

502. RATED SAIL AREA (RSA) is the calculated rated sail area.

503. The TOTAL RSA to be used for each rig is the sum of the RSA for each sail or area as defined below:—
(1) *For Cat Rig* = Mainsail only.
(2) *For Sloop or Cutter* = Mainsail + Fore Triangle.
(3) *For Yawl or Ketch* = Mainsail + Fore Triangle + Mizzen + Mizzen Staysail.
(4) *For Schooner (2-masted)*
= Fore Triangle RSA + RSA bet. masts +
Mainsail RSA $\left(\dfrac{\text{Mainsail RSA}}{\text{Mainsail RSA} + \text{MSA bet. masts}}\right)$
(5) *For Other Rigs.* A study of details for measurement of rigs specifically covered above should point the way to appropriate measurement of other rigs.

504. BASE SAIL AREA (BSA):—
$\sqrt{\text{BSA}} = 4 \cdot 3 \, (\cdot 179 \, L + \cdot 8)$ (See 608)

505. MAINSAIL MSA. A yacht must be rated with a mainsail. Mainsail MSA for rating purposes shall not be less than
(1) $\cdot 15 \, P^2$ for jib headed sloops, yawls and ketches, and $\cdot 15 \, P_2{}^2$ for gaff rigged sloops, yawls and ketches. P will be determined in accordance with 403 (b) and 506 (3).
(2) $\cdot 15 \, P_3{}^2$ for schooners.

506. MAINSAIL RATED SAIL AREA:—
(1) *Jib Headed Mainsail*
RSA $= \cdot 35 \, P \times B + \cdot 3 \, B \, (P - 2 \, B)$
(a) For jib headed mainsails the maximum width of the headboard shall be limited to 3 per cent of B.
Any excess width shall be multiplied by $\dfrac{P}{B}$ and added to P in computing mainsail rated area.
(b) The aspect ratio correction in the above formula may not be taken as a minus quantity.
(2) *Gaff Mainsail*
RSA $= \cdot 3 \, H \times B + \cdot 3 \, G\sqrt{H^2 + B^2} + \cdot 3 \, B \, (H - 2 \, B)$
(a) The aspect ratio correction in the above formula may not be taken as a minus quantity.
(b) If topsail is used, add 60 per cent of topsail MSA to Mainsail RSA. Topsail MSA shall be the area calculated from the measurement of the three sides by taking the height from the upper point of the mainsail hoist to the highest point to which the topsail may be set, including sprit, if any; the length of gaff (G) to which it is sheeted, plus extension of club, if any; and the length of leach measured from the sail when dry and stretched hard taut.
(3) Mainsails are subject to the following:—
(a) The upper point for measuring P shall not be lower than $\cdot 04 \, P_2$ below the upper point of P_2 or $\cdot 04 \, P_3$ below the upper point of P_3 for schooners.
(b) In case the minimum MSA under 505 is greater than the actual MSA, then $\cdot 7 \times$ Min. MSA shall be substituted for $\cdot 35 \, P \times B$ or $\cdot 6$ Min. MSA shall be substituted for $\cdot 3 \, H \times B + \cdot 3 \, G\sqrt{H^2 + B^2}$ in the RSA formula to calculate the mainsail RSA.
(c) The number of battens in any single sail shall be limited to four, except that when B exceeds 40 ft., five battens may be used. Battens must be spaced approximately evenly between head and clew.
The length of battens shall not exceed:—
For upper and lower battens $= \cdot 10 \, B + 1$ ft.
For intermediate battens $= \cdot 12 \, B + 1$ ft.
In case of any excess length, one-half of the total excess shall be multiplied by $\dfrac{P}{B}$ and added to P in computing mainsail rated area, or for gaff rigged mainsails, any excess shall be added to H in computing mainsail rated area.
(4) *Rating of Unusual Mainsails or Mizzens*
(a) Mainsail RSA of Staysail Ketch =
$\cdot 3 \, B \, (P + P_{miz}) + \cdot 3 \, B \, (P - 2 \, B)$
Distance between the masts to be used as B, and for gaff rigged mizzen $P_{miz} = H_{miz} + \cdot 5 \, G_{miz}$.
(b) Rated area of Quadrilateral Mainsail (other than Gaff sail) or other unusual mainsail, shall be taken as $\cdot 7$ MSA $+ \cdot 3 \, B \, (P - 2 \, B)$.

(c) Mainsails or Mizzens Without Booms: Where these are used, the B or B_{miz} measurement is the maximum measurement of the sail when new, and the dimensions should be marked and initialed on the sail by the measurer.
(d) Main Backstay Sails (Mules) as used on jib headed ketches or yawls, shall have 50 per cent of their MSA as determined by the maximum limits of halyard, tack, and sheeting points added to the otherwise determined mainsail rated area, to arrive at final mainsail rated area to be used for these rigs. The Mule will be classified as a Main Topsail. Mizzen staysail may be carried in addition.
(e) Gaff Mainsails. If gaff is less than $\cdot 6$ B or peaks higher than 70 degrees above horizontal, mainsail RSA will be calculated as a jib headed mainsail, 506 (1), using P = H + G.
(f) The aspect ratio correction in (a) or (b) above may not be taken as a minus quantity.

507. FORE TRIANGLE RATED SAIL AREA
RSA $= \cdot 55 \, P_2 B_2 + \dfrac{B_2}{LP} \, [(\cdot 55 \, LL \times LP) - \cdot 55 \, P_2 B_2]$
$\qquad\qquad + \cdot 3 \, B_2 \, (P_2 - 2 \, B_2)$
(a) The aspect ratio correction in the above formula may not be taken as a minus quantity.
(b) LL—shall be $\cdot 95\sqrt{P_2{}^2 + B_2{}^2}$
LP—shall be the greatest of
(1) the largest length of any jib to be carried measured on the perpendicular from luff to clew, or
(2) the length calculated as in (c) below, or
(3) $1 \cdot 5 \, B_2$.
(c) If any headsail is to be carried which
(1) is tacked aft of the forward point of J, and
(2) is set inside another headsail, and
(3) has (when sheeted flat on the wind) the position of its clew abaft a line parallel to the headstay and running through the clew of the jib with the largest LP as in (a) (1),
then the LP of this combination of sails shall be the length from the headstay to the clew of the inside headsail, measured on the perpendicular from headstay to clew.
(d) Battens may be used in jibs and fore staysails only if
(1) their length is not more than $\cdot 08$ J, and
(2) their forward end is forward of the centreline of the mainmast or foremast. The number of battens shall be limited to four (4) and battens must be spaced approximately evenly between head and clew.
(e) No headboards or clewboards may be used in jibs.
(f) A headsail may not be measured as a spinnaker unless the midgirth is 70 per cent or more of the foot length. No jib may have a midgirth measurement of more than 60 per cent of the foot length.

508. MIZZEN RATED SAIL AREA (YAWLS AND KETCHES)
(1) For jib headed
$\qquad\qquad$ RSA $= k \, (P_{miz} \times B_{miz})$
where
$k = \cdot 1 + \cdot 25\left(\dfrac{\cdot 5 \, P_{miz} \times B_{miz}}{\text{Main RSA} + \text{Fore Tri RSA}} - \cdot 1\right)$
(2) For gaff rigged
RSA $= k \, (H_{miz} \times B_{miz} + G_{miz}\sqrt{H^2{}_{miz} + B^2{}_{miz}})$
where
$k = \cdot 08 +$
$\cdot 2 \left(\dfrac{\cdot 5 \, H_{miz} \times B_{miz} + \cdot 5 \, G_{miz}\sqrt{H^2{}_{miz} + B^2{}_{miz}}}{\text{Main RSA} + \text{Fore Tri RSA}} - \cdot 1\right)$
(3) If mizzen MSA exceeds 50 per cent of the sum of Main RSA and Fore Triangle RSA, the yacht shall be measured as a schooner.
(4) Mizzens are subject to the following limitations:—
(a) For jib headed mizzens the maximum width of the headboard shall be limited to 5 per cent of B_{miz}.
Any excess width shall be multiplied by $\dfrac{P_{miz}}{B_{miz}}$ and added to P_{miz} in computing Mizzen RSA.

(b) The number of battens shall be limited to four. Length of battens shall not exceed:—

For upper and lower battens $= \cdot 10\ B_{miz} + 1$ ft.

For intermediate battens $= \cdot 12\ B_{miz} + 1$ ft.

In case of excess length, one-half of the total excess shall be multiplied by $\dfrac{P_{miz}}{B_{miz}}$ and added to P_{miz} in computing Mizzen RSA, or in case of gaff rigged mizzens, any excess shall be added to H_{miz} in computing Mizzen RSA.

Battens must be spaced approximately evenly between head and clew.

(c) A sail set on the main permanent backstay of a single masted yacht shall be classified as a mizzen and P_{miz} shall be the measured length of the luff on the stay.

No mizzen staysail may be carried with this rig.

509. RATED AND MEASURED SAIL AREA BETWEEN MASTS (2-MASTED SCHOONERS)

(1) RSA and MSA are dependent on type and number of sails used between masts as follows:

(a) For staysail rigged schooners and gaff or jib headed foresail schooners not subject to restriction on size and number of sails between the masts, RSA between the masts shall be taken as 100 per cent of the nominal area between masts and calculated as follows:—

$$RSA = \cdot 5\ B_1\ (P_1 + P_3)$$
$$MSA = \cdot 5\ B_1\ (P_1 + P_3)$$

(b) For gaff or jib headed foresail schooners accepting a limitation of two staysails, as provided in (2) (b) below, RSA between masts shall be taken as 80 per cent of the nominal area between masts and calculated as follows:—

$$RSA = \cdot 4\ B_1\ (P_1 + P_3)$$
$$MSA = \cdot 5\ B_1\ (P_1 + P_3)$$

(c) For gaff or jib headed foresail schooners where no other sails are used between the masts (except a topsail)

RSA = RSA of foresail taken as for a gaff or jib headed mainsail in 506

MSA $= 2 \times$ RSA

(d) MSA between the masts shall not be less than $\cdot 15\ P_2{}^2$.

(2) SAIL LIMITATIONS

(a) Foresails are subject to restrictions similar to those specifically listed for mainsails in 506, regarding headboard and batten limitations and in 703 regarding loose footed and light weight mainsails. Overlapping foresails are subject to foot measurements as in 412.

(b) When 80 per cent charge is accepted as in (1) (b) above, only two topmast staysails may be carried, one of which must be a bona fide Fisherman staysail and the other of which must be materially larger and suitable for downwind work. When the smaller staysail is used, the regular foresail must be set when the larger staysail is being used. With the exception of boats rated for a fore topsail, which may then be carried, no other sails may be used in the space between the masts.

(c) When area between masts is rated as in (1) (c) above, the foresail and topsail, if any, as declared at time of measurement are the only sails that may be carried between the masts.

510. MIZZEN STAYSAIL RSA

Shall be the largest RSA of any mizzen staysail carried.

RSA $= \cdot 2$ (Mizzen Staysail MSA $- 2\cdot 8$ (Miz. MSA).

Mizzen staysail RSA may not be taken as a minus quantity.

Mizzen staysail MSA shall be Shortest Distance Head to Foot $\times \dfrac{(Foot\ Length + Mid\text{-}girth)}{3}$.

511. S (SAIL AREA CORRECTION) is determined as follows:—

(1) If $\sqrt{RSA}$ *exceeds* $\sqrt{Base\ SA}$, multiply the excess by $1\cdot 15$ to get S, and insert as a *plus* quantity.

(2) If $\sqrt{RSA}$ is *less* than $\sqrt{Base\ SA}$, the difference equals S, and is inserted as a *minus* quantity.

PART VI

MEASUREMENTS AND CALCULATIONS BASED ON DATA GENERALLY OBTAINED FROM DESIGNER OR FROM PLANS

601. GENERAL. The measurements for this section are normally obtained from the designer. If plans are not available, the data must be obtained from the boat. If a boat is weighed or measurements of her are taken, these weights and measurements must be followed, even if they conflict with the plans.

602. MEAS. DRA. (MEASURED DRAFT) is the actual maximum draft (not including centreboard) below the measured load waterline plane.

This can be taken from the designer's certification after the designer has been given the measurer's figures which establish the measured plane of flotation. Where plans are not available, draft measurements must be taken from the yacht.

603. BASE DRAFT $= \cdot 147\ L + 1\cdot 5$.

604. CENTREBOARD FACTOR (CBF).

$$CBF = \frac{\text{Max. Exposed Area of Centreboard(s) in sq. ft.}}{\cdot 167\ L}$$

605. RATED DRA. (RATED DRAFT).

(a) In keel yachts = Meas. Dra.

(b) In centreboard yachts = Meas. Dra. + CBF.

606. DRA. (DRAFT CORRECTION).

(a) *For keel yachts*

(1) If Rated Dra. exceeds Base Dra., multiply excess by $\cdot 85$ and insert as a plus quantity.

(2) If Rated Dra. is less than Base Dra., multiply difference by $\cdot 75$ to get Dra. and insert as a minus quantity.

(b) *For centreboard yachts*

(1) If Meas. Dra. exceeds Base Dra, multiply the excess by $\cdot 85$ and add $\cdot 5$ CBF to get Dra. and insert the sum as a plus quantity.

(2) If Meas. Dra. is less than Base Dra., but Rated Dra. exceeds Base Dra., multiply the excess of Rated Dra. by $\cdot 5$ to get Dra. and insert as a plus quantity.

(3) If Rated Dra. is less than Base Dra., multiply difference by $\cdot 75$ to get Dra. and insert as a minus quantity.

607. MEAS. DISP. (MEASURED DISPLACEMENT). Measured displacement is the displacement below the LWL in cubic feet and is normally obtained by weighing the yacht and converting pounds to cubic feet, taking into account the specific gravity of the water at the time of measurement.

In special cases displacement may be determined by means other than by weighing.

(1) Where weighing facilities are not reasonably available for large boats, a waiver may be made by the Measurement Rule Committee. In such case displacement shall be obtained from the designer's certification after the designer has been furnished with the load water line plane figures by the measurer; or where the designer's certification is not available the yacht shall be measured for hull lines and have displacement figured from them.

(2) Where displacement has been previously determined by weighing, displacement in cubic feet may be calculated for a change in flotation that results in displacement within 4 per cent of the last weighed displacement.

608. CUBE ROOT OF BASE DISPLACEMENT

$$\sqrt[3]{Base\ Disp.} = \cdot 179\ L + \cdot 8$$

609. DISP. (DISPLACEMENT CORRECTION)

If $\sqrt[3]{Meas.\ Disp.}$ is:—

(a) Less than $\sqrt[3]{Base\ Disp.}$, the difference shall be multiplied by $4\cdot 5$ to get Disp. and inserted as a plus quantity.

(b) More than $\sqrt[3]{Base\ Disp.}$, but not more than $1\cdot 115\ \sqrt[3]{Base\ Disp.}$, the difference shall be multiplied by $3\cdot 5$ to get Disp. and inserted as a minus quantity.

(c) More than $1\cdot 115\ \sqrt[3]{Base\ Disp.}$, then Disp. will be a minus quantity equal to

$$\cdot 4\sqrt[3]{Base\ Disp.} + 2(\sqrt[3]{Meas.\ Disp.} - 1\cdot 115\sqrt[3]{Base\ Disp.})$$

610. STAB F (STABILITY FACTOR). This factor represents the

effect on rating for any difference in stability between that of the measured boat and a standard or base boat.

To derive Stab F, it is first necessary to obtain the Inclined Righting Moment (Inclined RM) at one degree heel, directions for which are contained in a separate booklet entitled 'Instructions to Measurers'. The data for determination of this Inclined RM is obtained by the measurer and is entered on the Measurement Certificate along with the other required measurement data.

The other necessary factors used to derive Stab F are determined from measurements by the measurer as described elsewhere in this rule.

Stability Factor (Stab F) is derived from the ratio of Adjusted Righting Moment (Adj. RM) and Base Righting Moment (Base RM).

(1) $Base\ RM = \cdot04\ L\ (Base\ Beam)^3$

(2) $Adj.\ RM = Incl.\ RM \times Flare\ Factor\ (FF)$
$\times Arm\ Factor\ (AF)$

(a) $FF = \cdot7 + \cdot3 \left(\dfrac{Meas.\ 4\%\ WL\ Beam}{Meas.\ WL\ Beam} \right)^3$

FF shall be taken as $1\cdot0$ if it is less than $1\cdot0$.

(b) Where Meas. WL Beam is equal to or less than Base Beam,

$$AF = \left(\frac{Base\ Beam}{Meas.\ WL\ Beam} \right)^2$$

(c) Where Meas. WL Beam exceeds Base Beam,

$$AF = \cdot1 + \cdot9 \left(\frac{Base\ Beam}{Meas.\ WL\ Beam} \right)^2$$

(3) (a) Where Adj. RM equals or exceeds Base RM,

$$Stab\ F = \cdot85 + \cdot15 \left(\frac{Adj\ RM}{Base\ RM} \right)$$

(b) Where Adj. RM is less than Base RM,

(i) and displacement weight equals or exceeds 10,000 lbs.,

$$Stab\ F = \cdot9 + \cdot1 \left(\frac{Adj.\ RM}{Base\ RM} \right) = X$$

(ii) or where displacement weight is less than 10,000 lbs. but more than 4,000 lbs.,
$Stab\ F = X$ [see (i) above]
$$+ \frac{10,000\text{-}weight}{6,000} (1\text{-}X)$$

(iii) or where displacement weight is 4,000 lbs. or less,
$Stab\ F = 1\cdot000$

611. PROP. (PROPELLER DRAG CORRECTION)

$$Prop. = \frac{1 - Prop.\ Factor \times \sqrt{Depth\ in\ ft.} \times Diameter\ in\ ft.}{14\sqrt{Base\ Draft} \times \sqrt[3]{Meas.\ Disp.}}$$

(1) *Accuracy of Data:* The owner has the burden to establish accurately and to the satisfaction of the measurer all data relating to propellers. A designer's certificate will suffice where pertinent conditions on the yacht have not changed since construction or are otherwise within the personal knowledge of the designer (see, for example, 602). Where any doubt exists, personal inspection and measurement by a certified measurer must be made. To avoid delay and inconvenience, particularly where propellers are changed, owners should arrange for a measurer to verify propeller data prior to the yacht's launching.

(2) *Prop. Factor* in the above formula is taken from the following table on the basis of type of propeller, number of blades and type of installation, namely: out of aperture without strut, in aperture, or out of aperture with strut (see also sub-paragraphs (3), (4), (5) and (6)):

		Prop. Factor		
Type	*No. Blades*	*Out of Aperture Without Strut*	*In Aperture*	*Out of Aperture With Strut*
Folding	Any	0·50	1·50	2·50
Feathering	2	1·00	2·00	3·00
Feathering	3 or more	1·50	2·50	3·50
Solid	2	4·00	5·00	6·00
Solid	3	6·00	7·00	8·00
Solid	4 or more	8·00	9·00	10·00

11*

(3) *Solid Propellers:* To qualify as a solid propeller, each of the blades must have a normal elliptical shape or such shape as disposes the area of the blade so as to reasonably approximate the same; otherwise, the propeller will be rated as a feathering propeller. A solid propeller with abnormally high pitch will be rated as a feathering propeller. In case of doubt or an unusual propeller, the measurer shall submit a detailed report, complete with measurements and sketch.

(4) *Struts:* To rate 'Out of Aperture With Strut', the strut itself must protrude from the hull a distance at least equal to 80 per cent of the radius of the propeller plus a reasonable clearance between the blade tip and the hull.

(5) *Twin Screws:* If a yacht has two permanently installed propellers the Prop. Factor in the above table shall be doubled.

(6) *Depth:* Depth is measured in feet from the centre of the propeller hub to the established LWL plane. The designer may certify to this measurement from the measurer's figures of plane of flotation.

(7) *Diameter:* Diameter is measured in feet. Diameter may not be taken as greater than 4 times the blade width across the widest part of the driving face of the blade on the chord at right angle to the radius from the propeller centre. Diameter of a folding propeller may not be taken as greater than 1·0 foot, regardless of actual diameter.

(8) *Secured While Racing:* Propellers must be locked or otherwise secured to prevent rotation while racing.

PART VII

SAIL, SAIL TRIMMING AND RIG LIMITATIONS

701. GENERAL. There are certain conflicts between the N.A.Y.R.U. and the C.C.A. Rules governing Sail Trimming and Rig Limitations. Where these conflicts exist, the C.C.A. Measurement Rule will govern in races conducted under this rule.

702. TRIMMING TO SPARS. Sheets of Spinnakers, headsails, mizzen staysails, and loosefooted sails *may not be trimmed to spars outside the measurement points*, except that such sheets may be trimmed to the usual bale or fitting on the after end of a *normal* length boom.

703. MAINSAILS
(a) *Loose-Footed Mainsails:* These are permitted only when they are the regular mainsail normally used for the boat in question. Under these conditions, when a loosefooted mainsail is used, it is not permissible to carry on board a second mainsail that is not loose-footed, nor is it permissible to shift back and forth between a loosefooted and a secured foot mainsail for various races. Rather, the selection must be made regarding mainsail type at the time the measurement certificate is issued.

(b) *Light-Weight Mainsails:* These are not permitted and it is the intent of the Rule that a second mainsail may not be carried aboard as a supplement to maximum performance that would be expected from the regular mainsail, but rather, *a second mainsail can only be carried as a spare for emergency replacement.*

(c) *Storm Trysails:* These must be materially smaller than a normal close reefed mainsail and of strength consistent with their intended purpose, viz., use in extremely severe weather.

704. HEADSAILS
(a) Headsails may be sheeted from only one point on the sail (thus excluding quadrilateral or similar sails).

(b) Headsails may be sheeted to any part of the rail or deck (or to the main boom *when the mainsail is set*) and to spinnaker pole when pole is set on opposite side from main boom, but may not be sheeted to any other spar or outrigger.

(c) No jib headsail will be permitted, whether hanked on to a stay or set flying, which has a luff length including tack pennant greater than $\cdot98\sqrt{P_2^2 + B_2^2}$.

(d) No headsail shall be set to fly out and over mainsail and/or spinnaker by sheeting over main boom or by any other means.

705. SPINNAKERS, SPINNAKER POLES AND SPECIAL DOWNWIND SAILS

(a) *Spinnaker Sheeting:* Spinnakers may be sheeted from only one point on the sail.

Spinnakers may be sheeted to any part of the rail or deck or to the main boom, *when the mainsail is set,* but to no other spar or outrigger. (See (f), below.)

(b) Any bona fide headsail otherwise permitted, may be used as a spare spinnaker without reverence to spinnaker measurement requirements. Such a sail may be tacked to or sheeted to the spinnaker pole when the spinnaker is not set.

(c) *Spinnaker Pole Limitations:* A spinnaker pole may be carried only on the windward side of the foremost mast. The inboard end must be carried on the mast, and may not be set higher than $\cdot 18\, P_2 + 2$ feet above main deck.

(d) *Spinnaker Tack:* Must be close to spinnaker pole on side opposite to main boom. (Spinnaker may not be carried without spinnaker pole.)

(e) *Squaresail:* A yacht may carry a squaresail, square topsail, raffee, or a twin spinnaker rig, instead of a spinnaker. The actual area of such sails may not exceed the rated fore triangle area, nor may the total length of their boom or booms exceed the length of the spinnaker pole.

(f) *Running Sails:* When mainsail is not set, two spinnaker poles, or one spinnaker pole and main boom may be simultaneously used without violating the last paragraph of 705 (a) or the first sentence of 705 (c) and two jibs may be set, neither of which may exceed the area of the biggest jib for which the boat is measured.

(g) Struts, spools or similar devices used solely for the purpose of keeping the spinnaker guy away from the windward main or foremost shrouds are permitted but are not to be used for any other purposes.

706. MIZZEN STAYSAIL ON YAWL OR KETCH

(a) *Sheet Leads:* Mizzen staysails may be sheeted to the rail or hull, and to the mizzen boom (whether or not the mizzen is set) but they may not be sheeted to any other spar or outrigger.

(b) Mizzen staysails must be three-cornered (head, tack and clew). The tack or tack pennant must be secured abaft the point of intersection of the after side of the mainmast with the main deck and also must be secured directly to and no higher than the rail cap, deck or cabin top (includes dog house top).

(c) There are no restrictions on the number of mizzen staysails on board but not more than one may be set at the same time.

(d) No mizzen staysail may be carried on a yawl or ketch whose mizzen is set on a permanent backstay in lieu of a mizzen mast (see 508 (c)).

707. SAILS BETWEEN THE MASTS IN SCHOONERS

(a) Sails Set Between the Masts may be trimmed to any part of the rail or the deck, or to the main boom. However, when the mainsail is not set, the area of any sail set between the masts must not exceed the total measured areas of the mainsail and of the area between the masts.

(b) Double clewed sails are not permitted.

(c) No sail set between the masts may extend below the base points used in establishment of P_1 and P_3 measurements (see 413 and 414).

708. SUMMARY OF PERMISSIBLE SAILS. Part IV, together with the foregoing paragraphs in Part VII outline the measurements and restrictions for sails which may be used. Sails which exceed the confines which are measured and described, such as sails which could be extended above the highest points measured, or which are extended by unmeasured portable spars or outriggers except as permitted in 705 (g), or which are tacked below the low limit of measurements, are not permitted. Following is a condensed summary of sails which are permitted:

(a) *Cat Rig:* Mainsail or storm trysail and main topsail if rated for same.

(b) *Sloop or Cutter:* A cat rig plus headsails (see 704 above); plus spinnakers or equivalent (see 705 above).

(c) *Yawl or Ketch:* A sloop or cutter rig plus mizzen or mizzen storm trysail and mizzen topsail if rated for same, plus mizzen staysail (see 706 above).

(d) *Two-Masted Schooners:* A sloop or cutter rig plus sails between the masts (see 707 above).

(e) *Miscellaneous:* A cat rig may not carry a spinnaker unless accepting this as a basis for fore triangle measurement, in which case classification and measurement would be as for a sloop or a cutter. Conversely, a schooner, yawl, or ketch which carries neither headsails nor spinnakers, may be rated without fore triangle measurement by following the normal procedures outlined in the foregoing but using zero for the fore triangle rated area.

709. MISCELLANEOUS RESTRICTIONS. Double luffed sails (other than spinnakers or squaresails), rotating masts, mechanically or permanently bent spars or other similar contrivances, are excluded for yachts measured under this Rule. Mainsails, foresails and mizzens may be reefed at the foot only. Roach, slab or flattening reefs are permitted along the foot only.

PART VIII

OWNER'S RESPONSIBILITY AFTER MEASUREMENT

801. OWNER'S RESPONSIBILITY. Owners of boats measured under this Rule should study the Rule carefully, to be thoroughly familiar with the numerous factors that affect rating. *Subsequent to measurement, owners must conscientiously avoid making any changes which would affect the rating, as such changes, if made without remeasurement, would disqualify them for competition.* A few typical examples are listed below.

(a) Sails may not be replaced or altered, in a manner to increase their size beyond the measured limits on which the rating certificate is based, without being remeasured.

(b) *Black Bands, Stoppers and Halyard Markers:* These must be maintained accurately in place and, regardless of the circumstances, a boat is not entitled to exceed these limitations without remeasurement. If in the course of a race a sail stretches excessively, it is the owner's responsibility to take all steps necessary to be sure that the sail does not pass a point where limits have been imposed.

(c) *Trimming of Headsails and Spinnakers:* The restrictions to sheeting are clearly outlined in 702, 704 and 705. It is important that these restrictions be adhered to, particular attention being called to the requirements that *mainsail be set* when trimming to the main boom (exception 705 (f)).

(d) *Propellers:* These cannot be changed as to diameter or type for which the boat has been measured without remeasurement.

(e) The Selection of Sails where there is a restriction as to number or type which can be used: For example, the selection between a loose-footed or secured foot mainsail, etc.

(f) Ballast of any type and heavy deck gear, which affects the trim or stability of the boat and which is on board and in place when stability measurements are made, must not be changed in amount or location without remeasurement.

PART IX

TIME ALLOWANCE TABLES

901. TIME ALLOWANCE. As suggested in 101, it is recommended that N.A.Y.R.U., or similar time allowance tables be used, in conjunction with ratings calculated under this Rule for the length of the race in question. However, if other arrangements are desired, ratings figured under this Rule are entirely suitable as a basis for calculating time allowance on the basis of time consumed in the race, or on any other basis.

(As modified, effective 1 January 1960)

MEASUREMENT CERTIFICATE, CRUISING CLUB OF AMERICA 1960 RULE

OWNER . . . . YACHT NAME . . . .

Designer . . . . RIG . . . .

RACING NO. . . . .

SAILS		

					Meas. S.A.	Rated S.A.	Spcl. Fctrs.
Mainsail & Topsail							
B P	G	H	T	P abv. dk.			
Fore Triangle	Jib foot length exceeds	=		$X.4P_2$ =			
P_2	J	Spinnaker Pole		B_2			
Sails between Masts of Schooners							
B_1 P_1	P_3	H	G	P abv. dk.			
Mizzen Bmiz	Bmiz rated		Gmiz				
Pmiz	Pmiz abv. dk.	Hmiz	Tmiz				

Spinnaker: Max Luff or Leach $.95 \sqrt{(P_2)^2 + (B_2)^2} = (I) =$ | Total

Max. Girth = 1.80J = $P_2 = \sqrt{\left(\dfrac{I}{.95}\right) - (B_2)^2} =$ | $\sqrt{RSA}$

Ballast:	Keel (Lead, Iron) . . . . . . _____	Length Over All . . . . _____	Tc. =
	Inside, incl. gear . . . . . . _____	Bow Overhang . . . . _____	
	Weight of centerboard . _____	Stern Overhang . . . . _____	
	Excess weight of cb. X2 _____	Load Water Line . . . . _____	X.3 =
	Total weight—Mes. Bal. . _____	Extension 4% W.L. for'd . . _____	
	Displacement in lbs . . . . _____	Extension 4% W.L. aft . . . . _____	
	Ratio, Mes. Bal./Disp. . . . _____	4% W.L. . . . . _____	X.7 =

Beam   "L" +

"Bm" Max. L.W.L. . _____ | Mes. Bm. or .21 "L"+3.8 _____ | Mes. Bm. . _____

"Bm" 4% W.L. . . . _____ | Base Bm. (.187 "L" +3.2) _____ | .21 "L"+3.8 . . . _____

2) _____ | difference . . . . _____ | excess . . . . _____

Mes. Bm. . . . . _____ | diff. X(1.5 or 1.4) . . . . . _____ | + ... "Bm"= | + | −

"Dra."
Mes. Dra. . . . . _____
Centerboard factor: Max. *Exposed area of c.b. in sq. ft.*
      .167 "L"   _____
Rated dra. (sum) . . . . _____
Base dra. (.147 "L" + 1.5) . . . . _____
Difference (diff.) . . . .
Keel yachts: diff. x (.85 or .75) . . . . , Centerboard yachts: (see 606 b)   "Dra" = | + | −

"Disp."
$\sqrt[3]{}$ Mes. Disp. _____ | $\sqrt[3]{}$ Mes. Disp. . . _____ | Mes. Disp. (cu. ft.). = _____
$\sqrt[3]{}$ Base Disp. _____ | 1.115 $\sqrt[3]{}$ Base Disp. _____ | Base Disp. (.179"L"+.8)= _____
difference . . . _____ | difference . . . . _____ |
diff.X(4 or 3.5) _____ | diff. X 2 . . . . . _____ | +.4(.179"L"+.8) _____ "Disp." = | + | −

"S"
$\sqrt{}$ Rated Sail Area (R.S.A.) . . . . . . _____ | 4.3 (.179"L" + .8) . . _____
$\sqrt{}$ Base Sail Area 4.3.(.179"L"+.8) . _____ | $\sqrt{}$ R.S.A. . . . . _____
difference . . . . X1.15 | difference . . . . "S" = | + | −

"F"
freeboard at for'd end L.W.L. _____ | Base F(.0566"L"+1.1) _____ | Mes. F . . . . . . _____
freeboard at aft end L.W.L. . . _____ | Mes. F or (.069"L"+1.2) _____ | .069"L"+1.2 _____
Rail height for'd _____   2) _____ | difference . . . . _____ | excess . . . . . . _____
Rail height aft _____ | diff.X(2 or 1.5) . . . . . _____ | excessX.75 . . . _____
4) _____ . . . . _____ | | 1.5Xdiff. . . . _____
Mes. F . . . . _____ | | "F" = | + | −

"I"   .0185 "L" _____ X(Iron ballast/Total ballast) _____ = −   "I" = | | −

"Prop"
Type _____ Dia _____ ft. No. Blades _____ | + | −
Blade Width _____ Location _____ Depth _____ ft. | − |
"Prop" = $1 - \left(\dfrac{\text{Prop. Fctr x }\sqrt{}\text{ Depth x Dia.}}{14 \text{ x }\sqrt{}\text{ Base Draft x }\sqrt[3]{}\text{Mes. Disp.}}\right) = $ _____ | | = Corr. "L"

"Bal R"
Base Bal/Disp. = $.44 + .7\left(\dfrac{\text{Base Bm—Mes. Bm}}{\text{Base Bm}}\right) = $ _____
     or
     $= .44 - \left(\dfrac{\text{Mes. Bm—Base Bm}}{\text{Base Bm}}\right) = $ _____
"Bal R" = 1 + .7 (Mes. Bal/Disp.—Base Bal/Disp.) = _____
     or
     = 1 − .35 (Base Bal/Disp.—Mes. Bal/Disp.) = _____

I hereby certify that this measurement was made by me on—

_____, 196__

Signed

Measurer of

RATING = .93 x Corr."L" _____ x "Bal R" _____ x "Prop" _____ =

804. TIME ALLOWANCE TABLES

FOR ONE NAUTICAL MILE,
IN SECONDS AND DECIMALS.

Rating	Allowance	Rating	Allowance	Rating	Allowance	Rating	Allowance
15.0	381.35	18.0	332.75	21.0	294.98	24.0	264 55
.1	379.49	.1	331.33	.1	293.87	.1	263.64
.2	377.65	.2	329.93	.2	292.76	.2	262.73
.3	375.83	.3	328.54	.3	291.65	.3	261.82
.4	374.03	.4	327.17	.4	290.56	4	260.92
.5	372.26	.5	325.83	.5	289.48	5	260 03
.6	370.50	.6	324.48	.6	288.40	.6	259.14
.7	368.76	.7	323.14	.7	287.33	7	258.26
.8	367.03	.8	321.82	.8	286.26	.8	257 38
.9	365.31	.9	320.50	9	285.20	.9	256 51
16.0	363.64	19.0	319.19	22.0	284.15	25.0	255.65
.1	361.97	.1	317.89	.1	283.10	1	254.78
.2	360.31	.2	316.60	.2	282.07	.2	253 92
.3	358.66	.3	315.32	.3	281.04	.3	253 07
.4	357.02	.4	314.05	.4	280.02	.4	252 23
.5	355.39	.5	312.78	.5	279.00	.5	251 39
.6	353.79	.6	311.53	.6	277.99	6	250.55
.7	352.21	.7	310.29	.7	276 99	7	249 72
.8	350.64	.8	309.06	8	276.00	.8	248 89
.9	349.08	.9	307.84	9	275 01	9	248 07
17.0	347.52	20.0	306.62	23.0	274.03	26 0	247 25
.1	345.99	.1	305.42	.1	273.06	.1	246.44
.2	344.47	.2	304.24	.2	272.09	.2	245.63
.3	342.96	.3	303.05	.3	271 13	.3	244 82
.4	341.46	.4	301.87	.4	270.17	.4	244.02
.5	339.97	.5	300.71	.5	269.22	5	243 23
.6	338.50	.6	299.54	.6	268.27	6	212 44
.7	337.04	.7	298.39	7	267.33	7	241 66
.8	335.60	.8	297.25	.8	266.40	.8	240.88
.9	334.17	.9	296.11	9	265 48	9	240 10
27.0	239.33	31.0	211.61	35.0	188.76	39.0	169.52
.1	238.56	.1	210.98	.1	188.24	.1	169 08
.2	237.79	.2	210.36	.2	187.72	.2	168.64
.3	237.00	.3	209.74	.3	187.20	.3	168 19
.4	236.27	.4	209.11	.4	186.68	.4	167.75
.5	235.52	.5	208.50	.5	186.17	.5	167.31
.6	234.78	.6	207.89	.6	185.65	.6	166.88
.7	234.04	.7	207.28	.7	185.15	.7	166.45
.8	233.30	.8	206.68	.8	184.64	.8	166.02
.9	232.57	.9	206.08	.9	184.14	.9	165.60
28.0	231.84	32.0	205.48	36.0	183.64	40.0	165.18
.1	231.11	.1	204.88	.1	183.14	1	164.75
.2	230.39	.2	204.29	.2	182.64	.2	164 32
.3	229.67	.3	203.70	.3	182.15	.3	163.88
.4	228.95	.4	203.11	.4	181.66	.4	163 46
.5	228.24	.5	202.52	.5	181.16	5	163.04
.6	227.53	.6	201.94	.6	180.67	6	162.62
.7	226.82	.7	201.36	.7	180.19	.7	162.21
.8	226.12	.8	200.79	.8	179.71	.8	161.80
.9	225.43	.9	200.22	.9	179.23	9	161 39
29.0	224.74	33.0	199.65	37.0	178.75	41.0	160.98
.1	224.05	.1	199.08	.1	178.27	.1	160.56
.2	223.37	.2	198.51	.2	177.79	.2	160.15
.3	222.68	.3	197.95	.3	177.31	.3	159.74
.4	222.00	.4	197.39	.4	176.83	.4	159.34
.5	221.33	.5	196.83	.5	176.36	.5	158.93
.6	220.66	.6	196.27	.6	175.90	.6	158.52
.7	219.99	.7	195.72	.7	175.43	.7	158.12
.8	219.32	.8	195.17	.8	174.96	.8	157.73
.9	218.66	.9	194.63	9	174.50	.9	157.33
30.0	218.00	34.0	194.09	38.0	174.04	42.0	156.93
.1	217.34	.1	193.54	.1	173.58	1	156.53
.2	216.70	.2	193.00	.2	173.12	.2	156.13
.3	216.05	.3	192.46	.3	172.67	.3	155.74
.4	215.40	.4	191.92	.4	172.21	.4	155.35
.5	214.75	.5	191.38	.5	171.76	.5	154.96
.6	214.11	.6	190.85	.6	171.30	.6	154.57
.7	213.48	.7	190.32	.7	170.84	.7	154.19
.8	212.85	.8	189.79	.8	170.40	.8	153.80
.9	212.23	.9	189.28	.9	169.96	.9	153.42

Time Allowance.—*Continued.*

Rating	Allowance	Rating	Allowance	Rating	Allowance	Rating	Allowance
43.0	153.04	47.0	138.71	51.0	126.10	55.0	114.90
.1	152.66	.1	138.38	.1	125.81	.1	114.64
.2	152.28	.2	138.05	.2	125.51	.2	114.37
.3	151.90	.3	137.71	.3	125.21	.3	114.11
.4	151.52	.4	137.38	.4	124.92	.4	113.84
.5	151.14	.5	137.05	.5	124.62	.5	113.58
.6	150.76	.6	136.73	.6	124.33	.6	113.32
.7	150.38	.7	136.40	.7	124.04	.7	113.05
.8	150.01	.8	136.07	.8	123.76	.8	112.79
.9	149.65	.9	135.74	.9	123.47	.9	112.53
44.0	149.28	48.0	135.41	52.0	123.18	56.0	112.27
.1	148.91	.1	135.08	.1	122.89	.1	112.01
.2	148.54	.2	134.76	.2	122.60	.2	111.75
.3	148.17	.3	134.44	.3	122.32	.3	111.49
.4	147.80	.4	134.11	.4	122.03	.4	111.24
.5	147.43	.5	133.79	.5	121.74	.5	110.99
.6	147.07	.6	133.47	.6	121.45	.6	110.74
.7	146.71	.7	133.16	.7	121.17	.7	110.49
.7	146.35	.8	132.85	.8	120.89	.8	110.24
.9	145.99	.9	132.54	9	120.61	.9	109.99
45.0	145.64	49.0	132.22	53.0	120.33	57.0	109.74
1	145.28	.1	131.90	.1	120.05	.1	109.49
.2	144.92	.2	131.58	.2	119.77	.2	109.24
3	144.56	.3	131.27	.3	119.50	.3	108.99
.4	144.20	.4	130.96	.4	119.22	.4	108.74
.5	143.85	.5	130.64	.5	118.94	.5	108.49
.6	143.50	.6	130.33	.6	118.67	.6	108.24
.7	143.15	.7	130.03	.7	118.39	.7	108.00
.8	142.80	.8	129.72	.8	118.12	.8	107.76
.9	142.46	.9	129.42	.9	117.85	.9	107.52
46.0	142.12	50.0	129.12	54.0	117.58	58.0	107.28
.1	141.78	.1	128.81	.1	117.31	.1	107.03
.2	141.43	.2	128.50	.2	117.04	.2	106.78
.3	141.08	.3	128.20	.3	116.77	.3	106.52
.4	140.74	.4	127.89	.4	116.50	.4	106.28
.5	140.39	.5	127.58	.5	116.23	.5	106.04
.6	140.04	.6	127.28	.6	115.96	.6	105.80
.7	139.70	.7	126.98	.7	115.69	.7	105.56
.8	139.37	.8	126.68	.8	115.43	.8	105.32
.9	139.04	.9	126.39	.9	115.16	.9	105.08
59.0	104.84	63.0	95.78	67.0	87.52	71.0	79.99
.1	104.60	1	95.56	.1	87.32	.1	79.80
2	104.36	.2	95.34	.2	87.12	.2	79.62
3	104 12	.3	95.12	.3	86.92	.3	79.44
.4	103.89	.4	94.91	.4	86.73	.4	79.26
.5	103.66	.5	94.70	.5	86.54	.5	79.08
.6	103.42	.6	94.49	.6	86.35	.6	78.90
.7	103.19	.7	94.27	.7	86.16	.7	78.72
.8	102.96	.8	94.06	.8	85.97	.8	78.54
.9	102 73	9	93.85	.9	85.78	.9	78.37
60.0	102 50	64.0	93.64	68.0	85.59	72.0	78.20
1	102.26	.1	93.43	.1	85.40	.1	78.02
.2	102.03	.2	93.22	.2	85.21	.2	77.84
.3	101.80	.3	93.01	.3	85.02	.3	77.66
.4	101.57	.4	92.80	.4	84.83	.4	77.48
.5	101.34	.5	92.59	.5	84.64	.5	77.30
.6	101.1I	.6	92.38	.6	84.45	.6	77.13
7	100.88	.7	92.17	.7	84.26	.7	76.96
.8	100.66	.8	91.97	.8	84.07	.8	76.79
.9	100.43	9	91.76	.9	83.88	.9	76.62
61.0	100.21	65.0	91.55	69.0	83.69	73.0	76.45
.1	99.98	.1	91.34	.1	83.50	.1	76.27
.2	99.76	.2	91.14	.2	83.31	.2	76.10
.3	99.53	.3	90.94	.3	83.12	.3	75.93
.4	99.30	.4	90.73	.4	82.93	.4	75.76
.5	99.07	.5	90.53	.5	82.74	.5	75.59
.6	98.84	.6	90.32	.6	82.55	.6	75.42
.7	98.62	.7	90.12	.7	82.36	.7	75.25
.8	98.40	.8	89.92	.8	82.17	.8	75.08
.9	98.18	.9	89.72	.9	81.99	.9	74.91
62.0	97.96	66.0	89.52	70.0	81.82	74.0	74.74
.1	97.74	.1	89.32	.1	81.63	.1	74.57
.2	97.51	.2	89.12	.2	81.44	.2	74.39
.3	97.29	.3	88.92	.3	81.25	.3	74.22
.4	97.07	.4	88.72	.4	81.07	.4	74.05
.5	96.85	.5	88.52	.5	80.89	.5	73.88
.6	96.64	.6	88.32	.6	80.71	.6	73.72
.7	96.42	.7	88.12	.7	80.53	.7	73.55
.8	96.20	.8	87.92	.8	80.35	.8	73.39
.9	95.99	9	87 72	.9	80.17	.9	73.23

902. Use of Assumed Course Length Other Than Actual Course Length. Where experience in a certain race over a period of time indicates that time allowances figured in conjunction with N.A.Y.R.U., or other similar time allowance tables, favour boats of one size range over boats of another, it is thoroughly feasible, by using an assumed course length, to increase or decrease handicaps all along the line, as may be necessary to provide better competition. An assumed course length shorter than actual reduces handicaps and hence favours the larger boats, while an assumed course length longer than actual would tend to favour the smaller boats.

903. Method of Using the Table. The figures in the table show in seconds and hundredths of a second the allowance a yacht of the measurement opposite these figures would be allowed by one of 150 feet, in sailing one nautical mile.

To find the allowance a yacht of any given rating should receive from a larger one, take the figure to be found opposite the smaller rating; from this subtract the figure opposite the measurement of the larger yacht, and the difference multiplied by the number of nautical miles in the course is the amount of time allowance due the smaller vessel, in seconds and hundredths of a second.

Boat A—Rating 36.7
Boat B—Rating 42.3
Course length 675 nautical miles

Boat A allowance from table
  (for 36·7)   180·19 seconds per mile
Boat B allowance from table
  (for 42·3)   155·74 seconds per mile
Boat B allows Boat A (subtract
  B allowance from A allowance) 24·45 seconds per mile
In the race (675 nautical miles)
  B allows A 675 × 24·45 seconds or 4 hours 35 mins. 4 secs.

904. Time Allowance Tables. The tables are based upon the assumption that, under average racing conditions, a yacht of rating measurement, R, will sail one nautical mile in the number of seconds given by the formula.

$$\frac{2160}{\sqrt{R}} + 183\cdot64$$

The allowance per mile between yachts of different ratings will, therefore, be given by

$$\frac{2160}{\sqrt{r}} - \frac{2160}{\sqrt{R}}$$

in which R is the rating measurement of the larger yacht and r that of the smaller yacht.

The theoretical number of seconds required to sail one nautical mile under average conditions (as would be encountered in a triangular race) is obtained by adding 360 to the figure in the table opposite the yacht's rating measurement.

APPENDIX XIII

JUNIOR OFFSHORE GROUP

General Conditions: 1963

A. Eligibility of Yachts. The several classes of the J.O.G. shall include all suitable yachts of over 16 ft. and up to 24 ft. designed waterline length with ratings of 12 ft. or over. Any yacht within the above limits but with a rating of less than 12 ft. may enter, but shall sail at a rating of 12 ft.

B. Safety and Rating Rules. The J.O.G. Safety Rules are designed to prevent undue risk when racing in open waters; yachts not issued with J.O.G. Certificate of Inspection will not be acceptable to the Committee and will not be issued with J.O.G. Time Correction Factor. The Committee reserve the right to inspect a yacht at any time and to prohibit it from starting in a race, if, in their opinion, it is not properly equipped.

The Rating Formula and Rule for single-hulled yachts shall be as the R.O.R.C. 1957 Rule, with the exceptions that Rule V (22) i and Rule X, shall not apply. Rule V (22) i shall be amended for J.O.G. purposes to read: 'Spinnakers and squaresails shall not be carried, but any one headsail included in the measured sail area, normally set and tacked to deck, may be boomed out, to weather only, with a bearing out spar of any desired length.'

The J.O.G. Time Scale, based on R.O.R.C. Rating, has been evolved to bring together by time allowance yachts of varying types within the limits laid down by the Committee, but no attempt has been made to produce any class or to favour any one type. It is impossible for the Rule to cover every eventuality and the Committee therefore reserve the right to deal with any peculiarity of design in the spirit of the Rule and to give such Time Correction Factor as they consider equitable. Subject to the foregoing proviso, J.O.G. TCF shall be calculated by:

$$TCF = \frac{\sqrt{R.O.R.C. \text{ Rating}} + 1}{6}$$

C. Racing Rules. No unmeasured yacht shall compete in races organised by the J.O.G. Unmeasured yachts are invited to sail round the course. They will be timed where possible so that their owners can obtain an idea of the boat's potential.

It is an essential part of offshore racing that yachts sail at night and, at times, out of sight of one another. Therefore all rules must be observed in their spirit and in the light of the ordinary customs of the sea.

For the purpose of the Rules, the Sailing Committee shall be deemed to be the Committee of the J.O.G. and its officers.

Races will be started and sailed under I.Y.R.U. Racing Rules subject to modifications imposed by R.Y.A. Rules and J.O.G. Special Regulations but, at the time or place specified in sailing instructions, Part IV (Sailing Rules) of I.Y.R.U. Rules will cease to be applicable and will be replaced by Part C, Rule 17 of International Regulations for the Prevention of Collisions at Sea.

Special Regulations

These Special Regulations vary certain specific details of the I.Y.R.U. and R.Y.A. Rules. The variation of any rule applies only to those details actually mentioned, and in every other respect I.Y.R.U. and R.Y.A. Rules hold good and must be observed.

1. Rating (affecting Rule 3). All yachts must have been measured before the start of a race. The ratings and time correction factors of all competing yachts will be those in the hands of the Sailing Committee at the time of the race. These time correction factors shall be those by which the yachts' corrected time will be calculated and shall be final for that race.

2. Sailing Instructions (affecting Rule 6). As far as possible, the names and ratings of yachts competing in the race will be included in Sailing Instructions supplied to yachts but these will not necessarily be complete or exact. Recall numbers will not be included, nor will the time and place at which protests will be heard. In the event of a protest, the time and place for the hearing will be arranged and notified to those concerned with the utmost despatch.

3. Navigational Lights and Fog Signals (affecting Rule 21). A competing yacht, in addition to complying with the International Regulations for the Prevention of Collisions at Sea, must show port, starboard, and stern navigation lights from sunset to sunrise, and must carry a fog signal and red and white flares. A powerful light must be kept ready at night to be shown in case of necessity to give other vessels, both steamers and yachts, ample warning of the presence of the yacht.

Showing a continuous white light, or lights, at the masthead or spreaders whilst under sail is contrary to Regulations for the Prevention of Collisions at Sea. Owners must see that these lights are used in such a manner as not to contravene the Regulations or confuse other ships.

4. NAVIGATIONAL AIDS. Competitors may not use yacht-borne radar, nor any form of wireless transmitter, nor yacht-borne receiving sets for use with hyperbolic navigational aids. The use of receiving sets for consol and direction finding stations is permitted. Prearranged signals, radio transmission, and the like for the benefit of individual competitors are prohibited.

5. SOUNDING (*affecting Rule* 25). Echo sounding is permitted.

6. RECALLS (*affecting Rule* 10). Recall numbers will not be displayed. If any part of a yacht or yachts be on or across the starting line when the signal to start is made, a gun will be fired or suitable sound signal made as soon as possible and the Numeral Pennant O (yellow and red) will be broken out. Any yacht that is over the starting line too soon shall return across the line or its extension and start again in accordance with Rule 10. If she fails so to do to the satisfaction of the Sailing Committee, two hours shall be added to her corrected time in the race unless she be disqualified by the Sailing Committee.

7. YACHTS ARRIVING LATE (*affecting Rule* 9). In races of not less than 25 miles, a yacht which has not been able to arrive in the vicinity of the starting line when the starting signal is made, may use her engine or be towed towards the vicinity of the starting line. She may not use her engine or be towed during the five minutes between the preparatory signal and the starting signal unless she is then out of sight and earshot of the starting line and the preparatory signals.

A yacht availing herself of this privilege shall, before she crosses the starting line, cease to use her engine, or be towed, and shall then turn through not less than 360 degrees or lie to an anchor keeping out of the way of all competing yachts which are starting or have started correctly, and shall then regain her rights of way. A yacht so competing must report the circumstances after the race to the Sailing Committee, who shall decide whether she be regarded as a bona fide starter.

8. DECLARATION FORMS (*affecting Rule* 16). A Declaration Form, completed with the yacht's finishing time and signed by the owner or owner's representative, shall be lodged with the Sailing Committee as soon as possible after the yacht has completed the race. If there is any undue delay in lodging this Declaration, the yacht may be treated as having failed to complete the course.

9. SAIL NUMBERS (*affecting Rule* 17 (1) (*d*) ii). Sail numbers shall not be of smaller size than prescribed by the I.Y.R.U. ($18 \times 12 \times 3$ in.) and must be displayed by alternative means if the mainsail is down.

10. OWNERSHIP OF YACHTS (*affecting Rule* 2 (3)). The Sailing Committee shall be deemed to have given their consent if the entries of two or more yachts owned wholly, or in part, by the same person or body are accepted for the same race.

11. OWNER STEERING ANOTHER YACHT (*affecting Rule* 5 (4)). If an owner steers any other yacht than his own in a race wherein his own yacht competes, the Sailing Committee may at their discretion take no action under Rule 5 (4).

12. UNMEASURED SAILS. Sails shall be set only in those areas which have been measured or declared for inclusion in sail area and must not exceed the limits specified.

13. SETTING AND SHEETING SAILS (*affecting Rule* 28). Sails may be sheeted to the main, fore, or mizzen boom, but will incur a penalty if sheeted more than 6 in. outside the clew outhaul or the after black band on either the main or mizzen booms.

14. HARD-WEATHER RUNNING SAILS. Two hard-weather running sails may be carried, set on spinnaker booms forward of the mast, provided (i) the sum of the areas of the two running sails does not exceed 100 per cent of the yacht's measured sail area; (ii) the mainsail is not set at the same time as the leeward running sail; (iii) neither spinnaker boom is longer,

nor mounted further forward than is permitted by the rule of measurement for the yacht's rating.

15. CANCELLATION OR POSTPONEMENT OF RACES (*affecting Rules* 12, 23). No race shall be re-sailed or declared void, except at the discretion of the Sailing Committee.

16. JOINING, LEAVING, AND GOING ASHORE DURING A RACE (*affecting Rule* 23). Within two hours of the start of a race, members of the yacht's company may join the yacht, in which case shore transport may be used. No restriction is placed upon persons leaving the yacht in order to take no further part in the race, but otherwise crew, gear, or stores may be taken to or from the shore only in the yacht's dinghy propelled by oars.

17. SEAWORTHINESS, SAFETY PRECAUTIONS, AND EQUIPMENT. Every competing yacht must be seaworthy and be fitted and sailed with proper precaution.

SAFETY RULES AND RECOMMENDATIONS

APPLICATION. The degree of compliance required of competing yachts will be clear from the text of each Rule. Where the word 'Must' is used, non-compliance will entail non-acceptance. In the case of recommendations, non-compliance will not necessarily entail non-acceptance, the Committee dealing with each case upon its merits, acting upon the advice of the inspecting officer and reserving the right to exclude any yacht considered unsuitable. *It is upon the Owner*, acting with commonsense and good seamanship and guided where necessary by these Rules, that the seaworthiness and ultimate safety of the boat must depend.

Rule I. The yacht must be self-righting (*i.e.* must possess an adequate range of stability) and, as a guide, the product of the following formula should exceed 1·10:

$$\frac{B + 2F}{L} + \frac{DR}{2}$$

where B is Maximum beam
　　　F is Freeboard at 50 per cent LWL
　　　D is Maximum draft excluding centreboard
　　　L is Length on waterline in measurement trim
　　　R is Ballast ratio, *i.e.*

$$\frac{\text{ballast lb.}}{\text{Displacement in measurement trim, lb.}}$$

B, F, D, and L are to be measured in feet to two places of decimals. In computing R, inside ballast will be reckoned at 50 per cent its actual weight. Metal centreplates, *i.e.* other than wood boards, will be reckoned as outside ballast but draft will be taken without reference to the plate.

To be acceptable, a yacht fitted with a centreboard or boards must be self-righting (*vide* self-righting test) with its plate or plates fully raised; and the Committee must be satisfied that, when the plate or plates are fully lowered or in any intermediate position, the boat is not likely to be strained in a seaway.

In cases where the inspecting officer is not satisfied with the safety of the boat, he may ask for a self-righting test. During this, after closing hatches, scuttles, and vents as necessary, the boat will be hove down on her beam ends, when a satisfactory righting moment must be developed.

It is emphasised that the above test and Rule (I) are designed to ensure that a yacht has the ability to recover from a severe knockdown in a seaway. This ability may be only distantly related to her ability to carry sail, and is a prime pre-requisite in a boat intended to keep the seas.

Rule II. Hull, decks and upperworks, mast, rigging and fittings must be sufficiently strong to withstand the weight of a heavy sea upon them or the stresses imposed by the vessel being rolled on her side.

Rule III. It is strongly recommended that the cockpit be watertight with any hatches in it sealed for racing; and as a guide, its volume be limited by the following formula, the product of which should not exceed 7·00:

$$\frac{100\,V}{F\,B\,\left(LWL + \dfrac{LOA - LWL}{3}\right)}$$

where   V is Volume of cockpit in cu. ft. up to deck level
i.e. excluding coamings
F is Freeboard as in Rule (I)
B is Beam as in Rule (I)
LOA is Overall length in feet excluding bowsprit or bumpkin
LWL is L as in Rule (I).

Locker space in the cockpit should count as part of the cockpit volume unless these lockers are emptied and made watertight when racing.

Rule IV. It is recommended that, especially in the smaller yachts, the yacht should carry sufficient positive buoyancy to support herself together with keel, stores, crew, and a reserve of at least 250 lb. In all cases where this is not practicable, an adequate inflatable dinghy with bottle inflation should be carried, in such a way that it may readily be used in an emergency.

Rule V. It is recommended that the area of the mainhatch or forehatch in plan should not exceed 3 sq. ft. in the smaller yachts or 4 sq. ft. in the larger; and that the hatches should not open below a point 3 in. above deck level.

Rule VI. Adequate ventilators should be fitted to cabins and should have efficient water traps.

Rule VII. Owners are reminded that they must anticipate spending longish periods at sea where there may be no harbour or refuge within easy reach and no means of obtaining assistance. Apart from assuring themselves of the soundness of the yacht and its gear, they should look to such matters as rudder hangings, chainplates, deck fittings, etc. They should make sure that glass in deck openings, etc., can be protected easily and secured if broken; that openings in the hull have seacocks on the flange of the opening; that propeller shafts are properly secured and cannot withdraw; that pumps are adequate and in good condition, can be worked at sea and can be cleared easily in the event of choking. And they must 'then know the sea, know that they know it, and not forget that it was made to be sailed over'.

Rule VIII. The following items of equipment are mandatory requirements and must be carried:
(a) Two serviceable bunks not less than 6 ft. long.
(b) Cooking stove capable of safe operation at sea.
(c) Adequate chart table or plotting board.

(d) W.C. or fitted bucket.
(e) Anchor and suitable cable. Where an anchor warp is used, a short length of chain should be fitted between warp and anchor.
(f) An efficient compass.
(g) At least one efficient fire extinguisher.
(h) First Aid box and instructions.
(i) Suitable storm canvas. Alternatively, the working canvas must be suitable for reducing in area and withstanding storm conditions.
(j) Internationally recognised distress signals. (Rockets flares, smoke floats, etc.)
(k) Internationally prescribed navigation lights, and two powerful electric torches.
(l) A lifejacket for each member of the crew.
(m) Efficient personal lifelines for each member of the crew on deck, with a line for properly securing to a strong point. *N.B.* These are regarded as being the most valuable single items of safety equipment and should be worn whenever risk of falling overboard exists.
(n) Adequate handholds about deck and cabin top.
(o) Taut and efficient grab wires or lifelines, properly supported at a height of not less than 2 in. clear of the rail for the full effective length of the vessel, on each side. *N.B.* It is recommended that a proper guard rail be fitted at a height of 12 to 18 in.
(p) A life belt with self-operating light or flare of approved type, carried on deck and able to be jettisoned readily.

EXPERIMENTAL ADDENDUM TO SAFETY RULES
(*To remain in force until further notice.*)

Where, in the special case of multihulls, the self-righting requirement of Rule (I) cannot be met, a boat may nevertheless be accepted, provided that all other safety rules are complied with and the following conditions are fulfilled, to the satisfaction of the Committee.
(a) Sufficient positive buoyancy be provided in each hull to meet the requirements of safety Rule (IV).
(b) Properly supported masthead or above-deck buoyancy be provided, sufficient to restrain a knockdown to an angle not greater than that at which the masthead is at water level, and capable of maintaining this attitude in gale conditions.
(c) It be proved by demonstration that the action of the crew on the centreboard(s), fin(s), or hull(s) is sufficient to right the boat from the above attitude, and that this righting operation can be performed with reasonable ease; or that some other effective means of righting the boat is available and can readily be used and operated.

APPENDIX XIV

TOOLS AND REPAIR MATERIALS FOR AN OCEAN RACING YACHT

Note.—The tools indicated * are only necessary for large yachts. Special tools for engines are not included.

*Hand saw—20 in. fine-toothed.
*Tenon saw—9 in. brass back.
Pad saw handle and 10-in. blade.
Carpenter's ratchet brace and set of bits for wood $\frac{1}{2}$ in., $\frac{5}{8}$ in., $\frac{3}{4}$ in., 1 in.; screwdriver bits $\frac{3}{8}$ in. and $\frac{1}{2}$ in.; countersink bits, 1 each for wood, *brass and *iron.
*Spokeshave.
2 in. smooth plane (iron).
*Raw-hide faced hammer.
Steel hammer, one end round-nosed.
3 bradawls, different sizes.
3 gimlets, different sizes.
2 carpenter's pencils.
*8-in. steel square.
*1 pair pincers, 7 in.
1 pair combination pliers 7 in. and one pair small.
1 half-round rasp, 10 in. and handle.
Selection of files for metal, and handles (quantity to suit size of yacht).
1 2-ft. four-fold boxwood rule.

Firmer chisels, $\frac{1}{4}$ in., *$\frac{1}{2}$ in., *$\frac{3}{4}$ in., and 1 in., with handles.
Firmer gauges, *$\frac{1}{2}$ in., $\frac{3}{4}$ in., *1 in., with handles.
Screwdrivers, small, medium, and large.
Small carborundum hone—one side coarse, the other fine.
2 non-leak oil cans, one filled with 3-in-1 oil, one with engine oil.
3 large tubes (or tin) Durofix cement.
*Breast drill, 2-speed, to take up to $\frac{1}{2}$ in. drill.
Hand drill to take up to $\frac{1}{4}$ in. drill.
*Vice, 4 in., $3\frac{1}{2}$ in., or 3 in., according to boat size.
Hand vice (small yachts).
*Set of fixed spanners $\frac{5}{16}$ in. to $\frac{3}{4}$ in.
Turit drills 'high speed' steel, set $\frac{1}{16}$ in. to $\frac{1}{2}$ in. by 32nd's in tin box.
*1 pair callipers—inside.
1 centre punch.
*Set nail punches ('Nail Sets').
Saddlers' punches, $\frac{1}{8}$ in., $\frac{5}{16}$ in., $\frac{1}{4}$ in., $\frac{3}{8}$ in., $\frac{1}{2}$ in.
Adjustable spanners, small, *medium, and large.
Footprint wrench, 5 in. long and *11 in. long.
Hacksaw frame for 9 in. blades.
Hacksaws, 9 in. long, 1 doz. each fine, medium, and *coarse toothed.
*Midget hacksaw frame and 1 doz. blades.
Copper rivets and washers—assortment.
Brass wood-screws—wide assortment, 1 doz. of each flat heads.
Brass wood-screws—half quantities, round-headed.
Assortment of soft stainless steel or galvanised iron wire.
Timber—mahogany, an assortment of odd pieces ⎫
Bolts and nuts, brass or galvanised iron—assortment ⎬ quantity to suit size of boat.
Copper nails and tacks, small assortment ⎪
Brass gimp pins and pond pins, assortment ⎭
Nails—iron (galvanised), assortment. Quantity to suit size of boat.
Cotter pins, brass—assorted box.
*Cold chisels, $\frac{1}{2}$ in., $\frac{3}{4}$ in., and *1 in.
Tin of lanolin grease.
Strip of felt 2 ft. $\times$ 1 ft.
Sheet of copper for tingles 2 ft. $\times$ 1 ft. (two-thirds the size for small boats).
Electric light cable gland filler or other leak stopping compound.
Bosun's chair of minimum width (18 in. between slings).
Aluminium alloy strip of Birmabright, say 1 ft. $\times$ 2 ft. $\times$ $\frac{1}{8}$ in.
Small tin Kanvo (for proofing canvas) (half size for small yacht).
*30 ft. twin electric light flex (15 ft. for small yacht, or flex wandering lead).
Tin Certus cold water glue.
Spare bulbs for each size of light, torches, compass light, hand bearing compass.
Spare torch batteries.
Insulating tape.
Thin special binding sticky tape $1\frac{1}{2}$ in.

Sail Repair Outfit to include:
6 sail needles (4 fine and 2 average).
2 sewing palms.
Fine cotton sailmakers' thread.
Medium cotton sailmakers' thread.
Standard sailmakers' thread.
Nylon thread (if provided with nylon sails).
Supply of large pins.
Beeswax, lump of.
Sailmakers' hook and lanyard.
Pieces of canvas applicable to each weight of sail carried.
Note.—Three weights are generally sufficient for a small boat, the heaviest being the mainsail and the lightest the light genoa.
    About 2 sq. ft., in long strips, in each case; double quantity for a medium and triple quantity for a large boat.
Fid.

Extra Gear for Larger Yachts:

Additional palm.
Double quantity of needles.

APPENDIX XV

OFFSHORE COOKING

Sandwiches and a Thermos of hot coffee may be all right in some cases; but if you are going to be at sea for three to five days and nights, this is not enough; and a good hard-working crew deserves to be fed well.

Most of our offshore races start in the evening. The member of the crew who is in charge of the galley should get everything checked and stowed well in advance.

Before leaving the moorings for the starting line, a mug of tea and some cake or biscuits are usually welcome.

Once under way the watch should be woken and fed in good time to relieve the others who will get their meal when they come below. Eating in the cockpit should be discouraged, as this distracts the helmsman. The food should be simple and easy to eat so that no time is lost in getting the boys fed and off to sleep.

During the night, bread, Ryvita, soup, chocolate, fruit, sweets, etc., should be left where everyone can help themselves easily. The watch should be encouraged, very firmly, to leave mugs and saucepans clean for the following watch. It is also very important that they should make as little noise as possible, and shade lights from the sleepers. There is nothing so maddening as to be woken up an hour or so before you are due to go on watch by an avalanche of saucepans, or the whistling of *La Traviata*, offkey.

A good and simple breakfast is scrambled or poached eggs and bacon. While this is in progress a glass of fruit juice goes down rather well.

For luncheon, one can usually keep roast chicken, cold beef or ham for the first two days, and have this with salad. Cheese and fruit are a good follow up. Later on (unless one has a deep freeze), one must use tinned meat, tongue, crab, lobster, etc. If lettuce is fresh (and can be stowed where it does not get squashed), it should keep for four or five days. After this one must fall back on tins again.

Most hard-working crewmen are ready for bread and jam and cake by tea-time. But stews have to appear with rather monotonous regularity for dinner. Using imagination one can vary these in many ways, with the addition of wine, sherry, curry powder, dried onion, spaghetti, or rice.

It is good for the cook's morale if he is given a hand with the washing-up.

More General Hints. The cheapest milk keeps longer than the very creamy; and after the second day it is as well to pour off any cream that has formed. If possible stow the milk upright in the bilges, but not where it will get submerged.

It is best to get marmalade and jam in screw-top jars. I always ask the grocer to take the rind off the bacon for me—he doesn't have to do it with a pair of rusty scissors in a shop at an angle of 35 degrees.

Brown bread (well wrapped) seems to keep best: if it is already sliced, this saves a lot of trouble and crumbs on board.

Some liquid soaps do well in sea water. Soap powder is apt to fall over and spill, and it has sometimes been mistaken for sugar. Lump sugar is easiest to deal with in bad weather.

Eggs seldom get broken if they are stowed with egg containers top and bottom. I always mix the salad dressing (oil and vinegar type) at home and take it on board in screw-top jars.

Pots and Pans. Normally two saucepans should be enough; one small and one large. Both should be fairly small in diameter with high sides. Apart from this a fairly large frying-pan, and a whistling kettle. It is important to have a frying-pan and kettle that will both fit on the cooker at the same time. I find it very necessary to have on board a soup ladle, egg-lifter, and wooden spoon. Also two spare tin-openers and bottle-openers; two or three plastic screw-top jars for the sugar, tea bags, etc., and some small polythene bags to keep matches, etc., dry.

In the days of the square-riggers, damp chamois leather was widely used to prevent plates and mugs from sliding off tables: today I find Wetex equally good—and half the price.

Six or seven tea-cloths are useful, and can be tucked in amongst the jam-jars and things to keep them from sliding about and rattling. A cook's belt is essential, and can be used even in moderate weather; it takes the weight off one's feet, and also leaves both hands free.

FOOD LIST FOR THREE DAY RACE

(CREW OF TEN)

Typical provisioning list for a crew of ten for a 250-mile race.

Item	Full stowage	Quantity remaining	Quantity required
Large sliced bread	8 loaves		
Butter	6 pkts.		
Marmalade	2 jars		
Sugar	6 lb.		
Tea Bags	1 pkt. (large)		
Milk (Marvel)	1 tin		
Nescafe—medium size	1 tin		
Bovril	4 oz.		
Matches—NOT ALLOWING FOR SMOKERS	6 boxes		
Cocoa or Chocolate	1 tin		
Cooking oil	1 bottle		
Vinegar	1 bottle		
Mustard	1 tin		
Salt	1 pkt.		
Pepper	1 tub		
Ryvita	4 pkts.		
Andrex and Polly roll	3 and 1		
Hard biscuits or Water biscuits	1 tin 2 pkts.		
Cakes	3		
Chocolate	6 pkts.		
Barley sugar	1 lb.		
Salad cream	1 jar		
Kraft sliced cheese	3 pkts.		
Mousetrap cheese	2 lb.		
Oxo or other cubes	1 pkt.		
Dried fruit	2 pkts.		
Spaghetti	3 tins		
Baked beans Curry beans	3 tins 1 tin		
Asparagus Celery	2 tins 2 tins		
Bully beef Luncheon meat	2 tins 2 tins		
Stewed steak	5 tins		
Sausages	5 tins		

Soups	6 tins		
Peas	3 tins (or dehydrated, in pkts.)		
Butter beans	2 tins		
French beans	2 tins		
Carrots	2 tins		
Potatoes or puree New Potatoes	3 pkts. 4 tins		
Rice—quick type	2 pkts.		
Fruit	6 tins		
Fruit juice	6 tins		
Lemon squash Orange squash	1 bottle 1 bottle		
Lemons—fresh	2		
Chickens—cooked	4		
Sliced ham or beef	2 lb.		
Bacon—thin slice and rind taken off	$2\frac{1}{2}$ lb.		
Eggs	4 doz.		
Milk in cartons—otherwise silver top	6 pints		
Lettuces	5		
Tomatoes	2 lb.		
Curry powder	1 pkt.		
Porridge oats	1 pkt.		
Biscuits—sweet			
Chutney Worcester sauce			
Apples Oranges	3 lb. 15		
Whisky			
Beer	2 doz.		
Liquid soap Ajax			
Gas or paraffin			
Water			

MEDICAL

Aspirins
Elastoplast
Surgical spirit
Cotton wool and bandages
Scissors

Marzine
Beechams pills
Dr. Collis Browns mixture
Anti-burn vaseline
Ether

APPENDIX XVI

Example of an Owner's Preliminary Specification

MYTH OF MALHAM

GENERAL — L.W.L. say 33·6 ft. Displacement about 8 tons. Beam say 9 ft. 4 in. Rating to be aimed at 27·7 ft. sailing without propeller.

LINES — Snubbed bow and after body to suit. Canoe stern well drawn out to suit ketch rig.
Note.—Roller reefing to mizzen is an important asset, and to work this it is desirable to reach leech of sail.

DRAFT — Limit or near limit under the R.O.R.C. rule.

SCANTLINGS — As necessary for sea-going strength subject to no penalty being incurred on scantling allowance. Eight-metre scantlings may be taken as a basis modified to suit the materials in use.

FREEBOARD — To be about 3 in. more than rule minimum (sum of freeboards) being considerably greater forward.

SHEER — To be virtually straight between girth stations in order (1) to take advantage of D measurements, (2) to give reasonable accommodation in a light displacement hull.

SAIL PLAN — J.H.I. will work out ketch rig with two working headsails with NS + 23, *i.e.* S + 529. Mainsail and fore triangle aspect ratios about 3 : 1. Mainmast approx. 44 ft. Mizzen 24 ft. or 24 ft. 6 in.
Note (1).—As soon as lines plan is sufficiently advanced L.G. & P. to inform J.H.I. of L.O.A.; position of mainmast relative to stemhead; position of after W.L. ending relative to stern.
Note (2).—Should the rating on measurement come out below 27·5 ft. the size of the mainsail will be adjusted, and allowance for this will be made in sail plan.

MAINMAST — Mainmast strength should assume that considerable use will be made of genoas on the wind up to Force 3. (Arrangements have been made to have nylon available in two weights for a working genoa as well as a lighter genoa.)
Note.—As regards sheeting *vis-a-vis* the rigging, no trouble is likely with genoas which will sheet outside everything. The sheeting of the staysail will be studied when sail plan is complete, which may determine choice between 3 cross and 2 cross-trees.

FORESTAY — To be detachable and single. If found feasible lever to be in fo'c'sle, to flex wire whip being led from the hook on deck. Leading through deck to lineable sheave on keel to an (off centre ?) lever on cabin sole near W.C.

FORE TOPMAST STAY — To be single. Consideration may be given if the stay is sufficiently inboard to fitting the bottle screw under deck (in order (*a*) to enable the standby sail to be hanked on and stowed close to the deck; (*b*) reduce windage on deck; (*c*) lower weight of screw; (*d*) relieve deck of load. Consideration (*a*) is the important one).

CHAIN PLATES — Four to be provided. Forward three to be used with the ketch rig in the first instance.

SHROUDS — May be linked type, to reduce windage, of solid strand wire if available. To be proof tested after fitting the end fittings. (Include in building specification.) Bottle screws aloft as necessary. The after lower shrouds to be lighter than the forward lowers. Consideration may be given to bringing lower three shrouds through deck, but this will probably prove impracticable.
Note.—The 2 headsail sail plan probably demands the staysail sheeting inside the cap shrouds, which presumably involves cap shrouds going to ship's side. Accommodation difficulty will probably arise also, and again measurers may consider that these fittings interfere with the reasonable comfort and utility of the vessel.

RUNNING BACKSTAYS — Should be given approximately the same drift as the forestay. Operated by improved levers.

PREVENTER BACKSTAYS — Twin stays should be led to ship's side with the minimum drift to clear the boom with a small margin at its highest topped position: heel say 5 ft. from deck. To be operated by 'Improved Highfield' type levers.
Note.—Twin as opposed to single preventers give better support to the masthead, and also reduce the initial *compressive stress in the mast*. Two preventers can be of smaller wire than a single preventer backstay since extension is not critical. The *minimum* preventer drift is desired so as to get the stays well out from centre-line. Twin preventers also allow the mizzen staysail to be tacked to windward of centre-line—important. The levers allow the lee preventer to be slacked to clear the mizzen staysail. Slacking without casting off should be sufficient.

MAST STEPS — Arrangements to be provided to enable main and mizzen masts to be moved aft if necessary for conversion to cutter or yawl.

MIZZEN MAST — Tentatively propose: 2 cross-trees; light triatic stay (between mastheads); running backstays from upper cross-tree worked by small levers (which only need slacking on a reach, *i.e.* not when turning to windward); light jumper stay, single strut on upper cross-tree; single lower shroud; chain plates, additional pair to be provided abaft working ones for conversion to yawl.
Note.—The principal loading of mizzen mast will be due to the 250 sq. ft. of staysail when reaching hard.

COACHROOF

Assuming that coachroof is about 14 ft. 6 in. in length propose to divide this: after space, 5 ft. 6 in.; saloon, 6 ft. 3 in.; fo'c'sle, remainder.
Coachroof to be of light construction and fairly well arched. Sides parallel to ship's side. Fixed lights in side only. Usual hand grip rails.

AFTER HATCH

Propose small twin after hatches; with central fore and aft beam between, carrying main sheet block and cleat.
Note.—These hatches would constitute virtually forward extensions to the cockpit for inshore racing, or with full ocean racing crew on deck. A step below them to be at a height convenient for a standing hand to work (say) the runner levers on side deck. The presence of these hatches may reduce the tendency of hands to crowd aft, putting the stern down, or sit on deck causing undue windage. This arrangement should also enable central steering compass to be used conveniently. The transom of pram dinghy to be cut away to take hatch slides (and portable piece fitted to transom before launching).

ARRANGEMENT OF FLOORS Steel floors are much preferred to keelson arrangement.
Note.—Preferred on the grounds of space since (a) headroom is critical and (b) following require low storage in boat to lower their weight: battery, water tanks, anchors, calor gas bottle, all tinned food. Propose if feasible steel floors be alternated some deep and some shallow; deep ones being located say two in way of mast, one between after compartment and saloon, one towards after end of after compartment, forward of engine. This should allow increased headroom: (a) at forward end of after compartment; (b) at after end of saloon; (c) under fore-hatch.

STOWAGES UNDER CABIN SOLE

ENGINE

Assume Stuart type R3MC will be used. Weight complete installation about 95 lb. Maximum installation angle 10 degrees. Hand start by standard raised handle above flywheel at front of engine. Presume engine will be on or near centre-line (as necessary to clear runner tube) as low as possible under cockpit fore end. Makers' particulars are: propeller pipe $\frac{3}{4}$ in.; leading dimensions, height overall $15\frac{11}{16}$ in. Length overall, including clutch, $20\frac{3}{4}$ in. Width overall $12\frac{1}{4}$ in.; distance between holding-down bolts (four) athwartships, 6 in.; fore and aft, $5\frac{1}{2}$ in.

BATTERY

As hand starting is fitted this may be disposed anywhere as convenient under cabin sole in waterproof well, of hardwood or copper or zinc. Say 50 amp. hrs., weight 50 lb.; 12 volts.

WATER

Assume 37 gal. carried (8 person at $\frac{1}{2}$ gal. per day for 9 days). Stowed in not less than 2 tanks, one fresh-water pump only in galley space. Light gauge piping to connect.

TINS

Stowage under sole. Normal consumption including soups is about 8 tins per day. Stow for 7 days—say 55 small tins.

ANCHORS

Kedge and main—3 fathoms of chain on main. Remainder nylon rope. No navel pipe is required.

STOWAGE LOCKERS

In laying out accommodation care to be taken to keep lockers in lower half of the accommodation principally under bunks and settees. (To keep weights low.)

SEATS

Cook's seat—hinged flap on bulkhead abaft galley if feasible. Settees in cabin to be about 13 in. wide and sloped up at inboard edges; lockers under. Seat flap to drop over W.C. pan in fo'c'sle forward.

FO'C'SLE

One narrow opening only required between saloon and fo'c'sle. (Required as this is the head.) Hanging cupboard one side 36 in. high. A chest of drawers opposite with simple enamelled wash basin on top, flap down over. Toilet article (small) cupboard behind. Fore-hatch to have slightly raised coaming above coachroof to give extra headroom. To have hinged wings for partial opening. Fo'c'sle bunks, permanent (use as sail racks at sea). Lockers or drawers under.

SALOON

May consider L-shaped settee, slightly wider at fore end starboard side (this giving two lounging corners). Lockers under settee, in three portions each side, with flap-up tops. Bunks outboard of settees says 24 in. wide at head (aft). Shallow drawers (in three portions) under each bunk. False side boards over forward end of bunks. Small cupboards outboard of these. One fitted for glasses. Small flap-up tables attach to mast for harbour use. (J.H.I. will supply sketch.) Abreast mast provide small hatch in cabin sole covering beer and wine bottle rack (emergency water when racing).

AFTER SPACE

Length allowed for galley, 3 ft. fore and aft. L.G. & P. asked to submit rough layout in due course. No fixed sink is required. Propose two aluminium buckets partly under stove, one for dirty crocks and other for refuse (both removable but in deep recesses).
Small gimballed two-burner calor gas stove (no oven).
Rack for crocks—8 large mugs and 12 tin soup-plates appear sufficient.
Chart table. Located as high under side deck as is feasible. 3 ft. fore and aft length and minimum 2 ft. 3 in. depth. Small book rack over for sailing directions and rack for instruments.
Chart drawers under. Small tool drawer under these. Small rack to take patent log box and sextant. Small settee lockers, say 11 in. wide, inboard of quarter bunks (bosun's gear).
Under cockpit, engine, oilskin stowage each side, and wet clothes drawer or bag.
Bronze quality diaphragm type bilge pump fitted in after space. Strainer to be fine meshed and fitted on end of stout rubber-canvas suction hose (readily brought up from bilge).
Canvas screens to let down over quarter berth fronts. Top edge permanently secured round a batten. Bottom edge aluminium tube, on which screen can be rolled up to show, and which can be secured in place at ends, by bunk occupant or from outside; one end in socket, other end turn button or similar.

COCKPIT

Rudder tube to end of self-draining cockpit floor. Coamings to taper in width fairly sharply from forward to aft (to reduce ingress of quarter seas). Sides of cockpit well can be run approximately parallel to ship's side. Seat, level to be below that of the deck, tapering nearly to 'nothing' in width under bridge deck. Portion of seat each side abaft quarter oilskin locker to form small bosun's locker. Main sheet slide to be mounted on bridge deck, forward edge. Single jib sheet winch to be mounted also on bridge deck amidships (if on drawing sail plan and leads this appears feasible). Single athwartship seat at after end of cockpit, to form access to after peak.

LIFE-LINES

Birmabright tube stanchions, 22 in. Single flex wire life-line. Rubber tube over wire in way of main sheet P. & S. Life-line to be lashed to main and mizzen shrouds port and starboard (eliminating necessity of stanchion in way of mast).

DECK GENERAL

No anchor winch (break out with staysail sheet winches if necessary).
Rail at ship's side to be about $2\frac{1}{2}$ in. with aluminium track on top for sheet leads. (*Note.*—Important that inboard side be vertical and not rounded at top.)
Note.—It appears better to run the track, so, since fastenings can then be common to bulwark and track saving weight, etc.

FORE GUYS

Permanent nylon whips. Require fixed fairleads worked into bulwarks P. & S. approx. abreast fore topmast stay on deck.

DECK WINCHES

Winch each to staysail and jib halyards, each side of mast, mounted fairly low. (Special attention to through fastenings securing.) No winch to main halyard—single moving block and hemp whip.
Staysail winch each side of forward end of cockpit. Single jib winch mounted amidships on bridge deck over tiller head abaft main sheet. Winches to be Bradford type made by U.S.M.P. Co. small size for mast, medium size for staysail.
Main sheet winch. Lead as in *Maid of Malham*.

ELECTRIC LIGHTING

Following points required (10 in all):
    Navigational side lights. (Boards built into the coachroof to clear the special pram dinghy.)

Owner's starboard quarter bunk	4 watt
Chart table	6 watt
Galley	4 watt
Saloon	8 watt
Fo'c'sle	4 watt
Forepeak	4 watt
Foredeck flood light	12 watt (through usual type fixed light in coachroof).

Compass lead
One spare fused point in box.

VENTILATORS

Ventilators having large projecting surfaces are not acceptable. In the course of the design the possibility may, however, be borne in mind of incorporating small box type splashless vents with the coachroof structure, *e.g.* it may be possible to combine small vents with the light boards, P. & S., the orifices being just forward of the lights in the boards. A very small vent in the stemhead may be combined with the rail, a triangular shallow box being used, with small orifices on each bow.

APPENDIX XVII

MOUSE OF MALHAM

Comments on Design and Detail

Class III R.O.R.C. Racer—Cruiser, Designed and Built 1954/55 by Aero Marine of Emsworth
for Peter Green, Esq., and Captain J. H. Illingworth

Length overall 32 ft.; Waterline 24 ft.; Beam 8 ft.; Draft 5 ft. 9 in. Displacement 2·4 tons; Thames tonnage 6;
Ballast ·94 tons. Sail area measured 260 sq. ft.; R.O.R.C. rating 20·32 ft.

The object of this design was to produce a successful ocean racer of first-class construction at the minimum of cost. No concessions whatever were made concerning quality of workmanship or materials, and yet the final cost was only about half that of some current designs of the same waterline length. In this lies the interest of the design.

Expense is saved firstly by reducing the displacement and the weight of the materials used. The ballast keel for instance costs about half the normal amount, and the whole rig is reduced in size.

Secondly by making her hull dinghy fashion and bolting the keel on afterwards. This much simplifies planking and bending the timbers and enables the hull to be turned over by hand for finishing and the frames run from gunwale to gunwale, so that the garboards are much stronger than with conventional construction.

Thirdly by simplifying the internal joinery, using nets and kit-bag racks instead of lockers, drawers and cupboards; and canvas bunks covered with thin upholstery rather than full depth rubber.

This boat was originally drawn as a reverse sheer design—which I personally recommend as it can eliminate the forward coach roof and give full sitting headroom over the bunks, as well as 6 in. more overall headroom. However, by way of a change we built her with the 'older fashioned' inverse sheer, which slightly reduces windage and rating. Incidentally with a reverse sheer one can build two extra berths into the after lazaret which in company with a special after hatch makes this a very good family cruiser.

It should be noted however that a low freeboard does not make a light boat as wet as a heavy one, because the gunwale rises more when the light boat is heeled.

She is built with 'bolted-on fins', the forward one cast iron, and the after one in wood, on which the rudder is hung. From a handling point of view this has the important advantage that for a given total fin area she will be steadier with two fins, or put another way, one can achieve steady running in a seaway without unduly lengthening the keel, thus avoiding unnecessary wetted surface.

It results also in the rudder being in an efficient vertical position, and the rudder post comes out where it is wanted; and a much shorter tiller can be used enabling a hatch to be fitted between the rudder head and the mizzen.

Reverting to the construction, a stout keelson is fitted through most of the boat over the timbers and wooden floors which gives the keel bolts a good long shank in the boat. This keelson forms part of the cabin sole.

Three special timbers are run from coach roof carlin, right round the ship inside the bilge stringers to the carlin on the other side in one length. They are packed out between the stringers; and in way of the gunwale with a bracket curved on its inboard face. They are fastened and glued to the normal timbers, making loop frames-cum-knees of some strength, but simple to run.

The coach roof sides and the cockpit coamings are of special ply which I feel is preferable to the more usual teak or mahogany on the score of strength. It should guard against the dangers of splitting horizontally when hit by a big sea, and without incurring undue weight or complexity.

The lights in the coach roof sides are worthy of mention. Normally these, especially when of ample size in the modern manner, can be a serious weakness in the coach roof; particularly when they are recessed into the wood. In the *Mouse* we have used perspex and fastened this to the outside of the roof, with multi-washered bolts and nuts, instead of clamping the light by a ring. Thus the perspex is itself stressed and becomes an integral part of the roof side. The cost and weight of special brass rings are also saved.

The extra 6 in. of beam compared with the R.N.S.A. Twenty-Four *Minx of Malham* forms an interesting comparison. It has enabled us to have wide cockpit seats in conjunction with a high coaming, resulting in a pit which feels secure and protected. The capping of the coamings is wide for comfortable sitting when so needed, and is 'all outside' to avoid catching one's back and also to help keep the water in the side deck from slopping into the pit when she is well heeled. The supports to the jib winches are in bronze and arranged well away from the cockpit sides so as to allow free passage of water down the weather deck.

The small displacement has enabled a big saving to be

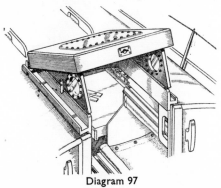

Diagram 97
Hinged companion hatch with lights in sides.

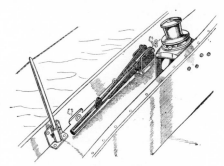

Diagram 98
Runner lever with traveller in handle.

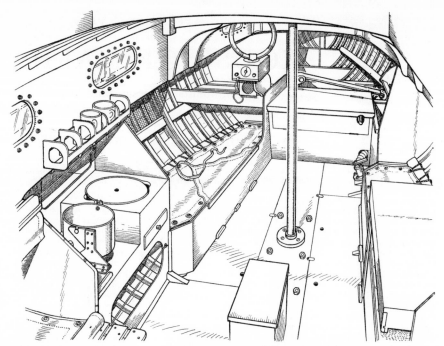

Diagram 99
Looking forward. Mast pillar stepped on hog which is flush with cabin sole. Cook's/navigator's seat cum bosun's locker in foreground.

made in the rig; her measured sail area is 260 compared to 450 of a R.N.S.A. Twenty-Four. And she is no sluggard in light weather. Since sail makers charge by area there is a 40 per cent saving in the initial and renewal cost of sails. The sail plan is illustrated on page 56.

To achieve these savings one sacrifices headroom in the cabin. The *Mouse* has 4 ft. 10 in., the reverse sheer model 5 ft. 4 in. Fortunately, the 8-ft. beam permits one to have benches inside the quarter berths, with plenty of sitting headroom, and with the splash curtains acting as backs to the seats. These curtains are in plastic so as to let some light into the bunk, and as there is a gap between the pit and the foot of the bunk, one gets plenty of air in too. The alloy tube in the top hem of the curtain takes in brackets at each end rather like a

root berth fixing, and the top is sealed against water by a flap coming down from a shelf on the side of the roof.

The bunk upholstery is in a synthetic lightweight foam material. It is very soft, half the weight of foam rubber, and rather less costly. It does not absorb water into its texture, so it dries quickly. However, the red Dulon coverings are splash proof in any case.

Moving forward in the accommodation the galley is to port. There is a special Calor gas single-burner stove, the burner being accommodated in a cylindrical alloy gimballed container which shields the flame and should make it impossible for the pan or kettle to get adrift. It will boil a kettle in under five minutes. Three light-weight gas cylinders are provided, so that one can readily keep a check on one's consumption.

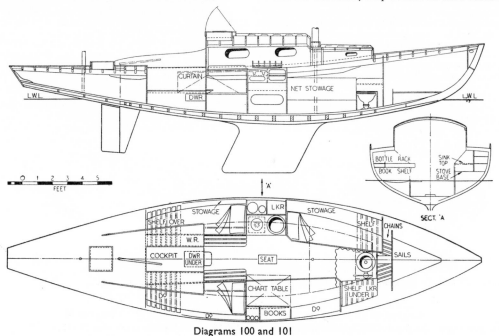

Diagrams 100 and 101

Opposite the galley is the chart table which is illustrated in the drawing. It is a good big one and placed so that when one is seated on the central stool, which is the bosun's tool box, one get get one's knees under the table and be really chocked off and secure in a seaway with both hands free for plotting. It is placed over the bunk head, and removed to the forecastle in harbour if the fourth berth is required.

As I have already mentioned there are no clothes lockers or clothes drawers, which saves weight and cost. Instead we have several racks for kit-bags, and a big clothes-net against the ship's side over each bunk; a system which, apart from its simplicity, has much to commend it. The sides and top of the nets are contained by elastic shock cord, which keeps the net tidy and makes for easy access. Personally I prefer keeping my things in a kit-bag, rather than having to stow everything afresh on arrival on board.

Coats and oilskins are hung in the space between the cockpit and the quarter berth. Seaboots and shoes go under the pit.

The head is a light-weight Baby Blake. Forward of this is a really big sail store. Here and in the locker in the counter one has a big reserve of storage space for extra gear for cruising; this due to the deliberate concentration of the accommodation in the middle of the length, which reduces the shift of crew weights when sailing and avoids the need to place bunks uncomfortably far forward.

We have no fore hatch; this with a view to reducing leaks, keeping the deck clear and to reduce cost and weight. I think these advantages far outweigh the slight extra trouble of getting sails out on deck, and for an English climate the extra aperture is not much needed. Anyway, when one is battened down and most needing air, it can't be used.

We have two baffled vent boxes. The first is formed by a watertight bulkhead close to the stem head, fed by false hawse pipe apertures on either bow. Five holes in the bulkhead near the deck head admit air to the boat, there is a drain hole, outboard through the stem. There are rubber plugs for these, but the indications are that they can remain open in any weather.

Abreast the mast heel is another vent box in which are forward-facing slots baffled from holes in the fore side of the after coach roof. In the wings of this box are the navigation side lights. With a view to avoiding the difficulty of keeping

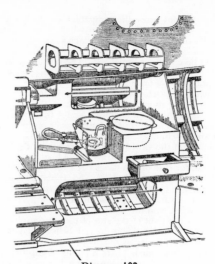

Diagram 102
Galley showing gimballed shielded gas burner and rack for mugs in which they can be filled while stowed.

the normal side lights watertight and the wiring and deck terminals in working order, dry battery-operated lights are completely enclosed in watertight plastic translucent containers. A complete spare lamp can then be carried against possible trouble.

The companionway hatch cover is hinged and beds on to soft rubber. This is likely to be much more watertight than the sliding type of hatch. But it has two other important advantages; the dinghy can lie on the coach roof without being cocked up to clear the companionway slides and as big folding wedge-shaped wings are fitted to the hinged cover, it can remain part open in most weather and forms a sort of baby doghouse, in which someone can sit and look out of Perspex lights fitted in the hatch or wings.

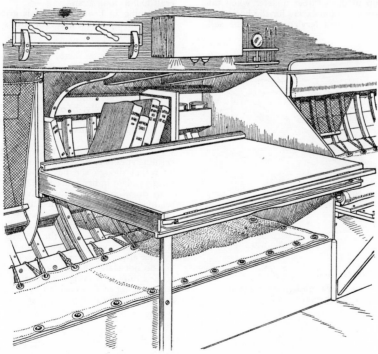

Diagram 103 Large chart table can be removed, and stowed forward, in harbour.

One small point here—the companionway lock is arranged with a special barrel-shaped hasp which comes away with padlock, leaving no projection on which to catch one's head.

The bunk leeboards are triangular canvas flaps which, when not in use, lie under the upholstery. The inboard edges of the canvas berth bottoms can be unbuttoned from studs for access to the storage spaces under the bunks.

The after box hatch cover is hinged at its forward end and fitted with heavy shock cord running from the centre of the hatch down to the hatch coaming, and 3 ft. forward, under the deck above. This keeps the hatch cover on its seat at sea without any catch.

The details of the yawl rig will be seen from the sail plan. I think most people would, in this size of boat, prefer a single headsail rig, for ease of handling, but I have got used to two headsails as fitted in *Maid, Myth,* and *Wista,* and so I have used it here. The big yankee and the genoa staysail need careful design to ensure that they set in a mutually compatible way on the wind, and the whole staying of the mast needs to be studied in the light of the run of the overlapping leaches of these sails. Provided this is done, I believe that the cutter rig is just as close winded as the sloop, and the loading on the mast is better distributed. There is plenty of gap between the leech of the main and the mizzen, which does enable the latter to set properly on the wind, and also helps the mizzen staysail to set nicely on the reach.

Both masts are of aluminium alloy with integral tracks. They are stepped on deck and can easily be shipped without the use of a crane; a great convenience to the amateur doing his own laying up and fitting out, and an economy of time and labour even to the equipped shipyard. The main mast can be lifted with one hand.

The runner backstays are operated by U.S.M.P. Co. tubular aluminium alloy levers, which incorporate plenty of adjustment, and need no bottle screws. For cruising or short tacking these levers need not be set up at all. The topmast backstays are well into the boat and the better staying which results from this wide base is a big help in keeping the jib luff taut. The boom clears these but a small lever is used to slacken them off when the mizzen staysail is to be set.

The mizzen mast has an ample fore and aft section so that there are no stays, only shrouds to this mast. The mizzen staysail halyard is set up to the weather quarter when this sail is in use. The sails are all cotton except for the horizontal cut nylon spinnaker and the light terylene mizzen staysail.

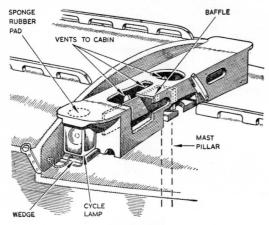

Diagram 104

Combined vent box and navigation light stowage at break in coach roof.

The storm jib can be used as a mizzen staysail when conditions are too breezy for the light sail. Incidentally this sail is cut high in the foot with a view to avoiding the need for any sheet leads on deck, when it is set as a jib.

The spinnaker boom is a tubular aluminium one by the U.S.M.P. Co. This small diameter boom stows very easily on deck. The same firm have supplied the sheet winches and the '$\frac{1}{4}$-ton clips' which are fitted to all sail tacks, halyards, and guys. These clips weigh very little and so even in light airs are no great burden on the clew of a spinnaker, and aloft on the head of a sail weigh no more than the ordinary shackle which they replace. As an aid to changing headsails I believe these quick clips constitute a real advance, compared with one's usual cold-fingered struggle with shackles, and holding the pin in one's teeth maybe. They come in various sizes, but as these small ones have a breaking strain of over $\frac{1}{2}$ ton, they match a $\frac{5}{8}$-in. circ. halyard whose splice will probably fail at about $\frac{3}{4}$ ton.

On a small yacht carrying a dinghy must always be a problem. In a yawl the counter is not available. The choice then rests between the cabin top and the fore deck where it causes least windage but is in the way when working round the mast; and it means the staysail must be set a foot higher up its stay.

The *Mouse*'s pram has been tailored to fit the cabin top; the after transom drops over the front of the roof and rests on the vent box, the forward sloping transom is against the companionway. To make up its short length it has a 4-ft. beam.

Finally a few words about *Mouse*'s performance at sea, which turned out to be just about what we had hoped and expected, which is not always the case—often the best point of sailing and the best weather is not what the designer expected.

She feels very alive to sail—a genuine fast dinghy feeling. With such a cut-down waterline she is very responsive to the tiller and the steering needs concentrated attention to get the best out of her when racing. In a cruising version I would alter the ballast keel by lengthening it fore and aft; a thing very easily done in this type, which would make her steadier and need less attention.

She is fast running and specially fast on the reach—she will in moderate weather reach boat for boat with many modern craft half as long again.

Running in heavy weather is great fun. She wave rides rather prettily and a great foam of spray drives back nearly level with the deck.

To windward in smooth water she sails her rating with ease. In broken water, as might be expected with such a very light boat, certain sorts of seas will set her back appreciably. In a long rough turn to windward the best of the medium heavy boats (such as *Favona*) may have the better of her.

In gale conditions she heaves to, with someone at the helm, very happily. She is not unduly wet, and at the end of one spell of about 24 hrs. in strong and gale winds there was still insufficient water in the bilge for the bilge pump to suck.

All fast boats pound somewhat going to windward in certain types of seaway and *Mouse* is no exception. But taken all round though she has a buoyant motion; she is by no means violent in her movement.

In drawing her lines we have been at pains to give her relatively easy sections. I feel that some designs of displacement yachts which have in the past taken advantage of the dinghy type of construction have failed because they have been too full and hard in the sections, and too flat in the run. A type which works well enough in a dinghy sailed upright but not always in a sea-going yacht.

I do not claim the *Mouse* type to be necessarily the yacht of the future, nor everyone's boat. I think, however, that for ocean racing or fast cruising at a minimum of cost, and for the enthusiast, this type offers something very likeable.

APPENDIX XVIII

BELMORE

Design and Detail

SAIL AREAS

Sail areas are: main 317 sq. ft.; C.C.A. genoa 460 sq. ft.; R.O.R.C. genoa 372 sq. ft.; ghoster 396 sq. ft.; working jib 236 sq. ft.; heavy weather jib 114 sq. ft.; spitfire jib 60 sq. ft.; staysail 42 sq. ft.; quad jib 430 sq. ft.; trysail 110 sq. ft.

R.O.R.C. rating details: I is 40 ft.; J is 14·35 ft. giving an area of 287 sq. ft.; B is 15·2 ft.; P is 41·5 ft. giving an area of 316 sq. ft. Rated total 603 sq. ft. C.C.A. rated total 687 sq. ft.

DIMENSIONS

Dimensions: L.O.A. 36 ft. 4 in.; L.W.L. 26 ft. 6 in.; Beam 9 ft. 6 in.; Draft 5 ft. 11½ in.

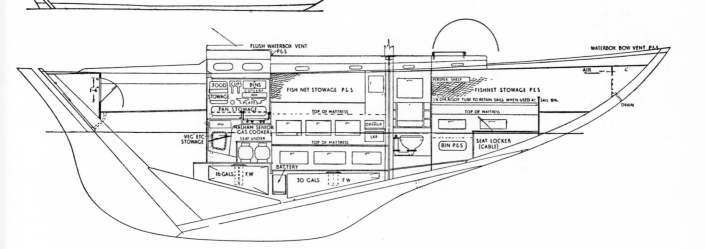

Diagram 105
The Sloop *Belmore*, designed by Aero Marine to the C.C.A. and R.O.R.C. rating rules.

This sloop has been designed by Aero Marine to the C.C.A. rule as well as the often R.O.R.C. rating rule. It seems clear that this is only the second time that a British-owned yacht has been planned from the start for entry in American offshore races. The first boat to this specification was Lloyd's Y.C.' *Lutine*. The plans are therefore of special interest.

The transom stern is not seen much among the Bermuda Race fleet, but it cuts down the overall length. This is important when the yacht has to be shipped abroad, quite apart from the saving in total cost. The draft is not to the R.O.R.C. limit and the bottom of the keel is rounded. This gives an easier driven form but one that is not quite so good to windward. The flat-bottomed keel presents a sharp edge at the maximum draft when heeled, which in theory at least, reduces the water flow from the lee to the windward side of the keel. Also the flat-bottomed keel does not lose quite so much draft when heeled as the round-bottomed one.

Belmore is designed for close reaching, as this occurs a good deal in the Bermuda, but she will not use her quadrilateral jib for C.C.A. races. The trouble with these sails has been mainly confined to the difficulty of sheeting correctly. Without a counter it is often hard to get the best sheet lead.

The low inner forestay is a feature that is gaining popularity. On it a baby staysail is set which helps to keep the yacht going during those few seconds when one headsail is lowered and another is going up. In bad weather it is a useful, easily handled bit of canvas. Under the spinnaker it catches a dollop of wind that would otherwise slither past the yacht without doing any useful work.

There is a $1\frac{1}{2}$-oz. terylene spinnaker for light weather, a $2\frac{1}{2}$-oz. nylon one for stiffer breezes, and a 3-oz. storm spinnaker. All have very light wire luff and leech lines, and these sails are striped in different colours so that they are easy to recognise in the fo'c'sle. A track for the spinnaker pole socket is fitted on either side of the mast.

The heavy-weather jib, spitfire jib, and small staysail have Tufnol battens sewn in permanently. All the sails are marked on both sides at the corners with the reference number, and the tack is identified by a 3-in. black spot. All these sails are kept on the two forward berths which have no leeboards. These bunks are not tenanted at sea because the motion

forward is often too fierce for proper resting. To keep the sails in place there is a portable $1\frac{1}{4}$-in. diameter alloy tube inboard of each bunk.

Outboard of these berths there are big areas of fish netting against the ship's side. This makes fine stowage for clothes, especially if polythene bags are used to keep the gear dry. In the fo'c'sle there are shelves with Perspex fiddles so that the contents of the shelves are easily seen. The stowage throughout the yacht is just what is wanted for serious racing and cruising offshore. There are two oilskin lockers, one each side of the companionway. Opposite the toilet there is a big hanging locker for the crew's shore-going clothes.

Those two important people, the navigator and cook, have special seats by their working spaces. These seats are set facing athwartships, and extend the full length of the galley and chart table. There is ample foot-room outboard of them, and there is more chart stowage space than usual beneath the chart table. There are ply bulkheads at each end of the chart and cooking departments. Those $\frac{3}{4}$-in. bulkheads add to the strength of the ship, and are positioned at each end of the toilet compartment, as well as forward and aft of the cockpit. In this way the whole hull is stiffened at short intervals throughout its length.

The mast is deck stepped. To support it there are four steel pillars, in pairs either side of the centre gangway. These rest on a big oak floor. All the other floors are wrought iron, one on each frame except at the ends of the ship where none are needed. The English oak keel supports the 7,400-lb. iron keel with eight keel bolts which are staggered to port and starboard of the centreline.

The $\frac{7}{8}$-in. planking is larch and, higher, mahogany, fastened to rock elm timbers. The shelf is larch, $1\frac{3}{4}$ in. thick throughout, $4\frac{5}{8}$ in. deep for most of the length but tapering to $3\frac{1}{2}$ in. at the end. The same material is used for the clamp which is well tapered, and is 6 in. by $1\frac{1}{4}$ in. in the middle.

The alloy extruded mast has no standing rigging at the top except the permanent backstay. Only a single lower shroud is fitted each side. From the permanent backstay a harbour topping-lift is fitted to the boom end. This saves the weight of a boom gallows. The mainsail has roller reefing.

APPENDIX XIX

VANE SELF-STEERING GEARS

I am very indebted to M. F. Gunning and to the *Yachting Monthly* for permission to quote from their January 1967 issue and to permission from M. S. Gibb to quote from their publications.

Marin Marie-Durand was probably the first yachtsman to cross an ocean with self wind steering—in *Winabelle* in about 1933—and vane-operated steering gears serve to keep a vessel sailing at a constant angle to the apparent wind by means of a linkage or gears which make the wind control the main or an auxiliary rudder. Many different types have been evolved, complicated and simple, cheap and expensive. Most work reasonably well, some very well indeed, and comparisons are difficult. The principal types are:

A: Gears which operate the main rudder directly. Miranda of *Gipsy Moth III* (1960) is perhaps the best-known example of this type.

B: Gears which operate a small auxiliary rudder directly. Tabarly used a gear of this type on *Pen Duick II*. On both these types the vane steers the ship directly.

C: Gears where the vane is used to steer an auxiliary rudder or tab attached to the main rudder. The vane steers the tab, the tab steers the main rudder, and the rudder steers the ship. This sounds complicated, but is, in fact, quite simple. The obvious drawback to this gear is that it can only be used on yachts with a transom stern having an outside hung rudder.

D: Gears where the vane again is used to steer a tab, this tab being an independent unit, free to swing round a horizontal axis, the so-called pendulum gear introduced by Lt.-Col. (Blondie) Hasler. Its great advantage lies in the fact that it can be fitted to yachts with a counter.

As regards vanes, the great majority of these are of the simple windvane type which swing round a vertical shaft. Tabarly, however, used a vane swinging round a horizontal axis, for which he claims advantages.

Before discussing these gears more in detail, it may be worth while to examine some factors that may cause trouble in all of them. I am thinking of friction, inertia, apparent wind, and wind speed.

As regards friction, one must remember that, roller bearings excepted, friction at rest may be up to ten times greater than the friction once motion is started. So in light winds a considerable angle of incidence of wind on the vane may be required before it starts the vane, and the tab, moving. Once started, it is apt to rush off like a slow-witted helmsman. Inertia has much the same effect. A gear with a great built-in inertia will be slow to start, and, once started, slow to stop. However, on occasion inertia may be beneficial.

The effect of apparent wind is more complicated. Take an example of a yacht sailing at 45° off a 10 knot breeze doing 3 knots, and at 60° off the wind at 4 knots. As the yacht alters course from 45° to 60° (a change of course of 15°) the apparent wind changes only 8°. It is this latter change which governs the setting of the vane. This example does overstate the case for clarity's sake, and the phenomenon will be less marked in strong winds when the difference between real and apparent wind is smaller. Nevertheless, it is felt that it must be possible to set the vane to very fine limits.

As regards wind speed, say a gear works satisfactorily with a wind Force 3 (10 knots), the yacht doing 5 knots. Now increase the wind to a Force 5–6 (20 knots), the yacht doing 7 knots. Forces on vane and rudder vary roughly with the square of speed, and are almost doubled for the rudder (25 : 49) but quadrupled for the vane (100 : 400). It is surprising that most gears are able to cope with this difference, but some means of roughly adapting vane size to the force of the wind seems desirable.

Now consider the working of the usual vane with vertical shaft. Suppose the wind veers 10°, and so will strike the vane at that angle forcing it over, taking the tab (or auxiliary rudder) with it. By the time they have moved 5°, the angle of incidence and with it the force on the vane will be halved. It is obvious that either the vane must be very large, or else the gear will be slow to respond.

As regards the setting of the vane we have seen that this must be done to very fine limits. Some gears do this by means of friction clutches which are apt to slip and are difficult to operate from a distance. Most gears therefore have a gearwheel fitted to the vane and a little tumbler to the tab shaft, which can lock the vane to the shaft, and be lifted by means of a line led to within easy reach of the helmsman. The yacht is brought on course with a little bias as indicated by practice, and the vane will set itself to the wind. Then the tumbler is released and engages with one of the teeth of the gearwheel, thus locking the vane in the desired position.

It all sounds delightfully simple, but the snag lies in the fact that these gearwheels usual do not seem to have more than 36 teeth (more would make the wheel too large or the teeth too small). That means setting to within 10° only, and that is not good enough.

The action of the Tabarly vane is somewhat difficult to understand. Imagine the vane, and the horizontal axis round which it pivots, heading directly into the wind. When the wind veers it will strike one side of the vane, forcing it over. But in doing so the vane will *not* lose the wind, at least not during the relatively small angles we are dealing with. It acts like a windmill with the sails set at a very small angle. It will go over, taking the tab with it, until the latter really bites. The vane, with its long leading edge and high aspect ratio, is sensitive to wind striking it at small angles, and thus it is quick to react, like a keen helmsman.

The Tabarly vane has other advantages. It will easily clear the backstay. It can be fitted half-way between the bearings on which it pivots, thus reducing friction to a minimum. It can easily be removed altogether, so that two vanes may be carried, for light and heavy weather. Being more effective it can be smaller and lighter, with smaller counterweights and greatly reduced inertia. A final great advantage is that it is set at a fixed bearing relative to the *ship*, as opposed to the ordinary vane which is set relative to the *tab*. This makes continuous and remote control a far easier proposition.

I have no doubt that the Tabarly vane is much better than the other type. Unfortunately, it is not a simple proposition to connect it to the tab; Tabarly is silent on this score, beyond saying that it is a matter for the engineers to solve.

Examining now some existing types in more detail, little need be said about type A, operating the rudder directly. Most people will have read of Chichester's Miranda, 45 sq. ft. of it, hard to control, hard to reef in a gale, altogether impractical although it won the race. But I have seen it work perfectly on a little J.O.G. type 20-footer, and the gear developed by Michael Henderson for the Prout Catamaran Ranger I appears also to be of this type.

The same gear can be used to work a small auxiliary rudder, say one-quarter of the size of the main one, and operating independently of it. This reduces the size of the vane, and the gear in general, in proportion. It may be asked why a small rudder will do the job; does this mean that the average yacht's main rudder is hopelessly oversize? In fact, the main rudder has to do many things which will not be required of the auxiliary one, notably bringing the yacht about, and controlling her when her bottom needs a scrub when the rudder becomes much less effective. Also it is possible to give some bias to the main rudder by means of a tiller line or some shockcord, taking part of the load. But this may cause trouble, say in a quartering breeze, when a rogue sea may cause the yacht to bear away and quick action is required to prevent a gybe. Otherwise the auxiliary rudder's main advantage is that it is small, so that violent movements of the vane will not greatly affect the ship, thus reducing oversteer.

Turning now to the various tab gears, the most common of these fit the tab on the after edge of the main rudder, the area of the tab being perhaps one-fifth (20 per cent) of the main rudder area. However it should be remembered that the tab exerts a force *opposite* to that of the rudder; this force is transmitted to the ship, giving it a wrong turning moment equal to, say, one-quarter (25 per cent) of that exercised by the main rudder; so 25 per cent of the rudder must be used to compensate, leaving it only 75 per cent effective. The answer is to move the tab away from the rudder stock, increasing its leverage and so reducing its size. The Tubornet gear does this in a simple and elegant way.

If we now take a look at the Hasler pendulum gear the first feature that claims our attention is that it doubles, in a small way, as an auxiliary rudder. That is, it does not oppose the action of the main rudder, but assists it. This, of course, is simply the manner in which the vane is linked to the tab, and the pendulum linked to the rudder. In practice the pendulum carries a quadrant above the horizontal main shaft. When the ship is to be steered to port, and consequently the stern pushed to starboard, the tab is so set that it swings also to starboard. This raises the starboard side of the quadrant, and pulls on the starboard tiller line. The main horizontal shaft is fixed at about deck level, giving the pendulum a long leverage, so that the tab, and with it the vane, can be relatively small.

This gear has been used with great success on a variety of yachts. Hasler has probably designed more vane-steering gear than anyone; at the date of writing some 130 have been fitted. Blondie has the special advantage of being not only a designer but an ocean-going user; he has made four Atlantic crossings with his gear. M. S. Gibb supplies the sets of standard parts. Special advice can be obtained from: Colonel H. G. Hasler, The Old Forge, Curdridge, Southampton; Telephone: Botley 2918. (In addition to the special system described briefly above, many sets of trim tab gear have been made; applicable to outboard rudders.) The sensitivity of the pendulum-servo type gear is extraordinary; in the merest of zephyrs I have found it will properly control the yacht.

Gunning found a simple way to transmit the movement of the Tabarly vane to the tab, and improved the pendulum gear by splitting the blade into a fixed skeg, and a rear part which can be turned, the two forming an airfoil section. This enabled placing the blade between two lightly loaded bearings fixed to the skeg, and to attach stays to the skeg, supporting it at waterline level. The stays double as tiller lines and are led over ordinary spreaders, giving great leverage with corresponding reduction in forces in the tiller lines.

The connection of vane to tab consists of two thin wires led over a quadrant on the vane over sheaves down the centre of the mast (a $1\frac{1}{2}$-in. tube) on which the latter is fitted, and so over further sheaves to the quadrant on the stock of the tab. When the fitting supporting the vane is turned to set the vane to the wind the wires are twisted, but as the movement is restricted to 180° each way, this does not matter. The head is fitted with a grooved flange, round which a wire is wound. By pulling one end or the other of this line the vane can be turned and set to fine limits, if needs be from the doghouse.

A lock is fitted which keeps the vane amidships when not in use. When it is to be used the ship is brought on course and the vane set to head into the wind. Then the lock is released and the vane takes over, final correction being made by adjusting the vane-setting lines.

The gear has been fitted to *Myth* and well reported on after a long offshore voyage.

Further details of the gear from M. F. Gunning, M.R.I.N.A., Little Hawsted, Steep, Petersfield, Hampshire.

Among U.K. suppliers of other vane-operated steering gears are:

AUTOMATE PRODUCTS, Pitt Lane, Binstead, Ryde, Isle of Wight. Small gears made to designs by J. R. Flewitt, A.M.R.I.N.A., suitable for yachts up 19-ft. waterline whose rudder is inboard of transom including Caprice, Mystic, Westerly, Audacity, etc.

M. S. GIBB LTD., Clock Tower Buildings, Warsash, Hants. Hasler design of trim-tab and pendulum-servo type suitable for a variety of yachts with inboard and outboard rudders. Two sizes of gear available.

HENDERSON PUMPS AND EQUIPMENT LTD., 38 Medina Road, Cowes, Isle of Wight. Designers of special vane gears for a wide variety of types of yacht, including Pionieer, Twister, Horizon, and Prout Ranger class catamarans.

BINGLEY, SON AND FOLLIT LTD., 50 Minerva Road, London, N.W.10. Manufacturers of the Quartermaster vane gear designed by H. K. Wiles for Folkboats and other outboard rudder yachts of similar size.

APPENDIX XX

GLOSSARY OF TERMS IN FRENCH, GERMAN, ITALIAN, SPANISH

English	French	German	Italian	Spanish
RIGS	Gréement	Takelung		Aparejos
ASPECT RATIO, of sail or triangle	Proportion longueur-largeur (voile)	Verhältnis Höhe zu Breite des Segels	Rapporto Altezza a Base	Proporción
BERMUDAN RIGGED	En Marconi; en bermudien	Hochgetakelt	Attrezzato alla Marconi	Aparejo bermudiano o Marconi
BERMUDAN RIG		Hochtakelung		
CUTTER	Cotre	Kutter	Cutter	Aparejo de cuter
CUTTER RIGGED	En cotre	Kuttergetakelt		
CUTTER RIG		Kuttertakelung		
FORE TRIANGLE	Triangle avant	Vorsegeldreieck	Triangolo di prua	Triangola se proa
GAFF RIGGED	En houari	Gaffelgetakelt	Attrezzato a picco	Aparejo de cangreja ó cangrejo Queche
GAFF RIG	Gréement aurique	Gaffeltakelung		
KETCH	Ketch	Ketsch	Ketch	Aparejo de Queche
KETCH RIG	Gréement ketch	Ketschtakelung		
SCHOONER	Goélette	Schoner	Goletta	Goleta
SLIDING GUNTER	En houari vertical	Steilgaffelsegel	Alla portoghese	Guairo
SLOOP, single headsail	Sloop	Schlup (mostly written as in English: sloop)	Sloop	Balandro
SLUTTER, cutter sometimes sailed as a sloop	Gréement intermédiaire entre sloop et cotre	Kutter, der manchmal als Sloop gesegelt wird	Mista sloop cutter	'Slutter'
STAYSAIL SCHOONER	Goélette à voile d'étai	Stagsegel-Schoner	Goletta americana	Goleta de estais
TOPSAIL SCHOONER	Goélette à doub e huniers	Topsegel-Schoner	Goletta a gabbiola	Goleta con escondalosas o simplemente Goleta
WISHBONE RIG	En wishbone	Spreizgaffel oder Wishbone-Takelung	A wishbone	Aparejo wishbone
YAWL	Yole	Yawl	Yawl	Yole
SAILS	Voile	Segel	Vele	Velas
BATTEN	Latte	Latte	Stecca	Sable
CLEW (of sail)	Point d'écoute	Schoothorn (eines Segels)	Bugna	Puño de escota
CRINGLE, eye	Crosse	Kausch	Brancarella	Guardacabo
FISHERMAN STAYSAIL, large between-mast sail	Fisherman	Viereckige-Stagsegel (zwischen den Masten)	Vela di strallo	Vela de estay, carbonera
FOOT (of sail)	Fond (de voile)	Unterliek	Bordame-Base	Pujamen
FORESAIL (Schooner)	Misaine	Vorsegel	Trinchetto	Trinquete
GENOA JIB, low cut overlapping jib set in a sloop or from masthead	Genois: Foc recouvrant	Genua-Fock	Fiocco Genova	Genova, foque de largos
To HAND (a sail) take in	Amener (une voile)	Ein Segel bergen bezw. wegnehmen	Dare una vela	Arriar; meter dentro
HEAD (of sail)	Tête de voile	Kopf (des Segels)	Penna	Puño de driza
HANK	Pistolet	Stagrutscher	Garroccio	mosquetones
HEADBOARD	Planchet têtière	Kopfholz	Tavoletta	Tabla de gratil
HEADSAIL	Voile d'avant; foc	Vorsegel	Fiocco	Vela de proa
(To) HOIST (A SAIL), make sail	Hisser	Ein Segel heissen	Alzare (una vela)	Izar
(To) SET (A SAIL)	Établir une voile	ein Segel setzen		
JACKYARD TOPSAIL	Flèche à vergue, flèche carrée	Rah-Topsegel	Freccia con asta	Escandalosa de cuatro puños
JIB	Foc	Klüver (Fock)	Fiocco	Foque
JIBHEADED TOPSAIL	Flèche à foc ou flèche pointue	Dreikant Topsegel	Contro fiocco	Escandalosa
LEECH (of sail)	Chute	Liek (Achterliek)	Balumina	Baluma ó caida de popa
LIGHT-WEATHER SAIL Extras (ghosters)	Voiles de petit temps	Leichtwetter-Segel (zusätzliche)	Vele de vento leggero	Velas ligeras
LUFF (of sail)	Envergure	Vorlick	Ghinda-Inferitura	Amura á caida de proa.
MAINSAIL	Grand'voile	Grossegel	Randa	Mayor
MAINSAIL track SLIDE	Chemin de fer	Grossegel-Rutscher	Rotaia	Guia, carril de la mayor
MIZZEN	Artimon	Besan	Mezzana	Mesana
OVERLAP (of sail)	Recouvrement	Ueberlappung	Incrocio	Superposición
QUAD JIB	Foc quadrilatéral	Vierkant-Vorsegel	Fiocco a quadrilatero	Foque cudrilátero

English	French	German	Italian	Spanish
QUEEN STAYSAIL Staysail schooner's largest between-mast sail	Voile d'étai Maitresse	Grosstagsegel (zwischen den Masten)	Vela di strallo Cavalla	Vela de estay Mayor
RAFFEE	Raffiot	Breitfockobersegel	Coltellaccio	Juanete triangular
(TO) REEF	Prendre un ris	Reffen	Terzarolare	Rizar
REEF POINTS	Bande de ris	Reffbändsel	Matafioni	Pantos de tomar prizos
ROACH	Rond (d'une daute, d'une voile)	Rundung des Achterlieks	Tondo	Alunamiento
ROLLER REEFING	Système à rouleau	Patentreff	Terzaroli a rullino	Maquina de rizar
SAIL HANK (spring hank)	Pistolet	Legel	Garrocci	Mosquetones
SPINNAKER	Spinnaker	Spinnaker	Spinnaker-forza di vele	Balón, spinnaker
SQUARE SAIL	Voile carrée; fard carré	Rahsegel	Vela quadra	Vela cuadra
STAYSAIL	Voile d'étai; trinquette	Stagsegel	Vela di strallo	Trinqueta
(TO) STOP UP	Étayer	Aufstoppen	ingiuncaze	Enjuncar
STORM SAIL	Voile de cape	Sturmsegel	Fiocco di Cappa o mangiavento	Vela de mal tiempo, o vela de cap
TACK (of sail)	Pointe d'amure	Hals (eines Segels)	Mura	Puño de amura
TOP UP, raise end of (say) boom	Apiquer	Auftoppen	Alzare a picco	Izar del amantillo
(TO) TRIM (A SAIL), to adjust a sail	Border une voile	Ein Segel trimmen	Bordare	Cazar
TRYSAIL, storm sail set abaft mast	Voile de cape	Trysegel	Randa di Cappa	Mayor de capa
YANKEE JIB, jib set to masthead	Foc Yankee	grosser Klüver (zum Masttop)	Fiocco alto Yankee	Yanqui
STANDING RIGGING	Gréement dormant	Stehendes Gut	Manovre Dormienti	Jarcia firme
BOBSTAY, stay under bowsprit	Sous-barbe de beaupré	Wasserstag	Briglia di bompresso	Baupres o Botalon
BOWSPRIT SHROUDS	Haubans de beaupré	Klüverbaumwanten	Sartie di bompresso	
CAP SHROUDS	Haubans	Eselshaupt-Wanten	Venti di bompresso	Zuncho de loss obenques
CHAIN PLATE	Cadène	Rüsteisen	Lande	Cadenote
DIAMOND SHROUD	Hauben en losange	Topwant, das über obere Saling zum Mast in Höhe der unteren Saling zurückgefuhrt wird	Sartie a Losanga	Obenque en diamante, o violin
FORESTAY	Étai avant	Vorstag	Strallo della Trinchettina	Estay de proa
FORE TOPMAST STAY	Étai de tête de mât	Vorstengestag	Strallo del Fiocco (in testa d'albero)	Estay de cabeza o de galop
JUMPER STAY	Galhauban	Jumpstag	Paterazzi (del Pennaccino)	Violin
LIFT (TO SPREADER)	Balancine	Topnant (der Saling)	Amantiglio	Amantillo
LOWER SHROUD	Hauban de bas mât	Unterwant	Sartie Basse	Obenque bajo
RIGGING SCREW, turn buckle	Ridoir	Wantenspanner (spannschraube)	Arridatoi a Tornichetto	Tensor
RUNNING BACKSTAY	Bastaque	lfd. Backstag	Sartie volanti	Borda volante
SHACKLE	Manille	Schakel	Maniglione-Grillo	Grillete
SPREADER, cross trees	Barre de flèche	Saling	Crocetta	Cruceta
STANDING BACKSTAY	Pataras	Achterstag	Strallo di Poppa	Borda
(MAST) TANG Strip of metal secured to mast	Ferrure de mât pour fixation des étais haubans	(Mast) Beschlag	Ferramenta d'albero	Zuncho
TRIATIC STAY, between mastheads	Étai de cougue	Knickstag	Strallo di contro velaccio	Estay triático
UPPER SHROUDS	Haubans de tête de mât	Oberwanten	Sartie alte	Obenques altos
RUNNING RIGGING	Gréement courant	Lfd. Gut	Manovre correnti	Jarcia de labor
AFTER GUY (after brace), e.g. to spinnaker	Retenue arrière du tangon de spinnaker	Achtergei	Braccetto di poppa—Scotta sopravento del tangeone	Braza
BLOCK	Poulie	Block	Bozzello	Moton
COIR (Grass)	Coco	Grastauwerk (Kokos)	Cocco	Fibra
CORDAGE	Cordage	Tauwerk	Cima-Cordami	Cabulleria
DOWNHAUL	Halebas	Niederholer	Caricabasso Alabasso	Cargadera
FOREGUY (Forebrace), e.g. to spinnaker	Retenue avant du tangon de spinnaker	Vorgei	Braccetto di Prora—Caricabasso tangone	Contrabraza
HALYARD	Drisse	Fall	Drizza	Driza
HANDY BILLY (Small purchase)	Palan	Kleine Talje	Paranchetto	Aparejuelo

English	French	German	Italian	Spanish
Italian Hemp	Chanvre	Ital. Hanf	Canapa	Cáñamo italiano
Kicking Strap, boom downhaul	Halebas de bôme	Niederhalter (Bullentalje)	Caricabasso del boma	Estrobo de la contraescota de la botavara
Lanyard	Bout; brin	Taljereep	Arridatoi a Bigotta	Acollador, rebenque
Lift, to boom or cross-trees supporting rope	Balancine	Dirk	Amantiglio	Amantillo
Manilla	Manille (cable en)	Manila	Manilla	Abacá
Outhaul	Hale-reliers	Ausholer	Butta fuori	Empunidora
Parrel Ball wood balls on heel of gaff yard	Pomme de racage	Rack Roller	Raccaggio	
Purchase, tackle	Palan	Talje	Paranco	Aparejo
Reef Racing Line	Bande de ris	Reihleine	Mano di Terzaroli	Culebra
Reef Pennants	Itague de ris	Reffbandsel Lfd. Gut	Barose di Terzarolo	Culebra
Sheave	Réa	Scheibe	Puleggia	Roldana
Sheet	Écoute	Schoot	Scotta	Escota
Sisal	Sisal	Sisal	Sisal	Sisal
(To) Splice (a Rope)	Épisser	(ein Tau) spleissen	Impiombare (un cavo)	Ayustar
Strop	Estrope	Stropp	Stroppo	Estrovo
Twofold Purchase	Palan double	Doppeltalje (vierscheibige (Talje)	Paranco Doppio	Cuadernal
Vang	Mas ou Palan de garde	Gaffelgeer	Ostino	Osta
Wire Rope	Fil d'acier	Drahttau	Cavo d'acciaio	Cable

SPARS AND OTHER FITTINGS

English	French	German	Italian	Spanish
	Matériaux et leurs garnitures	Spieren und Beschläge	Antenne e Guarniture	Palos y sus Herrajes
Boom	Bôme	Baum	Boma	Botavara
Boom Crutch	Axe de bôme	Baumstütze (Scheere)	Capra del Boma	Descanso de la botavara
Bowsprit	Beaupré	Bugspriet	Bompresso	Bauprés
Bumkin, sprit facing aft	Balestan	Heckausleger	Buttafuori di poppa	
Cross-trees, spreader	Barres de flèche	Saling	Crocette	Crucetas
Dolphin Striker, to extend bobstay		Stampfstock	Pennaccino	Moco
Foremast	Mât de misaine	Fockmast	Albero di Trinchetto	Trinquete
Gaff	Corne ou pic	Gaffel	Picco	Pico
Gallows (for boom)	Axe de bôme	Baumstütze	Capra	Calzos
Gooseneck	Vit-de-mulet	Halsbeschlag am Grossbaum	Trozza (Attacco Boma-Albero)	Zuncho de la botavara
Heel (of a spar)	Pied	Fuss (einer Spiere)	Rabazza	Coz
Inboard End (of a spar)	Bout à bord	Innenbordende (einer spiere)	Estremita a Bordo	Coz
Jackyard	Vergue de Flèche	Topsegel-Spiere	Freccia	escandalosa
Jaws	Joue	Backen (einer Klau)	Gola	Boca de cagrejo
Mainmast	Grand mât	Grossmast	Albero Maestro	Palo mayor
Mast	Mât	Mast	Albero	Palo
Mast Head	Tête de mât	Masttop	Testa d' albero; formaggetta	Topedel palo
Mast Heel	Pied du mât	Mastfuss	Miccia	Coz del palo
Mast Track	Chemin de fer	Mastschiene	Rotaia	Guia del palo
Mizzen Mast	Mât d'artimon	Besanmast	Albero di Mezzana	Palo mesana
Outboard End (of spar)	Bout au large	Aussenbordsende	Varea	Penol
Rake (of a mast)	Quête	Mastfall	Aggolettamento	Caida
Sheave	Réa	Scheibe	Puleggia	Roldana
Spinnaker Pole, spinnaker boom	Tangon de spi	Spinnakerbaum	Tangone	Tangon del balon
Tang, steel strip to supporting rigging	Ferrure	Beschlag	Ferramenta di albero	Zuncho
Topmast	Mât de hune	Stenge	Alberetto	Mastelero
Track Slides	Glissière	Rutscher	Garrocci della rotaia	Garruchos
Yard	Vergue	Rah	Pennone	Verga

ANCHORS, WARPS, ETC.

English	French	German	Italian	Spanish
		Anker, Trossen usw.	Ancore, Cavi	Ancla, Cabos
Anchor	Ancre	Anker	Ancora	Ancla
Anchor Chain Cable	Chaine d'ancre	Ankerkette	Catena del l'ancora Cablotto del l'ancora	Cadena del ancla
Anchor Warp	Corde d'ancre	Ankertrosse	Cavo del l'ancora	Cabo del ancla
Bits, cable-securing device on deck	Bitte	Poller	Bitte	Bitas
Capstan	Cabestan	Spill	Argano	Cabrestante
Catting Davit	Bossoir	Ankerdavit	Gru di capone	Serviola, pescante del ancla
Cotton Rope	Manoeuvre de cotton	Baumwoll-Tau	Cavo di cotone	Cabo de algodon
Crown, of anchor	Diamant d'ancre	Ankerkreuz	Diamante	Cruz

12

English	French	German	Italian	Spanish
FLUKE	Patte	Flunken	Patta	Uña
GRASS WARP (Coir warp)	Aussière en pitte	Grastrosse (Kokos)	Cavo di pitta (Vegetale)	Cabo de coco
HAWSE PIPE	Manchon d'écubier	Klüse	Cubia	Escobén
HEAVING LINE	Ligne d'attrape	Wurfleine	Sacchetto	Virador
HEMP WARP	Aussière en chanvre	Hanftrosse	Cavo di canapa	Cabo de cañamo
MANILLA WARP	Aussière manille	Manila-Trosse	Cavo di manilla	Cabo de abacá
NAVEL PIPE	Écubier de pont	Klüsenrohr, kettenrohr	Pozzo delle catene	Bocina del escobén
SHANK	Verge	Schaft	Fuso	Cara del ancla
STOCK, crossbar of an anchor	Jas	Ankerstock	Ceppo	Cepo
DECK AND EQUIPMENT		Deck und Ausrüstung	Coperta	Cubierta y equipaje
BOOM CRUTCH (see under SPARS)	Axe de bôme	Baumstütze	Capra del Boma	Horquilla de la botavara
CLEAT, for securing rope	Taquet	Klampe	Galloccia	Cornamusa
DEAD EYE, lead without sheave for hemp or lanyard	Cap de mouton	Juffer	Bigotta	Vigota
HORSE	Barre d'écoute	Leitwagen	Archetto	Cazaescotas
EYEBOLT, ring bolt	Piton à oeil	Augbolen	Golfare	Cáncamo
(RUNNER) LEVER, for tautening rigging	Levier	Backstaghebel	Leva per Sartie Volanti	Palanca
LIFE LINE	Filière	Strecktau	Battagliola	Guardamancebos, guia
LIGHT BOARD	Ecran de feu	Lampenbrett	Fanali di via	Pantallas de las luces de los costados
PIN RAIL	Ratelier	Nagelbank	Chiavetta della Rotaia	Cabilla
SHEET LEAD (Fairlead)	Conduit d'écoute	Schootführung	Passascotte	Escotero
SHEET LEAD TRACK	Chemin de fer de pont	Schootleitschiene	Rotaia passascotte	Guia del escotero
SKY LIGHTS	Hublot de pont	Oberlichter	Osteriggi	Lumbrera
STANCHION, deck support for lifeline or rail	Chandelier, étanson	Stutze	Candelieri	Candelero
STEERING GEAR	Appareil à gouverner; gouvernail	Steuergeschirr	Timoneria	Maguina de gobierno
TILLER	Barre	Pinne	Barra	Caña
STEERING WHEEL	Roue	Steuerrad	Ruota	Volante
SHEET WINCH	Winch	Schootenwinde	Arganello Verricello	Chigre o winche Chigre de mano
WINCH HANDLE	Manivelle poignée	Windenkurbel	Leva del l'arganello	Palanca de winche
HULL AND CONSTRUCTION	Coque et Construction	Rumpf und Konstruktion	Scafo e costruzione	Casco y construccion
ANTI-FOULING (Paint)	Antifouling	Anwuchsverhütend	Antivegetativo	Pintura anti-incrustante o patente
BALLAST KEEL	Lest	Ballastkiel	Zavorra di Chiglia	Quilla de lastre
BEAM	Bau, largeur	Breite	Baglio	Bao
BILGE	Bouchain	Bilge	Sentina	Pantoque
BREAST HOOK	Guirlande	Bugband	Gola	Buzarda
BULK HEAD	Cloison	Schott	Paratia	Mamparo
CARLING, frame of an opening in deck	Élongis; carlingue	Schlinge	Anguilla	Curva
CLAMP, for and aft member next to shelf	Serre bauquière	Unterbalkweger	Controdormiente	Ilurmiente
COACH ROOF	Roof	Kajütsdach	Tuga	Tambucho
COAMING	Hiloire	Süll	Mastra	Brazola
COCKPIT	Cockpit	Kockpit	Pozzetto	Bánera
COMPANIONWAY	Descente	Niedergang	Boccaporto della tuga	Escotilla
COUNTER	Voûte	Spiegel	(Carega) Volta	Bovedilla, aleta
CRADLE (Shipping)	Ber	Verladebock	Slitta Invasatura	Cuna
DEADWOOD	Massif	Totholz	Tacco	Dormido
DECK BEAM	Barrot de pont	Decksbalken	Baglio di Coperta	Bao de cubierta
DECK PLANKING	Virures de pont	Decksbeplankung	Comenti di Coperta	Cubierta, tablazon de cubierta
DEPTH (of hull)	Creux, profondeur de la coque	Seitenhöhe	Puntale	Puntal
DISPLACEMENT (of a hull)	Déplacement	Verdrängung	Dislocamento	Desplazamiento
DRAFT or DRAUGHT (of water	Tirant d'eau	Tiefgang	Immersione	Calado
DROP KEEL, Centreboard	Dérive	Schwert	Deriva mobile	Orza
FASHION PIECE, e.g. frame round counter	Estain	Randsomholz	Anello-Angolo	Gambota

English	French	German	Italian	Spanish
FLOOR, frame below cabin sole	Varangue	Bodenwrange	Madiere	Varenga
FLUSH DECK	Flush deck	Glattdeck	Coperta continua	Cubierta corrida
FRAMES (Timbers)	Members, membrures	Spanten	Costole-ossature	Cuaderna
FREEBOARD	Franc-bord	Freibord	Bordo libero	Franco bordo
GARBOARD STRAKE	Virure de galbord	Kielplanke	Corso del torello	Tablon de aparadura
HAND RAIL	Main courante	Schandeckel	Bordino	Regala
HATCH	Panneau	Luke	Boccaporto	Cuartel o escotilla
HOG	Arc	Strebe	Archetto	Brusca
HULL	Coque	Rumpf	Scafo-carena	Casco
INSIDE BALLAST	Lest intérieur, gueuses	Innenballast	Zavorra interna	Lastre interior
KEEL	Quille	Kiel	Chiglia	Quilla
KING PLANK, centre plank of deck		Fischplanke	Suola centrale	Tabla de crujia
KNEE	Gousset	Knie	Bracciolo	Curra angular
OVERHANG	Élancement	Ueberhang	Slancio	Lanzamiento
PLYWOOD	Contreplaqué	Sperrholz	Compensato	Contraplacada
RAIL (Bulwark)	Lisse	Reeling (Schanzkleid)	Falchetta	Batayola, cairel regala
REVERSE SHEER	Tonture inversée	Negativer Sprung	Cavallino rovescio	Quebranto
RUDDER	Gouvernail	Ruder	Timone	Timon
SECTION (of a hull)	Section, coupe	Bauspant	Sezione	Seccion
SHEERLINE	Tonture	Deckstrak	Cavallino-insellatura	Linea de cubierta
SHEER STRAKE	Virure de carreau	Scheergang	Corso della cinta	Cinta
SHELF, member under deck near ship's side	Étagère	Hauptweger	Stipetto Scaffale	
SIDE PLANKING	Bordé, bordage	Seitenbeplankung	Fasciame di murata	Tablazon de costado
SLIPWAY	Slip	Slip (Aufschlepp-helling)	Slitta	Varadero
SOLE (CABIN), cabin floor	Sol	Kajütsfussboden	Pagliolo	Piso de la camara
STEM	Étrave	Vorsteven	Dritto di prora	Roda
STERN POST	Étambot	Achtersteven	Dritto di poppa	Cadaste
STEP, portion under mast heel	Emplanture	Mastspur	Scassa	Carlinga
STOP WATER		Dübel (Schernagel)		
STRINGERS, fore and aft strength members in bilge	Serres	Stringer	Correnti; serrette	Vagras
TRANSOM STERN	Tableau	Spiegelheck	Specchio di poppa	Yugo del escudo de popa
TUMBLEHOME, inboard slope of a topside	Rentrèe	Seiteneinfall	Rientranza delle murate	Entrante
WATERLINE LENGTH	Longueur de flottaison	Länge Wasserlinie	Lunghezza al galleggiamento	Eslora de la flotacion

YACHT HANDLING

English	French	German	Italian	Spanish
YACHT HANDLING	Manoeuvre	Yachthandhabung (Führung)	Manovra	Maniobra
AHEAD	En l'avant	Vorwärts	Avanti	Avante por la proa
ASTERN	En arrière	Ruckwärts	Indietro	Atras por la popa
BY THE LEE (Sailing)	Sous le vent	Unter Lee	Navigare sottovento	A sotavento
CLOSE FETCH	Un bord de justesse	hoch am Winde	Stringere il vento	Barloventear
CLOSE HAULED	Au plus près	Schooten dicht-gehot	Di Bolina	Cinendo de bolina
CLOSE WINDED	Un bateau de près	hoch am Winde	Che Bolina bene	Bolinero
EASY MOTION	Mouvement doux	Leichte Bewegung	Movimento dolce	De muevimiento sauve
GYBE	Empanner gambeyer	Halsen	Virare in poppa Strambare	Trasluchar virar por
(TO) HAND (A SAIL), take down	Descendre (une voile)	ein Segel niederholen, wegnehmen	Ammainare	Arriar
HANK ON, a sail. Fix to stay	Endrailler; Crocher un mousqueton	Anschlagen	Ingarrocciare	Envergar
HEEL	Citer; prendre de la bande	uberliegen	Sbandare	Escorar
HELMSMAN	Barreur	Rudersmann	Timoniere	Timonel
IN IRONS, head to wind	Dans le vent	im Wind liegen	Prua al vento	Proa al viento o encantado
JUST FREE	Porter bon plein	voll und bei	Di buon braccio	Cenir abierto
LEEWARD	Sous le vent	leewärts	Sottovento	A sotavento
LEEWAY	Dérive	Leeweg	Scarroccio	Abatimiento
ON THE BOW	Par l'avant	Vorlich	Al mascone; in prua	Por la amura
ON THE QUARTER	Par l'arrière du travers	Achterlich	Al Giardinetto; al lasco	Por la aleta

English	French	German	Italian	Spanish
PITCH	Tanguer	Stampfen	Imbarcare acqua di poppa	Cabecear
POOPED, wave over stern	Embarqué par l'arrière	See übers Heck	Impoppata	Golpe de mar por la popa
POUND, of a craft Bump in a sea	Marteler	stampfen (hart aufschlagen)	Picchiare sull'onda	Dar pantocazos
REACHING	Au largue	raumschoots segeln	Al lasco	A un descuartolar
(To) REEF	Prendre des ris	reffen	Terzarolare	Tomar rizos, rizar
(To) ROLL (of a ship)	Rouler	rollen	Rollare—rollio	Balancear o tumbar
RUNNING	Au vent arrière	vor dem Winde segelnlenzen	In poppa	Viento en popa
RHYTHMIC ROLLING	Roulis rythmique	gleichmässiges Rollen	Rollio Ritmico	Balanceo ritmico
(To) SET (A SAIL), to put up a sail	Hisser	ein Segel setzen	Alzare Bordare	Izar
To SET UP	Raidir	ausholen	Cazzare-Tesare	
(To) TACK SHIP	Virer de bord	wenden, über Stag gehen	Virare in prua	Virar
VIOLENT MOTION	Mouvements violents	heftige Bewegung	Movimenti violenti	Movimiento violento
WATCH BELOW	Quart en bas	Freiwache	Guardia Franca	Reten
WATCH ON DECK	Quart sur le pont	Wache an Deck	Guardia in coperta	Guardia
WINDAGE, wind resistance resistance	Resistance du vent	Windwiderstand	Resistenza al vento	Resistencia del viento
(To) WINDWARD	Au près, remontant au vent	luvwärts	Bolinare	Barloventear a Barlovento
YAW ABOUT	Embarder	gieren	Straorzare	Guinar guinada
NAVIGATION	Navigation	Navigation	Navigazione	Navegacion
A FIX	Point	Ortsbestimmung	Punto	Una situacion
A RUNNING FIX	Point Courant	Laufende Ortsbestimmung	Punto trasportato	Situacion trasladada
A SIGHT (Celestial observation)	Hauteur	Beobachtung (eines Himmelskorpers)	Altezza	Observacion
BAROMETRIC FRONT	Front atmosphérique	Wetterfront	Fronte Barometrico	Frente barometrico
CHART ROOM	Chambre à cartes	Kartenraum	Sala nautica	Camara de navegacion
CHART TABLE	Table à carte	Kartentisch	Tavola da Carteggio	Mesa de derrota
CROSS BEARINGS	Relèvements croiés	Kreuzpeilung	Rilevamenti	Situacion de dosomas marcaciones
DEAD RECKONING POSITION (D.R.P.)	Point estimé	Position nach Koppel-kursrechnung	Punto stimato	Situacion de estima Posicion de estima
DECK LOG	Livre de bord. Journal de bord. Journal de mer	Schiffstagebuch	Giornale di Chiesuola	Borrador de bitacora
DEPRESSION, barometric low	Depression	Tief	Bassa pressione	Depresion
DISTANCE METER (Station keeper)		Entfernungsmesser		
DIVIDERS	Compas	Teilzirkel	Compasso	Compases de puntas
HAND BEARING COMPASS	Compas de relèvement à main	Hand-Peilkompass	Bussola da Rilevamenti portatile	Aguja acimutal de mano
LEAD AND LINE	Plomb et ligne de sonde	Lot und Leine	Scandaglio a sagola	Escandallo y sondaleza
LINE SQUALL	Ligne de cumulo-nimbus	Böe	Groppo	Chubasco de viento
NEAP TIDE	Marée de morte eau	Nipptide	Marea delle quadrature	Mareas muertas
OFFSHORE	Au large	Auf See	Alto Mare	Alta mar, mar adentro fuera
ONSHORE	Le cap sur terre	an Land	Costiero	En la costa, hacia tierra, cerca de tierra, barajando la costa
PARALLEL RULE	Règle parallele	Parallel-Lineal	Parallela a rulli	Reglas paralelas
PATENT LOG	Loch breveté	Patentlog	Solcometro a elica	Corredera mecanica o de patente
RHUMB LINE	Loxodromie	Loxodrom	Lossodromia	Rumbo
SEAWAY (WAVES)	De la mer	Seegang	Mare mosso	Marcha las olas
SEXTANT	Sextant	Sextant	Sestante	Sextante
SOUNDING MACHINE, depth finder	Sondeur	Echolot	Ecometro Scandaglio	Sondador mecanico
SPEED METER	Sillometre	Geschwindigkeits-messer	Tachimetro	Corredera de velocidad
SPRING TIDE	Marée de vive eau	Springflut	Marea delle sizigie	Marea viva
SWELL	Houle	Dünung	Mare Lungo; Risacca	Mar tendida; mar de leva

English	French	German	Italian	Spanish
TIDAL ATLAS, tidal charts	Atlas des marées; cartes des marées	Gezeitentafel	Atlante di maree	Atlas de mareas
TIDAL STREAM	Courant	Gezeitenstrom	Corrente di marea	Corriente de marea
ACCOMMODATION	Emménagements	Einrichtung	Arredamento; sistemazione degli alloggi	Acomodacion Acomodacion dojamiento
BUNK	Couchette	Koje	cuccetta	Litera
BUNK LEEBOARD	Planche à roulis ou anti-roulis	Schlingerbrett fur Koje	Tavola di sostegno laterale	Balancera
CABIN	Cabine	Kabine	Camerino; Cabina	Camarote camara
CHART TABLE	Table à carte	Kartentisch	Tavola da Carteggio	Mesa de derrota
COMPANIONWAY	Descente	Niedergang	Discesa della tuga	Bajada escotilla
FORECASTLE	Poste	Raum im Vorschiff	Castello	Castillo
GIMBAL (Swung between centres)	à la cardan	kardanische Aufhängung	Sospensione Cardanica	Suspension cardan
HEAD (W.C.)	W.C. ou Le water		Vaso; Gabinetto	Vater
OILSKIN LOCKER	Armoire ou placard cirés	Olzeugschrank	Armadio per le cerate	Ropa de agua
THE QUARTER BERTH	Couchette arrière en partie contigue au cockpit	Hundekoje	Cuccetta di poppa	Camarate Litera de popa
ROOT BERTH, folding canvas berths	Cadre pliant	Klappkoje	Branda pieghesole	Litera plegable
SALOON	Carré	Salon	Quadrato	Cámara ol salon
TABLE FIDDLES	Cadre mobile	Schlingerleisten		
MEASUREMENT	La jauge	Vermessung	Stazza	Arqueo
AMIDSHIPS	Au milieu du bateau	mittschiffs	Al centro nave; mezzeria	Almedio del barco
CORRECTED TIME	Temps compensé	Verbesserte Zeit	Tempo compensato	Tiempo corregido
DRAUGHT LIMIT	Limite de flottaison	Tiefgangsbegrenzung	Limite di galleggiamento	Limite de calado
ELAPSED TIME	Temps réel	Verstrichene Zeit	Tempo reale	Tiempo invertido
FREEBOARD BONUS	Détaxe de franc-bord	Freibordvergütung	Abbuono del Bordo libero	Bonificacion por francabordo
GIRTH STATION	Position de la chaine	Spant an dem der Umfang gemessen wird	Sezione ti catena	Seccion
QUARTER BEAM DEPTH	Profondeur à un Quart de largeur	Viertelbreiten Tiefe	Puntale al quarto del Baglio	Puntal a un cuarto del bao o de la manga
RATING	Rating	Messwert	Stazza	Clasificacion rating
SCANTLINGS, weight and size of parts	Echantillonage	Materialabmessungen	Dimensionamento delle Strutture	Escantillones
SHEER	Tonture	Sprung	Cavallino; insellamento	Arrufo
SNUB BOW, rounded bow	Avant canard	Runder Steven	Prua rotonda	Proa chata redondeada
TIME CORRECTION FACTOR	Coéfficient	Zeitvergütungsfaktor	Coefficiente di correzione tempo	Factor de correccion de tiempos
TOPSIDES	Partie émergée	Ueberwasserrumpf	Franchi dell' opera morta	Obra muerta
WOOD	Bois	Hölzer	Legni	Maderas
ASH	Frêne	Esche	Frassino	Fresno
BEECH	Hêtre	Buche	Faggio	Haya
BIRCH	Bouleau	Birke	Betulla	Abedul a'lamo
CEDAR PORT ORFORD	Cèdre américain	Port-Orford Zeder	Cedro Port Orford	Cedro Port Orford
CEDAR RED	Cèdre rouge	Rote Zeder	Cedro Rosso	Cedro rojo
CEDAR WHITE	Cèdre blanc	Weisse Zeder	Cedro Bianco	Cedro blanco
CHESTNUT	Chataignier	Kastanie	Castagno	Castano
ELM	Orme	Ulme	Olmo	Olmo
GREEN HEART	Green Heart	Greenheart	Sipiri	Green Heart
LARCH	Mélèze	Lärche	Larice	Alerce
MAHOGANY	Acajou	Mahagoni	Mogano	Caoba
OAK	Chêne	Eiche	Quercia Rovere	Roble
PINE WHITE	Pin	Weisstanne	Pino Bianco Abete	Pino blanco
PINE YELLOW	Pin jaune	Gelbtanne	Pino Giallo	Pino amarillo
PITCH PINE	Pichepin	Pechtanne	Pitch Pine	Pino de tea
ROCK ELM	Orme Américain	Felsenulme	Olmo di roccia	Olmo American
SPRUCE	Spruce	Spruce	Spruce	Abeto de Canada
TEAK	Teck	Teak	Tek	Teca

INDEX

(Page numbers in bold type indicate illustrations.)

Accommodation, 182–99, *see also* under Hulls
  berths and bunks, 186, 189, 190, 194, 247, 249
  J O G boats, 244, 247, 248, 249, **250**
  lighting, 196, 252
  Stowage, see 'Stowage'
  ventilation, 192–**195**
  windage, 208
Admiralty Lists,
  lights, 43–4
  W/T signals, 43–4
Aerials, wireless, 136
Aitken, Hon Max, 164
Akka, 260
Alcina, 170
Alcohol, effects of, 25–6
Alita (Griffin II), 169
Alloys,
  constructional use, 179
  insulation, 179
  masts and fittings, 62, 102–4, 134, **139**
  paints for, 104–5, 179
  spars, 105
  stanchions, 208
  strengths of, 267
  yacht fittings, 137–8
Almanac, nautical, 44
Alpa, 8, 134
Altitude and azimuth tables, 43
Anchor cable, nylon, 131
Ancolan, 22
Angela, 238
Anitra, 170
Annapolis Race, 2
Argentine Club, 235
Artica II, 41, 54, 173, 179
Aspect ratio, 54, 203, 288
Associacoa Naval Race, 3
Astro Stars for Navigation, 43
Atlantic, 1
Atlas, tidal, 43, 50
Auxiliary engines, 211–3
  alternator, 212
  engine drag, 213
  exhaust, 213
  propellers, see 'Propellers'
  type, 213
  weight, 212
Avomine, 22
Awnings, 242

Backstays, 112, 120
Balance of hull, 41, 69, 167, 171
Ballast, 23, 167, 168, 262
Bands, black, 109, 270, 286, 297
Barometers, 215, 218, 239
Battens, sail, 73, 81, 83, 91, 256, 278, 288
Batteries, 196, 212
Beam of boat (see also under 'Hulls'), 168, 272, 285, 297, 315
Bearing-out spars, 248
Beaufort Wind Scale, 220, 265
Becket for genoas, 92
Belmore, 38, 41, 43
  chart table, **50**, 54, 170, **208**, 230
  design and detail, **319**

Benadryl, 22
Bermuda Race, **112**, 229–35
  chart for, 234
  details of, 1, 229
  eligibility for, 2, 229–30
  equipment, 231
  fresh water requirements, 24
  Gulf Stream, allowance for, 234
  import regulations, 232–4
  preparation for, 231
  sails and rating, 59, 230–1
  shipment to USA, 232, **233**
  tactics and nagigation, 234
  time allowances, 230
  trophies, 229–30
  weather conditions, 34
  winds, 234–5
Berths, 183, 184, 186, 189, 194, 249
Bilge stringers, 249
Binding wire, 208
'Biscay' design, 168
Blocks, 133
Bloodhound, 5, 41, 69, 72, **119**, 167, **188**
Blue Charm, **112**, 143, 169, 184
Blue Disa, 39, 235
Bombard, Dr, 24
Booms, 74–7
  crutch, 38, **207**
  gallows, 206, **207**
  guy, 83
  hollow, 76
  layout, 76–7
  limits, 40
  position, 82
  sheeting (see 'Sheets and sheeting')
  spinnaker, 40–1, 78, 93, 126, 287, 302
Bottom, ship's—maintenance, 17
Bowsprit
  allowance, 287
  net, 92
Bow vents (see 'Ventilation')
Breezes (see 'Winds')
Brigantine, 57, **68**, 170
Bruce, Commander Erroll, 24
Bubble sextant, 50
Buckley, Mr R. McLean, 1
Buenos Aires Race (see 'Rio Race')
Bulkheads, JOG boats, 249
Bulwarks, 171
Bunks (see 'Berths' and 'Accommodation')

California to Honolulu Race, 3
Calliope, 169
Canvas, (see 'Sails')
Cardinal Virtue, 259
CCA (see 'Crusing Club of America')
Chain plates, 101, 135
Championship, Inter-Club, 2, 11
Channel Race, 10, 30, 55
Chart gear, 43
Chart, plotting on, 30–1, 45–50
Chart table, 42–3, 50, 190, **198**, 249, **316**, **317**
Cheers, 260
Chiar di Luna, 237, 238
Chichestr, Sir Francis, 258, 264
Chin Blu, 111, 255

Choosing a boat, 4–5
Circe, **145**
Classes and Divisions, RORC, 2, **13**, 170
Clearance, headsails, 63–4, 72
Clew position, 69
Close fetching, 33
Cloth Cap, 248
Clothing, 10, 21, 26–7, 197, 252
Clouds, 215, 221–2
Clubs, racing (see 'Racing')
Cockpit details, 17, 181, **182**
Code flags, 44
Cohoe, 10, 243
Cohoe II and III, 95, 169
Coir rope, 130
Cold fronts, 219, 223
Coles, Mr Adlard, 243
Comite International des Courses, 237
Companionways, (see 'Accommodation')
Compass, 200–3
  bowl design, 201
  deviation, 48–50
  fitments, **251**
  handbearing, 45, 48, 203
  lighting, 202
  mounting, 182
  positions, 200
Compressive loading on masts, 101, 106, **107**
Consol, bearings by, 48
Cooking and Diet, 22–4, 191, 242, 309–11
  stove, 197
Cordage, 130–132
  coir, 130
  deterioration, 131
  sisal, 130
  strength of, 266
  Terylene and nylon, 130, 131
  types compared, 130, 266
Course, (see 'Steering')
Crankshaw Bowl trophy, 2
Crew, 18–27
  clothing, 10, 26–7
  exhaustion, 12
  fitness, 24–5
  instruction sheet, 269
  numerical strength, 18
  rest periods, 10, 12
  sea-sickness, 12, 21–2
  training, 25
  watches, 10, 18, 19, 20
  weight, 248
Croce, Beppe, 237, 255
Crosstrees, 98, 106, 109, 137
Cruiser/Racers, 255
Cruising Club of America, 1, 168, 229
  certificate, 303
  headsails, 72
  measurement rule, 295–305
  rating, 295–305
  time allowance tables, 304
Cruising Yacht Club of Australia, 1, **2**, 75
Crusade, **240**
Crutch, boom, **207**
Customs regulations (Bermuda Race), 232
Cutter rig (see also 'Rigs and Rigging') 38–9, 51, 54, 57, 69, 72, 85
Cynthia, 4

What the Press said about the previous editions of *Offshore*:

'. . . Only once or twice in a decade does a genuine creative work book appear, and when it does it shines out like a diamond among a collection of bits of glass. *Offshore* is such a book. It is unquestionably the greatest contribution to yachting knowledge since Claud Worth and to many people it will be more valuable even than *Yacht Cruising*. It is impossible to praise Captain Illingworth's book too highly. It is, like everything he does, supremely competent, ruthlessly efficient and outstandingly successful.' *Little Ship Club Journal*

'. . . It is pleasant to hail a book that is completely new in its aims and that at once assumes stature as a classic in the library of yachting works. *Offshore* is the only technical book that has been written exclusively for the delectation and edification of blue water racing and cruising men. . . Will rank with the finest standard volumes on seamanship.' *Yachting*

'. . . John Illingworth is the most successful ocean racing skipper in Britain today, if not in the world, and he is writing with twenty years of ocean racing experience behind him. . . . It is at once, and I am convinced will remain for many years, the standard work on the sport. It is so detailed that it is difficult to think of any point which the author has failed to cover.' *Yachting World*

'. . . Technically the book is superb, perhaps the best yet written on all those aspects of rig, hull design, handling and tactics so vital in this fine sport now.

The illustrations and photographs, the detailed expositions, the tables and line drawings are quite first-class, and little escapes his eagle eye.' *Motor Boat and Yachting*

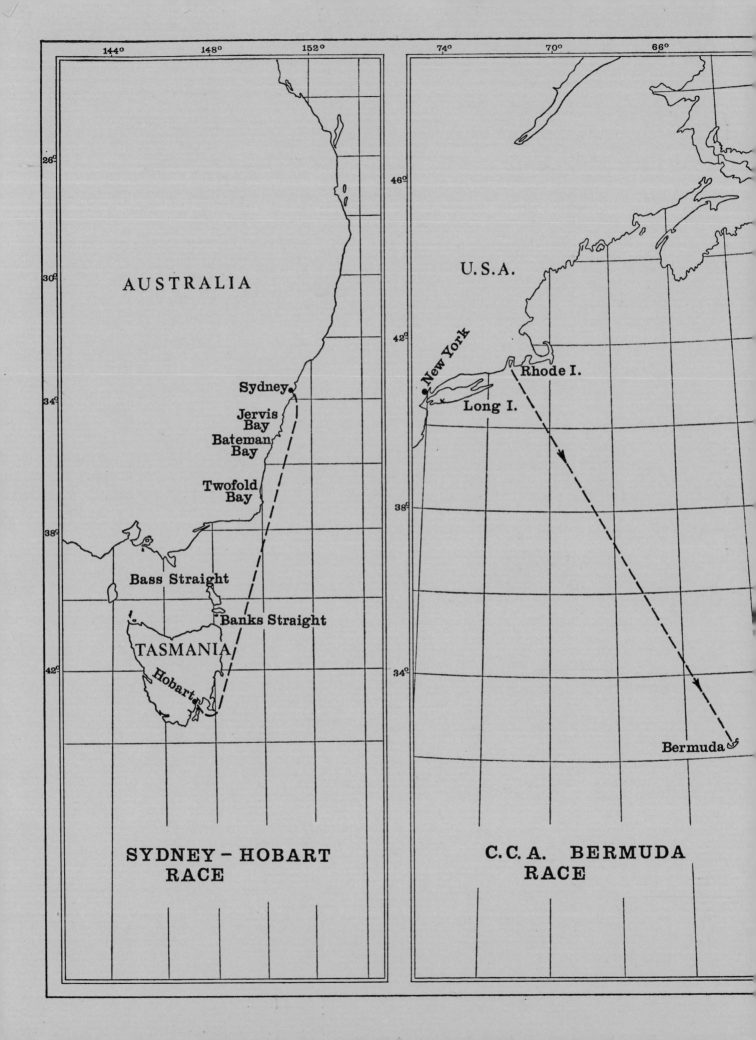

SYDNEY – HOBART
RACE

C.C.A. BERMUDA
RACE